D0032153

IDAHO

JAMES PATRICK KELLY

Contents

Idaho

daho is often misunderstood. When this rugged northwestern state is not being confused with Iowa, it's usually the brunt of some bad potato joke. True, farmers here do grow more spuds than any other state in the country, but Idaho goes beyond russet potatoes.

It's hard to fathom the varied landscapes of Idaho and the events that caused such a geologic spectacle. I strive to comprehend this beautiful state every time I head out in search of the perfect fishing hole in Hagerman Valley or when I'm crunching across a frozen lake in the Sawtooths on my snowshoes. The intense volcanic activity and major floods that helped to shape Idaho are evident at almost every bend. The basalt-hemmed cliffs along the Snake River Canyon seem like a different planet than the cedar-ringed glacial lakes in the northern Panhandle.

Central Idaho's Rocky Mountains have numerous wild rivers that vein the largest roadless area in the Lower 48. The few roads that do exist in the Frank Church-River of No Return Wilderness are jaw-chattering routes better suited for mountain bikes and bighorn sheep than they are for the family minivan. This craggy terrain poses the same challenges for modern-day explorers,

Clockwise from top left: Fall Creek Falls; Sawtooth National Recreation Area; sheep grazing in the grasslands; Bruneau Dunes State Park; a snowy road near Cambridge; Perrine Bridge in Twin Falls.

decked out in high-tech clothing and holding GPS devices, as it did for the Lewis and Clark expedition more than 200 years ago. But in today's world, the Salmon River is praised by white-water rafters and not cursed for its turbulence, as it was by those early explorers in their primitive dugout canoes.

Juxtaposed with Idaho's remote wilderness are thriving urban areas. Boise, the state capital, has a surprisingly mellow vibe for a city with the third-largest metropolitan population in the Northwest. The City of Trees has an exciting arts and entertainment scene, and it boasts the largest Basque population outside Spain. The Basque Block, a thriving ethnic enclave with restaurants, bars, and a museum, adds greatly to the city's cultural identity. Not far from Boise is the Snake River Valley, one of the country's newest wine-producing appellations.

The people of Idaho are as varied as the land itself. Conservative farmers, intellectual liberals, eco-rednecks, and antigovernment types may not have much in common, yet their adoration for the remarkable landscape that surrounds them is the only common thread they need.

Clockwise from top left: the Tetons near Driggs; Craters of the Moon National Monument; Snake River Valley wine country; fisherman on the Boise River.

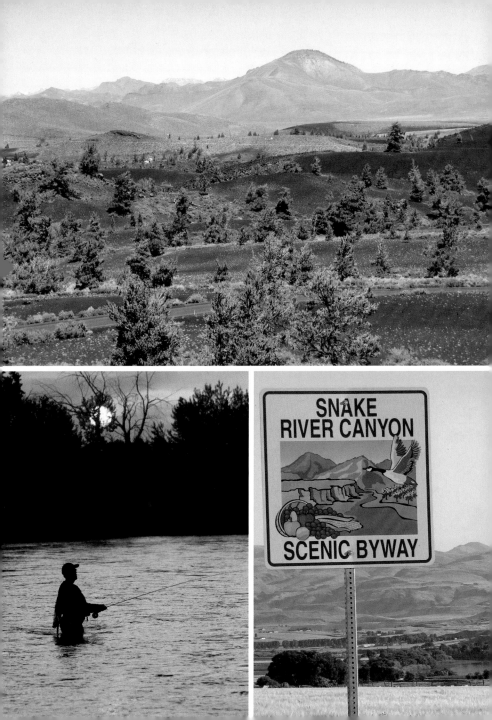

Planning Your Trip

Where to Go

Boise

This little river city has grown leaps and bounds in recent years, making it the third-largest metropolitan area in the Northwest. Boise boasts a **hip downtown** area, lots of parks with big shade trees, and a major urban university. Newer urban developments, like **BoDo** and the **Linen District,** mesh well with the beautifully preserved **historic neighborhoods.** Boiseans are an active set thanks to the **Boise River Greenbelt,** a 25-mile recreational path, and nearby **Bogus Basin Ski Resort.**

Southwest Idaho

Mountains, cities, remote desert, and vinifera grapes: This diverse region has it all. **Snake River Valley wine country** is the focal point for oenophiles who come to taste remarkable vintages made from grapes grown in the **Sunny Slope** area. Downtown **Nampa**'s historic Belle District contains used bookstores, antiques shops, coffeehouses, restaurants, and pubs.

Magic Valley

South-central Idaho is a strange and wonderful place. The **Snake River** defines the arid landscape. **Hagerman Valley** is a high-desert oasis with a profusion of fishing spots and commercial hot springs. At **Thousand Springs,** water from an ancient aquifer gushes out of the massive basalt cliffs like a faucet left on full blast. And rock climbers will surely enjoy

Idaho State Capitol and downtown Boise

Boise Depot

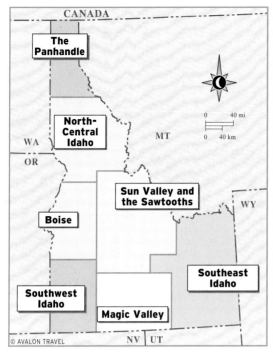

excellent place to get away from it all, but not before you go through the ritzy **Sun Valley-Ketchum** area. This fabled resort community boasts world-class **skiing,** top-notch restaurants, and attractive lodges. A few miles north, the buildings become few and far between as jagged mountain ranges dictate the scenery. The lovably rustic town of **Stanley** is a fun base camp for outdoor excursions.

North-Central Idaho

Hells Canyon marks the spot where the Snake River is furiously funneled through the deepest river gorge in North America en route to its confluence with the Columbia River. A few miles east, the resort town of **McCall** enjoys prime real estate on the southern shores of Payette Lake. Just outside town, **Brundage Mountain** beckons skiers and snowboarders to its powdery slopes. Traveling north on U.S. 95, the mountainous terrain eventually straightens out, giving way to a patchwork quilt of dryland farms near **Moscow.**

The Panhandle

The tip-top of Idaho is home to the **state's largest lakes,** Coeur d'Alene and Pend Oreille. This region may only be 45 miles wide at its skinniest point, but recreation abounds. The bustling resort towns of **Coeur d'Alene** and **Sandpoint** give travelers a place to relax after ripping through fresh powder at the **Silver Mountain** and **Schweitzer Mountain** ski resorts. During summer, the lakes buzz with activity as people flock here for boating, fishing, and general aquatic fun.

the imposing granite pinnacles at the **City of Rocks** near Almo.

Southeast Idaho

Framed by the majestic Tetons looming just over the border in Wyoming, this spectacular region is a veritable playground for anglers, backpackers, and skiers. The fabled Henrys Fork of the Snake River is pure **fly-fishing** paradise. **Pocatello** and **Idaho Falls** offer travelers urban amenities within a few miles of remote backcountry. This part of the state also boasts the largest **potato farms** in North America.

Sun Valley and the Sawtooths

The high country of Idaho's central Rockies is an

northern Idaho landscape, near the border with Montana

Know Before You Go

When to Go

Idaho offers year-round fun. Summer activities include white-water rafting, backpacking, fishing, mountain biking, and boating on the state's many scenic lakes. Wintertime brings tons of snow to the mountains, making Idaho a popular destination for skiers and snowboarders.

Summer is peak season in most resort communities in Idaho. Places like Coeur d'Alene, the Sawtooths, and Island Park in southeast Idaho are quiet during the winter months. As a matter of fact, most fishing and backcountry lodges are closed in winter due to heavy snow. Coeur d'Alene, on the other hand, may be slow in the off-season, but many of the hotels offer reduced rates and special package deals.

Mountain resort communities, like Sun Valley, McCall, and Kellogg, have two distinct peak seasons, winter and summer, when rates are the highest. The ski season generally runs from Thanksgiving weekend to around the end of March. Hotels, lodges, and restaurants are usually open year-round in these places. If skiing is not your thing but you like biking, fishing, and hiking, spring and fall are also good times to visit the mountain resort towns, when the streets are less crowded and room rates can drop as much as 25-30 percent.

Getting There and Around

Since Idaho is bordered by six states (Washington, Oregon, Nevada, Utah, Wyoming, and Montana) and one country (Canada), many people get here by car, especially along the I-84, I-15, and I-90 corridors.

Folks coming from areas outside the region generally fly into Boise, Salt Lake City, and Spokane. Renting a car makes the most sense and offers the most freedom because public transportation can be spotty in Idaho. Not to say there aren't shuttles to and from the airports and popular resort destinations, but you're on your own after that. Boise, Ketchum, Lewiston, and Coeur d'Alene have local transit systems, yet that won't help much if you plan on exploring the hinterlands.

With **winter** snow comes hazardous **driving conditions.** Getting to Idaho's numerous ski resorts and other winter recreation areas is generally not a problem, but it's important to check current weather advisories and road reports before embarking on a winter trip to the Gem State. Road conditions aren't a major consideration during the warmer months, except for errant rangeland livestock and an occasional late-spring snowstorm.

What to Pack

Once the mercury drops in Idaho, it's imperative that you bring along a **snow parka,** wick-away **thermal underwear, gloves,** and a warm **hat.** And regardless of where you are in the state, a well-insulated pair of **snow boots** will get you a long way during the frigid winter months, as will a pair of sturdy **hiking boots** in summer.

It doesn't rain much in Idaho, especially along the Snake River Plain and in Idaho's central Rockies. But the Panhandle does receive measurable annual rainfall, so you might want to pack a **rain-resistant jacket** if you're headed to north Idaho during the fall and spring months.

In general, the **dress code** is decidedly **casual** in Idaho, meaning you can get away with wearing a Carhartt jacket with your John Fluevog boots.

a barn south of Council along the Weiser River Trail

Idaho's Best Road Trips

Everywhere you go in Idaho, you'll encounter a postcard-perfect moment. The Gem State is multifaceted, like several states in one, making it a wonderful destination for a serious road trip. It takes some time and a little work to get to the different parts of the state, but the jaw-dropping sights you'll see along the way make it well worth the effort. This itinerary is separated into seven legs, spanning two weeks, but feel free to just take on one or two of them at a time.

Leg 1: Boise and Southwest Idaho

DAY 1

Upon arrival in **Boise,** stretch your getaway sticks with a stroll or a bike ride along the **Boise River Greenbelt,** before heading to the **State Capitol** and **Basque Block** for a few local history lessons. After checking out the city, enjoy some wine and Basque pub fare at **Bar Gernika,** and then call it a night at the **Modern Hotel,** but not before having a cocktail in the Euro-chic bar.

DAY 2

After breakfast in Boise, get in the car (or book a trip with a wine country tour company) and drive **35 miles** west on **I-84** and **Highway 55** to the **Sunny Slope** area of Caldwell. This is the beating heart of Idaho's wine country, the **Snake River Valley,** where you will find about a dozen wineries with tasting rooms. After hitting a few wineries and taking in the beautiful scenery near this ambling stretch of the Snake River, head back to Boise for dinner at **The Dish,** where you can enjoy more Idaho wine.

Leg 2: Southeast Idaho

DAY 3

Get up early and grab some breakfast in Boise before jumping in the car for the **five-hour drive** to **Driggs** on the Idaho-Wyoming border. It's some **353 miles** from Boise to Driggs, eastbound on **I-84, I-86, U.S. 26,** and **Highways 31 and 33,** respectively, but you'll be rewarded with stunning views of the Tetons upon arrival.

center of Boise

You can stop for lunch in **Idaho Falls** along the way, and maybe check out a museum. Once in Driggs, grab a burger and a beer at **The Royal Wolf** before retiring for the night at the **Teton Valley Cabins,** where there's an outdoor fire ring for roasting marshmallows.

DAY 4

Go to **Pendl's Bakery** in Driggs for pastries and coffee before heading out to explore the area. Make sure to stop by the shiny, new **Teton Geotourism Center** along the main drag for recreation information. One sure bet for alpine fun is a mountain-biking excursion (or skiing in winter) at **Grand Targhee Resort,** a mere **12 miles** up into the Tetons from Driggs. After tiring yourself on the labyrinth of single-track trails, grab dinner at one of the resort's eateries before heading back down the hill to your cozy cabin.

Leg 3: Sun Valley and the Sawtooths

DAY 5

Hit the road early and head back toward Idaho Falls, where you can jump on **U.S. 20** westbound

to **Highway 75,** about **120 miles,** on your way to the Ketchum-Sun Valley area. Along the way, stop and check out the bizarre landscapes at the **Craters of the Moon National Monument.** After arriving in **Ketchum,** you can shop for souvenirs and grab lunch before getting back in the car and continuing north on Highway 75, known as the **Sawtooth Scenic Byway,** for another **61 miles** to **Stanley.** Here you can grab a pizza at **Papa Brunee's,** and then check in to **Mountain Village Resort,** a friendly hotel with a natural hot springs spa.

DAY 6

After breakfast at the **Stanley Baking Company,** stretch your muscles and take a day hike to **Sawtooth Lake,** a scenic alpine lake at the sheer granite face of 10,190-foot Mount Regan. The **five-mile hike** may be strenuous, but you'll be rewarded with a long, graceful waterfall and bird's-eye views of the **Stanley Basin** below. After soaking in the hot springs tubs at Mountain Village Resort, head down to **Redfish Lake Lodge** for dinner and a stunning sunset over Mount Heyburn.

Salmon River near Stanley in the Sawtooth National Recreation Area

Leg 4: North-Central Idaho (McCall Area)

DAY 7

Get up early and travel west from Stanley on **Highway 21,** also known as the **Ponderosa Pine Scenic Byway.** Stop at **Kirkham Hot Springs** near **Lowman,** about **55 miles** from Stanley, for a relaxing soak in these scenic natural springs. In Lowman, head west on **Banks-Lowman Road** for about **35 miles** until you come to Banks. Go north on **Highway 55** for **65 miles** to **McCall** and check into your reserved cabin at **Ponderosa State Park.** Spend the rest of the day hiking and biking around the wooded park that juts out on a 1,000-acre peninsula into Payette Lake.

DAY 8

This would be a good day to sleep in a wee bit, considering the itinerary mostly includes **hanging out on the beach** and possibly **renting a canoe** for a mellow paddle around the mountain-ringed **Payette Lake.** Or you could continue exploring Ponderosa State Park, looking for wildflower-filled meadows and old-growth Douglas fir. After a day of relaxation (and you'll need it for what's coming up the next day), stop by **Salmon River Brewery** in McCall for dinner and some handcrafted beers.

Leg 5: North-Central Idaho (The Hells Canyon Corridor)

DAY 9

Get up early and take **Highway 55** to the **U.S. 95** junction at New Meadows, where you can stop at **Zim's Hot Springs** for a morning soak, and then head north for about **35 miles** to **Riggins.** Along the way you can take a little side trip down a bumpy road to Windy Saddle, a vantage point high in the **Seven Devils Range** that affords spectacular views of **Hells Canyon.** After sightseeing, head to Riggins and check into the **Salmon Rapids Lodge.** You'll want to get some sleep because the next day includes a white-water

rafting adventure (make sure to have a reservation for both the hotel and river guide).

DAY 10

The **Salmon River** in Riggins is world-famous for its wild rapids, which run north of town from the Lucile put-in. Expect to get a little wet along the way, but the river professionals who work this stretch of the river are good at keeping the rafts upright. Or you could **book a trip on a wooden dory** with **Wapiti River Guides.** After shooting the tube all day, head to the **Back Eddy Grill** for an elk burger and a few microbrews. Here you can swap tall river tales with fellow rafters on the patio.

Leg 6: The Panhandle (Coeur d'Alene)

DAY 11

After breakfast, travel north on **U.S. 95,** past Grangeville, until you come to the Clearwater River near Lewiston, about **110 miles** from Riggins. Here you'll find the interpretive center for the **Nez Perce National Historic Park,** adjacent to the Spalding Mission site. This is an excellent spot for a picnic and to soak in some of Idaho's Native American history. Lewis and Clark's Corps of Discovery also famously traveled through this area on their way to and from the Pacific Ocean in the early 19th century. After a history lesson, continue heading north on U.S. 95 for **116 miles** until you reach the shores of **Coeur d'Alene Lake.** Check in to the **Flamingo Motel** and head to Sherman Avenue for dinner.

DAY 12

Spend the day in **Coeur d'Alene** frolicking in the lake and relaxing on a lawn chair at **City Beach.** Nearby, Sherman Avenue has a multitude of cool shops and art galleries to peruse, with a few strategically placed ice cream shops along the way. Go to dinner at **Scratch,** a contemporary restaurant that sources lots of local foodstuffs, after which you can watch the fiery sunset on **Tubbs Hill,** a

Coeur d'Alene Lake

view of the landscape surrounding Hells Canyon

nature preserve with scenic hiking trails next to Coeur d'Alene Resort.

Leg 7: The Panhandle (The Silver Valley)

DAY 13

Take a short drive east on I-90, for 48 miles, to weird and wonderful Wallace. Along the way, you'll probably want to stop at the historic Cataldo Mission, at Old Mission State Park, a Greek Revival-style building constructed in 1853 by a Jesuit priest and a crew of converted Coeur d'Alene Indians. These resourceful people used mostly local materials in the construction of the mission, perched on a grassy hill overlooking the South Fork of the Coeur d'Alene River. The ceiling was even stained with huckleberry juice. Later, grab a room at the Beale House B&B in nearby Wallace and cruise the funky antiques shops, museums, and saloons in this Victorian-era mining town that flaunts its checkered past like a flag.

DAY 14

Finish your trip with a 15-mile ride along the Route of the Hiawatha trail, one of the most scenic bike rides in the Northwest. This rails-to-trails conversion of the old Milwaukee Road railway starts at the Idaho-Montana border (about 12 miles east of Wallace on I-90) and runs through a series of tunnels and over several high trestles. You can park your car at the Lookout Pass Ski Area and jump on your mountain bike (or rent one at Lookout Pass) at the trailhead, which is the starting and ending point. After a nice bike ride, go to The Fainting Goat in downtown Wallace for a well-deserved glass of wine and some appetizers.

The Gem State is a geologic wonderland. Ancient floods of massive proportion shaped this rugged topography, leaving behind strange rock formations and deep river gorges, as did a series of volcanic events that created a caldera that's still active today. Where does one even begin to choose the seven most interesting natural features of this incredibly beautiful and diverse state? It wasn't an easy decision, but here's a rundown of the Seven Wonders of Idaho as this author sees it.

- **City of Rocks:** You'll think that you've stepped onto another planet at this bizarre rockscape in the far reaches of **south-central Idaho.** Castles of eroded granite, some more than 600 feet tall, stick up like stony skyscrapers, creating a natural playground for climbers and rock-hoppers alike. You'll find two recreation areas near the Western-themed town of Almo: **City of Rocks National Reserve** and **Castle Rocks State Park.**

- **Craters of the Moon:** This amazing moonscape in **southeast Idaho** near Arco looks completely out of place in the mostly rust-and-sage-colored desert. A 250,000-acre swath of black lava scarred the earth here after some serious bouts of volcanism took place over geologic time. Now, it's the **Craters of the Moon National Monument,** a lava wonderland with cinder cones, spatter cones, lava tubes, and scenic hikes that loop around the charred hills and hinterlands of the Great Rift.

- **The Sawtooths:** These jagged mountains **north of Sun Valley** stretch into the sky like busted saw blades, thus the name. Pushed upward by the incredible force of plate tectonics, the pinnacled Sawtooths hold several ranges, including the **Boulder Mountains** and the lofty **White Cloud Peaks.** This postcard-perfect area boasts an impressive spectacle of granite faces and wooded river valleys. As a matter of fact, more than 50 peaks in the **Sawtooth National Recreation Area** stand over 10,000 feet.

- **Salmon River/Frank Church-River of No Return Wilderness:** The various forks of the wild and scenic Salmon River vein the craggy, batholithic core of the state, which comprises a majority of **central Idaho.** Elk outnumber people in this vast wilderness. Expect to see geologic wonders at every twist and turn. The Salmon River is known for its world-class whitewater rafting. Thrill seekers show up every summer for the never-ending churning rapids, which slice through some of the most beautiful high country in the United States.

- **Hells Canyon:** The western side of **north-central Idaho** borders with Oregon and Washington, but Hells Canyon, the deepest river gorge in North America, makes a border crossing here virtually impossible. The high-walled cliffs, carved out by the furious Snake River on its way to its confluence with the Columbia River in Washington, are most certainly hellish looking, especially at dusk when the sky burns bright orange. The **Hells Canyon National Recreation Area** contains, or at

Wine Country Weekend

The Snake River Valley wine country is an astonishing 8,263 square miles, but most of the state's 50-plus wineries are on the west side of the appellation. The high-desert terrain boasts rich volcanic soil, which makes for exceptional fruit. Wines produced in this region have pronounced tannins and well-balanced acidity. Syrah, cabernet sauvignon, malbec, viognier, chardonnay, and riesling are the leading varietals in the Snake River Valley.

It's important to keep in mind that most tasting rooms are typically open Friday-Sunday spring-fall, while other wineries are only open by appointment. Make sure to have a designated driver, or just sign up for a guided winery tour (described in the *Southwest Idaho* chapter).

Boise makes an excellent base camp for your wine country excursions. Good lodging picks include Hotel 43, the Modern Hotel, and Leku rock formations at City of Rocks National Reserve

least tries to contain, the **Seven Devils Range,** which hems the gorge to the east like a broken spine.

· **Lochsa River:** This densely forested wonderland in **north-central Idaho** is a veritable high-mountain playground for white-water rafters and anglers. But the Lewis and Clark expedition didn't see it that way; these early explorers ran into all kinds of problems here when they tried to cross **Lolo Pass** westward in the fall of 1805. The **Lochsa Face,** a super-steep 73,000-acre swath of land between the river and the Selway-Bitterroot Wilderness, runs parallel to the Lochsa's south bank. It's an impressive sight indeed.

· **Priest Lake:** Lakes don't get much more scenic than they do in **Idaho's Panhandle,** especially remote Priest Lake near the Canadian border. Snow-tipped peaks loom over this cedar-ringed lake (pocked out by widespread glaciers that once covered this part of North America) as it shines like a jewel down below. Two units of **Priest Lake State Park** are situated right on the shores, and there's a string of small islands with remote campgrounds. You won't be able to get the beauty of this place out of your head.

Ona Hotel, the latter of which is a good budget option.

Friday

Start your weekend of wine tasting in downtown **Boise** by checking out some vintages at the **Snake River Winery** tasting room in BoDo. This small winery produces syrah, grenache, barbera, malbec, and chardonnay, to name a few. Across town, in Garden City, is one of the best wineries in the state, **Cinder Wines.** Here you can taste syrah, chardonnay, viognier, and nearly perfect dry rosé. Next door, you'll find the **44th Street Wineries,** a co-op of smaller wineries like **Telaya Wine Company** and **Coiled Wines.** Continue on to the bedroom community of **Eagle** (about **10 miles** west of downtown Boise), where you can taste wines at **3 Horse Ranch Vineyards,** an organic winery specializing in syrah, merlot, and an extremely drinkable roussanne-viognier blend. When you're done, head to **Gino's Ristorante** in Meridian for succulent wild boar shanks and big glasses of Sangiovese.

Hells Canyon Winery

vineyard near Nampa

Saturday

After breakfast, head to the Sunny Slope area of Caldwell, which is about 35 miles west of Boise. This is the epicenter of winemaking activity in the Snake River Valley. Most of the wineries and vineyards are situated on south-facing steps near the Snake River. West of Highway 55, you should stop by Koenig Vineyards for the winery's remarkable syrah, viognier, cabernet sauvignon, and ice wine made from riesling grapes. Right up the road is Bitner Vineyards, which makes bone-dry riesling, cabernet sauvignon, and excellent chardonnay. The winery also has a small bed-and-breakfast inn if you want to stay in wine country. East of Highway 55, you'll find Ste. Chapelle Winery, a large corporate operation, and Hells Canyon Winery, a boutique winery that produces top-notch estate wines, including syrah, cabernet sauvignon, merlot, and chardonnay. You can continue to taste Idaho wines during dinner at Brick 29 Bistro, a contemporary restaurant in downtown Nampa.

Sunday

To get to the east side of the Snake River Valley from Boise, take I-84 eastbound past Mountain Home to Hammett (about 62 miles). This is where you'll find Cold Springs Winery, a small operation that makes varietal wines and blends like Hot Rod Red. Then continue east on I-84 to Glenns Ferry and stop by Crossings Winery, a good place to try wines and have brunch at the full-service restaurant overlooking the vines. Get back on I-84 eastbound and head to Bliss, then jump on U.S. 30 southbound. Take this scenic drive through the Hagerman Valley en route to Buhl, home to Holesinsky Winery, which makes excellent organic wines, and Snyder Winery, where you can taste cabernet sauvignon, syrah, chardonnay, and riesling.

Rest and Relaxation

A trip to Idaho doesn't always have to include running the rapids of a wild river or bombing down a steep single-track on a mountain bike. What about just relaxing in some hot springs or spending a lazy day checking out a museum or two? Southeast Idaho is a mellow place to pursue those activities. Pocatello and Idaho Falls are good base camps, and affordable hotel rates can be found in these sleepy burgs. This five-day itinerary will surely take care of the knots in your neck.

Day 1

Start your southeast Idaho getaway with a stay over in **Pocatello,** a college town with a handful of interesting museums. First off, check out the **Idaho Museum of Natural History** on the Idaho State University campus. Here you will be treated to a gamut of dinosaur bones, including the remains of a Columbian mammoth unearthed near Grangeville. The germaphobe in your car will surely get a kick out of the **Museum of Clean,** a repository of all things spotless. This new museum houses an extensive collection of vacuum cleaners, washing machines, toilets, mops, and more cleaning items than you could possibly shake a broom at. Afterward, take a mellow stroll along the **Portneuf Greenway,** an 11-mile interconnected recreational path that runs through town. There are several decent eateries and hotels in the downtown area.

Day 2

After breakfast, get in the car for the short drive to **Lava Hot Springs,** just off **U.S. 30,** about **36 miles** southeast of Pocatello. This is where you'll find the **Lava Recreation Complex,** a sprawling facility with three large geothermal swimming pools surrounded by a shady picnic area. After relaxing in the steamy water for a long spell, get a rubdown from one of the on-site massage therapists. You'll feel like Jell-O driving back to Pocatello.

Lava Recreations Complex at Lava Hot Springs

Day 3

Go north of Pocatello on **I-15** for **52 miles** to **Idaho Falls.** This little city has several good museums, including the **Museum of Idaho** and the **Art Museum of Eastern Idaho.** And it's hard to miss the **Mormon Temple** that punctuates the sky like a big wedding cake near the Snake River. The downtown corridor has a multitude of antiques shops, restaurants, and pubs. Most of the hotels are on the west side of the Snake River, just over the bridge from downtown.

Day 4

Get up early and head to **Heise Hot Springs,** which is about **20 miles** east of Idaho Falls on **U.S. 26** near Ririe. Locals have been hanging out at this hot springs resort for more than a century. And who can blame them? This idyllic spot along the **Snake River** in Kelly Canyon boasts a big hot springs-fed swimming pool and a row of rooms with private tubs. The park-like grounds have lots of grass and picnic benches under a canopy of shade trees. There's also a small snack bar (with pinball and air hockey machines) that serves pizzas and burgers.

Day 5

Leaving Idaho Falls, go northeast on **U.S. 20** for **53 miles** to **Ashton,** a good place to stop for lunch. Walk off all those calories with a day hike along the meandering nature trails at nearby **Harriman State Park.** Here you also can fly-fish for cutthroat trout on the fabled **Henrys Fork,** or just hang out by the river and read a book. Either way, this is a tranquil spot to decompress from the trappings of modern society.

High-Country Adventures in the Sawtooths

The Sawtooth country of central Idaho is a dreamland for outdoor enthusiasts. With a profusion of choices for backpackers, white-water rafters, mountain bikers, and anglers, this gorgeous mountain region has got you covered. Here are two suggested summer trips guaranteed to raise your heart rate and soothe your soul.

Backpacking the White Clouds

DAY 1

Take a three-day backpacking trip (or bring your mountain bike) in the White Clouds near Stanley. To access the **Boulder Chain Lakes,** head east from Stanley on **Highway 75** for about **30 miles** until you come to **East Fork Salmon River Road,** and then travel southwest on this road for **22 miles** until you arrive at the Little Boulder Creek trailhead. Don your backpack and follow the trail, which ascends next to the creek for about seven miles to the lakes. Scoop Lake is a wonderful place to camp, and fishing is excellent at this scenic locale.

DAY 2

First thing in the morning, cast a line in the tranquil lake for a hungry rainbow trout. After a healthy breakfast of pan-fried trout and eggs, explore a few of the 13 subalpine and alpine lakes that dot the map near majestic **Castle Peak.** After getting a strenuous workout and enjoying the remarkable scenery, set up camp at Castle Lake, where you can do some more fishing and sing campfire songs.

DAY 3

Strike camp and make your way back to the trailhead, taking your time along the way to enjoy the stunning vistas of the **Stanley Basin** spread out below like a verdant quilt. Travel west on **Highway 75** back to **Stanley,** where you can grab a hotel room and take a much-needed hot fishing from an inflatable boat on the Salmon River

shower then have dinner before turning in for the night.

White-Water Rafting the Salmon River
DAYS 1-3

Book a white-water rafting trip (well in advance) down the main Salmon River with Kookaburra Rafting in Salmon. A two-night, three-day rafting excursion will take you along a 45-mile stretch of this wild and scenic river, where you will be treated to rapids galore, stunningly beautiful riparian campsites, hearty meals, and wine and brews around the campfire. The trip starts at North Fork, just north of Salmon, and ends three days later at Corn Creek. Since you won't get back to Salmon until around 5:30pm on the last day, it's best to grab a hotel room there. And, once again, a hot shower will never feel so good.

The Quest for Perfect Powder

The Gem State boasts some of the best skiing in the country. Skiers and snowboarders love Idaho for its killer powder and relatively short lift lines. Here's a look at several ski resorts worth checking out.

BOISE

Sixteen miles north of Boise is **Bogus Basin Ski Resort,** which has 2,600 acres of skiable runs and a vertical drop of 1,800 feet. The resort can get crowded at times, but the views of Boise from the top are spectacular.

SOUTHEAST IDAHO

overlooking Sun Valley

Just over the Idaho border in Alta, Wyoming, **Grand Targhee Resort** boasts some of the fluffiest powder in the region. This beautiful resort has 1,500 acres of lift-served skiable terrain, with a 2,212-foot vertical drop and a base elevation of 8,000 feet.

SUN VALLEY AND THE SAWTOOTHS

Hands down the most popular ski destination in Idaho is the ultrachic **Sun Valley Resort,** which has more than 2,000 acres of skiable runs and a vertical drop of 3,400 feet. The only bummer about this place is the long lift lines and crowded slopes during peak season.

Nearby, you'll find excellent powder and much shorter lift lines at **Soldier Mountain Ski Area.** This small winter resort, just off U.S. 20 near Fairfield, has a vertical drop of 1,425 feet and 1,150 skiable acres.

NORTH-CENTRAL IDAHO

For remarkable powder and great views of Payette Lake, head to **Brundage Mountain** just outside McCall. This small resort, which can be somewhat empty if you come mid-week, has a vertical drop of 1,800 feet and 1,500 skiable acres.

Tamarack Resort, nestled in the West-Central Mountains near Donnelly, is an up-and-coming all-season resort with panoramic views of Lake Cascade. Here you will find a vertical drop of 2,800 feet and around 1,000 acres of lift-accessed runs.

THE PANHANDLE

The Panhandle has become well known for its ski resorts. While **Lookout Pass Ski and Recreation Area,** just off I-90 near the Montana border, may not get much press, it still offers shredders lots of fresh powder and beautiful alpine views. Here you'll find uncrowded slopes, 540 skiable acres, and a vertical drop of 1,150 feet.

Nearby in Kellogg, it's hard to miss **Silver Mountain Ski Resort,** mostly because the gondola—the longest of its kind in the world, at 3.1 miles—comes down the mountain right into town. The resort boasts 1,590 acres of skiable runs and a vertical drop of 2,200 feet.

Eleven miles north of Sandpoint is **Schweitzer Mountain Resort,** which earns the award for the ski resort with the best view in Idaho. From the top, you'll be treated to a 2,400-foot vertical drop, 92 excellent runs, and breathtaking panoramas of Lake Pend Oreille and a ring of mountain ranges.

Boise

Look for ★ to find recommended
sights, activities, dining, and lodging.

Highlights

© AVALON TRAVEL

★ **The Basque Block:** Boise is home to the largest Basque population in the United States. This vibrant cultural group has its own enclave in downtown Boise, with a cultural center, a museum, and a handful of Basque eateries (page 32).

★ **Idaho State Capitol:** The state capitol building recently underwent major renovation, adding two underground wings and restoring much of the original interior. It's open to the public for self-guided tours (page 33).

★ **MK Nature Center:** Area residents adore this 4.6-acre wildlife preserve and botanical garden near downtown Boise. Stroll along the shady walkways and peek through glass windows at several fish species in various stages of life (page 39).

★ **Old Idaho Penitentiary:** The Old Pen is one of only four U.S. territorial prisons still

standing. The inmates are long gone, and you can tour this medieval-looking penitentiary that's surrounded by an imposing sandstone wall (page 39).

★ **Boise River Greenbelt:** Join the locals for bicycling, running, walking, and fishing along this paved recreational path that hugs the Boise River for more than 25 miles (page 44).

★ **Bogus Basin:** Skiers and snowboarders flock to this nearby winter recreation area for fresh powder and spectacular views of Boise (page 54).

★ **Idaho Shakespeare Festival:** Fans of the bard converge every summer season at an outdoor theater near the Boise River. With a spectacular desert backdrop, the talented troupe brings to life Shakespeare's comedies and tragedies as well as contemporary plays (page 57).

Boise is hardly the little river city that it used to be, but this burgeoning capital city hasn't forgotten its storied past, as evidenced by the attractive historic districts that thrive alongside ongoing urban renewal.

The metro population is fast approaching the 650,000 mark, making Boise the third-largest city in the Northwest behind Seattle and Portland. Several gentrification projects and recently constructed high-rises have remarkably changed the city's look in the new millennium.

Boise (pronounced BOY-see, not BOY-zee) is home to a thriving high-tech industry anchored by Micron Technology, a worldwide manufacturer of semiconductor devices. Boise State University is another local institution where great minds collide, and its football team has become one of the top Division 1-A programs in the country.

The City of Trees is also a hotspot in the region for entertainment, shopping, and dining. People come from miles around, especially from the outlying rural areas, to take in all the city has to offer. Boise may be a growing urban mecca, yet it still has a mellow vibe—some even say that it's similar to how America used to be 30 years ago—and a relatively low crime rate. In other words, you are more likely to be panhandled by transients than fall victim to street crime, unless you're out stumbling the streets at 3am.

Bicycling is a popular mode of transportation here thanks to the numerous bike lanes and the Boise River Greenbelt, an urban recreation trail that runs along this scenic river for 25 miles. Many Boiseans would rather ride bicycles than drive cars. Don't be surprised to see lots of mountain bikes, fat-tired cruisers, vintage rides, and sleek road bikes zipping around town.

The lines between town and country definitely blur in Boise due to its close proximity to the northern front of the Rocky Mountains, which offers an impressive backdrop to the always-changing skyline. Locals are an active set, and they stay busy kayaking, mountain biking, skiing, and hiking in the nearby Boise Foothills and Owyhee Canyonlands.

Previous: downtown Boise; Boise Farmers Market. **Above:** Boise Depot.

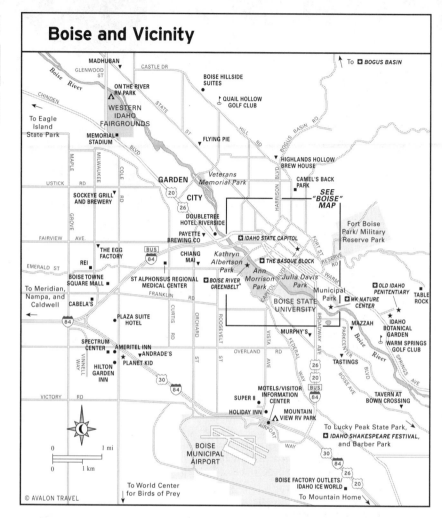

Boise and Vicinity

© AVALON TRAVEL

HISTORY

Early 19th-century French Canadian explorers were among the first nonnatives to see the location of present-day Boise, where the sprawling high desert gives way to the Boise Front of the Rocky Mountains. Can you imagine their surprise when they dropped into this scenic valley after laboring for days in the wide-open terrain of the Snake River Plain? An oft-told story is that members of this ragtag group reportedly said, *"Les bois! Les bois!"* ("The woods! The woods!") upon seeing the clusters of cottonwoods and other indigenous trees that skirted the Boise River.

About a half century later, around 1863, Fort Boise was relocated here from near present-day Parma, and these first settlers started to plant a large variety of nonnative trees that the city is now known for. These early residents seeking shady reprieve from the blazing desert sun are why Boise is called "The City of Trees." The Oregon Trail ran right down Main Street, but most of those folks were headed for the greener pastures of Oregon's Willamette Valley.

In 1865, Boise became the official capital of the Idaho Territory, designated by President Abraham Lincoln two years earlier. The City of Trees wrestled the distinction away from Lewiston, which had served as the capital for a little more than a year. Some people in the north part of the state are still sore about this shift of power.

During this period of the mid-19th century, Boise grew tremendously, from a fur-trading post to a bustling center of commerce for the nearby boomtowns in the Boise Basin and Silver City mining districts.

PLANNING YOUR TIME

Boise may be growing at a fast rate, but it's still a small city in terms of getting around town. It's easy to visit the city's most popular sites, like the Idaho State Capitol, the Basque Block and the historic Hyde Park neighborhood, in one day. But allow yourself a few extra days to fully experience Idaho's largest city and its hinterlands.

Check out the burgeoning craft-beer scene and wine-tasting rooms, where winemakers from the nearby Snake River Valley vineyards put forth their best vintages. Or you can stick with the old standbys, like taking in an al fresco play at the Idaho Shakespeare Festival, or enjoying a free Wednesday-night concert at The Grove as part of the city's summer concert series. The Boise area has a rich agricultural history, as well as a booming artisanal food scene, which you can discover at the two farmers markets that flourish with local color on Saturdays.

Boise is an excellent place for those who like to stay active while on vacation. You could spend the morning fly-fishing on the Boise River before jumping on a mountain bike and hitting the labyrinth of single-track trails in the Foothills, after which you could play a round of disc-golf at Ann Morrison Park, followed by a leisurely stroll along the Boise River Greenbelt at sunset. This may seem like a lot to do in one day, but it's definitely feasible in the City of Trees.

Year-round recreation abounds because Boise boasts a moderate climate and around 250 days of sunshine per year. Sure, winter brings a little snow and ice to the valley floor, but that generally melts away by noon. For those wanting to frolic in deep snow, head up to nearby Bogus Basin for steep alpine runs, cross-country ski and snowshoe trails, and one helluva ride down the massive tubing hill.

Sights

DOWNTOWN

Most of Boise's worthwhile sights are in or near the downtown corridor, meaning you can walk or ride a bike to these places without breaking much of a sweat. The transit system around town is in dire need of an overhaul, but during the day you can find a fairly steady stream of buses going to popular destinations. Check out www.valleyride.org for routes and schedules.

Besides the historic Old Boise and Hyde Park districts, Boise has several new districts to explore. BoDo and the Linen District, not to mention many other renewal and new construction projects, are helping to rejuvenate the downtown core. For instance, downtown Boise's skyline recently got much more pronounced thanks to the completion of the 18-story **8th & Main building,** which is now the tallest high-rise in Idaho. The new building is home to Zions Bank and has several retail shops and restaurants, including **Ruth's Chris Steak House, Flatbread Neapolitan Pizzeria,** and **On the Fly,** an upscale rotisserie-style deli.

Construction is under way on City Center Plaza, a new convention center and underground transit center next to the U.S. Bank Plaza, kitty-corner from the 8th & Main building. This project will greatly change the

Boise

face of downtown, and it will finally give the city a much-needed public transportation hub and more convention space. Construction should be completed by 2016. Check out www.boisetopia.com for a photorealistic virtual view of all the projects around town.

The Grove

Next to the U.S. Bank Plaza, south of Main Street between 8th and 9th Streets, you'll find **The Grove,** a large brick plaza with public art that many consider to be the beating heart of the city. The focal point of the plaza is a large water fountain that offers kids (and adults) a cascading reprieve from the scorching summer weather. The Grove fills with revelers every Wednesday evening during the warmer months for Alive After Five—an open-air festival with live music, dancing, and a beer garden with local microbrews.

The construction of the new convention center and transit hub will cause some disruption for events in The Grove. This might affect the happenings at Alive After Five, which is

Downtown Boise

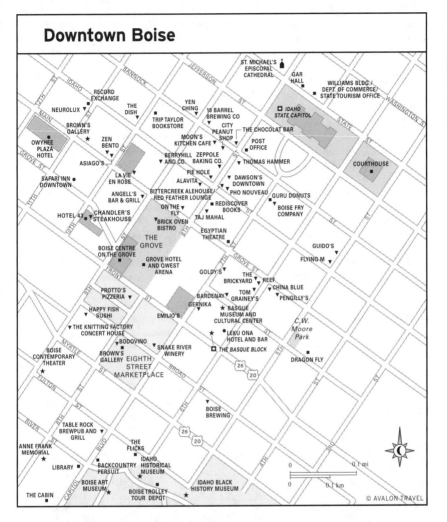

still slated to take place in The Grove (albeit in a smaller space) during this time. For updated information and concert schedules, go to www.downtownboise.org.

On one corner of the plaza is the **Grove Hotel** and **CenturyLink Arena,** a multipurpose venue that accommodates concerts and home games of the Idaho Steelheads pro hockey team and Idaho Stampede pro basketball team. Just across the way, it's hard not to notice the gargantuan **Boise Centre,** the original convention center in town that brings in thousands of people annually for conferences and local gala events.

BoDo

BoDo, Boise's latest entertainment and shopping district, consolidates the historic 8th Street Marketplace with an array of newly constructed buildings that house upscale boutiques, restaurants, and specialty shops.

BoDo is as glitzy as it gets in Boise. Boutique stores such as **Ann Taylor Loft, Urban Outfitters,** and **Helly Hansen** bring in droves of people looking for an urban shopping experience. Corporate restaurants such as **P. F. Chang's** and **Bonefish Grill** anchor the restaurant scene, but you will also find several independent eateries and bars such as **Happy Fish Sushi** and **Ha' Penny Bridge Irish Pub.** Just down the brick-clad alley, the **Knitting Factory** books an endless flurry of national touring bands.

Wine enthusiasts will surely enjoy the **Snake River Winery** tasting room and **Bodovino,** a modernized wine bar featuring 144 wines from around the globe. Have a glass of cabernet franc and some artisanal cheeses before catching a flick at BoDo's theater complex, **Edwards Cinemas Stadium 9.**

Old Boise Historic District

The **Old Boise Historic District,** on the east side of downtown, boasts a multitude of beautifully restored buildings, many of which are on the National Register of Historic Places.

Shortly after Boise was platted in 1863, this side of town soon became the premier commercial and residential district. Back then you could hop on a streetcar that ran down Main Street and out Warm Springs Avenue.

Today, Old Boise remains a beautiful and vibrant district, but the streetcar is long gone.

Coffeehouses, restaurants, bars, art galleries, and shops hum with activity day and night in buildings that once housed the city's pioneer businesses and residents. The area around 6th and Main Streets gets a little rowdy at night because of all the bars that bring in droves of college-aged partyers.

For those with an eye for classic architecture, it's hard not to miss the imposing 1904 Belgravia Building, a beautiful Romanesque structure (made with large blocks of local sandstone), at the corner of 5th and Main Streets, the city's first bona fide apartment building. In modern times, the building has been converted into offices.

Next door, **C.W. Moore Park,** named after one of Boise's most prominent denizens, is an excellent place to sip coffee and soak in some of the city's history—thanks to a gamut of relocated architectural artifacts—like a turret from the W.E. Pierce Building and a stone entrance arch from the Bush Building. There's even an antique waterwheel over a small canal on the south side of the small park, adding to the tranquility.

★ The Basque Block

Basques began settling here in significant numbers in the late 1890s. Today, Boise's

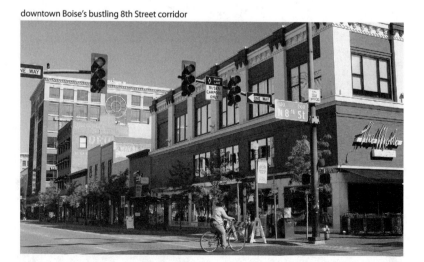

downtown Boise's bustling 8th Street corridor

Basque culture is a colorful part of the city's identity. Locals call the 600 block of Grove Street the "Basque Block." On the corner of Grove and 6th Streets is the **Basque Center,** built by Basques for Basques in 1952. The building serves as a center for Basque culture and a social center for older Basques who play cards and converse in their native tongue, but the bar is open to the public, and the sidewalk patio is a great spot to soak in the culture while enjoying a glass of Rioja.

The **Basque Museum and Cultural Center** (611 Grove St., 208/343-2671, www. basquemuseum.com, 10am-4pm Tues.-Fri., 11am-3pm Sat., $5 adults, $4 seniors, $3 ages 6-12, free under age 6) is two doors down, adjacent to the Cyrus Jacobs-Uberuaga House, Boise's oldest surviving brick building. The house was built in 1864 by Cyrus Jacobs, an early Boise merchant who eventually became mayor, and later purchased by Jose Uberuaga, a Basque who turned the residence into a boardinghouse for Basque sheepherders. Famous Idaho statesman William Borah, a longtime friend to the Basques, was married here in 1895. The museum's exhibits, including musical instruments, crafts, and other items unique to the Basques, provide a historical overview of the Basque culture in their homeland and in the United States.

On the end of the block is **Bar Gernika,** one of Boise's classic pubs. It's a great place to get a taste of Basque cuisine and culture intertwined with a hip modern scene.

Linen District

Located on the western fringe of downtown, bounded by Main and Front Streets and 13th and 16th Streets, the **Linen District** blends trendy with everyday useful. Here, carpet warehouses and industry supply stores are mingled with hip eateries, specialty shops, and the **Modern Hotel,** a mid-20th-century-inspired boutique hotel, restaurant, and bar.

The focal point is along Grove Street, where you will also find **Big City Coffee, Mouvance Winery,** and a stylish Italian-inspired market and café called **A 'Tavola.**

★ Idaho State Capitol

Just after the turn of the 20th century, prominent Boise architect J. E. Tourtelloutte was commissioned to draw up plans for the state capitol. He came up with a neoclassic design modeled after the U.S. Capitol, albeit on a smaller scale. Construction on the **Idaho State Capitol** began in 1905 and was

Take a break at C.W. Moore Park.

completed in 1920. It's the only capitol building in the country heated with geothermal hot water.

Outside, the building is a rather drab tan color due to the exterior use of Boise sandstone; multi-ton blocks were quarried behind the old Idaho State Penitentiary and hauled to the site by convicts. Inside, however, the impressive rotunda sports vast amounts of marble from Alaska (gray), Georgia (red), Vermont (green), and Italy (black). Sixty-foot-high faux-marble pillars support the dome. Around the four-story interior are changing exhibits put together by many state agencies and special-interest groups. The 1st floor holds a portrait gallery of Idaho's territorial governors, while the 4th floor is home to the Statuary Hall, where a replica of the *Winged Victory of Samothrace,* a gift from the French following World War II, is prominently displayed. Also on the 4th floor are the entrances to the House and Senate galleries, where you can watch Idaho's lawmakers in action when the legislature is in session. The 2nd and 3rd floors house the executive-branch offices and the legislative chambers, respectively.

Back outside, a circuit of the grounds reveals some interesting finds. Across Jefferson Street stands a bronze statue of former governor Frank Steunenberg, assassinated in 1905, supposedly in retaliation for his use of federal troops to squelch the Silver Valley mining riots some six years earlier. On the front steps of the capitol is a replica of the Liberty Bell, sans crack, and nearby you'll spot a seacoast cannon that was used by the Confederacy in the Civil War.

The capitol is open for **self-guided tours** (6am-6pm Mon.-Fri., 9am-5pm weekends). A free walking-tour booklet is available at the visitor information desk on the 1st floor. One-hour **guided tours** (208/332-1012, 10am-1pm Mon.-Fri., minimum five people, reserve at least two weeks in advance) are also available.

Jack's Urban Meeting Place

Jack's Urban Meeting Place (www.jacksurbanmeetingplace.org), referred to as JUMP, is slated to open in 2016 in downtown Boise. This nonprofit, interactive community center, bounded by 9th and 11th Streets and Broad and Myrtle Streets, pays homage to Jack Simplot, a potato farmer who became a billionaire after landing the frozen fries contract with McDonald's in the 1960s. He passed away in 2008, but his legacy lives on with this beautiful new building (funded by the Simplot family) that features public studio spaces for

the Basque Block

Idaho's Basque Country

The Boise area is home to more than 10,000 Basque Americans, the largest population in one city outside the Basque country of Spain. A Basque bar, Basque restaurants, Basque dancers, and a vibrant Basque block add cultural spice to Idaho's capital city.

Basques first began coming to Boise soon after the city was founded; by 1910 the city's Basque population was sizable. In traditional Basque culture, only one child inherits all the family wealth. The others—drawn by stories of goldfield bonanzas and high wages—made their way to the western United States. Many found work as miners, others as ranch hands. A large number became sheepherders, though it wasn't their experience back home that got them that job. Some of them had never tended sheep before; others had run small herds in their homeland, but nothing the size of the operations common to Idaho and the West. But it was a job that they could get without needing to speak English and that few others were willing to take because of its solitary nature.

Jaialdi festival

The Basque shepherds quickly gained a reputation for hard work and reliability.

Basques eventually assimilated into American culture and today are intertwined into Boise's social fabric. Most of the sheepherders now hail from Peru, but they still use the same rustic-looking camp wagons that the Basques once used, and blue heelers and border collies are still the preferred dog breeds for herding sheep.

On Boise's Basque Block, you can taste Basque cuisine at **Gernika, Leku Ona,** and the **Basque Market;** see traditional Basque dances performed by the **Oinkari Basque Dancers;** and get an overview of the unique culture at the **Basque Museum and Cultural Center.** If you're in town for the annual **Festival of San Inazio** at the end of July, you can get a full-blown introduction to Basque life. And if that suits your fancy, make plans to attend the next **Jaialdi,** an international Basque cultural festival organized by the **Basque Museum** (208/343-2671, www.jaialdi.com) that brings to town more than 40,000 people every five years, slated to take place next in late July 2020.

artists, public art, an urban park with an outdoor amphitheater, and a museum of antique tractors. The J.R. Simplot Company will be relocating its corporate offices to this location as well.

Capital City Public Market

Eighth Street in downtown Boise explodes in a flourish of color every Saturday April-November. The **Capital City Public Market** (www.capitalcitypublicmarket.com, 9:30am-1:30pm) is the state's largest Saturday market. Expect to find lots of fresh organic produce, farm-fresh eggs, natural meats, and prepared goodies such as crepes and flaky breakfast pastries. There is also a plethora of nonfood artisans selling handcrafted soap, photography, pottery, jewelry, and fused-glass art.

Boise Farmers Market

Serious foodies do their weekly shopping at this new farmers market in downtown Boise, held on the same day and just two blocks away (in a big parking lot at the corner of 10th and Grove Streets) from the Capital City Public Market. **Boise Farmers Market** (www.theboisefarmersmarket.com, 9am-1pm Sat., early Apr.-late Dec.) focuses on food and wine, so don't expect to find any duct tape wallets and fused-glass earrings here. What you will find is a profusion of seasonally fresh local foodstuffs, ranging from farmstead goat cheese to American Kobe beef to a bevy of organic produce. Several Snake River Valley boutique wineries show up weekly as well. The market also has mobile food vendors, like stone-oven pizza and fusion tacos, to feed the hungry masses.

NORTH END AND HYDE PARK

Some of Boise's most appealing architecture is found in the city's quiet **North End,** between State Street and the foothills. The tree-canopied streets are lined with beautiful Victorian homes and craftsman-era bungalows.

Bounded by 8th and 14th Streets and Hays and State Streets, numerous historic churches vie with one another for eye appeal, including the ivy-covered English Gothic **St. Michael's Episcopal Cathedral** (518 N. 8th St. at W. State St.), which first organized a congregation in 1864, just after the city itself was established. The magnificent **First United Methodist Church** (11th St. and W. Franklin St.) is called the "Cathedral of the Rockies." The modern Gothic steeple and its ornate stonework can be seen from some distance in

all directions, and it's an impressive edifice from any angle.

Hyde Park was Boise's first suburb, dating back to 1891. It's an attractive historic neighborhood located about a mile north of downtown. Growth in the district really spiked in the early 20th century once a Boise Rapid Transit trolley line was added to the 13th Street corridor.

The trolley line was removed years ago, but Hyde Park's main drag (North 13th Street between Alturas and Brumback Streets) is still a thriving business district where you will find a string of restaurants, coffeehouses, and antiques shops. Grab an ice-cream cone at **Goody's Soda Fountain** or a big burrito and a local brew at **Parrilla Grill.** The **Dunia Marketplace** is also worth checking out. This nonprofit store specializes in fair-trade artisan handicrafts from around the world. To get to Hyde Park, hop on the bus (Rte. 14) from downtown.

JULIA DAVIS PARK AND VICINITY

Thomas Jefferson Davis was one of Boise's earliest pioneer settlers. He and his brother homesteaded 360 acres here in 1863, raising vegetables that they sold to the Boise Basin

fall squash at the Boise Farmers Market

BAM members and under age 6) is growing in reputation with each passing exhibit. A gamut of major traveling exhibitions have been shown here over the years, like sculptures by Edward Degas, landscape paintings by Georgia O'Keeffe, and blown-glass art by Dale Chihuly. Its permanent collection includes the Glenn C. Janss collection of American realism, featuring some absolutely amazing photorealist works. A small store sells arts and crafts, art-related books, and art postcards. In addition to providing Boiseans a visual feast, the museum also hosts events year-round, plus the big Art in the Park festival each September.

Idaho Historical Museum

The **Idaho Historical Museum** (610 N. Julia Davis Dr., 208/334-2120, www.idahohistory. net) is also housed in Julia Davis Park, but it's currently closed and undergoing extensive renovation and expansion, which will add around 13,000 square feet to the existing Cold War-era building. This will allow thousands of artifacts that have been gathering dust in storage to be seen by the general public for the first time, in addition to the historical objects of significance already in the permanent collection. The museum plans to reopen in 2017.

Zoo Boise

Zoo Boise (355 N. Julia Davis Dr., 208/384-4260, www.zooboise.org, 9am-5pm daily, closed major holidays, $10 ages 12-61, $8 over age 62, $7 ages 3-11, free under age 3) is a great place to take the kids when they start to get bored. The more than 80 species include red pandas, penguins, zebras, giraffes, meerkats, birds of prey, and monkeys galore, to name a few. The zoo is open year-round, but many of the larger animals are moved inside during the winter and not available for viewing. But the steamy indoor rain forest exhibit is not a bad spot to hang out on a frigid day.

Discovery Center of Idaho

On the park's northern fringe is the **Discovery Center of Idaho** (131 Myrtle

historic Hyde Park

mining communities. On July 7, 1863, Davis and a handful of men got together in Davis's log cabin to lay out the city of Boise. In 1871, Davis married Julia McCrum of Ontario, Canada. The new couple's agricultural empire grew over the years, and they continued to add to their real estate holdings in the valley. In their retirement they offered the city about 40 acres along the river for a park. It took awhile to settle the arrangements, but in 1907 **Julia Davis Park** (700 S. Capitol Blvd.) became a reality. Today, the park is the queen of Boise's park system, home to many of the city's major attractions and plenty of open space. Plus, the park has the most beautiful rose garden in town.

Boise Art Museum

Beautiful inside and out, the **Boise Art Museum** (670 S. Julia Davis Dr., 208/345-8330, www.boiseartmuseum.org, 10am-5pm Tues.-Sat., noon-5pm Sun., closed Mon. and holidays, $6 adults, $4 seniors, $3 kids grades 1-12 and college students with ID, free to

Extreme Capitol Makeover

In 2010, a major capitol restoration project was completed at the cost of $120 million to state taxpayers. Besides extensive renovation to the original exterior, the interior was given lots of love, including refinished marble and wood flooring, upgraded lighting, hardware restoration, and the addition of a new passenger elevator. Speaking of elevators, construction workers found a nice surprise when they tore down a wall-sized bookcase on the 1st floor, unveiling a beautifully preserved electric elevator from the early 20th century. The shaft was plugged long ago, but the birdcage-like elevator is now part of the capitol tour.

Idaho State Capitol after major renovation

There was much more than restoration going on while the building was closed to the general public for two years. The project also included the construction of two 25,000-square-foot underground wings. These subterranean structures (barely visible from the street) are used for additional legislative offices and hearing rooms. The only downside to the construction was that 11 century-old trees had to be cut down to make way for the digging. Unfortunately, these included an oak tree planted by Benjamin Harrison and an Ohio buckeye planted by William Taft.

A creative caveat to this tree felling is that more than 4,000 board feet of wood was made available to local artists for various projects. Idaho State Rep. Max Black, an ardent woodworker and Republican lawmaker who spearheaded the drive, carved out a wooden replica of an Oregon Short Line steam engine, which has been part of a rotating display in the Statuary Hall on the 4th floor. A permanent Idaho history exhibit was also installed four flights down the marble steps on the garden level.

St., 208/343-9895, www.dcidaho.org, 10am-8pm Mon.-Fri., 10am-5pm Sat.- Sun., closed major holidays, $15 adults, $10 seniors, $10 ages 3-17, free for members and under age 3). More than 100 wild, wacky, and amazing hands-on exhibits—a spelling robot, an air-brake chair, and a seven-foot tornado, to name just a few—fill this huge, mad-scientist-in-training's classroom. Kids love this place, and it's popular with adults too.

WARM SPRINGS AVENUE

Warm Springs Avenue was one of early Boise's most prestigious addresses, and many beautifully restored Victorian and Queen Anne-style homes can be seen as you cruise down the shady tree-lined avenue. The street didn't get its name for nothing: Boise's abundant geothermal resources were developed early in the city's history. Today, many of the homes here continue to be heated with naturally hot water, as is the state capitol.

Pioneer Cemetery

Boise founders Julia Davis and Thomas Jefferson Davis, early Idaho governor George Shoup, and pioneer notables and nobodies alike share this final resting place in **Pioneer Cemetery,** near the intersection of Warm Springs and Broadway Avenues. The simple, poignant graves remain unadulterated by modern historical plaques or keep-away-from-the-history barriers. It's a nice spot for a picnic amid the ghosts of Boise's forefathers and foremothers.

★ MK Nature Center

Squirrels chatter in the trees, rainbow trout cruise sheltered pools, birds practice avian arias, and brightly colored flowers face the sun to shout off the morning dew. It's all at the **MK Nature Center** (600 S. Walnut St., 208/334-2225 or 208/368-6060, trails sunrise-sunset, free; visitors center 9am-5pm Tues.-Fri., 11am-5pm Sat.-Sun., free), a miniature 4.6-acre wildlife preserve and botanical garden a couple of blocks south of Warm Springs Avenue. Trails lead past a rushing stream and a tranquil glade to unique exhibits like a cut-away glass-walled stream where you can watch many of Idaho's native fish species cavorting in their underwater realm. The visitors center holds additional exhibits and a gift shop.

★ Old Idaho Penitentiary

The **Old Idaho Penitentiary** (2445 Old Penitentiary Rd., 208/334-2844, noon-5pm daily, $5 adults, $4 seniors, $3 ages 6-12, free under age 6) is one of only four U.S. territorial prisons still standing. It was built in 1870 and remained in use for more than a century. Among its famous tenants: Harry Orchard, convicted for the 1905 assassination of Governor Frank Steunenberg; and Lyda "Lady Bluebeard" Southard, convicted of killing her fourth husband for insurance money and suspected of doing away with the first three as well.

The Old Pen looks like something from another time—part Wild West military fortification, part medieval castle. It's hard to imagine that a 19th-century cellblock with no internal plumbing ("night buckets" were used) served inmates until the 1970s. Not surprisingly, the antiquated conditions led to a riot in 1973 that resulted in the gutting of a couple of buildings. That event helped convince the powers that be to move the prison to a new facility more appropriate to the 20th century. Now you can tour this State Historic Site, which boasts a beautiful rose garden that juxtaposes the original prison gallows, where numerous unfortunate convicts were dispatched to their final resting places. The self-guided walking tour takes approximately 90 minutes.

Idaho Botanical Garden

In the shadow of the Old Pen you'll find the **Idaho Botanical Garden** (2355 Old Penitentiary Rd., 208/343-8649, www.idaho-botanicalgarden.org, 9am- 9pm daily Mar. 15-Nov. 15, $7 adults, $5 seniors and ages 5-12, free under age 5). One species or another will be in bloom late April-mid-October. A humble

MK Nature Center

labor of love relying heavily on memberships and volunteer efforts, the gardens provide an always-welcome oasis of tranquil greenery. Various trails snake around the grounds, with picnic tables and benches placed strategically. The Idaho Botanical Garden has turned into a popular summer concert venue in recent years, aptly called Outlaw Field. Big-name acts like Willie Nelson, Bob Dylan, Modest Mouse, and Steely Dan have brought in big crowds to this otherwise sleepy part of town. And during the holiday season, Winter Garden aGlow beautifully illuminates the desert.

BOISE STATE UNIVERSITY

More than 22,000 students pursue undergraduate and graduate degrees at **Boise State University** (BSU, 208/426-1011, www.boise-state.edu), making it the largest university in Idaho and one of the West's fastest-growing schools. This vibrant urban university is situated right on the banks of the Boise River. Don't be surprised to see professors and students fly-fishing in between classes below the Friendship Bridge, which connects the campus to Julia Davis Park.

Campus Highlights

On the west end of campus along the river is **Morrison Center for the Performing Arts** (tickets 208/426-1609 or 208/426-1110). Considered one of the country's most acoustically perfect performance halls, the award-winning Morrison Center schedules musical and cultural events throughout the year. Tours of the 2,000-seat facility are offered by advance arrangement.

The **Hemingway Western Studies Center** (208/426-1999) focuses on the works and study of Western writers and other artists. The center also holds Hemingway memorabilia, including pictures of Papa's Ketchum home and a magazine article reprinting a letter Hemingway wrote to his editor grousing about young wannabe writers dropping by uninvited and interrupting his work. It also houses the **Idaho Film Collection,** an

the stone walls at the Old Idaho Penitentiary

archive of films made in the Gem State that includes the works of silent filmmaker Nell Shipman. A small **art gallery** (10am-5pm Mon.-Fri., noon-5pm Sat., free) presents student projects and exhibits related to the West.

Centennial Amphitheater is a delightful open and grassy 800-seat amphitheater within earshot of the Boise River. It's a great place to have a picnic. The adjacent road heading away from the river into the heart of campus leads to **Taco Bell Arena** (tickets 208/426-1494, www.broncosports.com). A variety of events—from BSU Broncos basketball games to major concerts like Macklemore and Lady Antebellum—are staged in this 13,000-seat arena. Looking east from the arena, you can't miss the imposing **Albertsons Stadium** (tickets 208/426-1494, www.broncosports.com) on the east edge of campus. For better or worse, this 37,000-seat stadium is known throughout the country not only as the home of the BSU Broncos football team but for its bright blue artificial turf, known to some as "Smurf Turf." Thanks to the incredible success of the university's football team in recent years, the stadium recently underwent a series of major expansion projects—adding glitzy skyboxes, more season ticket seating, a 97,000-square-foot indoor practice facility, and a **Bronco Shop** (208/426-4887), a ground-level store with shelves full of blue-and-orange BSU gear.

The **Student Union Building,** the on-campus social hub, contains the **university bookstore** (208/426-2665), an art gallery, a food court, pool tables, and even a small bowling alley. Adjacent is the **Special Events Center,** a theater used for seminars and performances, and across the parking lot on the 1st floor of the Liberal Arts Building is the **Visual Arts Center Gallery** (daily during the school year, free).

BSU has a **recreation center** (1515 University Dr., 208/426-5641), but unfortunately, most of it is only open to Boise State students, employees, and alumni. There are exceptions, though, like the outdoor program's equipment rental center, where guests of people associated with the university are allowed to check out gear. The newish **Cycle Learning Center** (www.rec.boisestate.edu/clc/rentals), located across the street in the Lincoln Garage building, offers cruiser bike and mountain bike rentals to the general public, as well as bike repairs and accessories.

Tours and Information

Tours leave the **New Student Information Center** (208/426-1820) in the Student Union Building at 10am and 1pm Monday-Friday during the school year. The center can also provide campus maps and further information about the university.

Parking

Metered parking is available all around campus, and pay parking is available for visitors in two relatively new parking garages (University Dr. and Lincoln Ave., and University Dr. near Capitol Blvd.). For more information, call the **Parking Office** (208/426-7275). The BSU campus is a short walk from downtown, and the city transit system operates a shuttle bus around campus.

EAST BOISE

East of the university, ParkCenter Boulevard runs close to the Boise River Greenbelt. Here you will see the headquarters of two corporations that helped to define Boise's reputation in the business world: URS Corporation (formerly Morrison-Knudsen) and the Albertsons

Boise State University

grocery chain. Near these corporate campuses there are several restaurants, hotels, and other businesses, as well as the **ParkCenter Pond,** a popular urban fishing hole.

Bown Crossing

Travel southeast on ParkCenter Boulevard and you will eventually come to **Bown Crossing,** a startup district that places an emphasis on pedestrian traffic. This 35-acre development has nearly 100 residences—craftsman patio homes, townhouses, and apartment lofts—mixed in with restaurants, boutiques, and specialty shops. History buffs will like the informative Oregon Trail markers that run down Boise Avenue adjacent to the district.

Leaving Bown Crossing, cruising north, you will cross over the Boise River on the ParkCenter Bridge. Immediately on the right is **Marianne Williams Park,** a public green space that opened in 2012.

Harris Ranch

Heading north on East ParkCenter Boulevard will lead you to the **Harris Ranch** neighborhood (on E. Warm Springs Ave.), where housing developments have replaced a sprawling cattle ranch that once dominated Barber Valley. Besides lots of upscale houses, Harris Ranch is also home to **Lucky 13,** a popular pizza and sandwich joint that relocated here from Hyde Park a few years back.

Continue traveling east on Warm Springs Avenue and you will find the **Idaho Parks and Recreation Department** (5657 Warm Springs Ave., 208/334-4199, www. parksandrecreation.idaho.gov) and the **Idaho Shakespeare Festival** en route to Highway 21.

OTHER SIGHTS
Idaho Anne Frank Human Rights Memorial

In 2002, Idaho dedicated the **Idaho Anne Frank Human Rights Memorial,** a moving tribute to the teenage author whose family hid from the Nazis during World War II. A statue of Anne Frank is next to the United Nations Universal Declaration of Human Rights and powerful quotes from human rights advocates through history. A series of educational voice boxes were recently installed that can be heard in English and Spanish. The monument is accessible from the Greenbelt between Capitol Boulevard and 9th Street, or by walking behind The Cabin Literary Center (801 S. Capitol Blvd.).

Bown Crossing in East Boise

farther; look for the sign on the right). It's on a hilltop only 15 minutes from the city but a world away—worth the trip just to experience the wind blowing across the sage and grasses, unimpeded by gas stations and shopping malls.

The Peregrine Fund started in 1970 from efforts to save the peregrine falcon, whose populations were on the decline before this nonprofit organization decided to step in. The peregrine was removed from the endangered species list in 1999. The Peregrine Fund continues its work to restore viable populations of other endangered raptors worldwide.

The **Velma Morrison Interpretive Center** (10am-5pm daily June-Aug., 10am-5pm Tues.-Sun. Sept.-May, $7 adults, $6 seniors, $5 ages 4-16, free under age 4) has slide presentations to fill you in on the status of endangered raptors worldwide as well as the fund's efforts to preserve them. You'll see a couple of individuals up close and personal, perhaps a harpy eagle headed for the jungles of South and Central America, or a huge California condor. Outside are several birds of prey species, all incapable of surviving life in the wild for one reason or another.

Idaho Anne Frank Human Rights Memorial

Boise Depot and Platt Gardens

The city of Boise owns the **Boise Depot** (2603 Eastover Terr., 208/384-9591, open to the public 11am-5pm Sun. and Mon., free), the beautiful old Union Pacific station perched on a bench at the south end of Capitol Boulevard. The Amtrak route that once stopped here was abandoned in 1997. The depot's Great Hall holds railroad memorabilia. Climb up into the bell tower for a great view of the capitol and downtown. Outside the depot you'll see "Big Mike," a Japanese-made steam engine from the early 20th century, as well as **Platt Gardens,** a small landscaped hillside with fountains, koi ponds, and trees.

Peregrine Fund World Center for Birds of Prey

The **Peregrine Fund World Center for Birds of Prey** (5668 W. Flying Hawk Ln., 208/362-8687, www.peregrinefund.org) lies six miles south of I-84 (take S. Cole Rd. south to the end and continue straight ahead a bit

SIGHTSEEING TOURS
Boise Trolley Tours

Boise Trolley Tours (208/433-0849, www. americanheritagetrolleytours.com, tours 11am Mon.-Fri., 2pm Sat.-Sun., $18 adults, $16 seniors and ages 13-18, $8 ages 3-12, $4 under age 3) provides a reasonable way to get an overview and background on some of the key parts of the city. All tours depart from Joe's Crab Shack (2288 N. Garden St.) next to the Riverside Hotel. It's not actually a trolley on tracks but a bus that's gussied up to look like a trolley. It'll take you around Boise for a one-hour narrated tour, introducing you to Julia Davis Park, the historic Warm Springs neighborhood, the Old Idaho Penitentiary, the capitol area, and the Old Boise Historic District. An informative narration reels off the history and fun facts of the city.

Flightseeing

SP Aircraft (4888 W. Aeronca St., 208/383-3323, www.spaircraft.com), a scenic and charter air service based near the airport, will take passengers up in a Cessna 172 on a one-hour air tour for around $260 per hour (up to three people). They also offer backcountry flight packages.

Sports and Recreation

This is an outdoors-oriented town. As soon as the spring rains end, Boise's hills come alive with a profusion of wildflowers and the sounds of ratcheting derailleurs. Mountain bikers are everywhere—up on the Boise Front, along the Greenbelt, in the streets downtown. Warm spring and summer evenings find the streets crowded with walkers and joggers, getting after-work exercise or just enjoying the City of Trees. And come the dog days of summer, the Boise River and local reservoirs draw water-sports enthusiasts by the thousands. You can float the Boise right through downtown, past park after verdant park. Or go white-water rafting on the Payette River, less than an hour outside town. When winter snows blanket the Boise Mountains, the skis come out of the closets, bound for Bogus Basin Ski Area. Both alpine and cross-country skiing there is close enough to get to after work or even on a long lunch hour.

CITY PARKS

No matter which part of town you're in, you'll almost certainly be near one of the more than 90 parks maintained by the City of Boise. The parks range in size from the grand Julia Davis and Ann Morrison Parks to smaller pocket parks dotting the city. Several of the most popular parks are described below. For a complete list of parks and their respective facilities, contact the **Boise Parks and Recreation Department** (1104 Royal Blvd., 208/384-4240, www.cityofboise.org/parks).

All city parks are open sunrise to sunset. Dogs must be kept on a leash and are not allowed at Municipal Park off Warm Springs Avenue or at Platt Gardens adjacent to the Boise Depot. (Dogs can play off-leash in a designated dog park at Fort Boise Park, as long as they're under your control.) Beer and wine are permitted at most of the parks, except where expressly prohibited. (Hard alcohol and glass containers are not permitted.) The Parks Department asks that you not feed the waterfowl or any other wildlife you might encounter.

★ Boise River Greenbelt

The beautiful, modestly sized Boise River flows through the heart of the city. Its lushly lined banks have been preserved as the city's signature park, the 25-mile **Boise River Greenbelt** that connects 850 acres of parks and riparian wetlands. Here you will find paved trails on either side of the river that wind along the banks, drawing strollers, bicyclists, joggers, and skaters. Several small piers jut out into the river in places, some half hidden by luxuriant greenery, while benches overlooking the water provide ideal places for quiet contemplation.

Wildlife also enjoys this riparian oasis. You'll see abundant waterfowl, and if you get lucky, you might spy bald eagles, blue herons, great horned owls, muskrats, beavers, deer, foxes, or even a cougar cruising the bushes. At some points along the trails, the downtown skyline comes into view, reminding you just how close this tranquil escape is to the urban core. The Greenbelt runs from Garden City in the west (with plans to eventually expand onto Eagle Island) to the Discovery Unit of Lucky Peak State Park in the east. Other major access points include Veterans Memorial Park, Ann Morrison Park (enter from Americana Blvd.), and Julia Davis Park, off Capitol Boulevard. But head down to the river anywhere in town and you should be able to find the Greenbelt trails with no difficulty.

Ann Morrison Park

The 153-acre **Ann Morrison Park** lines the south side of the Boise River between Americana and Capitol Boulevards. It's mostly level and grassy, suitable for kite-flying and pickup soccer games. There's also an 18-hole disc-golf course, plus nice picnic areas and a big playground. Tubers generally haul out here after floating down from Barber Park.

Julia Davis Park

Julia Davis Park is the "sights" park, home of Zoo Boise, the Boise Art Museum, the Idaho Historical Museum, a rose garden, and a band shell. The tennis courts here see a lot of use, as do the pedal boats you can rent for a cruise around the park's pond. The park is bounded by Capitol Boulevard on the west, Front Street on the north, Broadway Avenue on the east, and the Boise River on the south.

Kathryn Albertson Park

You can't miss the entrance sign for **Kathryn Albertson Park,** the tranquil, 40-acre wildlife preserve just across Americana Boulevard

from Ann Morrison Park; its name is chiseled into 11 huge sandstone boulders that look like something out of *The Flintstones.* Paved trails wind around ponds, where many species of birds and other animals can be seen. The park was specifically designed to encourage wildlife. This park is a great spot for quiet meditation, a relaxing picnic, or an outdoor wedding. Swimming and fishing are prohibited, and dogs must be kept on a leash.

Marianne Williams Park

The newest in the string of Boise's female-named parks, fondly referred to as the "Ribbon of Jewels," the 70-acre **Marianne Williams Park** debuted in 2011 on East ParkCenter Boulevard near Bown Crossing. Prominent Boise businessman Larry Williams, who once operated a lumber mill on the site, donated the property to the city; the park is named after his wife, Marianne. Expect to find lots of green space, paved walkways, picnic areas, and a fishing dock. As an added bonus, an offshoot of the Greenbelt runs right through it.

Camel's Back Park and Reserve

North of Hyde Park out along 13th Street, **Camel's Back Park and Reserve** has two

the grand entrance to Ann Morrison Park

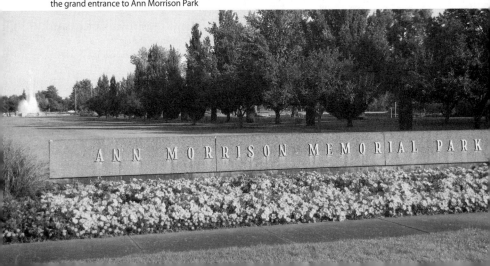

components. The corner lot at 13th and Heron offers an expanse of green grass with a soccer field, tennis courts, trees, and a large children's play area with some neat equipment. Behind this area is the camel's back itself—a couple of humps of hills rising up about 100 feet. Hike up to the top for a great view of the city; this is a popular place to watch fireworks. On the other side of the humps, trails continue down to the 8th Street trailhead.

Fort Boise Park and Military Reserve Park

Fort Boise was built in 1863 as a base from which the U.S. 9th Cavalry could protect Oregon Trail emigrants from attack by hostile Native Americans. The guardhouse at 5th and Fort Streets is the original sandstone structure. In addition to the many original buildings and parade grounds, a number of newer government buildings have been added, including Veterans' Hospital and the Idaho Veterans' Home. A historic officer's row sits on the hill above the hospital.

A trail leads to the top of Camel's Back Park.

Fort Boise Park is also the hub of Boise Parks and Recreation activities. The **Fort Boise Community Center** (700 Robbins Rd., 208/384-4486) houses the city recreation office, a community weight room and gym, an art center, and lots more. Fort Boise Park also has a skate park, tennis courts, and ball fields. The **Boise Little Theater** (100 E. Fort St., 208/342-5104) is here too.

Military Reserve Park encompasses 466 acres of brush-covered foothills behind Fort Boise Park, where there's also an old cemetery with headstone after headstone of Civil War veterans from different parts of the country. Only a few dirt roads cross the park, but dozens of hiking and biking trails lace the hills. It's a quick-access wild area just three blocks from the city. Sagebrush scents and some great city views make the park a good place for a day hike or a trail run.

ParkCenter Pond

This eight-acre pond amid the hotels and offices of **ParkCenter** is a favorite spot for float-tube fishing and windsurfing. Sand volleyball courts and picnic tables round out the offerings. Hatchery-raised rainbow trout get planted here throughout the year.

Municipal Park

Your basic picnic venue, **Municipal Park** has large grassy areas that make it a natural for family reunions or employee get-togethers. But anyone can enjoy the shade and tranquility. Off Warm Springs Avenue, it's near the MK Nature Center.

Veterans Memorial Park

The front half of **Veterans Memorial Park** (36th St. and State St., west of town, sunrise-sunset) has neatly trimmed lawns, stately evergreens, a small amphitheater, and a solemn memorial to Idaho's fallen veterans. But head down to the back half and the park turns wild: The river flows through it, bringing swamps and riverine jungles that attract would-be Huck Finns with fishing poles as well as bicyclists and joggers who work up a sweat doing laps on the cool, quiet trails. A large lake separated from the river by a narrow isthmus provides calm water for swimming or floating around on a raft.

COUNTY AND STATE PARKS
Barber Park

East of town, 87-acre **Barber Park** (Eckert Rd., off Warm Springs Ave., 208/343-1328) draws tubers in summer for the six-mile float down the Boise River to Ann Morrison Park. You can rent tubes and rafts (208/577-4584) in the summertime. In addition, the park offers fishing access, trees and grass, and shaded picnic areas. A $5 parking fee is charged in the summer floating season to offset the cost of keeping this tidy, well-maintained Ada County park in such good shape. The park is on the Greenbelt bike path and makes a nice destination for a half-day bike ride out from downtown.

Lucky Peak State Park

Lucky Peak Reservoir, about a 15-minute drive east of downtown, is Boise's premier place to escape the heat of summer. **Lucky Peak State Park** (208/334-4199, day-use only, Memorial Day-Labor Day) comprises three different units, one on the reservoir and two downstream from Lucky Peak Dam.

Coming from downtown Boise, take Warm Springs Avenue east. Eventually it turns into Highway 21. The first part of the park, about eight miles from town, is the **Discovery Unit** (day-use $5). The beautiful grassy park along the riverbank offers plenty of sun and shade, picnic tables, and some barbecue grills. No lifeguards are on duty, and some tricky currents in places make swimming potentially dangerous and certainly not recommended for small children.

Take the kids instead a bit farther upstream to the 25-acre **Sandy Point Unit** (208/334-2679, 7am-9pm daily summer, lifeguards on duty 11am-6pm daily summer, day-use $5), right below the dam. A calm cove here surrounds a fountain and makes a great place to float around on tubes or rafts, both of which can be rented from the concessionaire.

Finally, the **Spring Shores Unit** (day-use $5) is nine miles farther up the highway toward Idaho City on Lucky Peak Reservoir. The road curves over Highland Pass, past hillsides blanketed with arrowleaf balsamroot—brilliantly yellow in spring—and then drops down to the reservoir (turn right off the highway just across Mores Creek Bridge).

Lucky Peak State Park

Bicycle City USA

Tour de Fat-Boise bike parade

It doesn't take long after arriving in Boise to figure out that those who live here have bicycles on their brains. You'll see people whizzing around on cool cruisers, tricked-out mountain bikes, and really nice road bikes.

If you're lucky, you might even spot Olympic gold medalist Kristin Armstrong, who lives in Boise, taking a morning ride along Hill Road. (Armstrong is no relation to Lance Armstrong or his ex-wife, who also happens to be named Kristin.) She is a University of Idaho graduate and three-time national champion road racer. Her biggest achievements came when she won gold in the Women's Time Trial at the 2008 and 2012 Summer Olympics. Needless to say, she came home both times to a hero's welcome and a grand bike parade in downtown Boise.

On the benevolent side of biking, the **Boise Bicycle Project** (1027 Lusk St., 208/429-6520, www.boisebicycleproject.org) is a nonprofit community-run bicycle cooperative that fixes up donated bikes and gives them to low-income families. BBP also offers bike repair workshops, teaching people how to work on their own rides.

Boise hosts several exciting bicycling events, like the July **Twilight Criterium,** which brings in more than 100 professional road racers for a nighttime sprint through the streets of downtown Boise. Twenty thousand screaming fans line the sidewalks for this annual race, which has a Kid's Ride (led by Kristin Armstrong, no less) earlier in the day. If you like suds and bikes, check out **Tour de Fat-Boise,** a beer and bicycle blowout, sponsored by New Belgium Brewing Company, that happens every August in Ann Morrison Park. The costumed bike parade is a hoot. Please drink and ride responsibly.

This is the boaters' unit of the park—water-skiers, Jet Skiers, bass boaters, sailboarders, and even a few sailboaters come here to do their thing in the high-desert lake rimmed by mountains. Anglers try their luck at pulling rainbow trout, smallmouth bass, kokanee, perch, and whitefish from the glimmering waters. The large **marina** (208/336-9505) offers numerous slips and a boat-launching ramp.

The concessionaire also runs a small snack bar, sells boating supplies, and rents boats. A few picnic tables line the shore.

BICYCLING

Boise is a great bicycling town. In addition to the **Greenbelt,** the "Ridge to Rivers" trail system (www.ridgetorivers.org) provides for on-road and off-road cyclists alike and continues to expand under municipal planning efforts. Boise also has plenty of bike lanes to offer cyclists an added margin of safety and comfort by keeping them a little farther away from traffic.

Mountain biking claims a big niche, and no wonder. Just north of the city lies the **Boise Front,** a vast tract of foothill wilderness—part Bureau of Land Management, part Forest Service land—laced with both primitive roads and single-track trails. You can ride right from downtown and in minutes be out in the sage and rabbitbrush with no other sound than the wind whistling through your ears. This is an immensely popular after-work and weekend destination for Boiseans, and the heavy use is beginning to result in some erosion problems in the area's fragile soil. With the increased bike traffic, collisions at blind corners have unfortunately become a common occurrence.

To get there from downtown, head north on 8th Street and just keep going. Other access points in the same general area include Crestline Road (off Brumback St.) and Bogus Basin Road, just past the Highlands Hollow brewpub. A little farther south, Military Reserve Park, Rocky Canyon Road (at the end of Shaw Mountain Rd.), and Table Rock Road

are other gateways to the Front's trail system. Military Reserve Park has many trails that are well used in summer.

Here are a few of Boise's bike laws worth mentioning: Bicyclists must slow down and use caution at stop signs, but need not stop if it isn't necessary for safety. Bicyclists must stop at all red traffic lights. Also, it's legal to ride on the sidewalks unless specifically prohibited by signs; pedestrians have the right-of-way, however.

FISHING

How many cities this size—how many state capitals—offer good fishing right within the city limits? Start with the **Boise River** that flows through town. Its cold waters hold rainbow and brown trout and whitefish. Popular access points include (west to east) Glenwood Bridge, Veterans Park, Capitol Bridge, and Barber Park. The river is stocked with rainbows monthly, and it's stocked with steelhead for a brief time during the fall.

In addition to the river, many urban ponds are frequently stocked. Near the Glenwood Bridge, **Riverside Pond** holds rainbow trout and bluegill. **Veterans Park Pond** holds rainbows, largemouth bass, crappie, bullhead, and bluegill. **ParkCenter Pond** provides a

fly-fishing on the Boise River

home to rainbow trout, largemouth bass, crappie, bluegill, bullhead, and channel catfish. The ponds make ideal spots for youngsters to try fishing for the first time.

For more information on fishing the waters in and around town, you can pick up literature and find resources at the **Idaho Department of Fish and Game** office (600 S. Walnut St., 208/334-3700). Among the several fishing supply stores in town are **Anglers** (7097 Overland Rd., 208/323-6768) and **Idaho Angler** (1682 S. Vista Ave., 208/389-9957).

GOLF

Several courses in the vicinity keep Boise golfers swinging year-round, weather permitting—usually about 325 days a year. All the major courses offer club and cart rentals.

A perennial local favorite for its course, pro shop, and 19th hole is **Shadow Valley Golf Course** (15711 Hwy. 55, 208/939-6699, greens fees $20-42). Length for the 18-hole, par-72 course runs 5,514-6,433 yards. Many Boise golfers pick Shadow Valley's short, scenic, and unforgiving hole two as the best in town. Also look out for holes 13 and 14 on the back nine. Hole 13 is a 525-yard, par-five dogleg with what many consider the most difficult drive in the city, while hole 14's green has water on both sides. To get there, take State Street northwest from downtown and turn right on Highway 55 toward McCall.

On the north side of town you'll find **Quail Hollow Golf Club** (4520 N. 36th St., 208/344-7807, greens fees $23-32). Hole 1 at this challenging 18-hole course sets the tone for what could be a very long afternoon; it's a 293-yard, par-four nightmare that seems to be made up of equal parts sand, water, and grass. Hole seven provides a great view of the city. The length of the par-70 course runs 4,557-6,394 yards.

On the east side of town you'll find **Warm Springs Golf Course** (2495 Warm Springs Ave., 208/343-5661, greens fees $22-31). One side of the picturesque municipal course runs alongside the beautiful Boise River—also known as "Old Man Watertrap" to those who hook left on hole two. The 18-hole, par-72 course runs 5,660-6,719 yards.

HIKING

Most bike trails in the Boise Front are open to hikers as well as bikers, and the **Hull's Gulch National Recreation Trail** is open to hikers exclusively. Of the two Hull's Gulch trailheads, the lower one is 3.5 miles from the end of the pavement at the north end of 8th Street; the upper trailhead is three miles farther up the road. The primitive road is easily traversed in the Oldsmobile; just take it slowly. Both trailheads are on the right and well marked. From the lower trailhead, the 3.5-mile Bureau of Land Management (BLM) foot trail rounds a ridge and drops into Hull's Gulch—a deep, brushy canyon sliced down its center by the proverbial babbling brook. In spring, the wildflowers and butterflies try to outdo each other for your attention. Watch out for ticks during the spring months. The gradually ascending trail eventually reaches the lower limit of the pines, where a few magnificent ponderosas inhabit the sunny slopes.

All along the way, BLM signs identify some of the common botanical species and offer some basic ecology lessons. Among the plants you'll see: willow, rabbitbrush, Rocky Mountain maple, chokecherry, and syringa, the state flower. In spring, wildflowers brightening the gulch include arrowleaf balsamroot, phlox, lupine, and larkspur. Among the animals you might catch a glimpse of are rabbits, lizards, porcupines, badgers, and coyotes. A 2.5-mile loop at the top lets you come back on a slightly different path, or you might want to leave the gulch behind at the upper trailhead and just hike back down the dirt road. This route doesn't have quite the same wilderness feel, but it's atop the ridge and provides great views of Boise, the Owyhee Mountains, and a large chunk of southwestern Idaho. For more information on the Hull's Gulch Trail, contact the BLM's **Boise district office** (3948 Development Ave., 208/384-3300).

HOT-AIR BALLOONING

Dawn over the Treasure Valley, the perfect desert stillness broken only intermittently by the blast of a propane burner lighting off a couple of feet over your head as you float over the scenic valley. Enjoy this experience by booking a hot-air balloon flight with **Idaho Hot Air Lines** (4049 W. Plum St., 208/344-8462, www.idhotairlines.com).

ROCK CLIMBING

Several climbing gyms in town and a good toprope area out near Lucky Peak help keep local climbers in shape. **Urban Ascent** (308 S. 25th St., 208/363-7325, www.urbanascent.com, 4pm-10pm Mon., Wed., and Fri., noon-10pm Tues. and Thurs., noon-7pm Sat.-Sun., day pass $8-15) is an indoor climbing gym near downtown, just off the I-84 Connector. Shoe, harness, and chalk-bag rentals are available. Both the **West Family YMCA** (5959 N. Discovery Pl., 208/377-9622) and the downtown **Boise Family YMCA** (1050 W. State St., 208/344-5501) have climbing walls.

On the **BSU campus** you'll find a state-of-the-art climbing gym in the **Student Recreation Center** (1515 University Dr., across from the Student Union, 208/426-1946, 6pm-10pm Mon.-Thurs., 3pm-7pm Sun., closed school holidays), but you'll have to be a guest of a student, faculty, or alumni in order to climb here. Equipment rental is available. Climbers must pass a mandatory belay test ($5); free belay classes are offered periodically throughout the week.

The most popular outdoor climbing area in the vicinity is **Black Cliffs,** a 1-2-pitch basalt outcropping on the north side of Warm Springs Avenue (Hwy. 21), across from the diversion dam. You can't miss the roadside cliffs, a little less than a mile past the Beaver Dick and Oregon Trail twin historical markers, about seven miles east of downtown. Other popular areas include the old quarry behind the Old Pen, and Rocky Canyon—a small but scenic area north of Table Rock. To get to Rocky Canyon, take Reserve Road to Shaw Mountain Road as if you were going to Table Rock, but at the Y at the top of the hill, bear left on Shaw Mountain Road. A blue sign at the Y reads "To Rocky Canyon Road." Follow the road to the end of the pavement and continue about another 0.25 mile on a good gravel road.

RUNNING

The city is full of great places to go jogging. Start with the **Greenbelt,** where you can enjoy a car-free workout of up to 25 miles, past the rushing waters and lushly vegetated banks of the Boise River. At any time of year, you'll find Boiseans out for exercise on the Greenbelt's paths. All the major parks are great places to run. You can loop through **Ann Morrison Park,** using the Greenbelt as one side of the loop and the park's walkways as the other side. Or head over to **Veterans Memorial Park** on the west end of town—trails there wind down to the Boise River and around a marsh and a large pond.

Racers will find an event scheduled almost every weekend April-October; this is a runner's town. The annual **Race to Robie Creek,** considered by many to be the hardest half marathon in the Northwest, is held in mid-April. Thousands of runners start at Fort Boise Park and work their way up Rocky Canyon and over Aldape Summit in this grueling backcountry race.

SKATEBOARDING AND SKATING

Skateboarders and hard-core in-line skaters alike go to **Rhodes Park** (15th St. and Front St.), under the Connector, to fly up the quarter-pipes and other fun features at this industrial skate park. **Fort Boise Skate Park** also has bowls and quarter-pipes, and the **Greenbelt** is a prime place for in-line skating.

Those who prefer skating on ice can head to **Idaho Ice World** (7072 S. Eisenman Rd., 208/331-0044, $7 adults, $6 under age 13 and over age 59), next to the Boise Factory Outlets. Public skating sessions are held daily; call for times. Skate rentals are $3, and

Boise Sports Outfitters

The great outdoors is at your doorstep in Boise, and you'll want to get out there and enjoy it. Here's a list of some outfitters that rent the gear you'll need. First look up the type of gear you want to rent in the chart on top, then match the numbers listed there to the outfitter list.

Backpacks: 6, 10
Bikes: 3, 6, 8
Canoes: 7
Inner tubes: 1
Kayaks: 4 (inflatable), 7
Rafts: 1, 4, 7
Rock-climbing shoes: 2, 6, 10
Skates: 8, 9
Skis:
  Alpine: 5, 8
  Cross-country: 2, 6, 8, 10
  Telemark/backcountry: 2, 6, 10
Snowboards: 3, 5, 6, 8, 9
Snowshoes: 2, 5, 6, 8, 9, 10
Tennis rackets: 8
Tents: 2, 6, 10

1. **Epley's Boise River Rentals** (Barber Park on Eckert Rd., upstream end of the Greenbelt, 208/577-4584), July 1-Labor Day
2. **The Benchmark** (625 Vista Ave., 208/338-1700)
3. **Bikes2Boards** (3525 W. State St., 208/343-0208)
4. **Boise Army-Navy** (4924 Chinden Blvd., 208/322-0660)
5. **Sports Authority** (1301 N. Milwaukee St., 208/378-9590)
6. **Idaho Mountain Touring** (1310 W. Main St., 208/336-3854)
7. **Idaho River Sports** (601 Whitewater Park Blvd., 208/336-4844)
8. **McU Sports** (822 W. Jefferson St., 208/342-7734; 2314 Bogus Basin Rd., 208/336-2300)
9. **Newt & Harold's** (1021 Broadway, 208/385-9300)
10. **REI** (8300 W. Emerald St. at Milwaukee St., 208/322-1141)

Boise State University's Outdoor Program, located in the Student Recreation Center (1515 University Dr.), has a large selection of four-season rental gear. If you're a BSU student, staffer, or alum, or if you're attending a BSU conference, you qualify to rent gear here. For more information on equipment rentals or eligibility, call 208/426-1946.

lessons are available. Idaho Ice World also offers open curling (7pm-10pm Sun.) during the winter months.

SWIMMING

The Boise River and Lucky Peak Reservoir are suitable for summer swimming, but Boise offers a number of swimming pools too. For indoor swimming, the **Boise Aquatics Center** at the West Family YMCA (5959 N. Discovery Pl., 208/377-9622, $9 adults, $4 children, family rates available) has a 50-meter pool for lap swimming as well as a children's pool, a waterslide, and a hydrotherapy pool.

Outdoor city swimming pools can be found during the summer months at **Borah Park** (801 Aurora Dr., 208/375-8373), **Fairmont Park** (7929 W. Northview St., 208/375-3011), **Ivywild** (2250 Leadville Ave., 208/384-1697), **Lowell School** (1601 N. 28th St., 208/345-7918), and the **Natatorium/Hydrotube** (1811 Warm Springs Ave., 208/345-9270).

Admission varies from pool to pool but averages $3.50 adults, $2.50 ages 12-18, $2 under age 12, free for seniors.

TUBING AND FLOATING

Each summer, some 300,000 people start at Barber Park and float their way down the Boise River to Ann Morrison Park, a six-mile trip that takes about an hour and a half. You can bring your own gear (air is available at Barber Park 10am-7pm daily) or rent it at the park's **rental office** (208/577-4584, noon-5pm Mon.-Thurs., noon-6pm Fri., 11am-6pm Sat.-Sun. and holidays summer, tubes $12, rafts $45-58, inflatable kayaks $37). A **shuttle bus** (1pm-8pm Mon.-Fri., 1pm-9pm Sat.-Sun. and holidays, $3 pp per trip) leaves Ann Morrison Park every hour on the hour and Barber Park every hour on the half hour. Neither the rental office nor the shuttle operates if forecast temperatures fall below 80°F. It's important to note that alcohol consumption has been banned for those floating the Boise River, and it's strictly enforced by Boise's finest. Also, Idaho law states that rafters ages 14 and under must wear a life vest. Tubers are exempt from this law, but wearing a life vest is strongly recommended. It's also recommended that rafters and tubers take out at Ann Morrison Park because there's a dangerous diversion dam just past the park that has claimed several lives in recent years.

WALKING

One nice aspect about walking in Boise: By and large, the city is flat. The **Greenbelt,** Boise's premier walking path, meanders along the lush banks of the Boise River, providing plenty of spots along the way for quiet contemplation of the natural beauty. It also connects a string of parks from one end of town to the other and passes by Boise State University. BSU students often park off-campus and walk to class on the Greenbelt. You can pick up the path just about anywhere—just head for the river—but Julia Davis Park and Ann Morrison Park are two of the most popular access points.

One particularly wonderful spot on the Greenbelt for a stroll is at the east end, where you'll find the **Greenbelt Wildlife Preserve** (ParkCenter Blvd. and River Run Dr.), open only to pedestrians and wildlife. You can't park at the access point, which is located in a residential area; park on ParkCenter Boulevard somewhere, or just budget enough time to mosey down the Greenbelt from points farther west.

Downtown itself is generally a safe and pleasant place to walk, day and night. Evenings are especially nice here, after all the business traffic has migrated back to suburbia and the setting sun casts a warm glow on the numerous beautiful buildings.

WHITE-WATER RAFTING AND KAYAKING

The **Payette River,** less than an hour outside Boise, drops down out of the mountains in world-class white water that draws thrill-seekers from all over the country. Summer weekends see hundreds of rafters and kayakers on the river. The rapids here range from moderate Class III all the way up to unrunnable Class VI.

The **Boise River Park** (3900 W. Pleasanton Ave.), located on the Boise River between Main Street and Veterans Memorial Parkway, recently opened to the delight of local kayakers and river surfers. This urban river park is under the auspice of Boise Parks and Recreation, and it offers adjustable wave-shapers and pneumatically operated air bladders that inflate to control the upstream water levels. The best part: It's free to boaters.

ATHLETIC CLUBS

Boise has two **YMCAs,** both open to the public for a day-use fee ($13.25 adults, $6.75 ages 7-18). Here's a hot tip for road warriors on a tight budget: The Y charges just $2 for use of its showers, but you'll need to check the schedule to find out the available times.

The extensive facilities at the downtown **Boise Family YMCA** (1050 W. State St., 208/344-5501, 5am-10pm Mon.-Fri., 7am-8pm

Sat., 10am-6pm Sun., pool closes a half hour earlier) include pools, basketball and racquetball courts, cardio equipment and free weights, a climbing wall, and child care. The **West Family YMCA** (5959 N. Discovery Pl., south of W. Chinden Blvd. and west of Cloverdale Rd., 208/377-9622, 5am-10pm Mon.-Fri., 7am-8pm Sat., 10am-6pm Sun., pool closes a half hour earlier) has racquetball courts, a gym, a teen center, a climbing wall, a child-care center, basketball and volleyball courts, and an indoor running track. The facility also houses the Boise Aquatics Center.

SPECTATOR SPORTS
Baseball

Memorial Stadium (5600 Glenwood Ave.), adjacent to the fairgrounds, is home to the Single-A **Boise Hawks** (208/322-5000, www.boisehawks.com, mid-June-early Sept., $7-15), a farm team of the Colorado Rockies.

Basketball

Idaho Stampede (tickets 208/331-8497, www.centurylinkarenaboise.com, Nov.-Mar., $9-25) is an NBA Development League team that plays its home games at CenturyLink Arena. The basketball team is affiliated with the Utah Jazz.

Hockey

The **Idaho Steelheads** (208/424-2200, tickets 208/331-8497, www.idahosteelheads.com, Oct.-Mar., $17-50), affiliated with the Dallas Stars, bring East Coast Hockey League action to CenturyLink Arena.

Boise State University Sports

BSU fields intercollegiate athletes in seven men's sports and 10 women's sports, most competing in the Mountain West Conference. Division 1-A **Boise State Broncos** football games are a huge draw, held at the often sold-out Albertsons Stadium. The BSU athletic ticket office (208/426-1494, www.broncosports.com) is on the south end of the stadium.

Famous Idaho Potato Bowl

The annual **Famous Idaho Potato Bowl** is Boise's single biggest sporting event, held at Albertsons Stadium in December during the college football bowl season. The bowl game usually pairs mid-tier teams from the Mid-American and Mountain West Conferences. For tickets, visit www.famousidahopotatobowl.com or call 208/426-4737.

Treasure Valley Rollergirls

If you like hard-hitting women on roller skates, check out the **Treasure Valley Rollergirls** (www.tvrderby.com), who host bouts throughout the year at CenturyLink Arena. These tattooed ruffians take on clubs from other cities in the region. You can buy tickets ($10-25) at the door or at various locations around town, like The Record Exchange (1105 W. Idaho St., 208/344-8010).

★ BOGUS BASIN

Boise skiers are lucky to have superb skiing just 16 miles north of town.

Skiing and Snowboarding

Bogus Basin Ski Resort (2600 Bogus Basin Rd., 208/332-5100 or 800/367-4397, snow report 208/342-2100, www.bogusbasin.org, lifts 10am-10pm Mon.-Fri., 9am-10pm Sat.-Sun., full-day lift tickets $25, 4pm-10pm lift tickets $20) has a base elevation of 5,800 feet and rises to a peak of 7,582 feet—high enough to provide featherweight powder when a cold front blows through. On the resort's 2,600 acres are two quad chairs, a triple chair, four double chairs, and a rope tow, serving 52 trails with a maximum vertical drop of 1,800 feet and a longest run of 1.5 miles—not bad for Boise's "local hill." Snowboarders are welcome anywhere on the mountain, and a separate snowboard park offers a mogul field, half-pipes, quarter-pipes, and rail slides. There's also an 800-foot tubing hill ($12 for two hours, reservations recommended) that's accessible by a rope tow.

Night skiing here is one of the resort's highlights, with 165 acres open until 10pm nightly. Weather can often be better at night than during the day, and a peaceful, uncrowded feeling settles over the area. The views on a clear night are something special.

Down near the lower day lodge, a **cross-country ski area** offers skating and traditional cross-country tracks on more than 12 miles of developed trails. Snowshoers will also find lots of trails that skirt the ridge, most of which offer great views of a major chunk of southwestern Idaho, from the Boise Front foothills in the foreground out across the Snake River Plain to the Owyhee Mountains in the background. A snowshoe trail ticket will cost you $7. Backcountry telemarkers who don't mind some hiking should ask the staff about Mores Mountain (trail fee $14 adults, $7 ages 7-11, free under age 7 and over age 69). Rentals and lessons are available. For more information, call the **Frontier Point Nordic Lodge** (208/332-5390).

The resort's skier-service facilities include two day lodges, cafés, rental and retail shops, a ski school, a racing program, ski programs for children and physically challenged skiers, and day care. The season here usually starts around Thanksgiving or early December and continues through the end of spring break.

Buses (208/459-6612, $13 round-trip, $8 one-way) serve the mountain from Boise and some neighboring communities; call for routes and schedules.

Sleigh Rides

Bogus Creek Outfitters (208/278-7000, www.boguscreek.com) will bundle you up in wool blankets and take you for a horse-drawn sleigh ride from the Bogus Basin Nordic Area to a cozy cabin a mile deep in the woods. There you'll be served hot drinks by a roaring fire followed by a three-course dinner. The 2.5-hour dinner rides (6pm and 8:30pm daily, $80 pp) are offered November 28-mid-March.

Mountain Lodging

Sure, it's only a half-hour drive back to Boise, but to guarantee first crack at that untracked powder, you might want to book a room in the **Pioneer Condominiums** (208/332-5200, www.pioneercondos.com, $129-149, reserve in advance), which lie at mid-mountain, just steps from the slopes—you could ski right to your door if you wanted. Many of the plush yet unpretentious units offer fireplaces, with kindling and firewood provided. A hot tub and sauna can work après-ski wonders on those knots in your quads. Other amenities include free laundry and free transportation to the lower base area in ski season. You can get special rates for weekly stays and large groups. The condos are immediately adjacent to Pioneer Lodge—the upper day lodge of the alpine ski area—where the bar and grill is open until 11pm nightly.

Bogus Basin also operates a yurt (208/332-5100, sleeps up to 12, $125), but reservations need to be made far in advance because it's popular during the winter months. No maid service here—you pack it in and pack it out.

Entertainment and Events

Boise has a vibrant arts and entertainment scene, with several outstanding mainstays leading the way. The City of Trees boasts a high concentration of actors, dancers, writers, and visual artists, giving it an artsy feel. Musicians flourish here too; indie superstars Built to Spill hail from these parts, as does Hillfolk Noir, an alternative bluegrass trio, and Americana sweetheart Eilen Jewell.

PERFORMING ARTS

Tickets for many Boise-area performing arts events, especially those at Boise State University's Morrison Center and Taco Bell Arena, are available through **Idaho Tickets** (www.idahotickets.org), or stop at any of the dozens of outlets, which include the **BSU Student Union Building** (1700 University Dr.) and Albertsons stores across southern Idaho and eastern Oregon.

Boise Philharmonic

One of the Northwest's premier symphony orchestras, the **Boise Philharmonic** (ticket office in Esther Simplot Performing Arts Academy, 516 S. 9th St., 208/344-7849, www.boisephilharmonic.org, $15-40) is the state's largest performing arts organization and the oldest as well, dating back more than 100 years. Symphony season runs mid-September-mid-April, with performances at the Morrison Center on the BSU campus, Swayne Auditorium at Northwest Nazarene University in Nampa, as well as other venues around town. Numerous internationally acclaimed guest artists perform with the symphony each year.

Opera Idaho

See Madame Butterfly get the shaft! See Don Giovanni meet his just reward! **Opera Idaho** (513 S. 8th St., 208/345-3531, tickets 208/387-1273, www.operaidaho.org, $15-40) performs several masterworks throughout the year.

Boise performances often take place at the **Egyptian Theatre** (700 W. Main St.).

Ballet Idaho

Squeeze into those toe shoes and plié on down to the Morrison Center for a performance by **Ballet Idaho** (501 S. 8th St., 208/343-0556, www.balletidaho.org, Oct.-Apr., $38-58). The company teams up with the Boise Philharmonic in December for the perennial holiday favorite, *The Nutcracker.*

Oinkari Basque Dancers

The story of the Oinkari Basque Dancers starts in 1949 with Basque Boisean Juanita "Jay" Uberuaga Hormaechea, who could dance the *jota* like a house afire. She decided that all Basque American children should have the chance to learn the dances of the old country and began teaching them. In 1960 a group of her students went to Europe to see the homeland firsthand. In San Sebastian they met and studied with a local troupe named Oinkari, loosely translated as "check out those flying feet!" The two groups danced together a few times a week, developing close bonds. When the Boiseans were ready to return to the United States and form their own troupe, the San Sebastian Oinkaris asked the Boiseans to do them the honor of naming the fledgling American troupe Oinkari as well, in effect creating sister dance companies.

Boise's **Oinkari Basque Dancers** (208/557-1960, www.oinkari.org) went on to perform at four World's Fairs and in the rotunda of the capitol in Washington, DC. Today, the company performs at the international Jaialdi festival, at the annual Festival of San Inazio, and at other times throughout the year. Members wear traditional Basque costumes and dance the *jota*—a quick-step that has been around in one variation or another since the 12th century—and other traditional dances. The company remains a vital part of

Boise's Basque community; dancers must be of Basque descent to join the troupe.

★ Idaho Shakespeare Festival

Boise's bard-based **Idaho Shakespeare Festival** (box office 208/336-9221, www.idahoshakespeare.org, $25-42) troupe ranks among the city's shiniest cultural gems. From mid-June through September, Will's works and other dramatic delights come alive in an **outdoor amphitheater** (5657 Warm Springs Ave.) along the river east of downtown. The festival grounds are a wonderful place to picnic before the show; bring your own or sample fare from Café Shakespeare.

Other Theater and Dance Troupes

Boise now has about 10 professional and community theater groups, so drama fans often have several playbills to choose from each week. **Boise Little Theater** (100 E. Fort St., 208/342-5104, www.boiselittletheater.org, Sept.-June, $9-16) is a community theater group that was organized in 1948. Performances take place at the Boise Little Theater in Fort Boise Park.

As its name implies, **Boise Contemporary Theater** (854 Fulton St., 208/331-9224, www.bctheater.org, four productions Oct.-May, $15-35) presents fare by such current-day playwrights as David Sedaris and Steve Martin. But don't be surprised to see some classics by the likes of Anton Chekhov and Samuel Beckett, all in an intimate "black box" environment at the Fulton Street Theater.

Boise has a thriving modern dance scene as well. Check out **Idaho Dance Theatre** (405 S. 8th St., 208/331-9592, www.idahodancetheatre.org, Nov.-Apr.), a local troupe that puts on performances at the Special Events Center on the BSU campus.

LITERARY ARTS
Writers in Residence

Many notable authors have made Boise their home over the years. Most of these writers come to Idaho to teach at BSU's Masters of Fine Arts Creative Writing program. In the past, Robert Olmstead and Elise Blackwell have taught classes at the university. Currently, Brady Udall *(The Lonely Polygamist, Letting Loose the Hounds)* and up-and-comer Alan Heathcock *(VOLT)* teach fiction writing here.

Anthony Doerr also lives in Boise. He is the author of several short-story collections, novellas, and a popular creative nonfiction book, *Four Seasons in Rome.* Doerr is a recipient of the O. Henry Prize and the Pushcart Prize for fiction.

The Cabin

Considered to be the beating heart of Boise's literary world, **The Cabin** (801 S. Capitol Blvd., 208/331-8000, www.thecabinidaho.org) is based in an old log cabin next to the Idaho Anne Frank Human Rights Memorial. The literary center offers writing workshops and hosts a continuous stream of readings and author discussions. Over the years, The Cabin has brought to town famous writers such as T. C. Boyle, Elizabeth Gilbert, and Ruth Reichl, to name a few.

VISUAL ARTS
Public Art

One of the treats of exploring Boise is the discovery of art where you least expect it. Besides a profusion of art galleries around town, there are dozens of pieces of public art in an ever-growing collection that can be found throughout the City of Trees, including *Homage to the Pedestrian* (Patrick Zentz, 2002), an interactive walkway where motion detectors set off sounds, on the west side of The Grove. Across 9th Street in front of Hotel 43, *Grove Street Illuminated & Boise Canal* (Amy Westover, 2003) offers some glimpses into local history through silkscreened vintage photos and engraved text that observers can see as they walk amid steel and cast-glass circles. The Boise Department of Arts and History recently started a new public art project that commissions local artists to cover traffic light utility boxes with original artwork. There are currently around 40 of these colorful boxes in the downtown area.

Galleries

Stewart Gallery (2230 W. Main St., 208/433-0593, www.stewartgallery.com) is an attractive space that exhibits and sells the works of local and regional artists. Expect to find lots of contemporary paintings, eye-catching photography, and mixed-media pieces. Another noteworthy gallery in the downtown area is **Boise Art Glass** (1124 W. Front St., 208/345-1825, www.boiseartglass.com), a blown-glass studio that offers classes and sells jewelry, marbles, vases, bowls, and lighting fixtures. The in-house gallery exhibits a rotating selection of fused and hand-blown glass art.

Hipsters like to hang out at the **Visual Arts Collective** (VAC, 3638 Osage St., 208/424-8297, www.visualartscollective.com), just off Chinden Boulevard in nearby Garden City. Here you will find a constantly changing display of locally produced contemporary art, ranging from surrealistic paintings to bizarro mixed-media offerings. The VAC also has a bar, and it features live music and cutting-edge performance art on a weekly basis. You must be 21 to enter.

Boise State University has several galleries scattered around campus, including one in the Liberal Arts Building, one in the Student Union, and another in the Hemingway Center. For current shows, see www.boisestate.edu/art.

CINEMA

The Flicks (646 Fulton St., 208/342-4288, www.theflicksboise.com), near Capitol Boulevard and Myrtle Street, is Boise's art film house. Its four screens show independent and foreign films as well as some of the more intelligent first-runs. In addition to the theater, a deli-style café serves panini sandwiches, pasta dishes, and scratch soups. You can get a microbrew or glass of wine from the café and take it out onto the patio or even into the theater with you. You'll also find a good selection of art and foreign films in the DVD rental store.

The restored **Egyptian Theatre** (700 W. Main St., 208/345-0454, www.egyptiantheatre.net) is the city's most historic and beautiful movie house. Built in 1927, its Egyptian design was inspired by the discovery of King Tut's tomb not long before. Check out the ornamental sphinxes up near the roof. In addition to first-run films, the Egyptian regularly screens black-and-white classics and hosts a gamut of intimate concerts.

Elsewhere downtown, you can watch current-run movies in BoDo at the newish **Edwards Cinemas Stadium 9** (760 Broad St., 208/338-3821).

NIGHTLIFE

The local music scene in Boise is undeniably rich. The town has a lot of musicians and a lot of places for them to play. Boise fervently supports its homegrown musicians, to the extent that many locals can actually support themselves with their music. It's not uncommon for local bands to draw bigger crowds at the clubs than the nationally famous touring bands that come through town. And big-name acts show up in Boise with some regularity. Here's a look at a few concert houses, nightclubs, and cocktail lounges worth checking out. It's important to note that Boise recently passed a citywide smoking ban inside bars and restaurants, so the air is a lot cleaner in venues around town these days.

The **Knitting Factory Concert House** (416 S. 9th St., 208/367-1212, www.bo.knittingfactory.com) is one of the top live-music venues in town, with a never-ending onslaught of national touring acts. Don't be surprised to see bands like the Smashing Pumpkins, the Robert Cray Band, David Allan Coe, and The Misfits.

The **Revolution Concert House** (4983 N. Glenwood St., Garden City, 208/938-2933, www.cttouringid.com) is a new concert venue in neighboring Garden City that brings to town big-name acts throughout the year. This 17,000-square-foot facility lures in bands that can no longer fill arenas, but are still too big for smaller venues such as the Knitting Factory.

Neurolux (111 N. 11th St., 208/343-0886, www.neurolux.com, open nightly, cover charge for live music) is undeniably Boise's hippest watering hole. The bar's tattoo-clad clientele comes here to enjoy stiff drinks, a good jukebox, DJ music, and lots of local bands. Edgy touring acts, like Jerry Joseph and the Jackmormons and The Sword, occasionally grace the stage.

Old Boise, near the corner of 6th and Main Streets, is the epicenter of nightlife in downtown. Here you will find several live music venues, including **Pengilly's Saloon** (513 W. Main St., 208/345-6344), a historic bar that frequently features live acoustic music, and **Tom Grainey's** (109 S. 6th St., 208/345-2505), which has a pair of bars, upstairs and down, spotlighting local and touring rock bands. If you desire a tropical experience, check out the **Reef** (105 S. 6th St., 208/287-9200, www.reefboise.com), upstairs at the corner of 6th and Main Streets. This Polynesian-inspired restaurant and lounge has a palm-thatched roof over the bar and a spacious rooftop patio that's lit up with tiki torches. Besides tropical drinks and pupu platters, the Reef also has live music on weekends.

Elsewhere downtown, get your groove on at **The Balcony Club** (150 N. 8th St., 208/336-1313), a happening dance club in the Capitol Terrace complex that's popular with both gays and straights (and everyone in between), with near-nightly DJ music.

For craft cocktails and hip bar food, check out **The Mode Lounge** (800 W. Idaho St., 208/342-6633, www.themodelounge.com), at the corner of 8th and Idaho Streets. Here you can enjoy inventive drinks—mixed with house-made syrups and aromatic tinctures—and gastrolounge dishes like steak tartare and deviled ham with crostini.

In BoDo, **Liquid** (405 S. 8th St., 208/287-5379, www.liquidboise.com), located in the alley between 8th and 9th Streets, is also a good place to grab some cocktails and listen to hip DJ music.

Locals like to hang out at the **Spacebar Arcade** (200 N. Capitol Blvd., 208/918-0597, www.spacebararcade.com), a fun arcade near the state capitol that features a multitude of old-school video games and pinball machines. The Spacebar, downstairs from Guru Donuts and the Boise Fry Company, serves a good selection of local microbrews and has a small wine list.

EVENTS
Year-Round

Boise is a party town, and one event or another happens just about every weekend year-round. The delightful **First Thursday** series (5pm-9pm first Thurs. of every month), run by the Downtown Boise Association (208/472-5200, www.downtownboise.org), turns downtown Boise into a street fair. Galleries hold open houses, musicians play on the sidewalks, and seemingly all of Boise is out strolling downtown.

Spring

Fans of indie music should check out the **Treefort Music Fest** (www.treefortmusicfest.com), held in late March at various venues around town. This five-day music festival brings in dozens of cutting-edge bands and musicians from around the country. There's even a beer garden set up near the main stage that pours local microbrews.

In mid-April, the **BSU/Gene Harris Jazz Festival** (www.geneharris.org) pays tribute to the late great Idaho jazzman, with various performances by international acts around town. Mid-April also brings more than 2,000 runners to the **Race to Robie Creek** (www.robiecreek.com), a 13.1-mile test of strength and will that starts in Fort Boise Park and climbs Rocky Canyon up and over Adalpe Summit—a gain of 2,000 vertical feet followed by a loss of more than 1,000 feet.

You know summer's on the way when **Alive After Five** (www.downtownboise.org, 5pm-8pm Wed.) kicks off in early June at The Grove, which becomes a city party. Crowds pack the outdoor plaza to sample microbrews and food from local restaurants while listening or dancing to live bands. The concert series runs through September.

The first weekend in June is the **Greek Festival** (St. Helen's Church Park, 27th St. and Bannock St., behind the church, 208/345-6147) sponsored by Saints Constantine and Helen Greek Orthodox Church. More Greek food than you can possibly imagine—dolmas, souvlaki, spanakopita—will be spread out by Boise's Greek community, while Greek dancing and revelry continue all weekend. Foodies will also like **Savor Idaho** (www.savoridaho. org), a local food and wine showcase that takes place in early June at the Idaho Botanical Garden. This one-day festival features more than 25 Idaho wineries and about 20 area restaurants and food artisans.

Summer

At the end of June, Boise's Jewish community sets the table for **Deli Days,** held at the Ahavath Beth Israel Synagogue (11 N. Latah St., 208/343-6601). Here you can nosh on potato knishes, delicious baked goods, and fat pastrami sandwiches served with a pickle that actually has a crunch. Also at the end of the month is the **Boise Music Festival** (www. boisemusicfestival.com), a one-day affair held

at the Expo Idaho fairgrounds in Garden City. Past performers have included Train, Sir Mixa-Lot, and Macy Gray, to name a few.

Boise celebrates **Independence Day** on July 4 with fireworks and a parade. The last weekend of July, Boise's Basque community comes out in force for the **Festival of San Inazio of Loyola;** St. Ignatius, a native of Spanish Basque country, died July 31, 1556. The festivities include a performance by the Oinkari Basque dancers, Basque athletic contests, and an abundance of local Basque food and drink. For more information, call the Basque Museum (208/343-2671). **Jaialdi,** an international Basque festival, is held every five years at various locales around town; the next one is in 2020.

The **Western Idaho Fair** (208/287-5650) comes to the Expo Idaho (Chinden Blvd. and Glenwood St.) for 10 days in mid-August, bringing with it a carnival midway, livestock shows, eclectic exhibits, food galore, and lots of entertainers.

Hot-air balloons take to the air over Ann Morrison Park on four mornings in early September for the **Spirit of Boise Balloon Classic** (www.spiritofboise.com). The Night Glow is a beautiful sight as well, when dozens of illuminated balloons light up the evening sky.

Hyde Park Street Fair

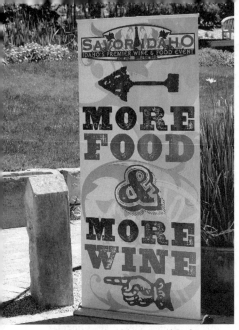

Savor Idaho at the Idaho Botanical Garden

and one of Idaho's largest and most elaborate arts and crafts shows, with hats, drums, candles, toys, fine arts, and lots of food. The "gallery" for this event is beautiful Julia Davis Park.

One of the coolest neighborhood bashes in the Northwest can be found in mid-September at the **Hyde Park Street Fair** (www.north-end.org), a weekend full of live music, kids' activities, and community conviviality. It's at Camel's Back Park in the city's North End.

Winter

Late November through January, the Idaho Botanical Garden's **Winter Garden aGlow** (208/343-8649) features thousands of twinkling lights decked artistically amid the garden grounds, along with bonfires and hot beverages.

Kids and adults alike will enjoy the collaborative efforts of Ballet Idaho and the Boise Philharmonic in bringing performances of Tchaikovsky's masterpiece *The Nutcracker* to Morrison Center. Call 208/426-1110 for schedule and ticket information. And if you're lucky, in early December, you might hit The Grove at the right time for **Tuba Christmas,** where upward of 60 tuba and baritone horn players oompah their way through traditional Christmas music and more. The tuba parade makes its way into the state capitol rotunda for a big grand finale.

Fall

Autumn brings colorful trees and the opening of a colorful cultural calendar as the Boise Philharmonic, Ballet Idaho, and Opera Idaho open their seasons.

The weekend after Labor Day brings **Art in the Park,** run by the Boise Art Museum (208/345-8330, www.boiseartmuseum.org)

Shopping

BOOKS

When it comes to new books, Boise doesn't have many options beyond corporate bookstores. **Barnes & Noble Booksellers** (1315 N. Milwaukee St., 208/375-4454), near Boise Towne Square mall, offers a large selection of books, stationery, and CDs.

The **Boise State Bookstore** (1910 University Dr., 208/426-2665), in the Student Union Building on campus, stocks more than

just textbooks. Also expect to find other books (Idaho authors, recreation, travel guides), stationery, and office supplies.

For used books, check out **Trip Taylor Bookseller** (210 N. 10th St., 208/344-3311). This downtown bookstore has lots of great titles and rare editions. The **Rediscovered Bookshop** (180 N. 8th St., 208/376-4229) is another place where you can find high-quality used books, mixed in with new titles.

OUTDOOR GEAR

If you need a new carabiner or hiking boots, **REI** (8300 W. Emerald St., 208/322-1141, www. rei.com) can help you out. This Seattle-based cooperative outdoor store has everything from maps to clothing to skis to tents and much more.

Hunters, anglers, and car-campers will find everything they need at **Cabela's** (8109 W. Franklin Rd., 208/672-7900) near the Boise Towne Square mall. Besides having a multitude of fishing rods, tackle, and hunting gear, this giant store also carries clothing, accessories, and an array of cast-iron Dutch ovens and other outdoor cooking supplies. It's something of a museum and nature center too, meaning you'll find wall tanks filled with live trout and sturgeon, and there's an impressive "mountain" with taxidermy wild game animals. Watch out for bears!

For used outdoor gear in good condition, head to **Backcountry Pursuit** (671 S. Capitol Blvd., 208/429-1124, www.backcountrypursuit.com), a consignment store across from Julia Davis Park that sells bikes, skis, snowboards, outdoor clothing, kayaks, and camping and backpacking gear.

SPECIALTY SHOPS

Downtown Boise has several locally owned and operated retail shops. In the Linen District, **Eyes of the World Imports** (1576 W. Grove St., 208/331-1212) sells cool handcrafted, imported items from around the globe, and it's also where you can score a box of Nag Champa incense.

The Record Exchange (1105 W. Idaho St., 208/344-8010, www.therecordexchange. com) occupies the corner of the funky block that also holds the hip bar Neurolux. It's the oldest music seller in town, where you'll find new and used CDs, old vinyl records, and a friendly, knowledgeable staff who can fill you in on the latest news in the Boise music scene.

Dragonfly (414 W. Main St., 208/338-9234) is a popular boutique and gift shop in Old Boise that stocks hippy-chic clothing, greeting cards, and fun figurines, like Gumby and Buddy Christ.

Satiate your sweet tooth at **The Chocolat Bar** (805 W. Bannock St., 208/338-7771, www. thechocolatbar.com), a little shop that specializes in handcrafted truffles, turtles, barks, and dipped fruit. Next door, you'll find the **City Peanut Shop** (803 W. Bannock St., 208/433-3931, www.citypeanut.com). This old-style

Check out the vinyl at the Record Exchange.

store turns out freshly roasted nuts, handmade brittles, and incredible caramel corn.

Just down the way, at the corner of Capitol Boulevard and Idaho Street, you can continue your sweet journey of the downtown area at **Guru Donuts** (204 N. Capitol Blvd.,

208/571-7792, www.gurudonuts.com), which shares a space with the Boise Fry Company in a Victorian-era building near the state capitol. Here you can score artisan donuts with a serious attitude. How does a donut with sangria frosting sound?

Accommodations

Boise has an abundance of corporate hotels and motels, most toward the high end of the $50-100 price range. The major hotel areas are downtown, around the university, around the airport, around the Boise Towne Square mall, and in the ParkCenter business district. The downtown places are mostly upscale, though a few less-expensive independents are available there as well. The university area is close to downtown and both Ann Morrison and Julia Davis Parks, though most of the lodgings here tend to be along busy thoroughfares. The airport area is convenient to I-84 and is where most of the national chain motels are located, but it's a long walk to downtown. The ParkCenter area is hoofable from downtown for those with time and a reasonable fitness level, and it's close to the Boise River. The mall area is on major bus routes. If you have a favorite chain, call its 800 number and chances are it'll have a place in Boise. A number of possibilities, including historic bed-and-breakfast inns and stylish boutique hotels, are listed below.

$50-100

Downtown, you can find clean and comfortable lodging at the **Safari Inn Downtown** (1070 Grove St., 208/344-6556, www.safariinndowntown.com, from $69 d). This motor inn has amenities like high-speed Internet, free continental breakfast, and an outdoor pool and spa. Also downtown is the small **Leku Ona Hotel** (117 S. 6th St., 208/345-6665, www.lekuonaid.com, $65-85), a Basque-run establishment that's next door to Leku Ona restaurant and bar. The rustic hotel may

only have five guest rooms, but it's smack-dab in the middle of Boise's nightclub district. You could literally crawl back to your room after a night of reveling.

The best thing about staying at the somewhat scruffy **Shilo Inn Riverside** (3031 Main St., 208/344-3521 or 800/222-2244, from $74 d) is its location right on the Greenbelt. Avid walkers and cyclists will have no trouble making it downtown or to BSU, and by car it takes less than five minutes. Amenities include a big indoor pool and continental breakfast.

If you're into historic bed-and-breakfast inns, the downtown area has two worth mentioning. The ★ **Idaho Heritage Inn** (109 W. Idaho St., 208/342-8066, www.idheritageinn.com, $75-120) more than lives up to its name. It's an exquisitely lovely lodging in a turn-of-the-20th-century home that once belonged to Governor Chase Clark and later was the residence of his daughter Bethine and son-in-law Senator Frank Church. How's that for heritage? Needless to say, the inn is listed on the National Register of Historic Places. The location can't be beat, within walking distance of Old Boise, BoDo, and the capitol; to help you extend your explorations, mountain bikes are available for rent. The inn's six guest rooms all have private baths, queen beds, air-conditioning, and in-room phones. A full gourmet breakfast is included in the price, as is an evening glass of wine. No smoking or pets are allowed.

The Pink Guest House (716 W. Franklin St., 208/880-8670, from $79 d, three-night minimum), behind the state capitol, offers

The Idanha

Although you can no longer stay here, the grande dame of downtown buildings remains the 1901 **Idanha Hotel** (pronounced EYE-din-ha, 928 W. Main St.), whose tall corner turrets are an impressive sight from blocks away. Famed architect W. S. Campbell designed the French château-style masterpiece, Idaho's first six-story building and the first in the state to have an electric elevator. When it was completed, it was considered the finest hotel west of the Mississippi and featured bay windows, claw-foot tubs, and the finest furnishings. In the hotel's glory days, Teddy Roosevelt, John and Ethel Barrymore, Buffalo Bill, William Borah, and Clarence Darrow all spent nights here. The Idanha's rooms were converted to apartments a few years back, but an Indian restaurant (with a good lunch buffet) on the ground floor is open to the public.

six furnished apartments with kitchens that are great for extended stays. This friendly inn is popular with foreign and domestic travelers who enjoy the independence of an apartment-like lodging experience.

Boise has no shortage of corporate hotels in this price range. On the east side of the BSU campus and across Broadway is **Courtyard by Marriott** (222 S. Broadway Ave., 208/331-2700 or 800/321-2211, from $89 d). It's a big, newish place about a mile from downtown and has an indoor pool, a hot tub, and a fitness center. Nearby in the ParkCenter area is the **Springhill Suites by Marriott** (424 E. ParkCenter Blvd., 208/342-1044, from $89 d), a pet-friendly hotel near the Greenbelt with an outdoor pool and free breakfast.

A variety of places in this price range are out by the airport, including the **Best Western Airport Inn** (2660 Airport Way, 208/384-5000 or 800/727-5004, from $70 d) and **Boise Hotel** (3300 Vista Ave., 208/343-4900, from $79 d), a clean place with a reputable restaurant and bar.

$100-150

The **Grove Hotel** (245 S. Capitol Blvd., 208/333-8000, www.grovehotelboise.com, from $100 d) has the best location in town, adjacent to The Grove, but this high-rise hotel is considered by many to be an urban eyesore. The drab sandstone-hued edifice appears uninviting from the street, and it epitomizes a lack of pedestrian vision in architecture—the hotel and connected CenturyLink Arena

don't offer much sidewalk space, and watch out for delivery trucks and tour buses around the building. That said, the well-appointed guest rooms boast wonderful views of downtown and the Boise Front. You'll find a cocktail lounge and a contemporary restaurant on the ground level.

Also downtown, you'll find the newly constructed **Hampton Inn & Suites** (495 S. Capitol Blvd., 208/331-1900, from $100 d), an 11-story hotel in BoDo that has complimentary breakfast, a coin-operated laundry, and an indoor pool and fitness center. Its central location makes walking around town a breeze.

One of downtown Boise's swankiest new places to sleep is **Hotel 43** (981 W. Grove St., 208/342-4622 or 800/243-4622, www.hotel43. com, from $119 d). This boutique hotel, formerly the Statehouse Inn, boasts 112 stylishly renovated guest rooms with excellent views of the city. Expect to be pampered here with room service, free Wi-Fi, valet parking and an airport shuttle service. Chandler's Steakhouse, on the 1st floor, offers upscale contemporary dining and a top-notch martini bar. In the morning, head to the espresso shop near the lobby for a morning cappuccino and freshly baked pastries.

For a B&B-type experience in this price range, go to the **Boise Guest House** (614 N. 5th St., 208/761-6798, www.boiseguest-house.com, $90-159) near Fort Boise Park. The inn's location next to the Foothills makes for easy access to mountain biking and hiking, and it takes less than five minutes to walk downtown. The guest suites are literally apartments, with private showers, kitchens, and flat-screen televisions, not typical little B&B guest rooms. Besides waking up to a big breakfast, the place also offers free parking and high-speed Internet.

Boise Hillside Suites (4480 N. Kitsap Way, 208/336-6502, www.boisehillsidesuites.com, $85-139) is a beautiful but small boutique hotel nestled in the foothills of Boise's tranquil North End. Here you will find three luxurious suites with individual hot tubs, fireplaces, and private entrances.

On the west side of Capitol Boulevard, backing up against Ann Morrison Park, is **Marriott Residence Inn** (1401 S. Lusk Ave., 208/344-1200, from $100 d). Its 104 suites are more like apartments than motel rooms; all have full kitchens, and many have fireplaces and living rooms. The nicely landscaped complex sits just far enough off Capitol Boulevard to be quiet. Amenities and services include cable TV with HBO, a free airport shuttle, an outdoor pool, spas, and a sport court. A large complimentary breakfast buffet is served in the spacious lobby, and if that doesn't fill you up, you can head to Elmer's next door.

The Riverside Hotel (2900 W. Chinden Blvd., 208/343-1871, from $99 d) has good Greenbelt access west of downtown, in the same area as the Shilo Inn in the previous price category, but catering to a higher-end business clientele. This is Boise's largest hotel, with 304 guest rooms, and the amenities include an outdoor pool and fitness center. Bikes are available for rent too. There's also a restaurant and lounge with a great view of the river.

On the fringe of downtown, the seven-story **Red Lion Hotel Boise Downtowner** (1800 Fairview Ave., 208/344-7691, $79-169) is a popular spot for conferences and business meetings.

$150-250

Boise doesn't have many hotels and inns that cost more than $150 a night. Of course, some of the aforementioned hotels have larger suites in the $175-225 range, but not many places exceed that limit. The ★ **Modern Hotel** (1314 Grove St., 208/424-8244 or 866/780-6012, www.themodernhotel.com, $99-200) in the Linen District, a revamped old-school Travelodge, is as posh as it gets in Boise. The Modern, as everyone calls it, has lots of post-postmodern touches, like contemporary Euro furniture and glass-tiled spa baths. All rooms are accentuated with splashes of bold color, and they have 32-inch flat-screen televisions, free Wi-Fi, and iPod docks. Grab a cocktail at the 1st-floor bar and take it outside to the hip fireplace seating area, where local artists often hang out. The restaurant turns out inventive fare that spotlights locally sourced foodstuffs.

The themed guest rooms at the **Anniversary Inn** (1575 S. Lusk Ave., 208/387-4900, www.anniversaryinn.com, suites $119-299) are among the most expensive lodging options in town, but where else are you going to find a "Jungle Safari" room or a "Biker Roadhouse" room? There's also a room called "Bronco Nights"—for diehard Boise State football fans—all decked out in blue and orange. The hotel may be cheesy, but it remains popular for those desiring a fantasy getaway.

RV PARKS

Boise has some good in-town options for RV campers, though tenters will find slimmer pickings. Unfortunately, the nearby state parks are day-use only, but there is plenty of dispersed camping in the Boise Front. For more information, drop by the **Boise National Forest headquarters** (1249 S. Vinnell Way, 208/373-4100). Here are two good picks if you are driving an RV and want water and electricity hookups.

Tenters are welcome at the **Boise Riverside RV Park** (6000 N. Glenwood St., 208/375-7432, www.boiseriversidervpark.com, RVs $28-35, tents $25) in Garden City. The 215 spaces have Good Sam and AARP discounts. Amenities include a Greenbelt location, high-speed wireless Internet access, and a neat laundry and shower building. The park abuts the Expo Idaho fairgrounds and the baseball stadium where the Boise Hawks play, so expect a bit of noise when games or other fairground events take place.

Hi Valley RV Park (10555 Horseshoe Bend Rd., 208/939-8080, $35) is on the way out of town heading toward McCall on Highway 55.

The big park, about eight miles from downtown Boise in Eagle, has 192 spaces with full hookups, and there are discounts for AAA and Good Sam members. No tents are allowed, but the park has two rental cabins ($81). The clubhouse has a large-screen TV, a full kitchen, spacious shower rooms, a laundry, and a billiard room.

Food and Drink

Boise's restaurant scene took a big hit back in 2008 when a dozen or so of the city's best locally owned eateries closed during the Great Recession. Things are looking up, though, with a recent spate of new openings around town. Here's a snapshot of several venerable restaurants and some new establishments that are helping to redefine the dining scene here.

UPSCALE STEAKHOUSES

If you're into upscale dining in a swanky environment, head to ★ **Chandler's Steakhouse** (981 W. Grove St., 208/383-4300, www.chandlersboise.com, from 4pm daily, appetizers $11-18, entrées $29-50) inside Hotel 43. Restaurateur Rex Chandler debuted this Northwest-influenced steakhouse in 2008 after relocating from Ketchum, where he ran Chandler's and Baci for many years. Success seems to follow Chandler because his Boise restaurant was met with resounding applause by those craving big steaks, seafood, and vintages from one of the best wine lists in town. The kitchen here likes to source Idaho foodstuffs, like Kobe-style beef, Kurobuta pork, Hagerman Valley trout, and local grass-fed lamb. Start out with house-made gravlax, baked oysters, clam chowder, and a delicious roasted artichoke. The entrée menu is mostly à la carte, but the restaurant offers a tasting menu that comes with three courses for around $30. The other

route includes a large list of steaks, like New York strips, rib eyes, and filet mignon, served with chosen sides such as pommes frites and asparagus with hollandaise. Chandler's also has a martini bar (from 4pm daily) that puts out inventive cocktails in a lively setting. Local jazz musicians play in the lounge on a weekly basis.

The Brickyard (601 W. Main St., 208/287-2121, www.brickyardboise.com, 11am-10pm Mon.-Wed., 11am-midnight Thurs., 11am-2am Fri., 5pm-2am Sat., appetizers $6-14, entrées $20-37) is located smack dab in the middle of Boise's nightclub district, at the corner of 6th and Main Streets. Here you can score classic steakhouse fare with a modern twist. Noteworthy appetizer picks include oysters Rockefeller and baked Brie with apples and cashews. The steakhouse specializes in hand-cut steaks and lamb chops, but there's also a good selection of poultry, seafood, and pasta dishes. Plus, there are dueling pianos in the lounge area, a fun place to have a martini and some appetizers.

Locals file into **Lock Stock & Barrel** (1100 W. Jefferson St., 208/336-4266, www.lsbboise.com, 11am-9pm Mon., 11am-10pm Tues.-Sat., 4pm-9pm Sun., entrées $16-42) for the slow-roasted prime rib, but a large variety of steaks, seafood dishes, and classic surf and turf combos round out the menu. Plus, there's an old-school salad bar. Remember those? The casual decor with low lights and candles is suitable for dates and good conversation.

CONTEMPORARY FINE DINING

Local foodies were excited when ★ **The Dish** (205 N. 10th St., 208/344-4231, www. thedishboise.com, 5pm-10pm Mon.-Sat., appetizers $8-12, entrées $12-25) debuted a few years ago on the ground floor of the historic Empire Building, at the corner of 10th and Idaho Streets. Chef Jered Couch is known for his whimsical New American fare, which draws influences from Latin and Asian flavor profiles. He also has a penchant for sourcing local foodstuffs such as goat cheese, buffalo, and seasonal produce. Don't be surprised to see appetizers like crispy beet home fries and pork belly lettuce cups with Bing cherry sambal. Entrées range from blueberry prawns on a jasmine rice waffle to a double-cut pork chop with balsamic-fig jam. The Dish also serves fat burgers made with select ingredients. How does a Brie burger with truffle aioli and red onion marmalade sound? The menu also offers inventive vegetarian, vegan, and gluten-free options daily. Plus, the restaurant has a wine list that boasts lots of Northwest labels, and it pours a rotating array of local microbrews on draft.

Fork (199 N. 8th St., 208/287-1700, www. boisefork.com, 11:30am-10pm Mon.-Thurs., 11:30am-11pm Fri., 9:30am-11pm Sat., 9:30am-9pm Sun., appetizers $4-13, entrées $14-28) is another eatery downtown that focuses on local foodstuffs. This farm-to-fork restaurant changes its menu with the seasons. Start with the fried local cheese curds and pan-fried wild mushrooms atop grilled polenta. Bigger plates include pan-seared Idaho trout with tomato vinaigrette and beef short ribs braised with local ale. Fork also offers a good weekend brunch, and it serves craft cocktails, Northwest wines, and local draft brews.

The restaurant at the ★ **Modern Hotel** (1314 W. Grove St., 208/424-8244, www.the-modernhotel.com, 5pm-10pm Sun.-Wed., 5pm-11pm Thurs.-Sat., brunch 9am-2pm Fri.-Sun., appetizers $6-16, entrées $14-20) recently underwent renovation to expand the kitchen. Now diners can get more than just swanky bar appetizers and craft cocktails at this hip boutique hotel in the Linen District. Chef Nate Whitley's French-tinged menus follow the seasons closely, and he has built solid relationships with local farmers over the years. Expect to find appetizers like smoked Hagerman Valley sturgeon with tarragon crème fraîche and fragrant lamb meatballs bathed in red wine demi-glace. Good entrée picks include a grilled flatiron steak with pickled chanterelles and ultra-tender gnocchi with cherry tomatoes and lemon ricotta.

Berryhill & Co. (121 N. 9th St., 208/387-3553, www.johnberryhillrestaurants.com, 11:30am-9pm Mon.-Thurs., 11:30am-10pm Fri., 5pm-10pm Sat., brunch 10am-2pm Sun., $8-32) is a casual yet stylish restaurant and bar downtown that's full of personality, thanks to a modern design and the eccentricities of its owner, chef John Berryhill. You'll often see him roaming the dining room, cracking jokes and schmoozing the guests. Sit on the happening patio and enjoy starters like shrimp cocktail and chipotle-fried calamari—washed down with a glass of local chardonnay from the expansive wine list. Larger plates include Parmesan-Brie cassoulet, chicken potpie, and a pan-seared Kurobuta pork chop smothered with brandied leeks.

Red Feather Lounge (246 N. 8th St., 208/429-6340, www.bcrfl.com, lunch Mon.-Fri., dinner from 5pm daily, brunch 8:30am-2pm Sat.-Sun., $10-30) is another downtown mainstay known for its excellent New American fare. Even though the place has a bar-like name, it's actually one of the better contemporary restaurants in town. Don't get me wrong, the Red Feather has a great lounge where you can indulge in craft cocktails, local microbrews, and wines from the largest cellar in Boise (more than 5,500 bottles are kept in a towering glass wine storage area). But the seasonal cuisine takes center stage at this stylish restaurant. Restaurateur Dave Krick, who also owns Bittercreek Alehouse next door, is passionate about sourcing local foodstuffs.

On any given night, you might see dishes like grilled halloumi (squeaky Greek cheese) with basil and fresh tomato, braised lamb riblets with harissa (spicy North African sauce), and fried chicken atop savory corn waffles. The bar stays open till 2 am most nights.

For more inventive New American cuisine, check out **Emilio's** (245 S. Capitol Blvd., 208/333-8002, www.grovehotelboise.com, breakfast, lunch, dinner from 5pm daily, entrées $16-35) at the Grove Hotel. This is a true hotel restaurant, and the nighttime menu really shines with a bevy of seasonal offerings. Expect to find appetizers such as artisanal cheese plates and wood-fired flatbread with Tasso ham, tomatoes, basil, and fresh mozzarella. Seal the deal with entrées like pan-seared Alaskan halibut with coconut rice risotto and a roasted rack of lamb with cipollini onion marmalade. The wine list spans the globe, with lots of Northwest and European labels.

On the ground floor of a modern office building, **Cottonwood Grille** (913 W. River St., 208/333-9800, www.cottonwoodgrille. com, 11am-10pm Mon.-Sat., 11am-9pm Sun., $8-35) hides its charms from passersby. Inside, you'll discover that the dining room backs right onto the Greenbelt and the Boise River. In summer, the large patio, replete with pond and waterfall, offers a great place to dine in a riparian setting. The extensive menu at this venerable restaurant includes veggie dishes, soups and salads, pastas, seafood, and all the usual upscale meat dishes—many of which are made with local foodstuffs. Expect to find Northwest-inspired items such as crab cakes, house-smoked trout, and a braised lamb shank with garlicky mashed spuds.

GASTROPUBS

The City of Trees could easily be called the City of Pubs, yet most watering holes here miss the mark in the culinary department. Foodies need not fret, though, because there are a few pubs where the food is just as good if not better than the drinks. ★ **Bittercreek Alehouse** (246 N. 8th St., 208/345-1813, www.bcrfl.com, 11am-late daily, $6-16), next

to the Red Feather Lounge and owned by the same people, has been wildly popular since it opened in 1995. Besides having more than 30 microbrews and imported beers on draft, the kitchen produces some of the best pub grub in town. Expect to find Northwestern offerings like grilled wild sockeye salmon with sweet hazelnut butter, clam chowder, and big burgers topped with local artisanal cheeses.

While **Bardenay** (610 W. Grove St, 208/426-0538, www.bardenay.com, lunch and dinner daily, $7-25), with other branches in Eagle and Coeur d'Alene, may not be a pub per se, this microdistillery on the Basque Block has a stellar reputation for serving creative pub fare to go along with cocktails mixed with its house-made vodka, gin, and rum. The large menu spans the globe with offerings like Thai salmon cakes, cider-brined pork chops, and grilled Hagerman Valley trout with balsamic reduction.

Saint Lawrence Gridiron (705 W. Bannock St., 208/433-5598, www.saintlawrencegridiron.com, 11am-11pm Mon.-Sat., $7-12) is the place to go for quirky Americana pub fare. This little gastropub near the state capitol specializes in applewood-smoked barbecue dishes and entrées with a Southern twist. Don't be surprised to find shrimp and grits, pulled pork sandwiches, sweet corn bisque and a smoked brisket sandwich with pickled onions, arugula, and horseradish-spiked Gorgonzola sauce. Wash everything down with a local microbrew, a glass of Idaho wine, or some bourbon.

The **Tavern at Bown Crossing** (3111 S. Bown Way, 208/345-2277, www.tavernatbown.com, from 11am Mon.-Sat., from 9am Sun., $8-36), in southeast Boise, not only pours cocktails, microbrews, and wines, it also puts out a creative menu of upscale pub fare in a contemporary environment. Standouts include the pot roast nachos, fried calamari with kung pao sauce, warm artichoke heart dip, and grilled filet mignon with potatoes au gratin. Did I mention that it also has a sushi bar? The restaurant has a popular Sunday brunch (9am-3pm) as well.

Boise's burgeoning craft-beer scene

BREWPUBS AND TAPROOMS

Boise's craft-beer scene has skyrocketed in recent years. Several new microbreweries have popped up around town as of late—some with better results than others—to the delight of local beer geeks. Here's a look at a few brewpubs and taprooms where you can enjoy tasty handcrafted beers.

Brewpubs

10 Barrel Brewing Company (826 W. Bannock St., 208/344-5870, www.10barrel. com, 11am-midnight daily, $8-23), at the corner of 9th and Bannock Streets, offers around 15 handcrafted draft beers on any given day. This Bend, Oregon-based microbrewery is known for its big hoppy ales and seasonal stouts and porters. The upscale pub menu plays well with the selection of brews. Expect to find lots of appetizers, big burgers, and stone-oven pizzas.

Crooked Fence Brewing (taproom at 5242 Chinden Blvd., 208/890-4120, www. crookedfencebrewing.com) recently opened a brewpub near its brewery in Garden City called the ★ **Barrelhouse** (5181 Glenwood St., 208/376-4200, www.crookedfencebrewing.com/locations/barrelhouse, lunch and dinner daily, brunch 9am-2pm Sat.-Sun., $6-19), at the corner of Glenwood Street and Chinden Boulevard. Here you can quaff a variety of craft brews, like porters, pale ales, and wheat ales, while playing shuffleboard or pinball in the brewpub's game room. The whimsical menu features items like Frito chili pie, corned beef tacos, and a glazed donut cheeseburger with candied bacon.

Highlands Hollow Brewhouse (2455 Harrison Hollow Ln., 208/343-6820, www. highlandshollow.com, 11am-late daily, $8-17), just off Bogus Basin Road, produces some extremely quaffable microbrews, including golden ale, pale ale, ginger wheat ale, and robust stout. The food here is above average as well, with appetizers like steamer clams, grilled polenta, and pan-fried oysters.

In Boise's Winstead Park neighborhood, you'll find **Sockeye Grill & Brewery** (3019 N. Cole Rd., 208/658-1533, www.sockeyebrew.com, 11am-late daily, $8-18), a long-time brewpub that turns out excellent India pale ale, espresso stout, porter, and various seasonal ales, many of which are now sold in cans at stores around the state. The menu has a typical array of sandwiches, wraps, salads, and rice bowls. Sockeye recently opened a second location (12542 W. Fairview Ave., 208/322-5200, 11am-late daily) in West Boise.

Taprooms

In downtown Boise, check out the aptly named **Boise Brewing** (521 W. Broad St., 208/342-7655, www.boisebrewing.com, 3pm-11pm Mon.-Thurs., 3pm-midnight Fri., noon-midnight Sat., noon-10pm Sun.), next to the *Boise Weekly* offices. This small, community-supported brewery (it used Kickstarter to find investors), near the corner of 6th and Broad Streets, turns out hoppy pale ales and Belgian-style farmhouse ales. The industrial-looking taproom also hosts lots of spoken word events, live music, and visual art shows.

Woodland Empire Ale Craft (1114 W. Front St., 208/602-9318, www.woodlandempire.com, 3pm-10pm Tues.-Thurs., 3pm-11pm Fri., noon-11pm Sat., noon-9pm Sun.), next to Boise Art Glass, is another small brewery downtown that used Kickstarter to raise money for start-up costs. Here you can enjoy a lineup of English-inspired ales, Belgian ales, pale ales, and seasonal brews. The brewery brings in local food trucks to feed its customers.

Next door, you'll find **PreFunk** (1100 W. Front St., 208/331-3865, www.prefunkbar.com, 11am-10pm Mon.-Thurs., 10am-midnight Fri.-Sat., noon-9pm Sun.), a fun craft-beer bar (housed in an old service station) that keeps lots of kegs of select local and regional handcrafted beers. Fill up a growler and head back to your hotel room, or hang out on the patio and quaff a few ales. PreFunk schedules a steady stream of food trucks and beer-related events throughout the year.

Payette Brewing Company (111 W. 33rd St., 208/344-0011, www.payettebrewing.com, 3pm-10pm Mon.-Thurs., noon-10pm Fri.-Sat., noon-6pm Sun.) has made quite the name for itself since it opened in 2011 on the industrial fringe of Boise. Payette's taproom fills up on most nights with people looking to get a taste of the microbrewery's handcrafted flagship and seasonal brews. The brewery puts out India pale ale, brown ale, lager, and stout, all of which are also sold in cans.

For more local craft-beer information, visit **www.boisealetrail.com,** a fairly reliable beer blog where you can get updates, maps, and listings for the breweries around town. You also can read fresh brew news at **www.idahostatesman.com/beer.**

WINE BARS AND WINERY TASTING ROOMS
Wine Bars
Bodovino (404 S. 8th St., 208/336-8466, www.bodovino.com, 11am-11pm Mon.-Thurs., 11am-1am Fri.-Sat., noon-8pm Sun., $7-16), a modernized wine bar in BoDo, lets wine drinkers get interactive by offering 18 self-serve wine dispensing machines (with eight different wines in each unit) filled with bottles from around the globe, including select labels from Idaho's Snake River Valley. The wine-friendly menu features inventive flatbreads, sandwiches, small plates, and a gamut of artisanal cheeses, sold in flights of three. There's also a bottle shop with an extensive selection.

Tastings (2447 Apple St., 208/385-9463, www.tastingsboise.com, noon-9pm Mon.-Sat., $5-15) is a wine bar and bottle shop in East Boise that offers wines from just about everywhere. Expect to find noshes like steamer clams, charcuterie, flatbread pizzas, and assorted cheese plates.

Winery Tasting Rooms
Several local wineries have set up tasting rooms in the downtown area in recent years. These boutique-level producers grow their grapes in the Snake River Valley, Idaho's wine appellation. In BoDo, you can sample some excellent vintages at the aptly named **Snake River Winery** (786 W. Broad St., 208/345-9463, www.snakeriverwinery.com, 10:30am-7:30pm Tues.-Sat., noon-5pm Sun.). This winery grows its grapes at Arena Valley Vineyard in Parma. Chef-turned-winemaker Scott DeSeelhorst produces several remarkable small-batch wines, including syrah, chardonnay, riesling, grenache, barbera, and malbec.

Mouvance Winery (1414 W. Grove St., 208/629-7781, www.mouvancewinery.com, noon-7pm Fri.-Sat., noon-5pm Sun.) is a small operation out of Oregon's Willamette Valley that recently opened a tasting room in the Linen District. This boutique winery specializes in pinot noir, a varietal that doesn't grow well in the high desert, but thrives in the wetter climes of western Oregon.

You can taste some excellent wines on Chinden Boulevard in Garden City at the **44th Street Wineries** (107 E. 44th St.), where you will find **Telaya Wine Company** (208/557-9463, www.telayawine.com, noon-6pm Sat.) and **Coiled Wines** (707/480-4919, www.coiledwines.com, noon-6pm Sat.), the latter of which is the brainchild of winemaker Leslie Preston, who turns out small lots of dry riesling, syrah, and an outstanding red blend called Black Mamba. **Cinder Wines** (107 E. 44th St., 208/376-4023, www.cinderwines.com, 11am-5pm daily) also has a tasting room in the same building. Winemaker Melanie Krause opened this small winery in 2008, after cutting her winemaking teeth at Chateau Ste. Michelle in Washington. Considered one of the best winemakers in Idaho, Krause turns out chardonnay, syrah, viognier, and a wonderfully dry rosé made from grapes grown at various Snake River Valley vineyards.

INTERNATIONAL CUISINE
Basque

More than 10,000 Basques live in the Boise area, so Basque food is fairly embedded into the mainstream culture. In other words, your average Joe can easily identify a croqueta. You'll find two Basque eateries and bars as well as one import market on the Basque Block.

★ **Bar Gernika** (202 S. Capitol Blvd., 208/344-2175, www.bargernika.com, 11am-11pm Mon., 11am-midnight Tues.-Thurs., 11am-1am Fri., 11:30am-1am Sat., $5-10), a tiny place that borrows its name from a city in the Basque region of Spain, is a popular hangout for people from all walks of life. You'll see bifocal-wearing college professors next to visiting Basques (conversing in their tongue-twisting language) next to tattooed 20-something locals—all enjoying big glasses of Rioja (Basque red wine) and draft microbrews. But this bar focuses just as much attention on food as it does on drink. (The Basques love to eat, and talking about food and wine is a favorite pastime as well.) The vibe here is casual, and the kitchen puts out everything from Basque-influenced sandwiches and traditional dishes to American-style burgers and melts. Try an order of croquetas (crunchy fritters made with chicken stock and roux) and a solomo sandwich (marinated pork loin with pimentos) served with hand-cut fries. Other noteworthy dishes include the lamb dip (dripping with jus on a crusty roll), paella, and delicious braised beef tongue—the latter dish is only served on Saturday, and it usually runs out by midday.

Leku Ona (117 S. 6th St., 208/345-6665, www.lekuonaid.com, 11am-late Mon.-Sat., $8-30) sits on the east side of the Basque Block. This restaurant and bar, in a historic brick building, used to be a Basque boardinghouse and social club. It's once again a social hub for Basques and non-Basques alike. It boasts three floors of restaurant and bar space: two separate lounge areas, a downstairs banquet room near the wine cellar, and an elegant 3rd-floor dining room with a rooftop terrace overlooking the Leku Ona Hotel. Whether you're into tapas and Rioja in the bar or a full-service dinner upstairs, Leku Ona has got you covered with a gamut of traditional Basque dishes. Start the night with ham *croquetas,* shrimp-filled piquillo peppers, and escargot baked in zesty butter. Many of the entrées are also made with tried-and-true recipes from the homeland. Expect to see dishes such as braised lamb shank, stewed beef tongue, and pepper-stuffed squid cooked in its own ink. The menu also has lots of grilled steaks and pork chops. (Basques love their meat almost as much as they adore seafood; there aren't many vegetarians in this culture.)

Next door, **The Basque Market** (608 W. Grove St., 208/433-1208, www.thebasquemarket.com, 10am-8pm Mon.-Sat.) is the place to go for all things Basque, like imported wines, cured meats, cheeses, chocolate, good olive oil, house-brined green olives, and more. The market has shifted gears into the restaurant realm in recent years. You can now score paella, sandwiches, and various tapas/pintxos dishes and take them to a table on the sidewalk patio. The Basque Market also sells freshly baked bread and tubs of house-made soups as well as delicious rice pudding.

Italian

Boise has a typical profusion of corporate Italian places out in the burbs, yet there are a few restaurants in the downtown area that make Italian food from scratch. **Asiago's** (1002 Main St., 208/336-5552, www.asiagos. com, lunch 11am-4pm Mon.-Fri., dinner 4pm-10pm daily, $9-28), in the historic Gem-Noble Building, has earned a loyal following for its creative regional Italian offerings. The exposed-brick dining room and wine bar quickly fills up on most nights with people craving big glasses of Sangiovese and dishes like herb-crusted veal loin with sweet vermouth-lemon reduction and grilled flatbread with pesto, artichoke hearts, and arugula. Pasta is made fresh daily, and the list might include rosemary gnocchi, shrimp and clam linguine, and spinach fettuccine with smoked tomato cream sauce.

Richard's Café Vicino (808 W. Fort St., 208/472-1463, www.cafevicino.com, lunch 11:30am-2:30pm Mon.-Fri., dinner from 5pm daily, $6-30) in the city's North End dishes up remarkable Italian fare in a casual setting. Chef Richard Langston's decidedly Mediterranean menu changes with the season and his whimsy. Expect to find entrées like cioppino, cheese ravioli with brown butter-sage sauce, and pan-seared New York strip steak served with Gorgonzola soufflé. Smaller plates might include prosciutto-wrapped figs, grilled shrimp on risotto cakes, and bruschetta with artichoke tapenade. The wine list has plenty of Italian and regional American labels, including some from Idaho's Snake River Valley.

Alavita (807 W. Idaho St., 208/780-1100, www.alavitaboise.com, 11:30am-10pm Mon.-Thurs., 11:30am-11pm Fri., 4pm-11pm Sat., $8-29) is the sister restaurant to Fork, right around the corner in the same building, at the corner of 8th and Idaho Streets. The contemporary Italian restaurant turns out lots of dishes made with scratch sauces and housemade pastas, not to mention an array of small plates, salads, and seasonal soups. The broiled halibut with gremolata, butternut squash ravioli, and Barolo-braised beef short ribs are solid picks. There's an extensive wine list, with an emphasis on labels from various regions in Italy, and plenty of cocktails.

Mediterranean

For tasty Lebanese fare, check out **Mazzah** (404 E. ParkCenter Blvd., 208/333-2223, and 1772 W. State St., 208/333-2566, www.mazzahboise.com, lunch and dinner daily, $5-13). This local fast-food restaurant sells falafel sandwiches, gyros, lamb kabobs, and dolmas (stuffed grape leaves). Also expect to find tabbouleh salad, baba ghanoush, and hummus, served with warm flatbread. Finish with some jolting Turkish coffee and a wedge of flaky baklava.

Chinese

At one time, more than a century ago, Boise had a large Chinatown with many Chinese restaurants. Now the city only has a few worth mentioning, unless you're into mediocre Chinese buffets.

Yen Ching (305 N. 9th St., at Bannock St., 208/384-0384, www.yenchingboise.com, lunch and dinner daily) is a local favorite. Here you can enjoy recognizable Chinese cuisine in a pleasant setting. The dining room is accented with stylish art and ornate Asian screens. Sit in a comfy booth and peruse the large menu of Hunan, Szechuan, and Cantonese offerings—all cooked in the eye-catching Mandarin style. The dinner menu ($10-14) has barbecued spareribs, egg drop soup, fried rice, and roasted duck. The twice-cooked pork and kung pao chicken are good choices as well. Vegetarians won't feel left out; there are plenty of properly cooked tofu and veggie options for them. The restaurant also serves dim sum, like barbecued pork buns and silky shrimp dumplings. Wash everything down with a cold Chinese beer or a cocktail from the lounge.

In the Bench Depot neighborhood, you can take care of that craving for Chinese food at **Panda Garden** (2801 Overland Rd., 208/433-1188, www.pandagardenboise.com,

10:30am-10:30pm Sun.-Thurs., 10:30am-11pm Fri.-Sat., $6-12). This small Chinese restaurant, which also serves sushi and sashimi, puts out decent Cantonese and Hunan-inspired food. Expect to see lots of egg rolls, soups, stir-fried dishes, and moo shu in every conceivable form, as well as more Americanized fare like egg foo yong and chow mein. Vegetarians should try the tofu and broccoli with brown rice. The service is friendly and swift, and they will deliver to your hotel room.

Thai

If you've got a hankering for nose-clearing curries and wok-seared noodles, head to ★ **Pad Thai House** (1473 S. Five Mile Rd., 208/375-6014, www.padthaihouseboise.com, lunch and dinner daily, $7-14), near the corner of Five Mile and Overland Roads. This popular Thai restaurant may be situated in an innocuous-looking strip mall, but the inside is beautifully designed with Thai woodcarvings and elegant furniture. Plus, service is incredibly friendly and efficient. The menu has Thai offerings from the country's four culinary regions, including coconut milk-infused curries (red, green, and golden) and soups, satay, and sweet and spicy pad thai as the name suggests. The honey-roasted duck and green papaya salad are also noteworthy dishes.

Chiang Mai (4898 W. Emerald St., at Orchard St., 208/342-4051, lunch and dinner daily, $6-14) puts out excellent Thai cuisine from the northern reaches of Siam. Besides fresh rolls, green papaya salad, and Panang curry, the menu also has dishes from other regions in Thailand, like chicken and pork satay, southern-style curries and soups, and a delicious beef salad redolent of lime, ginger, and red chili paste. Don't worry, though, Chiang Mai serves ice-cold Thai beer and creamy iced tea to put out the fire.

Vietnamese

Unlike Portland and Seattle, Boise is not known for having good Vietnamese food. (This may have something to do with the fact that only about 1,000 Vietnamese people live in the area.) But a few decent Vietnamese restaurants have opened here in recent years. **Pho Nouveau** (780 W. Idaho St., 208/367-1111, www.phonouveau.com, lunch and dinner daily, $6-15) dishes up big bowls of pho (beef noodle soup), served with fresh basil, bean sprouts, sliced peppers, and lime. Also expect to find other traditional Vietnamese specialties like Saigon-style crepes, shaken beef salad, and crispy spring rolls (cha gio).

For Vietnamese-style sandwiches, check out the **Baguette Deli** (5204 W. Franklin Rd., 208/336-2989, lunch and dinner daily, sandwiches around $6), next to the Fred Meyer department store on Orchard Street. This affordable restaurant specializes in banh mi, Vietnamese sandwiches (grilled beef, shrimp, pork loaf, roasted chicken, and veggie "ham") made on crusty baguette rolls with pickled radish, cilantro, and jalapeño. Besides banh mi, also expect to see pork and shrimp spring rolls, sweet pastries, Vietnamese coffee (with sweet condensed milk), and bubble tea.

Japanese

For a city that's about an eight-hour drive from the nearest ocean, Boise sure has a lot of sushi joints, but not all of them are noteworthy. One sure bet is ★ **Shige** (100 N. 8th St., 208/338-8423, lunch and dinner Mon.-Sat., $10-30) on the 2nd floor of the Capitol Terrace building. This downtown sushi bar is as authentic as it gets in Boise, and the interior design is straight out of Tokyo, with its wraparound counter, rice-paper lanterns, and glass case packed with relatively fresh fish. Chef Shigeki Matsuzawa and his crew turn out a large array of sushi and sashimi, including maki rolls (traditional and fusion), hand rolls, nigiri, and Kumamoto oysters on the half-shell. If raw fish isn't to your liking, go for the hot dishes such as shrimp tempura, chicken tonkatsu, and miso soup. Expect the usual array of sake, rice lagers, and sweet plum wine.

In BoDo, **Happy Fish Sushi** (855 Broad St., 208/343-4810, www.happyfishsushi.com, lunch and dinner daily, $6-20), in the alley next to the Knitting Factory Concert House, is a popular hangout for young hipsters who come here for sushi, sashimi, and martinis. The menu has lots of fusion rolls, nigiri, and other Japanese specialties such as beef tataki and poke, a martini glass filled with cubed raw tuna and spicy sesame sauce. Hot items include rice bowls, tempura, miso-glazed salmon, and edamame (blanched soybeans) sprinkled with sea salt.

Zen Bento (1000 W. Main St., 208/388-8808, www.zenbento.com, 11am-7pm Mon.-Sat., $7-10) is a downtown take-out place that focuses on teriyaki rice bowls and salads. Walk up to the counter and pick your protein (grilled chicken, beef, salmon, ahi, tofu) and they'll plop it in a bowl with steamed rice and crisp veggies. Sauces come on the side, and they include regular teriyaki, ginger-soy, and a zippy chili-garlic sauce, to name a few. There's also a Zen Bento (342 E. State St., 208/938-4277, 11am-8pm Mon.-Sat.) in nearby Eagle.

Indian

Boise has two noteworthy Indian restaurants. **Taj Mahal** (150 N. 8th St., 208/473-7200, www.tajmahalofboise.com, lunch buffet 11:30am-2:30pm Mon.-Sat., dinner 5pm-10pm Mon.-Sat., $6-20), across the terrace from Shige, leans to Pakistan and northern India for inspiration. The menu has everything from saucy curry dishes to tandoori chicken specialties to flatbreads like naan, kulcha, and roti. Start out with samosas (little meat pies), kebabs, and pakora (crunchy veggie fritters) washed down with an Indian beer or aromatic chai tea. Standout main dishes include chicken biryani (seasoned basmati rice) and vindaloo lamb, a spicy Goan curry guaranteed to open your nasal passages. Cool your palate with a bowl of rice pudding spiked with cardamom and almonds (kheer). Like most Indian restaurants, Taj Mahal offers a lunch buffet that's packed with all the Indian standards.

Madhuban (6930 W. State St., near Glenwood St., 208/853-8215, lunch and dinner daily, $7-16) also serves good Indian cuisine. Here you can choose from a large selection of traditional dishes such as chicken tikka masala, lamb vindaloo, and shrimp cooked with spinach and fresh herbs. Noteworthy vegetarian dishes include aloo chana (chickpeas and potatoes) and tarka dal (lentils stewed with spices). There's plenty of freshly baked naan bread to soak up the sauces. Madhuban puts out an excellent lunch buffet spread daily.

Mexican

Most locals would agree that nearby Canyon County has the best Mexican food in the area thanks to a large Hispanic population in Nampa and Caldwell. In Boise, Mexican cuisine is hit or miss, but here's a good place that doesn't melt orange cheese on everything: **Andrade's** (4903 W. Overland Rd., 208/344-1234, www.andradesboise.com, lunch and dinner daily, $7-12) serves authentic Mexican fare such as chiles rellenos, tamales, torta sandwiches, and tacos galore. Carnitas (fried pork butt) and carne asada (marinated, grilled skirt steak) are good choices if you're into tacos. Most dishes include rice and refried beans, not to mention chips and salsa. The beverage list boasts a good lineup of Mexican beers and sodas.

In Hyde Park, check out **Parrilla Grill** (1512 N. 13th St., 208/323-4688, www.parrillagrillhydepark.com, restaurant 7am-10pm daily, cantina 11am-late daily, $5-10), a funky Tex-Mex joint with a rockin' outdoor cantina. This place serves mission-style burritos and globally inspired wraps morning, noon, and night. Also expect to find tacos, nachos, and lots of freshly made salsas. The bar patio is so much fun you won't want to leave.

PIZZA

★ **Pie Hole** (www.pieholeusa.com) is a pizza joint that's popular with locals, especially the nighttime bar crowd. With two Boise locations, one downtown (205 N. 8th St., 208/344-7783, 11am-3am Mon.-Thurs., 11am-4am Fri.-Sat., noon-3am Sun.) and one by the university (1016 Broadway, 208/424-2225, 11am-3am Mon.-Thurs., 11am-4am Fri.-Sat., noon-3am Sun.), Pie Hole serves whole pies and pizza by the slice (around $2). Expect to see New York-style pizzas, ranging from a tasty potato and bacon pie to a meaty creation called the "Tritalian," loaded with pepperoni, salami, and Italian sausage. The meatless crowd will surely like the four-cheese and veggie pizzas.

In BoDo, **Proto's Pizzeria Napoletana** (345 S. 8th St., 208/331-1400, www.proto-spizza.com, 11am-9:30pm daily, $6-18) also makes thin-crust pizzas with premium toppings like hearts of palm, kalamata olives, and prosciutto. For dessert, try the classic cannoli and lemon gelato.

Guido's Pizzeria (235 N. 5th St., 208/345-9011, and 12375 Chinden Blvd., 208/376-1008, 11am-9pm Sun.-Thurs., 11am-10pm Fri.-Sat.) dishes up true New York-style pizza, served with a Big Apple attitude that borders on rude at times. Here you can score salads, sausage rolls, stromboli, whole pizzas (a 20-inch cheese pie is around $12), and pizza by the slice.

Another longtime local favorite is **Flying Pie** (6508 Fairview Ave., 208/345-0000, and 4320 W. State St., 208/384-0000, www.flying-pie.com, lunch and dinner daily), a friendly pizzeria that serves decent pizzas with typical toppings. It's a great place for families, and they deliver all over town.

BURGER JOINTS AND SANDWICH SHOPS
Burgers

Without a doubt, ★ **Big Jud's** (1289 S. Protest Rd., 208/343-4439, www.bigjudsboise.com, 11am-9pm Mon.-Sat., under $10) makes the best and biggest burgers in town. Known for its one-pound and two-pound gut-bombs (made with hand-formed beef patties), this burger joint near BSU is an institution in these parts. Don't worry, though, Big Jud's also sells smaller burgers, served with hand-cut fries and real ice-cream milkshakes.

Westside Drive-In (1929 W. State St., 208/342-2957, and 1113 ParkCenter Blvd., 208/424-0000, www.cheflou.com, lunch and dinner daily) is a classic burger joint operated by Lou Aaron, a local chef known for his great food and big personality. Expect to find big burgers, fries, shakes, and even prime rib with the works on weekends.

Downtown, ★ **Boise Fry Company** (204 N. Capitol Blvd., 208/495-3858, www.boise-frycompany.com, 11am-9pm daily, $4-10) is the place to go for twice-cooked, Belgian-style fries. Not only do you get to choose what kind of potato you want (russet, Yukon gold, sweet potato, white, Peruvian purple), you also get to pick the cut, ranging from traditional to shoestring to curly. House-made sauces, like smoky chipotle and blueberry ketchup, are there for dipping. You would be remiss not to try the wonderful burgers as well. Boise Fry Co. has three other Treasure Valley locations.

Also downtown, you should try **Grind Modern Burger** (705 W. Fulton St., 208/342-0944, www.grindmodernburger.com, lunch and dinner daily, $6-12), a new eatery that puts out inventive burgers in the former Table Rock Brewpub spot. Actually, Grind also makes small batches of handcrafted beers, using the existing equipment. Don't be surprised to find wild and wacky burgers, like one called the "DMZ," made with pork belly, Asian slaw, and spicy Saigon sauce, and fun appetizers such as sweet potato tots with maple aioli and a big pretzel with an ale-cheese sauce. Besides the house-made brews, expect to find a multitude of other local beers on tap, as well as craft cocktails and wines by the glass. The friendly folks who own Grind also operate a bustling beer market in the same building called Brewforia, meaning you can grab a bottle of your favorite beer (and they probably have it, even if it's rare) and take it to your table.

Sandwiches

Like most cities, Boise has no shortage of sandwich shops. Here's a look at a few locally owned delis that get it right. **Cobby's** (1030 Broadway, 208/345-0990, and 6899 Overland Rd., 208/323-0606, www.cobbys.com, lunch and dinner daily, sandwiches $5-13) is definitely the place to go for old-school submarine sandwiches. Recommended are the hot meatball sub and Italian sandwich made with capicolla ham, Genoa salami, mortadella, and provolone. They also make decent veggie subs.

★ **On the Fly** (800 W. Main St., 208/344-6833, www.ontheflydeli.com, 8am-6pm Mon.-Fri., $4-13) recently debuted in the new 8th & Main building in downtown Boise. As the name suggests, this rotisserie-style deli, owned by chef Dustan Bristol of Brick 29 Bistro in Nampa, is fast and efficient, thanks to a row of reach-in coolers packed with freshly made sandwiches, seasonal salads, and small bites. You can also get panini sandwiches, soups, and baked goods from behind the counter. The deli makes its own rotisserie-roasted chicken, ham, and roast beef. How does a chicken salad sandwich with fresh tarragon sound? How about an egg salad sandwich with sweet and smoky bacon jam?

Zeppole Baking Co. (217 N. 8th St., 208/345-2149, www.zeppolebakery.com, breakfast and lunch Mon.-Sat.) is a local bakery that turns out freshly baked baguettes and other loaves of artisanal bread. But they also have a café downtown that serves sandwiches (around $5), house-made soups, and salads. Most sandwiches are made on crusty focaccia rolls, and Zeppole is also known for its cookies and long breadsticks coated with pesto and Parmesan. The veggie sandwich (with roasted red pepper, spinach, olives, and feta and provolone cheeses) will keep you coming back.

SEAFOOD

Reel Foods Fish Market (611 S. Capitol Blvd., 208/342-2727, www.reelfoodsfish.net, 11am-3pm Mon.-Sat., $4-15) is a longtime seafood shop—next to Grind Modern Burger—that recently opened a small oyster bar and lunch counter. Here you can get fresh-as-can-be oysters on the half shell, sushi, and other raw items like a poke tuna bowl with zesty sesame dressing. Noteworthy hot items include seafood chowder, fish and chips, and an oyster po' boy on a crusty roll. The market also serves a good selection of bottled microbrews and Idaho wines.

Nearby, in BoDo, you can also enjoy classic seafood offerings at **Fresh Off the Hook** (401 S. 8th St., 208/343-0220, www.freshoffthehookseafood.com, 11am-9pm daily, $5-20). This is where locals go for steamer clams, crab cakes, and ultra-creamy clam chowder. Also expect to find baked salmon, pasta dishes, fish and chips, assorted seafood sandwiches, and more.

BREAKFAST

Don't be surprised to see a line out the door on weekends at ★ **Goldy's Breakfast Bistro** (108 S. Capitol Blvd., 208/345-4100, www.goldysbreakfastbistro.com, 6:30am-2pm Mon.-Fri., 7:30am-2pm Sat. and Sun., $6-12). This breakfast hotspot, kitty-corner from the Egyptian Theatre, is known for its funky dining room (the balcony is a great spot to watch people) and creative menu, with dishes like banana French toast, red flannel hash, eggs Benedict, and a delish red potato-dill frittata. You can also fire up your morning with a plate of habanero sausage and eggs. They pour a good cup of coffee to boot.

Bacon (915 W. Idaho St., 208/387-3553, www.johnberryhillrestaurants.com, breakfast and lunch daily, $6-12), owned by chef John Berryhill, and just around the corner from his flagship restaurant, Berryhill & Co., is all about beloved bacon. The restaurant offers eight different kinds of bacon, including chocolate-covered bacon, pancetta bacon, and even tempeh bacon for vegetarians. The kitchen puts out various egg dishes, sandwiches, and entrée salads, many of which, you guessed it, feature bacon. Bacon is also known for its large variety of Bloody Marys.

★ **Janjou Patisserie** (1754 W. State St., 208/297-5853, www.janjou.com, 7am-5pm Tues.-Sat., 8am-2pm Sun., $4-8) is a French-inspired boutique bakery in the North End that turns out freshly baked croissants, fruit tarts, chocolate éclairs, cookies, and excellent quiche. Try the quiche with sautéed leeks and goat cheese, washed down with a latte made with locally roasted espresso beans.

Up on Fairview Avenue, you'll find a

popular restaurant that serve breakfast all day. **The Egg Factory** (8061 W. Fairview Ave., 208/322-0191, 6:30am-3pm daily, under $10), at the corner of Milwaukee Street and Fairview Avenue, serves a large variety of creative egg dishes and other breakfast items. The expansive menu is full of food puns, like "Strawberry Fields Pancakes," "Buenos Dias Burrito," and "Are You Yolkin' Egg Sandwich."

COFFEEHOUSES

Corporate coffee chains (primarily Starbucks and Dutch Bros.) are widespread in the Boise area. But if you're looking for indie coffeehouses, The City of Trees has plenty of options.

The big, comfortable ★ **Flying M Coffee House** (500 W. Idaho St., 208/345-4320, www.flyingmcoffee.com, 6:30am-11pm Mon.-Fri., 7:30am-11pm Sat., 7:30am-6pm Sun.) is popular with locals who like to kick back here on the old sofas while reading or chatting with friends. The menu has the usual array of coffeehouse concoctions as well as light egg dishes and baked goods. Flying M, which also has a coffeehouse in downtown Nampa, features live acoustic music and art shows on occasion.

Dawson Taylor is a local coffee roaster with several locations in the Treasure Valley. The company's flagship coffeehouse, **Dawson's Downtown** (219 N. 8th St. near Bannock St., 208/336-5633, www.dawsontaylor.com, 6am-10pm Mon.-Thurs., 6am-11pm Fri.-Sat., 7am-9pm Sun.), is a hip place that serves a wide variety of coffee made from fairtrade beans sourced throughout the world, some of which are organically grown. Expect to find espresso blends, Vienna roast, French roast, and several signature blends.

In the Linen District, ★ **Big City Coffee & Café** (1416 W. Grove St., 208/345-3145, 6am-6pm Mon.-Sat., 6am-4pm Sun.) has earned a reputation for making excellent espresso drinks and baked goods, like apricot scones, bear claws, cinnamon rolls, and pumpkin chai muffins. Big City also serves breakfast sandwiches and steamed egg dishes as well as soup and sandwiches during lunchtime.

Another local favorite is **Java** (6am-9pm Mon.-Fri., 7am-9pm Sat., 7am-6pm Sun.) with two Boise locations: downtown (223 N. 6th St., 208/345-0777) and Hyde Park (1612 N. 13th St., 208/345-4777). This Ketchum-based coffeehouse uses organic fair-trade beans for its espresso drinks that boast clever names like Bowl of Soul, a Mexican mocha with a hint of cinnamon, and Keith Richards, a four-shot concoction that will have you jittering like the rock star himself. Java isn't all about coffee, though. The place also dishes up breakfast sandwiches, huevos rancheros, steel-cut oatmeal, and tasty baked goods.

GROCERIES

Boise Co-op (888 W. Fort St., 208/472-4500, www.boisecoop.com, 7am-10pm daily) in the North End is Boise's oldest natural food store. In addition to locally grown organic produce, soymilk, yogurt, vitamins, and other staples of a healthy diet, you'll find a large selection of cheeses, artisanal bread, a deli offering sandwiches and salads, and a great selection of microbrews. Across the parking lot is the co-op's wine shop (915 N. 8th St., 208/472-4519), where you can choose from a large variety of labels from around the world.

Downtown, there's a **Whole Foods Market** (401 S. Broadway Ave., 208/287-4600), between Myrtle and Front Streets, and a **Trader Joe's** (300 S. Capitol Blvd., 208/336-7282), if you really must have some wasabi peas and a bottle of "Two Buck Chuck."

For a good deal on everyday groceries, head to **Winco,** an employee-owned local grocery chain with two Boise locations (110 E. Myrtle St., 208/424-1634, and 8200 W. Fairview Ave., 208/377-9840, open 24 hours daily).

Information and Services

TOURIST INFORMATION

The **Boise Convention and Visitors Bureau** (250 S. 5th St., 208/344-7777, www. boise.org, 8:30am-5pm Mon.-Fri.) offers resources for inquiring minds. The **Boise Centre Visitors Center** (850 W. Front St., 208/336-8900, 10am-4pm Mon.-Fri.), at the corner of 9th and Front Streets, provides racks of free literature as well.

The **Boise Metro Chamber of Commerce** (250 S. 5th St., 208/472-5200) can also tell you what's going on around town. The **Idaho Department of Commerce** (700 W. State St., 208/334-2470, www.visitidaho.org) offers tourism information for all parts of the state, and it has a great website.

The **Idaho Outfitters & Guides Association** (711 N. 5th St., 208/342-1438, www.ioga.org) can hook you up with various outfitters and guides throughout the state. The **National Weather Service** (208/334-9860) can keep you up to date with local weather conditions. Log onto www.wrh.noaa. gov/boi for current weather information in the region.

MEDIA

The *Idaho Statesman* (www.idahostatesman.com), part of the McClatchy Company, is the largest-circulation daily in Idaho. Scene (Fridays), the newspaper's entertainment weekly, has concert and event previews, restaurant reviews, and an entertainment calendar. The Outdoors section (Thursdays) offers lots of great tips and articles about fun stuff to do out in the wilds. The *Boise Weekly* (www.boiseweekly.com) is a good liberal rag that acts as a watchdog on the establishment; it'll also direct you to the heart of Boise's hip arts and entertainment scene. *The Arbiter* (www.arbiteronline.com), Boise State University's twice-weekly student newspaper,

is available on campus and at other locations around town.

KBSU (www.radio.boisestate.edu), the city's NPR affiliate, has three signals: jazz and news at 90.3 FM; classical music, news, and information at 91.5 FM; and jazz at 730 AM. Programming schedules can be seen on the website. For local and national talk radio, dial up **KIDO** (580 AM) or **KBOI** (670 AM). **Radio Boise** (89.9 FM and 93.5 FM) is a community-powered radio station that plays an eclectic mix of music. Expect to hear everything from indie rock to gospel to world beats.

Libraries

The main branch of the **Boise Public Library** (715 S. Capitol Blvd., 208/384-4076, www.boisepubliclibrary.org, 10am-9pm Mon.-Thurs., 10am-6pm Fri., 10am-5pm Sat., noon-5pm Sun.) is located across from the Boise Art Museum and Julia Davis Park. Boise State's **Albertsons Library** (208/426-1204) is a good place to do some research and look at periodicals, but you can't check out anything unless you're a student or faculty.

POST OFFICES

Visit the **main post office** (770 S. 13th St., 800/275-8777) or the **Borah Station** post office (750 W. Bannock St.) in the old Federal Building.

HOSPITALS

If you pull an "endo" over your mountain bike handlebars and need to get stitched up, Boise has two main hospitals: **St. Luke's Boise Medical Center** (190 E. Bannock St., 208/381-2222), near the intersection of Warm Springs and Broadway Avenues, and **Saint Alphonsus Regional Medical Center** (1055 N. Curtis Rd., 208/367-2121) just off the Curtis Road exit on the I-84 Connector.

Getting There and Around

GETTING THERE
By Air
The **Boise Airport** (BOI, 3201 Airport Way, 208/383-3110, www.iflyboise.com) is on the southeast edge of town at I-84 Exit 53 (Vista Ave.).

Airlines serving the city include **Delta/SkyWest** (800/221-1212), which offers daily flights (through its Salt Lake City hub) to Minneapolis, Los Angeles, and Salt Lake City; **Southwest** (800/435-9792), offering direct daily flights between Boise and Denver, Las Vegas, Phoenix, Oakland, and Spokane; and **United** (800/241-6522), with direct daily flights to and from San Francisco, Chicago, Houston, Denver, and Los Angeles. **Alaska Airlines/Horizon Air** (800/654-5669) offers nonstop daily flights between Boise and Portland, Sacramento, San Diego, San Jose, Seattle, and Lewiston. **US Airways** (800/428-4322) offers nonstop daily flights to and from Phoenix.

The airport, which boasts of beautiful artwork throughout the concourse, recently went hyper-local when it replaced all its corporate food and beverage services with local businesses, including Big City Coffee, Boise Co-op, Bardenay, and Parrilla Grill. Besides food and drink, you'll also find a convenient business center with phones, fax machines, photocopiers, and both FedEx and UPS courier drops.

Car-rental companies with offices in the airport include **Avis** (208/383-3350 or 800/331-1212), **Budget** (208/383-3090 or 800/527-0700), **Enterprise** (208/381-0650 or 800/736-8222), **Hertz** (208/383-3100 or 800/654-3131), and **National** (208/383-3210 or 800/227-7368).

Those heading directly from Boise's airport to the Sun Valley area can catch the **Sun Valley Express** bus (877/622-8267, $69 each way with advance purchase), which offers two round-trips daily. Many Boise hotels and motels run free shuttle buses to the airport. You can catch a cab out front if need be; cab fare to downtown (four miles) costs about $12. The budget alternative is the **Valley Ride** city bus (208/345-7433, www.valleyride.org); Route 3 connects the airport with downtown for $1. Go online for bus schedules and information.

By Bus
Downtown, you'll find an old, scuffed-up **Greyhound** terminal (1212 W. Bannock St., 208/343-3681, www.greyhound.com), where three buses daily connect Boise with Portland as well as Salt Lake City. Sharing the Greyhound terminal is **Northwestern Trailways** (509/838-4029, www.northwesterntrailways.com), which offers one bus daily to McCall, Grangeville, Lewiston, Coeur d'Alene, and Spokane (with onward connections to Seattle).

By Car
I-84 runs east-west across southern Idaho, connecting Portland (430 miles; about a seven-hour drive) to the west and Salt Lake City (345 miles; about a five-hour drive) to the southeast. Highway 55 leaves Boise headed north to New Meadows, where it joins U.S. 95, the only north-south route traversing the entire state. It takes about seven hours (380 miles) to drive to Coeur d'Alene from Boise on the winding, two-lane U.S. 95. South of Boise, Highway 55 rejoins U.S. 95 for its run across the desert to Winnemucca, Nevada, and points south. For 24-hour **road conditions** in Idaho, dial 511 or visit www.511.idaho.gov. You can download a free app for your mobile device at this website.

It's important to note that the speed limit was recently increased to 80 mph on several of Idaho's interstates, including the western stretch of I-84. But the speed limit drops to

65 mph once you enter Oregon at Ontario, where you will often see Oregon State Police hanging out looking for speeders. Speaking of law enforcement, the Idaho State Police and other agencies in Idaho appear to be profiling cars with Colorado, Washington, Oregon, and California plates (states that have legalized marijuana in one capacity or another), looking for people transporting pot across state lines. Idaho is not a marijuana-friendly state, and don't be surprised to see K-9 police cruisers parked alongside the road at the Idaho-Oregon line.

GETTING AROUND
Driving and Parking

Driving around downtown Boise could give you fits; the one-way streets always seem to go the wrong way. It's best just to find a place to park and hoof it or bike around town. Both those nonpolluting modes of transportation are safe and practical downtown.

Municipal pay-parking lots are scattered throughout downtown; many downtown merchants validate parking. Metered spaces line the streets, and empty ones aren't too difficult to find, even in the heart of downtown. Look for the blue button on most meters; press it and you'll get 20 free minutes, which makes those quick trips much less of a hassle. You will only need to plug these meters 8am-6pm Monday-Friday. Weekends are free for now. Make sure to read the hours on the meters in case things change. There's been

talk recently about adding Saturdays to the pay schedule.

Bicycling

Bicycling isn't just a Boise passion—it's probably the most efficient mode of transportation here. The city, even out to the limits of the greater urban area, is still small enough to get around by bike without requiring a major time commitment. In the downtown area, biking (or even walking) is often faster than driving for most trips. Many streets are designated bike routes, with wide lanes marked specifically for cyclists. Even better than the bike lanes is the Boise Greenbelt, a multiple-use car-free path that follows the beautiful Boise River from one end of the city to the other. Using the Greenbelt and the bike lanes, you can get around town in a jiffy.

City Bus

Valley Ride (208/345-7433, www.valleyride. org), part of the Valley Regional Transit system, operates more than 20 bus routes in Boise and Garden City—radiating out from the downtown transit mall bordered by Capitol Boulevard, 9th Street, Main Street, and Idaho Street. Fare is $1; an all-day pass costs $3. You can pick up route brochures at Boise City Hall (N. Capitol Blvd. and W. Idaho St.) and at area Albertsons grocery stores, or simply go online to download current schedules. Valley Ride's new underground transit center in downtown Boise should be completed by the end of 2016.

Southwest Idaho

Look for ★ to find recommended sights, activities, dining, and lodging.

Highlights

★ **Sunny Slope Wineries:** In 2007 the U.S. government approved the Snake River Valley American Viticultural Area, opening the door to major growth in the state's winemaking industry, especially in the Sunny Slope area (page 87).

★ **Deer Flat National Wildlife Refuge:** This expansive wildlife refuge south of Nampa is one of the oldest of its kind in the United States, thanks in part to President Theodore Roosevelt. The 11,430-acre refuge is a watery safe haven for migratory birds such as mallards and Canada geese (page 93).

★ **National Oldtime Fiddlers' Contest and Festival:** Thousands of people show up in the small town of Weiser every June for the best hoedown this side of the Mississippi (page 107).

★ **Silver City:** To call Silver City a ghost town wouldn't be entirely accurate. This former mining town still has some year-round residents who live in the historic buildings, one of which is the operational Idaho Hotel (page 113).

★ **Bruneau Dunes State Park:** Bruneau Dunes State Park is a spectacle to behold as two prominent sand mounds rise nearly 500 feet from the sagebrush-dotted desert floor. The park is also known for its night-sky observatory that boasts a 25-inch telescope (page 116).

★ **Idaho City:** Travelers get a true Wild West experience in the heart of the Boise Mountains in this former boomtown, which has beautifully preserved its many historical sights (page 117).

★ **Thunder Mountain Line:** An excursion railroad company based in Horseshoe Bend, the line offers several scenic train rides along the steep grades of the Payette River (page 125).

S outhwest Idaho's scenery is geographically diverse—colorful desert canyon lands and ponderosa pine-studded mountains—and it is the most densely populated area in the Gem State.

The Boise suburbs of Eagle, Meridian, and Nampa have recently experienced major growth as housing developments quickly replace old farms that once dotted the high-desert landscape. But it doesn't take long to go from busy streets to remote blue highways in this western swath of the Snake River Plain, commonly referred to as the Treasure Valley.

The ominous Owyhee Mountains loom in the near distance along the Oregon border, beckoning adventurous types who desire extreme desert remoteness. To the north, the dry desert floor runs up against the shadowy foothills of the Boise Mountains, rising dramatically to a panorama of granite peaks and ponderosa pine forests. This rugged region, known as the Boise Basin, was a hotbed of gold-mining activity during the mid-19th century.

A few miles north, white-water rafters and kayakers converge every summer in the Banks area, where the rapid-laden Payette River rushes toward its confluence with the Boise and Snake Rivers.

HISTORY

The Snake River has long been the lifeblood for those living in southwest Idaho. From 19th-century fur trappers to modern-day farmers who harness the big river's endless flow of water, the occupants of this region have always been integrally tied to the Snake. The first nonnative settlement appeared in 1834, when the Hudson's Bay Company built a fur-trading post close to the confluence of the Snake and Boise Rivers. This bustling British post was originally called Snake Fort, but the name was later changed to Fort Boise. The fur trade brought a constant stream of river commerce to the developing region.

The fort later became safe haven for the convoys of wagons navigating the Oregon Trail before it was moved to present-day Boise. The fur trade eventually fizzled out, and the

Previous: Bruneau Dunes State Park; Snake River Birds of Prey National Conservation Area. **Above:** Nampa Train Depot.

Southwest Idaho

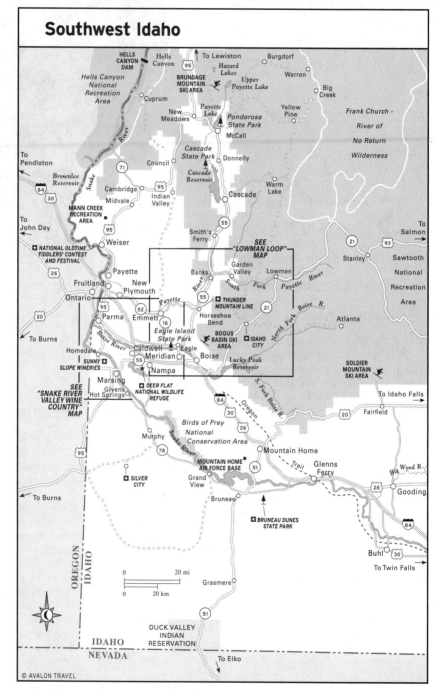

westward migration across this unforgiving portion of the Snake River Plain tapered off.

Twenty years later, human activity once again picked up in the region after gold was discovered in the Mores Creek area of the Boise Mountains. The Boise Basin mining towns of Idaho City, Placerville, and Centerville literally popped up overnight, and the frenzied rush lasted for the better part of 10 years until the pickings became slim. At this point, the miners shifted their attention to Silver City, nestled in the high-desert Owyhee Mountains on the southern fringe of the Snake River Valley.

After the mining heyday ended, farming and ranching became the primary business in the area during the early 20th century, when newly built irrigation canals brought water to the once-arid fields.

PLANNING YOUR TIME

You should afford yourself at least a week to explore this diverse part of the state. The suburbs don't offer travelers much—unless you're into big-box stores and corporate restaurants, of which there are many—but nearby there's plethora of fun stuff to do.

Idaho's burgeoning wine country, aptly called the Snake River Valley, situated along the Snake River near Marsing, is one of the biggest draws in these parts. Here you will find a concentration of vineyards and wineries with tasting rooms along the Sunny Slope Wine Trail, where there are also lots of orchards and fruit stands. The Snake River Canyon Scenic Byway runs right through this scenic viticultural area.

Not far away, downtown Nampa boasts a thriving historic neighborhood where you can nosh on inventive cuisine and shop for used books and antiques in the century-old Belle District.

The Treasure Valley, which is crowned by mountains to the north and south, makes a great base camp for your outdoor excursions. You would be hard-pressed to see another human being in the Owyhee Mountains while taking a three-day rafting trip through these basalt-rimmed chasms long ago carved out by the gurgling Owyhee River and its tributaries.

North of there, in the Boise Mountains, Idaho City is a lovable ramshackle of a town. For a spell, back in the 1860s, it was the largest city in the Northwest, before the boom ended and the miners left town to pursue other ventures. Today, this colorful mining town wears its rough-and-tumble past like an old hat. Many of the rustic buildings still boast their original boardwalks and decorative wood facades. And yes, the kindly locals are colorful as well. It's a great place to spend the day taking in the town's history.

The various forks of the Payette River are known for their world-class rapids. You can find several rafting companies—along the Highway 55 between Horseshoe Bend and Banks—that can take you out for a day of whitewater fun.

Sunny Slope and Snake River Valley Wine Country

Even though the Snake River Valley Appellation spans nine southern Idaho counties, Canyon County is undeniably the heart of wine country. This agricultural area is known for its big crops of sugar beets, yellow onions, mint, hops, and sweet-corn seed. But area farmers also produce tons of apples, cherries, apricots, peaches, and pears. And where tree fruit grows well, so do vinifera grapes. Grapegrowing and winemaking are hardly new concepts in the region, though. Winemakers have produced vintages here since the late 1970s, but the industry has grown tremendously in recent years thanks to the Snake River Valley American Viticultural Area (AVA), created in 2007.

Snake River Valley Wine Country

To ◼ NATIONAL OLDTIME FIDDLERS' CONTEST AND FESTIVAL

EMMETT

52

3 HORSE RANCH VINEYARDS

PEARL RD

84
30

95

201

PARMA

MARKET RD

16

95

84
30

SIMPLOT BLVD

44   W STATE ST   44

FUJISHIN FAMILY CELLARS

19   CALDWELL   20   W CHINDEN BLVD   20 26

SUNNY SLOPE WINERIES ◼

EAGLE

SEE "NAMPA" MAP

BOUNDARY RD   USTICK RD

MERIDIAN
W FRANKLIN RD

HUSTON   HOMEDALE RD

BITNER VINEYARDS   HUSTON VINEYARDS

84

30   W VICTORY RD

HOMEDALE

HAT RANCH WINERY   WILLIAMSON VINEYARD   55

69   W COLUMBIA RD

KOENIG VINEYARDS   STE. CHAPELLE WINERY   HELLS CANYON WINERY   Lake Lowell

OREGON   IDAHO

95   MARSING RD   NAMPA

DEER FLAT NATIONAL WILDLIFE REFUGE   E LOCUST LN

MARSING

LAKESHORE DR   INDIAN CREEK WINERY   KUNA

PERCH RD   DEER FLAT RD   KING RD   KUNA RD

78

0   4 mi
0   4 km

SAWTOOTH WINERY

BOWMONT

BIG FOOT RD

45

To ◼ SILVER CITY and ◼ BRUNEAU DUNES STATE PARK

© AVALON TRAVEL

The Sunny Slope area (called "The Slope" by locals), south of downtown Caldwell, has emerged as the epicenter of the Snake River Valley wine country. This spot is home to several century-old fruit orchards, and you will also see acres upon acres of new vineyards situated on south-facing steps near the Snake River, mixed in with vines that were planted many moons ago.

WINE TASTING AND TOURING

Most of Idaho's wineries (with the exception of the larger corporate ones) are only open on weekends for tours and wine tasting—generally spring-late fall. And many of the smaller boutique wineries are open by appointment only. It's also important to note that some of the smaller wineries are closed during the harvest and crush season, which typically runs mid-September-mid-October; all those tractors and forklifts buzzing around can be dangerous for visitors.

Idaho Winery Tours (208/407-9244, www.idahowinerytours.com) conducts Snake River Valley wine country tours for those interested in just kicking back and enjoying the ride. The packages include half-day tours, full-day tours, and custom tours. Call for rates and more information. **Winery Seekers** (888/581-7768, www.wineryseekers.com) also offers tours of Idaho's wine country.

If you're interested in taking a self-guided tour, contact the **Idaho Wine Commission** (821 W. State St., Boise, 208/332-1538, www.wine.idaho.gov). This agency provides maps

Snake River Valley AVA: Legitimizing Idaho Wines

In 2007, the Alcohol and Tobacco Tax and Trade Bureau, the U.S. government agency responsible for designating regional wine appellations, approved the Snake River Valley's application to become an American Viticultural Area, making it the first official AVA in the Gem State.

This heightened status has paved the way for more wineries to set up shop in Idaho. The state now has more than 50 wineries, and this number is expected to hit 100 by the early 2020s. The AVA designation has also greatly helped the marketing of Idaho wines, which is the next step in the evolution of this burgeoning wine country.

In sheer size, the Snake River Valley AVA is one of the largest in the nation, an astonishing 5.27 million acres, nearly the size of New Jersey. It stretches from about 30 miles inside the Oregon border, on the western fringe of the Snake River Plain, well into south-central Idaho. The Snake River Valley's high-desert terrain, with its long, hot days and cool nights, makes for exceptional fruit. When winemakers speak of *terroir* in this region, they usually talk about the high elevation at which the grapes are grown and the richness of the volcanic soil, lending itself to fruit-forward wines with pronounced tannins and well-balanced acidity. Hearty Rhône varietals such as syrah and viognier thrive, but this area has a long-standing tradition of growing Bordeaux-style varietals like cabernet sauvignon, merlot, and cabernet franc. Riesling and chardonnay grapes have also been grown in the Snake River Valley for more than 30 years. (Sorry, you won't find any potato wine, but there's spud vodka made in the area.)

and other winery information that you can simply download from its website.

SUNNY SLOPE

Expect to find about a dozen wineries clustered along this scenic stretch of Highway 55, eight miles south of downtown Caldwell en route to Marsing.

★ Sunny Slope Wineries

Winemaking is a family affair at **Hells Canyon Winery** (18835 Symms Rd., Caldwell, 208/454-3300, www.hellscanyonwine.com, www.zhoozhoo.com, tasting room noon-5pm Sat.-Sun. Apr.-Dec.), at the corner of Chicken Dinner and Symms Roads, where winemaker Steve Robertson and his daughter, assistant winemaker Bijou Robertson, turn out two brands: Hells Canyon and Zhoo Zhoo. This estate winery has been in business since 1981, and it specializes in cabernet sauvignon, chardonnay, merlot, syrah, fruit-forward rosé, and Bordeaux red blends, which you can try for a small fee at the tasting room and wine lounge. The shady patio boasts stunning views of the Owyhee Mountains, making it a great

place to hang out. Plus, they offer local goat cheese, olives, and baguette.

Koenig Vineyards and Distillery (20928 Grape Ln., Caldwell, 208/455-8386, www.koenigdistilleryandwinery.com, tasting room noon-5pm Wed.-Sun. year-round) produces various wines and brandies, as well as vodka and small batches of whiskey. Winemaker Greg Koenig is a busy guy: He also makes wines for three other local wineries. This winery and distillery boasts an attractive Tuscan-inspired building that overlooks the Snake River. Koenig Vineyards is well known for its exceptional wines, including reserve syrah, viognier, Bordeaux blends, and ice wine made from riesling grapes. Greg's brother, Andrew, is in charge of making eau-de-vie-style fruit brandies and clean, crisp potato vodka, produced in an ornate copper-pot still. A small tasting fee applies, but it generally gets waived if you buy wine from the upstairs bottle shop.

Bitner Vineyards (16645 Plum Rd., Caldwell, 208/455-1870, www.bitnervineyards.com, tasting room noon-5pm Fri.-Sun. year-round) undeniably has the best view in the Sunny Slope area. Ron Bitner, an entomologist turned vintner, was instrumental in landing Idaho's only American Viticultural Area (AVA). He was involved in writing the official application, first drafted in 2001. Bitner spent several years studying leaf-cutter bees in Australia, which might help to explain why his estate winery turns out bone-dry riesling and a cabernet-shiraz blend as well as excellent cabernet sauvignon, chardonnay, and a silky merlot-petit verdot blend, which are made by his friend and neighbor Greg Koenig. Bitner first planted chardonnay vines in the early 1980s, and since then he and his wife, Mary, have added a hilltop tasting room (with a spacious deck) that boasts a sweeping panorama of the Snake River and Owyhee Mountains. Foodies will like the fact that Bitner has hazelnut and oak trees on his property that have been inoculated with black truffle spores; he will be harvesting his first crop of truffles soon. Bitner Vineyards also operates a bed-and-breakfast next to the winery. Situated in the basement of the main house, this small inn has two guest rooms ($149-169) with queen beds and a private patio. Fill up on a farm-fresh continental breakfast before heading out to tour the wineries.

Ste. Chapelle Winery (19348 Lowell Rd., Caldwell, 208/453-7840, www.stechapelle.com, tasting room 10am-5pm Mon.-Sat., noon-5pm Sun. year-round) is the oldest and largest winery in Idaho. It has produced a large array of wines since 1976. This corporate winery, on the west side of Highway 55, quickly became known for turning out big lots of fruity riesling. In recent times, head winemaker Maurine Johnson has added many other wines to the repertoire, including sauvignon blanc, ice wines, and various red varietals. The destination winery boasts a remarkable French-inspired château (with Gothic architecture, no less) that sits perched atop the hill. This is where you can find the gift shop and tasting room (small fee), and it's often a starting point for people's wine country tours. Ste. Chapelle Winery has beautifully landscaped grounds, making the grassy terraces a great spot for a picnic and enjoying the popular concert series held every summer.

Williamson Vineyard (19692 Williamson Ln., Caldwell, 208/459-7333, www.willorch.com, tasting room 10am-6pm Mon.-Fri., 10am-4pm Sat. June-Oct.) is a small boutique winery affiliated with Williamson Orchards, a local fruit company and fruit stand next to Ste. Chapelle Winery. Roger Williamson is in charge of growing the grapes, which are

Hells Canyon Winery

then made into wine by, you guessed it, Greg Koenig. Among the orchards and vines you can taste a lineup of exceptional estate wines that includes viognier, syrah, sangiovese, and cabernet sauvignon. The tasting room is situated in an old barn near the produce stand.

Fujishin Family Cellars (15593 Sunnyslope Rd., Caldwell, 208/649-5389, www.ffcwine.com, tasting room noon-6pm Wed.-Mon. May-Oct.) is a boutique winery that has earned a good reputation in recent years. Winemaker Martin Fujishin produces an array of fruit-forward wines, including viognier, syrah, merlot, petite sirah, and late-harvest chardonnay. The tasting room is situated in an old fruit stand along Highway 55.

Huston Vineyards (16473 Chicken Dinner Rd., Caldwell, 208/455-7975, www.hustonvineyards.com, tasting room noon-5pm Fri.-Mon.) is one of Idaho's newest estate wineries. This small operation grows cabernet sauvignon, chardonnay, merlot, syrah, and malbec, which winemaker Melanie Krause (from Cinder Wines) turns into various wines, like Chicken Dinner Red, a blended red table wine. The winery has an attractive tasting room with a small patch of lawn out front, making it a good place for a picnic.

Hat Ranch Winery (15343 Plum Rd., Caldwell, 208/994-6416, www.hatranchwinery.com, tasting room noon-5pm Fri.-Sun.) is another boutique winery in the Slope that's putting out good wines, including unoaked chardonnay, merlot, tempranillo, and off-dry riesling. The winery also has a guest suite ($169 May-Dec.), a bed-and-breakfast inn, if you will, with a balcony that overlooks the vineyards and orchards.

Food

The Orchard House (14949 Sunnyslope Rd., Caldwell, 208/459-8200, breakfast, lunch, and dinner daily, dinner entrées $10-23) is the Slope's only bona fide restaurant. Take reprieve from the scorching sun on the restaurant's shady patio and enjoy some hand-cut steaks and a bottle of Snake River Valley wine. The dinner menu has plenty of appetizers, like bacon-stuffed mushrooms and salt-and-pepper prawns, alongside burgers and entrée salads. It's a popular place for breakfast as well, considering there aren't any other options in the area.

Produce Stands

The Sunny Slope area has several produce stands that are packed with local fruit and vegetables early summer-late fall. **Symms Fruit**

Koenig Vineyards and Distillery

Ranch (14068 Sunnyslope Rd., Caldwell, 208/459-4821, www.symmsfruit.com, 11am-5pm Mon.-Fri., 7am-noon Sat.), located on the east side of Highway 55 between Lowell Road and Williamson Lane, has been selling tree-ripened fruit for nearly a century. Even though the farm specializes in peaches, you can also find lots of cherries, nectarines, plums, pears, and apples as well as asparagus and onions in the spring and early summer. **Williamson Orchards** (19692 Williamson Ln., Caldwell, 208/459-7333, www.willorch.com, 10am-6pm Mon.-Fri., 10am-4pm Sat. June-Dec.) recently celebrated its 100th anniversary. This family-run orchard and winery sells a large variety of stone fruit, garden-fresh vegetables (tomatoes, eggplants, and pumpkins), and more than 20 varieties of apples, including Criterion, Honeycrisp, and Empire.

CALDWELL

Caldwell (population 46,000) was called Bugtown in the late 19th century when Oregon Short Line Railroad trains frequently steamed through the area. The town acquired this unsavory name because it was known for having many mosquitoes, red ants, grass-hoppers, and flies. Luckily the name didn't stick, but the bugs are still around in this part of Canyon County during the dog days of summer.

Situated near the hustle and bustle of I-84 (Exits 26-29), Caldwell offers basic services to travelers, and it has a nice little downtown area that's unfortunately still feeling the ill effects of the recent economic downtown. A few blocks from downtown, just off Blaine Street, you'll find a top-notch liberal arts college and the **Steunenberg Residential Historic District,** an attractive neighbor-hood with more than 300 historic homes, many of which are on the National Register of Historic Places.

College of Idaho

The **College of Idaho** (2112 E. Cleveland Blvd., Caldwell, 208/459-5011, www.college-ofidaho.edu) enjoys a solid reputation and

alumni who include grocery magnate Joe Albertson, two former governors, a Pulitzer Prize-winning historian, an Academy Award-winning musician, and many Rhodes Scholars. It's also the state's oldest four-year college, founded by the Wood River Presbytery in 1891.

Among the buildings on the beautiful 43-acre campus are the 850-seat **Jewett Auditorium,** which hosts concerts, lec-tures, and meetings; the 54,000-square-foot **Langroise Center for the Performing and Fine Arts,** housing the college's music, drama, dance, and visual arts departments; the **Rosenthal Gallery of Art,** which pres-ents a half-dozen exhibitions each academic year and also serves as a venue for poetry readings and performance art; and the **Orma J. Smith Museum of Natural History,** containing a sizable collection of animal and plant specimens, minerals, fossils, and Native American artifacts.

Events

The **Caldwell Night Rodeo** (2301 Blaine St., Caldwell, 208/459-2060, www.caldwell-nightrodeo.com) is one of the country's top 20 Professional Rodeo Cowboys Association-sanctioned rodeos, drawing almost 40,000 fans to the rodeo grounds (near Simplot Stadium) for a weeklong run in mid-August. On the last Saturday in September, College of Idaho hosts **Taste of the Harvest,** an an-nual event that celebrates the area's prolific bounty. Here you can nosh on creatively pre-pared seasonal dishes made with local food-stuffs paired with select wines from the Snake River Valley.

Accommodations

Unfortunately the Caldwell area doesn't offer travelers much in the way of lodging beyond the corporate hotels that line the interstate.

Most of the hotels in the Caldwell area are located near I-84 Exit 29. **Best Western Caldwell Inn and Suites** (908 Specht Ave., Caldwell, 208/454-7225, www.bestwesterni-daho.com, from $89 d) is a newer hotel with amenities such as an indoor swimming pool, a workout room, free Wi-Fi, and a hot breakfast buffet. Just down the road, **La Quinta Inn** (901 Specht Ave., 208/454-2222, from $59 d) offers clean guest rooms with all the amenities, including a complimentary breakfast.

Elegant bed-and-breakfast-style guest suites can be found at **Wild Rose Manor** (5800 Oasis Rd., Caldwell, 208/454-3331 or 866/399-3331, www.wildrosemanor.com, $139-189), just off I-84 Exit 17. This beautiful mansion, a popular spot for weddings, sits high atop a hill with commanding views of the Boise Front. Expect to be pampered with early-evening appetizers and wine, jetted tubs, and a multicourse breakfast.

If you are driving an RV or towing a trailer, check out the **Ambassador RV Resort** (615 S. Smeed Pkwy., Caldwell, 208/454-8584, $32 with hookups) near I-84 Exit 29.

Food

Caldwell has some of the best Mexican restaurants in the state, thanks to a large Hispanic population that thrives in Canyon County. One such place is **Tacos Y Mariscos El Compa** (605 N. 5th Ave., Caldwell, 208/459-2470, lunch and dinner Wed.-Mon., $8-14) in downtown Caldwell. It's hard to miss this eatery, which specializes in Mexican seafood, because a colorful mural of a tropical beach scene adorns the side of the building. Expect to find a big menu packed with shrimp tacos, breaded fish tacos, seafood cocktail (with shrimp and squid), and fresh-as-can-be oysters on the half shell. You can also get non-seafood items (carnitas and carne asada) in the form of tacos, enchiladas, and torta sandwiches. The restaurant has a full bar that offers a large selection of Mexican beers. For freshly baked Mexican goodies and lots of smiles from the friendly staff, head to **La Esperanza Bakery** (5216 Cleveland Blvd., Caldwell, 208/459-6812, 6am-10pm daily), where you can score flaky pastries, cakes, and cookies. The bakery also sells savory items such as crusty *telera* rolls (for making torta sandwiches) and tasty tamales.

NAMPA

Nampa (population 82,000), located between Caldwell and Meridian on I-84, has come a long way since its humble days as an Oregon Short Line rail stop. The town was originally platted in 1886 on land owned by Alexander Duffes, a pious man who refused to sell property to anyone planning to open a saloon. Financial pressures must have got the better of him because the town, mockingly called "New Jerusalem," eventually had a few drinking establishments. Ironically, Duffes's house was moved 20 years later to make room for a brewery.

Colonel William Dewey was another central figure in Nampa's history. This affluent mining baron, who made his riches in the nearby boomtown of Silver City, dumped oodles of money into the development of Nampa. In 1901 he built the luxurious Dewey's Palace, a grand hotel that was unfortunately torn down in 1963 after it fell into disrepair. Dewey turned Nampa into a major railroad town by establishing a busy terminus for the Boise, Nampa, and Owyhee Railroad.Today, Nampa is the thirdToday, Nampa is the third-largest city in Idaho and is still a busy railroad hub; the ground often shakes with train activity, and blasting horns are frequently heard in the downtown area, where you will find a vibrant historic neighborhood affectionately called the Belle District, in which there are lots of interesting antiques shops and used bookstores mixed in with hip coffeehouses and restaurants. Nampa is also home to a highly recognized Christian college and several museums. But unfortunately the rest of the city is a suburban blur of newer housing developments and big-box stores.

Hispanic Cultural Center of Idaho

Get an eyeful: Not only is the **Hispanic Cultural Center of Idaho** (315 Stampede Dr., Caldwell, 208/442-0823, www.hccidaho. org, 9am-5pm Mon.-Fri., free) a real architectural standout with its vibrant-hued building, but it also houses an impressive array of

Nampa

work by contemporary Hispanic artists. This cultural center is an integral part of Canyon County's flourishing Hispanic scene, and it hosts all kinds of educational programs and events throughout the year.

Warhawk Air Museum

Fans of World War II-era aviation will enjoy the **Warhawk Air Museum** (201 Municipal Dr., Caldwell, 208/465-6446, www.warhawkairmuseum.org, 10am-5pm Tues.-Sat., 11am-4pm Sun., $10 adults, $8 seniors, military, and veterans, $4 ages 5-12), where you'll find two Curtiss P-40 fighters used in the movie *Pearl Harbor* along with many other vintage aircraft. Surrounding the planes are aircraft engines, armaments, uniforms, old photos, and other World War II memorabilia.

Nampa Train Depot Museum

The **Nampa Train Depot Museum** (1200 Front St., Caldwell, 208/467-7611, 11am-3pm Thurs.-Fri., 10am-2pm Sat., $3 adults, $2 ages 13-18, $1 ages 6-12, under 5 free), operated by the Canyon County Historical Society, is a great place to learn about local history. The history lesson begins with the building itself: The museum is housed in the beautiful old Oregon Short Line Depot, built in 1902. Its architecture is unique and impressive—an ornate design in dark brick with white trim. The building was abandoned in 1972 but saved and restored a year later; it is now listed on the National Register of Historic Places. Inside you'll find railroad memorabilia, old newspapers dating back to 1881, photographs from as early as 1891, and pictures of the old Dewey Palace Hotel in its glory days.

Northwest Nazarene University

Northwest Nazarene University (NNU, 623 S. University Blvd., Caldwell, 208/467-8011, www.nnu.edu) is a top-rated four-year Christian liberal-arts school subscribing to the Wesleyan doctrines of the Church of the Nazarene. The park-like campus lies south of downtown on the east side of Highway 45 (12th Avenue Rd.) at Lake Lowell Avenue.

★ Deer Flat National Wildlife Refuge

If you're into birds, check out **Deer Flat National Wildlife Refuge,** an 11,430-acre refuge four miles southwest of town. The refuge, managed by the U.S. Fish and Wildlife Service, is a stop on the Pacific Flyway, an avian route for migratory species. During peak migration in early December, roughly 12,000 geese and 100,000 ducks honk and quack their way around the refuge's two units. The first unit—8,800-acre artificial Lake Lowell—was part of a 1906 irrigation project and was designated a national wildlife refuge by President Theodore Roosevelt in 1909. The second unit comprises the 107 islands in the Snake River between Swan Falls and Farewell Bend, Oregon.

Mallard ducks and Canada geese are the dominant species, but more than 200 other species have been observed on the refuge, among them loons, grebes, pelicans, cormorants, bitterns, herons, egrets, ducks such as the northern pintail and the cinnamon teal, raptors—bald eagles, red-tailed hawks, and peregrine falcons—and eight different species of sandpipers. A complete birding checklist is available at the visitors center.

Birding is just one of the many forms of recreation available here. Boating, swimming, waterskiing, fishing, horseback riding, and cross-country skiing can all be enjoyed at one time of year or another, with certain restrictions in place to protect the refuge's winged inhabitants. No boating is allowed on Lake Lowell October 1-April 14, and fishing from the shores of the Snake River islands is prohibited February 1-May 31 when the geese are nesting.

The refuge headquarters and **visitors center** (13751 Upper Embankment Rd., Nampa, 208/467-9278, 8am-4pm Mon.-Fri., 10am-4pm Sat. mid-Apr.-Sept.) is on the northeast shore of Lake Lowell near the intersection of Lake and Lake Lowell Avenues. Lake Avenue turns south off Highway 55, on the way out of town toward Marsing; the

historic Nampa Train Depot

The Amazing Comeback of the Peregrine Falcon

A trainer at Boise's Peregrine Fund World Center for Birds of Prey holds a peregrine falcon.

The peregrine falcon *(Falco peregrinus)* has bounced back from the cusp of extinction worldwide. Herbicides and pesticides were the main cause of the species' drastic decline, which started during the 1950s. By 1975 it was estimated that there were only 324 nesting pairs remaining in the world. Harsh chemicals, including DDT, caused the female falcons to lay eggs with paper-thin shells that easily broke, killing the embryos. DDT was banned in the United States in 1972.

With this harmful chemical reduced, peregrine populations have risen dramatically in recent years. It is believed that there are now 2,000-3,000 nesting pairs in North America, and the Peregrine Fund has released 4,000 captive-raised falcons in the United States in the last 25 years.

The peregrine, the fastest animal on the planet, reaching speeds up to 200 mph, has a wide distribution, from frozen tundra to the tropics. They have adapted specifically to cityscapes, where the tall buildings act as a safe haven and where they help to keep pigeon populations from getting out of control.

Idaho has a love affair with this colorful bird, which has a distinct yellow hue and a dark gray-and-white pattern. The peregrine is the state's official raptor, and it was recently commemorated on the state quarter.

turnoff is marked. Inside are informative exhibits focusing on the natural history of the refuge. Outside, a short self-guided nature trail winds down to the lakeshore and back; a pamphlet introduces some of the plant and animal species commonly seen along the way. The rest of the refuge is open dawn-dusk; no overnight camping is permitted.

Sawtooth Winery

Even though Nampa is smack-dab in wine country, it only has one winery to show for it. **Sawtooth Winery** (13750 Surrey Ln., Nampa, 208/467-1200, www.sawtoothwinery.com, tasting room noon-5pm Wed.-Sun.) is Idaho's second-largest winery in terms of production, and it has turned out good wines since 1987. Sawtooth makes a large variety of estate wines, including cabernet sauvignon, merlot, chardonnay, riesling, syrah, and viognier. The winery sits high atop a hill overlooking Hidden Valley, Skyline Vineyard, and the foreboding Owyhee Mountains. It can be tricky to find if you are not from these parts. To get there, take Exit 36 off I-84 to 11th Avenue North, and then hang a right to 3rd Street South. Travel just one block to 12th Avenue South (Hwy. 45) and turn right. Continue on Highway 45 for 8 miles to Missouri Avenue, where you take a right and follow the signs to the winery.

Entertainment

Grab dinner and a movie all in one spot at **Northern Lights Cinema Grill** (1509 Caldwell Blvd., Nampa, 208/475-2999, www. northernlightscinemagrill.com, movies $3) near Karcher Mall. This establishment has two large theaters equipped for dining. Buy a ticket and order some food and draft brews, and it's delivered to you in the theater. Don't quaff too much ale, though, or you will miss half the movie making frequent trips to the restroom. The theater shows second-run movies, and it serves pizza, burgers, and burritos.

The **Ford Idaho Center** (16200 Idaho Center Blvd., Nampa, 208/468-1000, www.for-didahocenter.com) has both an indoor arena and an outdoor amphitheater where major sports and entertainment events are held. The arena is home to the Snake River Stampede pro rodeo. Most of the big-name bands that come through the Boise area play this venue. The Rolling Stones even rocked the house a few years back.

Snake River Stampede

This professional rodeo, the **Snake River Stampede** (208/466-8497, www.snakeriver-stampede.com, $10-35), bucks into the Ford Idaho Center every year around the third week of July. The Professional Rodeo Cowboys Association-sanctioned stampede is one of the country's top 25 rodeos, attracting some 500 world-champion pros competing in bareback and saddle bronc riding, bull riding, steer wrestling, individual and team roping, and barrel racing. Even the rodeo clowns compete, in a "bullfight" competition, while kids ages 5-7 compete in Mutton Busting. The week kicks off with one of the West's largest horse parades and a buckaroo breakfast.

Shopping

Downtown Nampa is a veritable treasure trove of collectibles, used books, and antiques thanks to a profusion of shops in the Belle District. The **Yesteryear Shoppe** (1211 1st St. S., Nampa, 208/467-3581) is a wonderful spot to lollygag in time. This spacious used bookstore has thousands of titles neatly arranged in easy-to-follow sections, including history, general fiction, science, and beyond. Rare editions are kept under glass near the front of the store beside an impressive collection of old vinyl records. The shop specializes in jazz and blues, but you can probably score an old Iron Maiden album too.

Across the street, grab an espresso drink and peruse the dusty rooms at the **Old Town Antique Mall and Coffee** (1212 1st St. S., Nampa, 208/463-4555), where there is a multitude of 20th-century collectibles and antiques ranging from old G.I. Joes to retro dishware.

Karcher Mall (1509 Caldwell Blvd., Nampa, 208/465-7845, www.shopkar-chermall.com) is located on the "Boulevard," as locals call it, the bustling road that connects Nampa and Caldwell. The indoor mall, the first of its kind in Idaho, was recently given a makeover. Expect to find typical chain stores and restaurants.

Accommodations

With a country setting just a mile north of the Ford Idaho Center, **Hostel Boise** (17322 Can-Ada Rd., Nampa, 208/467-6858, www. hostelboise.com, $21-40) is a friendly and inexpensive base for exploring the area. A clean kitchen, a peaceful back patio, and a comfortable living room make guests feel at home, as does owner Elsa Freeman, who has practically made it her mission to bring this hostel, a Hostelling International affiliate, to southwest Idaho. Hostel Boise offers private and dorm-style rooms. Check-in is 5pm-10pm, check out by 9:30am. Reservations are advised.

Nampa has a string of motels along the Boulevard near downtown, but many of them are filthy and rife with illegal-drug activity. For clean and safe lodging, check out these two hotels: **Hampton Inn and Suites at the Idaho Center** (5750 E. Franklin Rd., Nampa, 208/442-0036, www.hamptoninn.com, from $99 d) is near I-84 Exit 38. This chain hotel is completely nonsmoking, and it offers all the amenities—an indoor swimming pool, a fitness room, and complimentary hot breakfast. A few miles west on I-84, near Exit 33, you'll find **Fairfield Inn and Suites** (16150 Midland Blvd., Nampa, 208/467-5888, from $79 d), which offers clean guest rooms. There's no pool but there is a workout room, a business center, and complimentary breakfast.

Food

Nampa has experienced something of a restaurant renaissance in recent years. Of course, there is the typical profusion of corporate restaurants on the Boulevard, but the downtown area now has several noteworthy food and beverage establishments.

★ **Brick 29 Bistro** (320 11th Ave. S., Nampa, 208/468-0029, www.brick29.com, 11am-9pm Mon.-Thurs., 11am-10pm Fri., 4pm-10pm Sat., brunch 10am-2pm Sun., dinner entrées $12-29) is a contemporary Northwest restaurant owned and operated by chef Dustan Bristol, who has been nominated three times for a prestigious James Beard Award in the Best Chef Northwest category. Locavores will love this place—housed in a historic Masonic Temple building on the edge of downtown—because Bristol sources lots of local foodstuffs that end up on his creative seasonal menus. Brick 29 offers whimsical yet recognizable dishes, like pear pizza with pesto, braised lamb shank with smoked mushroom risotto, and a scrumptious Kobe beef burger served on a crusty bun with jalapeño aioli. There are lots of Snake River Valley wines and inventive cocktails to wash everything down.

Messenger Pizza (1224 1st St. S., Nampa, 208/461-0081, www.messengerpizza.com, lunch and dinner daily, whole pizzas $15-30, slices $3) is the place to go in the Belle District for thin-crusted pizzas. The inside boasts the building's original brick walls and long, upholstered church pews. It's a comfortable place to hang out. Besides inventive pies, you'll also find calzones, bruschetta made with house-baked baguette, and a well-stocked salad bar. Try the Drunken Goat pizza topped with goat cheese, figs, bacon, and arugula. The pizzeria serves local beers on draft and wines by the glass.

A few doors down, **PreFunk** (1214 1st St. S., Nampa, www.prefunkbar.com, 11am-10pm Mon.-Thurs., 10am-midnight Fri.-Sat., noon-9pm Sun.) recently set up shop in a former sushi joint. These beer geeks, who also have a bar in downtown Boise, decided it was time to let Nampa in on the craft-beer fun. Here you can quaff ales from an always-changing array of local and regional draft brews. You can even take a growler of fresh brew with you.

Hipsters will definitely get a kick out of the ★ **Flying M Coffee Garage** (1314 2nd St. S., Nampa, 208/467-5533, www.flyingmcoffee.com, 6:30am-11pm Mon.-Fri., 7:30am-11pm Sat., 7:30am-6pm Sun.), a funky coffeehouse in a former tire shop. Surf the Web while enjoying an espresso drink and house-baked pastries. The walls are adorned with local art, and the place features live music throughout the year.

The **Nampa Farmers Market** (1350 Front St., www.nampafarmersmarket.com, 9am-1pm Sat. mid-Apr.-Oct.) is held at Lloyd Square in the Belle District. Here more than 20 produce vendors sell an assortment of impeccably fresh seasonal vegetables and fruit. Shoppers can also pick up artisanal bread, honey, fresh salsa, and locally roasted coffee, to name a few. There is live music every weekend as well as occasional chef demonstrations.

Information

The **Nampa Chamber of Commerce** (315 11th Ave. S., Nampa, 208/466-4641, www.nampa.com) offers brochures, maps, and general information about the area. The **Idaho Department of Fish and Game** (3101 S. Powerline Rd., Nampa, 208/465-8465) has resources for travelers and some wildlife and nature exhibits. Nearby, you'll find stocked fishing ponds and a trout hatchery.

KUNA

Kuna (pronounced Q-nuh) is a charmless little hamlet located seven miles southeast of Nampa on the edge of Ada County. The downtown area is not much more than a strip of unattractive buildings that look like they were slapped together overnight. And they probably were, considering the town was once a whistle stop for the Union Pacific Railroad's Oregon Short Line. If you like real-deal cowboy and biker bars, though, Kuna is definitely the place to go. Expect to see several beat-up saloons along the main drag, which are known for warm beer and tremendous bar fights. Don't be surprised to hear, "Are you looking at me?" if you spend any time at these places.

Kuna still holds onto its small railroad-town roots, but the new housing developments surrounding the downtown core tell a different story. Many people who work in nearby Boise choose to live here because of its small-town feel. This may help to explain the profusion of drive-through espresso shops that have popped up here in the new millennium. Head south of Kuna on the Western Heritage Historical Byway and it will feel like you're in the middle of nowhere. The desert hinterlands roll and dip as far as the eye can see until they reach the imposing basalt cliffs of the Snake River Canyon—home to the Snake River Birds of Prey National Conservation Area—and the remote Owyhee Mountains.

Indian Creek Winery

Indian Creek Winery (1000 N. McDermott Rd., Kuna, 208/922-4791, www.indiancreekwinery.com, tasting room noon-5pm Thurs.-Sun.) is owned and operated by Bill Stowe and his family, who produce remarkable pinot noir (yes, pinot in Idaho), chardonnay, cabernet sauvignon, malbec, and red blends, most of which are made with grapes grown in the winery's vineyard. Indian Creek has a tasting room and gift shop where you can sample wines free of charge. Plus, they host live music and other fun events during the warmer months. To get to the winery from Nampa, follow Greenhurst Road (southeast) toward Kuna until you cross McDermott Road, and then turn right (south) and continue three miles to the winery.

Snake River Canyon near Kuna

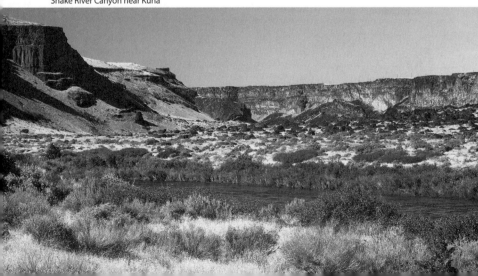

Snake River Birds of Prey National Conservation Area

Ada County is skirted by the Snake River to the south, and the big river at this undeveloped high-desert spot has been designated the **Snake River Birds of Prey National Conservation Area** (NCA). The chaparral along the riverbank is home to large populations of rodents and small mammals that constitute the prime diet for a variety of birds of prey. Among the raptors permanently residing here or just passing through are short-eared owls, burrowing owls, northern harriers, kestrels, Swainson's hawks, red-tailed hawks, sharp-shinned hawks, golden eagles, and the largest nesting concentration of prairie falcons in the country.

The NCA boundary is three miles south of Kuna on Swan Falls Road. On your way down to the river—another 16 miles farther—you'll see the raised lava butte of **Initial Point** on the east side of the road. In addition to being a great viewpoint over the vast plain and the Owyhee Mountains to the south, the point is significant in that it marked the starting point for Idaho Territory's first official land survey, begun in 1867. The base meridian for the survey ran due north from here, through what would become the town of Meridian. It's just

a short hike up to the top of the butte, which is a mellow spot for a picnic (provided the locals aren't using the adjacent hillside for target practice, as they often do).

The road continues down to the canyon rim and a pullout parking area at **Dedication Point.** A 0.25-mile nature trail leads to the edge of the abyss, and interpretive signs provide information about the various birds of prey, flora, and geology of the area.

The road continues southeast for a moment before making a hairpin turn and dropping precipitously into the canyon, to the road's end at **Swan Falls Dam.** The dam was the brainchild of Colonel William Dewey, a pioneering southwest Idaho entrepreneur who intended to use the hydroelectric power generated at the dam to run an electric railway up to his mine near Silver City. His plan never materialized, but the dam did supply electricity to Murphy and to Silver City as well until World War II. The dam, built in 1901, was the first hydroelectric project on the Snake River. A grassy picnic area and restrooms make this a good place for a stop. For more information on the Snake River Birds of Prey National Conservation Area, contact the Bureau of Land Management's **Lower Snake River**

Swan Falls Dam

district office (3948 Development Ave., Boise, 208/384-3300).

Recreation

Bernard Fisher Veterans Memorial Park, on the main drag, has a picnic area, a playground, and some scuffed-up skateboard bowls in the shadow of the water tower. Adjacent to the park is the aptly named **Indian Creek Greenbelt,** a short walking trail that meanders alongside a swift-flowing creek on the north side of the busy railroad tracks.

Falcon Crest Golf Club (11102 S. Cloverdale Rd., Kuna, 208/362-8897, www.falconcrestgolf.com, greens fees $30-40) is one of the nicest public golf courses in the area. With 36 holes of playable golf greens (one 18-hole course, two nine-holes, and a driving range), this expansive complex boasts incredible views of the Boise Front and sprawling desert landscape. The golf club also operates a small grill where you can grab a burger after hitting the links.

Food

Kuna does not have much in the way of food, but it does have a beloved Mexican restaurant that brings in droves of people. ★ **Enrique's** (482 W. Main St., Kuna, 208/922-5169, www.

elgallogirokuna.com, 10am-10pm Mon.-Sat., 10am-9pm Sun., entrées $8-15) is a colorful place with great grub, cold *cerveza,* and exceptionally friendly service. This family-run restaurant puts out an extensive menu of Mexican offerings such as chicken mole, carnitas, chili verde, enchiladas, and the best damn beef tongue (simmered in a peppery tomato sauce) this side of the Rio Grande, or at least the Snake.

MERIDIAN AND EAGLE

Meridian (population 85,000), seven miles north of Kuna on Meridian Road and sharing a border with Boise to the east, is the fastest growing city in Idaho, which has brought multilane boulevards dotted with big-box stores and corporate restaurants. Once a bustling milk hub, Meridian now is a hodgepodge of innocuous strip malls and office parks that have gobbled up the old dairy farms.

The behemoth Roaring Springs Water Park greets travelers at I-84 Exit 44. Take the off-ramps and head north on Meridian Road, and it will lead you past the Meridian Speedway and into an attractive little downtown area. Here you'll find an excellent Basque restaurant, among other good eateries and little shops.

fishing at Eagle Island State Park

It's hard to tell where Meridian ends and Eagle (population 20,000) begins as you travel north on Eagle Road. After crossing Chinden Boulevard, Eagle Road drops into a pleasant little valley and crosses the Boise River into downtown Eagle. This affluent river city, in the shadow of the foothills, has a multitude of locally owned restaurants and shops, many of which are along the cute downtown strip. These places cater to well-heeled customers who live in the nearby McMansions. Eagle Island State Park is a scenic riparian spot where you can take a dip or a shady hike in the trees near the Boise River during the sweltering days of summer.

Recreation

Race fans would be remiss if they didn't check out **Meridian Speedway** (335 S. Main St., Meridian, 208/888-2813, www.meridianspeedway.com, Apr.-Sept., $5-18), a 0.25-mile oval track that features winged sprint cars, late-model stock cars, and an occasional smash-up derby. The track has spawned many professional racers over the years, including Indy driver Davey Hamilton, whose family operates the speedway.

Summer brings something for everyone at **Eagle Island State Park** (4000 W. Hatchery Rd., Eagle, 208/939-0696, parking $5, pedestrians free), a beautiful spot about two miles west of downtown Eagle. A 15-acre lake makes a good swimming hole, and a nice sandy beach draws sun worshippers. Kids head right to the waterslide (noon-8pm Thurs.-Sun., $8 for 10 rides, $12 all day), while picnickers will find expansive grassy areas and numerous picnic tables. There's also an 18-hole disc golf course and plenty of hiking trails, which get shared with horses.

Shopping

Bargain hunters will surely like the **Sierra Trading Post** outlet store (530 E. Sonata Ln., Meridian, 208/898-0261, www.sierratradingpost.com) next to I-84 Exit 44 in Meridian. This Wyoming-based company, specializing in online mail-order sales, has a cultlike following. The superstore has tons of great deals on name-brand clothes, hiking boots, GPS devices, and other outdoor gear.

Before hitting one of Idaho's many rivers, fill your tackle box at **Sportsman's Warehouse** (3797 E. Fairview Ave., near Eagle Rd., Meridian, 208/884-3000, www.sportsmanswarehouse.com), but beware: This is the busiest intersection in the state. The large chain store carries all things related to fishing, hunting, and camping. There is row upon row of fishing poles, tackle, and accessories.

If you are looking to buy wines from around the world, **Erickson Fine Wines** (150 E. Riverside St., Eagle, 208/938-3698, www.ericksonfinewines.com, 10am-7pm Mon.-Sat.) near downtown Eagle is the place to go. This small yet well-stocked wine store near the Hilton Garden Inn has labels from Argentina, Chile, Spain, France, and Italy as well as California, Washington, Oregon, and Idaho. Owner Brian Erickson is a knowledgeable guy who can steer you in the right direction.

Accommodations

Meridian is the land of corporate hotels, especially along I-84, where you will find a plethora of choices. Here are two good picks at Exit 46 (Eagle Rd.): **Courtyard by Marriott-Boise West** (1789 S. Eagle Rd., Meridian, 208/888-0800, www.marriott.com, from $89 d) is easily Meridian's largest hotel. The four-story hotel has a nice indoor pool, a business center, an exercise room, and a complimentary breakfast buffet in the small restaurant just off the lobby. **Holiday Inn Express** (2610 E. Freeway Dr., Meridian, 208/288-2060, from $89 d) is a newish hotel with the usual amenities. It's located on the north side of I-84.

Hilton Garden Inn (145 E. Riverside Dr., Eagle, 208/938-9600, www.hiltongardeninn.com, from $109 d) is Eagle's only lodging option, but with the local wine industry booming, don't be surprised to see some bed-and-breakfast inns and other hotels opening up here in the coming years. The hotel (six miles north of Exit 46 on Eagle Rd.) is set on the Boise River and has an indoor pool, a fitness room, and a hot breakfast buffet.

Food

Both Meridian and Eagle have a frenzied blur of typical corporate restaurants, but here are a few independently owned gems worth checking out. ★ **Epi's** (1115 N. Main St., Meridian, 208/884-0142, dinner at 5pm Tues.-Sat., entrées $11-30) offers outstanding traditional Basque fare in a comfortable and friendly atmosphere. Basque music fills the air, and Basque art and family photos line the walls. You can choose from dishes such as stewed beef tongue in a pepper-tomato sauce or baby squid cooked in a sauce of its own ink. Or stick with something slightly less adventurous but equally as wonderful, like the lamb stew and marinated solomo pork loin. Reservations are highly recommended at this popular eatery.

For a true taste of regional Italian fare, head to **Gino's Ristorante and Bar** (3015 W. McMillan Rd., at Ten Mile Rd., Meridian, 208/887-7710, 11am-10pm Mon.-Sat., entrées $10-26), where chef Gino Vuolo puts out food with a southern Italian bent. Prime your palate with starters like beef carpaccio, antipasto, and bruschetta with smoked trout. Choose from a large selection of pasta and meatier dishes like a delightful braised boar shank and pan-seared veal chop. The wine list makes its way around Italy.

Sa-Wad-Dee (1890 E. Fairview Ave., Meridian, 208/884-0701, www.sawaddeethai. com, lunch and dinner daily, $7-19) is the best Thai restaurant outside Boise. This ornately designed place has great food and friendly service, and the menu runs the gamut of typical Southeast Asian offerings such as chicken satay, silky shrimp dumplings, fresh basil rolls, vibrant curries, stir-fried noodles, and colorful seafood dishes. Vegetarians will have much luck here.

Locals adore **Bardenay** (155 E. Riverside Dr., Eagle, 208/938-5093, www.bardenay. com, lunch and dinner daily, entrées $9-23), a microdistillery and restaurant next to

the Hilton Garden Inn. Walk past the towering still near the front door and the large dining room opens up onto a comfortable riverside patio where you can try the house-made spirits and appetizers from the expansive menu. Noteworthy picks include spicy plum-glazed chicken wings, smoked trout spread, and an artisanal cheeseboard. If you are really hungry, try a burger, beer-battered cod and chips, or the beef tenderloin with smoked tomato sauce.

Everyone in town goes to ★ **Rembrandt's Coffee House** (93 S. Eagle Rd., Eagle, 208/938-1564, www.rembrandtscoffeehouse. net, 6:30am-7pm Mon.-Fri., 8am-7pm Sat., 8am-2pm Sun.) for morning java, loose-leaf tea, and light breakfast and lunch fare. Located in a former church in downtown Eagle, this comfy coffeehouse has lots of big chairs and couches where you can kick back and sip an espresso drink made from fair-trade coffee beans while nibbling on a house-baked pastry.

Porterhouse Market (600 S. Rivershore Ln., Eagle, 208/938-1441, www.porterhouse-market.com, 10am-6pm Mon.-Sat.) is a specialty food store, butcher, and deli near the intersection of Eagle Road and State Street. Besides cases filled with ready-to-grill Kobe-style beef, house-made sausages, seafood, and natural chicken and lamb, the market also keeps hot barbecue items such as Kansas City-inspired baby back ribs, pulled pork, and beef brisket in a small case by the deli. You can also score fat sandwiches and tasty salads.

Dine 16 Gastropub at Crooked Flats (3705 Hwy. 16, Eagle, 208/258-6882, 4pm-10pm Wed.-Fri., 11am-11pm Sat., 10am-8pm Sun., $8-12) is a new brewpub on a five-acre spread along Highway 16 that was previously the site of a winery. Crooked Flats is owned by Crooked Fence Brewing Co., so expect to find the same great brews, like 3 Picket Porter and Rusty Nail Pale Ale, and inventive pub fare that gets served at the brewery's Barrelhouse in nearby Garden City. The menu has lots of fun appetizers, soups, burgers, and flatbread pizzas. Don't be surprised to taste a little beer in your food because the kitchen uses the various ales in several dishes, including a tasty turkey chili spiked with porter. Brunch is offered on Sunday 10am-1pm. The brewpub also has an outdoor music venue and bocce ball courts.

3 Horse Ranch Vineyards

The boutique winery **3 Horse Ranch Vineyards** (5900 Pearl Rd., Eagle, 208/863-6561, www.3horseranchvineyards.com, tasting room 11am-6pm Thurs.-Sun., small

tasting fee) has made quite a name for itself in recent years. Owner Gary Cunningham started the small organic winery in 2003 after planting vines in the vast rolling hills west of downtown Eagle. Expect to taste robust syrah, merlot, riesling, and a superb roussanne-viognier blend (made by Greg Koenig). To get here, go north on Highway 16 at the SR-44 junction for about six miles until you arrive at West Chaparral Road. Take a right here and travel three miles. Hang a left at Pearl Road and go 2.5 miles to the winery. You'll see the vineyards and the three horses.

U.S. 95: North to Weiser

U.S. 95 is Idaho's main arterial linking southern Idaho to northern Idaho. This long and winding two-lane road skirts the Oregon and Washington borders on its way to the Panhandle. In southwest Idaho, out on the flats of the Snake River Plain, U.S. 95 leads through mile after mile of rural farmland. During summer, the smell of yellow onions (the biggest crop in the area) lingers in the air. Most of these pungent alliums are sold to Ore-Ida in nearby Ontario, Oregon, a company that makes frozen onion rings and fries.

The small town of Parma is the western starting point for the Snake River Canyon Scenic Byway, a beautiful route that winds its way along the big river en route to the Owyhee Canyonlands. Just up the highway on the north side of I-84 are the small towns of Payette and Fruitland, which are known for having large fruit orchards. Continue due north on U.S. 95 and you will eventually come to Weiser, a town that hosts a famous fiddle festival every summer.

PARMA

Even though Parma is in the Snake River Valley Appellation, there's not much going on here in terms of viticulture. Local farmers grow large cash crops of onions, potatoes, wheat, hops, and table grapes. Raising cattle is also big business around these parts. Parma is also home to a replica of Fort Boise and one of the only operational drive-in movie theaters in the state.

Fort Boise, four miles west of present-day Parma near the confluence of the Boise and Snake Rivers, was the first nonnative settlement in southwest Idaho. In 1834, Thomas McKay of the Hudson's Bay Company built this fur-trading post in an effort to compete with the brisk business being conducted at Fort Hall on the southeast edge of the Snake River Plain. By 1863, Fort Boise had been moved to what is now downtown Boise, and it quickly fell into disrepair and was eventually washed away by the spring's rushing waters. Thirty years later, settlers started to file land claims in the area, one of whom was F. R. Fouch, a man with a penchant for classical history: He named the town after Parma, Italy.

Over the years, Parma has had several colorful residents, including Edgar Rice Burroughs, author of *Tarzan of the Apes,* who tried his hand at cattle ranching here during the early 19th century. He was even on the city council for a short time.

Snake River Canyon Scenic Byway

vineyards in Sunny Slope

The newly designated Snake River Canyon Scenic Byway winds its way through 53 miles of bountiful agricultural land, ranging from near the Oregon border to Walter's Ferry in the Owyhee hinterlands. Parma is the western starting point for the byway. From this spot, the route meanders southeast along the Snake River on a series of well-marked rural roads, passing by family-run farms, fruit orchards, and vineyards. You'll go through the winery district of Sunny Slope before ascending onto a sagebrush-dotted bench that skirts the river canyon, where Map Rock near Walter's Ferry shows ancient petroglyphs. Up here, dormant cinder cones punctuate the landscape, and the deep-canyon rim—long ago carved out by the Bonneville Flood—offers dramatic views of the Owyhee Mountains. Besides cattle, bison, and sheep, also expect to see abundant wildlife, like deer, coyotes, badgers, and red-tailed hawks, along this spectacular drive.

Fort Boise Replica

Although the original Fort Boise long ago succumbed to the elements, a re-creation has been built along U.S. 95 in downtown Parma. The new old fort contains a museum and a pioneer cabin. The **Fort Boise Replica** (208/722-6477, 1pm-3pm Fri.-Sun. June-Aug., other times by appointment, free, donations appreciated) hosts **Old Fort Boise Days** in mid-June, featuring a parade, a crafts fair, period costumes, and a chili cook-off. The adjacent Old Fort Boise Park has a picnic area, restrooms, and a small campground (208/722-5900, fee box at the park) with RV spots ($13) and tent sites ($7).

Recreation

At the site of the original Fort Boise is the 1,500-acre **Fort Boise Wildlife Management Area** (30845 Old Fort Boise Rd., Parma, 208/722-5888), a popular fishing and bird-hunting spot managed by the Idaho Department of Fish and Game. To reach the site, take Old Fort Boise Road west off the highway, just north of town.

Drive-in Theater

Remember drive-in movie theaters? Well, one still exists in Parma. **Parma Motor-Vu** (29522 U.S. 95, Parma, 208/722-6401, www.parmamotorvu.com, $8 general, free for children under 12) is located northwest of town en route to Nyssa, Oregon. This classic drive-in, operated by the same family that opened it in 1953, gives people a blast from the past by showing current-run movies on its large screen during the summertime. Fans of all things retro will get a kick out of the cool neon sign that draws people in like a bug zapper. Speaking of bugs, the only downside to the theater is that mosquitoes tend to swarm around the marshy grounds. (Careful: Don't get bug spray in your popcorn.)

Food

Next to Old Fort Boise Park, you'll find **Boy's Better Burgers** (911 E. Grove Ave., Parma, 208/722-5463, 11am-9pm Mon.-Sat.), a fast-food joint that brings in droves of locals for cheesy gut-bombs, fries, and shakes. In the quaint downtown area, try **Peg Leg Bistro** (215 Main St., Parma, 208/722-5444, 6am-3pm daily, under $10). This casual café serves espresso drinks, light breakfast fare, sandwiches, wraps, and house-made soups.

Some of the best farmstead goat cheese in the Northwest is produced in Parma at **Rollingstone Chévre** (27349 Shelton Rd., Parma, 208/722-6460, www.rollingstonechevre.com). Cheesemaker Karen Evans puts out an array of impressive goat cheeses with help from her flock of snowy Saanen goats, a breed that's known for having high-fat milk. She makes everything from herb-rolled logs of fresh goat cheese to mold-ripened aged cheeses, like Bleu Agé and Snake River Mist, a Camembert-like creation with a band of wine barrel ash running through it. There's a seasonal retail shop (1pm-4pm Thurs., Fri., and Sun. May-Sept. or by appointment) at the farm where you can buy cheeses, or stop by and visit her on Saturdays at the Boise Farmers Market. The farm is not set up for tours, and don't expect to find a petting zoo here.

PAYETTE AND FRUITLAND

Soon after crossing over to the north side of I-84 (at Exit 3), you will hit the small towns of Payette and Fruitland near Ontario, Oregon.

Parma Motor-Vu drive-in theater

It's hard to tell the difference between these two agricultural burgs while driving northbound on U.S. 95 because they kind of blur together along this stretch. The area is known for having several large fruit packing companies and produce stands that sell locally grown fruit and vegetables.

Payette, the seat of Payette County, has an attractive downtown district with several buildings on the National Register of Historic Places, making it a worthwhile stop for lunch or simply to stretch your getaway sticks. Major League Baseball great Harmon Killebrew, who played 22 seasons in the big leagues for the Washington Senators and Minnesota Twins, grew up in these parts. With 573 career home runs and a lifetime batting average of .256, he was inducted into the Baseball Hall of Fame in 1984. Killebrew passed away in 2011.

Payette County Museum

Delve into local history at the **Payette County Museum** (90 S. 9th St., Payette, 208/642-4883, noon-4pm Wed.-Sat., free), located in a former Episcopal church near downtown. Beautiful stained-glass windows refract the light in a kaleidoscope of colors as you walk through the front doors. The museum houses an array of local photos and artifacts, a Civil War-era cannon, and lots of Harmon Killebrew memorabilia such as old jerseys, bats, and photos from his high school days and time spent in the pros.

Recreation

Local golfers head to **Scotch Pines Golf Course** (10610 Scotch Pines Rd., Payette, 208/642-1829, www.scotchpinesgolf.com, greens fees $20-34), a scenic 18-hole course nestled in the foothills that's open spring-fall. After a day on the links, take refuge in the restaurant and bar at **The Pine Room** (208/642-4866), an air-conditioned 19th hole that serves chicken wings, burgers, beers, and stiff cocktails. To get here, head east off U.S. 95, take 7th Avenue North, turn left on Iowa Avenue, and right on Scotch Pines Road.

Anglers can try their luck on **Paddock Valley Reservoir;** take Little Willow Road off Highway 52, northeast of Fruitland or southeast of Payette. According to the Idaho Department of Fish and Game, the reservoir is a great spot for crappie fishing as well as other warm-water species. You'll find a boat ramp at the end of the road on the south edge of the reservoir.

Food

Bossman's Smokehouse BBQ (1619 N. Whitley Dr., Fruitland, 208/739-4436, 11am-9pm Mon.-Thurs., 11am-10pm Fri.-Sat., $8-20) has been a big hit since it opened in 2012 near downtown Fruitland. This barbecue joint boasts a rustic Americana decor with lots of retro signs, patches of sheet metal, and locally cut wood panels and tables. Here you can get Texas-style barbecue—brisket, tri-tip, chicken, saucy baby back ribs, and pulled pork sandwiches—served with sides of creamy spud salad, baked beans, and slaw.

Locals also convene at **Kloys Pizza** (120 N. Main St., Payette, 208/642-1877, lunch and dinner daily, $6-18) in downtown Payette for big pizza pies, hot sandwiches, and fried ravioli bathed in marinara sauce. Kids love this place thanks to a blinking video game room right off the main dining room.

For fresh seasonal fruit and veggies, head to **AC&D Farms** (6525 U.S. 95, Fruitland, 208/407-7533, 10am-7pm daily mid-April-Oct.), a big, red produce barn on U.S. 95 about a mile north of I-84 Exit 3. Expect to

Payette County Museum

find asparagus, cherries, strawberries, corn, peaches, apricots, apples, local alfalfa honey, and more. The folks at this family-run farm are friendly and can give you information about other agricultural offerings in the area as well.

Information and Services

Just past Fruitland, traveling north on U.S. 95, is the NW 16th Street junction. Take a left (west) and you will cross over the Snake River and enter Ontario, Oregon. This humdrum town has lots of chain hotels, big-box stores, and fast-food joints. For more information about the Payette and Fruitland area, contact the **Payette Chamber of Commerce** (34 S. Main St., Payette, 208/642-2362).

WEISER

The seat of Washington County, Weiser (pronounced WEE-zur) lies just north of the confluence of the Snake and Weiser Rivers. North of here the Snake rolls northwest toward its drop through Hells Canyon, while U.S. 95 bears north and east, climbing slowly up the Weiser River watershed.

This agricultural town in its glory days of the late 19th century was a major terminus for the Oregon Short Line Railroad. Weiser has definitely seen better times, but it's not without

charm. Besides a meticulously restored train depot, stately Victorian-era homes—some in better shape than others—and other historic buildings with interesting architecture can be seen all around town. The dusty downtown area has lots of affordable antiques shops and junk stores where the picking is good.

Weiser was once home to famed pro baseball player Walter "Big Train" Johnson, who pitched for the Washington Senators. Over the course of his 21-year pro career, Johnson won 666 games, making him the second-winningest pitcher in history behind Cy Young. But the town's biggest claim to fame is its world-famous fiddle festival and competition held every June.

Historic Buildings

Weiser's early wood-framed commercial district was rebuilt in brick after an 1890 fire reduced much of the town to ashes. Before the fire, the town core had been farther east, but rebuilding efforts centered the new downtown around the **Oregon Short Line Depot.** The Queen Anne-style depot, at the south end of State Street, recently received a much-needed makeover. It's now primarily used for fund-raising events. The building that currently houses **Matthews Grain**

Oregon Short Line Depot in Weiser

otherwise sleepy town for the **National Oldtime Fiddlers' Contest and Festival** (2235 Paddock Ave., Weiser, 208/414-0255, www.fiddlecontest.org), one of the most prestigious fiddle contests in the United States. All week long, all over town, the sounds of fiddles, guitars, mandolins, and banjos waft through the air.

The competition itself is staged in the air-conditioned Weiser High School gymnasium (W. 7th St. and Indianhead Rd.). Each contestant has four minutes to play a breakdown (fast hoedown), a waltz, and a third tune of the contestant's choice. Judges can hear but not see the contestants so they're not swayed by aesthetics. Every year about 350 fiddlers compete in eight divisions, including a swing category, ranging from Small Fry (8 and younger) to Senior-Senior (75 and older). The mature players are expectably masterful, but as you walk by the warm-up rooms and through the campgrounds, what may impress you more are the kids, who possess the same passion and technical abilities as their older counterparts.

Some of the best music at this event happens in the sprawling, makeshift campground behind the high school, aptly called Fiddle Town, where you will hear impromptu jamming day and night. Food and beverage vendors are typically set up here (in front of the Snake River Heritage Center) to feed the hungry masses. Free live musical performances get scheduled throughout the week at the City Park Bluegrass Village Stage in downtown Weiser. More food vendors and hawkers of arts and crafts relating to bluegrass and old-timey fiddle music can be found at this venue.

Tickets for the competition range in price from $5 for adults and $3 for children under age 13 (for daytime and weeknight contests) to $25 for the final rounds on Friday and Saturday. Six-day passes cost $50 for adults and $30 for children.

warming up for the National Oldtime Fiddlers' Contest

& Storage (Commercial St. and E. 1st St.) was once a house of ill repute known as the Clinton Rooms. According to local legend, a mailman delivering a COD package to the Clinton Rooms was one day offered payment in services instead of cash.

Did you know Weiser has a Welsh-inspired castle? It's strange but true. The local Knights of Pythias began building the storybook **Pythian Castle** (E. Idaho St. between State St. and E. 1st St.) in 1904, modeling it after a château in Wales. The stone blocks of the facade were quarried north of town, hauled here by wagon, and cut on-site. For a guide to these and other historic buildings downtown, pick up a free walking-tour pamphlet at the chamber of commerce office (309 State St., 208/414-0452).

Events
★ NATIONAL OLDTIME FIDDLERS' CONTEST AND FESTIVAL
Each year during the third full week of June, thousands of fiddle fans converge on this

Accommodations
Lodging in Weiser is not known to be the

cleanest. I would not recommend staying in any downtown motels for this reason.

Indianhead Motel & RV Park (747 Hillcrest Ave., Weiser, 208/549-0331), near the west side of the highway as you head north out of town, offers eight relatively clean, non-smoking rooms ($65-95) and eight RV spaces ($25) with water and electricity hookups. Amenities include a laundry room, a picnic area, showers, and horseshoe pits. Tent camping and pets are not allowed.

Weiser has two bed-and-breakfast inns that are both in historic homes. **Galloway House Inn** (1120 E. 2nd St., Weiser, 208/549-1719, www.gallowayhouseinn.com, $90 with private bath, $70 shared bath) is in a Victorian mansion near downtown. Relax in one of the many parlor-like common areas or sip iced tea on the veranda. ★ **Pioneer Guest House** (1203 W. 3rd St., Weiser, 208/414-0728, $50-65) is a clean and comfortable bed-and-breakfast inn operated by Mary Chavez and Ron Glenn. This attractive house was built in the early 20th century, and it has four Western-themed rooms chock-full of antiques. Expect to wake up to a continental breakfast that includes pastries, jam, juice, and coffee.

Food

Weiser Classic Candy (449 State St., Weiser, 208/414-2850, www.weiserclassiccandy.com, 10am-5:30pm Mon.-Fri., 10am-4pm Sat.), an old-school candy store in a Bavarian-inspired storefront downtown, is the spot to go for freshly made chocolates and specialty candies, like chai tea truffles, champagne truffles, almond bark, fudge, and apricot bonbons. The store also has a full-service deli that puts out above-average soups, salads, and sandwiches ($5-7). Try a delicious Monte Cristo.

Homestead Cafe (813 State St., Weiser, 208/414-3962, breakfast, lunch, and dinner daily, $6-18) is where you can get a cup of coffee and a slice of pie. The homespun restaurant also serves standard egg breakfasts, flapjacks, burgers, chicken-fried steaks, and prime rib with big baked potatoes on weekends. Don't be surprised if the waitresses call you "honey" at this friendly café.

Load up on fresh fruit at **Kelley Orchards** (53 Hill Rd., Weiser, 208/642-7265, www.kelleyorchards.com, barn store 8am-6pm Mon.-Sat. June-Sept.), a u-pick farm owned and operated by Ron and Kimi Kelley, who grow apples, apricots, nectarines, peaches, pears, plums, and berries. The farm also sells bags of yummy dried fruit. Kelley Orchards is located off U.S. 95 (at Cox Rd.) between Payette and Weiser. There are lots of roadside signs that will steer you to the red barn on the east side of the highway.

You can score late-summer fruit and vegetables, as well as baked goods, jams, and honey, at the **Weiser Farmers Market** (9am-noon Sat. Aug.-Sept.), which takes place at the Weiser Train Depot. The market doesn't have many vendors, but there are enough offerings to make a visit worthwhile.

Information

The **Weiser Chamber of Commerce** (309 State St., Weiser, 208/414-0452, www.weiserchamber.org) can tell you more about the town. For information about the area's recreational possibilities, drop by the Payette National Forest's **Weiser Ranger District** (851 E. 9th St., Weiser, 208/549-4200).

WEISER RIVER TRAIL

Weiser is the southern starting point for the Weiser River Trail, a dirt and cobblestone recreation trail that hugs the river along an abandoned Union Pacific and Idaho Northern Railroad grade for 85 miles from Weiser up to New Meadows. Some sections flank civilization, while other spots are blissfully remote along this scenic stretch of pastoral land. The landscape turns from rolling hills to high-desert canyons to pine tree-studded mountains as you travel north on the trail, which is best suited for mountain bikes and not road bikes with skinny tires. Hikers, runners, and horseback riders also use the pathway, as do cross-country skiers in winter. The trailhead is on Main Street, about a half-mile east of U.S. 95.

Most people ride the trail from start to finish in two days, but it's also great for shorter day trips on select sections. Here's a look at a few services and fun things to do along the way.

Midvale is the first town you will come to traveling north. It doesn't offer much in terms of services, but you'll find a grassy park area with big shade trees right off the trail along U.S. 95. The trail then winds through a basalt-rimmed canyon and drops into **Cambridge,** a small town with a handful of motels, restaurants, and an old-style market called **Loveland's General Store** (35 N. Superior St., Cambridge, 208/257-3813, 8am-8pm Mon.-Sat.), where you can fill up your paniers with provisions. Three miles north of town, you can soak your sore muscles in the big, naturally heated pool at **Mundo Idaho** (3016 Goodrich Rd., Cambridge, 208/257-3849, 10am-8pm Wed.-Sun., $6 general, $5 seniors and kids under 12), a commercial hot springs operation less than a mile off the trail with a hostel ($16), a campground (tent sites $13), showers, and a small restaurant. This is a good spot to spend the night, even if the place does look like a trailer park.

After jumping back on the trail, you will continue through rolling hills that are skirted by mountains to the east and west. The trail veers northeast at this point toward the high country. **Council,** a gateway to several access points in Hells Canyon, is a little burg that offers general services and a park with relatively clean restrooms. Jump off the trail here and grab a double mocha at **Hartlands Coffee Kitchen** (401 N. Dartmouth St., Council, 208-253-1154, daily), a little coffee shop that also serves tea, fruit smoothies, ice cream, and baked goods.

North of Council, the trail continues its climb toward the evergreen forests, through an area called **Mesa** that was once home to prolific fruit orchards. Most of the orchards are long gone, but you'll still see a few leftover apple trees here and there. Much of the trail borders private property so it's important to stay on track, even if a ripe apple calls your name. (Note: Some landowners aren't happy about the trail's easement going through their property, and they don't want people milling around on their land.) The trail goes into the forest soon after leaving the Mesa area. At this point, you'll be right next to the river again as it makes its high-elevation ascent northward. Expect to feel a burn in your legs and lungs from here on up. Don't worry, though, there are lots of little trestles and bridges along this stretch where you can take a dip

view from the Weiser River Trail

in the river and chillax for a spell. Or you can call it a night at the aptly named **Evergreen Campground,** operated by the Payette National Forest (208/634-0100). Even though the campground, 14 miles north of Council, is situated right next to U.S. 95 and the river and trail itself, it's relatively quiet thanks to a barrier of ponderosa pines, Douglas firs, and lush spruce trees. Campsites ($10-15) have picnic tables and recessed fire rings with grills. Fire restrictions may be in effect in late-summer months. The campground, which is open until the snow falls, has new vault toilets, potable water, and a friendly camp host who can hook you up with firewood. Make reservations at www.recreation.gov or pay at the site.

The remainder of the trail heading north is relatively steep until you pass by the company mill town of **Tamarack** en route to **New Meadows,** where the rocky, forested terrain starts to open up into a beautiful mountain-ringed valley. Of course, you can start your journey in New Meadows and go south, which a lot of people like to do because it's mostly downhill from here, with the exception of some elevation gains in the undulating hills along the southern stretches of the trail. (Information about New Meadows can be found in the *North-Central Idaho* chapter.)

For maps and current trail conditions and updates, visit the Friends of the Weiser River Trail's website at www.weiserrivertrail.org, or call the hotline at 888/698-7245. It's important to note that there aren't any bike shops along the trail, so make sure to have some extra tire tubes, a pump, and a small repair kit with you. **JDZ Bike Shop** (445 State St., Weiser, 208/414-4011), in the old Weiser Mini Mall, offers bike repairs, tune-ups, and parts, but it doesn't rent bikes.

Owyhee Mountains and Canyonlands

In many ways, life hasn't changed that drastically in Owyhee County in the last century or so. Ranchers now dial their trusty satellite phones (cell phone coverage is spotty out here) instead of riding their fastest horse into Murphy to dispatch an urgent message. But jackrabbits and rangeland cattle still outnumber people in this vast and desolate county, the second largest in the state at 7,639 square miles.

If you are lucky, a herd of wild horses will cross the dusty horizon as the high desert unfolds in front of you. Expect to see bighorn sheep, coyotes, rattlesnakes, peregrine falcons, and possibly an occasional cougar hanging out in a creekbed, stalking a wild turkey for dinner.

Named for Hawaiian fur trappers that frequented the area in the early 19th century, the Owyhee (loosely translated from the word *Hawaii*) Mountains and Canyonlands was once a rough-and-tumble place. Many train robberies and murders occurred here in the 1800s. Even the Hawaiian fur trappers mysteriously disappeared without a trace.

The ruggedly beautiful Owyhee Mountains run like a granite spine from the north to southeast, all the way into northern Nevada, splitting Idaho and Oregon into two distinct high-desert valleys. The mountain range rises to 8,403 feet at Hayden Peak. Back in the day, nearby Silver City was a bustling mining town, and in some respects it is still alive.

A few miles to the southeast, the undulating lower valley starts to straighten out until it reaches a pair of giant sand dunes that seem rather out of place among the sagebrush and basalt-streaked canyons.

MARSING

Marsing is a relatively new town, considering there was no bridge crossing the Snake River here until 1921. Before that, two different cable-ferries hauled travelers back and forth, and there wasn't much of a town here at all; it was actually platted about the same time the bridge was built.

Lizard Butte, a prominent basalt bluff that resembles a reptile's head, marks Marsing's north entrance, where the highway curves downward from Sunny Slope wine country and crosses the Snake into the town. **Island Park,** on the upriver side of the bridge, offers a grassy area with picnic tables, barbecue grills, and a dock. Anglers might try dropping a line in hopes of making the acquaintance of a smallmouth bass or two.

Dusty little Marsing seems as far removed as a city can be from Idaho's wine country, and it's only a mile or so away. But once you cross the bridge, it's as if you've entered a new dimension: Owyhee County, Idaho, the place time forgot. This is not such a bad thing, unless you're looking for a place to spend the night. Marsing does have a handful of decent eateries and a grocery store and gas station, but don't expect to find any shiny boutique hotels; in fact, you won't find any hotels or motels (at least ones I feel comfortable recommending). Instead, the downtown strip—Highway 55 slowed to a snail's pace—winds its way through town and up a big hill, eventually meeting U.S. 95 and continuing into the far reaches of southeastern Oregon and points south.

Jump Creek Falls

Jump Creek carves through the rugged Owyhee Canyonlands and forms a spectacular steep-walled box canyon where 60-foot **Jump Creek Falls** lunges into a deep, aquamarine pool. It's an idyllic spot—surrounded by big boulders, caves, and wedged crevices—for a refreshing summer swim, but people have been known to get swimmer's itch here. You'll also need to watch out for ticks, rattlesnakes, and poison ivy along the creek.

The Bureau of Land Management, who manages the site and maintains a vault toilet at the trailhead, has done a good job of keeping Jump Creek Falls and the surrounding environs clean in recent years. Locals for generations have had keggers at this spot, and they are known for leaving behind garbage and graffiti. To get here, take Jump Creek Road south from U.S. 95. At the Y just past the high-tension wires, go right. Just a little farther, you'll want to hang a left at the base of a small ridge. At the next Y you can go either way; from here on out, all roads lead to the parking area, which has a precarious paved strip leading to the lower parking lot. An easy

wild horses in the Owyhees

trail (0.25 mile) leads to the falls. Sorry, no overnight camping.

Food

Alejandra's Mexican Restaurant (208 Main St., Marsing, 208/896-5339, lunch and dinner daily, $6-12) is where you should go for tamales, chili verde, carnitas, enchiladas, and torta sandwiches. This small restaurant on the main drag also has a *mercado* that sells chicharrones (spicy pork rinds), fresh tortillas, and long-necked refrescos (Mexican soft drinks).

HIGHWAY 78 TO MURPHY
Givens Hot Springs

Nomadic Native Americans had been using the hot springs here, now known as **Givens Hot Springs,** for thousands of years when Oregon-bound Milford and Mattie Givens came upon the spot in 1879. The couple immediately abandoned their journey down the dusty Oregon Trail and set up housekeeping. In 1881 they built a home, and in the 1890s, with the help of their four sons, they added a bathhouse. Alas, marital bliss eluded the settlers, and they divorced. Mattie stayed in the family home and remarried, this time to Gus Yanke. Gus helped expand the home into a travelers' oasis that eventually included a hotel, a restaurant, an ice-cream parlor, tree-shaded picnic grounds, a barbershop, and a post office. In 1907, a school was established that apparently doubled as a matrimonial service, considering three of the four Givens boys married girls who came to teach.

The resort became known throughout the area and was well used by Oregon Trail pioneers, Silver City miners, and residents of the Treasure Valley. The hotel burned down in 1939 and was never rebuilt. In 1952 a new bathhouse was constructed. Although today only a small icehouse remains of Milford and Mattie's handiwork, the resort is still owned by their descendants, who have renovated the property in recent years.

The present **bathhouse** (208/495-2000, www.givenshotsprings.com, noon-10pm

Jump Creek Falls

Mon.-Sat. year-round) has an Olympic-size pool ($7 adults, $5 seniors and children, free under age 2 and over age 90), private soaking tubs ($7 pp per hour), and a small snack bar. Outside are picnic areas, horseshoe pits, and areas for baseball, volleyball, and fishing on the Snake River. Tent sites ($20-25) and RV sites ($30) are available, and cabins will cost you $65. The resort is on the south side of Highway 78, 11 miles south of Marsing.

Murphy

Although **Murphy** is the Owyhee County seat, it's not the largest town in the county. In fact, it's one of the smallest, with a population that lingers around 100. In the mining boom days at the turn of the century, Silver City was the county seat, but when metal prices dropped and the mines began to play out, a new site closer to the Snake River was proposed. At that time, Murphy had the county's only railroad terminal, the end of the line for the Boise, Nampa and Owyhee Railroad. Colonel William Dewey had hoped to build an electric continuation of the railroad from Murphy all the way up to his mine near Silver City, to be powered by electricity from the Swan Falls Dam hydroelectric plant he'd built, but the railroad never made it past Murphy. In the meantime, the county's extensive cattle and sheep industries had turned Murphy into the largest livestock shipping point in the Northwest, securing it as the county seat in 1934.

Murphy is semi-famous for its single parking meter in front of the courthouse. The meter was originally an unsubtle hint by locals to discourage people from parking in front of the courthouse gate. Now the lone meter highlights the fact that this little hamlet could well be the smallest county seat in the country. Facilities are limited; the town has no motels and just one small restaurant.

The **Owyhee County Museum** (17085 Basey St., Murphy, 208/495-2319, 10am-4pm Tues.-Sat. year-round, donation), one block south of the highway (look for the sign by the courthouse), includes several transplanted structures and a small historical research library. Among the historic buildings is a one-room schoolhouse, a homesteader's log cabin, and the old Marsing depot, outside of which sits a Union Pacific caboose. Much of the museum's exhibit space is devoted to the history of the Owyhee mines and includes a re-created stamp mill. Library archives hold microfilmed newspapers dating as far back as 1865 as well as more than 4,000 historic photographs of Owyhee County. On the first weekend of each June, the museum sponsors **Murphy Outpost Days,** a festival of folk art, cowboy poetry, country music, parades, food, a Saturday-night dance, and the culminating Horny Toad races.

★ SILVER CITY

Silver City lies in a draw on Jordan Creek, 6,200 feet high in the Owyhee Mountains. To get here, you have to negotiate a narrow winding road for 23 miles up from Murphy. The gravel and dirt road is usually blocked by snow more than half the year, and even in summer it's not recommended for trailers and large RVs. But if you think it's hard getting to Silver City today, just imagine what it was like trying to get here during the town's heyday, roughly 1860-1900. Back in those days, Silver City had a population of 2,500 along with some 75 businesses and 300 homes. Its prosperity led to its status as the county seat 1866-1934. By 1874 it boasted the first telegraph office and the first daily newspaper—*The Idaho Avalanche*—in Idaho Territory. Today, around a dozen people live here year-round. While modern-day residents are after nothing more than remote relaxation, the boomtown-era residents came for silver and gold.

The **Idaho Hotel** (208/583-4104, www. historicsilvercityidaho.com), built in 1863, is the gathering spot in Silver City. This historic hotel was falling down until someone brought it back to life in 1972. It has remained open since then under various owners. Go into the saloon, grab a cold one, and find your way across the sloping floor to a table by the back window. The restaurant serves breakfast, lunch, and dinner every day except Wednesday (the cook needs a day off). Rustic rooms range $80-175.

Besides the hotel, the town has some rental cabins in various price ranges and various states of entropy. You can inquire about these at the hotel. And just downhill from town, the Bureau of Land Management (BLM) oversees a free, 12-site primitive campground along Jordan Creek.

GRAND VIEW TO BRUNEAU
Owyhee Uplands National Backcountry Byway

If you're in need of solitude, the **Owyhee Uplands National Backcountry Byway** might be just the ticket. From east of Grand View, the gravel road loops out behind the Owyhee Mountains, leading back to Jordan Valley, Oregon, or Silver City. Along the way it passes through varied and spectacular high-desert terrain virtually devoid of people. Most cars will have no problem (unless they have really low clearance) navigating the gravel road when it's dry, which is usually June-October. Most of the land surrounding the road is public, managed by the BLM, so unless posted otherwise, you can set up your tent anywhere you want. Several creeks along the way provide an ample water supply, but much of this land is used for grazing cattle; make sure to boil or filter the water, or better yet, bring your own.

Heading south out of Grand View, you'll pass through arid ranchlands and then quickly leave civilization behind. Soon you'll reach the Owyhee foothills and begin ascending Poison Creek, where you'll find a small BLM picnic area. The road keeps climbing, and it won't be long before you'll have a sweeping, eagle's-eye view of the Snake River Plain. Onward and upward, the higher elevation brings new flora: first hills of mountain mahogany, and then high tablelands covered in dense juniper forest. Wildflowers brighten the interspersed grassy slopes until well into July. Keep your eyes peeled for wildlife. Mule deer, pronghorn, bighorn sheep, badgers, and coyotes inhabit this broad-brushed landscape, and looking skyward you might see golden eagles, red-tailed and ferruginous hawks, northern harriers, and short-eared owls. The road continues relatively level for miles through beautiful rolling terrain before suddenly dropping down into the canyon formed by the North Fork of the Owyhee River. A small BLM campground along the river here is a great spot to stop for the day and get wet while you explore the area. Upstream, the river rounds a bend to a hidden valley where large gravel bars along the banks make secluded sunning spots. Downstream, the river enters a dramatic gorge with red rock walls rising vertically huThe road continues relatively level for miles through beautiful rolling terrain before suddenly dropping down into the canyon formed by the North Fork of the Owyhee River. A small BLM campground along the river here is a great spot to stop for the day and get wet while you

explore the area. Upstream, the river rounds a bend to a hidden valley where large gravel bars along the banks make secluded sunning spots. Downstream, the river enters a dramatic gorge with red rock walls rising vertically hundreds of feet above the water.

Continuing past the campground, you'll pass through more cattle country. It's open range out here; there are no fences to keep bovines off the road. Drive carefully to avoid hitting any cattle. Plus, if you hit a rangeland animal in Idaho, and injure it or kill it, you're legally obligated to pay for it. And just think of the damage a Texas Longhorn would do to your rig. Anyway, you'll soon pass a little ranch called Cliffs and then descend through irrigated farmland and ranchland into Oregon and toward the turnoff to DeLamar and Silver City (it's marked with a huge sign for the Kinross DeLamar mine). Continuing straight on will take you into Jordan Valley, Oregon, where you can hook up with U.S. 95 and head north back into Idaho. If you head to Silver City from here, you'll have good road up to the DeLamar junction, then rougher road for the last eight miles into Silver City. From Silver City, you can descend the north side of the Owyhee Mountains into Murphy. Don't head up this way if the roads are wet. You might make it up to the top, but coming down the other side is steeper, slipperier, and more treacherous.

The length of the byway from Grand View to Jordan Valley is 103 miles, and you can figure on traveling about 35 mph or less en route. The road is well marked with directional signs and the special Backcountry Byway route markers, but obviously there are no services along the way, so make sure to top off the fuel tank and load up on water before you set out. For more information about the route, contact the BLM's **Boise Field Office** (3948 Development Ave., 208/384-3300).

Lawson's Emu-Z-Um

Sometimes you come across the strangest attractions where you least expect them. This is definitely the case at **Lawson's Emu-Z-Um**

(22142 River Rd., Grand View, 208/834-2397, www.emuzum.com, 9am-5pm Fri.-Sun., $10 adults, $5 children 6-12, free under age 6), a privately run historical museum situated by the Snake River near Grand View. Here, on a former emu ranch, thus the name, you'll find an extensive collection of relics from Silver City, Native American artifacts, and other reminders of Idaho's pioneer past. Expect to see a one-room schoolhouse, which was moved from Silver City a few years back, and the first automobile made in the area. There's even a replica of an old Western town on the property. The museum, owned and operated by Jack and Belva Lawson, may be a little pricey, but there's a grassy area with tables where you can have a picnic and make a day of it. To get here from Murphy, continue traveling southeast on Highway 78 until you come to mile marker 52. Hang a left and look for the museum on the north side of the highway near the river.

C. J. Strike Reservoir and Wildlife Management Area

Clifford J. Strike was the president of the Idaho Power Company from 1938 to 1948. The dam named after him, built in 1952, backs up 7,500-acre **C. J. Strike Reservoir,** a popular fishing hole with bass, bluegill, crappie, perch, catfish, and even the mighty sturgeon. The reservoir and the land surrounding it make up the 12,500-acre **C. J. Strike Wildlife Management Area** (WMA), protected habitat for migratory ducks and geese in winter. The WMA headquarters is near Jack's Creek, 12 miles east of Grand View on Highway 78. Several free BLM camping areas are spread along the southern shore of the reservoir. From east to west: **Jack's Creek Sportsman's Access Area; Cottonwood Sportsman's Access Area;** and **Cove Campground,** with 26 sites, fishing, swimming, and hiking trails.

Bruneau Canyon Overlook

If you pass through the blink-and-miss town of Bruneau and continue out on Hot Springs Road, it eventually turns into Clover-Three Creek Road and leads to a spur road to the scenic **Bruneau Canyon Overlook,** where the Bruneau River has sliced a deep slit in the earth. You can see the river glimmering down at the canyon bottom, but you can't get down to it. Rafters and kayakers, who put in southwest of here, across the river near Grasmere, run this wild stretch in the spring and early summer when the water levels are high.

Bruneau Dunes State Park

★ Bruneau Dunes State Park

One of the state's larger parks, **Bruneau Dunes State Park** (27608 Sand Dunes Rd., Mountain Home, 208/366-7919, $5 per vehicle) encompasses some 4,800 acres of southwestern Idaho desert. Two enormous interconnecting sand dunes—the tallest nearly 500 feet high—rise from the center of the park. Unlike most sand dunes, these don't shift much, thanks to prevailing winds that blow in opposite directions for roughly equal amounts of time. The pristine dunes are closed to motor vehicles, but you can hike right up to the top, where you'll find an interesting crater that the two dunes seem to spiral out of, along with great views across the Snake River Plain. Kids, and the more childlike adults among us, won't be able to resist rolling back down the giant sand hills. It's also an excellent spot to fly kites. Various hiking trails lead around the base of the dunes, past a couple of lakes that attract both wildlife and anglers, not to mention sheets of mosquitoes (bring DEET bug spray with you). Another feature of the park is an observatory with a 25-inch telescope and several smaller scopes. Stargazing programs (9:30pm Fri.-Sat. April-Oct., $3 general, free under age 6) are offered on weekends.

The park has two campground areas (standard and serviced sites $16-22). **Broken Wheel** is a grassy, 48-site campground with restrooms and a canopy of much-needed shade trees, while the newer Eagle Cove Campground, down the hill near the dunes, is better suited for RVs, and it doesn't offer much relief from the blistering sun. **Eagle Cove** has a large picnic shelter, restrooms, and showers, which you will need after rolling around in sand all day. Nearby, the park maintains two small cabins ($50) that face the dunes.

There's a small visitors center at the entrance to the park that displays fossils, mounted specimens of species native to the area, and lots of information about how the dunes came to be. They also keep a gift shop and store with basic provisions such as ice, water, firewood, and bug spray.

The Lowman Loop

Up in the northeast corner of the Treasure Valley, the desert finally surrenders to the pine-forested Boise Mountains. Amazing panoramas can be found just a short drive from Boise as you travel north on Highway 21. This curvy drive, known to locals as the Lowman Loop, connects three nationally designated scenic routes: Ponderosa Pine Scenic Byway, Wildlife Canyon Scenic Byway, and Payette River Scenic Byway.

Idaho City is 38 miles northeast of Boise. You can lick an ice-cream cone while taking a historic walking tour of the town's brick-clad buildings, many of which still have their original boardwalks. And Idaho City has the funkiest pioneer cemetery north of Tombstone, Arizona.

The South Fork of the Payette River near Lowman is a spectacular place to embark on a guided white-water rafting trip through a squeeze of impressive granite canyons. The area is also a hotbed of geothermal activity: Relax and take a soak in one of the many hot springs along this steamy stretch.

Leave the main highway at Lowman and head west through the deep recesses of South Fork Canyon on your way to beautiful Garden Valley. Continue west until you reach Banks and the North Fork of the Payette River, where you finish the loop by heading south to the small town of Horseshoe Bend, home to the Thunder Mountain Line.

HIGHWAY 21 TO IDAHO CITY
Arrowrock Reservoir and Middle Fork Boise River

Coming up Highway 21 from Boise, at the

upper end of Lucky Peak Reservoir, a turn-off to the right (Forest Rd. 268) leads along the northern arm of Lucky Peak Reservoir to Arrowrock Dam. Beyond the dam, the road follows the north shore of **Arrowrock Reservoir** to its inlet and continues up the **Middle Fork of the Boise River.** Numerous free Boise National Forest campgrounds are strung along the route. Heading upstream, you'll come to **Cottonwood** (3 sites), **Willow Creek** (10 sites), **Badger Creek** (5 sites), **Troutdale** (4 sites), and **Ninemeyer** (8 sites). For more information on the campgrounds, contact the **Mountain Home Ranger District** (2180 American Legion Blvd., Mountain Home, 208/587-7961).

Back out on the blacktop, heading north along a winding stretch of Highway 21 that clings to Mores Creek, it won't be long before you reach a popular commercial hot springs on the left-hand side of the road, and Idaho City is just a mile past the resort.

★ IDAHO CITY

After gold was discovered here in 1862, prospectors came flooding in seeking a share of the wealth, and many found it, while others just found misery and their place in the hillside cemetery. More gold was mined from the mountains of this area than from all of Alaska. Between August 1862 and December 1863 alone, the basin yielded more than $6 million in gold dust. By the time the miners were through, they'd reaped a glittering treasure estimated at $250 million (which would equate to around $4 billion today). Along with the miners came gamblers, ladies of the evening, lawmen, and lots of Chinese workers, who had a bustling Chinatown with restaurants, grocery stores, an herbalist, and a joss house. Looking at Idaho City today, it's hard to imagine that for a while this was the biggest city in the Northwest. By 1864 some 20,000 people inhabited the Boise Basin Mining District, with Idaho City as its booming hub. Today, the town's population is around 500, and the surrounding area—once full of mining camps—now has many more ghosts than people.

the Lowman Loop

The Lowman Loop

Banks
55
55
Lowman
21
BANKS-LOWMAN RD
52
Horseshoe
Bend
THUNDER
MOUNTAIN LINE
55
Boise
Emmett
21
National
Forest
21
IDAHO
CITY
Eagle
Star
44
44
Meridian
BOISE
30
Arrowrock
Reservoir
Nampa
30
Lucky Peak State
Recreation Area

0   5 mi
0   5 km

LOWMAN LOOP ROUTE

© AVALON TRAVEL

Historical Sights

Wandering through town on the many wooden sidewalks will take you past one historic "first" after another. Among them: the 1863 building where the *Idaho World*—Idaho's oldest newspaper—was first published; the 1864 **Idaho Territorial Penitentiary,** a hand-hewn log hoosegow that once held the killer of Idaho City's first marshal; the 1865 **Boise Basin Mercantile,** Idaho's first general store; and the 1867 **St. Joseph's Catholic Church,** successor to an 1863 church that was the state's first Catholic church for nonnative settlers. Out past the west end of town is the **Pioneer Cemetery.** Of the first 200 men and women buried here, it's said that only 28 died of natural causes. Yikes! To find out more about the town's Wild West history, visit the **Boise Basin Historical Museum** (Wall St. and Montgomery St., 208/392-4550, 11am-4pm daily Memorial Day-Labor Day, $2 adults, $1.50 seniors and students, $5 families), featuring old photos, mining tools, and other artifacts and memorabilia.

The Springs

People have soaked in the hot springs at this scenic spot next to Mores Creek since the mining days. There were even some notorious gunfights here back then. Things are considerably mellower in this day and age. **The Springs** (3742 Hwy. 21, Idaho City, 208/392-9500, www.thespringsid.com, 11am-10pm Wed.-Mon., $16 adults, $10 children 12 and under, reservations highly recommended), formerly known as Warm Springs Resort, recently underwent major renovation and construction. The resort's new owners run a clean and efficient operation, one with relaxation in mind and not six-shooters. The day resort features a large main pool, a much hotter soaking tub, a cold-water splash deck, and a spring water-fed steam room that holds about a dozen sweaty humans. There's also a small café where you can get snacks, small plates, salads, and grilled sandwiches, as well as espresso drinks and draft microbrews.

Recreation

Cross-country skiers and snowshoers will like the three Park N' Ski areas that lie along Highway 21 between Idaho City and Lowman. Thanks to their proximity to Boise—close enough for a day trip—the areas are the most heavily used and the best groomed in the state Park N' Ski system. Most of the trails are of intermediate difficulty. Both traditional and skating tracks are set, usually once a week on Thursday. That puts them in good shape for the weekend. By Wednesday they're usually pretty well thrashed. Park N' Ski permits ($25 for the season, $7.50 for three days) are required and are sold in Idaho City at Tom's Service (3889 Hwy. 21, 208/392-4900), or go to www.parksandrecreation.idaho.gov.

Eighteen miles north of Idaho City, **Whoop-Um-Up Creek Park N' Ski Area** offers four miles of marked but ungroomed

trails. Two loops are set on the west side of the highway, three on the east side. This is the place to bring Fido, as dogs are not permitted on groomed trails. Another three miles up the highway, **Gold Fork Park N' Ski Area** provides eight miles of marked and groomed trails in loops on both sides of the highway. Finally, 3.5 miles farther north is **Banner Ridge Park N' Ski Area,** where you'll find 16 miles of marked and groomed trails.

The Banner Ridge and Gold Fork systems are connected by a groomed trail, and both trailheads provide access to **Beaver Creek Cabin** ($45), a two-bedroom Forest Service cabin that rents by the night. You can make reservations through the Idaho City Ranger District (208/392-6681) or online at www.recreation.gov. Telemarkers can also ask at the ranger station for directions to great slopes off the Gold Fork and Banner Ridge systems.

The Idaho Department of Parks and Recreation (208/334-4199, www.parksandrecreation.idaho.gov) oversees six backcountry yurts ($65-100) in the area. (Just so you know, black bears are fairly active around here. I woke up one morning to find muddy paw prints all over my rig.)

For more information about the Park N' Ski trails, contact the **Idaho City Ranger**

historic Idaho City

District (3833 Hwy. 21, Idaho City, 208/392-6681), west of Idaho City on Highway 21. There you can also pick up the brochure *Park N' Ski—Idaho City Area,* which describes all the trails in the three systems.

For hiking and mountain biking, check out the **Crooked River Trail** just off Highway 21. This relatively easy trail (2.6 miles round-trip) skirts along the gurgling Crooked River. Just past the trailhead, you'll see the remnants of an old miner's cabin right before the trail starts its traverse through the steep-walled canyon. At 1.3 miles, you can continue on for another nine or so miles across a recently built bridge, or turn around and head back out. To get to the trailhead, take Highway 21 north of Idaho City to Forest Road 384 (Crooked River Rd.), and then take a right and head past the Edna Creek Campground until you see the pullout on the right.

If you continue going east on Crooked River Road for about 45 bumpy miles, you will eventually come to the old mining town of Atlanta, situated at the foot of the Sawtooths. (Information about the Atlanta area can be found in the *Sun Valley and the Sawtooths* chapter.)

Events

Idaho City hosts events throughout the year, but the biggest bash in town happens at the end of June. **Frontier Days** is an annual blowout that features a nighttime rodeo, a flea market (with lots of old cast-iron pans), and enough food and beer vendors to keep everyone happy. Chances are high that you'll also see staged gunfights and other quick-draw fun around town. For more information about this event and other happenings in Idaho City, call 208/392-6040.

Accommodations

The creaky old **Idaho City Lodge** (215 Montgomery St., Idaho City, 208/392-4499, $65-75), formerly known as the Idaho City Hotel, was built at the turn of the 20th century. Despite renovations over the years, the hotel's rustic character has been kept intact,

and there are reportedly some ghosts milling around in the upstairs hallways. The rooms are cramped in the main building, but the wraparound veranda is where you'll want to spend most of your time anyway. There's a two-bed bunkhouse out back for those who need a little more room.

Trudy's Cabins (3876 Hwy. 21, Idaho City, 208/392-4151) are near town on the highway next to Trudy's Kitchen. Here you will find two standard rental cabins ($79-99) and nine RV sites ($23) with hookups.

Camping

Between Idaho City and Lowman you'll find several Boise National Forest campgrounds. **Grayback Gulch** (20 sites, $15-30) is about three miles south of Idaho City on Highway 21. About halfway between Idaho City and Lowman along the highway is a cluster of three fee campgrounds all within a couple of miles of one another: **Ten Mile** (16 sites, $15), **Bad Bear** (6 sites, $15), and **Hayfork** (6 sites, $15). Farther north, just past the Whoop-Um-Up Creek Park N' Ski Area, is **Edna Creek** (9 sites, $15). For more information, contact the **Idaho City Ranger District** (3833 Hwy. 21, Idaho City, 208/392-6681).

Food

Everyone in these parts dines at ★ **Trudy's Kitchen** (3876 Hwy. 21, Idaho City, 208/392-4151, 8am-8pm daily, under $10). Expect homespun offerings such as biscuits and gravy, hot sandwiches, and chicken-fried steak served with mashed spuds and country gravy. They also dish up delicious huckleberry pie.

Sarsaparilla Ice Cream Parlor (205 Main St., Idaho City, 208/392-4484, open daily) is where tourists and locals alike go for ice-cream cones, milkshakes, frothy chocolate sundaes, and banana splits. You can also get espresso drinks here.

There are several other eateries along the main drag that offer big steaks and longneck beers, the preferred local diet.

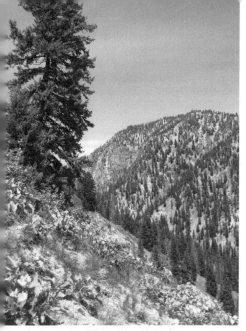
alpine wildflowers in Lowman

Information

The friendly folks at the year-round **Idaho City Visitor Center** (Main St. and Hwy. 21, 208/392-6040) can give you information about the town and its hinterlands. This is also where you can pick up a historic walking-tour map and inquire about a guided tour of the town.

LOWMAN

Lowman is about 35 miles northeast of Idaho City on Highway 21. While the mountainous area surrounding this hamlet abounds with recreational fun, it doesn't offer much in the way of services. There are several businesses along the South Fork of the Payette River that appear to be open but really aren't.

If you plan to continue driving on the Lowman Loop, this is where you'll need to leave Highway 21 and turn left (west) onto Banks-Lowman Road, also known as the Wildlife Canyon Scenic Byway. If you stay on Highway 21, which is sometimes closed in the winter months along this stretch due to heavy

snow, you will pass Grandjean en route to Stanley on the Ponderosa Pine Scenic Byway.

White-Water Rafting

Payette River Company (7655 Hwy. 21, Lowman, 208/259-3702, www.payetteriver-company.com) is a small outfit located along a stretch of the highway severely burned in 1989 when a lightning strike started a fast-moving fire that blackened 47,000 acres of pristine mountain-scape. The rafting company's building is not easy on the eyes either, but owners Sean and Ginger Glaccum have more than 20 years of combined experience as river-rafting guides. So who cares if the rafts are stored next to a rundown mobile home? You will be spending your time on the river anyway. Payette River Company offers half-day and full-day white-water rafting excursions ($60-100 pp); all-inclusive multiple-day trips range $300-500.

Accommodations and Food

Southfork Lodge was the nicest place to bed down in the Lowman area, but unfortunately it's currently closed and up for sale. This beautiful log lodge, with a restaurant, bar, and an assortment of cabins, could be yours for a cool $1.4 million. Keep your eye out for this place, near the junction of Highway 21 and Banks-Lowman Road, in case it reopens under new ownership.

But all is not lost. **Sourdough Lodge** (8406 Hwy. 21, Lowman, 208/259-3326, www.sourdoughlodge.com), 12 miles east of Lowman at mile marker 84, offers relatively clean lodging and friendly faces. This rustic resort has a full-service restaurant, a grocery store, a gas station, 13 guest rooms ($69-245), three small cabins ($99-129), and four RV sites ($20 with hookups).

Camping

Camping and hot springs go hand in hand in the Lowman area, considering that most of these steamy natural pools are next to established campgrounds. U.S. Forest Service campgrounds in the Lowman area include

Whitewater (5 sites, $15) and **Pine Flats** (24 sites, $15), with hot springs, both a short distance west down the Banks-Lowman Road; **Park Creek** (26 sites, $12), three miles north of Lowman up Clear Creek Road (Forest Rd. 582); **Mountain View** (14 sites, $15), right in Lowman; and three campgrounds east of Lowman on Highway 21 heading toward Stanley: **Kirkham** (15 sites, $15), **Helende** (10 sites, $15), and **Bonneville** (22 sites, $15). Kirkham is right at the roadside **Kirkham Hot Springs,** while Bonneville is within walking distance of the more secluded **Bonneville Hot Springs.**

Forest Service Rentals

In winter, Boise National Forest offers several ski-in guard stations for rent in the area, such as the **Warm Springs Guard Station** (sleeps six, $40) near Bonneville Hot Springs, a mile north of Highway 21 at mile marker 91. To reserve these cabins and for more information about other Forest Service fun in the area, call the **Lowman Ranger District** (7359 Hwy. 21) at 208/259-3361, or just stop by the office.

GARDEN VALLEY

Back on the Lowman Loop, heading west on Banks-Lowman Road, you'll quickly traverse the steep grade of **South Fork Canyon,** a deep chasm with weeping walls and visible mine shafts next to the road. After climbing up and over Grimes Pass, the twisting road continues to hug the river until the landscape opens up into a gorgeous valley.

Garden Valley was named for its prolific vegetable gardens in the late 19th century. Because of the valley's surprisingly mild temperatures, endless geothermal water, and fertile soil, many Chinese farmers grew produce here and hauled it to the Boise Basin mining camps. Today, there are only a few hothouses that grow specialty blooms for Boise-area florists.

After passing through a nondescript business district, look for Middle Fork Road. Hang a right here, and suddenly you'll be in

Crouch, a frontier-themed village with basic services. Many of the wood structures have similar red-tin roofs and a rustic appearance. This is a great spot to grab a burger and a beer, and perhaps a history lesson from a scruffy local.

Recreation

White-water fanatics looking for a thrill ride will definitely find it on the South Fork Canyon stretch of the river, which drops 475 feet in 13 miles. Along the way you'll have the chance to soak in a riverbank hot spring, portage around a 40-foot waterfall, and paddle for all you're worth through a slew of Class IV crunchers. Scenery is outstanding as you find yourself closed in by the canyon's steep granite walls.

Other boatable stretches on the South Fork in this area include a relatively easy float between Danskin Station and Garden Valley.

Idaho Whitewater Unlimited (787 Banks-Lowman Rd., 208/462-1900, www.idahowhitewaterunltd.com) operates on this portion of the river as well as on the North and Main Forks of the Payette River. The rafting company has several half-day and full-day packages ranging $25-85.

Golfers will rejoice in the natural beauty of the golf links at **Terrace Lakes Resort** (101 Holiday Dr., Garden Valley, 208/462-3250, www.terracelakes.com, greens fees $36-45), four miles north of town. The 18-hole golf course is situated amid the pine trees and mountainous terrain. Don't be surprised to see elk grazing on the fairway as you're teeing off. The resort also has a bar and grill, a motel ($59-85), and some rental cabins ($79).

Getting to **Silver Creek Plunge** (2345 Silver Creek Rd., Garden Valley, 208/739-3400, www.silvercreekplunge.com, 9am-10pm Thurs.-Tues., 7pm-10pm Wed., $10 adults, $8 seniors and children 12 and under) may be a long drive on washboard roads, but it's well worth the effort. Situated in Peace Valley, about 23 miles north of Crouch, this commercial hot springs resort is a great place to soak your sore muscles after fighting a current all day. Expect to find a 100°F outdoor swimming pool, cabins ($69-119), and several campsites ($15) along the meandering Silver Creek.

Accommodations and Food

In downtown Crouch, within stumbling distance of the bars, you'll find the **Wander Inn Motel & Cabins** (486 S. Middle Fork Rd., Crouch, 208/462-2305, $65-75). This ramshackle-looking place has two motel rooms and three marginally clean cabins.

For more comfortable lodging, try **Walk on the Wild Side Bed & Breakfast** (69 River Ranch Rd., Garden Valley, 208/462-2732, www.wildsidebb.com, $95-145), a ranch house-style inn on the banks of the Middle Fork that serves a big homespun breakfast.

If you're interested in renting a vacation home in the Garden Valley area, contact **Idaho Cabin Keepers** (522 S. Middle Fork Rd., Garden Valley, 877/322-2467, www.idahovacationcabins.com) for listings and pricing information.

Have a burger and a beer at **Two Rivers Grill** (1049 Old Crouch Rd., Crouch, 208/462-3770, www.tworiversgrill.com, dinner 4:30pm-9pm Mon.-Sat., lunch 11am-2pm Fri.-Sat., $9-25), or choose from a large menu that features globally inspired entrées such as Korean-style beef ribs, chicken Dijon, and crab cakes with aioli. Two Rivers also serves breakfast on Sundays (9am-1pm). Expect to find a good cup of coffee and blueberry pancakes, eggs Benedict, and French toast topped with candied bacon.

Camping

Past Crouch up Middle Fork Road (Forest Rd. 698), you'll enter the heart of Boise National Forest and find a number of hot springs and Forest Service campgrounds. Between Crouch and the Trail Creek Junction are **Tie Creek** (8 sites, $12), **Hardscrabble** (6 sites, $12), **Rattlesnake** (11 sites, $12), and at the junction of Forest Roads 698 and 671, **Trail Creek** (11 sites, $12). About 1.5 miles upriver from Hardscrabble Campground, across the river

from the road, you may see the steam rising out of **Rocky Canyon Hot Spring.** If you decide to soak, be careful fording the Middle Fork.

A left on Forest Road 698 at Trail Creek Junction reveals, in less than 0.5 mile, a spur leading off to the left; take it down to the river and **Fire Crew Hot Springs,** a good place for a soak after the peak spring runoff has passed. Seven miles or so farther north on Forest Road 698, you'll find **Boiling Springs Campground** (9 sites, $12) near some riverside hot springs that bear the same name.

Information

Load up on brochures and area maps at the **Garden Valley Ranger Station** (1219 Banks-Lowman Rd., Garden Valley, 208/462-3241).

BANKS AND VICINITY

Not long after leaving Garden Valley, traveling west along the South Fork on Banks-Lowman Road, you will come to the junction of Highway 55 at Banks. This stretch of the Lowman Loop, known as the Payette River Scenic Byway, clings to the river like a wet sock all the way to Horseshoe Bend. Banks doesn't have many facilities except for the small **Banks Store & Café** (7864 Hwy. 55, Banks, 208/793-2617), which doubles as a rafting company.

White-Water Rafting

Between Banks and Horseshoe Bend, the main Payette offers up the tamest water on the river, which isn't to say it's placid; three Class III rapids and several easier ones make for a thrilling ride, especially for white-water neophytes who might be a little nervous about offering themselves up to the river goddess. The river's highest flow rates are found here, peaking at around 8,000 cubic feet per second in June. That can make for some big waves. But the river is widest here as well, which tempers its ferocity. Between the rapids, you'll find plenty of time for relaxation on sandy beaches or in good swimming holes.

The South Fork

At Banks, the two major forks of the Payette River meet. The **South Fork,** coming in from the east, is the most prized stretch of the river for most boaters. The **Lower South Fork,** between the Deer Creek put-in and Banks, offers a five-mile thrill ride through three Class III rapids, the Class III+ Bronco Billy rapid, and the awesome waves of the Class IV Staircase. In high water, Staircase will put you into adrenaline overload. You need plenty of speed and concentrated paddling to make it through the string of waves that are nearly a boat-length high through this portion, and when it's done, you'll probably want to do it all over again. The great thing about the Payette is that you *can* do it again: Access is easy because the Banks-Lowman Road parallels the river, and the stretch is short, so you can run it three times in a day if you have the stamina.

The North Fork

Continuing north up Highway 55 past Banks, the **North Fork** of the Payette puts on quite a show. Incredible amounts of water funnel through the tight, rock-filled canyon in a raging flow no wider than a Winnebago. From just south of Smith's Ferry to Banks, the North Fork is, for all intents and purposes, just one long Class V rapid. Needless to say, it's not run commercially.

Above Smiths Ferry, the river returns to a descent once again suited to mere mortals. The **Cabarton run** from Cabarton Bridge to Smith's Ferry is a popular day trip through a canyon with some healthy but not too intimidating rapids. A bonus on this stretch is the abundant wildlife along the river, including bald eagles, ospreys, and deer.

River Guides

Several companies offer guided trips on the Payette River, among them **Bear Valley Rafting** (7864 Hwy. 55, Banks, 208/793-2272, www.bearvalleyrafting.com), next to the Banks Store & Café, which guides all the Payette's major runs as well as the Grandjean

stretch on the upper South Fork. **Cascade Raft & Kayak** (7050 Hwy. 55, Horseshoe Bend, 208/793-2221, www.cascaderaft.com) offers trips on all the major runs, and it has a kayak school.

Smiths Ferry

Smiths Ferry, about 25 miles north of Banks on Highway 55, is a good excursion off the Lowman Loop. Once you crest the rapid-laden canyon, the road and river flattens out through this tranquil high-mountain valley. This is where you will find **Cougar Mountain Lodge** (9738 Hwy. 55, 208/382-4464), a cozy roadhouse restaurant that offers seven guest rooms ($45-60).

West of Smiths Ferry, small but scenic **Sage Hen Reservoir** lies in a forested 4,800-foot-high basin; from Highway 55 at Smiths Ferry, take Forest Roads 644, 626, and 614. Forest Service campgrounds ring the lake, which offers good fishing for stocked trout. Small boats are permitted on the reservoir; Antelope and Sage Hen Creek Campgrounds offer docks and ramps.

Counterclockwise around the lake from the southeast shore, campgrounds include **Hollywood** (6 sites, $15), **Eastside** (6 sites, $15), **Sage Hen Creek** (15 sites, $15), and **Antelope** (20 sites, $15). All are open mid-May-mid-September. Reservations are taken for Antelope and Sage Hen at www.recreation.gov; the others are first-come, first-served. Also here at the west side of the reservoir is the **Sage Hen Dam Picnic Area,** which charges a $5 day-use fee. (Note: Keep your dogs close because a wolf pack in the area has recently killed a few pooches near the campgrounds.)

Hikers will find a trail (Joe's Creek Rd., then Joe's Creek Trail 137) between Sage Hen Creek and Antelope Campgrounds that leads north up Joe's Creek about five miles to great views at the top of West Peak (8,086 feet). In late spring, hikers should keep their eyes peeled for morel mushrooms, and again in summer for plump huckleberries.

HORSESHOE BEND

To complete the Lowman Loop, head south on Highway 55 along the main Payette River toward Boise. Eventually you arrive in Horseshoe Bend, a sleepy little community in a bowl-like valley. Here you will find a few restaurants and service stations as well as a popular scenic train ride.

★ Thunder Mountain Line

Horseshoe Bend is the home depot for the **Thunder Mountain Line** excursion railroad (120 Mill Rd., Horseshoe Bend, 208/331-1184, www.thundermountainline.com, $20-90, reservations advised). Three basic trips are offered: the Horseshoe Bend Express, a 2.5-hour tour from Horseshoe Bend to Banks and back; the Cabarton Flyer, a 2.5-hour round-trip from Cascade to Smiths Ferry; and the Cascade Limited, a five-hour trek from Horseshoe Bend to Cascade and back. Other offerings include a festive Christmas train, "river and rails" train-rafting combos, wine-tasting trips, and more.

Zip Idaho

Take a fast ride through the pine trees at **Zip Idaho** (101 Locust St., Horseshoe Bend, 208/793-2947, www.zipidaho.com, $90), a newish zipline company that offers several adrenaline-spiking tours. Scream your lungs out on the Wild Turkey, a 1,700-foot zipline that will have you reaching speeds up to 40 mph. You must weigh between 80 and 260 pounds to ride.

Food

Corner Cafe Bar & Grill (466 Hwy. 55, Horseshoe Bend, 208/793-3374, 6am-10pm daily, $6-20) serves pizza, burgers, smoked prime rib, and freshly baked fruit and cream pies. In the morning you can get espresso drinks and standard breakfast dishes.

If you're looking to load up on fresh produce, check out **Volcanic Farms** (457 Hwy. 55, Horseshoe Bend, 208/793-2882, May-Nov.). Here you can score a multitude of locally grown fruit and vegetables, like asparagus, cherries, peaches, melons, onions, and various potatoes.

Magic Valley

S een through a car window on I-84, the sprawling landscape of the Magic Valley in south-central Idaho may seem uninspiring. But take any exit and you will find oases of geologic wonder tucked away throughout this great rift.

Water, fed by an ancient aquifer, gushes in hundreds of streams falling from black-rimmed basalt cliffs. Bizarre rock outcroppings and boulders as big as minivans are scattered across the expanse, caused by the monumental Bonneville Flood about 15,000 years ago. Shoshone Falls, called the "Niagara of the West," is a hydro spectacle when it roars full force each spring. The Magic Valley is aptly named, both for its natural features and irrigation marvels that helped to reshape the land, with miles and miles of agricultural flatlands spread out like a patchwork sheet across the Snake River Plain.

Before this high-desert terrain was irrigated in the early 20th century with 2,600 miles of canals of water rerouted from the Snake River, a seemingly unending convoy of oxcarts and covered wagons passed through the arid region en route to greener pastures on the West Coast. It was here that these Oregon Trail emigrants faced some of their toughest challenges along the 2,000-plus-mile trail; most notably they had to get to the north side of the Snake River, but the region's deep gorges and turbulent waterfalls made the task perilous and nearly impossible. This wasn't a magic place for them at all. The wagons eventually found an easy spot to ford the river, at Three Island Crossing near present-day Glenns Ferry.

Today, the Magic Valley is more hospitable to humans, thanks in part to a series of bridges that connect both sides of the river.

PLANNING YOUR TIME

You can explore most of the Magic Valley in about three days. Twin Falls and Hagerman, both close to I-84, are good base camps for your high-desert adventures. The Hagerman and Buhl areas are home to numerous fish hatcheries and aquaculture farms as well as dairies and creameries where you can score the best ice cream for miles around. As an

Previous: Shoshone Falls; Snake River in Twin Falls. **Above:** City of Rocks National Reserve.

Look for ★ to find recommended sights, activities, dining, and lodging.

Highlights

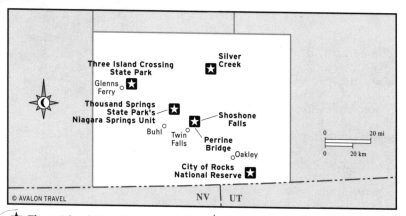

★ **Three Island Crossing State Park:** The 614-acre state park commemorates one of the most important historic sites on the Oregon Trail. Big shade trees and the air-conditioned interpretive center now offer relief from the blazing desert sun (page 130).

★ **Thousand Springs State Park's Niagara Springs Unit:** Here you will find an oasis in the desert, a magical place where high-rimmed canyon walls weep water at 250 cubic feet per second (page 139).

★ **Perrine Bridge:** This 486-foot-high metal bridge spans the scenic Snake River Canyon in Twin Falls. It has become a top destination for BASE jumpers, who show up here in droves during the summer months (page 143).

★ **Shoshone Falls:** Springtime is the right time to view these 212-foot-high falls, when a forceful torrent of water comes barreling over the giant rocks. It's a mere trickle the rest of the year (page 143).

★ **Silver Creek:** These alkaline springs near Picabo entice fly-fishers from around the world. Elusive wild rainbow and brown trout scurry about in the crystalline streams that intertwine through the spectacular high-desert landscape (page 153).

★ **City of Rocks National Reserve:** This out-of-the-way preserve near Almo is one of the country's top rock-climbing destinations. A city of monolithic granite rocks makes a veritable playground for the "chalky hand" crowd (page 158).

Magic Valley

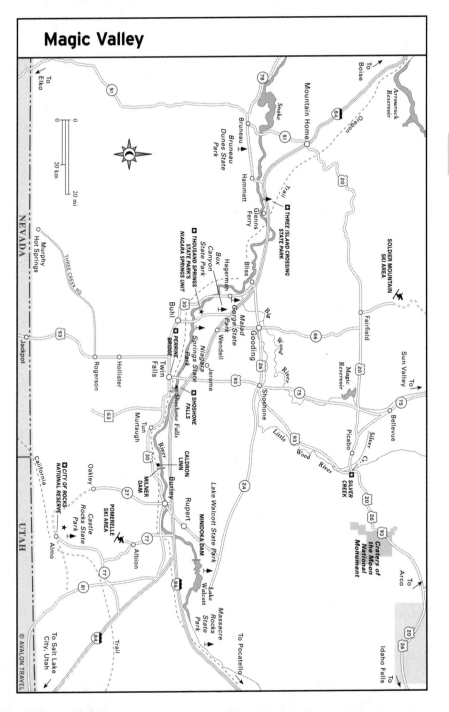

added bonus, several commercially operated hot springs are situated near the Snake River, giving travelers a place to unwind after a long day behind the wheel. You can also hit some tasting rooms at the local wineries, situated on the east side of the Snake River Valley Appellation.

Twin Falls, the largest city in the region, offers sojourners a wide variety of restaurants, lodging, and cultural activities. And thrill-seekers can leap off the 486-foot Perrine Bridge (with a parachute, of course), the only bridge in the United States where it's legal to BASE jump year-round.

Besides strapping on a chute, outdoor enthusiasts will find other exciting recreational opportunities throughout the region, like white-water rafting and kayaking, downhill skiing, premier fishing, and world-class rock climbing in the Almo area.

The West Side

Getting to the western fringe of the Magic Valley from Boise takes about an hour by car on I-84 east. There's not much to see between Boise and Hammett except for miles of sagebrush, ancient cinder cones, and newly erected wind turbines that strikingly punctuate the flat desert landscape.

You'll pass by Mountain Home along the way. This humdrum military town, home to the Air Force's 366th Fighter Wing squadron, is a good place to stop and fuel up the SUV, but that's about it. Several gas stations and fast-food chains are at Exit 95, along with the junction for U.S. 20, leading to the Sun Valley-Ketchum area. It's also the jumping-off point for Bruneau Dunes State Park, about 15 miles south on Highway 51. The barren desert on the way to the big dunes will have you thinking *Area 51*.

After leaving Mountain Home, I-84 drops into a tight canyon with black-hemmed buttes on both sides of the highway. Soon you will be in Hammett, but you may not know it, because there's not much here besides a wide swath of the Snake River, a few family-run farms, and a winery. Keep traveling east on I-84 to Glenns Ferry (Exit 120), an attractive little town that flaunts its rich Oregon Trail and railroad heritage.

HAMMETT
Cold Springs Winery
The boutique winery, **Cold Springs Winery**

(7853 W. Ringert Ln., Hammett, 208/366-7993, www.coldspringswinery.com, tasting room noon-5pm Sat.-Sun. or by appointment, $5 tasting fee), is perched on a butte on the north side of I-84. At Exit 112 look to the left and you'll see the winery's name plastered on a large potato-storage shed with a big arrow pointing up the hill. Owner Bill Ringert, a former lawyer and Idaho state senator, and his family operate the small winery and vineyard on a 33-acre spread overlooking the Snake River. Winemaker Jamie Martin produces an array of excellent wines, like chardonnay, viognier, merlot, syrah, and Hot Rod Red, a smooth blend of syrah, merlot, and cabernet franc.

GLENNS FERRY
In 1869, Gus Glenn built a ferry across the Snake River, putting an end to the dangerous ford that Oregon Trail emigrants had been forced to negotiate. By 1879, enough of a settlement had grown up around the ferry that a post office was established, but it wasn't until the arrival of the Oregon Short Line Railroad in 1883 that Glenns Ferry was formally platted into a town.

★ Three Island Crossing State Park
At one of the most important historic sites on the Oregon Trail, settlers faced a decision that could have life-or-death consequences.

Reaching this point from the south side of the river, they could either brave the ford—a dangerous undertaking in high water, but one that led to a shorter, easier route to Fort Boise—or continue down the longer, drier, and more sparsely vegetated south bank. The three somewhat level islands in the river served as steppingstones for those who attempted the crossing, but many wagons and their passengers were swept away by the swift current.

This perilous spot is now commemorated with 614-acre **Three Island Crossing State Park** (off W. Madison Ave., Glenns Ferry, 208/366-2394, $5 per vehicle). Here you will find 82 serviced campsites ($22-38) on the hill and eight camping cabins ($50) near the river, all of which have the usual state park amenities. There's also an Oregon Trail interpretive center featuring historical exhibits about the trail and the indigenous Shoshone people of this area, and a nearby interpretive path leads you down to the river past visible Oregon Trail wagon ruts. Check out the beautiful replica of a Conestoga wagon near the trailhead.

Crossings Winery

Crossings Winery (1289 W. Madison Ave., Glenns Ferry, 208/366-2313, www.crossingswinery.com, tasting room 11am-8pm

daily), an estate winery on a scenic stretch of the Snake River next to the state park, offers vines, wines, a nine-hole golf course, and more. Formerly known as Carmela Vineyards, the winery produces a large selection of varietal wines and blends, and it operates a restaurant (lunch and dinner daily, entrées $14-25) that serves an excellent brunch on Sunday 10:30am-1:30pm.

Vineyard Greens Golf Course (greens fees $16) at the winery surrounds the vineyard with a par-34 course stretching 4,378 yards. Hard-core golfers can park the RV at **Vineyard RV Park** ($25 with hookups) across the street. The winery also has a few camping cabins ($90) near the links.

Glenns Ferry Historical Museum

In an early 20th-century sandstone schoolhouse, the **Glenns Ferry Historical Museum** (161 W. Cleveland Ave., Glenns Ferry, 208/366-2320, noon-5pm Sat.-Sun. June-Sept., donation) has exhibits that provide insight into the town's early history alongside beautiful charcoal portraits by Glenns Ferry artist Frank Clark and football jerseys worn by Korey Hall, a local farm boy who recently played for the Green Bay Packers.

historic downtown Glenns Ferry

Gorby Opera House

On the main drag near the railroad tracks, you'll see the historic **Gorby Opera House** (148 E. Idaho St., Glenns Ferry, 208/366-7408, www.glennsferrytheatre.org), built in 1914. This classic theater house, designed by Tourtellotte and Hummel, the same architectural firm that designed the Egyptian Theatre in Boise, originally featured vaudeville acts and melodramas. Today, the theater still serves the community with a summer schedule of old-time musicals and plays (Fri.-Sat. night June-Aug., $7 adults, $6 seniors and under age 12, dinner show $25, reservations recommended). Whenever a train rumbles by (and this happens often), the performances stop momentarily, and everyone in the audience stands up and sings, "I've Been Working on the Railroad." It's a hoot.

Accommodations and Food

The **Redford Motel** (525 W. 1st Ave., Glenns Ferry, 208/366-2421, $35-62) is a well-kept place on the way into town that has 11 guest rooms—some in a historic main building and the rest across the street in a Cold War-era motor inn.

River Roads Bed & Breakfast (1882 E. Little Basin Rd., Glenns Ferry, 208/366-2974, $100) is east of town right on the river. This inn only has two guest rooms, but the view here is spectacular, and there's a hot tub. Wake up to a big homespun breakfast before heading out to explore the Oregon Trail. Pets are not allowed.

Besides the dining room at Crossings Winery, locals also eat downtown at the aptly named **Oregon Trail Cafe** (36 E. Idaho Ave., Glenns Ferry, 208/366-2280, breakfast, lunch, dinner daily). This rustic diner boasts an exaggerated Western motif. Expect standard breakfast dishes ($4-10) such as biscuits and gravy, flapjacks, French toast, and Three Eggs Garbage, a big egg-and-potato pile-up. Hopefully you don't mind a little guff with your morning eggs and coffee, because the waitresses here can be surly at times. The dinner menu has buffalo steaks, gizzards and fries, and pan-fried oysters. The restaurant also has a cocktail lounge called the De Rail Bar that stays open late.

wagon replica at Three Island Crossing State Park

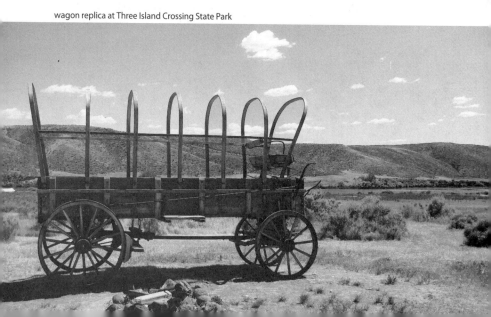

Hagerman Valley

Hagerman Valley, due east of Glenns Ferry, is a weird and wonderful place strewn with rounded boulders that were carried along by the great Bonneville Flood and then dropped in place when the waters receded. The valley's main topographic feature, however, is the series of springs gushing from the lava rock along the north rim. The springs are outflow from the Snake River Plain Aquifer, which begins some 100 miles northeast near Howe, where the waters of the Big and Little Lost Rivers, Birch Creek, and other smaller watercourses disappear into the lava of the Snake River Plain and begin a century-long journey to the Hagerman Valley. The water flows underground until the deep cut of the Snake River Gorge sets it free. This must have been a spectacular sight back when the springs flowed unimpeded from mile after mile of canyon wall. Today, most of the springs have either been despoiled by hydropower facilities or diverted to farmlands and fish hatcheries. Nevertheless, what's left still makes an unusual sight, and it's well worth the detour off I-84.

At I-84 Exit 137 is the small town of Bliss and the junction of U.S. 30, the northern starting point for the 68-mile **Thousand Springs Scenic Byway.** After dropping down the hill into Hagerman, this curvy road stays relatively close to the river along U.S. 30, which used to be the main highway before I-84 was built. Now it's a scenic back way into Twin Falls. If you want to go directly to Twin Falls, continue east on I-84.

HAGERMAN

Shoshone people spearfished for salmon on the Snake River here for centuries, until the nonnatives showed up and drove off first the Shoshone, then the salmon. The Oregon Trail passed near the site—wagon ruts are still visible across the river from town—which later became a stagecoach stop. Present-day Hagerman began in 1892, when Stanley Hegeman applied for a post office. The postal department got Hegeman's name wrong and granted the post office under the present spelling. Many Basques have called Hagerman home over the years. These sheepherders and their families started arriving in the early 20th century, and they soon became embedded into the fabric of the community.

In modern times, Hagerman offers anglers several good places to fish for trout and warm-water species like catfish, smallmouth bass, and yellow perch. The area also has two fish hatcheries (state and federal) and a string of aquaculture farms that raise rainbow trout, catfish, tilapia, and white sturgeon. Leo Ray, a biologist who operates a fish farm in Hagerman, produces world-class sturgeon caviar as well. Hagerman Valley is also known for its sweet melons—honeydews, cantaloupes, and watermelons—which everyone around here seems to grow in the peak of summer.

Hagerman has had its share of famous residents, including writer Vardis Fisher and Archie Teater, a renowned landscape artist who built a home that was designed by master architect Frank Lloyd Wright.

Hagerman Fossil Beds National Monument

The 4,300 acres of **Hagerman Fossil Beds National Monument** are not developed for visitor use, nor will they ever be. That's because the area is one of the world's foremost fossil beds, and indiscriminate trampling could destroy priceless archaeological remains. In addition to the Hagerman horse, fossils of more than 140 other species have been unearthed, including waterfowl, otters, muskrats, and 3.5-million-year-old beavers.

Details on this fascinating historical site are found at the national monument **visitor center** (221 N. State St., Hagerman,

The Hagerman Horse Was a Zebra?

Archaeological digs at the Hagerman Fossil Beds National Monument have yielded more than 125 full skeletons of a prehistoric, zebra-like horse from the Pliocene epoch that were found in one location. No hide samples made it through the last three million years, so no one knows for sure if the animals had stripes or not. Now called the Hagerman horse, *Equus simplicidens* is the earliest known member of the *Equus* genus and has been designated the Idaho state fossil. A local rancher first discovered the bones in 1928, and a major archaeological excavation led by paleontologists from the Smithsonian Institution began the following year. Two theories prevail as to why so many of these horses died in one place. One assumes the prehistoric watering hole turned into a mud bog, trapping the animals in sticky goo. The other holds that the horses drowned trying to cross the river during a flood. Either way, these ancient horses have been forever locked into local folklore.

208/933-4100, 9am-5pm daily Memorial Day-Labor Day, 9am-5pm Thurs.-Mon. Sept.-Memorial Day, free) in downtown Hagerman, across from the high school. When funding allows, rangers lead free tours of sites in the monument on weekends in summer; tours leave from the visitor center. Otherwise, a flyer describing a self-guided auto tour (22 miles, two hours) is available. The best view of the fossil area is from the Bell Rapids Sportsman's Access Area, on the Hagerman side of the river (follow the signs from U.S. 30). You won't see anything exciting, but your imagination can fill in the picture with thousands of prehistoric beasts.

You can also drive over to the other side of the river for a closer look. Continue south through Hagerman and turn right just after you cross the bridge over the Snake River. Alongside the fossil area you'll find a turnout with an interpretive sign, but you won't see giant dinosaur bones sticking out of the mud. Continue to the top of the hill and you'll find a meandering path that skirts a ridge above the rutted Oregon Trail.

Hagerman Valley Historical Society Museum

Like the national monument visitors center, the tiny **Hagerman Valley Historical Society Museum** (100 S. State St., Hagerman, 208/837-6288, 1pm-4pm Wed.-Sun. year-round, free) in a historic brick building holds a full-size cast replica of a Hagerman horse skeleton. You'll also see a colorful mural, old photos of the Hagerman Valley, and a bookshelf packed with Vardis Fisher first editions.

Hagerman Wildlife Management Area and Fish Hatcheries

On the north side of the Snake River, two miles south of Hagerman, the **Hagerman Wildlife Management Area** (WMA) preserves 880 acres of riverine wetlands as wildlife habitat. Fed by the constant-temperature spring water, the area stays ice-free all year long. This makes it a winter haven for ducks and geese by the thousands, as well as ospreys, peregrine falcons, and bald and golden eagles. The river also supports a healthy population of river otters.

Within the WMA is **Hagerman State Fish Hatchery** (1060 State Fish Hatchery Rd., 208/837-4892), which raises millions of trout annually to be stocked in waters across Idaho. Six miles of walking trails loop from the hatchery past many lakes and ponds. You can get a close look at various species of fish, including rainbow trout, white sturgeon, and tiger muskie, kept in cement raceways near the parking lot. There's even a gumball machine filled with fish pellets that you can feed to the fish, but you may want to wash up afterward to get rid of the nasty smell on your fingers.

Vardis Fisher: Hagerman's Literary Native Son

Hagerman writer Vardis Fisher was a permanent fixture in the valley until his death in 1968. With more than 30 published works of fiction and nonfiction, Fisher was hands-down the most prolific Idaho author of his generation. Sure, Ernest Hemingway and Ezra Pound had more name recognition, but they didn't spend most of their lives in the Gem State, as Fisher did. He was born in 1895 near Rigby in southeast Idaho and raised in a Mormon household. Later in life Fisher became an avowed and outspoken atheist.

He's probably best known for his novel *Mountain Man,* the basis for the 1972 Robert Redford movie *Jeremiah Johnson.* But Fisher also wrote many other historical novels, including the epic series *Testament of Man* and *The Mothers: An American Saga of Courage,* depicting the tragic story of the Donner Party. He was also a columnist at the *Idaho Statesman* and the director of the Idaho Writer's Project for the Works Progress Administration, who commissioned him to write *Idaho: A Guide in Word and Picture,* a historically based travel book about the Gem State that came out in 1937.

Fisher built his own home north of town on a secluded knoll overlooking a vodka-clear pond fed by cold springs. Sadly, the house fell into disrepair after his death, and it eventually burned down; only the lava-rock chimney stands today. (The undeveloped Vardis Fisher Home Site, once managed by the Idaho Parks and Recreation Department, was closed to the public in 2015.)

Nearby, you will find the **Hagerman National Fish Hatchery** (3059 National Fish Hatchery Rd., 208/837-4896), a federal facility that raises 1.5 million steelhead smolts each year. Visit in March-April for the best look.

Recreation

Anglers can try their luck at catching trout and bass at the Hagerman WMA, where there are several big ponds (July-Oct.) with easy access. Before you cast a line, check with the **Idaho Department of Fish and Game** (324 S. 417 E., Jerome, 208/324-4359) for restrictions and possible closures. If you like battling feisty bass, head to the **Bell Rapids Sportsman's Access Area** on the Snake River just south of Hagerman (follow the sign on U.S. 30). There are some restrictions at this year-round spot near the Lower Salmon Falls Dam: catch-and-release January-June, and a bag limit of two fish per day July-December. The river also holds white sturgeon, but there's currently no harvest allowed on these massive prehistoric fish.

You can fish for rainbow trout (some of which are the hybrid blue and gold variety) in Billingsley Creek, north of Hagerman. You must use artificial flies or lures (no worms) and barbless hooks. There's a daily limit of two fish, and they must be at least 20 inches long.

Take in the spectacular scenery of the Hagerman Valley on the back of a horse. **Across the River Horse Ranch** (6252 King Hill Canal Rd., Bliss, 208/961-1911, www.acrosstheriverhorseranch.com) conducts guided trail rides ($25 pp per hour) and lessons. Owner Amita Smith keeps her stables full of mild-mannered horses, ranging from humongous draft horses all the way down to pinto ponies (great for kids), and everything in between. The ranch also offers wagon rides and summer camps for children ages 10 and up.

Accommodations and Food

The 16-room **Hagerman Valley Inn** (661 Frogs Landing, Hagerman, 208/837-6196, www.hagermanvalleyinn.com, from $68 d) is a relatively clean motel on the south side of downtown. All rooms are nonsmoking, and amenities include cable TV and a covered patio area downstairs. Pets are allowed.

★ **Billingsley Creek Lodge** (17940 U.S.

30, Hagerman, 208/837-4822, www.billings-leycreeklodge.com) is on U.S. 30 about a mile north of town. It has been around since 1928 and boasts a distinguished literary history: Ernest Hemingway and Vardis Fisher both stayed here. Although it's right along the highway, the resort is well landscaped and has a tranquil little picnic area on the creek. Choose from six lodge rooms ($60-80) or five private cabins ($90-115).

★ **Snake River Grill** (611 Frogs Landing, Hagerman, 208/837-6227, www.snakeriver-grill.com, dinner entrées $12-23), next to the Hagerman Valley Inn, is where to go in town for an upscale dining experience, and the restaurant also serves good breakfast and lunch. Chef Kirt Martin, a classically trained chef and all-around nice guy, uses lots of local farm-raised fish on his menu, which includes sturgeon nuggets, pan-seared rainbow trout, and grilled catfish. Also expect to see barbecued pork ribs and steaks smothered with sautéed cremini mushrooms. Wash everything down with a bottle of Idaho wine.

Camping and RVing

Hagerman RV Village (18049 U.S. 30, Hagerman, 208/837-4906) offers 60 RV sites with hookups ($30), five cabins ($40-60), and several tent sites ($20). Amenities include a laundry room, restrooms, showers, an exercise room, and a sauna.

Information

The friendly folks at the **Hagerman Valley Chamber of Commerce** (191 N. State St., Hagerman, 208/837-9131, 9am-noon and 1pm-4pm Mon.-Fri.) would be happy to give you more information about the area.

THOUSAND SPRINGS AREA

Along this stretch of the Snake River south of Hagerman, a torrent of waterfalls emerges from the black basalt cliffs on the river's north side. This extensive lineup of springs—there may be more than 1,000—gushes forth clean, crystal-clear water at a constant 58°F.

Thousand Springs State Park

Thousand Springs State Park has five major units in the Hagerman and Buhl areas: **Malad Gorge, Billingsley Creek, Niagara Springs, Earl M. Hardy Box Canyon,** and **Ritter Island,** formerly The Nature Conservancy's Thousand Springs Preserve. Be aware that the Thousand Springs State Park system (main office at Malad Gorge, 1074 E.

Thousand Springs area near Hagerman

2350 S., Hagerman, 208/837-4505, $5 per vehicle) can be confusing because it's always morphing into new units, and some of them are only open on a limited basis.

Near Hagerman, you'll find three units of the park, including the small but interesting Billingsley Creek unit (north of town), the Earl M. Hardy Box Canyon, and Ritter Island, a 400-acre spread that The Nature Conservancy recently turned over to the state. Ritter Island can be a challenge to find. From the west side of the river, you can look right across at the power plant and the unbridled springs on either side, but getting over to those springs is quite another matter. To get there from Hagerman, take U.S. 30 south to Hagerman-Wendell Road, hang a left (east), and travel about four miles until you come to County Road 1500 East. Take a right and go about two miles to County Road 3200, where you'll hang a right and follow the road down the hill past a massive waterfall and into an Idaho Power facility parking lot, where there's a little picnic area with restrooms.

The preserve occupies the former Minnie Miller ranch, purchased by businesswoman and dairy farmer Minnie Miller in 1918. For 36 years, Miller steadfastly protected her share of the Hagerman Valley springs from development, and upon her death she deeded the property to an equally staunch environmentalist. The property was sold to The Nature Conservancy in 1986. Among the highlights of the preserve are Minnie Miller Falls, which pours forth from the canyon wall and cascades down nearly 200 feet into crystalline pools, and Ritter Island, site of Miller's 1920 home. A 0.25-mile trail on the island leads north to the falls, the only totally undisturbed springs along the entire 40-mile width of the aquifer. Due to budget cuts, this unit of the park is only open periodically; call 208/837-4505 for details.

The newish Earl M. Hardy Box Canyon unit, which also used to be under the auspices of The Nature Conservancy, is east of town on the way to Wendell. This horseshoe-shaped canyon boasts a 20-foot waterfall that drops into a beautiful cold springs pool, the 11th largest spring of its kind in North America. Red-tailed hawks, falcons, owls, and eagles can be spotted perched on the cliffs, looking for little critters to munch on. The park is also home to an endangered snail species and the rare Shoshone sculpin, a spiny little fish with prehistoric ties. But this wide-open place doesn't offer much relief from the hot desert sun, so early mornings and early evenings are good times to take a hike along the canyon rim here. To get to Box Canyon, continue past the Ritter Island turnoff on County Road 1500 East for about a mile, until you see the parking lot on the right.

Snake River Boat Tours

Several outfitters conduct guided boat trips down the Snake River through Hagerman Valley. You can cruise up the river on a motorboat or shoot down the rapids in a raft. Due to the influx of spring water into the river, this section of the Snake can be run nearly year-round.

1000 Springs Tours (Hagerman, 208/837-9006, www.1000springs.com) offers two-hour cruises down the Snake River through Hagerman Valley aboard a 30-foot motorized pontoon boat. Along the way you'll see Blue Heart Springs, which gurgle their way up from the riverbed into a crystal-clear pool, and Riley Creek Falls. Tours (10am and 1pm Tues.-Sun., $25 pp, reservations advised) are offered year-round, weather permitting, but prime season is April-October. Also available are dinner cruises ($58 pp), catered by Kirt Martin of Snake River Grill, with a multicourse menu that includes wood-roasted prime rib with all the trimmings, as well as beer, wine, and cocktails. All tours leave from 1000 Springs Resort (18734 U.S. 30, Hagerman), on the river six miles south of Hagerman.

For those who prefer a raft to a motorboat, the Hagerman Reach of the Snake River churns through challenging Class II-III rapids, which are exciting but not dangerous when you ride with a skilled skipper. **Idaho**

Guide Service (563 Trotter Dr., Twin Falls, 208/734-4998, www.idahoguideservice.com, $50 pp, $70 pp with lunch) offers guided trips along the Hagerman Reach.

Commercial Hot Springs Resorts

The first of three resorts on the way south through Hagerman Valley is **1000 Springs Resort** (18734 U.S. 30, Hagerman, 208/837-4987, pools 10am-10pm Tues.-Sat., noon-8pm Sun. year-round, $7 adults, $6 ages 6-17, $3 under age 6). The resort offers a large, hot spring-fed indoor swimming pool, hot baths, and an RV park (year-round, $35 with full hookups, $25 without). Campers get a discount on the pools. Private hot baths are also available. Picnickers can drive in and use the grounds for a small fee.

The other two resorts are on opposite sides of the river but share the same turnoff from the highway. Turning left (east) will take you to a T intersection; turn right and follow Banbury Road for 1.5 miles over a small hill and down to **Banbury Hot Springs** (1128A Banbury Rd., Buhl, 208/543-4098, noon-9pm daily year-round). The venerable resort offers a crystal-clear outdoor swimming pool ($8 adults, $7 ages 6-13, $4.50 under age 6) fed by continuously flowing hot and cold springs; five hot tubs ($8 pp per hour, jetted tubs $9 pp per hour) that are drained, cleaned, and disinfected before each use; and picnic grounds and campsites ($15 tents, $20-30 RVs), luxuriously shaded under a profusion of mature trees. A boat-launching ramp and dock are down on the river, and campers can use the restrooms, showers, and laundry facilities as well.

The relaxed, low-key **Miracle Hot Springs** (19073A U.S. 30, Buhl, 208/543-6002, 8am-11pm Mon.-Sat. year-round, $10 adults, $8 seniors, $4 ages 4-15, $1 under age 4 includes swim diaper), on the west side of the highway, is a great place to soak. And you'll even see a few alligators. Don't worry; they are kept behind a fence. In addition to the regular soaking tubs ($4 per hour plus admission price), there are four VIP tubs ($8 per hour) that are large, private, temperature adjustable, and open to the stars. The swimming pool has spring water continuously flowing through it. Massage is available by appointment. As with the other two resorts, there's an RV park ($10-20); the sites are a little close to the highway but are nicely landscaped. Miracle also has several geodesic camping domes ($39-64) with comfy pads, but you'll need your own sleeping bag.

BUHL AND VICINITY

Buhl was founded in 1906 and named after Frank Buhl, a bigwig in the Twin Falls Land and Water Company. It's an agricultural center where you'll find fertilizer stores, tractor lots, Farm Bureau Insurance, Farmers National Bank, and a popular creamery that churns delicious ice cream. But this is also one funky farm town, with a great arts center, many alternative-health practitioners, and lots of cool junk stores.

Eighth Street Center

A few blocks off Buhl's main drag, the **Eighth Street Center** (200 N. 8th St., Buhl, 208/543-2888, www.buhlartscouncil.tripod.com) is home to the Buhl Arts Council and a cornucopia of arts classes, performances, and gallery space. "The arts" can mean everything from painting exhibitions to couples massage classes. Take a stroll through the tranquil garden across the alley from the center.

Bordewick Sportsman's Access Area

Idaho is chock-full of Sportsman's Access Areas, as evidenced by the numerous signs along every highway. **Bordewick Sportsman's Access Area** is spectacularly notable for its location on a stunning stretch of the Snake River where several species of large waterbirds nest and congregate. Great blue herons, white pelicans, and Canada geese can often be seen soaring above the riffles and around the many verdant islands. You'll also find good fishing, toe-dabbling, and primitive camping at this beautiful site, or at several other possible campsites along this stretch of the Snake. A little farther down the road is the state's **Magic Valley Fish Hatchery** (208/326-3230), which raises millions of steelhead from roe to fingerling size for release back into the Salmon River drainage. To get to the access area and the hatchery, head out of Buhl on Clear Lakes Road and turn right just before you cross the river.

Trout Farm

The world's largest commercial trout farm is just north of Buhl on Clear Lakes Road (turn off U.S. 30 at the big Buhl water tower). **Clear Springs Foods** (1585 Clear Lakes Rd., Buhl, 208/543-4316, www.clearsprings.com) produces millions of pounds of Idaho rainbow trout each year. Visitor facilities include a picnic area and a fish-viewing pond. The pond holds trout, of course, as well as a couple of big Snake River sturgeon. An underwater viewing window gives you a trout's-eye view of their riverine abode.

★ Thousand Springs State Park's Niagara Springs Unit

On the river's north side, across the water from the reaches of the Bordewick Sportsman's Access Area, is the **Thousand Springs State Park's Niagara Springs Unit** (2136 Niagara Springs Rd.). A National Natural Landmark, the springs gush out of the canyon wall at 250 cubic feet per second. It's a roundabout route to get there from Buhl and much easier from Wendell, to the north. From Buhl, after crossing the river on Clear Lakes Road, the road ascends to the north rim. Turn right on the Bob Barton Highway and continue past four intersections (1600 E., 1700 E., 1800 E., and 1900 E.); the next intersection you'll come to should be Rex Leland Highway (1950 E.). If you travel south from Wendell, this is the road you follow straight down the whole way. From Bob Barton Highway, turn right and follow the road down to the river and the park. It's a steep drop of 350 vertical feet to the canyon floor; the gravel road is not recommended for trailers or motor homes.

Two different areas make up the park. The Emerson Pugmire Memorial Recreation Area (day-use $5) has a shaded picnic area with restrooms. The area is well maintained and offers a large expanse of grass and a great location on a scenic stretch of the Snake River. Continuing a little farther down the road will take you to the Crystal Springs Area, where

Thousand Springs State Park's Niagara Springs Unit

you'll find springs as well as a small pond for year-round fishing.

Niagara Springs Wildlife Management Area

Just west of Thousand Springs State Park's Niagara Springs unit, the **Niagara Springs Wildlife Management Area** (WMA) protects 957 acres of habitat for waterfowl and other wildlife. Wildlife viewing and fishing are the most popular activities; bird-watchers and others can follow trails both up on the canyon rim and down along the water, where sightings of songbirds and mule deer are common. In winter, waterfowl arrive in large numbers. Anglers can try for rainbow trout in the Thompson-Mays Canal or for trout, catfish, and sturgeon (catch-and-release) in the Snake River.

To reach the WMA from Buhl, cross the river on Clear Lakes Road, which ascends to the north rim. Turn right on the Bob Barton Highway and continue past four intersections to Rex Leland Highway (1950 E.). If you travel south from Wendell, this is the road you follow straight down the whole way. From Bob Barton Highway, turn right and follow the road to the bottom of the river gorge, then turn right into one of several parking areas. Hiking trails follow the river east past Boulder Rapids and a couple of ponds. For more information, contact the **Idaho Department of Fish and Game** (324 S. 417 E., Jerome, 208/324-4359).

Balanced Rock

Balanced Rock, this huge question mark-shaped rock, 17 miles southwest of Buhl and west of Castleford, is balanced on a small point and looks as though a strong wind would blow it over. Apparently the thought of that happening scared the county's lawyers, and the wondrous natural feature has been reinforced with concrete around its base.

About a mile away, just down the hill from the precariously perched rock, you'll find **Balanced Rock Park,** a veritable oasis in the middle of the sprawling desert. This is a great spot—thanks to a row of big shade trees—for picnicking and swimming along Salmon Falls Creek. Rock climbers can find interesting climbing on the area's castle-like hoodoos, which gave the town of Castleford its name. And across the road on the river's north side, hot spring water pours out of a pipe, creating a semi-natural hot tub.

Balanced Rock near Buhl

Wineries

Buhl has two boutique wineries where you can taste varietal wines from the Snake River Valley Appellation. **Holesinsky Vineyard & Winery** (4477A Valley Steppe Dr., Buhl, 208/543-6940, tasting room by appointment only), just off Clear Lakes Road, is one of the only certified organic wineries in the state. Here winemaker-owner James Holesinsky produces wines from organic grapes grown in his 18-acre vineyard. His lineup includes syrah, dry rosé, riesling, and merlot.

Snyder Winery (4060 N. 1200 E., Buhl, 208/543-6938, www.snyderwinery.com, tasting room and wine bar 1pm-9pm Fri.-Sat., 1pm-5pm Sun.) boasts beautifully landscaped grounds, rows of grapevines, and a weekend-only steakhouse (5:30pm-9pm Fri.-Sat.). Owners Russ and Claudia Snyder produce small lots of estate wines, including cabernet franc, chardonnay, syrah, cabernet sauvignon, and riesling. They also operate a small bed-and-breakfast cabin ($145 with full breakfast). Did I mention there's a hot tub? To get here from downtown Buhl, head west on Burley Avenue (the road name quickly changes to E. 4100 N.) and turn left (south) onto North 1200 East; look for the winery on the left.

Accommodations and Food

Buhl has a few cutesy old motels around town.

One good pick is the **Oregon Trail Inn** (510 Broadway Ave., Buhl, 208/543-8814, www.oregontrailinn.com, from $54 d), a recently remodeled and impeccably clean motor inn with 17 nonsmoking guest rooms within walking distance of downtown.

Remember when milk came in glass bottles? It still does at ★ **Clover Leaf Creamery** (205 Broadway Ave., Buhl, 208/543-4272, 9am-7pm Mon.-Fri., 10am-7pm Sat., 1pm-7pm Sun.). Besides all-natural milk, this classic creamery makes the best ice cream and milkshakes in the Magic Valley. Choose from a large selection of flavors such as strawberry, peach, rocky road, and Elk Tracks, a chocolate and vanilla swirl with peanuts and big chunks of dark chocolate. Clover Leaf also sells local farmstead cheeses, made by Ballard Family Dairy in Gooding, frozen local trout, and other treats produced in the area.

Grab a cup of coffee at **Broadway Java** (500 Broadway Ave., Buhl, 208/543-9160, 6am-6pm Mon.-Sat., 6am-4pm Sun.), a few doors down from the Oregon Trail Inn. Here you can get the best espresso drinks in town, as well as chai tea, smoothies, and Italian sodas. The artsy little coffeehouse also serves freshly baked muffins and scones, breakfast sandwiches, and bowls of hearty oatmeal. Lunch items include pita sandwiches and salads.

Twin Falls

Twin Falls (population 45,000) was founded in 1904 as a hub for Carey Act settlers, who came flooding in to grab up 160-acre parcels for $25 per acre. The huge Snake River irrigation projects of the day turned the desert here into a livable, arable place. Potatoes, sugar beets, and alfalfa are among the crops grown locally, and cattle ranches and dairies also add to the agricultural scene. Chobani recently built a yogurt plant a few miles from town, the largest of its kind in the world. Yet Twin Falls is too big to be just a farm town. Diverse services, light industry, and a top-notch junior college with a nationally recognized basketball program contribute to the town's healthy mix of rural character and urban amenities.

The falls for which the city is named were supposedly once a sight, but dams have dimmed their glory. Just downstream, however, wide Niagara-like Shoshone Falls has been a tourist destination since the pioneer

Twin Falls

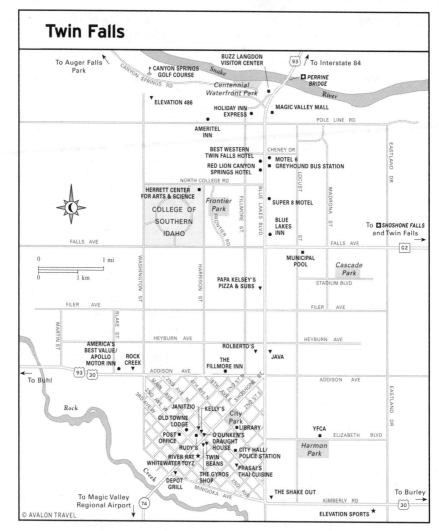

days and still is the city's prime sightseeing attraction.

Twin Falls perches on the rim of the Snake River Canyon, a spectacular gorge that daredevil Evel Knievel attempted to jump in 1974 on a steam-powered rocket cycle. He obviously didn't make it across the chasm (the jump ended anticlimatically with him and the cycle floating to the bottom of the canyon tethered to a parachute), but the event is still the town's greatest claim to fame. Several other daredevils have recently filed permits with the city and county to jump the canyon on rocket-propelled cycles. We'll just have to wait and see if one of them can take care of Knievel's unfinished business.

The Snake River Canyon offers all kinds of recreational activities. People here spend their time rafting, kayaking, fishing, hiking, mountain biking, and golfing on one of the wildest courses in the state. And let's not forget BASE jumping off the 486-foot Perrine Bridge.

Spending a summer day in Twin Falls will give you a clue as to why the westward-bound pioneers were so relieved to get to tree-filled Boise. Here the summer sun reflects off a city covered by miles of asphalt and concrete right up to the canyon rim and buffered by precious little shade. If you don't have air-conditioning in your vehicle, you'll regret it when the dog days of summer push the mercury past 100°F. The downtown area does have its charms, and a park with big trees where you can beat the heat.

SIGHTS
★ Perrine Bridge

Coming from I-84, you enter Twin Falls over 1,500-foot-long **Perrine Bridge.** It is named for I. B. Perrine, the region's biggest pioneer-era promoter and the man most responsible for bringing about the irrigation projects that turned much of the area green. The bridge ushers traffic across the river 486 feet above the glimmering waters. The town's main visitor information center is just across the bridge on the southwest side. From here, you can actually walk out onto the bridge on a pedestrian walkway—not for those with a fear of heights.

Hansen Bridge

Hansen Bridge crosses the Snake River east of the city. Until 1919 crossings were made via rowboat. Then a suspension bridge was built, and in 1966 the current bridge was put in. It's a 350-foot drop from the bridge to the river.

★ Shoshone Falls

East of town, **Shoshone Falls** (7am-10pm daily year-round, $3 per vehicle) has been called the "Niagara of the West." At 1,000 feet wide and 212 feet high, the horseshoe-shaped waterfall is 52 feet higher than Niagara. The falls are often a mere trickle, since much of the water is diverted to the region's irrigation system; spring is usually the best time to see a torrent of water going over the big boulders.

Fortunately, there's more to do if the falls aren't falling. Twin Falls's 2004 centennial year was celebrated with a new trail leading out of the canyon from Shoshone Falls Park. Also part of the same park complex, **Dierkes Lake** is a favorite haunt for fishing, swimming, paddling, and rock climbing. The swimming areas employ lifeguards in summer, and trails provide some nice

Perrine Bridge

hiking opportunities if you can ignore the ostentatious trophy homes perched on the canyon rim. To get to Shoshone Falls and Dierkes Lake, take Blue Lakes Boulevard to Falls Avenue and go three miles east—to 3300 East Road—and two miles north, following the ample signage.

College of Southern Idaho

A two-year junior college offering associate and vocational degrees, **College of Southern Idaho** (315 Falls Ave., Twin Falls, 208/733-9554, www.csi.edu) enrolls more than 9,000 students. One highlight for visitors to the 300-acre campus is the free **Herrett Center for Arts & Science** (www.herrett.csi.edu, 9:30am-9pm Tues. and Fri., 9:30am-4:30pm Wed.-Thurs., 1pm-9pm Sat. year-round, longer hours in summer), which boasts a collection of almost 20,000 pre-Columbian artifacts from North and Central America. The museum also has a gallery of contemporary art and the **Faulkner Planetarium** (shows $6 general, $5 seniors, $4 students, free children ages 2 and under). You can also catch a music laserium show at the planetarium; expect to see shows like *U2: Feel the Music, Ride the Light*.

Numerous public events are held in the school's Fine Arts Auditorium, and the rest of the nicely landscaped campus makes a pleasant spot for a picnic or a stroll. Twin Falls has a good jazz scene anchored by a strong music department at the College of Southern Idaho. (The college is also the home of the Boise State University Radio Network's statewide jazz feed, 89.3 FM.) Expect to see trios and quartets playing at coffeehouses and other venues around town. To find out who's playing where, keep an eye open for fliers, or call the CSI jazz studies program (208/732-6765).

RECREATION
Parks

Centennial Waterfront Park (free) lies practically at the base of Perrine Bridge and offers a dock and a boat ramp in addition to splendid views and some big rocks to crawl around on. It's at the bottom of Canyon Springs Road, a scenic drive in itself past a waterfall gushing forth from the canyon's south rim. Photographers will find this an excellent place to get a shot of the bridge.

Also down in the canyon, about four miles northwest of Centennial Waterfront Park on Canyon Springs Road, you'll discover **Auger Falls Park** (free), a 547-acre recreational area

Shoshone Falls

BASE Jumping

Twin Falls draws BASE jumpers from all over the world. BASE stands for "building, antenna, span (bridge), earth," and in the case of Twin Falls, the focus is on "span." BASE enthusiasts say the 486-foot-high Perrine Bridge over the Snake River Canyon is the only one in the United States where it's legal to jump year-round. BASE jumpers travel from around the world to plunge off the Perrine, and on summer holiday weekends as many as 150 people may be in town for the opportunity.

BASE experts say would-be jumpers need to become proficient in skydiving before attempting BASE jumps. After about 200 jumps from an airplane, parachutists should be ready for the more demanding BASE experience. (It's harder because you're closer to the ground and there's less room for error.) First-time jumpers are urged to take BASE jumping instruction, which is sometimes offered at the Perrine Bridge by Apex BASE (www.apexbase.com).

Twin Falls is exceptionally friendly to BASE jumpers. Many of the jumpers stay at hotels near the canyon rim. When night falls, you'll often find BASE enthusiasts swapping stories at restaurants and bars around town.

If you'd like to see BASE jumpers in action, stand on either end of the Perrine Bridge any day that has calm winds and you're likely to spot some. You can also watch jumpers preparing their gear on the lawn at the Buzz Langdon Visitors Center and in the canyon at Centennial Waterfront Park.

that's well suited for mountain biking, hiking, and fishing.

Downtown, **City Park** (Shoshone St. between 4th Ave. and 6th Ave.) was the original central-city park platted by the town founders in 1904. It's still a major venue for events throughout the year. The year-round **city pool** (756 Locust St., Twin Falls, 208/734-2336), managed by the YMCA, is a swimming facility that's open to the elements in the summer and covered the rest of the year.

For more information on the city's parks, contact the **Twin Falls Parks and Recreation Department** (136 Maxwell Ave., Twin Falls, 208/736-2265).

Guides and Gear

Visitors with a hankering to get out for some

Snake River Canyon in Twin Falls

serious adventure in the area can contact **Idaho Guide Service** (563 Trotter Dr., Twin Falls, 208/734-4998 or 888/734-3246, www.idahoguideservice.com), which offers guided canoe, raft, and kayak trips as well as hiking and biking trips. Fishing excursions and powerboat tours are also available.

Twin Falls has several stores where you can rent gear for paddle sports. **River & Adventure Toys** (701 2nd Ave. S., Twin Falls, 208/735-8697, www.riverrattwinfalls.com) can hook you up with kayaks, rafts, lifejackets, and more.

Golf

Down in the canyon, you'll find the 18-hole **Canyon Springs Golf Course** (199 Canyon Springs Rd., Twin Falls, 208/734-7609, greens fees $25-28), a beautifully rugged 6,770-yard, par-72 course that's laced with rock and water traps. There's also a driving range, a pro shop, a restaurant, and a lounge. The course is typically open year-round, unless there's snow on the ground.

THE ARTS

The **Magic Valley Arts Council** (195 River Vista Pl., Twin Falls, 208/734-2787, www.magicvalleyartscouncil.org) brings together and supports area artists from various mediums at the Twin Falls Center for the Arts. The organization's newish headquarters, spectacularly perched on the south canyon rim, includes an art gallery that exhibits and sells local artwork. The facility also features an upscale bar and grill. The council sponsors annual events like **Arts on Tour** and **Kids Arts in the Park.** Check the website for a calendar of events.

ACCOMMODATIONS

The two major motel districts in town are on the north end of Blue Lakes Boulevard and on the west end of Addison Avenue (U.S. 30). Both zones are busy thoroughfares. The Blue Lakes Boulevard accommodations are primarily the bigger chain motels, while the Addison Avenue establishments are mostly older but serviceable independents.

Under $50

Near the heart of downtown, **Old Towne Lodge** (248 2nd Ave. W., Twin Falls, 208/733-5630, $30-55) offers basic but inexpensive rooms with cable TV. **Monterey Motor Inn** (433 Addison Ave. W., Twin Falls, 208/733-5151, from $46 d) has 28 guest rooms—some nonsmoking—with queen and king beds. Amenities include cable TV and high-speed Internet.

$50-100

America's Best Value/Apollo Motor Inn

(296 Addison Ave. W., Twin Falls, 208/733-2010, from $59 d) offers a complimentary continental breakfast, cable TV, a pool, and a hot tub.

Red Lion Hotel Canyon Springs (1357 Blue Lakes Blvd. N., Twin Falls, 208/734-5000, from $79 d) features spacious guest rooms, all with king or queen beds, irons, hair dryers, phones, and Wi-Fi, along with a restaurant and lounge and an outdoor swimming pool.

Best Western Twin Falls Hotel (1377 Blue Lakes Blvd., Twin Falls, 208/736-8000, from $89 d) is another typical chain hotel with standard amenities.

$100-150

Amid the blur of corporate hotels along Blue Lakes Boulevard, you'll come across **Blue Lakes Inn** (952 Blue Lakes Blvd., Twin Falls, 208/933-2123, www.bluelakesinn.com, $99-120), an affordable boutique-style hotel with well-appointed rooms that offer plush bedding and linens, 40-inch flat-screen TVs, high-speed Internet, and gorgeous photography and other artwork by Boise artist Anna Gorin. Expect to find a big continental breakfast spread in the morning.

★ **The Fillmore Inn** (102 Fillmore St., Twin Falls, 208/736-4257, www.thefillmore-inn.com, $99-185) is a bed-and-breakfast inn situated in a beautiful redbrick house that features four guest rooms with hardwood floors and lots of antique furniture. Wake up to breakfast and coffee served in the elegant dining room, or you can enjoy it on the patio during the warmer months.

Camping

Oregon Trail Campground (2733 Kimberly Rd., Twin Falls, 208/733-0853, www.oregontrailcampground.com, $30-40 RVs, $30 tents) is on the way out of town heading east on Kimberly Road (U.S. 30). The 80-site RV park features a playground, restrooms and showers, a game room, a snack bar, and 24-hour guest laundry. RV sites have full hookups and cable TV.

FOOD

Twin Falls has just about every kind of chain restaurant imaginable, especially along the Blue Lakes strip, but I don't need to waste any space talking about those places. Here's a snapshot of some local favorites around town.

Upscale Fare

Elevation 486 (195 River Vista Pl., Twin Falls, 208/737-0486, www.elevation486.com, 11:30am-midnight Mon.-Sat., 11:30am-11pm Sun., entrées $10-29) borrows its name from the height of the Perrine Bridge. This stylish bar and grill, in the Twin Falls Center for the Arts, easily has the best view in town because of its position near the edge of the south rim. The menu is all over the globe in terms of influence, with dishes like Baja-style scallop ceviche and chicken Marsala, but it definitely has inroads to the American West. In other words, also expect to find grilled Oregon quail, saucy baby back ribs, and pan-seared Idaho ruby trout topped with smoked red pepper butter. The wine list pays close attention to Idaho labels and other select offerings from the Northwest, and the place also serves inventive cocktails and draft microbrews.

It's safe to say that nearly everyone in Twin Falls has dined at **Rock Creek** (200 Addison Ave. W., Twin Falls, 208/734-4154, dinner daily, entrées $12-24) at one time or another. The venerable steakhouse west of downtown is an institution around these parts. People

file in for hand-cut steaks and chops, and big slabs of slow-roasted prime rib served with fully loaded baked potatoes. Seafood items include smoked trout bruschetta, garlic shrimp, and classic fish and chips. There's even an old-school salad bar where you can load up on roughage. The friendly bar, with its subdued lighting and retro cocktail lounge ambience, is a great place to sip a martini before dinner.

International Cuisine

Thai one on at ★ **Prasai's Thai Cuisine** (428 2nd Ave. E., Twin Falls, 208/733-2222, lunch and dinner Mon.-Sat., entrées $10-15), where you will find traditional dishes like sweet and sour catfish, green curry with tofu, chicken satay, and various wok-seared noodles. In a meat-heavy town, vegetarians definitely won't starve at this friendly place. Wash everything down with a cold Thai beer.

The Gyros Shop (132 Main Ave. S., Twin Falls, 208/733-1425, 11am-4pm Mon.-Sat., sandwiches $4-7), in a small storefront downtown, serves, you guessed it, gyros. Get your Greek on with a gyros sandwich (lamb, beef, chicken, or veggie) made on fluffy, grilled pita bread lathered with garlicky cucumber yogurt. The lunch-only restaurant also serves Greek salads, flaky baklava, and a rotating selection of soups.

Twin Falls has no shortage of Mexican restaurants. Here are two places worth checking out. **Rolberto's** (275 Blue Lakes Blvd., near Addison Ave. E., Twin Falls, 208/733-5516, 24 hours daily, $4-8) seems to get it right with a large array of affordable and authentic Mexican fare served *mucho rapido*. The kitchen pumps out big burritos, tacos, tamales, and torta sandwiches, and you can also get Mexican sodas and *horchata*, a cinnamon-spiked rice drink.

If you're into a chips-and-salsa kind of place, try **Janitzio** (164 Main Ave. N., Twin Falls, 208/734-9910, lunch and dinner daily, $8-13). This family-style Mexican restaurant is festive, thanks in part to the constant *ranchera* music that blares from the speakers. Sink into a big booth and munch on fajitas, enchiladas, smothered burritos, and combination plates. Try the flan and churros for dessert.

Burgers and Sandwiches

Locals flock to **The Shake Out** (1186 Kimberly Rd., Twin Falls, 208/734-0300, 10:30am-9pm Mon.-Sat., $3.75-7.50) for big burgers, tater tots, and milkshakes. The restaurant has more than 50 flavors of shakes, like huckleberry, apple pie, peach, chocolate chip, and butterscotch.

Papa Kelsey's Pizza & Subs (637 Blue Lakes Blvd. N., Twin Falls, 208/733-9484, lunch and dinner daily, pizzas $12-20, sandwiches $6-10), along bustling Blue Lakes Boulevard, may be a pizza joint at heart, but it also dishes up oven-baked submarine sandwiches. Do yourself a favor and try the Italian meatball sub.

Pubs and Taprooms

O'Dunken's Draught House (102 Main Ave. N., Twin Falls, 208/733-8114, 11:30am-late daily), on a busy corner downtown, is a local watering hole with more than 20 draft microbrews, good pizza, and probably the most happening sidewalk patio in town. It's not only for adults, though; this nonsmoking establishment is open to people of all ages.

Twin Falls does have a microbrewery, called **Von Scheidt Brewing Company,** but it's somewhat clandestine and intermittently open to the public. The brewery and taproom (157 2nd Ave. W., Twin Falls, no phone or website available, 4pm-9pm Fri.-Sat.) is where you can quaff handcrafted brews such as Catalpa Brown Ale and Hollow Point Porter. Von Scheidt beers have earned a cult following since they debuted a few years ago, and maybe that's why the brewery likes to fly under the radar.

Breakfast

For a hearty breakfast downtown, ★ **Kelly's** (110 Main Ave. N., Twin Falls, 208/733-0466, breakfast and lunch daily, under $10) is a good choice. Plump omelets bursting with fresh veggies and crispy home-fried spuds are among the delights on the menu, and the coffee is pretty good too. The bright and cheery downtown eatery also serves sandwiches, burgers, and salads at lunchtime.

Night owls and insomniacs head to the **Depot Grill** (545 Shoshone St. S., Twin Falls, 208/733-0710, 24 hours Mon.-Sat., closes 9 pm Sun.). The Depot, which opened in 1927, serves breakfast around the clock. The venerable diner is known for its dollar-sized buckwheat cakes and buttermilk biscuits and sausage gravy. The Depot also serves lunch and dinner.

Coffee

The best coffee in town can be found at **Twin Beans** (144 Main Ave. S., Twin Falls, 208/749-0927, 7:30am-4pm Mon.-Fri., 9am-4pm Sat.), a downtown coffee roaster that puts out excellent espresso drinks made with beans from around the world. The coffeehouse also serves freshly baked pastries, sandwiches, soups, and seasonal salads.

Like its sister establishments in Hailey, Ketchum, Boise, and Coeur d'Alene, **Java** (228 Blue Lakes Blvd. N., Twin Falls, 208/733-9555, 6am-9pm Mon.-Sat., 7am-6pm Sun.) makes a good cup of coffee, and you can also get light breakfast and lunch offerings.

Groceries

Stop by the **Twin Falls Farmers Market** (N. College Rd., across from CSI's Herrett Center, 9am-1pm Sat. May-Oct.) for locally grown produce, eggs, alfalfa honey, and yummy fruit pies, to name a few. Also expect to see lots of jewelry, pottery, and other artisan crafts.

Rudy's: A Cook's Paradise (147 Main Ave. W., Twin Falls, 208/733-5477, 9am-6pm Mon.-Fri., 9am-5:30pm Sat.) is a specialty shop downtown that has the best wine selection in the Magic Valley. You'll also be able to load up on local farmstead cheeses, grass-fed buffalo products, fruit preserves, and more.

INFORMATION AND SERVICES

Information

The best spot to pick up visitor information is at the new and improved **Buzz Langdon Visitors Center** (3591 Blue Lakes Blvd. N., Twin Falls, 208/733-3974) on the southwest side of the Perrine Bridge. The friendly folks here can point you in the right direction; make sure to check out the vintage Evel Knievel lunchbox hanging on the wall.

For information on local recreation, contact the city **Parks and Recreation Department** (136 Maxwell Ave., Twin Falls, 208/736-2265). For adventures farther afield, the **Sawtooth National Forest** office (2647 Kimberly Rd. E., Twin Falls, 208/737-3200), east of downtown, also serves as the forest's Twin Falls Ranger District headquarters.

Services

Contact Twin Falls's main **post office** (253 2nd Ave. W., Twin Falls, 208/733-0702) for general delivery inquiries. Twin Falls recently opened a beautiful new **public library** (201 4th Ave. E., 208/733-2964) across from City Park. The periodicals section is a good place to escape the heat or the cold.

Just west of town you'll find emergency medical services at **St. Luke's Magic Valley**

Medical Center (801 Pole Line Rd. W., Twin Falls, 208/814-1000).

GETTING THERE AND AROUND

Getting There

Joslin Field-Magic Valley Regional Airport (TWF, 208/733-5215) is about four miles south of town on Blue Lakes Boulevard. Commercial air service is provided by **SkyWest** (800/325-8224, www.skywest. com), offering three flights daily to and from its Delta hub in Salt Lake City.

The **Greyhound Bus Station** is at the Oasis Stop-N-Go (1390 Blue Lakes Blvd. N., Twin Falls, 208/733-3002). Tickets can be purchased there 9:30am-5:30pm Monday-Friday. If you need tickets on weekends, go to www. greyhound.com.

Getting Around

At the airport, you can rent a car at **Budget** (208/735-8698, www.budget.com) and **Avis** (208/733-5527, www.avis.com).

Twin Falls doesn't have a true city transit system, but don't be surprised to see one in the coming years. College of Southern Idaho operates **Trans IV Buses** (208/736-2133), a limited fixed-route service that runs twice daily between Twin Falls and smaller towns in the outlying area.

North of the Snake River

West of Twin Falls on I-84 is Thousand Springs State Park's Malad Gorge unit, but first are two major routes that leave I-84 heading north. Highway 46 passes through Gooding on its way to the Camas Prairie and the town of Fairfield. U.S. 93 runs due north out of Twin Falls, passing near Jerome and continuing to Shoshone. There it veers northeast toward fly-fishing nirvana—the Little Wood River and the pristine, trout-filled waters of Silver Creek. Highway 75 continues

north out of Shoshone on its way to the Wood River Valley.

MALAD GORGE

The Big Wood and Little Wood Rivers meet near Gooding to form the Malad River. Today it would probably just be called the lower Big Wood if early fur trappers in the area hadn't experienced a culinary catastrophe. In 1819, Donald Mackenzie's expedition stopped at the river and dined on beaver meat. Many of the men subsequently fell ill, leading Mackenzie to christen the river with the French word for "sick." Subsequent expeditions in 1824 and 1830 reported similar fates. Before the fur trappers came along, Shoshone Indians had inhabited the area, hunting pronghorn and fishing for salmon. After the trappers, thousands of Oregon Trail pioneers passed by on the Kelton Road. The gorge was a major stop along that route.

When the Malad River reaches 2.5-mile-long Malad Gorge, it gets a boost of spring water flowing into it at 1,200 cubic feet per second. The supercharged river froths and foams in tormented torrents down through the narrow lava-rock chasm. It reaches the height of its fury at **Devil's Washbowl,** where it plunges over a 60-foot waterfall into calmer waters. Below Devil's Washbowl, the canyon widens. Standing on the rim surveying the scene, you are 250 feet above the shimmering river below. Springs pour out from the rim in places, cascading down the cliffs in ribbon-like waterfalls. Signs warn visitors about getting too close to the edge of the precipice; deep fissures run parallel to the rim, indicating another layer of rock getting ready to slough off into the canyon. It could happen tomorrow, or it might take 1,000 years.

Although there is some disagreement among geologists, prevailing opinion seems to have it that the modestly sized Malad River on its own wouldn't have been powerful enough to carve such a deep canyon. Rather, the gorge is most likely another example of the work of the Bonneville Flood, an apocalyptic wall of water that crashed across the Snake River Plain around 15,000 years ago, reconstructing the landscape dramatically as it went. Melon gravel seen in the area lends support to this theory.

Thousand Springs State Park's Malad Gorge Unit

The 652-acre **Thousand Springs State Park's Malad Gorge Unit** (office 1074 E. 2350 S., Hagerman, 208/837-4505) is a day-use

Devil's Washbowl at Malad Gorge

area ($5) on the south side of I-84 Exit 147. The center of activity is the Devil's Washbowl overlook and interpretive area. Here signs explain the human and geologic history of the site, and a footbridge allows visitors to take a breathtaking stroll out high above the gorge. It's definitely not for acrophobes. As you walk across the footbridge, which is within diesel-sniffing range of the highway, the rumbling of the big rigs roaring by on I-84 shakes the bridge and adds to the excitement. One odd feature—perhaps engendered by engineering requirements—is the placement of the overlook bridge directly above Devil's Washbowl; you can't actually see the falls well from the bridge. Continue across the iron bridge and on down the trail for better views of the turbulent cascade.

Elsewhere in the park proper, a green picnic area with restrooms makes a good place to break out the lunch, while a loop road continues down to the Snake River rim, past a couple of smaller gorges eroded out of the cliffs. Hiking trails let visitors get off the asphalt and see some of the park's wildlife, including lots of hawks and jackrabbits.

GOODING AND VICINITY

Gooding was originally a railroad stop named after local sheep baron Frank Gooding, who went on to become a successful career politician. He was first elected mayor of the town bearing his name, then elected governor of Idaho, and then elected to the U.S. Senate, where he served from 1921 until his death in 1928. In 1913, the town of Gooding was designated the Gooding County seat.

Cities of Rocks

North of town, Highway 46 climbs into the Bennett Hills, passing access roads to two different "city of rocks" areas, where you'll find patches of hoodoo formations carved by eons of erosion. The common mushroom-cap shapes are created because the layer of basalt (lava rock) on top is harder than the rhyolite (consolidated volcanic ash) underlying it and therefore less easily worn away by wind and water.

The first turnoff you'll come to heading north, 14 miles north of Gooding, is for **Little City of Rocks.** Four miles farther up the highway is the turnoff for **Gooding City of Rocks.** Their names seem to indicate the latter is the best area; actually, while both are worth exploring, Little City of Rocks is about a mile or less off the highway, allowing quick access to relatively tall, impressive formations. Gooding City of Rocks, on the other hand, lies at the end of a nine-mile dirt road, and the rocks—or those near the road, at least—are much more humble in size. But the Gooding City of Rocks area does offer great views of the Snake River Plain as well as opportunities for extended exploring; the Special Recreation Management Area here encompasses more than 20,000 acres where you might come upon Native American petroglyphs or a herd of desert-dwelling elk. Other residents in the area include deer, black bears, chukars, golden eagles, prairie falcons, red-tailed hawks, great horned owls, and an abundance

of range cattle. For more information, contact the **Bureau of Land Management Shoshone District** (400 W. F St., Shoshone, 208/732-7200).

Events

Gooding boasts a good-sized Basque community, which throws the annual **Basque Picnic** on the third Sunday in July at the Gooding County Fairgrounds. Here you can enjoy a big spread of Basque food that includes grilled lamb, fish, chorizo-pocked rice, red bean soup, and hearty bread. The event also features lots of Basque dancing and a weightlifting competition (Basques like to lift big rocks, anvils, and other heavy objects).

Accommodations and Food

The **Gooding Hotel Bed & Breakfast** (112 Main St., Gooding, 208/934-4374, www.goodinghotelbandb.com, $69-95) is a friendly little inn that's listed on the National Register of Historic Places. This beautiful B&B is actually run by Goodings, descendants of the town's founding family. It has two guest rooms with private baths and nine more with shared baths. Rates include a large country breakfast.

For big farm-style breakfasts, head to the ★ **Farmhouse Restaurant** (1955 Frontage Rd. S., Wendell, 208/536-6688, 7am-8pm Sun.-Thurs., 6:30am-9pm Fri.-Sat., under $10), right off I-84 Exit 157 in nearby Wendell. Besides homespun breakfast fare served with a smile, the restaurant also dishes up lunch and dinner. The Basque omelet—made with spicy chorizo and pimentos—is a tasty way to start the day.

Grab a burger and a shake at **Stampede Burger** (701 Main St., Gooding, 208/934-4202, 7am-9pm Mon.-Sat., $4-8), a classic drive-in just south of town where you can also get chili dogs, finger steaks, and a decent hot pastrami sandwich.

SHOSHONE AND VICINITY

Once a rowdy rail hub, Shoshone still seems to delight in its frisky heritage. The chamber of commerce pamphlets fairly gloat when relating the gory details surrounding the town's former brothels and speakeasies. Shoshone's layout also contributes to its Wild West ambience. Railroad tracks split the center of town, leaving the two main streets to face off across the tracks like a couple of gunfighters.

Architectural Highlights

The town's architecture is noteworthy for its extensive use of local lava rock. Construction with lava rock is a lost art. Somehow the pioneer masons learned how to fit the lightweight rocks together into solid foundations and walls. Adding to the architectural flavor are flaking signs for businesses long gone, painted on many exterior walls around town.

Right downtown on the north side of the tracks is the **McFall Hotel** (230 N. Rail St. W., Shoshone), an 1896 beauty that was recently restored. Now a private residence, the "haunted" hotel had a guest list that included Teddy Roosevelt, Ernest Hemingway, and Erle Stanley Gardner. Could one of the ghosts roaming the halls possibly be Papa Hemingway looking for some pickled herring and ale? You never know. Other fine original structures still standing include the Hotel Shoshone; the Nebraska Bar; the W. H.

Baugh Building, now housing the Shoshone Showhouse movie theater; and the Doncaster, once a Prohibition-era speakeasy that later became an animal museum.

Accommodations and Food

The scuffed-up **Governor's Mansion Bed and Breakfast** (315 S. Greenwood St., Shoshone, 208/886-2858, $30-65), a historic mansion that used to be owned by the Gooding family, has five nonsmoking guest rooms, and it offers a small breakfast spread. It's important to note that the inn is sometimes open and sometimes not.

People come from miles around for the large selection of house-baked pies at the **Manhattan Cafe** (133 S. Rail St., Shoshone, 208/886-2142, breakfast, lunch, and dinner daily), a diner that harkens back to earlier times in America. Expect your coffee cup to be kept full while working your way through a tall stack of blueberry pancakes. At lunch, try a club sandwich with fries. Chicken-fried steaks and mashed spuds rule the menu at night.

Information

Inquire about the highlights of the surrounding high desert at the **Bureau of Land**

historic downtown Shoshone

Management Shoshone District (400 W. F St., Shoshone, 208/732-7200). For information about area tourist attractions, stop by **2nd Time Around Antique Mall** (102 S. Rail St., Shoshone, 208/886-7787), a wonderful antiques and collectibles shop that doubles as a visitors center. Besides picking up some old Yellowstone National Park postcards and other cool stuff, you can get a free historic walking tour brochure and insight about the town from the shop's friendly owner, Claudia Reese.

NORTH OF SHOSHONE
Shoshone Indian Ice Caves

North of town on Highway 75 is the **Shoshone Indian Ice Caves** (1561 N. Hwy. 75, 208/886-2058, 8am-7pm daily May 1-Sept. 30, $10 adults, $8 seniors, $6 ages 4-12), which offers 40-minute guided tours through a lava tube with a fascinating history and geology. Water seeping into the tube from the Big Wood River as well as from percolating rainwater collects and freezes on the floor of the cave thanks to air currents that keep the cave perennially icy. The convenient, year-round source of ice was a boon for the early town of Shoshone, especially during the blazing summers. Outside the cave is a gift shop selling tourist-trap stuff, as well as a museum boasting an impressive collection of gems and minerals.

Magic Reservoir

Continuing north on Highway 75 you'll pass two turnoffs to **Magic Reservoir,** which lies out of sight to the west. The first turnoff, right at the Big Wood River, leads to the west shore, while a turnoff farther north leads to the east shore. Boat ramps are available at both areas.

The reservoir is five miles long, 1.5 miles wide, and about 120 feet deep at its deepest point. The fishing is good for rainbow trout and perch, and a few brown trout also lurk along the east side's rocky shore. Ice fishing is popular in winter, as is waterskiing in summer. Campers can pitch a tent anywhere around the shoreline (free). Lava Point, just north of West Magic, is the most heavily used primitive camping area.

★ Silver Creek

Silver Creek is born of crystal-pure alkaline springs in the high desert west of Picabo, and it meanders slowly down to the Little Wood River through wide-open meadows. The wild rainbow and brown trout here can see you coming a mile away and aren't easily fooled.

Silver Creek Preserve is a world-famous fly-fishing spot.

They're big and strong, and they lure fly fishers from around the world. To avid fly casters, this is nirvana.

One of the prime fishing areas along the creek is The Nature Conservancy's **Silver Creek Preserve** (208/788-2203). It's on the south side of U.S. 20, seven miles east of Highway 75 or four miles west of Picabo. The Nature Conservancy works constantly to keep the preserve and the surrounding lands in pristine shape, a difficult task given the ever-increasing usage of the area. At the heart of the 825-acre core area is a small visitors center with interpretive information and a store selling conservation-oriented items to support the preserve. The center is up on a small rise, offering sweeping views of the creek. It's also a trailhead for a 0.5-mile nature trail that loops down to and around the creek. Along the way is a boardwalk that takes you right out over the water, which is so clear you can see every grain of sand and piece of gravel on the bottom. Even if you're not a fishing fiend, this is a peaceful and pleasant place. If you *are* a fishing fiend, you can fish for free—catch-and-release fly-fishing only—but you'll have to sign in at the visitors center first. The preserve relies heavily on donations, so please feel free to leave some greenbacks while you're here.

Fishing-guide service to Silver Creek is offered by a number of companies, including **Silver Creek Outfitters** (500 N. Main St., Ketchum, 208/726-5282, www.silvercreek.com).

To reach Silver Creek from Shoshone, either head north up Highway 75 and turn east on U.S. 20 or take U.S. 26/93 northeast through Richfield to Carey and turn west on U.S. 20. The latter route follows the Little Wood River, a good brown-trout stream that was one of Ernest Hemingway's favorite fishing holes.

South of the Snake River

ROCK CREEK STAGE STATION

Southeast of Twin Falls you'll find Hansen and Rock Creek Road (County Road G3), which follows Rock Creek to its source in the heart of the South Hills, a remote mountain range that has get-away-from-it-all hiking, mountain biking, and skiing. For information about recreational opportunities, contact the U.S. Forest Service's **Twin Falls Ranger District** (208/737-3200).

Rock Creek Stage Station dates back to the 1860s when the hardscrabble pit stop was one of southern Idaho's major transportation hubs and the first trading post west of Fort Hall. Oregon Trail wagon trains, stage lines, cowboys, and Indians all passed by here on their way to somewhere else. Gone are the horses whinnying in the stables and the rowdy pioneers downing whiskey and carrying on in the saloon. Now the only sounds breaking the pervasive stillness of the Snake River Plain are the babbling waters of the creek and the birds chirping in the willows.

Herman Stricker bought the property in 1875, and he and his wife, Lucy, scratched a life out of the expansive Snake River Plain. The old store—the oldest building in southern Idaho—still stands, alongside a couple of sod-roofed underground cellars. The dry cellar was used to store supplies and as protection from Native Americans, while the "wet" cellar housed booze for the saloon. Nearby is the turn-of-the-20th-century house Lucy had built after the original home burned down in 1899, as well as a graveyard with the remains of a dozen or so pioneers.

The site is a great spot for a picnic, and you'll come away with a feeling for what it must have been like on the Oregon Trail so long ago. Rock Creek Stage Station is five miles south of Hansen, a bit west of County Road G3 (watch for signs), and the buildings are open (1pm-5pm Sun.) during summer for self-guided tours. Admission is free; donations are appreciated. For more information, call the Friends of Stricker Ranch (208/423-4000).

U.S. 93 TO NEVADA

Between Twin Falls and Buhl, U.S. 93 turns south and makes a beeline for the Nevada border, carrying busloads of gamblers through the high rangeland to the campy casinos in Jackpot, just over the state line. Along the way are a couple of points of interest as well as the turnoff for the route west to Murphy Hot Springs and the old mining town of Jarbidge, Nevada. Keep your eyes peeled for birds of prey as you head south on the highway; they're abundant (and big) down here.

Rogerson

There's not much in **Rogerson** besides a small store with gas and an old saloon. But that's all the town needs to supply the gamblers en route to Jackpot, or the anglers heading for either of the two reservoirs, Salmon Falls and Cedar Creek, west of town. The road to the reservoirs also continues past Three Creek to Murphy Hot Springs and Jarbidge, Nevada; it's paved all the way to the top of the downgrade into Murphy Hot Springs.

Murphy Hot Springs and Jarbidge

About 49 miles west of Rogerson via Three Creek Road, you get to **Murphy Hot Springs.** Native Americans from the Duck Valley Indian Reservation reportedly recognize this spot, where two forks of the Jarbidge River meet on their way down from the snow-covered Jarbidge Mountains, and where natural mineral water flows from the earth at 106°F, as a magic spot with healing powers. Those less metaphysically minded will appreciate Murphy Hot Springs simply as a remote and idyllic spot with rivers perfect for fishing or splashing, and picturesque canyon

walls leading the eye ever upward toward the Jarbidge massif.

Past Murphy Hot Springs, the narrow gravel road continues 15 more miles to **Jarbidge.** It first descends one fork of the Jarbidge, past several shaded primitive campsites, before turning back on itself and climbing alongside a more westerly fork. At the U-turn in the road is the Bureau of Land Management's **Jarbidge River Recreation Site,** which, when the river is flowing just right, serves as the put-in point for white-water rafters and kayakers. Primitive campsites are found on both sides of the river around the put-in.

The Jarbidge River offers a Class IV white-water run in its short spring season (May-June). The normal takeout is 29 miles downstream at the confluence of the West Fork Bruneau River at Indian Hot Springs. This is one of the remotest stretches of white water in the state, through steep-walled canyons filled with wildflowers, cacti, and junipers. Of course, the river is also full of rock gardens, and the shores are full of rattlesnakes. Those yearning for this kind of adventure can contact **Wilderness River Outfitters** (Lemhi, 800/252-6581, www.wildernessriver.com) and sign up for a trip. The six-day trip ($2,000 pp) includes a run down the Bruneau River as well. It's expensive due to the difficult logistics and the fact that each raft carries just one guest plus the guide.

Up the road toward the Nevada state line you'll climb a canyon that's surrounded by phallic hoodoos. Numerous sandy beaches and swimming holes line the river for the next many miles. At the top of the hill, the canyon opens out into a broader valley, at the head of which sits Jarbidge, Nevada. Once a booming gold-mining town, today it's a remote mountain enclave supporting about 50 year-round residents. Here you'll find **Tsawhawbitt's Lodge B&B** and the "world-famous" **Red Dog Saloon,** which boasts a portrait of Diamondtooth Lil, something of a "head madam" for the gaggles of working girls who once serviced the gold miners.

UP THE SNAKE RIVER

Murtaugh

The town of **Murtaugh** is a tiny farming hamlet set off from even the rural stretch of U.S. 30 that passes just to the south. Once a railroad town, Murtaugh retains some glimpses of its heritage. Check out the **Iron Rail Bar & Grill** (109 Archer St., Murtaugh, 208/432-5657) down by the tracks. The 1908 building used to be the railroad depot, and it later served as a Model T repair garage and a general store. Now it's a local watering hole where you can get burgers and longneck beers.

Murtaugh Reach

The bridge over the Snake River at Murtaugh is the put-in point for experienced rafters and kayakers attempting the **Murtaugh Reach.** At peak spring flows, this is one of the toughest stretches of white water in the state. The 15-mile section of river between Murtaugh and just above Twin Falls offers a number of Class III and IV rapids. Agricultural diversion in early summer makes for a short season, however. **Idaho Guide Service** (563 Trotter Dr., Twin Falls, 208/734-4998, www.idahoguideservice.com) leads guided day trips on the Murtaugh Reach. Expect to pay around $125 pp with lunch.

Caldron Linn

Even the worst rapids on the Murtaugh Reach can't compare to what lies just upriver from the bridge: the man-eating falls at **Caldron Linn,** which early settlers nicknamed the Devil's Scuttle Hole. Linn is the Scottish word for waterfall, and this one's resemblance to a boiling, bubbling witch's caldron earned the cascade its sinister moniker. To get to the site, cross the Murtaugh bridge and turn east on the far side of the river, following signs down to the falls.

Murtaugh Lake

Those who prefer placid water underneath their boat can cross U.S. 30 to the south and head down to **Murtaugh Lake,** a haven for anglers, water-skiers, and white pelicans in the middle of the arid desert.

Camping ($15 RVs, $5 tents) is available at two areas on the west shore of the lake. **Dean's Cove** has a small grassy patch next to a couple of docks, where you'll also find some tree-shaded picnic tables. The other area, **Murtaugh Lake Park,** is much bigger, and it offers lots of grass, a baseball field, docks, picnic tables and shelters, restrooms, and boat ramps.

Milner Dam and Recreation Area

Milner Dam was completed in 1905, and the newly backed-up waters were diverted into canals that irrigated some 360,000 acres of cropland. Twin Falls, Jerome, and other towns to the west subsequently grew up along the river. Along the south side of Milner Reservoir, history and recreation share the spotlight at the Bureau of Land Management's **Milner Historic Recreation Area** ($3 day-use, $5 camping). The 2,055-acre site provides easy access to the water for anglers, boaters, and water-skiers. It also preserves a stretch of Oregon Trail ruts. At this point the westward-bound Oregon Trail pioneers had journeyed 1,315 miles from their starting point in Independence, Missouri. A small interpretive gazebo marks the spot and provides details about the dusty trail through this stretch.

Mini-Cassia Country

Before the Snake River was dammed and the volcanic soil of the central Snake River Plain irrigated, communities such as Oakley and Albion developed along rivers in the higher valleys to the south. After the advent of irrigation, communities developed on the Snake River Plain as well. Rupert and Burley, both founded in 1905, were the biggest in this region. Today Rupert is the seat of Minidoka County, which extends north from I-84 out into the lava fields. Burley is the seat of Cassia County, which encompasses the original high-valley settlements and several interspersed mountain ranges south of I-84. Together the two are known as Mini-Cassia Country, a combination of the two counties' names.

BURLEY

Burley lies near the crossroads of five pioneer trails. The Oregon Trail ran east-west about one mile south of town. The California Trail branched off the Oregon Trail and turned south up the Raft River Valley. The Salt Lake City-Oregon Trail route used after 1838 crossed the California Trail nearby. And the Salt Lake-California Trail route joined the California Trail just south of the City of Rocks. Finally, the Hudspeth Cutoff, first taken in 1849, came straight west from Soda Springs.

The town is named after David Burley, an Oregon Short Line Railroad agent who also helped foster the region's potato-farming industry.

Cassia County Historical Society Museum

One of the finer specimens on the historical museum circuit, the **Cassia County Historical Society Museum** (1142 Hiland Ave., at E. Main St., Burley, 208/678-7172, 10am-5pm Tues.-Sat. Apr. 1-Oct. 1 or by appointment, donation) houses an impressive collection of artifacts. You'll find a number of re-created rooms, including a doctor's office, a photo studio, and a saloon; collections of saddles, guns, hand tools, sewing machines, dolls, toys, and more; and displays pertaining to the area's sheep, mining, and fur industries. Don't miss the collections of old newspapers and photographs, some of which depict Shoshone Falls and Twin Falls before the dams were built.

Recreation

The city's 20 miles of river frontage make for easy access to Snake River recreation. Waterskiing is popular, with boat landings on the north side of Burley Bridge and adjacent to Burley Golf Course.

Burley Municipal Golf Course (131 E. Hwy. 81, Burley, 208/878-9807, greens fees $20-27) offers 18 holes over 6,500 yards. The scenic par-72 course lies astride the Snake River. Also here are a driving range, a pro shop, and a snack bar. Take I-84 Exit 208 to Main Street and turn left; the course is straight ahead on your left.

Events

On the last weekend of June, speedboats thunder down the Snake River during the **Idaho Regatta.** The annual event draws powerboat fans out of the woodwork, temporarily doubling the town's population. It's held at the riverfront marina.

The last weekend in July brings to town more than 300 buffed athletes for the **Spudman Triathlon,** a popular event that's been covered by ESPN. For more information about area events, visit the **Mini-Cassia Chamber of Commerce** (1177 7th St., Heyburn, 208/679-4793, www.minicassia-chamber.com).

Accommodations and Food

Near I-84 Exit 208, **Budget Motel** (900 Overland Ave., Burley, 208/678-2200, $50-89) has 139 nicer-than-average guest rooms along with a pool, a jetted tub, cable TV, and a kids' playground. Right next door, the 126-room **Best Western Burley Inn & Convention Center** (800 Overland Ave., Burley, 208/678-3501, from $69 d) offers an outdoor heated pool, a guest laundry room, and an on-site restaurant and lounge.

★ **Morey's Steakhouse** (219 E. 3rd St. N., Burley, 208/679-1166, www.moreyssteakhouse.com, 4pm-9pm Mon., 11:30am-9pm Tues.-Fri., 4pm-9pm Sat., dinner entrées $15-25) is the nicest place in this neck of the sagebrush. The restaurant's exterior is unattractive, but the dining room is elegant and the menu has lots of traditional steak, seafood, and pasta dishes. Expect to see prime rib, chicken-fried steak, shrimp scampi, and center-cut pork chops. The lunch offerings include burgers, finger steaks, hot sandwiches, and a noteworthy Cobb salad.

THE CITY OF ROCKS LOOP
Oakley and Vicinity

Mormon pioneers laid claim to Oakley and its environs between 1878 and 1880, and these squeaky-clean Christians still remain dominant here today.

The entire town of **Oakley** has been designated a National Historic District, and a number of surviving turn-of-the-20th-century buildings are listed on the National Register of Historic Places. **Judge Benjamin Howells Mansion** (110 Blaine Ave.), a Queen Anne-style home built by the judge in 1909, is today a private residence that's occasionally open to the public. The nearby 1904 **Howells Opera House** (160 Blaine Ave.) was renovated in the 1980s to serve as an entertainment venue once again. The stone evident in much of the local construction—Oakley stone, a type of quartzite—is still quarried in the area and is shipped worldwide for use in construction and as flagstone.

Oakley's **City Park** (W. Main St.) provides a shady green with picnic tables, a playground, and the municipal pool (June 1-Labor Day).

Also in the park is the memorial jail cell that once imprisoned, rightly or wrongly, the legendary Diamondfield Jack Davis.

Seven miles southwest of town is **Goose Creek Reservoir,** where boating, fishing, and swimming help residents beat the summer heat.

★ City of Rocks National Reserve

Castles of eroded granite, some over 600 feet tall, create a mythic fairy-tale landscape at the out-of-the-way **City of Rocks National Reserve** (free entry). They also make this natural landmark one of the country's top rock-climbing destinations. As at Yosemite, Joshua Tree, and Smith Rocks, you'll hear the clink of climbing gear from sunup until sundown and a host of foreign languages being spoken in the campgrounds that dot the preserve. Rock jocks have put up more than 600 routes, ranging in difficulty from 5.4 up to supposedly a 5.14a.

The 14,300-acre preserve also lies at a major intersection of pioneer trails. What a sight this must have been for those early adventurers. Some of them were moved to record their passage in axle grease on Signature Rock alongside the trail. Today the signatures of these California-bound settlers and miners can still be seen on the rock, between the preserve and Almo. Another bit of history here concerns a famous heist. In 1878, bandits held up the Overland Stage near Almo. Supposedly they buried their loot somewhere out in the City of Rocks, but the granite towers remain silent as to its whereabouts.

Among the most impressive rock formations at City of Rocks is Twin Sisters, on the west side of the preserve. The elder sister is composed of 2.5-billion-year-old granite, while the younger one was formed just 25-30 million years ago. The two look similar, however, because for millions of years they've been subjected to the same forces of erosion.

The reserve's 78 primitive campsites ($12) are administered from the reserve headquarters (3035 Elba-Almo Rd., Almo,

208/824-5519, www.nps.gov/ciro), four miles to the east.

Sawtooth Mountain Guides (208/774-3324, www.sawtoothguides.com) holds climbing classes and guided trips at City of Rocks several times a year and also plans instruction at Castle Rocks State Park.

Castle Rocks State Park

Rock climbers also flock to **Castle Rocks State Park,** next door to City of Rocks. Not only is it the first major new climbing area in the United States to open in the last 25 years, it was designed by climbers for climbers. Once a private ranch, the Castle Rocks Ranch unit (day-use $5 per vehicle) includes many of the same sorts of challenging granite spires as its neighbor. Although crag climbing is the park's reason for being, it's not the only thing to do at the 1,240-acre preserve. Picnicking, horseback riding, hiking, and mountain biking are also popular here, and the wildlife watching is superb: You may see mule deer, bighorn sheep, and even mountain lions. The main unit of the park offers several lodging options, including a yurt ($53), a bunkhouse ($106), and a lodge ($159) that was once a ranch house.

The park has two other units near Almo:

Smoky Mountain, with 38 serviced campsites ($23), and an administrative area that it shares with the City of Rocks National Reserve. This day-use area has a visitors center, a picnic area with restrooms, a California Trail wagon exhibit, and park offices (208/824-5901). Camping reservations for both the reserve and state park can be made at www.reserveamerica.com.

Almo

Almo was founded in 1881 as a stage stop on the Kelton-to-Boise route. Neither the stage route nor any other major thoroughfare passes through town today. Yet down at **Tracy's Merc** (3001 Elba-Almo Rd., Almo, 208/824-5570) you'll see license plates from all over the United States, mostly because the town serves as the supply center for the City of Rocks. Tracy's, established in 1894, still uses a turn-of-the-20th-century National Cash Register to tally up the gallons of bottled water and other camping supplies it sells to climbers. You can hang your climbing gear for the night at the frontier-themed **Almo Inn** (3020 Elba-Almo Rd., Almo, 208/824-5577, $100-170) next door to the **Almo Creek Outpost** ($7-16), a rustic diner open morning, noon, and night.

City of Rocks National Reserve

Cache Peak Area

North of Almo, Highway 77 leads to the community of Elba, where you can turn west and head up into the highest reaches of the Albion Mountains: **Cache Peak Area.** These are the state's highest mountains south of the Snake River. Here you'll get an eyeful of glacially carved high-alpine scenery.

The four **Independence Lakes** sit in a high cirque between Mount Independence (9,950 feet) and Cache Peak (10,339 feet). It's a three-mile hike up to the lakes, the lower two of which offer good trout fishing. To get to the trailhead, take Forest Road 548 east from Elba (or west from Oakley) up to the Basin-Elba Pass, and then take Forest Road 562 south to Forest Road 728 east. A small parking area is at the trailhead on Dry Creek.

Mountaineers looking to bag Cache Peak will find a Class 2 route up the northwest ridge, which leaves from Independence Lakes and heads over the saddle between Cache Peak and Mount Independence.

For more information, contact the U.S. Forest Service's **Burley Ranger District** (3650 Overland Ave., Burley, 208/678-0430).

Howell Canyon Recreation Area

The popular **Howell Canyon Recreation Area** (free entry) in the Sawtooth National Forest above Albion offers year-round recreation opportunities ranging from camping, fishing, and hiking in summer to skiing and snowmobiling in winter. The road up the canyon leaves Highway 77 just south of Albion and winds its way up into the mountain heights. A good viewpoint pullout along the way puts the area's landscape into aerial perspective, and you can even see the craggy Tetons looming in the distance.

Heading up the mountain, you'll first encounter the short spur that leads down to **Bennett Springs Campground,** offering six free sites along an aspen-lined creek. Next up the hill comes the **Howell Canyon Snowmobile Area.** The trailhead parking area here serves 25-30 square miles of trails, mostly on snow-covered Forest Service roads.

Travel a little farther up the road and you'll come to **Pomerelle Mountain Resort** (208/673-5599, snow report 208/673-5555, daily mid-Nov.-mid-Apr., full-day $39 adults, $25 seniors, and $29 ages 7-12, free under age 7 with an adult, night pass $15). The 8,000-foot elevation here makes for plenty of fluffy-dry powder on the resort's 24 groomed runs, five of which are lit for night skiing (Tues.-Sat. late Dec.-mid-Mar.). A triple chair, a double chair, and a free rope tow serve 1,000 vertical feet. Snowboarders and stunt skiers will also like the terrain park, while skinny-skiers can skate off down the small **cross-country ski** trail system on the far side of the parking lot. Rentals, lessons, and food are available at the base area, and a shuttle bus runs weekends and holidays from Twin Falls, Burley, and Rupert. The resort is open for hiking and mountain biking in summer.

The ski area marks the end of the plowed road in winter. In summer, the road continues higher to the 20-site **Thompson Flat Campground** ($8), tucked away in a lodgepole pine grove near a high meadow filled with wildflowers and some meandering cattle.

A right fork in the road past Thompson Flat leads you to **Lake Cleveland,** a scenic cirque lake flanked on three sides by steep slopes, including some impressive granite walls. The high alpine feel makes the lake a favorite of Mini-Cassia anglers and campers. A small campground on the far (west) shore of the lake gets crowded in summer. A larger campground on the near side offers more room and fewer people, but it isn't right on the lake. Both sites charge a fee ($10) for overnight camping. Since you're up at 8,300 feet, hookups for RVs are out of the question. Fishing in the lake is good for rainbow trout, especially during the spring and early summer months.

Back at the fork in the road, bearing left will take you up a good graded road right to the summit of **Mount Harrison** (9,200 feet) and a Forest Service fire lookout. The irrigated farmlands down on the Snake River

Plain stretch out to the northern horizon like a patchwork quilt. To the south, many of the mountains are across the state line in Utah. Mount Harrison has become a popular **hang gliding** spot in recent years.

ALBION

Founded in 1868, Albion was a logging center for the timber cut in the Albion Mountains just outside town. The town enjoyed county-seat status until irrigation of the Snake River Plain drew most of the local populace down the hill. The county seat was moved to Burley in 1919. Albion gained particular notoriety in 1897 when Diamondfield Jack Davis was jailed, tried, and convicted for the murder of two local ranchers.

At the north end of town, a group of impressive old buildings stand on a hillock. They were constructed in 1893 for the campus of **Albion Normal School,** a state teacher's college that closed in 1951. The historic campus was taken over by Magic Valley Christian College, but that school also closed and moved to eastern Oregon. Eventually the state sold the 44-acre site and all the buildings to the city of Albion. It's currently home to the **Albion Campus Retreat** (437 E. North St., Albion, 208/430-6430, www.albioncampusretreat.

com), which books family reunions, weddings, and other large-group special events at Miller Hall and the surrounding campus grounds. To arrange a tour of the historic buildings, call 208/312-8484.

Accommodations and Food

★ **Marsh Creek Inn** (386 S. Main St., Albion, 208/673-6259, www.marshcreekinn.com, from $65 d) is a good base camp for your explorations of the area. This clean and comfy hotel has 12 nonsmoking rooms with campy mountain themes and cable TV. Outside you'll find a covered hot tub and park-like grounds with a picnic area next to the tranquil creek.

Albion Steakhouse (248 W. North St., Albion, 208/673-5066, www.albionsteakhouse.com, 4pm-9pm Mon.-Thurs., 4pm-10pm Fri.-Sat., entrées $12-26) is the only bona fide restaurant in town, but it's just open for dinner. Here you can get prime rib, chicken-fried steak, cedar-plank salmon, and fried shrimp with orange marmalade dipping sauce. Appetizers include hand-cut Idaho fries, deep-fried mushrooms, and, oddly enough, house-baked scones. The eatery is also known for its burgers and huge milkshakes.

Lake Cleveland high above Albion

RUPERT AND VICINITY

Kitty-corner from Burley on the north side of I-84, Rupert is the Minidoka County seat. The U.S. Bureau of Reclamation laid out the town in 1905 when it was building Minidoka Dam. The downtown area surrounds a beautiful town square, a feature seldom seen in this part of the country.

The town might be named for a Bureau of Reclamation engineer, or it might be named for a pioneer-era mail carrier. It's open to debate. To find out which is more likely, head to the **Minidoka County Historical Museum** (99 E. Baseline Rd., Rupert, 208/436-0336, 1pm-5pm Mon.-Sat., free), a mile east of town.

Minidoka Dam and Lake Walcott State Park

With the Reclamation Act of 1902, Congress authorized construction of dams along the Snake River and provided irrigated land to settlers to farm. The farmers would make annual payments to the government for a term, at the end of which they would receive title to the land along with water rights on it. **Minidoka Dam** was built in 1906, the first of the Reclamation Act projects on the Snake. After the dam was completed and irrigation began to turn the brown plains green, thousands of settlers disembarked at the Minidoka railroad station with hopes of sowing their dreams in southern Idaho's volcanic soil. Other dams on the Snake followed, eventually irrigating a total of one million acres of dry, high-desert chaparral.

A hydroelectric plant was soon added at Minidoka Dam; seven turbines weighing over five tons each were hauled in by horse-drawn wagon from the Minidoka rail station. Power from the plant—the first federal hydropower project in the Northwest—was used to pump water into the irrigation system, with the remainder delivered to surrounding towns. As a result, Rupert was one of the first towns in the country to be powered by electricity.

During construction of the 86-foot-high earth-filled dam, crews lived in an adjacent camp. When the dam was completed, their camp evolved into **Lake Walcott State Park** (208/436-1258, $5 entry fee), the focal point for recreation on the lake. The park was popular with the region's residents right from the start. On Fourth of July weekend in 1912, an estimated 500 revelers celebrated the holiday here. Today the 22-acre park is still popular with boaters, water-skiers, windsurfers, and anglers. The latter might come up with a trout, bass, or perch. Large expanses of grass and groves of mature shade trees make the park a picnickers' paradise, and beautiful walking or bike paths meander along the shoreline past cattails, cottonwoods, and willows. The campground offers tent sites ($12), RV sites with hookups ($22), and camping cabins ($50) that sleep up to five.

Minidoka National Wildlife Refuge

Lake Walcott is also the centerpiece of the **Minidoka National Wildlife Refuge** (208/436-3589), a 20,000-acre preserve established in 1909. Bird-watchers will have a field day; in fall, up to 250,000 ducks and geese pass through. You might also spot whistling swans, snowy egrets, and great blue herons. Winter brings bald eagles, ospreys, Canada geese, and mallards. In spring, look for tundra swans, common loons, and lots of ducks, including buffleheads, common goldeneyes, and common mergansers. Summertime brings western and Clark's grebes and white pelicans. In addition to the abundant birdlife, the refuge also supports a healthy population of mule deer.

The U.S. Fish and Wildlife Service's refuge headquarters is next to Lake Walcott State Park, where you'll find a campground with picnic areas and boat-launching facilities. Anglers heading out onto the water will find the fishing good for perch as well as rainbow and brown trout. Small populations of crappie and bass are also present.

Accommodations and Food

The **Uptown Motel** (102 S. Oneida St./ Hwy. 24, Rupert, 208/436-8383, $40-55) is an affordable and clean motor inn with 18 standard guest rooms. Amenities include cable TV and a complimentary continental breakfast.

If you're craving pizza and beer, go to **Doc's Pizza** (514 6th St., Rupert, 208/436-3300, lunch and dinner Mon.-Sat., $5-16). This family-friendly restaurant on the historic square dishes up big pizzas, nachos, and hot sandwiches. If that's not enough, take a trip through the soup and salad bar.

EXPLORING THE WAPI FLOW AND GREAT RIFT

Confirmed desert rats, spelunkers, and lava lovers will find outstanding exploring opportunities in the barren desert northeast of Rupert. A vast sea of lava, the **Wapi Flow,** oozed out of a shield volcano at Pillar Butte only a relatively recent 2,100 years ago. The intense volcanic activity in this hot spot also created the **Great Rift,** a crack in the earth's crust over 800 feet deep in places and stretching northwest all the way to Craters of the Moon National Monument. The Great Rift has been designated a National Natural Landmark.

Note that all the sights in this area are found on unimproved dirt roads, which are impassable when wet and challenging when dry. Make sure you have USGS topographic, Bureau of Land Management, or other good maps of the area. Top off your tank before you set out, and carry plenty of water with you. If ever a place called for carrying two spare tires, this is it. It's dry and desolate, and help is a long way off.

Area Highlights

The three **Baker Caves**—lava tubes, actually—were discovered in 1985 by local farmer Mark Baker and subsequently excavated by a team of archaeologists from Boise State University, the Idaho Archaeological Society, and the Bureau of Land Management (BLM). The caves held abundant evidence of human habitation dating to about 1,000 years ago. One contained the bones of some 17 bison butchered here. Also found at the site were a few stone pipes as well as evidence of cooking, bead-making, and reed arrow shafts.

The **Wood Road Kapuka** is an "island" of vegetation surrounded by pahoehoe lava. Here pioneers cut a road in to get to the abundant junipers growing in the area, which they cut down for firewood.

Bear Trap Cave is an impressive gaping mouth in the ground suitable for a role in a Steven Spielberg movie. It's a lava tube created when an outer skin formed on a stream of lava, cooling and solidifying while the molten magma in the center of the tube flowed out. The entry to the cave is a spot where the tube's ceiling collapsed.

Other area points of interest include **Pillar Butte,** source of the Wapi Flow; **Split Butte,** a prominent feature befitting its name; and **Higgins Blowout,** a craterlike depression in a butte near the Wood Road Kapuka.

If these descriptions have tempted you into further exploration of this unique and little-visited area, get directions and more information from the **BLM office** (15 E. 200 S., Burley, 208/677-6600).

EAST TOWARD AMERICAN FALLS
I-84 to Salt Lake City

East of the Rupert and Burley area, you'll soon come to a major interchange where I-84 splits off to the southeast heading toward Ogden, Utah, while I-86 continues eastward toward American Falls and Pocatello.

I-84 crosses the Raft River Valley and climbs gradually up the Black Pine Valley through desolate undeveloped rangeland flanked most of the way by the Black Pine Range to the west and the Sublett Range to the east. After cresting the pass, it's just a hop, skip, and a few gallons of gas to the Utah border.

One other note at this juncture: If time is not of the essence on your Utah-bound journey, you might consider continuing east on I-86 to the American Falls area, then turning south on one of the more rural and definitely more scenic roads that eventually meet I-84 just over the Utah line at Snowville. Highway 37 leaves I-86 just west of American Falls and drops through Rockland Valley, intersecting the Arbon Valley Highway outside Holbrook. The Arbon Valley Highway leaves I-86 east of American Falls and winds through beautiful wheat fields and through the Curlew National Grassland on its way to the state line.

Eastbound on I-86

As you cruise east down I-86 bound for American Falls, you can spot a number of interesting topographical features on either side of the highway. **Horse Butte** is that big golden formation to the south just after the freeway splits. The butte is a fault scarp, relatively young in geologic age. Also

to the south, you can make out three different mountain ranges along this stretch. The **Raft River Mountains** are the long, low range in the distance that seems to be running parallel to your direction of travel. They're located just across the border in Utah. The range that appears more like a single pyramid is the **Black Pine Range,** while farther east, the low, brown **Sublett Range** starts far to the south and runs north to almost directly in front of you.

On the north side of I-86, the vast black expanse of the Wapi Flow soon comes into view. The high point that you can see (a long butte with a little raised nipple toward its right edge) is **Pillar Butte,** the shield volcano that was the source of the flow.

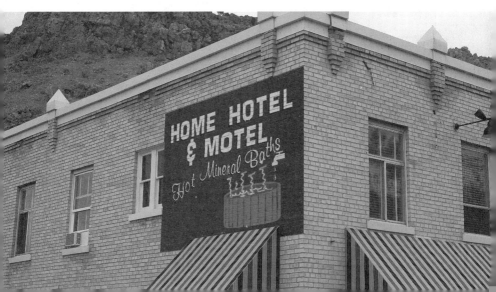

Southeast Idaho

Look for ★ to find recommended sights, activities, dining, and lodging.

Highlights

★ **Idaho Museum of Natural History:** Dinosaur fans should check out this museum on the campus of Idaho State University. It curates more than 500,000 cultural and natural artifacts, most notably the remains of a Columbian mammoth that was unearthed in Grangeville during the 1990s (page 175).

★ **Bear Lake State Park:** This park offers great access to gorgeous Bear Lake, which takes on a surrealistic turquoise hue thanks to the dissolved limestone deposits suspended in the water (page 190).

★ **Mormon Temple in Idaho Falls:** It's hard to miss the golden angel Moroni perched atop this prominent temple on the Snake River. The wedding cake-like structure is the regional spiritual center for the Mormons (page 191).

★ **Harriman State Park:** The fabled Henrys Fork runs through this state park, which used to be a cattle ranch for the Harriman family, who made their riches on the Union Pacific Railroad (page 210).

★ **Craters of the Moon National Monument:** Take a hike among the bizarre lava-rock outcroppings and cinder cones at this barren wilderness preserve near Arco. You'll think you're on the moon (page 217).

Potatoes often come to mind when people talk about Idaho. It's true, Idaho grows more russets than any other state, and most of these spud farms are in the high valleys that comprise this scenic swath of the Snake River Plain.

The snowmelt in the majestic Tetons—just to the east along the Wyoming border—gives birth to the Snake River, a flow of water that irrigates the largest potato farms in the world. The Gem State is so proud of its prized crop that it wears the moniker "Famous Potatoes" on its license plates.

This productive agricultural land, with its rich volcanic soil, offers more than just potatoes, though. The patchwork of family farms that dot the region are skirted by ancient lava flows, pinnacled peaks, and a caldera that is still very much alive. People flock to this part of Idaho for world-class trout fishing, especially at Henrys Fork, and recreational fun in the alpine hinterlands.

The cities of Idaho Falls and Pocatello are the region's urban centers. Pocatello boasts a colorful railroad history, and it's home to Idaho State University, the second-largest university in the state. Idaho Falls is a little tamer, due its strong Mormon upbringing. Here the

sky is punctuated by an alabaster temple—rising above the Snake River like a big wedding cake—letting everyone know they're in the land of Latter-day Saints.

Mormons have definitely made their presence known in these parts over the years. This corner of the state lays claim to the oldest nonnative settlement in Idaho. Franklin, near the Utah-Idaho border, was established by Mormon pioneers in 1860. These early immigrants thought they were still in Brigham Young's stronghold of Utah, but inadvertently ended up being Idaho's first settlers. The Mormons fanned out from Franklin, and today this conservative bunch contributes an unmistakable character to the region.

PLANNING YOUR TIME

You'll need the better part of a week to properly explore this expansive region. Island Park and Driggs are good base camps for year-round outdoor adventures, and you can

---

Previous: Craters of the Moon National Monument; Lava Hot Springs. **Above:** an old sign in Pocatello.

Southeast Idaho

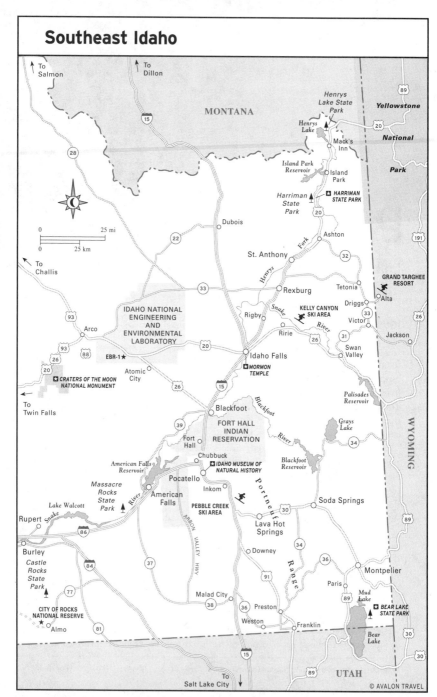

SOUTHEAST IDAHO

To Salmon

To Dillon

MONTANA

Henrys Lake State Park

Yellowstone

Henrys Lake

Mack's Inn

National

Island Park Reservoir

Island Park

Park

Harriman State Park

HARRIMAN STATE PARK

To Challis

Dubois

Ashton

St. Anthony

191

GRAND TARGHEE RESORT

Rexburg

Tetonia

Driggs

Alta

Rigby

Snake

KELLY CANYON SKI AREA

Victor

Arco

Ririe

River

Jackson

EBR-1

IDAHO NATIONAL ENGINEERING AND ENVIRONMENTAL LABORATORY

Idaho Falls

Swan Valley

Atomic City

MORMON TEMPLE

CRATERS OF THE MOON NATIONAL MONUMENT

Palisades Reservoir

To Twin Falls

Blackfoot

Blackfoot

WYOMING

Grays Lake

FORT HALL INDIAN RESERVATION

Fort Hall

River

Chubbuck

Blackfoot Reservoir

American Falls Reservoir

IDAHO MUSEUM OF NATURAL HISTORY

Massacre Rocks State Park

Pocatello

Inkom

Lake Walcott

American Falls

PEBBLE CREEK SKI AREA

Soda Springs

Rupert

Snake

River

Lava Hot Springs

Burley

Castle Rocks State Park

Downey

Montpelier

CITY OF ROCKS NATIONAL RESERVE

Malad City

Paris

Mud Lake

BEAR LAKE STATE PARK

Almo

Preston

Weston

Franklin

Bear Lake

To Salt Lake City

UTAH

© AVALON TRAVEL

0   25 mi

0   25 km

access remote backcountry within a few minutes from either Idaho Falls or Pocatello, both along I-15.

Pocatello and Idaho Falls are as cosmopolitan as it gets around here. Pocatello is the livelier of the two thanks to its college-town status. Pokey, as locals call it, has several good ethnic restaurants and a popular brewpub that puts out good handcrafted beers. You can get a history lesson and learn about present-day marvels in Idaho Falls at the Museum of Idaho, and the city also has a handful of pubs, coffeehouses, and decent eateries. Other noteworthy population centers include the Island Park area, where folks live to snowmobile in winter and fish the Henrys Fork in summer, and the Teton Valley, a rollicking fur-era rendezvous site that has retained a fun-loving spirit ever since.

Those looking to get away from civilization will find plenty of the big wide open. The landscape can be deceptive, especially in summer. Crossing the Snake River Plain on I-15 might lead you to think you're in low-altitude flatland, but both Pocatello and Idaho Falls lie at elevations of nearly 5,000 feet, and much of the lava-covered plain sleeps beneath a blanket of snow in winter. Not deceptive, however, are the mountains ringing southeast Idaho; they're unmistakably tall. The most prominent of them, visible across much of the region, are the famed Tetons, rising just across the border in Wyoming. These lofty peaks provide superb slopes for downhill skiers; powder hounds swarm to Grand Targhee, on the west side of the range near Driggs, as well as Jackson Hole, just a short drive to the east.

Massacre Rocks to American Falls

MASSACRE ROCKS STATE PARK

In August 1862, three small wagon trains were plodding down the dusty Oregon Trail east of here when the first two trains in the line—the Smart and Adams parties—were attacked by a band of Shoshone. Six emigrants were killed and several more wounded. The next day, 36 men from the third wagon train in the line boldly rode out in pursuit of the Indians. They actually managed to find the Indian camp and were quickly forced to flee for their lives. Four more of their number died in the process. All told, 10 pioneers were killed.

The "massacre rocks" themselves—not actually where the skirmishes took place—straddle I-86 just north of Exit 28. The Oregon Trail passed between the rocks, just as I-86 does now. The pioneers on the trail called the narrow passage Gate of Death or Devil's Gate, reflecting their fear of Indian ambush. The name Massacre Rocks was coined long after the 1862 skirmishes by an enterprising entrepreneur who built a gas station and store here

in the 1920s hoping to draw in tourists to find out more and perhaps buy a soda or two. The roadside stop also became a favorite gathering place for locals, but time eventually took its toll on the structures, which ended up being sold to the federal government and torn down.

Today Massacre Rocks State Park, set amid range grasses and junipers on a tranquil stretch of the Snake River, offers visitors a chance to study the area's Oregon Trail history as well as the much older history of the land itself. Evidence of the area's volcanic past abounds, as do telltale signs of the great Bonneville Flood, which roared down the river here some 14,500 years ago. Wildlife watchers and flora fans will also be enthralled; the park's 900 acres are home to more than 200 species of birds, including western grebes, white pelicans, and great blue herons, and almost 300 species of desert plants, among them locoweed, tumble mustard, and yarrow.

Geologic History

The Snake River Plain-Yellowstone geologic

province, which includes the park, is a volcanic swath that began to erupt 15 million years ago. At Massacre Rocks the eruptions took place some 6.5 million years ago. The volcanoes weren't the towering, exploding type like Vesuvius, Krakatoa, or Mount St. Helens. Rather they were shield volcanoes, cracks in the earth's skin through which molten lava flowed out like blood from a wound. At Massacre Rocks, as the 2,000°F molten lava rose toward the earth's surface, it came in contact with the water in the Snake River Plain Aquifer. The water instantly turned to steam and created lava geysers, spattering yellow-brown volcanic tuff in all directions. Subsequent flows covered the older ones. The lava rock you see across the river to the north is much younger than that on the south side; it's only 75,000 years old. By comparison, the youngest flows in Idaho were along the Great Rift, north of Massacre Rocks, where the lava oozed out of the earth just 2,100 years ago.

Long after the lava flows ceased, another cataclysmic event further altered the landscape. Utah's Great Salt Lake is still fairly large today, but it's just a small remnant of enormous Lake Bonneville, which once covered some 20,000 square miles of Utah, eastern Nevada, and southern Idaho. About 14,500 years ago, the lake overflowed its natural rock dam, which soon collapsed under the force of the rushing water. Some 1,000 cubic miles of water burst through Red Rock Pass, smashing down through today's Marsh Valley, Portneuf Narrows, and Pocatello. The flood lasted about eight weeks and was the second-largest known flood in history. It held more water than the total annual flow of all the major rivers in North America combined. The floodwaters carved out the Snake River channel, carrying boulders along with it. When the waters finally receded, these boulders were dropped downstream as "melon gravel." The flood also carved out secondary channels that today appear like hanging valleys along the Snake River rim.

Visitors Center

Start off at the park **visitors center** (3592 N. Park Ln., American Falls, 208/548-2672), where you pay the standard state park $5-per-vehicle entrance fee. The small center overlooks the Massacre Rocks and provides a multi-panel route map of the entire Oregon Trail from Independence, Missouri, to Oregon's Willamette Valley, showing highlights and major stops along the way. The visitors center's other exhibits focus on the area's

Massacre Rocks State Park

cultural and natural history. Many pioneer-era artifacts are on display. You'll find trailheads for the Geology Exhibit and Yahandeka Trails here as well.

Devil's Garden

A fenced-off area alongside the upper campground loop encloses **Devil's Garden,** a plot roughly 50 feet square holding numerous small pinnacles, each around six inches high. An interpretive sign theorizes that the pinnacles were formed when escaping gas vented through the volcanic ash, carrying silica up with it. The silica glued the ash together, creating hardened areas around each vent hole. The softer ash around the vents eventually eroded away, leaving the small pinnacles standing above the surrounding surface.

Register Rock

Along Rock Creek, a few miles west of the park proper, is **Register Rock,** a shady day-use area once popular with Oregon Trail wagon trains. Register Rock bears the carved-in signatures of dozens of emigrants who passed this way, including "H. Chestnut, Aug 20 1869." Now the rock is surrounded by a vandal-discouraging, seven-foot-high chain-link fence and sheltered by a gazebo. If you didn't pay the $5 entrance fee at the main park entrance, you'll have to pay it here. Mature shade trees and grassy lawns surround the rock, making the site a good spot for a picnic. To reach Register Rock, cross to the south side of the highway at the Massacre Rocks State Park exit and follow the signs.

Hiking Trails

Six different hiking trails thread their way through the park, one or another taking you down to the river, to high points overlooking the river, or to Oregon Trail ruts on the south side of the freeway. Start with the **Yahandeka Trail,** a 0.25-mile, self-guided interpretive trail that loops out from the visitors center. Interpretive signs along the way point out common vegetation in the area and explain some of the park's unique topography.

Along any of the trails you're likely to surprise a cottontail bounding through the brush or see a white pelican or two cruising elegantly through the sky above your head. Also of note is the short **Geology Exhibit** trail starting at the visitors center. The trail climbs up to a great viewpoint of river and rocks, where signs detail the park's volcanic origins and explain how the Bonneville Flood reshaped a large part of southern Idaho.

Campground Facilities

The park's 52 campsites ($22-38) are divided into two loops. The upper loop is less crowded but a little closer to I-86 and therefore noisier. The lower loop is closer to the water, quieter, but more crowded and susceptible to swarms of bloodthirsty bugs. Both loops have some pull-through sites, some double sites, water, and restrooms with showers. All sites have water faucets and power outlets. An RV dump station is available, and boaters can launch their watercraft at the ramp to the west of the interstate exit. The park is open for camping year-round, but facilities are limited in winter. Massacre Rocks also has several cabins ($50) that sleep up to five people.

To make campsite reservations, contact the **Massacre Rocks State Park office** (3592 N. Park Ln., American Falls, 208/548-2672) or call 888/922-6743.

AMERICAN FALLS AND VICINITY

Visitors coming to American Falls in search of a waterfall will be disappointed because they no longer exist. When American Falls Dam was built in 1925, it provided electricity to the city but obliterated the falls. The reservoir also inundated the original town site. The whole town was moved beforehand, but when the lake level drops in prime summer irrigation season, you can spy an old grain elevator and other evidence of southeast Idaho's Atlantis.

American Falls sits squarely in potato country, and farming drives its economy. Windsurfers come in droves during the summer months to take advantage of the strong winds that regularly rip across the Snake River Plain. Basic accommodations and food are available in town, but don't expect anything fancy.

American Falls Dam and Reservoir

The largest reservoir on the Snake River and the second largest in the state, the **American Falls Dam and Reservoir** offers recreation opportunities of all sorts, including fishing, waterskiing, sailing, and windsurfing. A Bureau of Reclamation **visitors center** (May-Oct.) on the dam's north side has historical photos and exhibits relating to the moving of the original town site and the dam's 1977 reconstruction as well as information on facilities around the reservoir. You'll also find a boat ramp and picnic areas.

Two marinas are on the reservoir near American Falls: **Willow Bay Recreation Area** is just north of town. It offers a boat-launch area, camping ($18-30), bike paths, picnic areas, ball fields, horseshoe pits, and a small burger shack. Farther east—take I-86 Exit 44 and wind around some dirt roads down to the water—is **Seagull Bay Yacht Club** (208/226-2086, www.seagullbayyc.com), a private marina where nonmembers are welcome for a small fee. The marina also has a grassy area with restrooms and a few RV spots with full hookups.

Just below the dam on the river's south side, you'll come to the Bureau of Reclamation's **Oregon Trail River Access,** offering boat ramps, docks, and restrooms. To get here, take Lincoln Street to Falls Avenue to Valdez Street.

Pocatello and Vicinity

Pocatello (population 55,000) began in 1864 as a stage stop named after Chief Pocataro of the region's Shoshones. Pocataro (meaning unknown) and his warriors were a thorn in the side of encroaching settlers in this area until 1863, when the U.S. Army finally forced them into submission. Pocataro signed a peace treaty and ended up on the Fort Hall Reservation, where he died in 1884. His gravesite unfortunately got flooded when American Falls Reservoir was created in 1925.

In 1879 the iron horse came to town, belching soot and putting Pocatello on the map when the Utah and Northern Railroad extended north from Salt Lake City and Franklin. Five years later, the Oregon Short Line came to town, pushing west from Wyoming into Oregon. Pocatello became a regional division point and the biggest rail hub west of the Mississippi. By 1920 it had grown into a bustling city of 15,000, with a lively mix of people and commerce that enabled it to become a libertine oasis in the land of the Latter-day Saints.

Today, despite the continued presence of the railroad and the added presence of the university, Pocatello is relatively quiet. You can actually find bars and coffeehouses here—not always a given in Mormon country—but the street scene after dark is minimal, and the clubs are relatively tame.

One worthwhile activity in Pocatello is watching the summer sunsets. The late-afternoon light comes shooting in low and bright off the northwestern horizon, rolling down the Snake River Plain. Head up to Red Hill on the Idaho State University campus for the best show.

SIGHTS
Historic Buildings
Downtown Pocatello's historic district, bounded roughly by Garfield Avenue and the railroad tracks and by Lander and Lewis Streets, holds a number of architectural delights dating back to the 19th century. Among the highlights: the 1898 **Trinity Episcopal Church** (248 N. Arthur Ave.); the 1916

Pocatello and Vicinity

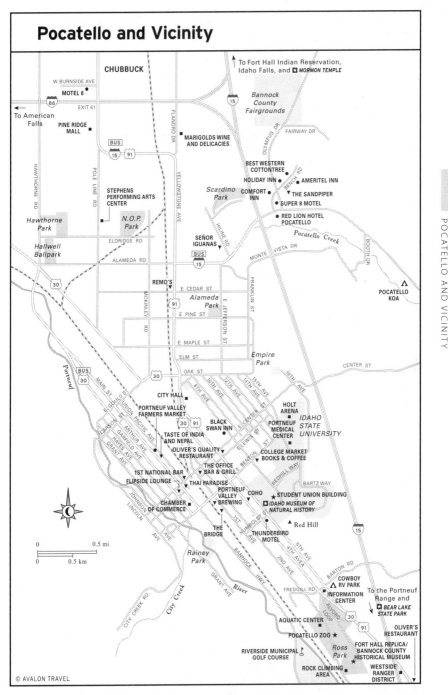

CHUBBUCK

To Fort Hall Indian Reservation,
Idaho Falls, and ✠ *MORMON TEMPLE*

W BURNSIDE AVE
MOTEL 6 ●

86

EXIT 61

← To American
Falls

Bannock
County
Fairgrounds

PINE RIDGE
MALL ■

OLYMPUS DR

FAIRWAY DR

15

BUS
15 91

MARIGOLDS WINE
AND DELICACIES

FLANDRO DR

HAWTHORNE RD

POLE LINE RD

STEPHENS
PERFORMING ARTS
CENTER

N.O.P.
Park

YELLOWSTONE AVE

BEST WESTERN
COTTONTREE

HOLIDAY INN ● ● AMERITEL INN

COMFORT ● ▼ THE SANDPIPER
INN

● SUPER 8 MOTEL

BENCH RD

Scardino
Park

● RED LION HOTEL
POCATELLO

Pocatello Creek

BOOTH DR

Hawthorne
Park

Hallwell
Ballpark

ELDRIDGE RD

HILINE RD

SEÑOR
IGUANAS ▼

MONTE VISTA DR

POCATELLO
KOA ⛰

ALAMEDA RD

BUS
15

REMO'S ●

E CEDAR ST

Alameda
Park

E PINE ST

E MAPLE ST

ELM ST

FRANKLIN ST

E JEFFERSON ST

Empire
Park

CENTER ST

30

91

MCKINLEY RD

OAK ST

BUS
30

30

MAIN ST

E GOULD ST

UNION PACIFIC

CARSON ST

ARTHUR AVE

GARFIELD AVE

HAYES AVE

GRANT AVE

Portneuf

CITY HALL ■

PORTNEUF VALLEY
FARMERS MARKET

30 91

TASTE OF INDIA
AND NEPAL

OLIVER'S QUALITY ▼
RESTAURANT

1ST NATIONAL BAR ■
FLIPSIDE LOUNGE ●

THAI PARADISE ▼

CHAMBER ■
OF COMMERCE

THE
BRIDGE

Rainey
Park

5TH AVE

10TH AVE

12TH AVE

14TH AVE

15TH AVE

19TH AVE

BLACK
SWAN INN ●

E CENTER ST

E LEWIS ST

BENTON ST

PORTNEUF
VALLEY ▼
BREWING

1ST AVE

HUMBOLDT AVE

THUNDERBIRD
MOTEL

HOLT
ARENA

PORTNEUF
MEDICAL
CENTER

COLLEGE MARKET
BOOKS & COFFEE

THE
OFFICE
BAR & GRILL

REDHILL WAY

COHO

✠ STUDENT UNION BUILDING

✠ IDAHO MUSEUM OF
NATURAL HISTORY

● Red Hill

*IDAHO
STATE
UNIVERSITY*

BARTZ WAY

▲ Red Hill

15

JOHNSON AVE

LINCOLN AVE

5TH AVE

4TH AVE

2ND AVE

BANNOCK HWY

GRANT AVE

City Creek

CITY CREEK RD

River

AQUATIC CENTER ●

POCATELLO ZOO ★

RIVERSIDE MUNICIPAL
GOLF COURSE ⛳

ROCK CLIMBING
AREA

ALVORD LOOP

BARTON RD

COWBOY ⛰
RV PARK

✠ INFORMATION
CENTER

FREDGILL RD

30

91

Ross
Park

COWBOY

To the Portneuf
Range and
✠ BEAR LAKE
STATE PARK

OLIVER'S
RESTAURANT

FORT HALL REPLICA/
BANNOCK COUNTY
HISTORICAL MUSEUM

WESTSIDE
RANGER
DISTRICT

0   0.5 mi

0   0.5 km

Valentine Building and the 1919 **Carlson Building,** kitty-corner from each other at Arthur Avenue and Center Street; and the 1916 **Yellowstone Hotel** (230 W. Bonneville St.), down by the Old Oregon Short Line-Union Pacific Depot at the east end of West Bonneville Street.

The most beautiful old building in town is the **Standrod Mansion** (648 N. Garfield Ave.), built in 1901. The gorgeous sandstone castle was designed by San Francisco architect Marcus Grundfor in a Classical Revival style; its interior is filled with oak, tile, and imported French marble.

Ross Park

Pocatello's biggest city park, **Ross Park,** has a number of attractions worth a visit. On the lower level of the park is **Pocatello Zoo** (2900 S. 2nd Ave., Pocatello, 208/234-6264, www.zoo.pocatello.us, 10am-6pm daily June 16-Labor Day, limited hours Apr. 15-June 16 and Labor Day-Oct. 31, $5.75 ages 12-59, $4.50 over age 59, $3.75 ages 3-11, free under age 3), home to a menagerie of bears, badgers, bobcats, bison, mountain goats, mountain lions, and more. The newish grizzly exhibit has been a big draw.

Also on the lower level of the park you'll find grassy and shaded picnic areas, horseshoe pits, volleyball courts, baseball fields, a playground, and the city's recently remodeled and expanded **Aquatic Center** (208/234-0472, $6 adults, $4 seniors, $5 ages 7-17, $2 ages 1-6), which offers lap pools, waterslides, water volleyball, and even inner-tubing on the "Lazy River." Lockers are available, but you'll need your own lock.

Upper Ross Park, accessed from Alvord Loop off South 5th Avenue, is where you'll find the **Fort Hall Replica** (208/234-1795, www.forthall.net, 10am-6pm Mon.-Sat., 1pm-5pm Sun. Memorial Day-Labor Day, check website for off-season hours, $4 adults, $3 seniors, $2 ages 3-17). Of course, this is just a reconstructed version of the famous fort that supplied Oregon Trail emigrants back in the day. Native Americans, fur trappers, and westward travelers all congregated at the fort, which stood north of today's Pocatello on what is now the Fort Hall Indian Reservation. The reconstruction—re-created from the original plans—allows you a look at life here circa 1830-1850. Within the thick adobe walls are blacksmith and carpentry shops, a large Native American exhibit, and exhibits on the fort's history and the Oregon Trail. You can often see the zoo's hoofed animals better from the parking lot of the old fort than you can from the walkways inside the zoo itself. Kids can get a free look at the bison, deer, pronghorn, and other ungulates from behind the fence.

Next to the fort is the **Bannock County Historical Museum** (3000 Alvord Loop, Pocatello, 208/233-0434, 10am-6pm Mon.-Sat., 1pm-5pm Sun. Memorial Day-Labor Day, $4 adults, $3 seniors, $2 children).

The cliffs separating Upper and Lower Ross Park are used for **rock-climbing** practice. Some 75 recorded single-pitch routes vary in difficulty from 5.7 to 5.12c. About one-third of the climbs are bolted. To reach the "shady side," head for Lower Ross Park as if you were going to the zoo, but continue past it. Look for a big, open parking area; the cliffs are clearly visible. To get out to the sunny side, head south of town on 5th Street until it joins with 4th Street to form Old Bannock Highway, then look for the cliffs on the right. Note: no dogs are allowed in the park.

Idaho State University

Idaho State University (ISU, University Relations 208/282-3620, www.isu.edu) began in 1901 as a two-year community and vocational college. By 1927 it had grown sufficiently large to warrant its designation as the southern branch of the University of Idaho. In 1947 it became Idaho State College, and in 1963 it gained its current status. Today, its enrollment is about 15,500. The 735-acre campus fronts South 5th Avenue, with its main entrance at South 5th Avenue and East Humbolt Street.

Several buildings on campus are worth a

special mention: **Holt Arena,** a large sports, concerts, and events venue; the recently re-modeled **Student Union Building,** which houses a movie theater, a bowling alley, a bookstore (208/282-3237), and ISU's Outdoor Adventure Center (208/282-3912); and the recently renovated and expanded Idaho Museum of Natural History.

★ IDAHO MUSEUM OF NATURAL HISTORY

The **Idaho Museum of Natural History** (S. 5th Ave. and E. Dillon St., Pocatello, 208/282-3168, 11am-5pm Tues.-Sat., $5 adults, $2 college students with ID, $1 grades K-12) offers displays focusing on important events in Idaho's natural history. This is the best place in the state to learn about dinosaurs and other prehistoric creatures that used to roam Idaho, including the remains of a Columbian mammoth found near Grangeville, which was excavated by ISU museum paleontologists in the mid-1990s.

At the museum you can also pick up a brochure detailing a guided walking tour to the **Idaho State Arboretum,** a collection of labeled trees and shrubs spread around the museum grounds. Among the 51 botanical

species you'll see are syringa, Idaho's fragrant state flower, and its cousin, the mock orange.

Museum of Clean

The impressive, new **Museum of Clean** (711 S. 2nd Ave., Pocatello, 208/236-6906, www.museumofclean.com, 10am-5pm Tues.-Sat., $6 general, $5 ages 3-11) in downtown Pokey is just the place for the germaphobe in your car. Owner Don Aslett, an all-around nice guy who became a millionaire selling cleaning supplies and services, has compiled his extensive vacuum cleaner collection and other items that scream clean in this beautiful 75,000-square-foot facility. Expect to see nearly 1,000 different vacuums throughout history, dating to the 1860s. There's also a plethora of vintage and antique tubs, brooms, washing machines, toilets, and much more. You won't be able to take your eyes off the impeccably restored 1940s-era cleaning supply delivery truck.

Fort Hall Indian Reservation

The Shoshone and Bannock of the **Fort Hall Indian Reservation** were two separate peoples speaking two different languages yet sharing many cultural similarities. Both groups were hunters and gatherers who

Idaho Museum of Natural History

roamed the Great Basin region of Nevada, Utah, Wyoming, and Idaho in search of fish and game. When the nonnatives arrived, the two tribes were muscled onto the Fort Hall Reservation, established in 1867. The reservation originally encompassed 1.8 million acres, but 20 years later the allotment process of the Dawes Act reduced the size of the reservation to about 540,000 acres, where many of the 3,900 enrolled tribe members live today.

The reservation is just north of Pocatello on I-15. To learn more about its history and people, head for the **Shoshone-Bannock Tribal Museum** (208/237-9791, 9:30am-5pm daily, $2.50 adults, $1 ages 6-18, free for tribe members with ID), just off I-15 Exit 80. You can view exhibits and historical photographs preserving their heritage and buy books, posters, and Native American art. You can also arrange tours of the Fort Hall Bottoms to view both the reservation's buffalo herd and the site of Nathaniel Wyeth's original 1834 Fort Hall trading post.

Across the street from the museum is the reservation's **Trading Post complex,** with a restaurant, a casino, and a gift shop selling Native American-made goods.

Some of the region's best **fishing** can be found on the reservation, on a stretch of the Snake River in the Fort Hall Bottoms, essentially the inlet waters of American Falls Reservoir. Few anglers compete for the plentiful 5-7-pound trout. To fish the Bottoms, you'll need to pick up a permit from the tribe, available at the truck stop at I-15 Exit 80. The fishing season usually runs April-October.

The spectacular **Shoshone-Bannock Indian Festival and Rodeo** (www.sb-tribes.com/festival) draws Native Americans and nonnatives from all over the United States and Canada. Traditional Indian dancing takes center stage, and multitudes of dancers and drummers come attired in intricate dress and face paint. In addition, the event features a rodeo, an arts and crafts show, and a softball tourney. It all takes place the second week of August at the Fort Hall rodeo grounds.

RECREATION
Portneuf Greenway

Portneuf Greenway (208/234-4929) has been a work in progress since its inception in the mid-1990s. The idea for this recreational path, which gives bicyclists, joggers, and walkers a place to play along the Portneuf River, was spearheaded by a local nonprofit organization. There are currently about 11 miles of connected paved trails, starting north of Pokey at Swanson Reach and running south through the heart of Old Town, and then over to the university en route to the Edson Fichter Trail and Nature Area. All the dots have yet to be connected, but look for big developments along this scenic path in the coming years. You can pick up a trail map at the community recreation center (144 Wilson Ave., Pocatello, 208/232-3901) or at the chamber of commerce (324 S. Main St., Pocatello, 208/233-1525).

Hiking and Mountain Biking

The **Gibson Jack Trailhead,** at the top of Gibson Jack Road off Bannock Highway, offers access to one of the nicest hiking opportunities in the Pocatello area. The trail follows Gibson Jack Creek into a Research Natural Area, closed to motorized vehicles. It's about four miles from the trailhead to a gate at the area boundary. You won't find a single head of cattle on this spread, and as a result, the watercourse is in excellent shape. The creek is too small to offer much in the way of a swimming hole, but a couple of "dabbling holes" can cool the feet on a hot summer day.

City Creek is a local favorite for hiking and mountain biking. Following the trail up the creek will eventually take you to the top of **Kinport Peak** (7,222 feet), a quick fix for local mountaineers when time doesn't permit a trip to more rarefied realms. To get to the trail, take West Center Street west to Lincoln Avenue and turn left, then right on City Creek Road. You can access the area from the Portneuf Greenway.

Mink Creek, south of town, provides a major focus for outdoor recreation in the area. The Bannock Highway, which originates on the southwest side of Pocatello, parallels the hills for several miles before veering right and climbing alongside Mink Creek. The road continues up and over Crystal Summit and down to the Arbon Valley on the other side of the range. Along the way it passes numerous trailheads offering gateways into the Bannock Range. The bottom of Mink Creek can also be accessed from the Portneuf Area exit of I-15 South (Exit 57). Starting at the bottom of the hill, **Cherry Springs Nature Area** is the first turnout, where you'll find a beautiful nature trail winding through the creekbed vegetation and breaking out onto the slopes on the far side. It's a day-use-only area. Continuing up Mink Creek, you'll pass trailheads to **Slate Mountain, West Mink Creek, Valve House Draw, Corral Creek-South Fork Mink Creek,** and **Porcelain Pot Gulch** before topping out at Crystal Summit, just under 6,000 feet in elevation. Some of these trailheads serve cross-country skiers and snowmobilers in winter.

Alpine Skiing

Pebble Creek Ski Area (3340 E. Green Canyon Rd., Inkom, 208/775-4452, snow report 208/775-4451, www.pebblecreekskiarea.com, Fri.-Sun. until Dec. 24, closed Dec. 25, daily Dec. 26-Feb., Wed.-Sun. Mar., Fri.-Sun. Apr., night skiing until 9:30pm Fri.-Sat. Jan.-mid-Mar., full-day lift tickets $43 adults, $29 ages 6-12 and over age 69, $3 under age 6) is up East Green Canyon Road, just a short drive south of town on I-15 (follow signs from the Inkom exits). With 1,100 acres on Mount Bonneville, the small resort offers 2,200 vertical feet served by two double chairs and one triple chair. Head for Al's Drop to get your adrenaline pumping. Skiing, telemarking, and snowboarding lessons are offered, and rentals are available; day care is also available.

Portneuf Range Yurt System

On Pocatello's eastern flank lies **Portneuf Range Yurt System,** a cross-country skier's

nirvana. Wide-open snow-covered wheat fields gradually give way to the high ridges and backcountry bowls of the Portneuf Range. As a bonus, the area has a public yurt and cabin system. Several of the canvas-topped Mongolian-style shelters ($30-90) and camping cabins ($40-70) are spread across the area from just east of town to just north of Pebble Creek Ski Area. Each yurt is equipped with plywood bunk beds, a woodstove, a cookstove, a lantern, pots, and a shovel. You'll need to bring all your own winter-camping gear as well as mantles for the lantern and Coleman propane cylinders (16.4 ounce) for both the lantern and the stove.

Idaho State University's Outdoor Program maintains the yurts and cabins, but all users are expected to help keep the shelters shoveled out and in good shape. Make reservations at the **Outdoor Adventure Center** (Student Union Building, S. 5th Ave. and E. Humbolt St., Pocatello, 208/282-3912), where you can also get maps and rent a wide variety of gear for rafting, kayaking, skiing, snowboarding, camping, and hiking. It's also an excellent place to learn about other recreational opportunities throughout southeast Idaho.

ENTERTAINMENT
Nightlife

The **1st National Bar** (232 W. Center St., Pocatello, 208/904-1033) is an old-school drinking establishment in Old Town where local and touring rock bands perform on weekends. The clientele is friendly and the drinks are strong here.

Nearby, college students and other younger folks frequent the **Flipside Lounge** (117 S. Main St., Pocatello, 208/233-2116), a subterranean club that brings to town alternative bands from around the Northwest. Also expect to find DJ music on weeknights and lots of cocktails and craft beers.

Just across the tracks from downtown, **The Office Bar & Grill** (251 E. Center St., Pocatello, 208/232-9816) is a popular weekend nightspot where middle-age types go on the lustful prowl. It's definitely a friendly place.

Performing Arts

Idaho State University's **Stephens Center** (1002 Sam Nixon Ave., Pocatello, 208/282-3595, www.isu.edu/stephens) is the beating heart of Pokey's performing arts scene. The impressive 123,000-square-foot building, perched on a hill above campus, boasts several venues, including the 1,200-seat Jensen Grand Concert Hall. Here the schedule is kept full with a gamut of national touring acts and campus concertos and plays. The center is also home to the **Idaho State Civic Symphony** (208/234-1587, www.thesymphony.us), which presents about nine classical performances September-April. In addition to the regular season, an annual pops concert features contemporary works.

ACCOMMODATIONS
Under $50

For affordable and relatively clean rooms, head to the **Thunderbird Motel** (1415 S. 5th Ave., Pocatello, 208/232-6330, www.thunderbirdmotelid.com, from $41 d), right across the street from the ISU campus and close to Ross Park and downtown. It has an outdoor pool in summer and a guest laundry year-round, and some rooms have refrigerators and microwaves. Pets are welcome.

$50-100

Clustered up against the hill on the east side of town (I-15 Exit 71) are most of the city's chain motels, including **Super 8** (1330 Bench Rd., Pocatello, 208/234-0888 or 866/378-7378, from $55 d), with 80 guest rooms and complimentary continental breakfast.

Red Lion Hotel Pocatello (1555 Pocatello Creek Rd., Pocatello, 208/233-2200 or 800/325-4000, from $79 d) offers 150 nonsmoking rooms, a restaurant and lounge, an indoor pool, a jetted tub and sauna, and a small exercise room. Pets are allowed with a deposit.

A little farther up the hill, you'll find **Best**

Western CottonTree Inn (1415 Bench Rd., Pocatello, 208/237-7650 or 800/662-6886, from $94 d). King beds, kitchenettes, and family rates are available, and 60 percent of the guest rooms are nonsmoking. Amenities include an indoor pool, cable TV, a guest laundry, and a free breakfast spread.

$100-250

Black Swan Inn (746 E. Center St., Pocatello, 208/233-3051, www.blackswaninn.com, $99-239) offers more than a dozen "Fantasy Theme Suites." Examples include the Caveman Suite, the Pirate's Suite, and the Jungle Falls Suite. The Sea Cave Suite is home to a lovely mermaid. It's a fine line between "fantasy" and "cheesy" at this place.

RV Parks

Pocatello KOA (9815 W. Pocatello Creek Rd., Pocatello, 208/233-6851, www.koa.com) is up Pocatello Creek Road past the cluster of motels and restaurants by I-15. The campground offers 40 RV sites with hookups ($37), two cabins ($48), and 18 tent sites ($23-28). A dump station is free to guests; nonguests can use it for a fee. Facilities include showers, a laundry, a game room, a playground, and a small grocery store that also sells gasoline and propane.

Cowboy RV Park (845 Barton Rd., Pocatello, 208/232-4587), on the south end of town near Ross Park, offers 41 RV sites with full hookups ($32-35) and a few tent sites ($15). Facilities at this Good Sam park include showers and laundry.

U.S. Forest Service Campground

Caribou-Targhee National Forest's Westside North Ranger District (4350 S. Cliffs Dr., Pocatello, 208/236-7500) supervises **Scout Mountain Campground** (25 sites, $10), perched at 6,500 feet on the shoulder of 8,700-foot Scout Mountain. Nearby is the East Mink trailhead, with trails that crisscross the mountains. To get to the campground, head south of town either on Bannock Highway or I-15 South (exit at the "Portneuf Area Recreation" sign, Exit 63). About five miles up the hill from the Bannock Highway-Portneuf Road junction, the East Fork road turns to the left. Follow the road to the campground at the end.

FOOD
Wine Bars and Brewpubs
★ **The Bridge** (815 S. 1st Ave., Pocatello, 208/234-7000, www.thebridgerestaurant.net, 11:30am-10pm Tues.-Sat., $8-26) is probably Pocatello's best restaurant in terms of contemporary cuisine. This stylish eatery and wine bar, downtown in an old brick warehouse, serves a large menu of wine-friendly fare. Expect to see small plates like hoisin-glazed pork ribs and cheese samplers. The kitchen uses Kobe-style beef and Kurobuta pork from Idaho's Snake River Farms, and you can also get pasta dishes and entrée salads. The extensive wine list plays well with the food.

For good pub grub and handcrafted ales, check out **Portneuf Valley Brewing** (615 S. 1st Ave., Pocatello, 208/232-1644, www.portneufvalleybrewing.com, 11am-10pm Mon.-Thurs., 11am-midnight Fri.-Sat., $7-16). Here you'll find nachos, hot wings, big burgers, and sandwiches, which you can wash down with Twisted Stick Amber Ale and Ligertown Lager. The brewpub hosts live music on a weekly basis.

International Cuisine
Señor Iguanas (961 Hiline Rd., Pocatello, 208/233-4422, lunch and dinner Mon.-Sat., $8-15) doesn't cloak its food with orange cheese the way many other Americanized Mexican restaurants do. Locals come in droves for chiles rellenos, tamales, burritos, enchiladas, and shrimp dishes. As an added bonus, the eatery serves lots of Mexican beers.

Fans of Southeast Asian food will surely enjoy **Thai Paradise** (140 S. Main St., Pocatello, 208/269-7313, lunch and dinner Mon.-Sat., $9-14) in Old Town. This friendly little Thai joint serves stir-fried noodles, hotpot soups, spring rolls, and aromatic curries. Good picks are the fried tofu in peanut sauce and spicy beef salad.

A few blocks away, you'll find ★ **Taste of India & Nepal** (330 N. Main St., Pocatello, 208/478-0172, www.tasteofindianepal.net, lunch and dinner Mon.-Sat., entrées $8-15), a restaurant that turns to the Himalayas for inspiration. Besides standard Indian fare, like samosas, chicken tikka, lamb vindaloo, and charred naan bread, the restaurant also dishes up Nepali classics such as veggie momo dumplings and lamb kothay. Beverages include mango lassis (yogurt drink) and creamy chai tea.

Breakfast and Coffee
Oliver's Restaurant (130 S. 5th Ave., Pocatello, 208/234-0672, breakfast, lunch, and dinner daily, $6-15) is a classic diner downtown that serves homespun fare with a twist. In the morning, try the trout and eggs or huevos rancheros. Fish and chips and chicken-fried steak are noteworthy picks later in the day. Vegetarians will find a breakout menu that features dishes like spinach lasagna and Southwestern-style stewed lentils.

CoHo (904 S. 4th Ave., Pocatello, 208/417-0074, www.cohothesmartbar.com, 6:30am-10pm Mon.-Sat., 8am-8pm Sun.), a happening little coffeehouse near ISU, serves excellent espresso drinks, boba teas, smoothies, and the largest selection of loose-leaf teas in town. You can also get freshly baked goodies in the morning and light lunch offerings in the afternoon.

Groceries
Marigolds Wine and Delicacies (1800 Flandro Dr., Pocatello, 208/237-9463, www.marigoldswine.com, 11am-9pm Tues.-Thurs., 11am-10pm Fri.-Sat.), in the Gold's Gym complex, is a specialty store with a large selection of wines from around the world. Marigolds also stocks artisanal cheeses, bread, and lots of bottled microbrews and imported beers.

Portneuf Valley Farmers Market (9am-1pm Sat., 5pm-8pm Wed. May-Oct.) sets up at the **Old Town Pavilion** (420 N. Main St.). Here you can pick up fresh produce, crusty breads, fruit preserves, and local sausages and other meats.

INFORMATION AND SERVICES

For more information about Pokey, drop by the **Greater Pocatello Chamber of Commerce** (324 S. Main St., Pocatello, 208/233-1525, www.pocatelloidaho.com).

To inquire about recreational activities, contact the **City of Pocatello Parks and Recreation Department** (911 N. 7th Ave., Pocatello, 208/234-6232) and Caribou-Targhee National Forest's **Westside North Ranger District** (4350 Cliffs Dr., Pocatello, 208/236-7500).

For emergency medical services, go to **Portneuf Medical Center** (777 Hospital Way, Pocatello, 208/239-1000) near the university.

GETTING THERE AND AROUND

Getting There

Greyhound Bus Lines (208/232-5365 or 800/231-2222) uses the city Transit Center (215 W. Bonneville St.) as its Pocatello terminal. Buses run south to Salt Lake City, northeast to Idaho Falls, and to Burley and points west.

Pocatello Regional Airport (PIH, 208/234-6154, www.iflypocatello.com) is west of town off I-86, and **SkyWest/Delta** (800/221-1212) provides four daily flights to and from its hub in Salt Lake City. Car rental companies at the airport include **Avis** (208/232-3244), **Budget** (208/233-0600), and **Hertz** (208/233-2970).

Getting Around

Pocatello Regional Transit (215 W. Bonneville St., Pocatello, 208/234-2287, www.pocatellotransit.com) operates city bus service ($0.90 general, $0.45 students and seniors). Check the website for schedules.

South to Utah

HEADING DOWN I-15

Leaving Pocatello and heading south on I-15, you'll flow like lava past the basalt cliffs displaying the Snake River Plain's volcanic history. Mountains flank the highway on both sides—the Portneuf Range on the left, the Bannock Range on the right—and straight ahead in the distance, the unique summit ridge of Oxford Peak reaches into the sky.

Those entering Idaho on I-15 from the south will find the **Gateway Southeast Idaho Visitor Center** (208/766-4788) at the Cherry Creek Rest Area, seven miles north of the Utah border. The center is well stocked with brochures covering all parts of the state.

Mormon Canyon

At I-15 Exit 47, U.S. 30 leads east toward Lava Hot Springs and Soda Springs, while the road to the west leads into the Bannock Range and the Bureau of Land Management's primitive **Mormon Canyon Campground.** To get to the campground, turn west at the Exit 47 off-ramp and follow the road to its junction with Marsh Creek Road. Turn left, then right on Green Road almost immediately thereafter. Follow Green Road straight up to the campground on the eastern edge of the Caribou-Targhee National Forest.

The site is actually in Goodenough Canyon, along Goodenough Creek. But Goodenough Canyon is a box canyon, while **Mormon Canyon,** just over a small ridge, provides access via a hiking and off-road vehicle trail up into the Bannocks—all the way to Scout Mountain, Mink Creek, and Pocatello if you so desire. The Mormon Canyon Trail crosses Goodenough Creek to the south. Alternately, a trail straight up Goodenough Creek leads past several primitive, secluded creek-side campsites. This dead-end trail makes a great day hike. To the north, a third trail leads to Bell Marsh Creek, and from there you can either go to Scout Mountain or back out to Marsh Creek Road. This latter trail in particular is great for relatively easy mountain biking; the Mormon Canyon Trail is more difficult. A loop trip connects the two trails. The free campground here is quiet and idyllic. Shade abounds under a magnificent mix of trees, and Goodenough Creek runs through it.

Devil Creek Reservoir

Anglers fish for planted rainbow trout and kokanee salmon at **Devil Creek Reservoir,** a small impoundment seven miles north of Malad City. Primitive camping is available along one end of the west shore, and an RV park with a boat ramp is at the other end, nearest the exit from I-15.

MALAD CITY AND VICINITY

French trappers named the Malad River in the 1830s after eating some local beaver meat that didn't agree with them (*malade* is the French word for "sick."). In 1843, a party led by John C. Frémont passed through the area and encountered a small band of emaciated Indians. Frémont noted that since the establishment of Fort Hall in 1834, trappers and buffalo hunters using the fort as a trading center and home base had devastated the Malad Valley's once-prolific buffalo herds, much to the dismay of local Native Americans.

On his first sight of the Malad River Valley in 1854, Brigham Young didn't think much of the area, but in 1856 he sent 15 families here to try to add another settlement to his Mormon empire. They found good land with plentiful grass for livestock, numerous streams full of fish, and abundant game in the vicinity. They also found Chief Pocatello and his people camped in the area, so they built a fort, but growth escaped the settlement until Henry Peck came to town in 1864 with a plan

to turn the valley's grasslands into a lucrative business. He planned to sell hay to the stage lines and freight wagons passing through the area as feed for their livestock. Peck began encouraging construction and growth in the valley and pushed for the county seat to be moved to Malad. In 1866 he went so far as to travel to Soda Springs, then the county seat, swipe the county records, and bring them back to Malad. History is unclear as to whether he had legislative authority to do so, but from that point on Malad took over as county seat.

Today, the sleepy little town has about 2,000 residents, and you will find basic accommodations and restaurants along the downtown strip.

Recreation

Several reservoirs on the outskirts of town make good fishing holes. **Daniels Reservoir,** 18 miles northwest of town on Bannock Street, offers camping, a dock, and plenty of trout. **St. John Reservoir** is the local kids' pond three miles northwest of town. It's full of bluegill, bass, perch, and rainbow trout. **Crowther Reservoir,** on the edge of town to the north, is stocked with rainbows. **Pleasantview Reservoir,** west of Malad on Lower St. John Road, offers two lakes and fishing for bass, rainbow trout, and tiger muskies.

U.S. 91
Downata Hot Springs

The popular, full-service resort **Downata Hot Springs** (25900 S. Downata Rd., Downey, 208/897-5736, www.downatahotsprings.com, noon-9pm Mon.-Thurs., 11am-9pm Fri.-Sat. Memorial Day-Labor Day, 11am-9pm Fri.-Sat. Labor Day-Memorial Day, $10 ages 3 and up, $1.50 under age 3), 3.5 miles south of Downey along U.S. 91, offers volleyball courts, horseshoe pits, picnic areas, wagon and sleigh rides, cabins, a restaurant, a campground, and more. The big draw in the arid reaches of Bannock County is the water. The resort's pure, 113°F natural hot springs feed a beautiful 300,000-gallon Olympic-size swimming

The Legend of the Iron Door

Thar's gold in them thar hills! Or at least there might be. One tale of treasure—in this case stolen, not mined—persists in the annals of Malad City folklore. Back when the stagecoach ran from Malad to Montana, holdups on the route were common. At some point during this era, three strangers showed up in a Utah town that had just been gutted by fire. The three men found a heavy iron door—off a bank vault, perhaps—among the ashes. They bought the door, loaded it on a wagon, and rode off to the north. It turns out the trio was a gang of stage-robbing desperados. They found a cave somewhere near Malad, installed the iron door over the mouth of the cave, and kept their considerable booty securely locked within.

As legend has it, the three of them had a falling out. Their disagreements led to a gunfight that ended with all three wounded in the cave. One of them got out, locked the other two inside, and crawled to a nearby ranch for help. Alas, the grim reaper was closer than the nearest doctor. Knowing he was on his deathbed, with his dying breath the gunman told the rancher the tale of the iron door. But he died before he revealed the door's location. People have been looking for it ever since.

A few years later, a local rancher by the name of Glipsy Waldron said he found the door, but it was during a storm and he never could relocate it. Others also found the door and tried to mark it for their return; one sheepherder supposedly tied a sheep to the door, in hopes that the animal's bleating would lead him back to it. No such luck.

In more recent times, Malad Valley miner Leo D. Williams and his partner, an Ogden doctor, found what looked like an old, abandoned mineshaft covered by rock and dirt. They had a hunch they might find the remains of the iron door inside, fallen to the bottom of the shaft. After digging a ways down, they found some humanlike bones, which jibed with the story about the two thieves who supposedly died inside the "cave." The doctor loaded the bones into his truck, intending to take them to Weber College for positive identification. But that same week he fell ill and died, and somewhere along the way the bones were lost. The mystery continues.

pool, a whirlpool tub, and a couple of hydrotubes. Summer is prime time.

The resort has RV sites with hookups ($24-30) and tent sites ($22). Other accommodations include a ranch house ($250) that can sleep up to 12, a bunkhouse ($165) with room for six, and some cabins and yurts ($75-150).

Bear River Massacre Site

Two historical signs, a few miles north of Preston on U.S. 91, mark **Bear River Massacre Site,** the spot of the single biggest massacre of Native Americans in U.S. history. This tragic event took place at dawn on January 29, 1863, when U.S. Army Colonel Patrick E. Connor and his California volunteers—assigned to suppress Native American resistance in the area—launched a surprise attack on a village of Northwestern Shoshone. An estimated 400 Shoshone were asleep that morning in Battle Creek Canyon when the thundering hooves of Connor's cavalry descended on the camp. A few people managed to escape by diving into the ice-choked Bear River and floating away; the rest—up to two-thirds of them women and children—were slaughtered. Only 14 bluecoats lost their lives in the one-sided battle.

PRESTON

The Franklin County seat, Preston was founded by Mormon pioneers in 1866. Originally called Worm Creek, it was later renamed for Mormon leader William B. Preston. Today, it's a hub of area farming; primary local crops include grains, hay, beans, and corn, and there are a number of dairy farms in the area.

Several beautiful examples of pioneer-era architecture still grace the town, among them the **Oneida Stake Academy** (151 E. 2nd St. S.), an early Mormon school, and the

Mathias Cowley home (100 S. 100 E.), built for an early Mormon leader.

Napoleon Dynamite

Preston was pushed into the global spotlight in 2004 after the debut of the independent smash hit **Napoleon Dynamite,** filmed around town in 2003. Writer-director Jared Hess, who grew up in Preston, taps into the colloquialisms of this little Mormon burg as seen through the eyes of Napoleon Dynamite (Jon Heder), a quirky, alienated teenager with a dysfunctional home life. Napoleon's language is indicative of the Mormon-influenced towns in the region, with a barrage of softened swear words such as "heck," "dang," and "frickin'." The film has grossed more than $44.5 million worldwide, not bad for a production that only cost $400,000 to make.

Preston Chamber of Commerce (49 N. State St., Preston, 208/852-2403, www. prestonidaho.org) operates a small gift shop where you can buy *Napoleon Dynamite* paraphernalia that includes tote bags, postcards, hats, and T-shirts labeled "Vote for Pedro" and "If You Vote for Me Your Wildest Dreams Will Come True." You can also pick up a map of the sites around town where the movie was filmed. Grab some "tots" at Big J Burgers or play a round of tetherball at the school playground.

Entertainment and Events

Worm Creek Opera House (70 S. State St., Preston, 208/852-0088, www.wormcreek.org) shows current-run movies and hosts live community-theater productions. Summer is prime season for the local thespian troupe.

The **Preston Night Rodeo** (www.prestonrodeo.com) at the end of July features various professional rodeo events and a carnival. Pretty much everyone in town shows up for this annual shindig, which has been going strong for more than 75 years.

Accommodations and Food

Plaza Motel (427 S. U.S. 91, Preston, 208/852-2020, from $52 d) is a well-kept motor inn on the edge of town with 31 nonsmoking guest rooms. Amenities include cable TV and a laundry facility; pets are allowed.

Get your *Napoleon Dynamite* fix at ★ **Big J Burgers** (196 N. Main St., Preston, 208/852-2800, lunch and dinner Mon.-Sat., under $10), a popular fast-food joint with some of the best burgers in the region. You can also get a thick milkshake and a side order of "tots." The restaurant has jumped on the *Napoleon Dynamite* bandwagon by offering its customers merchandise from the movie.

On the way up to the Bear River Range, **Deer Cliff Inn** (2016 N. Deer Cliff Rd., Preston, 208/852-0643, 5pm-9pm Mon.-Sat. June-Aug., 5pm-9pm Thurs.-Sat. May and Sept.-Oct., entrées $11-25) sits right along the road at the base of Deer Cliff. This rustic restaurant dishes up steaks, seafood, and pasta, and live music (small cover charge) gets the place hopping on Friday and Saturday nights. Four cabins ($45) are also available.

Bear River Range Recreation

Two national forest fee campgrounds can be found in the area. Closest to Preston, at lowest elevation, is **Albert Moser Campground** (9 sites, $10), along the Cub River. Farther up the road is the turnoff to **Willow Flat Campground** (51 sites, $12), which occupies a beautiful spot in a steep-walled box canyon. Here the Cub River meanders over riffles and through pools, much to the delight of anglers. From the campground, a hiking trail leads to Willow Spring and Bloomington Lake, and a jeep trail crosses the range east to the Bear Lake region.

Just before the Willow Flat Campground is Thomas Spring, once a popular stop on the Shoshone Indian trail between Cache Valley and Bear Lake. The Shoshone Trail was used as a mail route for many years. In summer it was probably a cushy route for the intrepid mail carriers, but in winter they must have cursed the glue right off their stamps as they slogged the mail over the mountains on snowshoes.

FRANKLIN

Thirteen Mormon pioneers arrived on the banks of the Cub River in April 1860 and immediately went to work establishing a town site. They had come north from Salt Lake City on the advice of Brigham Young and were under the mistaken impression that they were still in Utah. An official boundary survey in 1872 revealed that instead of founding just another Utah town, these pioneers had founded the very first town in Idaho. Later, Franklin enjoyed the first telephone and telegraph connections in Idaho and in 1874 the first railroad line into the state. Many buildings remain from the pioneer days, making for an interesting walking tour for students of history, especially that of the Mormons.

Historic Buildings

The log-cabin-style 1937 **Relic Hall** (113 E. Main St., Franklin, 208/646-2290, 11am-3pm Tues.-Sat. Memorial Day-Labor Day, donation) is what most towns would call a historical museum. Old portraits of the forefathers and mothers line the walls, most glaring down on visitors with dour expressions. Another interesting photo, for Mormon-history buffs, at least, shows the jail in Carthage, Illinois, where Mormon founders Joseph and Hyrum Smith were murdered by an angry mob. Old pioneer tools and artifacts fill the rest of the building.

Next door is a stone building dating from the 1860s that once housed the **FCMI store.** The FCMI (Franklin Cooperative Mercantile Institution) was one of the early branches of the Mormon ZCMI department store chain. Today, the FCMI building holds a collection of pioneer-era furniture.

Just down Main Street is the 1872 **Bishop Hatch House,** also constructed of locally quarried sandstone artfully carved by immigrant English stonemasons. Lorenzo Hill Hatch was the town's second Mormon bishop and its first mayor. Before settling in Franklin he served in the Utah legislature, and after his move to Idaho he became the first Mormon elected to the Idaho legislature. His house in Franklin was the largest in town when it was built to accommodate his three wives and 24 children. The Hatch home also became a popular guesthouse for visitors, including Brigham Young. Some say the house is the finest example of Greek Revival architecture in Idaho.

U.S. 30 to Bear Lake Country

LAVA HOT SPRINGS AND VICINITY

Today, the natural Lava Hot Springs alongside the Portneuf River draw tourists to this small resort town, but long before the first non-natives arrived, the Shoshone and Bannock people gathered here to partake of the waters. The Native American groups may have had their differences, but they considered the waters a gift of the Great Spirit and established a truce in the area so that all could benefit. The Hudspeth Cutoff on the Oregon Trail passed by here too. Perhaps that's one reason why the trail through this stretch became so popular with the weary pioneers. Settlers moved into the area in the 1880s, and the present town was platted in 1911. It was incorporated as Lava Hot Springs in 1915.

Lava Recreation Complex

The biggest attraction in Lava Hot Springs is the state-owned **Lava Recreation Complex** (430 E. Main St., 208/776-5221 or 800/423-8597, www.lavahotsprings.com), which consists of two sites: On the west end of town is the 25-acre **swimming facility** (8am-11pm daily mid-May-Labor Day, $9 over age 11, $8 ages 3-11, $1.50 under age 3) featuring three 86°F pools, one of which is enormous and offers two Olympic-height diving platforms.

Surrounding the pools is a large grassy expanse with volleyball courts and picnic tables. Down at the other end of town is the **hot springs** (9am-10pm daily Oct.-Apr., 8am-11pm daily May-Sept., closed Thanksgiving and Christmas, $9 ages 12-59, $8 ages 3-11 and over age 59, $1.50 under age 3), where several 110°F hot pools sit amid beautiful landscaping in a hollow between the highway and the Portneuf River. The hot pools are sulfur-free and thus have very little odor.

Weekend and holiday passes as well as combined passes to both the Olympic pool and the hot springs are available, as are Monday-Thursday family specials. If you need a swimsuit or towel, you can rent them at either place.

Tubing the Portneuf River

In summer, kids love **inner-tubing down the Portneuf River** from one end of town to the other. The run is short—less than a mile—and takes about 10-15 minutes, depending on how fast the water is flowing. The put-in point is at the convenience store at the east end of town, and the takeout is at the Center Street Bridge just before the swimming pool facility. Some of the many tube-rental companies in town will pick you up at the bottom and

shuttle you back to the top. But by the time you wait for the shuttle bus to arrive and load passengers, you'll probably find it nearly as fast just to walk back. The crux of the run is the "rapids" near downtown. The water is shallow there and flows pretty quickly over a rocky riverbed. You might want to consider renting one of the deluxe tubes with a padded bottom. Numerous tube companies hawk their wares right on the main drag through town. The going rate for a one-person tube is around $4 per hour; larger multi-person tubes are also available.

Historical Museum

The **South Bannock County Historical Center and Museum** (110 E. Main St., Lava Hot Springs, 208/776-5254, noon-5 pm daily year-round except Christmas and Thanksgiving, donation) offers interesting regional-history exhibits. One set of displays chronicles the history of each of the little communities in the area: Swan Lake, Virginia, Inkom, and McCammon, among others.

Accommodations

Lava Spa Motel & RV Park (359 E. Main St., Lava Hot Springs, 208/776-5589, from $49 d) is right across from the state hot

Take a soak at Lava Hot Springs.

springs. In addition to motel rooms, RV sites with full hookups ($30-40) are available. Tents are not permitted.

Riverside Hot Springs Inn (255 E. Portneuf Ave., Lava Hot Springs, 208/776-5504, www.riversidehotspringsinn.com, $59-159) was built in 1914 and restored in 1991. Twelve guest rooms with private baths and four guest rooms with shared baths all include continental breakfast and use of the private indoor or common outdoor hot tubs. You'll find a television and phone in the lobby but not in the guest rooms. Out back is a beautiful patio overlooking the river. All rooms are nonsmoking. **Greystone Manor B&B** (187 S. 2nd W., Lava Hot Springs, 208/776-5959, www.greystonelavahotsprings.com, $140-165) offers five B&B rooms, including a honeymoon suite with a private jetted tub. Amenities include a billiard room and an upright piano. The old 1917 **Royal Hotel** (11 E. Main St., Lava Hot Springs, 208/776-5216) has seven guest rooms ($110-150) with lots of antique furniture.

★ **Lava Hot Springs Inn** (94 E. Portneuf Ave., Lava Hot Springs, 208/776-2530, www.lavahotspringsinn.com, $79-250) occupies an old hospital-sanatorium just upriver from the Center Street Bridge. The inn's grounds feature five hot mineral pools, including a large one for swimming. The pools are every bit as nice as anything at the state complex up the street, so if you stay here you can save the admission price you would've paid at the state's pools. A lap pool and 10 private hot mineral-water tubs are out front. Inside the inn, the decor is casually elegant. Several honeymoon suites—complete with in-room jetted tubs—make for an ultimate romantic getaway. A full breakfast is included in the rates. Some less-expensive rooms with shared bathrooms are available too, as are larger family suites, massage therapy, and complete spa services.

Camping

⌐ch Inn Motel & Campground (9611 Lava Hot Springs, 208/776-9917) offers 25 RV sites with full hookups ($30-50) and 100 tent sites ($20-30). Amenities at the campground include showers, restrooms, horseshoe pits, volleyball courts, picnic areas with tables and barbecue grills, and a nice stretch of riverfront for fishing.

River's Edge Campground (101 W. Portneuf Ave., Lava Hot Springs, 208/776-5209), down by the river near the swimming pool complex, has 87 RV sites with full hookups ($40-45) and tent sites ($25). Shower and laundry facilities are available, and pets are allowed.

Food

The attractive restaurant at the **Royal Hotel** (11 E. Main St., Lava Hot Springs, 208/776-5216, lunch and dinner daily) serves good pizza, calzones, and pasta dishes galore. Also expect to find 16 beers on tap, cocktails, and wines by the glass.

Watering holes in town include the **Wagon Wheel Lounge** (225 E. Main St., Lava Hot Springs, 208/776-5224), which has a big beer garden with horseshoe pits and offers live music on weekends, and **Blue Moon Bar & Grill** (89 S. 1st St. E., Lava Hot Springs, 208/776-5077), where you can grab a burger and a beer and shoot some stick with the locals.

Information

For more information about the town, contact **Lava Hot Springs Chamber of Commerce** (208/776-5500, www.lavahotsprings.org).

SODA SPRINGS

The Caribou County seat, Soda Springs is named for the numerous naturally carbonated springs that well up in the vicinity. The area was something of a novelty to pioneers, who named one of the water holes Beer Springs for its fizzy-salty taste and dubbed another Steamboat Springs because it sounded like a churning steam engine. Both these springs are now submerged under Alexander Reservoir. Also beneath the reservoir lies the original Soda Springs town site, which grew around the Army fort established in 1863 by Colonel Patrick Connor of Bear River Massacre infamy. The present town didn't take hold, however, until Brigham Young visited and supported the establishment of a new town site at the current location.

The Geyser

In November 1937, a drilling crew probing for hot water to supply a proposed municipal swimming pool inadvertently tapped into a pressurized underground chamber of geothermal water. They capped off the resulting geyser, and now it's on a timer, erupting every hour on the hour. The stream of hot carbonated water shoots 150 feet into the air and runs down over a small, mineralized mound at its base. Pathways lead to various viewpoints all around the site, which is on the west side of downtown, at the west end of 1st Street South.

Hooper Spring

One of the naturally effervescent springs that gave the town its name is **Hooper Spring** (3rd St. E.). Oregon Trail pioneers stopped here to partake of the waters, and folks still come from all over to drink the water right out of the spring, claiming it helps their arthritis or other ailments. The city built a gazebo over the spring itself and a park around it. The park has basketball courts, horseshoe pits, picnic sites, and a playground.

City Parks

Corrigan Park (Main St. and 1st St. S.) downtown showcases two old locomotives. The Dinky Engine was used to haul supplies during the construction of Alexander Dam. When the water began to back up into the reservoir, the little engine was trapped and drowned at the bottom of the lake. It remained there until 1976, when the reservoir was drained for repairs. The Union Pacific Railroad retrieved and restored the Dinky and donated it to the city. The Galloping Goose carried mine workers and ore between Soda Springs and Conda from 1922 until 1936. The

park also offers tennis and basketball courts and lots of grass.

Oregon Trail Public Park and Marina (8am-10pm daily, free), west of town on Alexander Reservoir, offers a dock, a boat ramp, and picnic shelters. On the east edge of town, **Kelly Park** is a large, open recreation area with baseball diamonds, tennis courts, a fishing pond, and jogging paths.

Recreation

Oregon Trail Country Club (2525 U.S. 30, Soda Springs, 208/547-2204, closed winter, $11 for 9 holes, $18 for 18 holes), just west of town, offers a special thrill to golfers who also happen to be history buffs. The nine-hole, par-36 course surrounds the old Oregon Trail; wagon ruts can be seen on the course's south side between holes one, eight, and nine. The course managers don't mind if you walk from the clubhouse down between the fairways to take a look, but be careful not to get in the way of a drive.

Trail Canyon Park N' Ski Area, 12 miles northeast of Soda Springs on Trail Canyon Road, offers 10 miles of trails in five loops as well as a warming hut. The trails are groomed periodically and are suitable for all ability levels.

Accommodations and Food

Call it a night at the ★ **Largilliere Carriage House** (30 W. 2nd St. S., Soda Springs, 208/547-3663, www.largillierecarriagehouse. com), a recently restored early-19th-century home that features four bed-and-breakfast-style rooms ($79-99) with a shared kitchen and bathroom. Wake up to a big country breakfast before heading out to explore the Oregon Trail.

For some of the best Mexican eats in these parts, try **El Toro** (651 U.S. 30, Soda Springs, 208/547-4720, 11am-8pm Mon.-Fri, $7-14) near downtown. Here you can choose from a menu that includes a multitude of tacos, burritos, enchiladas, tamales, and spicy seafood dishes. And, of course, there are plenty of Mexican beers to extinguish the fire.

Forest Service Rentals

The **Soda Springs ranger station** (410 Hooper Ave., Soda Springs, 208/547-4356, or make reservations at www.recreation.gov) handles rentals for three guard stations (year-round, $35 per night) in the Caribou-Targhee National Forest. Northwest of Grays Lake National Wildlife Refuge, 45 miles northeast of Soda Springs, **Caribou Guard Station** lies along McCoy Creek in Caribou Basin. It sleeps up to eight people. **Johnson Guard Station** guards the Webster Range at the upper end of Upper Valley and sleeps six. And just two miles from the Wyoming border, **Stump Creek Guard Station** sleeps four and is reached most easily through Afton, Wyoming. All three are equipped with beds and mattresses as well as propane lights, heaters, and stoves.

HIGHWAY 34 TO WYOMING

Heading north out of Soda Springs, Highway 34 runs past Blackfoot Reservoir to Grays Lake, then makes a 90-degree turn east to Freedom, Wyoming. It's big, open country. Blackfoot Reservoir has a small fishing-village scene, but Grays Lake can be all but deserted, even in the peak summer travel season.

Grays Lake National Wildlife Refuge

The remote 20,000-acre **Grays Lake National Wildlife Refuge** (74 Grays Lake Rd., Wayan, 208/237-6615)—actually a large marsh rather than a lake—has the world's largest concentration of nesting sandhill cranes as well as a few rare and endangered whooping cranes. The whooping crane is the tallest bird in North America, standing nearly five feet from head to toe.

The perimeter road encircling the refuge makes a scenic drive. In addition to cranes, you'll likely see ducks, geese, white pelicans, herons, egrets, Franklin's gulls, grebes, bitterns, and phalaropes. Nonwinged species in the area include moose, elk, mule deer, muskrats, and badgers.

Refuge headquarters along the southeast side of the refuge has a **visitors center** (daily Apr. 1-Nov. 15) with interpretive exhibits, including a mounted whooping crane. A short road leads from the headquarters up to a nearby hilltop, where you'll find an observation point equipped in summer with a free spotting scope. Hiking and cross-country skiing are permitted on the northern half of the refuge October-March.

Camping

Up the Blackfoot River at a point called the Narrows is the U.S. Forest Service **Mill Canyon Campground** (10 sites, $8). It's unremarkable except for its proximity to the river for fishing.

Getting to the remote Forest Service **Gravel Creek Campground** (12 sites, $8) is definitely worth the extra effort. After climbing into the Grays Range, you'll enter a lush forest filled with a veritable arboretum of tree species. Catch a trail to the top of Henry Peak (8,319 feet) or just nap alongside Gravel Creek. To get to the campground, take Wayan Loop off Highway 34 and turn south up Forest Road 191.

MONTPELIER AND VICINITY

According to local legend, which some locals question, famous desperado **Butch Cassidy** and his Wild Bunch gang rode into Montpelier on August 13, 1896, and relieved the local bank of some $16,500 in gold, silver, and currency. The deputy sheriff on duty couldn't find his horse, so he grabbed a nearby bicycle and rode off after the gang as they headed up Montpelier Canyon. Needless to say, his pursuit efforts were futile. One of the Hole-in-the-Wall Gang, Bob Meeks, was eventually caught and jailed for his part in the robbery, but Butch and Sundance escaped scot-free for this one. The bank building that the gang held up still stands, but it's now a print shop.

National Oregon Trail and California Trail Center

The **National Oregon Trail and California Trail Center** (320 N. 4th St., Montpelier, 208/847-3800, www.oregontrailcenter.org, one-hour tours 9am-5pm daily May-Sept., $11 adults, $10 over age 59, $8 ages 8-15, $4 ages 4-7) houses interactive exhibits on life along the pioneer trails, among them a computer-controlled covered wagon. This interpretive center also offers regular living-history programs.

In the basement of the center is the **Bear Lake Rails and Trails Museum** (9am-5pm Mon.-Sat. May-Sept., free), offering some great regional-history displays. Among the topics covered are the wild and woolly Bear Lake Rendezvous of 1827; nearby Big Hill, the toughest grade on the Oregon Trail up to this point; and the Native American history of Bear Lake Valley. Artifacts on display include many items brought across the plains on wagon trains by the area's early settlers.

Accommodations and Food

Montpelier keeps several corporate hotels along the highway near downtown. But if you want to save some bucks, the town has a few locally owned and operated motels that are extremely affordable. One good pick is the **Park Motel** (745 Washington St., Montpelier, 208/847-1911, from $45 d), a surprisingly clean motor inn with 25 nonsmoking guest rooms with cable TV.

Craving breakfast? Head on over to the ★ **Ranch Hand Trail Stop** (23200 U.S. 30, Montpelier, 208/847-1180, open 24/7), about a mile north of downtown on U.S. 30, for corned beef hash and eggs, fat omelets, and tall stacks of blueberry pancakes. Breakfast gets served around the clock at this friendly truck stop, and your coffee cup won't stay empty for long. The restaurant also serves excellent burgers and homespun dinner entrées, like chicken-fried steak with mashed spuds and country gravy.

Information

To learn more about the area, contact **Bear Lake/Montpelier Chamber of Commerce** (925 Washington St., Montpelier, 208/847-0067, www.bearlakechamber.org), which stocks pamphlets and other literature about fun stuff to do in these parts. For Caribou-Targhee National Forest recreation information, stop by the **Montpelier Ranger District** (431 Clay St., Montpelier, 208/847-0375).

On to Wyoming

Heading east out of Montpelier on U.S. 89 North, you'll soon come to the turnoff to Montpelier Reservoir. Anglers can try their luck either in the reservoir, which doesn't allow motorboats, or just downstream from the dam, where clean and clear Montpelier Creek meanders through verdant meadows, in and out of thickets, over riffles, and through cool pools. The U.S. Forest Service's primitive Elbow Campground is just off the highway, right below the dam. Continuing east, you'll crest Geneva Summit (6,938 feet) and coast down the other side to the state line. From there it's another 30 miles to Afton, Wyoming.

U.S. 89 TO BEAR LAKE

Nonnatives first laid eyes on Bear Lake in 1812 when a party of trappers passed this way on a return trip from Astoria, Oregon. Trappers played a leading role in the area's history, and two of the annual fur-trading rendezvous were held here in 1826 and 1827.

Half in Idaho, half in Utah, Bear Lake is 20 miles long and seven miles wide. Dissolved limestone particles suspended in the water give the lake a surreal turquoise-blue color, especially intense at sunrise. Rainbow and cutthroat trout tease anglers, while another fish, the sardine-like Bonneville cisco, is found nowhere else in the world. Besides fishing, popular summer pastimes on the lake include sailing and powerboating. The nearest boat rentals are at the Bear Lake State Recreation

Area marina in Garden City, Utah, about three miles across the state line.

Ovid

On the way down to Bear Lake from Montpelier, you'll pass through the small town of **Ovid,** settled by Mormons in 1864. The town lies at the junction of Highway 36, which heads west to Preston, and U.S. 89, which continues south to Bear Lake and the Utah border. Twelve miles northwest of Ovid off Highway 36, the U.S. Forest Service **Emigration Campground** (23 sites, $10) occupies a delightful spot high on the east side of the Bear River Range at an elevation of 7,500 feet. Wildflowers are abundant here, and hiking trails lead to other parts of the range.

Paris

Paris was founded in 1863 by 30 Mormon families who thought they were still in Utah Territory, as was the case in nearby Franklin.

Presiding majestically over Main Street downtown is the red sandstone **Paris Stake Tabernacle,** a Romanesque Mormon temple designed by one of Brigham Young's sons. It was built 1884-1889 with stone quarried 18 miles away and hauled by horse cart to the site, where immigrant Swiss stonemasons carved the stunning edifice. Tours of the tabernacle are offered daily in summer. If you're hungry, go across the street to **The Paris Grill** (48 S. Main St., Paris, 208/945-1100, 9:30am-7pm Mon.-Sat.), a little diner that's known for its burgers, calzones, and house-baked pies.

Paris Springs Campground (12 sites, $12-22) is six miles up into the mountains west of town in a quiet spot near the namesake springs. No mere trickle, these springs gush profusely out of the ground at the head of a steep-walled box canyon. Ice-cave diehards can take the lower fork in the canyon and continue a few miles up a gravel road to the small **Paris Ice Cave.**

Bear Lake National Wildlife Refuge

The 18,000-acre **Bear Lake National Wildlife Refuge,** most of it marsh, is one of the largest Canada goose nesting grounds in the western United States and home to the country's largest nesting population of white-faced ibis. Scads of ducks pass through in spring and fall, and deer and moose roam the refuge as well.

Spring is the best time to view the greatest numbers of species. Most migratory species begin arriving in April and begin leaving in August. Access restrictions apply for much of the year; contact the refuge headquarters (370 Webster St., Montpelier, 208/847-1757) for complete regulations. The best viewing area is in the refuge's Salt Meadow Unit at the northern end. To get here, take Paris-Dingle Road east out of Paris and turn south just after crossing the canal. The canal road leads to a boat-launching ramp and several parking areas.

★ Bear Lake State Park

As Idaho's state parks go, **Bear Lake State Park** (208/945-2325) is pretty humble. You won't find interpretive information, campfire programs, or nature trails. The key attraction is beautiful Bear Lake itself. The park has two units: a day-use beach and boat ramp along the north shore, and a campground on the east shore. The normal state park motor vehicle entry fee of $5 applies. **East Beach Campground** ($14, $18 with electricity hookup) has 150 campsites.

St. Charles and Vicinity

For what it's worth, Gutzon Borglum, the painter and sculptor who carved Mount Rushmore, was born in **St. Charles** in 1867. Recreation opportunities abound in St. Charles Canyon, which climbs into the Bear River Range west of town. A paved road (Forest Rd. 412) leads all the way up to **Minnetonka Cave** (435/245-4422, tours every half hour 10am-5:30pm daily June-Labor Day, $8 adults, $6 ages 6-15, free under age 6, family rates available), one of the few federal show caves in the country. Those who have traveled in southern Idaho and expect every "cave" site to be a lava tube are in for a surprise, because this is an honest-to-goodness limestone cave, complete with stalagmites and stalactites. A half-mile guided tour takes you deep inside, up and down some 448 steps, and through nine rooms with formations with names like "the Seven Dwarfs" and "the Devil's Office." Bring a sweater; the cave is a constant 40°F.

On the way to the cave, you'll pass a string of U.S. Forest Service campgrounds administered by the **Montpelier Ranger District** (431 Clay St., Montpelier, 208/847-0375). First, lowest, and least interesting is **St. Charles Campground** (6 sites, $23),

followed by **Davis Canyon Campground** ($8), a primitive and unmarked site down on the creek where the main road climbs above the creek for a stretch. A spur leads down to the water. If you don't need a lot of amenities, this is an excellent place to spend a few nights. Next up is **Porcupine Campground** ($10), right on St. Charles Creek, where a newly added loop among lodgepole pines and aspens brings the total number of sites to 16. Continuing higher up the canyon, you'll come to **Cloverleaf Campground** ($10), which offers 20 sites in three cloverleaf loops near a trail that climbs up to Minnetonka Cave.

Idaho Falls and Vicinity

Idaho Falls, the Bonneville County seat, owes a great deal of its economy to the Idaho National Laboratory (INL), the U.S. Department of Energy's top nuclear research facility deep in the desert about 30 miles from town. You'll see a regular stream of innocuous white tour buses carrying the site's engineers and physicists to and from work and home.

Idaho Falls (population 57,000) was here long before INL, so it has an interesting mix of farmers and nuclear scientists. The two groups seem to coexist well enough. In any case, you'll find just enough culture—including the state's largest museum—to keep you entertained, along with plenty of that down-home charm that makes Idaho so great.

The city is not much to look at in terms of architecture, but there are a handful of old buildings that boast eye appeal, and an effort is under way to revitalize the downtown core to make it more attractive to tourists and denizens alike. Future plans include a large water feature by the Snake River Greenbelt that will be both visual and recreational (swimming in summer, ice skating in winter), a riverbank amphitheater for live concerts, and a grand gateway sign at Memorial Drive and B Street,

letting people know they have entered the historic downtown district. A later phase of the urban renewal project will include a walking bridge across the falls, connecting both sides of the river for pedestrian traffic.

SIGHTS
The Falls
The falls at Idaho Falls were just rapids until 1910, when work began on the hydroelectric power plant just south of the Broadway Bridge. The diversion dam resulted in the cascade you see today. The falls may not be natural, but they're still a pleasant sight and sound. A paved pedestrian trail winds along the riverbank right by the falls, making for scenic jogging, strolling, or picnicking.

★ Mormon Temple
The big Moroni-topped wedding-cake structure on the city's finest riverfront property is the **Idaho Falls Temple of the Mormon Church** (1000 Memorial Dr., Idaho Falls, 208/523-4504). The temple offers a place for non-Mormons to learn about the prevalent religion in southeast Idaho. A **visitors center** (9am-9pm daily, free) has displays and videos about the church.

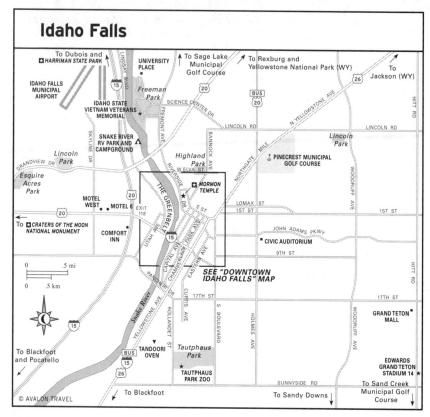

Idaho Falls

Museum of Idaho

The recently remodeled and expanded **Museum of Idaho** (200 N. Eastern Ave., Idaho Falls, 208/522-1400, www.museumofidaho.org, 9am-8pm Mon.-Tues., 9am-5pm Wed.-Sat., $8 adults, $7 seniors, $6 ages 4-17, free under age 4) has triple the space it did before, making it the largest museum in the state. A full-size fleshed-out replica of a Columbian mammoth is the centerpiece attraction, but you'll also find an informative exhibit showing Eagle Rock (Idaho Falls's original name) as it may have looked on a typical day in 1891. In addition to the permanent collection, the museum also books a full schedule of national touring exhibits.

Art Museum of Eastern Idaho

When you're out strolling the greenbelt,

make sure to stop by the **Art Museum of Eastern Idaho** (300 S. Capital Ave., Idaho Falls, 208/524-7777, www.theartmuseum.org, 11am-5pm Tues.-Sat., $4 adults, $2 ages 6-18). In addition to traveling exhibits and works by local adult and child artists, the museum/gallery hosts events throughout the year, like a holiday show the first weekend in December and a spring show in April.

Historic Architecture

Several of the city's original buildings are still standing. An exploratory stroll through downtown yields views of the 1917 **Hotel Idaho** (482 Constitution Way), which was in use until 1979; the 1918 **Underwood Hotel** (347 Constitution Way), built for early Idaho Falls entrepreneur Jennie Underwood; and the 1915 **Shane Building** (381 Shoup Ave.),

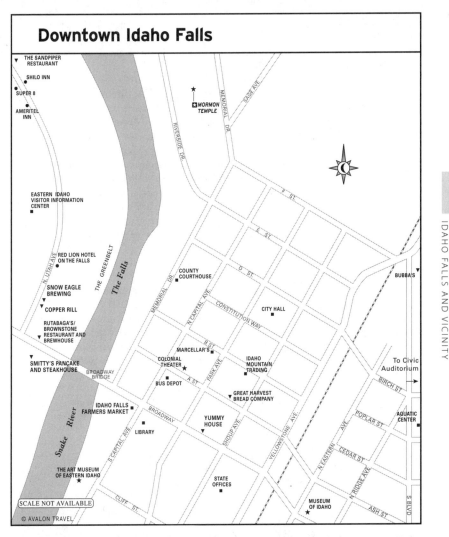

Downtown Idaho Falls

THE SANDPIPER RESTAURANT

SHILO INN

SUPER 8

AMERITEL INN

MORMON TEMPLE

RIVERSIDE DR.

MEMORIAL DR.

SAGE AVE.

F ST.

E ST.

D ST.

EASTERN IDAHO VISITOR INFORMATION CENTER

THE GREENBELT

The Falls

RED LION HOTEL ON THE FALLS

N. UTAH AVE.

SNOW EAGLE BREWING

COPPER RILL

RUTABAGA'S/ BROWNSTONE RESTAURANT AND BREWHOUSE

SMITTY'S PANCAKE AND STEAKHOUSE

COUNTY COURTHOUSE

MEMORIAL DR.

N. CAPITAL AVE.

CONSTITUTION WAY

CITY HALL

BUBBA'S

MARCELLAR'S

COLONIAL THEATER

BUS DEPOT

B ST.

A ST.

PARK AVE.

IDAHO MOUNTAIN TRADING

GREAT HARVEST BREAD COMPANY

To Civic Auditorium

BIRCH ST.

POPLAR ST.

N. EASTERN AVE.

AQUATIC CENTER

BROADWAY BRIDGE

BROADWAY

IDAHO FALLS FARMERS MARKET

S. CAPITAL AVE.

LIBRARY

YUMMY HOUSE

SHOUP AVE.

YELLOWSTONE AVE.

CEDAR ST.

N. RIDGE AVE.

S. BLVD.

Snake River

THE ART MUSEUM OF EASTERN IDAHO

STATE OFFICES

CLIFF ST.

MUSEUM OF IDAHO

ASH ST.

SCALE NOT AVAILABLE

© AVALON TRAVEL

a Renaissance Revival retail space with terracotta accents.

Across the railroad tracks on the east side of Yellowstone Avenue is the **Ridge Avenue Historic District,** once the city's prime residential neighborhood, which has Queen Anne, craftsman, and Colonial Revival houses surrounded by expansive lawns and large maple trees. Many are listed on the National Register of Historic Places. Among the most impressive: the 1896 A. D. Morrison house (258 Walnut St.); the 1916-1917 Tudor Gothic Trinity Methodist Church (237 N. Water Ave.); and the 1910 Fuller House (101 N. Placer Ave.), which once did double duty as a home and a hospital.

The city publishes detailed walking-tour guides to both the downtown and Ridge Avenue districts. Pick up copies at the **Eastern Idaho Visitor Information Center** (425 N. Capital Ave., Idaho Falls, 208/523-1010).

RECREATION
Snake River Greenbelt

One of the best ways to spend an hour or more in Idaho Falls is a stroll along the city's **Snake River Greenbelt,** a 29-acre park lining both sides of the Snake River. This scenic 2.3-mile pathway is popular with joggers, speed-walkers, and bicyclists, not to mention squadrons of ducks and Canada geese. In winter, the snow-covered landscape takes on a contemplative air, and the greenbelt becomes a whitebelt suitable for snowshoeing or cross-country skiing.

Tautphaus Park

Tautphaus Park (off Rollandet St.) is undeniably the crown jewel of the city's park system. Here you will find acres and acres of grassy expanses, an abundance of trees and flowers, a fountain, baseball fields, tennis courts, and a playground.

In addition, the **Idaho Falls Zoo at Tautphaus** (Rogers St. and Carnival Way, Idaho Falls, 208/612-8552, 9am-5pm daily Memorial Day-Labor Day, limited hours Apr.-May and Sept., closed Oct.-Mar., $7 adults, $5.50 over age 61, $4 ages 4-12, free under age 4) houses more than 250 animals in re-created natural habitats simulating the respective creatures' home turf. Among the rare and endangered species on display are snow leopards, red ruffed lemurs, and Amur tigers.

Other Parks and Recreation Facilities

At the west end of Science Center Drive at the river, 75-acre **Freeman Park** offers plenty of open space along with baseball diamonds, a disc golf course, picnic tables and shelters, a playground, and the **Idaho State Vietnam Veterans Memorial,** a stainless-steel sculpture engraved with the names of Idaho soldiers killed or missing in action in the Vietnam War.

The city's **Recreation Center** (520 Memorial Dr., Idaho Falls, 208/612-8480) offers racquetball courts, basketball courts, a weight room, showers, and lockers. The **Wes Deist Aquatic Center** (149 7th St., Idaho Falls, 208/612-8111) provides an indoor lap pool, hot tubs, and an outside wading pool open in summer. Call for hours and rates. You'll also find a municipal pool at **Reinhart Park** (1055 Washburn Ave., Idaho Falls, 208/612-8480).

Climbers in need of some good 5.11 can head to the **YMCA Climbing Gym** (755 S. Capital Ave., Idaho Falls, 208/528-8610), an

Mormon Temple in Idaho Falls

indoor facility with 6,500 square feet of climbing walls. Shoe and harness rentals are available. Call for current hours, which change monthly, but it's generally open most afternoons and evenings except for Sundays.

For more information on the city's municipal parks and recreation facilities, contact **Idaho Falls Parks and Recreation** (208/612-8480).

Spectator Sports

The **Idaho Falls Chukars** (tickets 208/522-8363), a Pioneer League team affiliated with the Kansas City Royals, play summer evenings at Melaleuca Field in Highland Park (Bannock Ave. and W. Elva St.).

Outfitters

To buy or rent backpacking, climbing, skiing, and skating gear, stop by and see the friendly folks at **Idaho Mountain Trading** (474 Shoup Ave., Idaho Falls, 208/523-6679, www.idahomountaintrading.com).

ENTERTAINMENT AND EVENTS

The renovated **Colonial Theater/Willard Arts Center** complex (450 A St., Idaho Falls, 208/522-0471, www.idahofallsarts.org), the beating heart of the city's art scene, hosts live shows on a weekly basis, including many touring acts. It's also the home of the Idaho Falls Arts Council, which can fill you in on all the arts events around town.

Mid-April brings the annual **East Idaho Fly Tying Expo** (www.srcexpo.com), with demonstrations by more than 100 top tiers. The website is packed with info both on the event and the region's great angling opportunities. The **Mountain Brewers Beer Festival** (www.northamericanbrewers.org) bubbles forth in early June at the Sandy Downs Rodeo Grounds, featuring more than 80 breweries in what has become the largest beer festival in the region. It is ironic, given that Idaho Falls is strong Mormon country. Teetotalers will find plenty of handcrafted root beers on tap too.

ACCOMMODATIONS

Idaho Falls is inundated with corporate hotels. The city desperately needs bed-and-breakfast inns, guesthouses, and hostels, the latter of which would be great for sojourners heading to and from the Yellowstone and Teton areas. But for now, you'll be staying at a chain establishment if you plan on spending the night here.

$50-100

Out by I-15 Exit 118, you'll find two motels with reasonable rates. **Motel 6** (1448 W. Broadway, Idaho Falls, 208/522-0112, from $65 d) offers 79 standard guest rooms with cable TV. **Motel West** (1540 W. Broadway, Idaho Falls, 208/522-1112, from $46 d) is another good budget choice, with an indoor pool and an on-site restaurant.

Most of the city's chain lodgings cozy up to each other on Lindsay Boulevard, along the west side of the Snake River near the falls. From south to north on the riverbank side of Lindsay, you'll find **Red Lion Hotel on the Falls** (475 River Pkwy., Idaho Falls, 208/523-8000, from $95 d); **Best Western Driftwood Inn** (575 River Pkwy., Idaho Falls, 208/523-2242, from $79 d); ★ **Shilo Inn** (780 Lindsay Blvd., 208/523-0088, from $79 d); and **Best Western CottonTree Inn** (900 Lindsay Blvd., Idaho Falls, 208/523-6000, from $69 d).

At all of these lodgings, you can get riverview guest rooms (worth the extra bucks, as the view in the opposite direction is less than exciting), and you'll be able to walk right out the door and onto the greenbelt for an evening stroll. The cylindrical-shaped Red Lion is the tallest and nearest to the falls, while the Shilo Inn probably has the best location and range of amenities.

CAMPING AND RVING

Snake River RV Park and Campground (1440 Lindsay Blvd., Idaho Falls, 208/523-3362) lies north of U.S. 20 in an industrial area dominated by a General Mills seed plant. But a long driveway and abundant trees provide a sufficient buffer against the sights and sounds out on the boulevard. Amenities, some seasonal, include a heated pool and jetted tub, a playground, and a camp store. The campground maintains 40 tent sites ($25), 120 RV sites with full hookups ($34-38), and 10 camping cabins ($40).

FOOD
Upscale Yet Casual

In a city riddled with corporate restaurants, local foodies were ecstatic when ★ **Copper Rill** (415 River Pkwy., Idaho Falls, 208/529-5800, www.copperrill.com, 5pm-9pm Mon., 11am-2pm and 5pm-9pm Tues.-Fri., 5pm-9pm Sat., entrées $12-28) debuted in 2013 near the Red Lion. Housed in an attractive brick building, this contemporary eatery boasts a stylish, comfortable dining room and a menu that bounces around the globe for inspiration. Start off with appetizers like pan-seared crab cakes with dill beurre blanc and curried chicken skewers. Larger plates include toothsome butternut squash ravioli and grilled flatiron steak smothered with sautéed wild mushrooms. Oh yes, there's a thoughtful wine list to boot. The restaurant also offers Sunday brunch (10am-2pm), where you will find a tasty egg frittata with bell pepper and Italian sausage, Danish-style pancakes with berry compote, and other Euro-inspired breakfast dishes.

The **Sandpiper Restaurant** (750 Lindsay Blvd., Idaho Falls, 208/524-3344, 4pm-10pm Mon.-Sat., entrées $13-28) is part of the small southern Idaho chain that offers consistently good food and atmosphere in a traditional, casually elegant setting. Entrées include chicken Oscar, seafood fettuccine, St. Louis-inspired pork ribs, and slow-roasted prime rib served with a big Idaho baked potato. The place makes a pretty mean martini too.

International Cuisine

For nose-clearing curries and garlicky naan bread, check out **Tandoori Oven** (3204 S. 25th St. E., Idaho Falls, 208/522-8263, 11am-2:30pm and 4:30pm-9:30pm Mon.-Sat., $6-14), a northern Indian and Paki restaurant in a strip mall on the east side of town. Enjoy a plate of properly charred chicken tikka masala and a frosty bottle of Indian beer. Or turn up the heat with an order of lamb vindaloo, a spicy red curry served with basmati rice. The meatless crowd will find plenty of options, like veggie curries, stewed lentils, and the likes.

If you're in the mood for kung pao chicken, fill your tummy at **Yummy House** (354 W. Broadway St., Idaho Falls, 208/524-6188, lunch and dinner Mon.-Sat., $7-13) in the historic downtown district. This storefront Chinese joint (think restaurant scene in *A Christmas Story*) offers a large menu of standard offerings, like egg rolls, lo mein, fried rice, egg drop soup, honey sesame chicken, wok-seared noodles, and roasted duck—minus the head. Plus, the restaurant delivers to most parts of town.

Barbecue and Brew

Got a hankering for barbecue? **Bubba's** (118 E. 1st St., Idaho Falls, 208/523-2822, lunch and dinner daily, $7-16) is the place for you then. Here you can get beef brisket, saucy baby back ribs, and pulled pork sandwiches, dished up with typical sides. For craft beers and inventive pub fare, stop by **Snow Eagle Brewing and Grill** (455 River Pkwy., Idaho Falls, 208/557-0455, www.snoweaglebrewing.com, lunch and dinner Mon.-Sat., $8-17) near Copper Rill. It's a clean, spacious brewpub with a menu that pairs well with the handcrafted flagship and seasonal ales. Expect to find burgers, grilled bratwurst, Baja-style fish tacos, and pizzas. Snow Eagle shares a space with its sister restaurant, **Wasabi Sushi Bar,** which supplements the brewpub menu with raw and hot Japanese items.

Breakfast and Coffee

The best breakfast in town can be found at ★ **Smitty's Pancake & Steak House** (645 W. Broadway St., Idaho Falls, 208/523-6450, 6am-9pm daily, breakfast dishes $5-10), an old-school diner near the Broadway Bridge. The booths are big, and your waitress will probably call you "honey" at this venerable eatery. The large menu features classic egg breakfasts, like omelets and scrambles, waffles, and pancakes galore. The banana pancakes and bacon-pocked waffles are noteworthy picks. At night, the restaurant shifts into dinner mode with homespun offerings like chicken-fried steak and grilled pork chops and applesauce, which you can also get in the morning with eggs.

Open your eyelids at the **Villa Coffeehouse** (344 Park Ave., Idaho Falls, 208/524-8882, 7am-5pm Mon.-Thurs., 7am-6pm Fri.-Sat., 9am-4pm Sun.). This comfy hangout downtown makes the tastiest espresso drinks in these parts. Relax on one of the overstuffed couches and enjoy a double latte. The coffeehouse also serves muffins, scones, and quiche in the morning, and later in the day you can get sandwiches and soups.

Groceries

The **Idaho Falls Farmers Market** (9am-1pm Apr.-Oct.) takes place downtown on Saturdays in the Key Bank parking lot (501 W. Broadway St.). Here you can score fresh veggies and fruit, baked goods, local meats, and prepared food items.

An imbiber's oasis in dry southeast Idaho, **MarCellar's Vintage Wines & Brews** (431 Park Ave., Idaho Falls, 208/523-0503) stocks a wide selection of premium wines and handcrafted beers from all around the world, with an emphasis on regional microbrews. This is a good place to load up the cooler before heading out into the wilds.

INFORMATION AND SERVICES

The **Eastern Idaho Visitor Information Center** (425 N. Capital Ave., Idaho Falls, 208/523-1010, www.idahofallschamber.com) offers interpretive displays about the region, sells related books and maps, and stocks free literature on everything from accommodations to recreation opportunities.

The headquarters of the **Caribou-Targhee National Forest** and the **Idaho Falls Bureau of Land Management** field office (both at 1405 Hollipark Dr., Idaho Falls, 208/524-7500) can provide additional recreational information about the area.

GETTING THERE

Idaho Falls Regional Airport (IDA, 2140 N. Skyline Dr., 208/612-8224) is served by **Delta** (800/221-1212), with daily flights to Salt Lake City, and **United** (800/864-8331), which offers weekend flights to Denver. **Allegiant Air** (702/505-8888) has Monday and Friday flights to and from Las Vegas.

Car rental agencies at the airport include **Avis** (208/522-4225), **Budget** (208/522-8800), and **Hertz** (208/529-3101).

I-15 NORTH TO MONTANA
Waterfowl Sanctuaries

As I-15 beelines north to the Montana border, it passes two separate preserves that serve as aqueous stepping-stones for migratory waterfowl on the Pacific Flyway. In spring and fall, the preserves draw vast numbers of snow geese and Canada geese; mallard, gadwall, and ring-necked ducks; green-winged and cinnamon teal; trumpeter swans; double-crested cormorants; herons; egrets; sandhill cranes; Franklin's gulls; white-faced ibises; and many other species. Numerous extras with important roles include shorebirds, songbirds, and raptors. These refuges are open year-round. Camping, fishing, and boating are permitted subject to seasonal restrictions; inquire at the respective headquarters.

Twenty miles north of Idaho Falls is **Market Lake Wildlife Management Area** (806 N. 2900 E., Roberts, 208/228-3131), a 5,000-acre area surrounding 1,700 acres of spring-fed marsh. A map and birder's checklist are available at the wildlife management area (WMA) headquarters. To reach the headquarters, take I-15 Exit 135 at Roberts and head east to Road 2880 East. Turn north on 2880 East and drive through the town of Roberts. At the fork in the road, bear right to Road 800 North and follow signs to the headquarters.

The huge **Camas National Wildlife Refuge** protects more than 10,000 acres of waterfowl-filled wetlands. The two largest lakes on the refuge cover 600 and 700 acres. In addition, Camas Creek winds through the area. During peak spring and fall migration periods, you might see up to 100,000 ducks. The birder's checklist for the refuge includes 177 species. Information and a map of the refuge are available at the **headquarters** (2150 E. 2350 N., Hamer, 208/662-5423). To get here, take the Hamer exit from I-15 into the town of Hamer, and then turn north on the old highway. Go three miles north, then two miles west to the headquarters.

Dubois

Dubois lies in high-desert terrain at 5,149 feet. Some 20 miles to the north, the Centennial and Beaverhead Mountains form the Continental Divide. Northwest of Dubois, Medicine Lodge Road follows Medicine Lodge Creek ever higher into the high peaks, eventually cresting at Medicine Lodge Pass (also called Bannock Pass) on the Montana border. Up Medicine Lodge Road, the U.S. Forest Service **Webber Creek Campground** (4 sites, free) lies at a lofty altitude of 7,000 feet. The trail leaving from the trailhead here ascends alongside the creek up into the Beaverheads along the Continental Divide. Mountaineers can make their way over to the scenic Italian Peaks area for a Class 2 ascent of Scott Peak (11,393 feet), the highest of the Beaverheads. To reach the campground, turn west off Medicine Lodge Road on Forest Road 196 at Edie Creek Ranch and follow the road about five miles to the end. For more information, stop by the Caribou-Targhee National Forest's **Dubois Ranger District** (98 N. Oakley St., Dubois, 208/374-5422).

Spencer

As soon as you get off the interstate at the little outpost of **Spencer,** you'll be bombarded with signs for a number of different businesses, all imploring you to buy the town's claim-to-fame product: opal. The first opal was discovered in the area in 1948 by a couple of deer hunters. Precious gem-quality opal is rare because a unique combination of geological circumstances is required for its formation; it only forms at the bottom of still pools of underground water. The mineral's layers of microscopic silica spheres reflect light like millions of miniature prisms, brilliantly flashing the colors of the rainbow.

Spencer Opal Mines (27 Opal Ave., Spencer, 208/374-5476, 9am-5pm daily Memorial Day-Labor Day, $10 over age 12, $5 ages 4-12) sells permits to dig for opal at its commercial mine that allows you to take up to one pound of rock; additional rock costs $10 per pound. You need to bring your own tools, including a rock hammer, sledgehammer, bucket, spray bottle, gloves, boots, and safety glasses.

A couple of U.S. Forest Service campgrounds are in the area. **Stoddard Creek Campground** (21 sites, $10) is three miles north of Spencer; take I-15 Exit 184, then turn west. The remote **Steel Creek Campground** (1-50 people, $50) is best suited for large groups, and it's in the Centennial Mountains northeast of Spencer, midway between Spencer and Kilgore on Forest Road 006. To get to Forest Road 006, head north from Spencer to the Stoddard Creek Campground exit on I-15 (Exit 184), then turn east (right). The road climbs up Miner's Creek, crests Porcupine Pass, and drops down West Camas Creek about six miles to the campground.

U.S. 26 to Wyoming

RIRIE AND VICINITY
Alpine Skiing

Kelly Canyon Ski Resort (5488 E. Kelly Canyon Rd., Ririe, 208/538-6251, www.skikelly.com, 12:30pm-9:30pm Mon.-Thurs., 9:30am-9:30pm Fri.-Sat., full-day lift tickets $40 ages 13-64, $32 seniors and ages 6-12) is about 25 miles from Idaho Falls. Take U.S. 26 toward Swan Valley and watch for a signed turn to the left, a mile or so past the turnoff to Ririe. After crossing the Snake River, the road turns up the canyon and leads to the ski area. A shuttle bus is available from Idaho Falls on Saturdays and holidays; call for current schedule and route.

This family-friendly ski area has reasonable prices and enough varied terrain to satisfy everyone. Four double chairs serve 27 runs on 640 acres with a maximum vertical drop of 1,000 feet. There's even a terrain park for stunt skiers and boarders. A day lodge has a cafeteria and plenty of space to thaw out.

Cross-Country Skiing and Mountain Biking

Just past Kelly Canyon Ski Resort, a network of cross-country ski trails laces the hills on Caribou-Targhee National Forest land administered by the **Palisades Ranger District** (3659 E. Ririe Hwy., Idaho Falls, 208/523-1412). Of the 20-some miles of trails, some are periodically groomed, while others are marked but not machine-tracked. There are trails of all ability levels. Easiest is the one-mile Tyro Loop, beginning and ending at the Y junction just above the ski lodge. Most difficult are the five-mile Hawley Gulch Loop, which leads to a remote area and offers lots of big ups and downs along the way, and the Kelly Mountain Trail, which offers advanced skiers a chance for panoramic views of the Snake River Valley. In summer, these old logging roads become prime mountain biking terrain.

Heise Hot Springs

Near Kelly Canyon Ski Resort, you can soak your sore muscles at **Heise Hot Springs**

Snake River near Ririe

(5116 E. Heise Rd., Ririe, 208/538-7312, daily, all-day pass $10 ages 12 and older, $7 seniors, $6 ages 2-11, swimsuit and towel rental available), a commercial hot springs resort where locals have congregated since the early 1900s. The resort's centerpiece is a century-old house next to a big, naturally heated pool and waterslide (both summer only), but there are smaller hot and warm pools (open year-round) as well. The tranquil park-like grounds are situated next to the Snake River, and the resort operates a campground with RV spots with full hookups ($32), tent sites ($20), and cabins ($75-130). If you get hungry, there's a pizza parlor next to the big pool, where you will also find a few pinball machines and video games. In addition, Heise runs a zipline business (208/538-6048) on the hill above the pools and offers guided fishing trips (208/538-7453).

Cress Creek Nature Trail

If you cross the Snake River headed toward Kelly Canyon but turn left instead of right just across the bridge, you'll soon come to a small parking area for the Bureau of Land Management's **Cress Creek Nature Trail.** The trail climbs steeply up a sage- and juniper-covered hillside and leads to sweeping views across southeast Idaho. Cress Creek is a sparkling clear spring, and its incessant babbling provides the perfect soundtrack for your picnic.

SWAN VALLEY

Named for the whistling swans that once frequented the area, idyllic Swan Valley lies between the lofty Snake River Range to the northeast and the lower Caribou Range to the southwest. The south fork of the Snake River—a blue-ribbon cutthroat trout stream—flows gently through the valley from Palisades Reservoir. The reservoir and river provide water recreation, while hiking possibilities abound in the mountains to either side.

Fall Creek Falls

Fall Creek makes a beeline down out of the Caribou Range, plunging 60 feet into the Snake River at **Fall Creek Falls.** The falls are on the southwest side of the Snake River, west of the town of Swan Valley. Coming from town, turn left onto Snake River-Palisades Dam Road, just after the highway crosses the Snake River. Follow the road a short distance just across Fall Creek to a small parking area. An overgrown trail leads to a view from the top of the falls.

Palisades Dam and Reservoir

At the time it was completed in 1959, **Palisades Dam** on the Snake River was the largest earthen dam ever built by the federal Bureau of Reclamation. An overlook at the outlet provides good views of the lake, dam, and spillway. The 16,100-acre lake has both wild and stocked cutthroat trout as well as smaller populations of brown trout, kokanee, and mackinaw. Ice fishing is popular in winter. Five boat ramps dot the east shore, and two more are found at either end of the west shore.

Fishing

While Henrys Fork gets all the press, fly-fishing for trout on the South Fork of the Snake River between Palisades Dam and the Henrys Fork is also outstanding and less crowded. You'll be chasing primarily cutthroats and browns. Both South Fork Lodge and The Lodge at Palisades Creek specialize in helping anglers hook the big one, offering fishing-only trips and fishing-lodging packages.

Hiking

Trails lace the Caribou-Targhee National Forest units surrounding Swan Valley. The most noteworthy hike in the region is to **Palisades Lakes,** high in the Snake River Range northeast of the reservoir. To get to the trailhead, take the highway north from Palisades Dam about four miles, then turn right onto Forest Road 255 and follow it three miles to the parking area. The trail climbs seven miles along Palisades Creek to the two lakes, both of which offer excellent fishing.

Upper Palisades Lake, the larger of the two, sits at an elevation of 7,000 feet. The Palisades Peaks add a majestic background to the high alpine setting, and the lake is a good base camp for a couple of side trips. Another two miles up in **Waterfall Canyon** is a beautiful waterfall. Ambitious mountaineers can continue from here up the canyon trail to its T junction with the Little Elk Creek trail, then scramble straight ahead up the Class 3 north ridge of **Mount Baird** (10,025 feet), the range's highest peak.

Float Boating

The South Fork of the Snake River—from below Palisades Dam to its confluence with the Henrys Fork near Menan—is a beautiful, 64-mile-long, trout-filled watercourse perfect for those who eschew white-knuckle white water in favor of calm currents and placid pools. It's an easy eight-hour float in your raft, canoe, or kayak from below the dam to Heise. Along the way you'll pass 39 islands— some suitable for camping—and float through a magnificent canyon with 100-foot-high walls. Glorious stands of cottonwoods line the banks, holding in their uppermost branches the nests of bald and golden eagles. Ducks and geese are plentiful, and you might also spot great blue herons, grouse, deer, moose, otters, beavers, and mountain goats. Side trails leading up Dry Canyon, Black Canyon, and Table Rock Canyon allow you to paddle ashore and explore terra firma if you so desire. The three canyons are linked by another trail that parallels the river's northern bank.

The river is floatable year-round, but some hazardous obstacles—notably canal diversions—do exist; be sure to pick up the *South Fork of the Snake River Boater's Guide* at the visitors center in Idaho Falls. The guide also describes the campsites available en route, some of which have use restrictions.

Camping

Numerous U.S. Forest Service campgrounds are scattered between Fall Creek Falls and the south end of Palisades Reservoir. **Falls Campground** ($10) provides 24 sites just south of Fall Creek Falls on Snake River-Palisades Dam Road. **Palisades Creek Campground** (8 sites, $10) is at the Palisades Lakes Trailhead at the top of Forest Road 255. It offers restrooms, trailer parking, and good fishing in the creek. **Calamity Campground** ($12) is the valley's largest, with 41 sites on the northwest shore of the reservoir near the dam. A boat ramp makes this campground convenient for campers heading out on the water. Continuing around the west shore of the reservoir, you'll come to the small and quiet **Bear Creek Campground** ($10). Its eight sites are on Bear Creek about a mile from an arm of the lake. Past Bear Creek, you can continue to follow the road as it winds west through the mountains and eventually circles back to the southern end of the lake and **McCoy Creek Campground** (18 sites, $10), next to a boat ramp. This one is more easily reached, however, from the south off U.S. 89 in Wyoming.

Coming back up the east shore, **Alpine Campground** ($10) offers 19 sites by a meandering lakeshore trail. The 16 sites at **Blowout Ramp Campground** ($10) are adjacent to the Blowout boat ramp. **Big Elk Creek Campground** ($10) offers 21 sites at the mouth of Big Elk Creek. From the trailhead here, you can hike up the creek into the heart of the Snake River Range.

All the Forest Service campgrounds open for the season around June 1; Alpine opens a little earlier, Palisades and Blowout a little later. Bear Creek and Blowout Ramp stay open through the end of October; the others all close for the season between Labor Day weekend and mid-September.

Fishing Lodges

Overlooking the Snake River, **South Fork Lodge** (40 Conant Valley Loop, Swan Valley, 208/483-3112, June-Oct., packages from $445) is one of the West's most plush angling lodges. It offers eight guest rooms in the main lodge plus two newish log buildings with five guest rooms each along with a restaurant and a tackle shop. Guided fishing is the specialty, and packages are available.

Just upstream from Swan Valley is the hamlet of Irwin and **The Lodge at Palisades Creek** (3720 U.S. 26, Irwin, 208/483-2222 or 866/393-1613, www.tlapc.com, cabins from $380). The lodge sits right along the highway, but also right along the Snake River at Palisades Creek. The log cabin-style

accommodations are upscale rustic. You'll be exceedingly comfortable whether lounging on the porch of your cabin overlooking the Snake River or enjoying a gourmet meal served alfresco on the beautiful lodge deck. A minimum four-night stay is requested. Rates include meals and many activities; fishing guides during peak season cost $525 per day for 1-2 people.

Teton Basin

Teton Basin was once known as Pierre's Hole after Iroquois trapper "Old Pierre" Tevanitagon. Old Pierre trapped here frequently until he got himself killed in Montana by Blackfoot Indians in 1827. In 1832, Pierre's Hole was the site of the annual rip-roarin' rendezvous of fur trappers, mountain men, and Native Americans, the West's original trade show.

The 6,000-foot-high valley is spectacularly situated between the Big Hole Mountains on the west and the Teton Mountains on the east. The Tetons are the youngest range in the Rockies; their steep granite faces tower over the landscape from just across the border in Wyoming. Beneath their western flanks lies the Grand Targhee ski area, one of the West's best ski and summer resorts.

Both the Tetons and the Big Holes are laced with hiking and mountain-biking trails. For a complete hiking guide to the area, stop by the Caribou-Targhee National Forest's **Teton Basin Ranger Station** (515 S. Main St., Driggs, 208/354-2312).

VICTOR

At the south end of the valley, Victor is an important crossroads, especially for skiers. Coming in on Highway 31 from Swan Valley, turn right to get to Jackson Hole, left to get to Grand Targhee. Victor is named for mail carrier George Victor Sherwood, who courageously made his appointed run from here over to Jackson at a time when the local

Indians were in a threatening and hostile mood. The bustling resort town is a lot tamer in this day and age.

Recreation

Among the almost endless hiking opportunities in the area, the **Moose Creek Trail** (Trail 038) follows Moose Creek up to the Teton Crest past a waterfall and alpine lakes. To get here, take Highway 33 southeast from Victor. Just before Mike Harris Campground, Forest Road 276 leads 1.5 miles east to the trailhead.

Across the valley in the Big Hole Mountains, the **Patterson Creek Trail** (Trail 054) climbs alongside Patterson Creek up to Mahogany Ridge and on to Red Mountain (8,715 feet) for panoramic views of the Tetons and the sprawling valley. To get to Patterson Creek, take Cedron Road west out of Victor. After several miles, the road bends north; continue north one mile and turn left to the trailhead.

Entertainment

Old Pierre Tevanitagon would no doubt enjoy knowing that Victor remembers him to this day. **Pierre's Playhouse** (37 N. Main St., Victor, 208/787-7469, www.pierresplayhouse. com) is the venue for old-fashioned melodrama presented by the Teton Valley Players. The playhouse also serves as a movie theater, showing current-run flicks, and it puts on an annual production of A Christmas Carol during the holidays.

Quaff some handcrafted ales with the locals at ★ **Grand Teton Brewing** (430 Old Jackson Hwy., Victor, 888/899-1656, www.grandtetonbrewing.com, noon-8pm Mon.-Fri., 1pm-8pm Sat.-Sun.). The taproom at this popular brewery pours a large selection of flagship and seasonal beers, including Old Faithful Pale Ale and Trout Hop Black IPA. You can also get kettle-brewed root beer and cream soda, which will surely keep the kids happy.

Camping

Teton Valley Campground (1208 W. Hwy. 31, Victor, 208/787-2647, www.tetonvalley-campground.com) is a tidy, pleasant, and friendly RV park just outside town. Amenities include a heated pool, a coin laundry, a rec room, restrooms, and showers. It has 60 RV sites with full hookups ($38-52), cabins ($59), and a few tent sites ($32).

U.S. Forest Service campgrounds in the area include **Pine Creek Campground** (9 sites, $10), back down toward Swan Valley on Highway 31, just on the Victor side of Pine Creek Pass, and **Mike Harris Campground** (12 sites, $10), about the same distance southeast of Victor on Highway 33.

DRIGGS

Driggs is the "urban" hub of Teton Basin, and it's the valley's largest town and a service and supply center for skiers, hikers, mountain bikers, and horse-packers heading off into the Tetons or the Big Hole Mountains. Its atmosphere carries vague reminders of the valley's wild rendezvous heritage; Driggs still feels like a remote party town, full of independent outdoors enthusiasts. Driggs has become popular with New Yorkers and Californians—who have adopted the town in recent years—as evidenced by all the vacation homes that now dot the valley.

Recreation

The road to the ski resort forks on the far side of Alta; the left fork takes you to Grand Targhee, the right fork to Teton Canyon. At the end of the road up Teton Canyon is the area's most popular trailhead. From here you can continue on foot up Trail 027 for 7.7 miles to the top of Teton Canyon and **Alaska Basin,** a scenic alpine valley with a number of gem-like lakes. The downside is that the area is heavily used. Another, shorter trail offering an exceptionally scenic hike is the **South Darby Trail** (Trail 033). This 2.7-mile

Welcome to Driggs, the hub of Teton Basin.

one-way hike begins at a trailhead at the end of Darby Canyon Road (Forest Rd. 012), which turns east off Highway 33 three miles south of Driggs. The trail climbs along the South Fork of Darby Creek, past waterfalls and beautiful wildflower-filled meadows.

If you think the Tetons and Teton Valley are impressive from the ground, wait till you see them from the air. **Teton Aviation** (208/354-3100, www.tetonaviation.com) can take you aloft from Teton Peaks Centennial Airport in Driggs for a scenic airplane or glider flight. Flights in the single-passenger gliders cost about $295 for an hour. Airplane flightseeing costs $275-375 per hour for a planeload of up to three passengers.

OUTFITTERS
Yöstmark Mountain Equipment (285 E. Little Ave., Driggs, 208/354-2828, www.yostmark.com, 9am-6pm daily) can set you up with gear for outdoor excursions. Plus, they offer guide services for the area. Telemark packages and snowshoes are the hot rental items in winter. In summer, the store rents paddleboards, tents, backpacks, stoves, sleeping bags, and bear-proof food containers. Yöstmark also manufactures the famous "Mountain Noodle" backcountry ski.

Entertainment and Events
Locals file into the **Spud Drive-In Theatre** (2175 S. Hwy. 33, Driggs, 208/354-2727, www.spuddrivein.com), which plays current-run movies May-Oct. Just look for the big potato on the back of a truck that sits out front; the massive screen is hard to miss as well.

Idaho has no shortage of hot-air balloon events, but the **Teton Valley Balloon Rally** has to be the tops. On Fourth of July weekend, more than 50 colorful balloons chase each other across the crystal-clear blue skies above the Tetons.

Accommodations
Pines Motel Guest Haus (105 S. Main St., Driggs, 208/354-2774, $45-100) offers seven guest rooms, six with private baths, in a refurbished and expanded turn-of-the-20th-century log cabin. Breakfast is available for an extra charge. Amenities include cable TV, a jetted tub, a large lawn for summer picnics and barbecues, and an ice-skating rink in winter. Pets are allowed.

Best Western Teton West (476 N. Main St., Driggs, 208/354-2363, from $70 d) offers a tidy and amenity-filled Best Western package, and it honors discounts for AAA members.

The Tetons loom just over the Wyoming border near Driggs.

Luxuries include an indoor heated pool and hot tub.

★ **Teton Valley Cabins** (34 Ski Hill Rd., Driggs, 208/354-8153, www.tetonvalleycabins.com, $79-119) are right on the road to the ski area. Here you'll find 20 cutesy cabins and a grassy area with a big fire pit for roasting marshmallows and hot dogs.

Food

★ **The Royal Wolf** (63 Depot St., Driggs, 208/354-8365, 11am-10pm daily, $8-15), in a converted house right off the main drag, is the place to go in Driggs for a burger and a beer. The Wolf, as locals call it, serves brew-friendly appetizers, big burgers, ribs, hot sandwiches, and plenty of hand-cut Idaho fries. The chimichurri steak sandwich is an excellent choice, washed down with a pint of ale from Grand Teton Brewing. After dinner, shoot a game of pool or just chillax on the deck and watch the birds go by.

In the morning, head over to **Pendl's Bakery** (40 Depot St., Driggs, 208/354-5623, breakfast and lunch daily, $4-9) for apple strudel and a steamy latte. This Austrian-inspired bakery is situated in an old red house, a stone's throw from The Wolf, with a grassy backyard that has lots of picnic tables. It's a great place to hang out while enjoying flaky pastries, cinnamon swirls, quiche, and steel-cut oatmeal. At lunch, you can get sandwiches and housemade soups. Pendl's hosts live acoustic music on Sundays.

Teton Valley Farmers Market takes place on Fridays (9am-1:30pm June-Sept.) in a grassy lot at the corner of Main and Depot Streets. This is a good spot to buy fresh produce, artisanal cheeses, baked goods, and local sausages. Do yourself a favor and pick up a wedge of "Yellowstone," a buttery alpine-style cheese made by Teton Valley Creamery.

Information

Stop by the shiny, new **Teton Geotourism Center** (60 S. Main St., Driggs, 208/354-2607, www.tetongeotourism.us, open 24/7) in downtown Driggs for information about the Teton and Yellowstone areas. The center, billed as the first of its kind in the world, offers literature, travel services, and interactive exhibits about fun stuff to do around these parts.

ALTA, WYOMING

Yes, technically both the little town of Alta and the Grand Targhee Resort are in Wyoming, but unless you're a hard-core mountaineer the only way to get to either of them is through Idaho. A handful of lodgings options, a restaurant, and a golf course are all you'll find in Alta; most services in the area are based in Driggs.

Golf

Targhee Village Golf Course (530 Perimeter Dr., Alta, 307/353-8577, Apr.-Oct., $18 for 9 holes, $24 for 18 holes) is a nine-hole, par-72 course stretching just over 6,000 yards. There is also a driving range and great views of the Tetons.

GRAND TARGHEE RESORT

The Tetons are some of the West's most magnificent mountains, and **Grand Targhee Resort** (3300 E. Ski Hill Rd., 307/353-2300, www.grandtarghee.com) is certainly one of the West's most magnificent resorts. It's also just far enough off the beaten track to make you feel as if you've discovered your own personal Shangri-la, and that's a feeling the resort's friendly staff are pleased to encourage.

Alpine Skiing

Often overshadowed by the mega-ski resorts in Utah and by its Wyoming neighbor Jackson Hole, **Grand Targhee** (full-day lift tickets $73 adults, $51 seniors, $32 ages 6-12, free under age 6) is an awesome spot to ski and snowboard in its own right. And what nice powder this place has! The 3,000-acre, two-mountain ski heaven gets more than 500 inches of snow per year. In one recent year, the total topped 650 inches.

Grand Targhee is by no means unknown, but you have to work a little to get to it. That fact automatically keeps the dilettantes at bay, leaving the slopes wide open on most days. Fred's Mountain has 2,000 vertical feet and 1,500 acres of groomed skiing. The resort has two quad chairs, one double, and an easy-on, easy-off "Magic Carpet" for beginners. The other mountain, Peaked, has 500 acres and 1,277 acres of lift-served terrain, but another 1,000 acres are reserved for powder skiing and riding. Snowboarders will find a terrain park as well as board rentals and lessons.

Cross-Country Skiing

Twelve miles of immaculately groomed cross-country tracks—both skating and traditional—leave from the resort's base area and head out into the surrounding glades. The farthest three-mile loop leads to a view of Grand Teton, and chances are good that you'll have the whole trail system to yourself. A full-day trail pass costs $10 for adults; lessons and rentals are available. To find out more about the mountain's cross-country scene, check in at the **Nordic Center** (9am-4:30pm daily winter) at the base of the Shoshone lift.

Summer Recreation

Grand Targhee is a great place to be in summer too, when the Tetons pierce the brilliant blue sky and wildflowers paint the alpine meadows in a rainbow of vivid colors. The resort offers **chairlift rides** (end of June-early Sept., $15 adults, $10 ages 6-12) up the mountain in summer for great views—including the backside of the Tetons—and a leisurely hike back down. **Mountain bikers** will appreciate the resort's trail system. You can even load your bike onto the chairlift ($35 all day) and ride down from the summit. Bike and helmet rentals are available at the resort's Activity Center.

Activity Center

The folks at the **Activity Center** (307/353-2300) in the base-area village can set you up with just about any activity that interests you, on or off the mountain, any time of year. In many cases they can handle all the arrangements for you right from the office.

Accommodations

Three separate lodging options are available right at the resort's base area. **Targhee Lodge** (from $125 d) offers standard guest rooms with two queens. The plush rooms of the exquisite **Teewinot Lodge** (from $179 d) are furnished and decorated in Southwestern and Native American motifs. Each room has two queen beds, and amenities include a hot tub and a large lobby with a fireplace and ski racks. The **Sioux Lodge Condominiums** come in various sizes that sleep anywhere from two (from $199 d) to eight (over $250). The midrise Sioux Lodge building lacks architectural character, but you get great views from each of the guest rooms, which have fireplaces and kitchenettes. Rates vary depending on the date, and various discount packages are available. Pets are not allowed.

Food

The resort's main dining room, the **Branding Iron Grill** (breakfast, lunch, and dinner daily, dinner entrées $14-26), is itself a work of art; a high open-beam ceiling caps two-story-high windows and a massive fireplace. The upscale menu plays well with the extensive wine list, which features select labels from Idaho, Oregon, Washington, and California. Other eateries include the **Trap Bar,** a favorite après-ski and evening spot, and **Snorkels,** with espresso, deli sandwiches, and pastries.

U.S. 20 to West Yellowstone

RIGBY TO ST. ANTHONY

Rigby

Rigby is known as the "Birthplace of Television." Inventor Philo T. Farnsworth (1906-1971), holder of more than 125 patents, first came up with the idea of the cathode ray tube while living in Rigby. You can find out more about Farnsworth and Rigby at the **Jefferson County Historical Society and Farnsworth TV & Pioneer Museum** (118 W. 1st S., Rigby, 208/745-8423, 1pm-5pm Tues.-Sat., $2 adults, $1 students, free under age 7).

Considering the strong Mormon influence around here, it's surprising that Rigby has become vodka central in recent years. Several potato vodka producers have set up shop in this sleepy burg, which will surely please martini fans. Rigby has a handful of restaurants and lodging options along the main drag.

Rexburg

The squeaky-clean lifestyle of the Latter-day Saints is ever present in **Rexburg,** home of the Mormon-owned Brigham Young University-Idaho. Established in 1888, the onetime junior college was originally named for Thomas Ricks, the Mormon leader who came north from Logan, Utah, in 1882 to found the town, but it got the Brigham Young University moniker and became a full-fledged university in 2001. Rexburg is also a favorite among "sunbirds," senior citizens who spend winters down south and summers in the cooler climes. Between the straitlaced Mormon collegians and the senior set, you might expect Rexburg to be one of Idaho's more sedate towns, and it most certainly is.

Rexburg is a nice place to get out of the car for a picnic in **Porter Park** (at 2nd W. and 1st S. Streets) near downtown. Here you will find a splash pool for the kiddies, a tranquil walking path, sports courts, and picnic shelters, not to mention an expanse of grass and big shade trees. The park is home to the **Idaho Centennial Carousel** (noon-7pm Mon.-Sat. Memorial Day-Labor Day, rides $1), a beautiful century-old horsey carousel that will put a smile on everyone's face.

St. Anthony Sand Dunes

Prevailing wind patterns have created **St. Anthony Sand Dunes,** a 35-mile-long, five-mile-wide desert of sand dunes a few miles west of St. Anthony. The 10,000 acres of dunes—some hundreds of feet high—constitute a playground for the off-road-vehicle set. Hiking and camping are possible in the area, but don't expect a wilderness experience; this is an area sacrificed to off-roading. The two hubs of dune-buggy and all-terrain vehicle activity are the scruffy **Sand Hills Resort** (865 Red Rd., St. Anthony, 208/624-4127, www.thesandhillsresort.com), on the east side of the dunes, which offers a bit of grass and RV spots with full hookups ($39-49) and tent sites ($19-23); and the **Egin Lakes Access Area** on the south side (off 500 N.), a free primitive camping area constantly abuzz with the sounds of internal combustion engines. For more information, contact the **Bureau of Land Management Idaho Falls District** (1405 Hollipark Dr., Idaho Falls, 208/524-7500).

ASHTON AND VICINITY

Ashton was founded in 1906 and named after William Ashton, chief engineer for the Oregon Short Line Railroad. As the world's largest seed-potato-producing area, Ashton's life revolves around the famous tuber. Surrounding the city are some 11,000 acres of potato fields, which produce about 10 tons per acre. In addition to spuds, local farmers also grow wheat, barley, canola, hay, hops, and peas.

Highway 47, designated by the state as the Mesa Falls Scenic Byway, is the scenic 25-mile back way between Ashton and Harriman State

Idaho Potato Vodka

The Gem State's prized potato crop gets turned into a multitude of products, like potato chips, french fries, instant mashed potatoes, potato soup, potatoes au gratin, hash browns, and even potato-based skin lotion. (OK, now I'm sounding like Bubba in *Forrest Gump*.) But did you know that potato vodka is also produced in Idaho? The little farming community of Rigby has turned into vodkaville in recent years. Local russets are used to make **Teton Glacier Vodka.** Master distiller Pat Wernimont employs modern techniques to produce this crystal-clear spirit. Instead of using the typical pot-still process, he distills the vodka in a four-column continuous distillation system that raises the alcohol level and removes all impurities. The filtration process involves running the spirits through charcoal and garnet crystals, giving the potato vodka a silky, smooth finish. **Silver Creek Distillers** (134 N. 3300 E., Rigby, 208/754-0042, www.glaciervodka.com) produces Teton Glacier, and they have been known to give occasional tours of the facility.

Also in Rigby, two vodka-loving guys turn out flavored potato vodka on a smaller scale. Distillers Ken Wyatt and Ron Zier produce Mountain Huckleberry and Rainier Cherry vodkas under the **44° North** label (www.44northvodka.com). Besides these fruity yet dry vodkas, they also make grain vodka called Magic Valley Wheat.

Over on the west side of the Snake River Plain, in the heart of Idaho's wine country at Sunny Slope, **Koenig Distillery** (20928 Grape Ln., Caldwell, 208/455-8386) makes exceptionally smooth potato vodka in ornate copper-pot stills. Distiller Andrew Koenig also makes Austrian-style fruit brandies and whiskey, while his brother, Greg, turns out award-winning varietal wines under the **Koenig Vineyards** label.

All these vodkas can be purchased at Idaho state liquor stores and at liquor stores throughout the country.

Park. Most of the sights listed below are on or near Highway 47.

Accommodations and Food

★ **Squirrel Creek Guest Ranch & Inn** (4587 E. 1200 N., Ashton, 208/652-3972, www.idahoranch.com), just east of town, is a good base camp for your explorations. This scenic ranch spread has all kinds of clean and comfortable lodging options, like a bunkhouse ($150), three cabins ($75-105), and a grand lodge ($465, sleeps 20). The park-like grounds also hold RV spots with full hookups ($25) and tent sites ($10) near a covered picnic area. The friendly folks who own and operate the resort can give you information about recreational opportunities in the area.

Everyone in these parts goes to **Big Jud's** (1370 U.S. 20, Ashton, 208/652-7806, 11am-9pm Mon.-Sat., $5-10), right along the highway, for big burgers, hand-cut fries, and ice-cream milkshakes. The fast-food joint is known for its mammoth half-pound and one-pound burgers. You can also get veggie burgers, chicken sandwiches, and fish and chips. The huckleberry milkshakes are especially good.

Mesa Falls

Continuing north up Highway 47 past Warm River, you'll soon come to two impressive waterfalls on the Henrys Fork. At **Lower Mesa Falls,** the river squeezes through a narrow gorge and drops 65 feet. A turnout at the lower falls offers good but distant views of the cascade. Nearby is the U.S. Forest Service **Grandview Campground** (8 sites, $20). Farther up the road, 114-foot **Upper Mesa Falls** offers a well-developed viewing area. Wheelchair-accessible walkways lead down to the top of the falls for close-up views. You'll also find the rustic old Big Falls Inn, which was a roadhouse back in the days before U.S. 20 was built. It's now a visitors center that's open seasonally.

Yellowstone National Park

Although nearly all of **Yellowstone**

National Park—including its major tourist facilities—is found in Wyoming, a thin strip along the western border of the park extends into Idaho. Cave Falls Road leads about 25 miles northeast from Ashton into the southwestern corner of the park. It's a dead-end road, isolated from the rest of the park; you can't keep driving to Old Faithful without going back to Ashton and taking other highways through Montana or Wyoming. But this stretch of the park, known as the "Cascade Corner," boasts an excellent backcountry trail system leading into the Bechler River drainage and more than half the park's waterfalls. From the end of the road at Cave Falls or from the nearby Bechler Ranger Station, you can hike to Dunanda Falls, Iris Falls, Ouzel Falls, Colonnade Falls, or Union Falls, among others. Pick up a map and a wilderness permit at the ranger station, which is up a spur road a few miles back toward Ashton from Cave Falls. The area didn't get torched in the 1988 firestorm that incinerated 36 percent of Yellowstone's forests; thus it remains heavily timbered. This is grizzly country, so take appropriate precautions and check with the rangers for news of recent sightings and for trail-condition updates.

Cave Falls is a low, broad, and beautiful cascade on the Falls River. The nearby U.S. Forest Service **Cave Falls Campground** (23 sites, $10, June 1-Oct. 1), just outside the Yellowstone park boundary, gets filled up in summer; come after Labor Day for more breathing room.

Jedediah Smith and Winegar Hole Wildernesses

Yellowstone National Park is north of Cave Falls Campground, but the beautiful backcountry knows no boundaries. An area south of the park, extending all the way to Teton Pass, Wyoming, with only one small gap, has also been protected in the **Jedediah Smith and Winegar Hole Wildernesses.** Both of these pristine areas hold large populations of grizzly bears, and both are located entirely within the state of Wyoming.

Cross-Country Skiing

At the **Bear Gulch-Mesa Falls Park N' Ski Area,** about five miles past Warm River on Highway 47 North, you'll find a trailhead for cross-country ski tracks leading to Upper Mesa Falls. The trailhead is at the old Bear Gulch Ski Area. It's 8.8 miles from Bear Gulch to the falls and back; the trail climbs steeply at first, but then becomes more moderate as it traverses the rim of Henrys Fork Canyon. On the way back you'll get great views of the Tetons, 30 miles away. Other shorter loops are also marked and groomed. You won't have the area all to yourself because snowmobile trails parallel the cross-country tracks.

Falls River Ridge Park N' Ski Area, 10 miles east of Ashton on Cave Falls Road (1400 N.), offers seven miles of beginner-intermediate trails that are periodically groomed. Loops of 2-6.1 miles are possible, and sections of the trail system are shared with snowmobilers. Some of the trails wind through groves of lodgepole pines and aspens, but most of the trails cross open terrain.

Forest Service Cabins

Caribou-Targhee National Forest's **Ashton-Island Park Ranger District** (46 U.S. 20, Ashton, 208/652-7442) offers three year-round rental cabins within a 30-mile radius of Ashton. Reservations can be made at www.reserveamerica.com.

To the northwest, the one-room **Bishop Mountain Lookout** ($30) overlooks Island Park Reservoir from atop 7,810-foot Bishop Mountain. It sleeps four in two sets of bunk beds and has a woodstove and outhouse but no water or lights. In winter you'll need a snowmobile for access.

The two-bedroom **Warm River cabin** ($50) lies 24 miles northeast of Ashton, about five miles east of Mesa Falls. It sleeps 10 in bunk beds and is furnished with a wood cookstove and a heater. Water must be taken from the creek and treated or brought in. You can cross-country ski to the cabin in winter.

Finally, 23 miles due east of Ashton on Forest Road 261, you'll find **Squirrel**

Trumpeter Swans

Harriman State Park is a prime wintering area for the Rocky Mountain trumpeter swan, a species that was close to extinction at the turn of the 20th century. Hunting and habitat changes brought about by human settlement had wiped out most of the swans. Only a few living in Alaska and the most remote areas of the Rockies survived. Those survivors wintered in this area, where hot springs feeding into the rivers keep the waters open and flowing even in the coldest times. Conservation efforts began in the 1930s. The wintering swans were fed grain at Red Rock Lakes National Wildlife Refuge 20 miles northwest of Harriman. The artificial feedings continued for almost 60 years until 1992. The feedings probably saved the swans from extinction, but they also created a problem of their own. The swans took to wintering only around the artificial-feeding areas and abandoned their migratory routes to points farther south. As a result, the southerly migratory routes were obliterated from the species' collective memory, and the Red Rock Lakes refuge and the area around Harriman State Park are now overcrowded with the beautiful swans in winter. The park's aquatic vegetation is insufficient to support their numbers, so once again the species is faced with a threat to its survival. Game wardens now encourage the swans to keep moving south in winter by persistently hazing them so they don't get too comfortable.

Meadows Guard Station ($40), a two-room affair with a woodstove and bunk beds that sleep up to six. Outside you'll find an outhouse and a hand pump for water. In winter you can ski in.

★ HARRIMAN STATE PARK

Eighteen miles north of Ashton, **Harriman State Park** (3489 Green Canyon Rd., Island Park, 208/558-7368, day-use $5) was formerly a 10,700-acre cattle ranch and private retreat owned by several bigwigs of the Union Pacific and Oregon Short Line Railroads. Edward H. Harriman, father of Sun Valley founder Averell Harriman, bought into the ranch in 1908, and eventually the entire Railroad Ranch, as it was known, ended up in the Harriman family. The family donated the land to the state in 1977, stipulating that the property be used as a wildlife preserve. The park opened to the public in 1982.

The Henrys Fork flows right through the ranch, offering superb fly-fishing for cutthroat trout. Elk, moose, beavers, muskrats, and sandhill cranes also call the park home, and some of the region's trumpeter swans winter on the park's lands. The park is primarily a day-use area, but there are two year-round yurts ($50) that sleep up to six, and a few of the old ranch houses and cabins ($100-200) are available for large-group lodging.

Hiking, Biking, and Skiing

Twenty-one miles of trails are open to hikers, mountain bikers, and equestrians in summer and to cross-country skiers in winter. No motorized vehicles or pets are permitted on the trails. The trails are particularly noteworthy in winter, as the park maintains one of the finest trail layouts in the state's Park N' Ski system. About half the trails are groomed; the side closest to the highway is the groomed side and has the easiest trails, most traversing wide-open meadows. Both skating and traditional lanes are set up where the terrain permits; traditional tracks are set up through the trees. All trails start from the visitors parking area just off the highway.

ISLAND PARK

In 1939, geologists studying the Island Park area realized that the surrounding landscape was a giant caldera. When this area passed over the Yellowstone hot spot about two million years ago, a huge volcano erupted, blowing rhyolite tuff over a 6,000-square-mile area and creating a crater 23 miles in diameter. The crater subsequently collapsed, forming the caldera. Just north of Ashton, U.S. 20

crosses Big Bend Ridge, part of the rim of this ancient crater.

In winter, under a glaze of snow, the area is especially beautiful. Unfortunately it's also incredibly popular with snowmobilers. The Big Springs snowmobiler parking lot is just up the road near Mack's Inn and serves a large trail system on national forest land. As a result, the tranquility of winter in Island Park is spoiled by the constant two-stroke din and stench of hundreds of snow machines. If you're here to cross-country ski, go to the snowmobile-free Harriman State Park, where you'll have the best chance of getting a little peace and quiet.

Island Park Reservoir

Island Park Dam was built on the Henrys Fork in 1938, creating 7,000-acre **Island Park Reservoir.** The lake supports a population of landlocked kokanee salmon and whitefish as well as brook, cutthroat, and rainbow trout. Ice fishing is popular in winter. In summer, the reservoir buzzes with boating activity.

Hiking and Mountain Biking

The **Box Canyon Trail** makes an easy six-mile round-trip day hike. Start at Box Canyon Campground and follow the Henrys Fork south for three miles along the canyon rim. The trail provides access to the river's trout heaven for fly-fishing and delights wildflower watchers with bursts of summer color.

Across the highway to the east, the old **Union Pacific Railroad bed** has been converted into a recreation trail running north-south past Island Park. It's a multiuse trail, so you'll be sharing it with motorized vehicles. The closest access road to Island Park is Chick Creek Road (Forest Rd. 291), which leads east off the highway about three miles south of Island Park. From the highway it's four miles down Chick Creek Road to the trail.

Float Boating

The **Henrys Fork** between Island Park Dam and Last Chance makes a pleasant two-hour float suitable for beginners, and the **Buffalo River** from its headwaters to U.S. 20 is equally placid and popular. To reach the Buffalo River headwaters, take Forest Road 291 east off U.S. 20 about 2.5 miles south of Ponds Lodge. Follow Forest Road 291 about seven miles to Forest Road 292 and turn north, then in another two miles turn west on Forest Road 1219 to the put-in. The put-in can also be reached out of Mack's Inn; take the Big Springs Loop to Forest Roads 082, 292, and 1219. Be careful of fences spanning the river.

Ponds Lodge

Right on the west side of the highway, **Ponds Lodge** (3757 N. U.S. 20, 208/558-7221, www.pondslodge.com) may not be the quintessential mountain resort, but it has a big restaurant serving homespun fare and a rustic saloon with a pool table, a jukebox, and a woodstove. The year-round lodge offers 14 cozy cabins ($85-295). The venerable Ponds is the bustling hub of Island Park activity, filled in summer with tourists en route to Yellowstone and in winter with boisterous snowmobilers. But the best part is that it's right next to the Brimstone Park N' Ski trailhead. The Brimstone trails are easy and flat, skirting the Buffalo River and the Henrys Fork, where trumpeter swans like to hang out in winter.

Camping

U.S. Forest Service campgrounds around Island Park Reservoir are administered by the **Ashton-Island Park Ranger District** (208/652-7442) and are accessed via Kilgore Road. They include the busy **McCrea Bridge Campground** (25 sites, $15), next to the boat ramp at the lake's inlet, and **Buttermilk Campground** (52 sites, $15), on the northeast shore of the lake next to a boat ramp. In the Ponds Lodge area are **Buffalo Campground** (105 sites, $15-40), on the Buffalo River on the east side of the highway, and **Box Canyon Campground** (17 sites, $15), also on the riverbank on the west side of the highway south of Ponds Lodge. To get there from U.S. 20, take Forest Road 134 and then Forest Road 284. **West End Campground** (19 sites, free) is reached via a long drive west on Green

Canyon Road (Forest Rd. 167), which turns west off U.S. 20 just south of Osborne Bridge near Harriman State Park.

MACK'S INN AREA
Big Springs

One of the country's largest springs, **Big Springs** pours 120 million gallons per day of super-clear water into the Henrys Fork. The constant-temperature 52°F water emerges from underground at 186 cubic feet per second and makes ideal spawning habitat for fish, especially cutthroat trout and kokanee salmon, but there's no fishing allowed at this spot. Also at the springs, a mile-long interpretive trail leads downstream to the Big Springs boat-launch area, and another short trail crosses Big Springs bridge and leads to **Johnny Sack cabin** (July 4-Labor Day), which was built by German immigrant Johnny Sack in the early 1930s. He also constructed a small waterwheel, using the flow of the springs to provide his cabin with electricity and water. The little waterwheel house is as artful as the cabin.

In summer, crowds of rafters, canoeists, and inner-tubers line up at the boat-launch area, 0.75 mile downstream from the springs, to put in on the **Big Springs National Recreation Water Trail.** It's a placid 2-hour float trip from here down the Henrys Fork to Mack's Inn. Both Big Springs and the boat launch are on Big Springs Loop Road (Forest Rd. 059), which leaves the highway at either Mack's Inn or Island Park village. At Mack's Inn Resort you can rent canoes and rafts, and they even provide a shuttle service.

Hiking

The **Coffee Pot Rapids Trail** offers an easy day hike on the west side of Mack's Inn. It begins from Upper Coffee Pot Campground and follows the Henrys Fork downstream for 2.5 miles, passing both placid pools and turbulent rapids. It's closed to motorized vehicles.

More difficult is the **Sawtell Peak-Rock Creek Basin Trail,** which starts near the top of 9,866-foot Sawtell Peak and crosses the Continental Divide on its way to Rock Creek Basin. The trail is six miles round-trip, some of it steep, and outstanding views are the norm. To reach the trailhead, take Sawtell Peak Road (Forest Rd. 024) west off the highway, about 1.75 miles north of Mack's Inn. Follow the road 11.5 miles to the trailhead, or 13 miles to the summit of Sawtell Peak.

the Henrys Fork of the Snake River near Mack's Inn Resort

Accommodations

Big, bustling **Mack's Inn Resort** (4292 N. U.S. 20, Island Park, 208/558-7272, www.macksinn.com) holds down the south bank of the Henrys Fork with accommodations and recreation options galore and hundreds of happy campers. Lodging options include an array of cabins ($69-200) and riverfront motel rooms (from $69 d). There's also a campground with RV spaces with full hookups ($30) and a few tent sites ($15). A rental shop offers rafts, canoes, and more. Other amenities include a restaurant, a general store, and a shower facility.

On the west side of U.S. 20, you'll find **Sawtelle Mountain Resort** (U.S. 20, milepost 395, 208/558-9366, www.sawtellemountainresort.com), which offers hotel rooms and cabins ($50-100), a hot tub, and an RV park ($35-50) with full hookups.

Camping

The Caribou-Targhee National Forest's **Big Springs Campground** (15 sites, $15) enjoys a prime location within walking distance of Big Springs and Johnny Sack cabin. Across the highway to the west are **Flat Rock Campground** (38 sites, $15) and **Upper Coffee Pot Campground** (14 sites, $15). For more information, contact the U.S. Forest Service's **Ashton-Island Park Ranger District** (208/652-7442), or make reservations at www.reserveamerica.com.

HENRYS LAKE AND VICINITY

In a high mountain bowl at an elevation of 6,740 feet, surrounded on three sides by the Continental Divide, Henrys Lake has been a historically important campsite. Major Andrew Henry was the first nonnative to see the lake when he passed by in 1810. Jim Bridger camped on the lake's shores with trappers and Flathead Indians in 1835, and the

Nez Perce camped here on their flight from General O. O. Howard during the Nez Perce War of 1877.

The lake is popular among anglers, who pursue rainbow-cutthroat hybrids, cutthroat and eastern brook trout, and mountain whitefish in the shallow waters.

Henrys Lake State Park

On the southeast shore of the lake, 586-acre **Henrys Lake State Park** (3917 E. 5100 N., Island Park, 208/558-7532, $5 day-use fee) provides anglers with a great base camp for fishing expeditions out on the water. The small park has a campground with 83 serviced sites ($18-31) as well as showers, restrooms, a boat ramp, boat docks, a nature trail, and a picnic area. There are also three camping cabins ($50) that can sleep up to six.

Backpacking

The 14-mile **Targhee Creek Loop Trail** begins north of U.S. 20 near Targhee Pass and leads through dense forests, across wide-open ridges with panoramic views, and past five alpine lakes perfect for camping and fishing. The trailhead is at the end of Targhee Creek Trail Road (Forest Rd. 057), midway between Targhee Pass and the junction of U.S. 20 and Highway 87. This is prime grizzly country, so be careful. Bear-proof food boxes are installed at many campsites for your convenience.

Howard Springs

Travelers continuing on to Yellowstone on U.S. 20 will find a historic rest stop along the east side of the highway at Howard Springs. General Oliver Howard passed these springs in hot pursuit of Chief Joseph and the Nez Perce in 1877.

Heading north on U.S. 20, you'll cross **Targhee Pass** into Montana. Targhee, a Bannock chief, is remembered for his peacemaking efforts during the turbulent 1860s.

Lava Land

North of Pocatello, I-15 stays close to the hills on one side and fronts the vast, wide-open Snake River Plain on the other. U.S. 26 and U.S. 20 head west from Blackfoot and Idaho Falls, respectively, forging bold straight paths out across the plain's lonely high-desert terrain. Not far from the lifeblood water of the Snake River, the plain doffs its irrigated mask of green to reveal the blacks, browns, grays, and reds of its volcanic origins.

BLACKFOOT AND VICINITY

Blackfoot, the Bingham County seat, is a working-class agricultural hub where spuds reign supreme; this is the number-one potato-producing county in the nation as well as Idaho's top grain producer. Founded in 1879, Blackfoot is the largest of the county's handful of small towns, most of which have declined in population in the last few decades.

Idaho Potato Museum

The **Idaho Potato Museum** (130 NW Main St., Blackfoot, 208/785-2517, www. idahopotatomuseum.com, 9:30am-5pm Mon.-Sat. Apr.-Sept., 9:30am-3pm Mon.-Fri. Oct.-Mar., $3 adults, $2.50 seniors, $1 ages 6-12), housed in the old Oregon Short Line Railroad Depot near downtown, pays homage to Idaho's prized crop. The spud-themed museum houses endless potato anecdotes and trivia. Here you'll see the world's largest potato chip, made by Procter & Gamble's Pringles division; a picture of Marilyn Monroe dressed in a burlap potato sack; and a copy of the 1992 letter sent by Idaho governor Cecil Andrus to U.S. Vice President Dan Quayle following Quayle's well-publicized spelling-bee faux pas. The letter, which accompanied a gift box of Idaho bakers, reads: "As far as we're concerned you can spell potato any way you want as long as it's genuine Idaho. P.S. There is no 'e' in Idaho either." Next door to the museum is a gift shop selling T-shirts (not made from potatoes), potato fudge, potato hand lotion, and other potato products.

Recreation

Jensen Grove Park is a great place to get

Idaho Potato Museum in Blackfoot

out of the car for a breather. A shady grove of cottonwoods gives the park its name and watches over an inviting picnic area. Water-skiers and summertime splashers make good use of the park's 55-acre lake. To get here, take I-15 Exit 93 east, then make the first left and follow it to the park. Golfers enjoy the adjacent 18-hole, 6,722-yard, par-72 **Blackfoot Municipal Golf Course** (3115 Teeples Dr., Blackfoot, 208/785-9960, Mar.-Oct., greens fees $18-26). Club and cart rentals are available.

HELL'S HALF ACRE

Hell's Half Acre, covering some 222 square miles, is a geologically brand-spanking-new lava flow—about 2,000 years old—which occupies almost the entire eastern half of the triangle formed by I-15, U.S. 20, and U.S. 26. You can get a pretty good look at the flow from the rest stop on I-15 just north of Blackfoot, but to really explore the flow, take U.S. 20 west of Idaho Falls for 20 miles, then turn south on a 0.25-mile gravel road to a parking area and trailhead. This is the Hell's Half Acre Wilderness Study Area, a 66,000-acre preserve managed by the Bureau of Land Management (BLM), Bonneville County, and the Idaho Alpine Club. From here you can head out across the lava on foot in any direction. A couple of suggested but unimproved trails are marked with colored poles. One of them is a half-hour loop that takes you past several different volcanic features; the other is a 4.5-mile route that leads to the volcanic vent itself, the spot from which the molten goo oozed. From the vent, at an elevation of 5,350 feet, the lava flowed south down to a point near today's I-15, at an elevation of 4,600 feet.

The best time to visit is in late spring or early summer, when the wildflowers are blooming brightly and the summer sun has yet to turn the Snake River Plain into Dante's *Inferno*. For more information on the Hell's Half Acre area, contact the **BLM Idaho Falls District** (1405 Hollipark Dr., Idaho Falls, 208/524-7500).

BIG SOUTHERN BUTTE

You can't miss this landmark rising nearly 2,500 feet above the surrounding plain. Like scores of other smaller buttes sprinkled across the Snake River Plain, Big Southern Butte was also created by the forces of volcanism, yet unlike the other smaller buttes, the molten rock that spewed from the earth here was not basalt but much more viscous rhyolite. Think of it like an upwelling of Elmer's glue instead of water. The rhyolite cooled and solidified before it had the chance to spread and flatten out across the plain. Unlike the more common black basalt, rhyolite is light colored, which helps Big Southern Butte stand out in contrast to its surroundings.

You can hike to the top of the 7,560-foot butte or even drive up in a 4WD. To get to the road to the summit, start from Atomic City on U.S. 26 and take Cox's Well-Atomic City Road west. Continue across the railroad tracks, bearing right at the Cedar Butte Road intersection and left at the Cedar-Big Butte Road intersection. From here, the idea is to follow roads clockwise around the south and west sides of the butte, ending up at Frenchman's Cabin (and landing strip) on the butte's northwest corner. From the major intersection at Frenchman's Cabin, the road to the butte leads off to the southeast. After 1.5 miles, you'll come to a gate. If it's locked, hike up the remaining 3.5 miles; if it's open and you have a 4WD vehicle, you have your choice of hoofing it or driving to the top. In either case, bring plenty of water. You'll pass through a Douglas fir forest on the way up, and there are spectacular views from the summit. Backpackers can bivouac on top to catch sunrise over the Tetons.

IDAHO NATIONAL LABORATORY

The U.S. government established the Idaho National Laboratory (INL) in 1949 to build and test nuclear reactors for both civilian and military purposes. Today, Department of Energy contractor Bechtel BWXT conducts a broad spectrum of nuclear-related studies here, including research and development of electric vehicles, medical radiation cancer treatments, environmental cleanup technologies, and nuclear waste volume-reduction systems, among others.

You won't see much of INL from most roads in southeast Idaho. That's totally by design: The 890-square-mile site was selected for its remote location. The barren desert out on the sparsely populated Snake River Plain seemed like the perfect place for this kind of nuclear scientific research. "The site," as many call it, has the nation's highest concentration of nuclear reactors; 52 have been built here over the years, and more than a dozen continue to operate. That's a scary thought given that the site is located in one of the nation's most geologically active areas and sits atop an aquifer that supplies drinking and irrigation water for much of southern Idaho. Many people see this as a nightmare in the making. INL is also the federal government's current repository for nuclear waste shipments from all over the country. Spent reactor fuel from the nuclear Navy is shipped here by rail from Mare Island, California, and Newport News, Virginia.

ARCO

Arco was the first city in the world to be lit by atomic power. On July 17, 1955, scientists at the National Reactor Testing Station (now INL), 18 miles east of town, threw a switch and sent two million watts of electricity from Boiling Water Reactor No. 3 (BORAX-III) into the living rooms of Arco for a little more than an hour. That's pretty much the town's claim to fame.

King Mountain

Consistent updrafts make the summit of **King Mountain,** north of town, a popular launching spot for hang gliders. On the south flanks of the peak, you'll see a natural bridge spanning 80 feet. The massive limestone arch frames the rugged spruce-covered terrain, making it a great spot for hiking. If you're gliding through town the second weekend in July, make sure to check out the **King Mountain Hang Gliding Championships** (www.flykingmountain.com). If you ask around, you might even be able to get a tandem ride on one.

Accommodations and Food

Arco keeps a handful of old-school motels along its main drag, some cleaner than others.

the atomic town of Arco

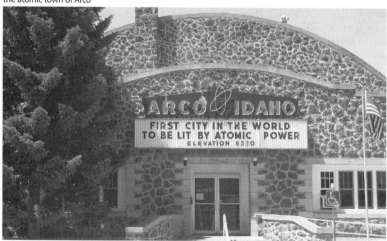

Call it a night at the **D-K Motel** (316 S. Front St., Arco, 208/527-8282, www.dkmotel.com, $38-80), a clean and cozy motor inn with 25 guest rooms. Amenities include cable TV, free Wi-Fi, and a laundry facility.

Nearby, grab some gut-bombs at ★ **Number Hill Grill** (242 S. Front St., Arco, 208/527-8224, 11am-9pm Mon.-Sat., 11am-6pm Sun., under $10), a little fast-food shack with a hard-to-miss red-and-white paint job. Here you can get burgers, chicken sandwiches, wraps, salads, and breaded finger steaks. The super-thick milkshakes are pretty good too.

★ CRATERS OF THE MOON NATIONAL MONUMENT

Eighteen miles southwest of Arco, U.S. 20/26/93 enters **Craters of the Moon National Monument** (208/527-1300, www.nps.gov/crmo), an eerie, otherworldly landscape pocked, cracked, contorted, and charred by lava flows and eruptions occurring at various times 2,100-15,000 years ago. When Oregon-bound pioneers passed by here on Goodale's Cutoff in the 1860s, they considered the area a forbidding wasteland and kept on moving, but the area soon caught the eye of geologists, who began studying it in the early 1900s. In 1921, U.S. Geological Survey geologist Harold T. Stearns described the area as resembling the craters of the moon and recommended the creation of a national monument at the site.

That idea, and the name, really took hold after Boise taxidermist-turned-explorer Robert Limbert made several long treks across the lava flows. He brought national attention to the area by describing his adventures in the March 1924 issue of *National Geographic* magazine. Later that year, President Calvin Coolidge designated the area Craters of the Moon National Monument. In August 2002 the monument was expanded from about 55,000 acres to more than 250,000 acres, now known as Craters of the Moon National Monument and Preserve, managed jointly by the National Park Service and the Bureau of Land Management.

Lava fields cover much of southeastern Idaho, but what makes this area unique is the concentration of different volcanic features. Craters of the Moon lies along the Great Rift, a 60-mile-long perforation in the earth's crust along which eruptions have occurred as recently as about 110 BC, practically yesterday on geologic time scales. The earth's crust is stretching apart, becoming thinner, and

SOUTHEAST IDAHO
LAVA LAND

Craters of the Moon National Monument

Craters of the Moon National Monument

developing deep cracks and fissures above hot rising magma deeper down. When the magma reaches the crust and finds the cracks, it erupts out onto the earth's surface—sometimes placidly oozing, sometimes spouting forth in geysers of molten rock. Scientists say the area is due for another eruption any day now, sometime in the next 1,000 years.

From the air, the Great Rift looks like a giant dashed line of enormous cracks, dotted here and there with cinder cones marking the sites of volcanic vents. This bizarre landscape tells the story of the Great Rift, where an entire textbook's worth of volcanic phenomena can be seen in one place.

A Lavaland Lexicon

Besides the alien moonscapes, visitors to Craters of the Moon will also be faced with an alien set of words used to describe the various volcanic features. Many of the words come from the Hawaiian language; those islands were built by similar volcanism, and the process continues today, so it's no surprise that Hawaiians were ahead of mainlanders in coming up with names for what they saw. Here are a few of the more common terms:

A'a (pronounced "AH-ah" and meaning "hard on the feet") lava is full of sharp edges that slice open both sneakers and bare skin. You can't walk barefoot on *a'a*, and you certainly don't want to fall down on the stuff.

Pahoehoe (pronounced "pa-HOY-hoy" and meaning "ropy") lava is smoother than *a'a* and won't make mincemeat of your shoes. It's also full of enclosed air pockets, so chunks of *pahoehoe* are far lighter than equivalently sized *a'a* chunks.

Cinder cones form when an eruption sprays lava into the air. The lava droplets cool on the way down, and the resultant cinders accumulate as big ash heaps, generally with shallow-sloped sides that are highest right around the vent. Since the cinders are light, cinder cones are often elongated in the direction of the prevailing wind. **Spatter cones** form where steam vents disgorge denser globs of lava into the air. The heavier globs clot together like a hollow chimney around the vent, generally forming cones that are smaller than cinder cones and with steeper sides. Large globs of lava thrown skyward often solidify in midair and land as **lava bombs.** The bombs come in several different common shapes, including spindle, ribbon, and bread crust, the latter looking like a fine pumpernickel *bâtard.*

Kipukas are areas where a lava flow surrounded, but didn't cover, either an older flow or an area yet untouched by lava. These "islands" of vegetation allow scientists a window on preflow vegetation in an area and allow them to compare that vegetation to postflow growth. Where lava flows into a tree, it makes a cast of the trunk, and then cools around it. The trees themselves are long gone—burned to a crisp—but the impression of their scorched bark remains etched in the lava.

A **lava tube** is formed when the surface of a river of *pahoehoe* lava cools and hardens into a skin, while the interior of the stream stays molten and pours through. After the molten flow drains away, the hardened outer skin forms a hollow tube, often loosely called a cave. Sometimes these "caves" can even have "stalactites," which in this case aren't calcite deposits left by dripping water but lava that hardened in the act of dripping off the ceiling of the tube.

Plants

Looking at the dry, blackened landscape, you wouldn't expect much life to be found at Craters of the Moon. The area receives a limited amount of precipitation to begin with, about 15-20 inches per year. Arid conditions are compounded by wind-exacerbated evaporation, and rainfall and snowmelt sink through the porous lava before the plants have much of a chance to make use of it. Nevertheless, many plants have adapted to these harsh conditions.

Of primary importance to all the other plants in this land of abundant rock is the minute **lichen,** a symbiotic association of an alga and a fungus. It attaches itself to rocks and over time breaks down the rock into soil in which other plants can get a start. What an odd but heroic life form, the lichen.

Drought-tolerant desert dwellers such as **sagebrush, antelope bitterbrush,** and **prickly pear cactus** also inhabit the monument, but probably the most striking plant species here is the **dwarf buckwheat.** This tiny plant grows only a few inches tall, but its root system spreads out across an underground area up to three feet in diameter. As a result, dwarf buckwheat plants are spaced out across the lava fields, looking more like a gardener's plantings than nature's handiwork. In summer, the white-foliaged plants look like snowflakes against the black lava.

The most prevalent tree in the monument is the hardy **limber pine.** Its limber branches bend easily but don't break in the heavy winds, and its very large seeds can germinate in cracks in the lava where other trees could never get started. In early summer, it's time for the wildflowers to show off; look for **monkeyflower, desert parsley, Indian paintbrush, bitterroot,** and **scabland penstemon,** among others.

Animals

Small mammals can make a home in and among the cracks in the lava flows. Don't be surprised to see mice, voles, squirrels, and chipmunks darting about waiting for you to drop some food. Of course, those little guys are food themselves for the local raptor population, which includes northern harriers, red-tailed and sharp-shinned hawks, and great horned and long-eared owls. Though you're unlikely to see them, gopher snakes and rattlesnakes are also found here.

Besides *Homo sapiens,* the **mule deer** is the largest mammal inhabiting the monument. The park's healthy herd of these big-eared deer has made remarkable adaptations to life on the lava. In spring, the herd turns up in the wilderness area south of the monument, where they find high-quality forage, but since the area provides no pools of open water they get all their water from dew, condensed fog, and the vegetation they eat. When summer comes and the wilderness area dries out, the herd moves north into the smaller monument proper, congregating in larger-than-normal population densities around the few water sources. In fall, the rains return and the herd heads back south into the wilderness area. When snow falls, the deer leave the park entirely, off to their wintering grounds. It's a complicated schedule as mule deer migrations go, but it seems to be working well for this ingenious herd.

Visitors Center and Campground

After turning off the highway, on the left you'll find the monument's **visitors center** (208/527-1335, 8am-6pm daily summer, 8am-4:30pm daily the rest of the year, closed federal holidays). Exhibits and videos explain the geology, flora and fauna, and history of the area, and National Park Service rangers answer questions and sell a variety of related science and history books.

Across the road from the visitors center is the monument's only **campground.** Its 52 sites ($10) are densely clustered in a relatively small area, but this is a blessing rather than a curse, because it means the rest of the monument is less crowded. Water and restrooms are available at the campground, but showers, hookups, groceries, and other amenities are not. Rangers lead interpretive walks by day

and present amphitheater programs in the evening.

The day-use fee is $8 per vehicle or $4 per person for those entering by bicycle, motorcycle, or on foot. Day use and camping are free October-May, but there's no running water, and the campsites aren't plowed. When the loop road gets covered in snow, rangers turn it into a groomed cross-country ski trail.

Around the Loop Road

From the campground, a seven-mile road loops south into the heart of the monument, past many sight-filled stops. Among the highlights: the **Devil's Orchard,** where a short, wheelchair-friendly interpretive trail loops through some bizarre formations; **Inferno Cone Viewpoint,** where you can hike up to the top of Inferno Cone for sweeping views across the lava flows and the Snake River Plain; the **Tree Molds** area, where a short hike leads to some prime examples of that phenomenon; and the **Cave Area,** where a trail leads to numerous lava tube "caves," most of which require a flashlight to explore. With multiple stops, a few short hikes, and a picnic lunch thrown in for good measure, plan a leisurely 3-4 hours to make your way around the loop.

Into the Wilderness

In 1970, Congress designated 43,000 acres south of the monument as **Craters of the Moon Wilderness.** You'll need a permit from a ranger at the visitors center to venture into this area, accessed past the end of the Tree Molds trail. Not surprisingly, the wilderness receives little use. In summer, temperatures are high and water is scarce. In addition, hiking on the lava chews up boots. In winter, it might seem tempting to head out into the snow-covered wilderness on cross-country skis, but unstable snow bridges can obscure deep cracks in the lava. A fall into the Great Rift would put an end to your cross-country ski vacation.

Sun Valley and the Sawtooths

Look for ★ to find recommended
sights, activities, dining, and lodging.

Highlights

0   40 mi

0   40 km

Salmon ○   MT

**Custer Motorway
Adventure Road**

Sunbeam ○ ★ ○ Challis

★ Stanley

★ Redfish Lake

★ Sun Valley Resort
Ketchum ○

Fairfield ○

★

**Camas Prairie
Centennial Marsh
Wildlife Management Area**

© AVALON TRAVEL

★ **Camas Prairie Centennial Marsh Wildlife Management Area:** Springtime is the right time to see wildflowers and waterfowl strut their stuff in the verdant marshlands of this high prairie, framed by the looming Soldier and Trinity Mountains (page 229).

★ **Sun Valley Resort:** Known as the country's first bona fide ski resort, this charming mountain getaway has been a popular destination for powder fanatics since it opened in 1936 (page 248).

★ **Redfish Lake:** Check out this gorgeous lake that's flanked by the massive granite faces of Mount Heyburn. Stay in the grand Redfish Lake Lodge or at one of the eight U.S. Forest Service campgrounds that surround the lake (page 255).

★ **Stanley:** This frontier-themed town is situated in a high-mountain valley surrounded by the imposing Sawtooth and White Cloud peaks. It's pure nirvana for outdoor recreationalists (page 257).

★ **Custer Motorway Adventure Road:** Fans of ghost towns will get a kick out of this scenic drive that leads to Custer and Bonanza, old mining towns in the Yankee Fork Historic Area (page 266).

The upper reaches of the Snake River Plain finally relent to central Idaho's Rocky Mountains, a postcard-perfect panorama of craggy peaks and pastoral high-mountain valleys.

Wood River Valley is home to the mountain-chic towns of Hailey, Ketchum, and Sun Valley, a fabled ski resort that was once party central for the likes of Clark Gable, Marilyn Monroe, Ernest Hemingway, and Errol Flynn. Today, it's still a playground for celebrities and titans of business who keep vacation homes in this recreational wonderland.

North of Sun Valley, the softly contoured mountains give way to the more jagged and much larger White Cloud, Boulder, and Sawtooth Ranges, stretching toward the sky like busted saw blades. The pinnacled mountains are veined with wild rivers that lure in white-water enthusiasts every summer for multiday rafting excursions. This rugged core of Idaho is defined by the Frank Church-River of No Return Wilderness, which happens to be the largest wilderness area in the Lower 48. Getting away from it all here is not a problem.

PLANNING YOUR TIME

Since much of this mountainous region is extremely remote, exploring the hinterlands generally takes the better part of a week. But you'll want to allow yourself a few extra days to get pampered in the Ketchum-Sun Valley area. Spring and fall are good times to visit this adjoined resort community, mostly because the crowds and hotel rates both go down. Expect to find designer boutiques, posh galleries, and upscale restaurants. The Wild West and Wilshire Boulevard most certainly come together in this isolated draw flanked by the Pioneer and Smoky Mountains.

The entire region abounds with recreational fun for the skilled and daring, and for properly briefed novices. You will find a long list of exciting things to do in these parts, one that includes exceptional alpine skiing, world-class white-water rafting and kayaking, backpacking, mountain biking, and remote backcountry skiing.

Stanley, a rustic and lovable little town crowned by massive peaks, is a wonderful spot to chillax after pushing your body to the limit. Grab a hotel room, some burgers and

---

Previous: skiiers at Sun Valley; Stanley Lake with Sawtooths in background. **Above:** a bald eagle perching over the Salmon River.

Sun Valley and the Sawtooths

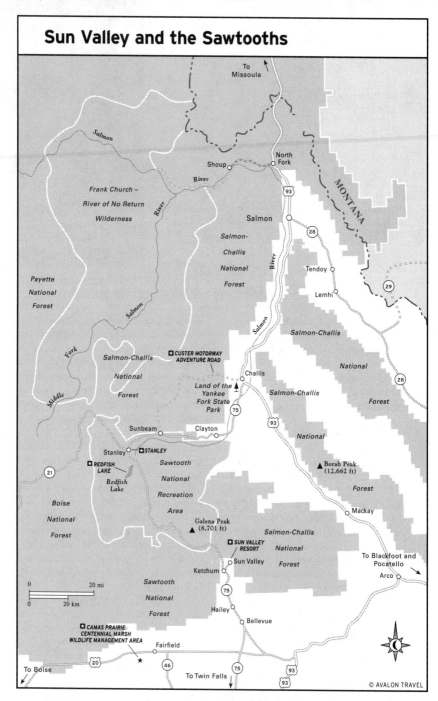

To Missoula

Salmon

Shoup

North Fork

MONTANA

93

Frank Church – River of No Return Wilderness

River

Salmon

Salmon-Challis National Forest

28

Tendoy

Lemhi

29

Payette National Forest

Salmon

Salmon

River

Salmon-Challis

National

Forest

28

Middle Fork

Salmon-Challis National Forest

CUSTER MOTORWAY ADVENTURE ROAD

Challis

Land of the Yankee Fork State Park

75

Salmon-Challis

National

Forest

93

Sunbeam

Clayton

STANLEY

Stanley

REDFISH LAKE

Redfish Lake

21

Sawtooth National Recreation Area

National

Borah Peak (12,662 ft)

Forest

Mackay

Boise National Forest

Galena Peak (8,701 ft)

Salmon-Challis

National

Forest

To Blackfoot and Pocatello

Arco

SUN VALLEY RESORT

Sun Valley

Ketchum

75

0   20 mi
0   20 km

Sawtooth National Forest

Hailey

Bellevue

CAMAS PRAIRIE CENTENNIAL MARSH WILDLIFE MANAGEMENT AREA

Fairfield

To Boise

20

46

75

To Twin Falls

93

93

© AVALON TRAVEL

beers, and then soak in a spring water-fed hot tub while watching the sunset over Potato Mountain.

The southwestern fringe of the Sawtooths is a land less traveled. The Camas Prairie explodes with color each spring when the marshes of blue camas lilies and other wildflowers sway in the gentle wind. The Soldier and Trinity Mountains offer quiet solitude, miles of remote trails, and a few nail-chewing drives on primitive roads, like the Rocky Bar-Atlanta stretch.

Anderson Ranch Reservoir to Atlanta

The southwestern stretch of the Sawtooths is actually in the Boise National Forest district. Here you will discover Idaho without all the trappings of out-of-state tourism. To access the area from Boise, head east on I-84 to Mountain Home and take the exit for U.S. 20 northbound, after which the road leaves the flats of the Snake River Plain and rises past Bennett Mountain. Soon you will catch glimpses of the high country to come, as mountain peaks and undulating valleys suddenly appear to the left. The highway eventually straightens out on the Camas Prairie, leading to the Wood River Valley and beyond.

ANDERSON RANCH RESERVOIR RECREATION AREA

Anglers come to scenic Anderson Ranch Reservoir Recreation Area to fish for kokanee, rainbow trout, yellow perch, and smallmouth bass. In addition, the **South Fork Boise River** below the dam offers blue-ribbon trout fishing. Waterskiing is popular on the reservoir in summer—there are several boat-launching ramps around the lake—as is snowmobiling in winter. Two different roads traverse the east and west shores. To reach the west shore, turn off U.S. 20 on Forest Road 134 and you'll soon drop precipitously down to the dam. The road crosses the spillway and continues north up the west side of the reservoir on a winding dirt road that clings to a sheer cliff. This drive will surely make your knuckles white. Eventually you'll come to Fall Creek, where you can calm your nerves with a cold beer.

An intense fire in 2013 blew through the Fall Creek drainage like a blowtorch, incinerating more than 50 vacation homes and cabins. Luckily, **Fall Creek Resort and Marina** (2147 S. Fall Creek Rd., Mountain Home, 208/653-2242) was spared from the devastation. This little fishing haven lies at the Fall Creek inlet to the reservoir, eight miles from the dam. It's a nice spot to hang out for a few days. The restaurant and bar offers typical pub grub and draft brews, and a downstairs fitness area has a small sauna and some exercise equipment. The marina rents paddleboats, sells marine fuel, and keeps a little store with groceries, tackle, and boating supplies. Ten guest rooms ($70) are available in the main building, and the resort maintains 30 RV sites ($15-30) with full hookups and a few tent sites ($15) down by the creek. Other facilities include a small game room, a gift shop, a boat ramp and moorage, and shower rooms.

Continuing up Forest Road 113, you climb to a beautiful wooded tableland before descending to the lake's main inlet at the little town of **Pine.** Here, Forest Road 113 joins the main road along the east shore. **Nester's Pine Resort** (12 N. Pine-Featherville Rd., Pine, 208/653-2210) offers RV sites ($25) with full hookups, 15 motel rooms ($63-110), and one cabin ($135). The resort also has a gift shop, a laundry facility, a bar, and a café that's open for three meals a day. Close by, the **Nitz Pine Store** (88 N. Pine-Featherville Rd., Pine, 208/653-2222) sells groceries, sundries, and fishing tackle.

To reach the east shore, continue east

on U.S. 20 three miles past **Little Camas Reservoir** and turn left onto Forest Road 152; follow it down to Forest Highway 61 and make a left. This side of the reservoir is busier than the more remote Fall Creek Resort side.

Deer Creek Lodge (730 S. Pine-Featherville Rd., Pine, 208/653-2454) offers a café, RV sites ($35) with hookups, and a few tent sites (around $15). About two miles north of Deer Creek Lodge, you'll meet the west-shore road at Pine.

JOHNSON'S SPRINGS HOT SPRINGS

Forest Highway 61 crosses the South Fork Boise River at Johnson's Bridge, where you'll no doubt see many cars parked along the north side. On the east bank of the river, just downstream from the bridge, Johnson's Springs Hot Springs send toasty water flowing down into riverside pools suitable for soaking. It's a popular spot with area campers; thus it tends to be crowded.

Anderson Ranch Dam near Pine

TRINITY MOUNTAINS

An alpine gem in southern Idaho, the Trinity Recreation Area has craggy peaks and numer-ous small lakes that often remain snowbound into August. Trinity Mountain (9,451 feet) crowns the area, providing panoramic views of the Sawtooths and Smoky Mountains to the northeast, and the Snake River Plain and Owyhee Mountains to the southwest. If you make it all the way up to the Forest Service fire lookout on top, you'll be at the highest lookout in the Boise National Forest.

This is great mountain-biking country. Forest roads weave through pine forests, aspen groves, and wildflower-filled mead-ows. One of the best hiking and backpack-ing trails in the area is the **Rainbow Basin Trail** (Trail 1174). It begins at Big Trinity Lake Campground and meanders south for about four miles past short spur trails to nine dif-ferent alpine lakes that have rainbow and cut-throat trout.

Big Trinity Lake Campground (17 sites,

$10) lies at the end of Forest Road 129E off Forest Road 129. Other U.S. Forest Service campgrounds in the vicinity include **Big Roaring Campground** (12 sites, $10) and **Little Roaring Campground** (4 sites, free). All the campgrounds are open July-September. For a bit more comfort, con-sider renting the Forest Service's **Big Trinity Guard Station** ($30, July 15-Sept. 30, res-ervations at www.reserveamerica.com), a rustic cabin that sleeps six. For more infor-mation on the guard station or the camp-grounds, contact the Boise National Forest's **Mountain Home Ranger District** (2180 American Legion Blvd., Mountain Home, 208/587-7961).

To reach Trinity Mountain and the Trinity Lakes, take Fall Creek Road (Forest Rd. 129) north from Fall Creek Resort on the west side of Anderson Ranch Reservoir, or take Trinity Creek Road (Forest Rd. 172) west off Featherville Road (Rte. 61) just south of Featherville.

FEATHERVILLE AND POINTS EAST

Featherville is an old mining town at the confluence of the small Feather River and the big South Fork of the Boise River. Here, Forest Road 227 heads east out of town and follows the South Fork of the Boise up to its headwaters, where there are numerous hot springs and U.S. Forest Service campgrounds. The following sites are listed from west (Featherville) to east (Big Smoky Creek).

Four small campgrounds (all $6) appear in rapid succession within the first seven miles east from Featherville. **Abbott Campground** (7 sites) comes first, followed closely by the like-sized **Chaparral Campground,** and 1.5 miles farther is **Bird Creek Campground** (5 sites). Nearby, you'll find **Willow Creek Campground** (5 sites), which is close to the little-used **Willow Creek Hot Springs.**

Baumgartner Campground ($10-20), about 12 miles from Featherville, is the main destination for most of the campers headed up the South Fork. John Baumgartner was a local miner who died in 1941 and left his mining claims to the federal government for a park; this campground is the result. The big attraction here is the Forest Service-developed hot-springs pool, a deluxe, concrete-lined number that can be crowded in summer. The large, 30-site campground lines the river amid groves of majestic ponderosa pines. A short nature trail starting near the hot pool loops across the hillside above the creek; signs explain aspects of the area's natural history along the way. There's a lot of bear activity in this area, so keep a clean campsite and don't smear kielbasa grease all over your shirt before crawling into your sleeping bag for the night. Make reservations at 877/444-6777 or www.recreation.gov.

Continuing east up the South Fork Boise, you'll pass the swampy and unappealing Lightfoot Hot Springs along the shoulder of the road near **Bowns Campground** (12 sites, $6).

Just past Bowns Campground, you'll come to some private cabins in the Big Smoky area, where there's a Forest Service guard station and the **Trapper's Inn** (208/764-3104), which keeps a few cabins ($50-70) next to a small store with ice, bait, and other necessities.

The road forks here; Forest Road 227 crosses Big Smoky Creek and heads out of the mountains down to Fairfield or to Ketchum.

OVER TO ATLANTA

If you go straight at Featherville instead of veering east, you are headed for the mining town of Atlanta, and there is a choice of two routes. **Phifer Creek** is the easier and longer way, and if you're headed to Atlanta after coming down from the Trinities, this is the road you'll be on. **James Creek** (Forest Rd. 072) is a lot shorter, but it's steeper and more demanding. This primitive route boasts incredible views and staircase waterfalls along the way. The decision point—in other words, the road junction—is at the mining ghost town of **Rocky Bar.** The right fork is the James Creek route, and the left goes via Phifer Creek. You can also get to Atlanta off Highway 21 near Idaho City.

ATLANTA

Although prospectors discovered precious metals around Atlanta in the 1860s, development of the area was hampered by its inaccessibility. Eventually the logistics problems were solved, and during 1932-1936 the Atlanta Mining District ran the most productive gold mines in Idaho. Today, there's still some gold mining going on in these parts, especially during the summer months. The little village of about 75 people lies at the south end of the Sawtooths, which rise just north of town. Greylock Mountain (9,317 feet) dominates the skyline, summoning backpackers up into the high reaches of the Sawtooth Wilderness.

Atlanta preserves its history in **Community Historic Park,** which features several pioneer-era buildings, among them the old jail. The town has basic services and several nice campgrounds, but there's nothing fancy here.

Hot Springs

Atlanta is blessed with two hot springs near the center of town. **Atlanta Hot Springs** is up the hill on the right as you drive east from town toward Power Plant Campground. It can get crowded in these steamy pools during the summer months. **Chattanooga Hot Springs** is one of the nicest in the state. It's in a much more secluded spot, unseen from the road, beneath bluffs lining the Middle Fork Boise River. The springs pour out of the bluff in a waterfall into riverside pools that have great views. When you start to get overheated, you're just steps from the cool water of the river. To get to Chattanooga, take the spur road heading north onto a grassy flat just west of Atlanta Hot Springs. Park on the bluff top and descend the steep trail to the springs.

Accommodations

Beaver Lodge (71 Main St., Atlanta, 208/864-2132), which also has a seasonal restaurant and bar, offers several guest rooms ($65-75) throughout the year, but don't expect to find any frills at this rustic establishment.

You can also make a reservation at the U.S. Forest Service's **Atlanta Guard Station** cabin ($45, May 31-Sept. 30), right in "downtown" Atlanta. It has electricity, a living room, a woodstove, a small kitchen, an indoor toilet and shower, and indoor drinking water. In recent years, the cabin has been used for fire crew lodging, so it may not be available every summer. To reserve it, contact the Boise National Forest's **Idaho City Ranger District** (3833 Hwy. 21, Idaho City, 208/392-6681).

Camping

Two U.S. Forest Service campgrounds are in the area: **Riverside Campground** (11 sites, $15) is closest to town, and the larger **Power Plant Campground** (24 sites, $15) is just down the road.

Camas Prairie and the Soldier Mountains

Camas Prairie is sacred ground for the Shoshone-Bannock people, who once came to this scenic spot every spring to hunt elk and stock up on camas lily bulbs, a starchy staple of their diet. The Soldier and Smoky Mountains frame the marshlands and sprawling prairie to the north. Pioneer emigrants on Goodale's Cutoff, a well-trodden spur of the Oregon Trail, traveled the entire length of the prairie in the shadow of these prominent mountains. Modern-day adventurers will discover many miles of backcountry solitude and a good ski area with short lift lines.

FAIRFIELD

This friendly little town offers basic services and a glimpse into the area's colorful history. In 1911 the Oregon Short Line Railroad completed its route across the Camas Prairie, giving birth to Fairfield. Trains no longer run, as they did for 70 years, but evidence of the railroad's existence is still present: An old caboose at the entrance to town serves as a visitors center, and the former depot has been turned into the **Camas County Historical Society Museum** (124 E. Camas Ave., Fairfield, 208/320-5994, 11am-4pm Sat. Memorial Day-Labor Day, free). The museum is packed with telegraph machines, farm equipment, pioneer clothing, railroad photos, and other artifacts.

Fairfield is not much to look at today, but it has an honest farm-town feel. Alfalfa farming and cattle ranching floats the economy. Most local kids are 4-H and FFA cardholders. But tourism is on the rise, and the town does have a handful of decent restaurants and lodging options for U.S. 20 travelers.

Accommodations

Prairie Inn (113 E. U.S. 20, 208/764-2247, from $69 d) is a rustic-looking hotel that sits right next to the highway. Most guest rooms have queen beds, satellite TV, and free wireless Internet. You can get family suites and rooms with jetted tubs for a few extra bucks.

For a little more money, you can stay at ★ **Soldier Mountain Ranch** (470 W. 500 N., Fairfield, 208/764-2506, www.soldiermountainranch.com). The Western-style resort has cabins ($145-200) and guest suites ($50-100) in the main lodge, not to mention an 18-hole public golf course (greens fees $18-22) with incredible views of the prairie and nearby mountains.

Food

The **Wrangler Drive-In** (105 W. U.S. 20, Fairfield, 208/764-2580, lunch and dinner daily, under $10) is where locals go for burgers and fries. Just look for the red building skirted with river rock just off the highway on the left as you come into town. This old-school drive-in serves big burgers, a large milkshake selection, and fries in all shapes and sizes. Try a Road Kill patty melt or a Powder Pig burger. The finger steaks are pretty good too.

Along the main drag, you'll find **Jim Dandy's Pizza** (505 Soldier Rd., Fairfield, 208/764-2030, 5pm-9 pm Wed.-Sun., $6-22) in a little storefront. The dinner-only restaurant puts out decent pizza, pasta dishes, calzones, and entrée salads. Treat yourself to a plate of Italian sausage fettuccine or a big pie with the works called the Kitchen Sink.

Information

For more information about campgrounds and recreational opportunities in the Sawtooth National Forest, stop by the **Fairfield Ranger District** (102 1st St., Fairfield, 208/764-3202), just off the highway. To learn more about the area in general, head to the **yellow caboose** (Soldier Rd. and Poplar St., Fairfield, 208/764-2660) for visitor brochures and advice from the friendly volunteers.

★ CAMAS PRAIRIE CENTENNIAL MARSH WILDLIFE MANAGEMENT AREA

Expect to see a variety of waterfowl at this tranquil marsh southwest of Fairfield.

Camas Prairie

Among the more interesting avian inhabitants are sandhill cranes, great blue herons, and sharp-beaked curlews. Several species of raptors, including golden eagles, prairie falcons, peregrine falcons, and great horned owls, also frequent the area, as do mule deer and pronghorn. During the spring months, the marsh makes a great spot to enjoy the bright blue camas blooms and other wildflowers like Indian paintbrush and clusters of yellow yarrow. To get here, travel 10 miles west of Fairfield on U.S. 20. The turnoff is marked with a big wooden sign. Make sure to have extra batteries for the camera; you don't want to miss these gorgeous shots.

NORTH OF FAIRFIELD

The Soldier and Smoky Mountains are laced with hiking trails and interesting spots to camp. The campgrounds can get crowded on weekends, but they're generally quiet during the week.

Next to Soldier Mountain Ski Resort, the U.S. Forest Service **Pioneer Campground** (May 20-Sept. 30, free) offers five sites. Just south of the ski resort, Forest Road 094 splits off to the east and winds up into the Soldier Mountains, over Couch Summit (7,008 feet) and down into the McHan Gulch drainage of Five Points Creek. Soon you'll come to the recently overhauled Forest Service **Five Points Campground** (3 sites, free) and, a little farther down the road, the confluence of Five Points Creek and the larger Little Smoky Creek. This point is also the junction of Forest Road 094 and Forest Road 227 (Little Smoky Rd.), which follows the babbling Little Smoky east to a few dispersed campsites along the creek (or "crick," as true Idahoans call them). **Worswick Hot Springs** is an idyllic spot where Worswick Creek flows down to join Little Smoky. Several pools have clear, sulfur-free water of various temperatures ranging up to *really* hot. Past Worswick, the road splits, with Forest Road 227 continuing over Dollarhide Summit and on to Ketchum, and Forest Road 015 heading southeast to the **Little Smoky Winter Recreation Area,** a snowmobile trailhead.

Forest Road 227 continues down the Little Smoky past **Preis Hot Springs,** an easy-to-miss one-person tub along the right side of the road. Eventually the road takes you to the confluence of Little Smoky and Big Smoky Creeks, which in turn feeds the South Fork of the Boise River.

wildflowers blooming at Centennial Marsh

SOLDIER MOUNTAIN SKI AREA

Twelve miles north of Fairfield up Soldier Creek Road, **Soldier Mountain Ski Area** (208/764-2526, www.soldiermountain.com, 9am-4pm Thurs.-Sun. Dec.-Apr., extended hours during Christmas break, full-day pass $38 adults, $22 ages 7-17 and 62-69, free under age 7 and over age 69) offers a friendly and inexpensive alternative to Sun Valley, some 60 miles to the east. The ski and snowboard area was once owned by Hollywood star Bruce Willis, who recently donated it to a nonprofit trust. The ski area boasts a 1,400-foot vertical drop that's served by two double chairs and two surface lifts. All 36 runs are groomed, and they boast fun names like "Wang Dang Doodle" and "Uh-Oh." Half-day passes, rentals, lessons, cat ski trips ($275), and a snowboard park are available. The base lodge is a good place to grab breakfast and lunch, or enjoy a brew after cutting through deep powder. A large, sunny deck provides good views of the slopes.

Bellevue and Hailey

At the junction of Highway 75 and U.S. 20, about 20 miles east of Fairfield, you can continue east on U.S. 20 to Craters of the Moon National Monument, or hang a right (south) at the junction to head to the Magic Valley and points south. If you take a left (north) on Highway 75, you'll soon enter the Wood River Valley, a slim draw flanked by the Smoky and Pioneer Mountains.

Coming into Bellevue, you can almost feel a buzz of excitement in the air of what lies ahead: the nation's first ski resort and playground for the rich and famous. And when you reach the airport at the south edge of Hailey, you'll see not only the expected Cessna 150s and crop dusters parked on the tarmac but also a formidable row of fancy corporate Learjets.

BELLEVUE

It's hard to tell where Bellevue (population 2,300) ends and Hailey begins. Bellevue's main drag (Hwy. 75), which moves at a snail's pace, is considerably shorter than Hailey's business district, yet it still has its charms. Bellevue was once called Biddyville, but the name was changed to make the town sound more attractive. As with most upscale resort communities, people are either rich or they work for the rich. That said, many residents of Bellevue work in service-related jobs (landscaping, restaurants, housekeeping) in the Ketchum-Sun Valley area, but more and more vacation homes are popping up around this gateway town. And with vacation homes come more restaurants and shops.

Accommodations and Food

Hang your hat for the night at the **High Country Motel** (766 S. Main St., Bellevue, 208/721-0067, from $65 d), one of the most affordable lodging options in the valley. This log cabin-style motor inn is clean and comfortable, and the owners are friendly. All rooms have queen-size beds, cable TV, small refrigerators, and microwaves.

People come from all over the valley for the pizza at **South Valley Pizzeria** (108 Elm St., Bellevue, 208/788-1456, 4pm-9pm daily, pizzas $16-$23). This tucked-away pizza joint specializes in thin-crust pies. You can either pick your own toppings or choose one of the restaurant's specialty pizzas, including a Basque creation with chorizo, green chiles, garlic, and asiago cheese.

HAILEY

Hailey (population 8,000), 12 miles south of Ketchum and Sun Valley, is a small, relatively quiet town living in the shadow of its famous neighbors up the road. But as the Blaine County seat, Hailey boasts its own share of Idaho history. The town is named after John Hailey, who founded it in 1881 and served two terms as a territorial delegate to the U.S. Congress. Hailey flourished as a mining boomtown 1881-1889, and at one point had the largest Chinese population in the state; meticulous Chinese miners worked abandoned claims profitably long after other miners had left the area. Hailey was also the birthplace of 20th-century poet Ezra Pound.

Blaine County Historical Museum

To learn more about the town's history, visit the **Blaine County Historical Museum** (218 N. Main St., Hailey, 208/788-1801, 11am-5pm Mon.-Sat., 1pm-5pm Sun. Memorial Day-Oct. 31, free). The museum has a large political button collection, old mining and farming tools, a walk-through mine tunnel, Idaho's first telephone switchboard, and a display of Chinese dishes and artifacts.

Birthplace of Ezra Pound

One of the 20th century's most influential poets, Ezra Loomis Pound was born in Hailey on October 30, 1885. His father was registrar of the U.S. Land Office in Hailey's boomtown days. Ezra didn't have much of a chance to become an Idahoan—the family moved from Hailey to Philadelphia when he was barely a year old. Yet as a young man Ezra clung to a fascination with his birthplace.

Pound, something of a boy genius, also developed a taste for defying convention, authority, and social norms. He mastered nine languages, got fired as a college professor, and then exiled himself to Europe for 40 years. He befriended William Butler Yeats, fostered the careers of a number of literary greats—among them T. S. Eliot, Robert Frost, Ford Madox Ford, Ernest Hemingway, James Joyce, Amy Lowell, and Marianne Moore—and developed an attraction to the politics of fascist Italian dictator Benito Mussolini. His irascible anti-Semitic, anti-American radio broadcasts from Italy in the early 1940s got him arrested for treason after that country fell to the Allies in World War II. Pound was ruled mentally incompetent to stand trial, despite having written the award-winning *Pisan Cantos* while incarcerated, and was committed to a mental hospital in Washington, DC. He was released after 12 years and moved back to Italy, where he died in 1971.

Recreation

The onetime Union Pacific Railroad

Hailey's main drag

right-of-way between Hailey and Sun Valley is now part of **Wood River Trails** (year-round, free), a system of paved paths available for jogging, strolling, horseback riding, bicycling, and rollerblading. In winter, cross-country skiing is popular along this scenic path. The highway is within earshot along much of the route, but so is the Big Wood River.

The **Hailey Skate Park** (free) boasts a 16-foot full-radius concrete pipe, tall walls, and lots of other challenges for the board set. It's right across from the airport entrance on the south end of town.

Entertainment

Company of Fools (208/788-6520, www.sunvalleycenter.org, $30 adults, $22 seniors, $10 students) is a Hailey-based theater company that presents about three productions a year. Its biggest claim to fame may be that part-time resident Bruce Willis serves on its board of directors, and he even shows up in its productions from time to time. (A few years back, I saw him play a riveting version of Lee in Sam Shepard's *True West*.) But even without the celebrity cachet, this is one of the state's most important arts organizations. It performs at the beautifully restored 1938 **Liberty Theatre** (110 N. Main St., Hailey) and at various venues around the state.

You can catch a flick at **Big Wood Cinemas** (801 N. Main St., Hailey, 208/578-0971, $8.75 adults, $6.50 seniors and ages 2-12) on the north end of town. This four-theater complex shows first-run movies as well as matinees and weekly special deals.

Accommodations

The 29-room **Airport Inn** (820 4th Ave. S., Hailey, 208/788-2477, from $80 d) is a stone's throw from the airport. Amenities include free Wi-Fi and a light breakfast. Suites and kitchenettes are available.

The **Wood River Inn** (603 N. Main St., Hailey, 208/578-0600 or 877/542-0600, www.woodriverinn.com, from $120 d) is a friendly hotel that offers all the amenities, including in-room refrigerators, microwave ovens, coffeemakers, and hair dryers. It also has an indoor pool. Rates include continental breakfast, and suites are available.

Food and Drink

★ **CK's Real Food** (320 N. Main St., Hailey, 208/788-1223, www.cksrealfood.com, lunch 11am-2pm Mon.-Fri., dinner 5pm-10pm daily, entrées around $25) is a deliciously funky restaurant in a gussied-up bungalow along the main drag. Chef-owner Chris Kastner uses lots of locally raised meat products and organic produce. The menu changes with the seasons and the whim of the kitchen staff. One night you might see a beautifully braised Lava Lake lamb shank, and another time it could be braised Cuban-style pork shoulder with buttermilk polenta. How about a grilled gaucho steak in a pool of verdant chimichurri sauce? Smaller plates are all over the culinary map too. Thai-inspired ceviche (with shrimp, finfish, and calamari) and a bright salad of broiled apricots, black figs, prosciutto, and hazelnuts also make appearances on the menu. The wine list boasts lots of Northwest labels.

McClain's Pizza and Spirits (103 S. Main St., Hailey, 208/788-0960, 11am-9pm daily, $9-26) is in the heart of downtown Hailey. This lively joint with a cocktail lounge serves hand-tossed pizzas as well as big salads, calzones, hot wings, and a mean meatball sandwich. The bar stays open late.

Sun Valley Brewing Company (202 N. Main St., Hailey, 208/788-0805, www.sunvalleybrewery.com, lunch and dinner daily) has a pub that offers 12 commendable handcrafted brews and a large menu of upscale bar food. Try an Asian-inspired appetizer (like calamari tempura and lemongrass chicken) before committing to the pub's more substantial offerings: hot sandwiches, steaks, salads, and thin-crust pizzas.

Open your tired eyes at the **Hailey Coffee Company** (219 S. Main St., Hailey, 208/788-8482, 6am-6pm Mon.-Fri., 6am-4pm Sat.-Sun.), a local roaster with a coffeehouse right on the main drag. Besides espresso drinks made from freshly roasted organic beans, you can also get in-house baked goodies such as flaky pastries, scones, and excellent banana bread.

Atkinsons' Market (93 E. Croy St., Hailey, 208/788-2294, 7am-9pm daily), with other stores in Ketchum and Bellevue, is the place to go for wine, artisanal breads, and specialty cheeses as well as everyday grocery items. The deli puts out a rotating menu of fresh sandwiches, soups, and salads. The market is in Alturas Plaza, east of the main drag.

The **Hailey Farmers Market** (2pm-6pm Thurs. June-Oct.) may be small, but it boasts a colorful profusion of seasonal produce and other foodstuffs. Besides oodles of organic produce, you'll also find freshly baked goods as well as locally produced meats, cheeses, honey, eggs, and fresh-cut flowers. The market sets up in downtown's Bullion Square.

Information

Stop by the Hailey Chamber of Commerce's **visitors center** (781 S. Main St., Hailey, 208/788-3484, 9am-5pm Mon.-Fri.) for brochures and information about the area. The **Blaine County Recreation District** (1050 Fox Acres Rd., Hailey, 208/578-2273) can give you the lowdown and brochures about recreational activities in the Wood River Valley.

Ketchum and Sun Valley

As Highway 75 slowly climbs alongside the Big Wood River from Bellevue to Ketchum, property values climb as well. Hailey, while by no means undeveloped, is relatively rural compared to Ketchum, where you'll find yourself awash in a sea of multimillion-dollar homes and glitzy art galleries, boutiques, and restaurants.

History

Among those impressed by the 1932 winter Olympics at Lake Placid, New York, was W. Averell Harriman, chairman of the board of the Union Pacific Railroad. An avid skier, he soon came up with a grand plan to build a remote resort that other affluent types would have to take the train to reach. This strategy had already proven enormously successful for the Canadian Pacific Railway, which started a luxury-lodging empire after its success building the Banff Springs Hotel. Harriman sent young Austrian Count Felix Schaffgotsch scouring the West in search of an ideal site for a destination ski resort that would draw the tourist throngs via the Union Pacific Railroad.

Schaffgotsch toured from the Cascades to Colorado, passing up many areas—including Aspen, Colorado—that would eventually be

Sun Valley

© AVALON TRAVEL

home to first-class ski resorts. When he saw the sleepy mining and sheep-ranching town of Ketchum, he wired Harriman with the news: "Among the many attractive spots I have visited, this combines more delightful features than any place I have seen in the United States, Switzerland, or Austria for a winter sports resort." Harriman was quickly on the scene to buy the 4,300-acre Brass Ranch. Construction of a no-expense-spared luxury lodge began in May 1936, and now Harriman needed to tell the world about his new baby. He came up with a stroke of genius: draw Hollywood stars and other celebrities, and the masses will follow. Shortly after the December 1936 opening of the lodge, Clark Gable and Errol Flynn swashbuckled their way through Ketchum to the delight of the paparazzi and the public, and the trend began that to this day marks the Wood River Valley as a playground for Hollywood luminaries and other high-profile celebrities.

When Harriman's Union Pacific mechanical engineers came up with the world's first chairlift on Dollar Mountain, styled after a hoist system used to load bananas into ships' holds, the resort's skiing legacy was firmly established.

Getting Oriented

The Ketchum-Sun Valley metropolitan area (if you want to call it that) consists of two main areas, each virtually self-contained. **Ketchum,** right on the highway, is the biggest and the most like a real city, with the essential services that keep life flowing smoothly for locals. Ketchum is the closest community to the ski resort's River Run lift.

Travel about a mile northeast of Ketchum, and you'll come to the idyllic **Sun Valley** area, essentially the resort's company town. Unlike Ketchum, Sun Valley (despite having more name recognition than its neighbors) is a small, Tyrolean-themed hamlet consisting primarily of the original Sun Valley Lodge and its sibling Sun Valley Inn, along with the company's restaurants and activity centers serving guests of those establishments.

The rest of the area is residential, with condos and homes galore, but other than a small pedestrian mall with shops in the village, you won't find much in the way of basic services. Interestingly enough, Sun Valley is actually farther from Bald Mountain recreation than Ketchum. If staying at Sun Valley Lodge and skiing Bald Mountain is your plan, realize that you won't be skiing out the door of your room or even walking to the lifts, but rather taking a short free bus ride first. Sun Valley, however, is close to the less challenging and less expensive Dollar Mountain ski area, also part of Sun Valley Company's operation.

Also of interest is the **Warm Springs** area, a short distance northwest of downtown Ketchum at the base of Bald Mountain. Warm Springs has a smaller, quieter feel than Ketchum proper, but it doesn't offer much beyond condos and coffee shops for the ski crowd. The resort's base area here features another plush day lodge and two detachable quads that will zoom you up the mountain.

SIGHTS
Sun Valley Museum of History
The **Sun Valley Museum of History** (180 1st St. E., Ketchum, 208/726-8118, 1pm-5pm Tues.-Sat. year-round, $5 adults, $2.50 students, seniors, and active military with ID, free under age 5), in Forest Service Park, offers exhibits focusing on the town's rich ski and railroad heritage. Highlights span the days of the fur trappers and the Tukudeka people all the way to the arrival of Sun Valley Lodge and the Hollywood glitterati. A self-guided walking-tour pamphlet to town is available here.

Ore Wagon Museum
A bit of Ketchum's mining heritage is kept behind glass at the **Ore Wagon Museum** (East Ave. and 5th St., Ketchum), where you can spy for free the giant ore cars that once hauled supplies and mining booty up and down the valley. The heavily laden wagons were often towed in strings, pulled by teams of eight or more mules. This isn't a staffed museum, just a walk-by and peek-in point of interest.

Hemingway Memorial

After Averell Harriman completed his Sun Valley Lodge in 1936, he offered complimentary stays to some of the era's most glamorous people. One of the invitees was 40-year-old writer Ernest Hemingway. By the time he first visited Sun Valley in 1939, he had written *The Sun Also Rises* and *A Farewell to Arms* and had been featured on the cover of *Time* magazine. He stayed in Sun Valley Lodge that fall, working on *For Whom the Bell Tolls*. He returned in fall 1940 and again in 1941. During these visits, Hemingway found his niche in the rich Sun Valley social scene: duck hunting with Gary Cooper and partying at the Trail Creek Cabin with Dorothy Parker and other luminaries. Although Hemingway enjoyed these trips to Ketchum, after World War II he settled in Cuba with his fourth wife, Mary Welsh. In 1953, he won a Pulitzer Prize for *The Old Man and the Sea*, and the following year he was honored with the Nobel Prize for Literature. The 1958 Cuban revolution along with Hemingway's deteriorating health led the couple to leave Cuba and become Ketchum homeowners in 1959. It was a short-lived residency: Plagued by depression and alcoholism, Hemingway slid into his final chapter. Ernest and Mary dined at Ketchum's Christiania Restaurant on July 1, 1961; early the next morning, Hemingway turned a shotgun on himself, ending his own life at the age of 61. When Mary Welsh Hemingway died in 1986, she left the couple's Ketchum home to The Nature Conservancy, but a gaggle of meddling neighbors have prevented the house from opening to the public for tours.

Meanwhile, Sun Valley's **Hemingway Memorial** to the great writer, a short distance up Trail Creek Road from the lodge, is as simple and eloquent as a Hemingway sentence. An obelisk topped with a bust sculpted by Robert Berks stands in a shady nook overlooking the tranquil babble of Trail Creek. It's inscribed with words written by Hemingway in 1939 as a eulogy for his friend Gene Van Guilder, who was killed in a hunting accident. Ironically enough, the words seem as

Stargazing in Sun Valley

The night sky above Idaho's mountains is bright with constellations, but if you spend any time in the Sun Valley area you might see other kinds of stars too. Over the years, Sun Valley has had many famous part-time residents, including Gary Cooper, Lucille Ball, Marilyn Monroe, some of the Kennedys, and Ernest Hemingway. This valley of sun and snow continues to draw celebrities to its mountain charms. Rockers Steve Miller and Peter Cetera have been longtime homeowners. Folk superwoman Carole King lives just up the road on a big spread near Stanley. Hollywood luminaries who hold part-time addresses in Sun Valley include Jamie Lee Curtis, Clint Eastwood, Tom Hanks, Bruce Willis, Jean-Claude Van Damme, and Arnold Schwarzenegger, to name a few.

Most everyday residents here don't pay much attention to these big-name stars, who are occasionally seen hanging out around town, so don't expect to find any maps to the stars' homes. These celebrities blend in well, which is just the way they like it. Sun Valley is a great place for people from all walks of life, including famous folks, to take a break from their hectic schedules.

though Hemingway could have written them for himself:

> Best of all he loved the fall. The leaves yellow on the cottonwoods. Leaves floating on the trout streams. And above the hills the high blue windless skies... now he will be a part of them forever.

Ketchum Cemetery

Ernest Miller Hemingway is buried at the **Ketchum Cemetery** (1026 N. Main St., Ketchum) in the Warm Springs area of town. A long, rectangular gravestone, often scattered with wine corks, coins, and other things fans leave behind, marks the place where Papa's earthly remains rest under two pine trees.

Sawtooth Botanical Garden

South of town, the **Sawtooth Botanical Garden** (11 Gimlet Rd., Ketchum, 208/726-9358, www.sbgarden.org, dawn-dusk daily, free but donations are suggested) is a nonprofit organization that teaches environmental stewardship. You can meander through beautiful gardens that delineate the region's five biomes, including a sagebrush xeriscape, a lava rock moonscape, and alpine, montane, and riparian gardens. It's a great spot for a picnic.

WINTER RECREATION
Alpine Skiing and Snowboarding

To the late Gretchen Fraser, the first U.S. Olympic skiing gold medalist (she won the slalom in 1948), Sun Valley's Bald Mountain was "the greatest mountain in the world." Following in her footsteps, local Olympic wunderkind Picabo Street (gold medalist in the Super G slalom in 1998) grew up carving through powder on the mountain's lofty summit, as did Olympic snowboarder Kaitlyn Farrington, who won gold on the half-pipe at the 2014 Winter Games.

This is one Olympic-size mountain, all right, or rather one big mountain and one small mountain; you get a choice of two at **Sun Valley Resort** (snow report 800/635-4150, tickets 208/622-6136, www.sunvalley.com, full-day lift tickets $109 adults, $80 seniors, $59 children). Bald Mountain, or "Baldy," as locals call it, offers runs up to three miles long down some 3,400 vertical feet from its 9,150-foot summit. What's more, the 2,054 skiable acres are served by a decidedly decadent array of fast lifts and luxurious day lodges. The resort recently debuted its new Roundhouse Gondola system, featuring 56 eight-passenger cars that zoom up and down 2,000 vertical feet in less than 10 minutes. The express gondola starts at the River Run base and travels up to the Top Terminal Plaza, where the Roundhouse Restaurant is located. Seven high-speed detachable quads web the mountain along with four triple chairs and

two double chairs. In addition to all the quads, the resort boasts a state-of-the-art computer-controlled snowmaking system to ensure optimum snow conditions throughout the season.

And then there are the three lodges: one each at Warm Springs and River Run base areas, and one high on a mid-mountain ridgetop overlooking the valley. They're all spectacular multimillion-dollar affairs designed in a beautiful mountain mega-cabin theme, including oversize logs, river rock, and sweeping expanses of glass. Their interiors are positively regal in their furnishings. Marble, chandeliers, and fine wines mix with trophy heads and fireplaces to give the lodges an air of high-mountain classiness.

As for skiing, Baldy might be the nation's ultimate mountain for cruisers. You'll find an incredible abundance of moderately steep, consistently pitched, and immaculately groomed intermediate runs, along with some excellent bowls, challenging tree skiing, and a half-pipe on Lower Warm Springs. But extreme skiers looking for serious airtime might be disappointed; the Limelight run off the Warm Springs quad is probably Sun Valley's biggest challenge. And while it's true that the lift system covers the entire mountain like a blanket and makes for short lift lines, that can have its own drawbacks. On a busy weekend the summit is like a circus: Multiple quads continually dump out skiers in batches, while paragliders jump off the mountaintop, photographers photograph the skiers, and everyone stands around aimlessly admiring the world-class view. Locals probably know a secret spot or two, but you may not be able to ferret them out. Finally, you have to pay top dollar for all those fancy quads, gondolas, and lodges. Half-day tickets and special deals are available for those on a tight budget.

The resort's other hill, Dollar Mountain, is on the Sun Valley side of Highway 75. It's a relatively uncrowded, wide-open beginner hill with three lifts and a handle tow on 628 vertical feet, great for floundering about on teleskis or for kids learning to snowplow. Tickets are about half the price of those on Baldy.

Heli-Skiing

Sun Valley Heli-Ski/EpicQuest (208/622-3108 or 800/872-3108, www.epicquest.com) offers a variety of chopper-drop packages that leave from the Sun Valley Gun Club across from Trail Creek Cabin. To go diving through the untracked fluff, all you'll need is intermediate or better skiing skills and a small trust fund. A full day (with 5-6 runs for a total of around 10,000 vertical feet) costs about $1,100 per person.

Cross-Country Skiing

The **Wood River Trails** system runs 19 miles from Hulen Meadows north of Ketchum all the way south to Bellevue along a former Union Pacific Railroad right-of-way. Three miles north of Ketchum, the **Lake Creek Trails** offer a 10-mile network of loops on the west side of the Big Wood River. The regularly groomed trails are part of the North Valley Trail System, which requires a $17 trail pass.

Sun Valley Resort's **Nordic Center** (208/622-2250, day passes $24 adults, $15 seniors, $10 ages 12 and under), just past the lodge up Trail Creek, has 25 miles of groomed trails on the snow-covered golf course and surrounding hills and canyons. The trails are meticulously groomed, including a set of narrow-spaced tracks provided especially for kids. The best steeps are on the Diamondback Trail across the road, as it climbs to a ridge for a good view of Ketchum. Rentals and lessons are available.

Backcountry Skiing

The joys of nearly unlimited skiable terrain in the mountains surrounding the Wood River Valley must be balanced against the backcountry's serious avalanche potential. Before setting out, visiting backcountry skiers should call the **Ketchum Ranger District** (208/622-5371) for avalanche updates to be on the safe side.

Sun Valley Trekking (Hailey, 208/788-1966, www.svtrek.com) offers guided tours to its cozy and comfortable backcountry huts in the Smoky and Sawtooth Mountains. The huts have woodstoves with plenty of firewood,

propane cookstoves, lanterns, toilets, wood-fired hot tubs or saunas, and bunk beds with sleeping pads. You can rent a hut and ski to it on your own, but first-time hut users are required to employ a guide for the first day. The company also offers classes in backcountry ski-touring, telemarking, and avalanche education. Full-day guided tours and overnight packages range $125-595 per person per day. The company also offers guided day hikes in the summer, and one of its huts is open for summer use by hikers and mountain bikers.

Sleigh Rides

Dinner sleigh rides out to historic **Trail Creek Cabin** are offered through Sun Valley Resort's sports and recreation office (208/622-2135, $35 pp). The 1937 log-and-stone cabin was a retreat popular with the Hollywood set back in the day, and it was Ernest Hemingway's favorite New Year's Eve party venue. Sleighs depart from the Sun Valley Inn several times a night for dinner as well. The ride to the cabin along Trail Creek takes about a half hour. Dress warmly; blankets are provided.

SUMMER RECREATION

Although Sun Valley started as a ski resort, a few decades ago the Sun Valley Company and local civic leaders pushed to convert the area into a year-round destination resort. They succeeded, and now the Sun Valley/Ketchum area does even more business in summer than in winter. Summer is an undeniably magnificent time of year here. Hundreds of square miles of the surrounding mountains (accessible in winter only to experienced mountaineers) open up for everyone to enjoy.

Trail Systems

The 10 miles of paved pedestrian and bike paths in the **Sun Valley Trail System** loop around Dollar Mountain from Ketchum to Sun Valley to Elkhorn and out along Elkhorn Road back to the highway. A spur trail follows Trail Creek from Sun Valley Lodge out to Boundary Campground. The Sun Valley system connects with the 20-mile-long **Wood**

River Trails system, which traces the old Union Pacific right-of-way from Lake Creek Road, north of Ketchum, down the valley to Bellevue. Ambitious long-term plans call for trails to eventually connect Stanley with Shoshone. For more information, contact the **Blaine County Recreation District** (1050 Fox Acres Rd., Hailey, 208/578-2273).

Hiking and Mountain Biking

You'll find no shortage of suitable ground for exercise; within a five-mile radius of Ketchum lie some 40 miles of unpaved hiking and mountain-biking trails, all of which get heavily used as workout terrain by area residents. West of downtown Ketchum, the **Bald Mountain Trail** (Trail 201) runs five miles up to the top of Baldy itself. The trailhead for the five-mile hike is at the bottom of the River Run lift. Or be lazy and take your bike up the lift with you, thanks to Sun Valley ski area's detachable quads that haul mountain bikers in summer.

In the Sun Valley area, several trails leave from Trail Creek Cabin, two miles east of Sun Valley Village up Trail Creek Road. The **Trail Creek Trail** (Trail 305) follows the creek for 1.5 miles one-way and is barrier free. The **Proctor Mountain Trail** (Trail 119) climbs to the summit of that peak for panoramic views of the valley. The easy 1.75-mile **Aspen Loop Trail** (Trail 119A) and the more difficult 3.5-mile one-way **Corral Creek Trail** (Trail 119B) wind through aspen and evergreen forest. No bikes are allowed on the Aspen Loop or Proctor Mountain Trails.

The Adams Gulch trails are 1.5 miles north of Ketchum; follow Adams Gulch Road 0.75 mile off Highway 75 to the trailhead. The network of trails ranges from the **Shadyside Trail** (Trail 177A), an easy 1.5-mile stroll, to the demanding **Adams Gulch Trail** (Trails 177 and 142), a 14-mile loop. Intermediate-length hikes are also possible. Bikes are permitted on the Adams Gulch trails.

The **Fox Creek-Oregon Gulch Trails** lie a bit farther up the west side of Highway 75 and are accessed by two separate trailheads:

The Lake Creek trailhead is right off Highway 75, four miles north of Ketchum; the Oregon Gulch trailhead is three miles farther north, off Highway 75 at Forest Road 143, just past the North Fork Store. These trails are more difficult than the Adams Gulch trails. Loops ranging 3-10 miles are possible, and bikes are allowed.

For more information on these hikes, pick up a trail brochure and map at the U.S. Forest Service **Ketchum Ranger District office** (206 Sun Valley Rd., Ketchum, 208/622-5371).

Horseback Riding

Sun Valley Stables (208/622-2387) offers one-hour guided trail rides in the area for $45 per person, or 90-minute rides for $54 per person. The rides leave the center on Sun Valley Road (between Ketchum and Sun Valley) starting at 9am daily in summer. Reservations are required; children must be at least eight years old and 52 inches tall. Spring and fall rides, group hayrides, winter sleigh rides, and stagecoach rides may also be available by appointment.

Golf

The **Sun Valley Resort Golf Course** (208/622-2251, 18 holes $110-169 peak season), designed by Robert Trent Jones Jr., is a scenic place to hit the links. The resort just added an extra nine on the north side of Trail Creek Road, stretching this par-72 course to 6,948 yards. Fairways on the main course follow Trail Creek, crossing it seven times on the front nine. Reservations for tee times are required.

For less expensive golfing, check out the nine-hole **Bigwood Golf Course** (115 Thunder Trail Rd., Ketchum, 208/726-4024, $40 for nine holes, $70 for 18 holes), on the hill between Highway 75 and Sun Valley. This par-36 course, designed by Robert Muir Graves, has more than 3,200 yards of gorgeous greens. Cart rentals are available.

Rafting

The local Big Wood River provides great

fishing but no boating. However, several raft companies based in the area offer guided trips on nearby white water. **White Otter Outdoor Adventures** (Stanley, 208/788-5005, www.whiteotter.com) runs the Salmon River day stretch out of Sunbeam as well as the Murtaugh and Hagerman reaches of the Snake River. Half-day Salmon River trips cost around $75 adults, $55 under age 13. Also running the Salmon day stretch is the Stanley-based **Sawtooth Adventure Company** (208/721-8772, www.sawtoothadventure.com).

Camping

Six U.S. Forest Service campgrounds south of the Sawtooth National Recreation Area boundary ring Ketchum and Sun Valley. Up Trail Creek Road about two miles past Sun Valley Village is **Boundary Campground** (8 sites, $10). Continuing on Trail Creek Road over Trail Creek Summit in the direction of Mackay are **Park Creek Campground** (12 sites, $12), 26 miles from Ketchum, and **Phi Kappa Campground** (21 sites, $10), 23 miles out.

Up the East Fork Wood River (Forest Rd. 118 east of Hwy. 75 between Ketchum and Hailey), you'll find **Federal Gulch Campground** (15 sites, free) and **Sawmill Campground** (3 sites, free). Finally, west of Highway 75 out Deer Creek Road is **Deer Creek Campground** (3 sites, free), 20 miles from Ketchum.

For more information and campground maps, contact the **Ketchum Ranger District** (206 Sun Valley Rd., Ketchum, 208/622-5371).

YEAR-ROUND RECREATION
Fishing

The beautiful Big Wood River flows the length of the valley, offering good trout fishing around every bend. Anglers also enjoy success up Warm Springs Creek (which flows into the Big Wood from the west side of Ketchum), Trail Creek (which flows down from the east), and other tributaries. Throughout the valley, many sections of riverbank are privately owned. Access points for the public portions are marked by signs and noted in a fishing brochure published by the Blaine County Recreation District, available at the Ketchum-Sun Valley visitors center and ranger station.

Trout fishing is open year-round on the Big Wood River and Little Wood River, but restrictions apply on certain stretches of both tributaries. For details, contact the **Idaho Department of Fish and Game** (208/334-3700, www.fishandgame.idaho.gov), or hire a trusty river guide to take you out into the riffles.

Local fishing guides include **Bill Mason Outfitters** (Sun Valley Village, 208/622-9305) and **Silver Creek Outfitters** (500 N. Main St., Ketchum, 208/726-5282, www.silver-creek.com). Expect guide service to run $300-450 per day for 1-2 anglers.

Hot Springs

The closest hot springs to Ketchum is **Frenchman's Hot Springs,** 10.5 miles west of town via Warm Springs Road (Forest Rd. 227). **Warfield Hot Springs** is just 0.5 mile farther down the road. North of Ketchum you'll discover **Easley Hot Springs** and **Russian John Hot Springs** in the Sawtooth National Recreation Area.

Ice Skating

Sun Valley Lodge offers a pair of rinks, one indoors in a separate building behind the lodge, the other right outside the back door of the lodge (208/622-2194, $12 adults, $10 ages 6-17, free under age 5 with a paid adult, skate rental $5). Lessons are available. In winter, you can also skate for free on the outdoor rink at **Atkinson Park** (8th St. and 3rd Ave.).

OUTFITTERS

Plenty of area shops rent the equipment you'll need to enjoy a big adventure. Some of them are listed below.

Ski, Snowboard, Mountain Bike, and Skate Rentals

Area rental shops include **Sturtevants Ski & Sports** (340 N. Main St., Ketchum,

208/726-4501), **Formula Sports** (460 N. Main St., Ketchum, 208/726-3194), and **Pete Lane's Mountain Sports** (River Run Plaza, Ketchum, 208/622-6123; Sun Valley Village, 208/622-2276).

Backcountry Shops

Mountaineering-oriented rental centers include **The Elephant's Perch** (280 East Ave., at Sun Valley Rd., Ketchum, 208/726-3497) and **Backwoods Mountain Sports** (711 N. Main St., at Warm Springs Rd., Ketchum, 208/726-8826). Both carry a full selection of cross-country ski gear, including touring, skating, and telemark skis, boots, and poles. They also carry climbing gear and rent a good selection of camping equipment, including packs, tents, sleeping bags, and the likes. Backwoods rents kayaks and rafts too.

EVENTS

Ketchum-Sun Valley's events calendar is huge, and something's always going on in the valley of the sun. Here's a look at some of the area's most noteworthy events. For details and a complete list, contact the **Sun Valley-Ketchum Chamber and Visitors Bureau** (491 Sun Valley Rd., Ketchum, 208/726-3423, www.visitsunvalley.com).

Summer

The world-class **Sun Valley Ice Show** (208/622-2135, dusk Sat. late June-early Sept., call for ticket information) presents Olympic medalists and other world-champion skaters and features a dinner package option. It all takes place at the Sun Valley Lodge ice rink just off the terrace.

Music fills the upper Wood River Valley during numerous summertime events. The **Ketch'em Alive** music series (7pm-9pm Tues. June-Aug.) presents bands from around the Northwest at Forest Service Park. The **Sun Valley Summer Symphony** (208/622-5607, www.svsummersymphony.com, July-Aug.) performs free outdoor concerts at Sun Valley Lodge. Also keep your eye peeled for

occasional **outdoor concerts** put on by the Sun Valley Center for the Arts (schedule and tickets 208/726-9491, www.sunvalleycenter.org). Shows in the past have included the likes of Willie Nelson, Lyle Lovett, James Taylor, and Carole King. This organization is also responsible for the annual **Sun Valley Arts and Crafts Festival,** held in August at Sun Valley Resort.

Labor Day weekend bring **Ketchum Wagon Days** (www.wagondays.org), a festival commemorating the town's mining history. Festivities include one of the West's largest nonmotorized parades, featuring those glassed-in ore wagons, along with pancake breakfasts, concerts, and street dances.

Fall

In mid-October, the saints come marchin' in to Sun Valley for the **Sun Valley Jazz Jamboree** (www.sunvalleyjazz.com). About 20 of the best Dixieland and ragtime jazz bands from the United States, Canada, and around the world re-create Bourbon Street and the Big Band era for the dancing crowds. The revelry takes place at Sun Valley Resort. If you'd rather see sheep marching than saints marching, look for the **Trailing of the Sheep Festival** (208/720-0585, www.trailingofthesheep.org), also in mid-October. This three-day shindig celebrates the Wood River Valley's sheepherding heritage at various locations around the valley, with sheepdog trials, Basque and Peruvian music and dancing, arts and crafts, food, and a big parade where thousands of sheep get herded down Ketchum's main drag on their way back from the high country.

Winter

Cross-country ski races fill the winter calendar. The biggest cross-country event in the valley comes in early February, when the huge **Sun Valley Nordic Festival** (www.nordictownusa.com) draws upward of 700 cross-country ski racers from all over the world. They race right down the Harriman Trail from Galena Lodge to the Sawtooth National

Recreation Area Headquarters, the very same 19-mile trail you can ski yourself on any other winter's day for $17.

Spring

The **Sun Valley Wellness Festival** (www.sunvalleywellness.org), held over Memorial Day weekend, features big-name speakers, intimate workshops, and a "Hands-on Hall" where you can try a variety of alternative and holistic health treatments.

KETCHUM

Ketchum (population 2,700) is the urban hub of the Wood River Valley. Although the town is not large, every block is packed with restaurants, bars, galleries, outdoor outfitters, and boutiques. It's important to note that Ketchum, along with Hailey, has two distinct monthlong breaks (Spring Slack and Fall Slack) between the busy summer and winter seasons, when some businesses are closed and others offer great deals. This is a mellow time

Ketchum

to visit the area, and enough places stay open to make a trip worthwhile.

Art Galleries

Ketchum is known for its multitude of art galleries, and most of them are within walking distance of each other.

The nonprofit **Sun Valley Center for the Arts** (191 5th St. E., Ketchum, 208/726-9491, www.sunvalleycenter.org) has been the hub of the valley's art world for more than 20 years, presenting exhibits, lectures, films, workshops, and more.

Frederic Boloix Fine Arts (351 Leadville Ave. N., Ketchum, 208/726-8810) is a sleek gallery that features contemporary art and occasionally works by 20th-century masters such as Picasso, Matisse, and Chagall. **Broschofsky Galleries** (360 East Ave., Ketchum, 208/726-4950) carries an eclectic mix of works from the 19th and 20th centuries, including Native American, Western, and contemporary paintings, jewelry, weavings, and pottery.

On the Baldy side of Main Street, **Gail Severn Gallery** (400 1st Ave. N., Ketchum, 208/726-5079) features a first-class collection of modern works by a distinguished list of artists, including the moody Morris Graves and photographer Edward S. Curtis. Nearby, **Friesen Gallery** (320 1st Ave. N., at Sun Valley Rd., Ketchum, 208/726-4174) deals in contemporary paintings, sculptures, and glass. **Kneeland Gallery** (271 1st Ave. N., Ketchum, 208/726-5512) presents and sells works in a wide range of styles and mediums by artists living and working in the western United States.

Entertainment

For nightlife involving libations and live music, head to the new and improved **Whiskey Jacques'** (251 N. Main St., Ketchum, 208/726-5297, 4pm-2am daily). A fire in 2008 gutted the original structure, but the establishment was quickly rebuilt at the same spot. It's the place to go in Ketchum for live music and dancing, as well as good hand-tossed pizzas, microbrews, and cocktails.

The Casino Club (220 N. Main St., Ketchum, 208/726-9901) has drawn its share of Ketchum characters over the years. It's a dark, unassuming, and somewhat mysterious place with lots of nooks and crannies. The bar also has pool tables, darts, foosball, and plenty of stiff drinks.

For a more mellow night out, catch a movie at **Magic Lantern Cinema** (100

Ketchum is packed with galleries, boutiques, and restaurants.

2nd St. W., Ketchum, 208/726-4274), a four-screen theater that shows current-run blockbusters, avant-garde indie films, and foreign flicks.

Shopping

Iconoclast Books (671 Sun Valley Rd., Ketchum, 208/726-1564) keeps 4,500 square feet of new, used, rare, and out-of-print books. The bookstore also operates a small café that serves espresso drinks, baked goods, and sandwiches.

Giacobbi Square (4th St. E. and Leadville Ave., Ketchum) is a small indoor mall with tourist gift shops, clothing stores, and **Atkinsons' Market** (208/726-2681), a boutique grocery store with a profusion of specialty foods along with wines and beers from around the globe. The **Ketchum Farmers Market** (2pm-6pm Tues. early June-early Oct.) sets up nearby, where you can score fresh organic produce and other locally produced natural foodstuffs and aromatherapy products.

Accommodations
$50-100

You won't find many double-occupancy lodging choices for under $100 in the Sun Valley area. One good pick for those on a budget is the ★ **Lift Tower Lodge** (703 S. Main St., Ketchum, 208/726-5163, from $85 d). It may not look like much as you drive by, but the guest rooms are clean, comfortable, and affordable. Out front is the restored 1939 Sun Valley lift tower that gives the lodge its name, but the best guest rooms are around back, where it's quiet and you'll find a hot tub and views of Baldy. The friendly and welcoming managers set out a complimentary continental breakfast in the lobby each morning.

$100-150

Best Western Kentwood Lodge (180 S. Main St., Ketchum, 208/726-4114 or 800/805-1001, from $100 d) lies along the highway at the south edge of downtown. Log and stone accents mark both the exterior and interior of the modern nonsmoking motel. Amenities include an indoor heated pool and spa, an on-site espresso bar, and microwaves and small refrigerators in each of the 57 guest rooms. Also available are guest rooms with full kitchens as well as spa suites.

The Austrian-styled **Best Western Tyrolean Lodge** (260 Cottonwood St., Ketchum, 208/726-5336 or 800/333-7912, from $120 d) is within easy walking distance

Pioneer Mountains near Ketchum

of the River Run lift. Amenities include a heated pool, two indoor spas, and a fireplace in the lobby. All the beds are topped with thick comforters, and many different suites are available, some with kitchens or in-room jetted tubs. Rates include continental breakfast and après-ski cider. Pets are allowed.

The nondescript yet modern **Clarion Inn of Sun Valley** (600 N. Main St., Ketchum, 208/726-5900, from $100 d) sits on the highway at the north end of town. It has a year-round outdoor heated pool and hot tub and offers free continental breakfast.

$150-250

Christophe Condominium Hotel (200 W. River St., Ketchum, 888/799-7294, $90-330), near downtown, has 18 nonsmoking condostyle guest rooms ranging from full suites with kitchens and laundry rooms to no-frills smaller units. It also has a year-round outdoor pool.

★ **Bald Mountain Lodge** (100 Picabo St., Ketchum, 208/726-4776, www.baldmountain-lodge.com) is the only hotel in town where you can nearly ski up to the front entrance. Located about 100 yards from the Challenger Lift at Warm Springs, this elegant lodge boasts amenities like ground-level ski lockers, an outdoor hot tub, a fitness room, and a roaring fireplace in the lobby. The lodge has some studio rooms for $90, but most of the larger suites here cost around $200.

OVER $250

★ **Knob Hill Inn** (960 N. Main St., Ketchum, 208/726-8010, www.knobhillinn.com, $200-649) is as plush as it gets in Ketchum. The foyer library and lobby area look out onto a lushly landscaped garden with a gurgling fountain. The 29 guest rooms feature marble-appointed bathrooms with tubs and separate shower stalls. Each room has its own private balcony with great mountain views. Amenities include a jetted tub, a sauna, a year-round lap pool, and free breakfast. There's also an upscale bar and grill near the lobby. Pets are not allowed.

Food

UPSCALE FARE

Michel's Christiania and Olympic Bar (303 Walnut Ave. N., Ketchum, 208/726-3388, dinner daily, entrées $20 and up) is an elegant restaurant that is reminiscent of a European ski chalet, with a cozy interior tastefully appointed in hardwoods and crisp white linen along with a flower-filled patio centered on a small fountain. The classic French menu boasts upscale dishes like garlicky escargot, beef bourguignon, lamb shank braised with red wine, and Idaho trout amandine. The Olympic Bar, where the walls are adorned with photos of famous skiers, is the best place in town to enjoy a quiet cognac with a friend, and the tall windows beautifully frame Bald Mountain. The restaurant has been around for more than 50 years, and it was one of Ernest Hemingway's favorite dining haunts. As a matter of fact, he dined here with friends the night before he committed suicide in 1961.

If you desire local foodstuffs presented in a contemporary manner, check out ★ **Ketchum Grill** (520 East Ave., Ketchum, 208/726-4660, www.ketchumgrill.com, from 5pm daily, entrées $16-29), downtown in a 120-year-old converted house. The restaurant's patio, only open in the warmer months, is the place to be seen, and it's a wonderful spot to enjoy chef-owner Scott Mason's inventive Northwest-inspired cuisine and the excellent wine list. During the winter, giant icicles hang from the eaves of this dinner house, accentuating the elegantly lit dining room. The menu follows the seasons closely, using organic local food whenever possible. Late-summer starters might include almond-crusted goat cheese with apple slaw or shrimp cakes in a pool of roasted red pepper coulis. Main dishes like pan-seared duck breast with cherry chutney and grilled elk loin with huckleberry-red wine reduction are typical summer offerings.

★ **Vintage Restaurant** (231 Leadville Ave., Ketchum, 208/726-9595, dinner from 6pm Mon.-Sat., entrées around $25) is another fine-dining establishment that uses local ingredients well on its seasonal New American menus. Chef-owner Jeff Keys even found time a few years back to pen a cookbook, aptly titled *Vintage Restaurant*. As in the pages of the book, the menu at this eatery (situated in a small house surrounded by pine and aspen trees) is globally influenced while at the same time rooted firmly in the Northwest. Expect to find dishes like a prawn-goat cheese tart and freshly made mozzarella with smoked tomatoes and balsamic caviar.

For upscale Italian fare, head to **Il Naso** (480 N. Washington Ave., Ketchum, 208/726-7776, 5pm-10pm daily, entrées around $22), a comfortable yet luxurious restaurant that dishes up Tuscan-influenced cuisine such as chilled melon-prosciutto soup, sautéed calamari, veal scaloppini, wild mushroom ravioli, and other seasonal pasta dishes. The wine list favors labels from Tuscany and Piedmont.

The Sawtooth Club (231 N. Main St., Ketchum, 208/726-5233, www.sawtoothclub. com, from 5:30pm daily, entrées $18-33) is a venerable Ketchum restaurant that offers spectacular mountain views, making it a great place to enjoy the restaurant's contemporary steakhouse offerings. Expect to find lots of mesquite-grilled steaks and seafood as well as inventive pasta and poultry dishes. Cocktails, microbrews, and a large wine list pair nicely with the menu.

CASUAL FINE DINING

There's a fine line between upscale dining and casual fine dining in Ketchum, considering most places around town don't have strict dress codes (after all, it's a resort town where sporty attire is the norm). And many of the restaurants in this category also use the same refined culinary concepts as the upscale eateries.

★ **Zinc** (230 Walnut Ave., Ketchum, 208/727-1800, www.zinc-ketchum.com, dinner from 5:30pm Tues.-Sun., $8-24) has garnered rave reviews since it debuted in 2014 in the Walnut Avenue Mall. The interior boasts a decidedly sleek and modern design, and the menu is just as sophisticated

and nuanced, thanks to chef Taite Pearson's inventive American grill menu. Start things off with smoked trout with lemon jam on grilled bread and a bowl of silky pumpkin soup dusted with rye crumbs. Larger plates include assorted wood-oven flatbreads and entrées like succulent baby back ribs bathed in huckleberry barbecue sauce. The restaurant also serves Sunday brunch 9am-1pm. Zinc maintains a rotating selection of draft microbrews and a wine list that is both approachable and affordable.

Also on the classy side of the pub-grub scene is the **Pioneer Saloon** (308 N. Main St., Ketchum, 208/726-3139, www.pioneersaloon.com, open nightly, $12-33), which puts out excellent burgers and prime rib. The bar is an old Ketchum landmark where trophy heads and pioneer artifacts line the walls, and locals can tell you stories about the town's glorious (and sometimes checkered) past.

Cornerstone Bar & Grill (211 N. Main St., Ketchum, 208/928-7777, 5pm-late daily, entrées from $17), in the historic Ketchum post office building, is a relative newcomer to the town's casual fine dining scene. Here you will find classic steakhouse preparations done with modern flair. Expect dishes like espresso-crusted buffalo rib eye, braised Alaskan halibut with Parmesan polenta, and decadent macaroni and cheese. The bar mixes big-city cocktails and pours an expected array of microbrews and wines.

WINE BARS AND TAPROOMS

Sun Valley Wine Company (360 N. Leadville Ave., Ketchum, 208/726-2442, www.sunvalleywineco.com, 10am-9pm Mon.-Sat., noon-6pm Sun.), above the liquor store, is an attractive spot to enjoy some stinky cheeses and a glass of wine. In winter you can eat indoors by a crackling fire, and in summer the deck is a popular place to hang out. The wine-friendly menu has light offerings like panini sandwiches, soups, salads, small pizzas, and an artisanal cheeseboard with fresh fruit and baguette. The wine bar also has a retail shop with the largest selection of wines in the valley as well as tasty stuff for your picnic basket.

Craft-beer geeks were literally foaming at the mouths when **Sawtooth Brewery** (600 N. Main St., Ketchum, 208/806-1368, www. sawtoothbrewery.com, taproom 4pm-10pm Mon.-Fri., 2pm-10pm Sat.-Sun.) opened downtown in 2011. The microbrewery has earned a loyal following since then with its array of seasonal and flagship beers. Stop by the taproom and quaff one of the ski mountain-inspired brews, with names like Flow Trail Pale Ale and Last Chair Nitro Stout. The brewery doesn't serve food, but they don't mind if you bring in pizzas and sandwiches from other places in the neighborhood.

INTERNATIONAL CUISINE

Rickshaw (460 N. Washington Ave., Ketchum, 208/726-8481, dinner from 5:30p.m. Tues.-Sun., $8-15), surrounded by art galleries in lower Ketchum, is a favorite for locals who enjoy the restaurant's upscale takes on Asian street food. This funky little eatery has a menu that bounces all over Asia, making stops in Vietnam, Korea, Thailand, and China. Expect to find everything from green papaya salad to Korean fried chicken to coconut milk-infused curried noodles.

Despo's (211 4th St., Ketchum, 208/726-3068, lunch and dinner Mon.-Sat.) is the place to go in town for Mexican eats. The restaurant, known for its zesty guacamole and freshly made salsas, has a large menu that includes chiles rellenos, tortilla soup, fish tacos, and tender pork carnitas, to name a few. Wash everything down with an icy margarita or a *cerveza*.

★ **Sushi on Second** (260 2nd St., Ketchum, 208/726-5181, www.sushionsecond.com, from 5:30pm daily, entrées around $20, sushi platters $30-35) boasts a chic Japanese interior with a long sushi bar and private tatami-mat rooms. Besides serving top-notch maki rolls, nigiri, and sashimi, the kitchen also has a flair for contemporary pan-Asian cuisine with dishes like ahi carpaccio and grilled Alaskan halibut brushed with a chile-lime glaze. Libations include Japanese rice lager, sake, and sparkling wines.

QUICK BITES

Wise Guy Pizza Pie (460 Sun Valley Rd., Ketchum, 208/726-0737, lunch and dinner daily), also with a store in Hailey, sells New York-style pizza by the slice (around $3). Pizzas include pesto, Margherita (tomato, basil, fresh mozzarella), and a meaty creation called the Fat Guy, a pie with salami, pepperoni, sausage, ham, and bacon. (Could somebody please get me a stretcher?) The restaurant is really a sit-down kind of place that also sells whole pies, calzones, big salads, and hot sandwiches, and it delivers.

If you're into really good hot dogs, check out **Irving's Red-Hots** (Ketchum, 208/720-1664), a red-and-white sausage shack specializing in Chicago gut-bombs. Besides red-hots, you can also score other Windy City dogs of the beef variety. Ask them to "drag it through the garden," meaning they'll top your dog with marinated sport peppers, green relish, onions, and chopped tomato. But don't even think about asking for ketchup. This hot dog shack spends its summers downtown at the corner of Main and 4th Streets and its winters at the Warm Springs chairlift; hours change with the season.

VEGAN EATS

If the thought of a meaty hot dog makes you queasy, Ketchum has got you covered with at least one good vegan place. ★ **Glow Live Food Café** (380 Washington Ave., Ketchum, 208/725-0314, www.glowlivefood.com, 10am-5pm Mon.-Sat., most dishes around $10) offers a completely raw vegan menu that favors local organic produce. You'll find lots of whole-grain dishes. A good choice is the Indian-inspired grain bowl with lightly steamed quinoa, kale, carrot, and a spicy cashew dressing. Also expect to see vegan sandwiches and wraps (with fillings such as almond hummus and a veggie terrine) made on "live" bread. The restaurant also makes desserts (no sugar, wheat, or dairy products) such as cookies, chocolates, and cakes that you can wash down with a spirulina-kicked fruit smoothie.

BREAKFAST AND COFFEE

The Kneadery (260 Leadville Ave., Ketchum, 208/726-9462, 7:30am-2pm daily, around $10) serves standard American breakfast fare. You can get big plates of Belgian waffles, corned beef hash, omelets, pancakes, and several variations of eggs Benny. At lunch the menu is supplemented with burgers, sandwiches, and salads.

The flagship store of the small regional Java chain is Ketchum's **Java on Fourth** (191 4th St. W., Ketchum, 208/726-2882, 6am-6pm Mon.-Fri., 7am-6pm Sat.-Sun.). The floor plan is as funky as the crowd in this small but immensely popular coffeehouse. You can't go wrong with either the food or the coffee, and it's a damn good place to watch people.

SUN VALLEY

The incorporated city of Sun Valley starts just outside Ketchum, less than a mile up Sun Valley Road. Besides the ubiquitous ski condos and impressive vacation homes, everything in Sun Valley proper revolves around Sun Valley Company's operations. You'll find the famous Sun Valley Lodge, the slightly lower-crust Sun Valley Inn, and Sun Valley Village, with its various shops and restaurants that primarily serve guests of the resort. Nightlife is more sedate, favoring martinis and piano bars over Ketchum's beer and rock and roll.

★ Sun Valley Resort

The grande dame of the Wood River Valley, **Sun Valley Resort** (1 Sun Valley Rd., Sun Valley, 208/622-4111 or 800/786-8259, www.sunvalley.com, $199-549) opened in 1936, the realization of Union Pacific director Averell Harriman's pet project to build a world-class ski resort in the American West. Harriman's intended motif for the resort was "roughing it in luxury," but it's difficult to see where the "roughing it" part comes in, especially after renovations in 1986, 1992, 2003, and 2015. Old-world elegance is the lodge's hallmark, retained in the newly upgraded country-French decor. But new furnishings can't conceal the patina of history gracing these venerable halls. Harriman still presides over the oak-paneled foyer living room in the form of a portrait hanging above the fireplace, and the ghost of Ernest Hemingway still haunts Room 206, where the author holed up while working on *For Whom the Bell Tolls.*

winter at the popular ski resort of Sun Valley

Amenities at the lodge include a year-round glass-enclosed heated pool, an indoor and an outdoor ice-skating rink, and four restaurants, among them the elegant Lodge Dining Room, which has the largest wine list in the region. A great many recreational facilities (in addition to world-class skiing) are available at the lodge or in the immediate area. The bowling alley, golf course, stables, tennis courts, and a trapshooting range are open to resort guests and nonguests alike. The resort's three swimming pools, including an Olympic-size pool adjacent to the tennis courts, and the sand volleyball courts are open to resort guests only.

In addition to the lodge, which underwent major renovation in 2015, the resort offers a number of other lodging options, including the **Sun Valley Inn** ($199-449); **condominium units** ($209-629); and for those who demand the most exclusive lodgings available, a number of **guest cottages** scattered about the expansive resort grounds, topping out at around $1,000 a night.

Recreation Center

The resort's **Recreation Center** in Sun Valley Village (208/622-2135) can arrange whatever activity you're interested in, either on the resort grounds or anywhere in southern and central Idaho. Examples of off-resort activities the center frequently arranges for guests include white-water rafting trips, glider flights, guided fishing excursions, and wilderness pack trips, to name a few.

Entertainment

The lodge's elegant **Duchin Lounge** (208/622-2145), just off the lobby, features swanky cocktails and the best live jazz for miles around. In Sun Valley Village, the **Opera House** offers current-run movies and free shows of *Sun Valley Serenade,* the 1941 Hollywood classic starring Sonja Henie and John Payne and featuring music by the Glenn Miller Orchestra, which was filmed on location at the resort.

Food

The best Sunday brunch (10am-2pm Sun., $30 adults, $20 ages 5-12) in the valley gets served at the resort's **Lodge Dining Room** (208/622-2150).

Downstairs from the Lodge Dining Room is **Gretchen's** (208/622-2800, breakfast, lunch, and dinner daily). In the morning, it's all about French toast, omelets, and eggs Benedict. At lunch, the restaurant dishes up club sandwiches, burgers, and salads, and during dinner the lights get dimmed and the menu features dishes such as baked halibut and grilled New York steak topped with locally foraged morels.

In Sun Valley Village, you can get good pizza and pasta at **Bald Mountain Pizza** (208/622-2143, 5pm-9pm daily, $12-20), which also serves calzones, salads, and an excellent chicken Parmesan. Around the corner, **The Ram Restaurant** (208/622-2225, 7am-9pm daily, dinner entrées $28-49) is the place to go for European bistro fare, served breakfast, lunch, and dinner. At night, settle into a big booth and enjoy a cauldron of cheese fondue, followed by pan-seared diver scallops with silky pumpkin risotto and beef tenderloin smeared with herby mushroom butter.

For a quintessential Sun Valley experience, sign up for a sleigh ride ($35 pp round-trip, not including food and beverage) out to dinner at the resort's historic ★ **Trail Creek Cabin** (208/622-2019, 5pm-9pm daily, entrées $24-33). After a brisk ride through the snow, you'll arrive to a crackling fire and a menu that includes cedar plank Idaho trout, braised buffalo short ribs, and bacon-wrapped lamb meatloaf with sautéed chanterelles.

INFORMATION AND SERVICES
Information

The **Sun Valley-Ketchum Chamber and Visitors Bureau** (491 Sun Valley Rd., Ketchum, 208/726-3423) has a well-stocked rack of brochures and area maps, but the employees can be snooty at times. The U.S. Forest

Service **Ketchum Ranger District** (206 Sun Valley Rd., Ketchum, 208/622-0090) offers good advice for both local recreation and backcountry exploration.

Services

If you need to mail a postcard or buy stamps, head to the Ketchum **post office** (151 4th St. W., Ketchum, 208/726-5161).

For emergency medical services, go to **St. Luke's Wood River Medical Center** (100 Hospital Dr., Ketchum, 208/727-8800), just off Highway 75 between Hailey and Ketchum.

GETTING THERE AND AROUND
Getting There

By air, you'll fly into Hailey's **Friedman Memorial Airport** (SUN, Hwy. 75, Hailey, 208/788-4956, www.iflysun.com). **SkyWest/Delta** (800/221-1212) offers daily flights from Salt Lake City; **Alaska Airlines** (800/252-7522) has nonstop flights from Seattle and Los Angeles; and **United** (800/864-8331) offers round-trip flights to and from Denver. Several car rental companies operate at the airport.

If you're coming by car, figure on a 2.5-hour drive from Boise or Idaho Falls, 1.5 hours from Twin Falls, and five hours from Salt Lake City. **Sun Valley Express** (877/622-8267, www.sunvalleyexpress.com) operates year-round shuttle bus service to and from Boise (one-way $69 adults).

Getting Around

Trying to walk across, or make a left turn across, one of the valley's main streets during the day can be a challenge. Unlike most of Idaho, you'll find traffic here. Fortunately, there is an excellent free bus service around Ketchum itself: **Mountain Rides** (208/788-7433, www.mountainrides.org) runs several bus routes connecting major Ketchum-Sun Valley destinations. It also offers bus service to Hailey and Bellevue (one-way $3 adults, $2 seniors and youth).

Sawtooth National Recreation Area

Driving north out of Ketchum on Highway 75, you don't need a sign to tell you when you've entered the 765,000-acre Sawtooth National Recreation Area (NRA). The houses suddenly disappear, and the grandeur of the mountains and the tranquility of the wooded river valley return. The dividing line between the two worlds is found at the Sawtooth NRA Headquarters and Visitor Information Center, seven miles north of Sun Valley on the east side of Highway 75. From here on up the valley, you'll see no more 4,000-square-foot "cabins," and traffic is much lighter.

The NRA, established in 1972, encompasses parts of four different mountain ranges. From the headquarters in the Wood River Valley, the Smoky Mountains are visible to the west, and the Boulder Mountains to the east. Across Galena Summit to the north,

the famous Sawtooth Mountains dominate the western skyline with a string of jagged summits, while the eastern horizon is shaped by the inscrutable White Cloud Peaks—more than 50 summits in the NRA stand over 10,000 feet.

Among these mountains are more than 300 alpine lakes, all suitable for fishing, some even big enough for boating and sailing (boat ramps are available on Alturas, Pettit, Redfish, and Stanley Lakes). And four major Idaho rivers, namely the Salmon, South Fork Payette, Boise, and Big Wood, start within the boundaries of the NRA.

Although the entire NRA is spectacular and wild, the centerpiece of the area is the 217,000-acre Sawtooth Wilderness, an alpine realm closed to motor vehicles and even mountain bikes. Hikers and horse-packers

Sawtooth National Recreation Area

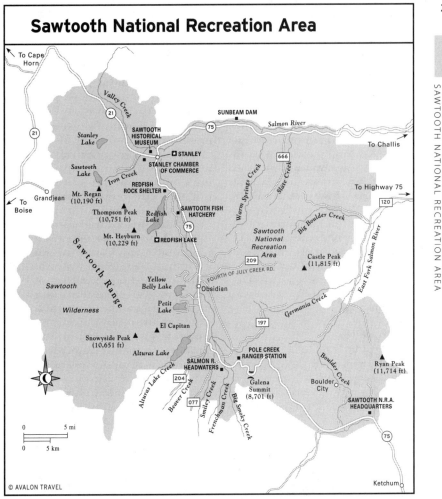

To Cape Horn

Valley Creek

21

SUNBEAM DAM

75

Salmon River

To Challis

Stanley Lake

SAWTOOTH HISTORICAL MUSEUM

21

STANLEY

STANLEY CHAMBER OF COMMERCE

Sawtooth Lake

Iron Creek

666

Slate Creek

Warm Springs Creek

120

To Highway 75

REDFISH ROCK SHELTER

To Boise

Grandjean

Mt. Regan (10,190 ft)

Thompson Peak (10,751 ft)

Redfish Lake

SAWTOOTH FISH HATCHERY

Mt. Heyburn (10,229 ft)

75

REDFISH LAKE

Sawtooth National Recreation Area

Big Boulder Creek

209

Castle Peak (11,815 ft)

East Fork Salmon River

Sawtooth Range

Yellow Belly Lake

FOURTH OF JULY CREEK RD.

Obsidian

Sawtooth Wilderness

Petit Lake

El Capitan

197

Germania Creek

Snowyside Peak (10,651 ft)

Alturas Lake

POLE CREEK RANGER STATION

Boulder Creek

Ryan Peak (11,714 ft)

SALMON R. HEADWATERS

204

Alturas Lake Creek

Beaver Creek

077

Smiley Creek

Frenchman Creek

Big Smoky Creek

Galena Summit (8,701 ft)

Boulder City

SAWTOOTH N.R.A. HEADQUARTERS

75

0   5 mi

0   5 km

Ketchum

© AVALON TRAVEL

here can enjoy some of the country's most magnificent scenery. Unlike most mountain ranges, the Sawtooths rise suddenly. They're not particularly tall, as far as peaks go (the tallest is just under 11,000 feet), but their steep relief and abundant granite walls and spires are a mountaineer's paradise. Birders can watch for many of the 214 bird species found here either year-round or part-time. You can pick up a checklist at NRA headquarters.

NRA HEADQUARTERS TO GALENA SUMMIT
Sawtooth NRA Headquarters and Visitors Center

Although most of the Sawtooth NRA lies north of Galena Summit, the NRA headquarters is on the south side, nearer the Wood River Valley's major population base. The **visitors center** (208/727-5000) is on the east side of Highway 75 just where all the fancy houses stop. Here you'll find lots of excellent natural-history books and copious exhibits and free informational flyers. In winter, there's an ice-skating pond and groomed cross-country ski trails as well. The visitors center is open year-round; in winter you can buy ski permits here for the North Valley Trail System.

From the visitors center, you can continue north up the **North Fork Big Wood River.** The road ends after about five miles, and trails head up high into the Boulder Mountains from here. Mountaineers can follow Trail 115 up to West Pass, and from there scramble up to the summit of **Ryan Peak** (South Ridge, Class 2); at 11,714 feet, it's the highest peak in the range. From trailhead to summit, the six-mile hike climbs 5,000 vertical feet.

A less vertiginous day hike in the area is the **Amber Gulch Trail** (Trails 129-130), which leads about 4.5 miles one-way to Amber Lakes and views of the North Fork and the Pioneer Mountains.

North Valley Cross-Country Trails

You'll find many superb places to go cross-country skiing in Idaho, but the upper Wood River Valley is one of the best. The Blaine County Recreation District (208/578-2273) grooms some 60 miles of trails between Lake Creek and Galena Lodge. You can ski anywhere you like on the trail system, as long as your legs and lungs will hold out, for $17 per day.

The **Boulder Mountain Trail** runs from Galena Summit down to the Sawtooth NRA visitors center. This is the route taken by the Boulder Mountain Tour, one of the country's largest cross-country ski events. The race draws upward of 700 participants annually, including world-class racers. If you can arrange a car shuttle, you can start at the top and ski all the way to the bottom, letting gravity do a lot of the work for you.

The Boulder Mountain Trail alone would be worth the trail fee, but there's more: Branching off the main trail are three separate side-trail systems on either side of the highway. At Prairie Creek, about halfway between Galena Lodge and the NRA headquarters (11 miles north of Ketchum), loops are set on both sides of the highway: On the east side, the **Billy's Bridge** system provides 4.3 miles of trails, while on the west side the **Prairie Creek** trails run another four miles up one side of the creek and down the other. Dogs are allowed on the Billy's Bridge trails but not on Prairie Creek. Both sides offer scenic views. At

Sawtooth National Recreation Area

the NRA headquarters, the **North Fork Trail System** offers 2.5 miles of easy trails along the North Fork Big Wood; dogs are allowed. This trail is recommended for beginners.

In addition to all these trails, Galena Lodge is the hub of a fantastic 31-mile trail system that's also included in the $17 fee.

Day passes are sold at Galena Lodge, the NRA headquarters, and in Ketchum at the visitors center, Backwoods Mountain Sports, and the Elephant's Perch. For up-to-the-minute trail grooming information, call the Rec District's **North Valley Trails Hotline** (208/578-9754).

Day Hikes

Recommended by the U.S. Forest Service are the **Lakes Trails,** a network accessing a half dozen or so named lakes in the Smoky Mountains on the west side of Highway 75. From a trailhead at the end of Baker Creek Road (Forest Rd. 162), it's a short two-mile hike up Trail 138 to the popular (and often crowded) fishing hole **Baker Lake.** A spur partway up Baker Creek Road takes you to a second trail from Trail 135, which leads two miles to **Norton Lakes.** The Forest Service recommends this trail for novice hikers; more athletic visitors might want to continue past Norton Lakes over Norton Saddle and down to **Miner Lake,** where you'll have great views of the Boulder Mountains.

Four miles farther up the highway, a third trailhead at the end of Prairie Creek Road (Forest Rd. 179) also provides access to the Lakes Trails. From here you can take Trail 136 up to shallow **Mill Lake,** a 2.5-mile one-way jaunt; or pick up Trail 134, which leads to a high-mountain loop that can take you to one or more of Miner, Norton, and **Prairie Lakes.** From this trailhead it's four miles and a steep climb to Miner Lake, and five moderate miles to Prairie Lakes. For a complete guide to the area, pick up a trail map at the NRA visitors center.

Galena Lodge

Almost to Galena Summit, 24 miles upstream from Ketchum, you'll come to the region's cross-country ski nirvana: the incomparable ★ **Galena Lodge** (15187 Hwy. 75, Ketchum, 208/726-4010, www.galenalodge.com), with the crown jewels of the Wood River Valley trails, a 31-mile network of loops winding through pristine high-mountain forests and glades, with no snowmobiles to disrupt winter's subtle songs, and all included in the North Valley Trails user fee.

The lodge itself, a day lodge with no accommodations, is intimate but not cramped, and the atmosphere is casual and friendly. A small restaurant serves homespun lunch and brunch (9:30am-3:30pm Sat.-Sun. summer only). The small bar keeps a variety of wines and a few microbrews on tap, and a store with a rental and repair shop handles all your equipment needs. Lessons are available as well. After a morning on the trails, it isn't too difficult to spend most of an afternoon out on the sunny lodge deck, serenaded by the quiet rhythm of snowmelt dripping off the roof.

The lodge also maintains popular **backcountry yurts** ($135-165). Three yurts are available in winter and one in summer. They are popular, and reservations must be booked and paid for at least 30 days in advance. The lodge also hosts several events and special dinners throughout the year.

In summer, the trails are open free to hikers, equestrians, and mountain bikers. The store is open daily, offering mountain-bike rentals and trail maps. Wildflower walks and a range of other interpretive programs keep the lodge's events calendar full. Summer or winter, Galena Lodge is a fantastic place.

Galena Summit

Galena Summit, at the crest of the hill, tops out at 8,701 feet. The summit marks the separation of two watersheds: the Big Wood to the south, and the Salmon to the north.

Mountain bikers can ride the **Old Toll Road** down into the Sawtooth Valley from the summit. The road was built in the 1880s and was the nightmare of early pioneers attempting to descend it with fully loaded wagons. The trail starts across the highway from the Galena Overlook, 0.25 mile north of the summit.

Camping

The **North Fork Campground** (28 sites, $14-28) lies across the highway and a bit farther up the road from the Sawtooth NRA Headquarters. Two miles farther up the valley is **Wood River Campground** (30 sites, $14-28). At Easley Hot Springs, the reservable **Easley Campground** (reservations 877/444-6777, 10 sites, $12-20) has the advantage of being next to this small hot-springs resort. All three of these U.S. Forest Service campgrounds are open approximately Memorial Day-Labor Day.

SAWTOOTH VALLEY

After cresting Galena Summit, you'll be dropping down to the headwaters of the Salmon River, the famous watercourse that flows undammed for more than 400 miles to its confluence with the Snake River in Hells Canyon. **Galena Overlook** is a must-stop turnout just down the north side from the summit, where you'll be awestruck by a magnificent panoramic view of the Sawtooths. The road continues down into **Sawtooth Valley,** a scenic spot that's rich with mining history.

Historic Sites

Not far from the bottom of Galena grade, Forest Road 194 turns east to the 1909 **Pole Creek Ranger Station,** the first structure built by the Forest Service in the Sawtooth National Forest. It was constructed and occupied by Bill Horton, a district ranger in this area for more than 20 years. Today the site is listed on the National Register of Historic Places. Farther up Pole Creek is a trailhead for hiking and biking into the Boulder Mountains and White Cloud Peaks.

A little farther north up the highway, a couple of tributaries (Smiley Creek and Beaver Creek) flow into the Salmon River from the west. These two streams and their surrounding lands supported a hive of early mining efforts in the Sawtooth Valley. Levi Smiley first found silver ore in this end of the valley in 1878, and other miners found gold on Beaver Creek in 1879. **Sawtooth City,** partway up Beaver Creek, boomed 1882-1886 and held on until the crumbs were exhausted around 1892. **Vienna** was the equivalent boomtown over on Smiley Creek that petered out around 1887. You can drive or mountain-bike to the former sites of these towns (Vienna is up Forest Road 077, and Sawtooth City is up Forest Road 204), both of which make for great places to picnic and get an Idaho history lesson.

Popular Lakes and Wilderness Trailheads

As Highway 75 continues north from Beaver Creek, it parallels the eastern boundary of the Sawtooth Wilderness, some three miles to the west. Between the highway and the wilderness lie several lakes popular with campers, anglers, hikers, bikers, and cross-country skiers. **Alturas Lake** (Forest Rd. 205) is the area's largest. Three **campgrounds** ($15-30) along the north shore of the lake have a total of 54 sites. In winter, **cross-country skiing** enthusiasts will find six miles of periodically groomed trails, rated easy to intermediate, that wind across open meadows and along a wooded creek.

Continuing north, **Pettit Lake** (Forest Rd. 208) has a small free campground and is the site of the Tin Cup trailhead, a well-used access point into the Sawtooth Wilderness. Backpackers head out from here on the Pettit-Toxaway Loop Trail, a two-day trip past several wilderness lakes. Undeveloped **Yellow Belly Lake** (Forest Rd. 365) is a favorite of anglers; no boat motors are allowed.

Off Forest Road 315 you'll find the trailhead to **Hell Roaring Lake.** The moderately difficult 10.4-mile round-trip trek to the lake makes a great day hike. Surrounded by the granite towers of Finger of Fate and the Arrowhead, Hell Roaring Lake lies in one of the most spectacular parts of the Sawtooth Wilderness.

Mountain Biking

On the south end of the Sawtooth Valley, **Valley Road** (Forest Rd. 194) more or less parallels the highway on the east. It begins at Sawtooth City. To get here, follow the route to Pole Creek Ranger Station, but at the junction of Forest Roads 194 and 197, continue north on 194. Of course, you could always swing up the extra half mile and back and check out the ranger station while you're in the area. The rest of the route north leads through pastures and ranchlands, and it rejoins Highway 75 about 0.5 mile south of Fourth of July Creek Road.

If you turn off Highway 75 on Forest Road 315, cross the Salmon River, and turn right, you'll find yourself on **Decker Flat Road** (Forest Rd. 210), an easy mountain-biking route that parallels the river for 14 miles north to Redfish Lake Road. The rangers recommend this scenic ride for families.

Just across the highway from Forest Road 315, **Fourth of July Creek Road** (Forest Rd. 209) leads east up into the White Cloud Peaks. This is the prime west-side access route into the White Clouds, a favored realm of mountain bikers.

Another popular trail begins 1.5 miles farther north on Highway 75. The 18-mile **Fisher Creek-Williams Creek Loop** starts at Fisher Creek Road (between mileposts 176 and 177 on Hwy. 75) and follows that road up to the old Aztec Mine, where it turns into singletrack. It then descends to the Warm Springs Creek drainage and turns back west, crossing a second saddle before descending Williams Creek to the highway. Hard-core bikers could instead follow Warm Springs Creek north, all the way down to the Salmon River at Robinson Bar east of Sunbeam.

Day Hikes

On the south end of the valley, **Horton Peak Lookout** provides a high vantage point overlooking the NRA. It's a strenuous eight-mile round-trip hike that gains 2,700 vertical feet. The trailhead is on Forest Road 459, which turns off Valley Road (Forest Rd. 194) about midway along its length.

In the Alturas Lake area, the **Cabin Creek Lakes** trail offers an easier trek. The eight-mile round-trip hike follows Cabin Creek up to a string of small lakes just inside the wilderness boundary. To reach the trailhead, take Cabin Creek Road (Forest Rd. 207) west from Highway 75, about 1.5 miles north of Alturas Lake Road. Stay on Forest Road 207 at every road junction and find the trailhead about 0.25 mile north of Cabin Creek. You can also reach the trailhead from the south by taking Forest Road 207 north off Alturas Lake Road about one mile.

Farther north, across the highway from the Sawtooth Hatchery, a 0.75-mile spur road leads to the trailhead to **Casino Lakes.** It's a heart-pounding, five-mile one-way hike up 3,000 vertical feet to the cluster of small lakes at the head of Big Casino Creek.

Sawtooth Fish Hatchery

At the **Sawtooth Fish Hatchery** (Hwy 75, 208/774-3684), Idaho Department of Fish and Game fisheries biologists are trying to undo the devastating effects of the lower Snake River dams on the Salmon River's anadromous chinook salmon population. The small visitors center has plenty of information about the endangered salmon and explains the hatchery process. Perhaps the most fascinating exhibit is the simple dry-erase board at the entrance listing the number of returning sockeye counted here, a number that has been growing in recent years. Several 45-minute guided tours are given daily during summer and by appointment the rest of the year. Self-guided tours are possible too.

★ REDFISH LAKE AREA

The largest lake in the Sawtooths is also the most developed and most popular. Besides a main lodge and cabins, the bustling Redfish Lake Lodge also offers several campgrounds, trailheads, and water-sports opportunities, and the landscape couldn't be more sublime. Mount Heyburn's granite walls rise nearly 4,000 feet over the far end of the lake, and views up into the heart of the Sawtooth

Wilderness will tempt you to don a backpack and hit the dusty trail.

The lake is aptly named for the sockeye salmon that once spawned heavily in Redfish Lake; the fish turn a brilliant orange-red when they spawn. Some sockeye exist in the lake, as do a few resident kokanee, which are essentially landlocked sockeye.

Redfish Rock Shelter

Near Highway 75 on the north side of Redfish Lake Road is **Redfish Rock Shelter,** a rock overhang that archaeologists believe was used by indigenous people for shelter as early as 9,500 years ago. Later, the Tukudeka band of Northern Shoshone, known as the sheep eaters, also camped here on their bighorn hunting forays into the area. A very short trail begins at a turnout between the north end of Little Redfish Lake and the highway and leads across the creek to the site.

Redfish Lake Visitors Center

The Forest Service's **Redfish Lake Visitors Center** (208/774-3376, summer only) provides interpretive information about Redfish Lake and the Sawtooth Wilderness and hosts guided hikes, campfire programs, slide shows, and children's activities. A short half-mile interpretive trail makes a great hike for the little ones. The visitors center is just a short distance from the lakeshore, just east of the lodge.

Day-Use Areas

The **Sandy Beach boat ramp and day-use area** ($5) on the lake's northeast shore attracts crowds of swimmers and sunbathers in summer. The **North Shore Picnic Area** near the visitors center also features a popular beach. Noncamping visitors are welcome to use the beaches at the Point and Outlet. All day-use areas are open 8am-10pm, and camping is not allowed.

Horseback Riding

Redfish Lake Corrals (208/774-3311), about halfway down the road to Redfish Lake, offers trail rides ranging in length from 1.5 hours ($56 pp) to a full day ($129 pp). The full-day rides head up to one or more of the Sawtooths' beautiful lakes and include a nice spread of food along the trail. Anglers are welcome.

Day Hikes

Two popular, one-way hiking trails begin at the Redfish trailhead parking area, just past the turnoff to the lodge on Redfish Lake Road. The **Fishhook Creek Trail** (Trail 186) leads west several miles upstream along Fishhook Creek with minimal elevation gain. A short distance from the parking area it meets **Redfish Lake Creek Trail** (Trail 101), which heads south to the trailhead at the far end of the lake (5.2 miles) and continues into the Sawtooth Wilderness. Partway along this trail, a turnoff switchbacks up to **Bench Lakes,** four miles from the trailhead, where you'll have a bird's-eye view of Redfish Lake.

You also might consider taking the lodge shuttle across the lake and starting your hike from the trailhead at the other side. The 10.5-mile round-trip hike from the boat dock up Redfish Lake Creek to **Alpine Lake** is particularly popular.

Out on the Water

Canoes, kayaks, fishing boats, sailboats, and ski boats ply Redfish Lake. **Boat rentals** of all sorts are available from the lodge; just wander down to the dock and find an attendant. Or sign up for one of the **Lady of the Lake Scenic Tours** ($15 adults, $5 children), a one-hour lake cruise aboard a pontoon boat. Hikers can get a **boat shuttle** (208/774-3536, $16 round-trip, $10 one-way) ride to the trailhead at the far end of the lake. (Note: The docks were destroyed by ice in 2015, but the resort is working hard to get everything operational again.)

Stanley Ranger Station

A couple of miles north of the Redfish Lake turnoff, you'll find **Stanley Ranger Station** (208/774-3000), the main ranger station serving the Sawtooths and White Clouds. Check in here before you venture into the wilderness. The rangers have up-to-date information on backcountry conditions and can answer any questions about routes or campsites. In winter, a four-mile **cross-country ski trail** loop runs through lodgepole pine forest.

Redfish Lake Lodge

Although its widespread reputation might lead you to expect something along the lines of the Sun Valley resort, **Redfish Lake Lodge** (208/774-3536 summer, www.redfishlake.com, mid-May-early Oct.) is instead down-home Idaho all the way. You'll find nothing grand or imposing, which isn't to say it isn't nice. But it's more rustic than regal, more folksy than aristocratic. It's like summer camp for the entire family. While Mom's out fishing on the lake, Dad can take the baby on a walk through the woods or a horseback ride along the creek.

Rather than one giant château-like lodge, this resort consists of a modest main lodge near the lakeshore and numerous outbuildings. Motel rooms ($84-199) in the lodge are available as well as private cabins ($182-579) that range from small cottages to larger lakeside gems. Facilities at the lodge include a dining room serving three meals a day, a cozy lounge where locals swap fish stories, a Laundromat, stables, a general store, a gas station, and a marina. Online reservations are strongly recommended, and the sooner you make them (like January), the better, because this place books up months in advance.

Camping

Eight separate U.S. Forest Service campgrounds ($16-36) with a total of 119 sites dot the Redfish Lake area: **Sockeye, Mount Heyburn, Outlet, Glacier View,** and **Point** ring the north end of the big lake; **Mountain View** and **Chinook Bay** are on Little Redfish Lake, closer to the highway; and **Sunny Gulch** is out on the far side of Highway 75. Reservable sites are offered in the Point, Outlet, and Glacier View Campgrounds (reservations 877/444-6777); Sockeye and Mount Heyburn are first-come, first-served. For more information, call the NRA headquarters at 208/727-5000.

★ STANLEY AND VICINITY

In 1864, Captain John Stanley led a party of miners into the Valley Creek area. The town that now bears his name started as a supply center for the gold-mining district that eventually dug in. The little town is the yin to Ketchum's yang: There are no fancy homes or cars; in fact, except for the two highways, the streets aren't even paved. Only about 70 people live here year-round, mostly because Stanley's harsh winters are among the coldest you'll encounter in the state. Recreation fuels the town's economy, which races in summer with rafters, anglers, campers, and backpackers, and stays idling in winter with the help of the few snowmobilers and skiers who venture up this way. Besides its decidedly down-home character, Stanley's biggest asset is its incredible view. The Sawtooths rise up like a giant picket fence just south of town; they're so dramatic that it's almost impossible to take your eyes off them.

Highway 75 intersects with Highway 21 near town. West on Highway 21 is the Ponderosa Pine Scenic Byway heading toward Lowman. Stanley is a wonderful place to hunker down for a few days, taking in the remarkable scenery and the frontier culture.

Stanley Museum

To find out more about the history of Stanley and the Sawtooths, stop by the **Stanley Museum** (208/774-3517, www.discoversawtooth.org, 11am-5pm daily June-Sept., free), on the west side of Highway 75 a short distance north of the Highway 21 junction. The museum is housed in a 1933 Forest Service ranger's cabin and offers exhibits focusing on pioneer life in the region.

Mountain Biking

Great views of the Sawtooths and White Clouds highlight the 6.5-mile ride down **Nip**

Robinson Bar Ranch:
A Slice of Idaho History

Bethine Clark Church, wife of the late U.S. Senator Frank Church, spent much of her childhood in the White Cloud Mountains near Stanley. Her father, Chase Clark, who later became the 18th governor of Idaho, acquired a chunk of prime Idaho wilderness in 1917 after a devastating car wreck left him in need of hydrotherapy. The Clark family purchased an abandoned stagecoach stop at the mouth of Warm Springs Creek, a tranquil spot where therapeutic steamy water bubbled up from deep within the earth. Chase, with the help of his entire family, homesteaded the 123-acre spread and turned it into a sublime mountain getaway, which they named **Robinson Bar Ranch,** although it was not a working ranch with livestock.

Over the years, the Clarks built a main lodge and several cabins on the property, and they even harnessed the natural spring water into two concrete-lined ponds the size of large swimming pools. Under the cobalt Sawtooth sky, the family spent many hours soaking away their pains. Chase enjoyed catching big salmon that were once prevalent in the nearby creek. The family eventually moved away from the ranch to Idaho Falls so Chase could pursue his law practice, and later to Boise after he won his Democratic gubernatorial bid in 1941. But the family always returned to Robinson Bar Ranch during the summer months to decompress in the steamy pools and enjoy each other's company in the unfettered wilderness.

As a young woman, Bethine started dating a gentleman by the name of Frank Church, a young man with a promising future in the Democratic Party. He had just earned his bachelor's degree at Stanford University, and the young couple felt that nuptials were in order. Frank and Bethine were married in 1947 at Robinson Bar Ranch. Bethine's father, an ardent Democrat himself, was impressed by his son-in-law's intelligence, charm, and the fact that Frank was about to enter law school at Harvard University. Frank, however, went on to earn his law degree from Stanford University after spending only one year at Harvard. Later he became a four-term U.S. senator from Idaho. Frank and Bethine had two sons, Frank Forrester and Chase, named after his grandfather.

During Frank's time in Washington, DC, he earned a reputation for being an environmental watchdog. He cosponsored the Wilderness Act in 1964, which designated federally protected status to a large portion of central Idaho's pristine mountains that should be, in Frank's words, "Untrammeled by man; where man is a visitor who does not remain." This controversial Senate Act (Republicans were in favor of continued mining and logging in the area) gave birth to the River of No Return Wilderness, a 2.2-million-acre protected beauty enjoyed by many low-impact recreationalists today.

He was also involved in several other pieces of senate legislation, like the 1968 Wild and Scenic Rivers Act and a 1972 bill that created the 756,000-acre Sawtooth National Recreation Area (NRA), the first of its kind in the country. This is when things got tricky for the Churches, who now owned Robinson Bar Ranch on the fringe of what would soon be the Sawtooth NRA. Senate Republicans were calling the Churches' property a conflict of interest, stating that the Churches were simply trying to preserve the area around the ranch and not really looking out for the best interests of Idahoans. They couldn't have been more wrong, but the Churches made the heart-wrenching decision to let the ranch go for a mere $140,000 in order to preserve the integrity of the upcoming Congress vote in 1972.

Just before Frank Church's death in 1984, the River of No Return Wilderness was renamed the Frank Church-River of No Return Wilderness, honoring a man who did so much to ensure that Idaho remains wild. Bethine Church passed away in 2013.

Carole King, the famous singer-songwriter, now owns Robinson Bar Ranch, but she currently has it up for sale for a cool $10 million. Hopefully whoever buys the property, with all its buildings and hot springs pools, has the same vision as its previous owners, meaning not to commercialize this gorgeous slice of Idaho history.

and Tuck Road. The old wagon road (Forest Rd. 633) follows an easy grade west up Nip and Tuck Creek from Lower Stanley, then crests the hill and descends to Stanley Creek, ending at the intersection of Valley Creek Road and Highway 21.

Mountain biking is prohibited in the Sawtooth Wilderness, but east of town the White Cloud Peaks constitute the Holy Land for area mountain bikers.

Floating the Upper Main Salmon

The stretch of the Salmon River just downstream from Stanley is popular for white-water day trips; between Stanley and Basin Creek it's an easy float suitable even for inner tubes, while between Basin Creek and Torrey's Hole the river throws two Class III and two Class IV tantrums. The lower segment is usually runnable May-September. The upper stretch draws most floaters in May-June, as after that it usually gets a tad shallow.

Guide services on the Salmon River day stretch include **The River Company** (1150 Eva Falls Ave., Stanley, 800/398-0346, www.therivercompany.com) and **White Otter Outdoor Adventures** (Stanley, 208/788-5005 or 877/788-5005, www.whiteotter.

com). Rates for a full-day guided trip on the river cost about $75 without lunch, $95 with lunch.

Outfitters

Next to the Mountain Village complex you'll find **Riverwear** (Hwy. 21, Stanley, 208/774-3592), a great outdoor store selling all the supplies you'll need for your raft or pack trip and renting a variety of gear as well. Sample rentals: bikes for $28 per day, wetsuits for $10 per day, kayaks for $30 per day, rafts for $75-125 per day.

White Otter Outdoor Adventures (208/788-5005) rents rafts, kayaks, and related equipment for private trips from its office at the Sunbeam put-in, 13 miles east of Stanley on Highway 75.

Accommodations

Mountain Village Resort (Hwy. 21 and Hwy. 75, Stanley, 208/774-3661 or 800/843-5475, www.mountainvillage.com, from $75 d) is the most obvious, well-established lodging in town. Guest rooms are modern rather than rustic, and the adjacent dining room serves no-frills breakfast, lunch, and dinner. Plus, there's a bar where you can quaff a microbrew. The motel's biggest plus is probably the

the Sawtooths near Stanley

natural hot springs spa on-site. Kitchenette suites are available.

Heading west on Highway 21 from the big junction, you'll pass a string of motels lining the highway. The motels on the north side front Valley Creek and have a nicer ambience than those on the south side.

Valley Creek Lodge (1060 Eva Falls Ave., Stanley, 208/774-3606, $80-150) sits on high ground, resulting in some of the best views in town. All guest rooms have queen beds, private baths, cable TV, and refrigerators. Valley Creek also offers a few basic RV sites ($28-30) with water, power, and sewer hookups.

Among the several accommodations in Lower Stanley, **Gunter's Salmon River Cabins** (208/774-2290 or 888/574-2290, closed winter, $75-120), about a mile and a half north of town on Highway 75, and **Redwood Cabins** (83 Hwy. 75, 208/774-3531, www.redwood-stanley.com, closed winter, $75-100) offer cabins right on the river.

Food

The **Kasino Club** (34 Ace of Diamonds St., Stanley, 208/774-3516, from 6pm daily, entrées $12-22) is regarded as the finest of dining in Stanley proper. The kitchen specializes in big, juicy steaks, fresh-as-can-be seafood, and pasta dishes. The bar, with a lineup of regional microbrews, is a good place to sit a spell.

Decent pizza is available downtown across from the post office at **Papa Brunee's** (37 Ace of Diamonds St., Stanley, 208/774-2536, hours vary), where you can also get deli salads, sandwiches, and lots of beer to wash it all down.

In the morning, head to the ★ **Stanley Baking Co. and Cafe** (250 Wall St., Stanley, 208/774-6573, www.stanleybakingco.com, 7am-2pm daily May-Oct., breakfast $6-12) for biscuits and gravy, sourdough pancakes, breakfast burritos, house-made granola, and supreme vegetarian items. You can also get freshly baked scones, cinnamon rolls, coffee cake, and sticky buns to go with your espresso drink made from organic beans. The restaurant serves sandwiches and burgers at lunch. Try the delish veggie burger (patties made in-house with shiitake mushrooms, tofu, and toasted pecans) plopped on a crusty bun with provolone, fresh tomato, and mixed greens.

Information

The **Stanley-Sawtooth Chamber of Commerce** (208/774-3411, www.stanleycc.org, 10am-6pm daily June-mid-Oct.), in the community building under a big flagpole, has all the information you'll need to know about the area. These friendly folks can also hook you up with backcountry outfitters and guides.

HIGHWAY 21 TO SAWTOOTH AND STANLEY LAKES

Spectacular mountain vistas and vast meadows awash in wildflowers combine to make this stretch of pavement, the Ponderosa Pine Scenic Byway, one of the most beautiful drives in Idaho. Several angler access roads branch off the highway and lead down to meandering Valley Creek, while other spur roads lead south off the highway to campgrounds at the foot of the Sawtooths.

Day Hike to Sawtooth Lake

A photographer's favorite, Sawtooth Lake enjoys the sheer granite face of 10,190-foot Mount Regan as a backdrop. The moderately strenuous five-mile trail takes you up past dramatic cliffs, a tall graceful waterfall, and gem-like Alpine Lake. Sawtooth Lake itself is one of the largest lakes in the Sawtooth Wilderness. Snow lingers in these heights until well into summer; don't be surprised to see miniature icebergs drifting across the lake even in July-August. On the hike back down, you'll get glimpses of Stanley on the valley floor below.

To reach the trailhead, take Iron Creek Road off Highway 21, three miles west of Stanley. The trailhead is at the end of the road. Also at the trailhead you'll find **Iron Creek Campground** (9 sites, $15).

Stanley Lake

Boating, fishing, and family camping are the prime pastimes at **Stanley Lake,** 2.5 miles off the highway on Stanley Lake Road (five miles west of Stanley). Three separate campgrounds line the lake's north shore: **Inlet** (14 sites, $15), **Lakeview** (6 sites, $15), and **Stanley Lake** (19 sites, $15). It's a beautiful spot offering access into the Sawtooth Wilderness along Stanley Creek, but it's also a dusty, relatively noisy, heavily used area best suited for those who don't like to be too far removed from their fellow human beings.

A challenging 12.5-mile **mountain-biking** trail loops from here north around Elk Mountain to Elk Meadows and back. Stay on Stanley Lake Road past the lake; turn off onto Trail 629, which leads to Elk Meadows and eventually intersects Forest Road 630; return to the lake on Forest Road 630. Elk Meadows is a good spot for watching wildlife.

Cross-Country Skiing

In winter, a short 2.5-mile loop is set at the **Park Creek** turnout, about three miles northeast of Stanley Lake Road on Highway 21. The trail winds through open meadows and is rated easy to intermediate. It's groomed only periodically.

HIGHWAY 75 TOWARD SUNBEAM

Heading first north then east out of Stanley, Highway 75 hugs the Salmon River downstream. There are a string of hot springs along the riverbank; west to east, look for **Elkhorn Hot Springs,** 0.7 mile east of mile marker 192; **Mormon Bend Hot Spring,** 350 yards downstream from Elkhorn at mile marker 193, on the far side of the river; **Basin Creek Campground Hot Spring,** next to the campground, seven miles east of Stanley; and **Kem Hot Springs,** 0.7 mile east of mile marker 197.

For panoramic views of Salmon River Canyon and the Sawtooths, make the 12-mile round-trip **day hike** up to **Lookout Mountain.** You'll climb 2,600 vertical feet to the lookout on the peak (9,954 feet). Bear left at each of the two forks along the way. The trailhead is at the end of Rough Creek Road (Forest Rd. 626), which turns off Highway 75, east 10 miles from Stanley.

Between Stanley and Sunbeam on Highway 75, U.S. Forest Service **campgrounds** on the Salmon River include **Salmon River** (30 sites, $15), **Riverside** (17 sites, $15), and **Mormon Bend** (16 sites, $12). All campsites are open June-September.

SAWTOOTH WILDERNESS

Although it's nowhere near the largest wilderness area in Idaho, the 217,000-acre Sawtooth Wilderness is a prime contender for the grandest. Three major Idaho rivers start here in snowy tarns beneath granite spires: the South Fork Payette River drains the northwest third of the wilderness; the North and Middle Forks of the Boise River drain the southwest third; and the mighty Salmon is born of the waters flowing off the east side of the wilderness.

Rock climbers have a field day here on the big-wall granite faces of Warbonnet Peak, Elephant's Perch, and the Finger of Fate, among others. Mountaineers come to bag more than a dozen summits rising over 10,000 feet, the tallest being 10,751-foot Thompson Peak. Hikers and horse-packers are content to keep their feet on the 300 miles of trails lacing the preserve, which lead the backcountry adventurer through awesome glacier-carved valleys, past nearly 200 trout-filled alpine lakes and meadows lush with summer wildflowers.

Access Guide

A list of primary access points into the Sawtooth Wilderness, starting at the northern tip of the wilderness and proceeding clockwise:

- **Stanley Lake** trailhead, on Stanley Lake Road (Forest Rd. 455), six miles west of Stanley on Highway 21; access along the western edge of the wilderness into Sawtooth Lake and Baron Creek drainage

- **Iron Creek** trailhead, on Iron Creek Road (Forest Rd. 619), three miles west of Stanley on Highway 21; access across the eastern boundary of the wilderness into Sawtooth Lake and Baron Creek drainage

- **Redfish Lake** trailheads, at the north or south sides of lake, on Redfish Lake Road, five miles south of Stanley on Highway 75; access into the heart of the wilderness up Redfish Lake Creek, and access to rock climbing on Mount Heyburn, Grand Mogul, and Elephant's Perch

- **Hell Roaring Creek** trailhead, on Forest Road 315 off Decker Flat Road (Forest Rd. 210), 17 miles south of Stanley off Highway 75; access to Hell Roaring Lake, Finger of Fate, the Arrowhead, and Imogene Lake

- **Pettit Lake** trailhead, on Pettit Lake Road (Forest Rd. 208), 20 miles south of Stanley on Highway 75; access to the Pettit-Toxaway Loop (a prime backpacking trail) and on into the South Fork Payette River drainage

- **Atlanta** trailhead, at the end of Middle Fork Boise River Road (Forest Rd. 268), about 60 miles northeast of Highway 21 (turn off Highway 21 at Lucky Peak Reservoir); access up Middle Fork Boise River drainage into the southern end of wilderness

- **Grandjean** trailhead, on Forest Road 524, about eight miles east of Highway 21 (turn off Highway 21 about 45 miles west of Stanley or 89 miles northeast of Boise); access up either Baron Creek drainage or South Fork Payette River drainage

Mountaineering Guides

The folks at **Sawtooth Mountain Guides** (Stanley, 208/774-3324, www.sawtooth-guides.com) know every nook and cranny in the Sawtooths. They offer rock climbing and mountaineering in summer and hut-to-hut ski touring in winter. The company has been in business for more than 30 years and regularly leads ascents of Mounts Heyburn, Thompson, Williams, and Warbonnet, the Finger of Fate, and the Elephant's Perch. Call for rates.

Information

To learn more about the Sawtooth Wilderness, contact the **Sawtooth NRA Headquarters** (208/727-5000), just north of Ketchum.

WHITE CLOUD PEAKS

From a distance, you might have to squint pretty hard to distinguish the white limestone peaks here from summer clouds; hence the name White Cloud Peaks. Unlike the Sawtooths on the other side of Highway 75, the White Clouds aren't within a designated wilderness area, so mountain bikes are permitted. And while the Sawtooths top out at about 10,700 feet, the White Clouds' tallest peaks tower more than 1,000 feet higher. The highest in the range, 11,815-foot Castle Peak, is highly coveted by mountaineers.

Before Congress established the Sawtooth NRA in 1972, mining companies were eyeing the molybdenum deposits in the White Clouds, and a large open-pit mine was proposed in the 1960s. Under the rules regulating the NRA, all lands within its boundaries are now closed to new mining claims. Pre-1972 claims can still be worked, however, provided they don't infringe on the area's prime mission as a recreational haven. Thankfully, all the old claims are currently dormant, and there's now a proposal to make Boulder-White Clouds a designated wilderness area.

The White Clouds receive less use than the Sawtooths. Those adventurers taking the time to seek out this pristine high country will find steep granite galore and water everywhere. As a matter of fact, more than 125 alpine lakes set the range aglitter in the summer sun. The lakes tend to be smaller than their Sawtooth counterparts but no less beautiful. Elk, deer, bighorn sheep, and mountain goats inhabit the lofty realm, keeping a sharp eye out for members of the area's small cougar population. Coyotes, foxes, beavers, badgers, and black bears add to the White Clouds' mix of resident wildlife.

Access Guide

Primary access routes are from the west, up Pole Creek-Germania Creek Road (Forest Rd. 197) and Fourth of July Creek Road (Forest Rd. 209); from the north, up Slate Creek Road (Forest Rd. 666), off Highway 75 about six miles west of Clayton Ranger Station; and from the northeast, up East Fork Salmon River Road (Forest Rd. 120), off Highway 75 about five miles east of Clayton.

Hiking

The west side's Fourth of July Road will take you from Highway 75 some 10 miles east into the heights before you'll have to park and continue on foot. From there, it's about 1.5 miles up Trail 109 to **Fourth of July Lake** and a mile farther to **Washington Lake.** The elevation gain is minimal. Both lakes are only a couple of crow-flapping miles to Castle Peak, the monarch of the White Clouds.

On the north side, six miles up Slate Creek Road, you'll come to a four-way intersection. Turn left and go a short distance to the trailhead for the **Crater Lake** trail. The trail follows Livingston Creek four miles and some 2,500 vertical feet up to the lake, from which you'll have views of the striking **Chinese Wall.**

The **Boulder Chain Lakes** attract a healthy share of the backpacking visitors to the range. The trail winds along the shores of eight lakes that lie at elevations averaging around 9,000 feet. Access is via the Little Boulder Creek trailhead, about 22 miles in on the East Fork Salmon Road. From there, Trail 682 ascends Little Boulder Creek about seven miles to the intersection of Trail 047. Turn right and continue another 1.5 miles to the first of the lakes.

Mountain Biking

Since all the trails in the area are open to mountain bikes, you can just get yourself a map and take off exploring. The prime access points for mountain bikers are **Fourth of July Creek Road** (Forest Rd. 209), which leads east up into the White Clouds from Highway 75; **Germania Creek Road** (Forest Rd. 197), which takes off from Pole Creek-Valley Road (Forest Rd. 194, off Hwy. 75 near Sawtooth City); and **East Fork Salmon River Road** (Forest Rd. 120), which heads south off Salmon River Road east of Clayton.

Mountaineering

The White Cloud Peaks aren't known for technical rock climbing; the predominant loose, friable limestone is a climber's nightmare. Still, many peak-baggers can't resist the allure of **Castle Peak** (11,815 feet), the highest in the range. All the routes to the summit are Class 3. Access is from Chamberlain Basin, reached via either Little Boulder Creek (Trails 682, 047, and 110) or Germania and Chamberlain Creeks (Trails 111 and 110). The approach to the north-side routes is via a cross-country trail from near the junction of the Wickiup Creek and Little Boulder Creek Trails (Trails 684 and 047).

Hot Springs

On the southeast side of the White Clouds, at the end of East Fork Salmon River Road, you'll find a couple of hot springs where you can soak in secluded privacy. **West Pass Hot Spring,** on a hillside above West Pass Creek, offers a pair of tubs with great views. Coming in on the East Fork Road, cross West Pass Creek (29 miles south of Hwy. 75) and almost immediately bear left on a road that climbs the hillside. Park on the flat and find the short trail past an old mine to the tubs. **Bowery Hot Spring** is in the same area. Continue straight up the East Fork at the West Pass Creek junction to the trailhead. Hike 100 yards up the road toward Bowery Guard Station, and at the bridge continue a short distance upstream to the spring.

FRANK CHURCH-RIVER OF NO RETURN WILDERNESS AREA

Access to Frank Church-River of No Return Wilderness Area, named for the late U.S. senator from Idaho and lifelong champion of Idaho's wild lands, is relatively easy, which may or may not be a positive attribute, depending on your perspective. When Congress established the wilderness, rather than just drawing a big box for a boundary and letting all the preexisting roads within it grow over, it instead made sure all existing mining and logging roads were grandfathered out of the wilderness. As a result, even in the deepest heart of the Frank Church, you're never too far from one of these "cherry-stemmed" roads. Although purists consider this an unwanted intrusion, the roads do permit you to drive to a plethora of trailheads on all sides of the area.

Frank Church-River of No Return Wilderness Area

© AVALON TRAVEL

For general information on the Frank Church wilderness, contact the **Salmon-Challis National Forest Supervisor's Office** (1206 S. Challis St., Salmon, 208/756-5100). Look for the big blue building right before you come into town.

Wilderness Trails

Backpackers with a map will be like kids in a candy store, with an astounding number of trails to explore. Backpackers entering the heart of the wilderness are certain to encounter solitude; there's an awful lot of land to get lost in. Favorite destinations are the Bighorn Crags (a magnificent area of jagged spires and alpine lakes on the east side of the wilderness) and the two big rivers, each of which offers a trail running alongside much of its length. Hot springs abound alongside those rivers and elsewhere in the wilderness, allowing the enterprising backpacker to do a multiday spring-to-spring trip and have a hot soak every night. Horse-packers also enjoy the wilderness. Mountain bikes are not allowed. A compromise that aided passage of the bill creating the Frank Church makes one exception to the no-mechanized-vehicles rule: Jetboats are permitted on the main Salmon.

White-Water Rafting

When the Lewis and Clark expedition came over Lemhi Pass looking for a route to the sea, they intended to follow the Lemhi River down to the **Salmon River,** then float the Salmon to the Columbia River. At camp in the Lemhi Valley, the local Shoshone told Captain Clark that the Salmon River Canyon was impassable, but Clark figured he'd go see for himself. Reaching a point 14 miles downstream from today's town of North Fork, Clark climbed high up the side of the canyon for a better view. From this high vantage point, he saw Pine Creek Rapids (Class III-IV) churning away downstream and nothing but a deep gorge with steep, rocky walls leading all the way to the horizon. Clark immediately opted for Plan B, and the expedition made a long detour to the north

rather than attempt a descent of the Salmon. Later pioneers managed to float some sections of the upper Salmon, but paddling back upstream against the swift current was impossible; hence the river's nickname, the "river of no return."

The Salmon River drains some 14,000 square miles and flows undammed for its entire 420 miles, from its headwaters in the southern Sawtooth Valley to its confluence with the Snake River. For more than 180 miles of its length it flows through a deep gorge rising over a mile on either side of the river. From North Fork to the normal take-out at Riggins, the river drops 1,910 feet, an average of more than 12 feet per mile. Rapids on the river for the most part range Class II-III+, although a few Class IVs (Pine Creek, Big Mallard, Elkhorn, Vinegar) challenge even the experts, and many of the Class IIIs go Class IV in high water. Permits (www.recreation.gov) are required for this stretch of the river.

The **Middle Fork of the Salmon** is one of the world's greatest and most popular white-water trips, drawing rafters and kayakers from around the globe. From the put-in at Boundary Creek, northwest of Stanley, the river flows 100 wet and wild miles through a wilderness little tarnished by human activity. Bighorn sheep, black bears, mountain goats, salmon and steelhead, bald eagles, and even wolves inhabit the area.

The river itself puts up a premier challenge at any flow level. More than 30 significant rapids line the route, almost a third of them running Class IV. From Velvet Falls on Day 1 to the wild roller coaster of Rubber Rapids on Day 6, the Middle Fork rarely lets up. Another delight of the river is the abundance of hot springs along its banks, making great places for midday breaks or stargazing soaks at day's end. Historic sites along the way include hermit cabins, Native American pictographs, and sites associated with the Sheepeater Campaign of 1879. Permits (www.recreation.gov) are required year-round for boaters here.

Of the two, the Middle Fork is a more technical river, particularly in its narrow upper reaches. The main Salmon has the biggest waves, the biggest holes, and the most adrenaline-inducing power. The Middle Fork is a wilderness river. Few roads lead to its banks, and only a handful of isolated ranches provide reminders of civilization. The main Salmon also flows past just a few roads and ranches; however, its wilderness quality is sullied somewhat by the permitted presence of jetboats. You'll see more people on the main Salmon, more wildlife on the Middle Fork. The Middle Fork has the lion's share of hot springs, while the main Salmon has most of the wide sandy beaches. Both rivers offer a lot of history: old mining claims, Indian camps, and pioneer cabins. Trips generally last 3-6 days on either river.

For specific details on boating the main Salmon River, contact the **North Fork Ranger District** (11 Casey Rd., North Fork, 208/865-2700). For information on Middle Fork float trips, contact the **Middle Fork Ranger District** (U.S. 93, Challis, 208/879-4101).

River Guides

If you go with an outfitter, which is recommended unless you've rafted these rivers before, you don't have to worry about getting a permit. Dozens of guide services offer trips on either or both rivers. Expect to pay $1,200-2,400 per person for an all-inclusive six-day trip. Here are several river outfitters and guides that can make it all possible:

- **Aggipah River Trips** (Salmon, 877/705-7370, www.salmonriverwhitewater.com)
- **Middle Fork River Tours** (Hailey, 208/788-6545 or 800/445-9738, www.middlefork.com)
- **North Fork Guides** (North Fork, 208/865-2534 or 800/259-6866, www.northforkguides.com)
- **River of No Return Outfitters** (Salmon, 208/756-7002, www.raftidaho.com)
- **Wilderness River Outfitters** (Lemhi, 800/252-6581, www.wildernessriver.com)

For more listings of outfitters, see the Idaho Outfitters and Guides Association website (www.ioga.org).

Yankee Fork Country

The Yankee Fork River flows into the Salmon River between the Frank Church-River of No Return Wilderness on the north and Highway 75 on the south. Around the river lies one of Idaho's major historic mining districts, the Land of the Yankee Fork Historic Area. Prospectors first began exploring the area in the 1860s, and mining of one sort or another has been taking place ever since.

★ CUSTER MOTORWAY ADVENTURE ROAD

When gold was discovered on the Yankee Fork, the boomtowns of Bonanza and Custer sprang to life. The miners needed equipment and supplies to work their claims, and the nearest supply center was at Challis.

Entrepreneur Alex Toponce saw a money-making opportunity. He won a charter from the Territorial Legislature to build a toll road between Challis and Bonanza. It was completed in 1879 and was the sole freight route into the Yankee Fork mines for a decade. In 1933, the Civilian Conservation Corps (CCC) restored the road, and today it's known as the Custer Motorway Adventure Road. It would be an unpleasant adventure to attempt the unpaved route with a trailer or a large RV. Also note that the road is subject to damage from spring runoff and is sometimes closed between Challis and Custer.

The organization of this chapter is from Stanley to Salmon, so the sights along the

46-mile Custer Motorway are listed below from southwest (Sunbeam) to northeast (Challis).

Bonanza

Turning north off Highway 75 at Sunbeam, onto Yankee Fork Road (Forest Rd. 013), you'll soon come to **Bonanza,** the first of the Yankee Fork boomtowns. It was founded in 1877 and by 1881 had a population of 600. Fires in 1889 and 1897 gutted much of the town, and most of the townsfolk moved to Custer as a result. Today, the site is a ghost town and less developed than Custer. A CCC-built Forest Service work camp presides over the slowly decaying miners' shacks. A short, dusty spur road (Forest Rd. 074) leads to two separate cemeteries. The first, **Bonanza Cemetery,** is the more typical of the two, with the graves of a town of souls who lived and died pursuing their glittering dreams. Among their causes of death: avalanche, black lung, blood poisoning, gunshot wound, heart attack, mining accident, pneumonia, scarlet fever, spinal meningitis, suicide, and typhoid fever.

Farther down the spur is **Boothill Cemetery,** where just three old wooden markers surrounded by a fence record the final resting places of Lizzie King and her two husbands. Husband number one, Richard King, came to Bonanza with Lizzie in 1878. He was subsequently shot and killed in an argument. Lizzie moved to Butte, Montana, where she met prospector Bob Hawthorne. The two ended up back in Bonanza (running the Yankee Fork Dance Hall and Saloon) and got married in 1880. Hawthorne told everyone in town that he was filthy rich and had a large estate in England. When the truth came out that he was actually dirt poor, he apparently couldn't bear the humiliation; he shot and killed Lizzie and then turned the gun on himself. Both Lizzie and Bob were buried at Boothill next to Rich King, who no doubt would have killed Bob himself if they both weren't already dead.

Custer

Established two years after Bonanza, **Custer** went on to become the more important of the two gold-rush towns. It reached its peak population of 600 in 1896, at which time it was home to the huge General Custer stamp mill, the Nevada Hotel, the Miner's Union Hall, a cathouse, a brewery, and a sizable Chinatown. It even had its own newspaper, *The Yankee Fork Herald,* which on April 28, 1880, reported: "There will be no religious services tomorrow; first, because there is no minister, and secondly, there is no church. But there will be several poker games running."

The mines all played out by 1911, and the town disappeared shortly thereafter. Today, it's a resurrected boomtown full of Nikons and out-of-state license plates. A museum (summer only) tells the story of the town's heyday, and a self-guided walking tour leads visitors past mining-equipment detritus and other points of interest.

To Challis

Continuing northeast from Custer, the historic sites along the route get fewer and farther between. You'll pass the sites of several way stations where meals, refreshments, and fresh horses were available and see the remains of the toll station where Toponce & Co. collected the tolls. The rate for a wagon and team was $4. The station operated 1879-1889. A few miles later, the road passes the U.S. Forest Service **Mill Creek Campground** (8 sites, June-Sept., $10), which has potable water.

A mile or so farther, Forest Road 080 turns off to the north and leads three miles to **Mosquito Flat Reservoir,** a popular fishing hole with primarily rainbow trout, a boat ramp, and drinking water. Just north of the reservoir is the **Mosquito Flat Campground** (9 sites, free).

CHALLIS

Alvah P. Challis surveyed and platted Challis as a mining and ranching supply town in 1876. Now it's the Custer County seat, but it's still a mining and ranching town. At the Forest

Service office on U.S. 93, history buffs can pick up a guide to the town's historic structures, including pioneer houses, the old jail, and the old schoolhouse, all of which were constructed between 1877 and 1914. The town claims to have the state's largest collection of pre-1900 log homes. Challis has a few motels, eateries, and basic services along the main drag.

Land of the Yankee Fork Interpretive Center

Travelers heading from Salmon toward Stanley are best poised to take advantage of the modern and informative **Land of the Yankee Fork Interpretive Center** (Hwy. 75 and U.S. 93, 208/879-5244, 9am-5pm Thurs.-Sun. Apr. 1-Oct. 15, $5) before starting out on the Custer Motorway over to Sunbeam. Travelers coming from Sunbeam on the Custer Motorway will get here last and can at least get answers to any questions they came up with on the way over. The center commemorates the area's mining history in well-designed educational exhibits. You'll find out about the ghost towns of Custer and Bonanza along with other sights along the Custer Motorway.

Challis Hot Springs

The large, developed **Challis Hot Springs** resort (5025 Hot Springs Rd., Challis, 208/879-4442, year-round, call for rates) has been around since the mining days, although those old sourdoughs missed out on the big swimming pool and a campground with RV sites ($35) and tent sites ($25). Fishing the nearby Salmon River keeps some guests occupied, while horseshoes and volleyball are on the agenda for others. You'll find it east of Challis, 4.5 miles north of U.S. 93 at the end of Hot Springs Road.

Backcountry Roads

A long cherry stem probing 25 miles into the Frank Church-River of No Return Wilderness, Sleeping Deer Road (Forest Rd. 086) traverses a long, high ridgeline between Twin Peaks and Sleeping Deer Mountain. A spur road at Twin Peaks (not for the new minivan) leads to the West's second-highest staffed fire lookout. Farther on, the road is dotted with picnic areas offering great views of the Frank Church and several trailheads leading into the wilderness. At the end-of-the-road trailhead, you're within a long day's hike of the Middle Fork. Numerous little lakes also pepper the area.

A bit farther north up U.S. 93, **Morgan Creek Road** (Forest Rd. 055) ascends Morgan Creek, crosses a divide, and descends Panther Creek, joining the Salmon River Road west of Shoup. Along the way you'll pass the Bureau of Land Management's **Morgan Creek Campground** and a turnoff (Forest Rd. 057) to the U.S. Forest Service **Little West Fork Campground.** Both are small, with no improved water source and no fees.

Salmon and Vicinity

At the confluence of the Lemhi and Salmon Rivers, the town of Salmon is the Lemhi County seat and another contender for honors as the state's white-water capital. It's the staging center for the start of float trips down the main Salmon River and the end of trips down the Middle Fork. Although filled in summer with more river rats than you can shake a paddle at, the town has none of the boisterous buzz of Riggins or even Stanley.

SIGHTS
Sacajawea Interpretive Cultural and Educational Center

The newish **Sacajawea Interpretive**

Cultural and Educational Center (110 Lewis and Clark St., Salmon, 208/756-1222, www.sacajaweacenter.org, 9am-5pm Mon.-Sat., 12:30pm-5pm Sun., end of May-early Sept., $5 over age 5, $12 family), one mile east of Salmon on Highway 28, mainly serves to pay homage to the young Shoshone woman, a Lemhi Valley native, who accompanied the Lewis and Clark expedition. Its many facets are still coming together, but right now you'll find a small interpretive facility, an amphitheater, and a walking trail. You might even see living-history demonstrations and reenactments too.

RECREATION
Rafting and Outfitters
In addition to the many weeklong raft trips that either begin or end in Salmon, the town is a base for several outfitters that offer shorter half-day to three-day Salmon River adventures. Salmon-based companies include **Kookaburra Rafting** (1115 U.S. 93, Salmon, 208/756-4386 or 888/654-4386, www.raft-4fun.com) and **Idaho Adventures** (6 Adventure Ln., Salmon, 800/789-9283, www.idahoadventures.com). Idaho Adventures also offers gentle three-hour scenic trips on a traditional Salmon River scow.

Elk Bend Hot Springs
Those who prefer their hot springs undeveloped and au naturel will find a treat at **Elk Bend Hot Springs** (also called Goldbug Hot Springs), about 22 miles south of Salmon on U.S. 93. Look for a turnoff to the east near mile marker 282. Follow the road a short way down to a well-marked trailhead. The springs are situated on a high bench overlooking the valley. It's a magical spot, but it can get crowded at times.

ACCOMMODATIONS
$50-100
Sacajawea Inn (705 Challis St., Salmon, 208/756-2294, from $65 d) is a recently revamped old motor inn with 21 small but clean guest rooms. Amenities include cable TV and an outdoor fire pit where you can roast marshmallows and wieners. Pets are allowed, and the motel is nonsmoking.

The biggest motel in town is the 100-room **Stagecoach Inn** (201 Riverfront Dr., Salmon, 208/756-2919, from $74 d), right at the Salmon River bridge. Queen beds are standard; some guest rooms with king beds are available. Amenities include a heated pool, free continental breakfast, and a coin laundry; pets are not allowed. Ask for a room facing the river.

rafting on the Salmon River near Salmon

Twelve miles south of Salmon on U.S. 93 is the ★ **Greyhouse Inn** (1115 U.S. 93 S., Salmon, 208/756-3968, www.greyhouseinn. com, $65-124), a beautifully restored 1894 Victorian farmhouse turned B&B with four guest rooms (two with shared bath) plus a few cabins and a carriage house. Rates include a full breakfast.

FOOD

★ **Bertram's Brewery & Restaurant** (101 S. Andrews St., Salmon, 208/756-3391, www. bertramsbrewery.com, 11am-9pm Mon.-Thurs., 11am-10pm Fri., 8am-10pm Sat., 8am-9pm Sun.) serves handcrafted microbrews and sodas in the grand old 1898 Redwine Building in downtown Salmon. Expect to find beer-friendly appetizers and burgers ($8-12) as well as big steaks, seafood, and pasta dishes ($16-24) in the evening. The restaurant is smoke-free, and kids are welcome.

Junkyard Bistro (405 Main St., Salmon, 208/756-2466, 11am-10pm Mon.-Sat., 11am-9pm Sun.) is a funky little beer and wine bar that dishes up tasty appetizers, sandwiches, and burgers. Try the Vietnamese pork sandwich and a cold microbrew.

NORTH TO MONTANA

Heading north of Salmon on U.S. 93, you'll soon pass through the small towns of North Fork and Gibbonsville before summiting Lost

Trail Pass (7,014 feet), at which point you'll be in Montana.

LEWIS AND CLARK NATIONAL BACKCOUNTRY BYWAY

About 20 miles southeast of Salmon on Highway 28, you'll come to a turnoff near Tendoy that leads to this well-marked loop road that lets you follow in the footsteps of Lewis and Clark. The unpaved but well-graded route first passes an interpretive display that fills you in on the history of the Corps of Discovery in this area. The road then climbs up and across a heavily logged plateau before dropping down to historic **Lemhi Pass,** where an advance party led by Meriwether Lewis first set eyes on the land that would eventually become the state of Idaho. Lewis planted the U.S. flag on the west side of the pass, claiming the land for the United States. When the expedition crossed the Continental Divide here in 1805, they were no longer in territory covered by the Louisiana Purchase, and Britain and the United States would jockey for control of the Pacific Northwest for many years to come.

Lemhi Pass is usually accessible June-September, but check with the Bureau of Land Management's **Salmon Field Office** (1206 S. Challis St., Salmon, 208/756-5400) for current road conditions.

Basin and Range Country

Southeast of the Challis-Salmon stretch of U.S. 93, three parallel mountain ranges separated by road-bearing valleys provide a great example of what geologists call a basin-and-range formation. As the earth's crust stretches apart at the rate of 0.5 inch per year, the ground breaks into blocks formed of peaks and valleys. The Lost River, Lemhi, and Beaverhead Ranges and the valleys between them are aligned as neatly as F to B-flat on a piano. The Beaverhead Range forms part of

the Continental Divide, while the Lost River Range is home to Idaho's highest mountain, 12,662-foot Borah Peak.

UP WARM SPRINGS CREEK

Turning southeast out of Challis down U.S. 93, you'll head up Warm Springs Creek and eventually enter the tight squeeze of **Grandview Canyon.** Past the impressive canyon you'll climb up to **Willow Creek Summit** (7,160 feet), a favored winter grazing area for elk. When you crest the pass, the road heads down into the **Big Lost River Valley.**

BORAH PEAK

As you head southeast down the Big Lost River Valley, the massive wall of the Lost River Range rises abruptly on the left. From along the highway, this range is nowhere nearly as exciting a sight as, say, the snowy Sawtooth Range. The terrain here is dry and relatively barren in comparison, and the mountains look not so much like high alpine spires as big hulking blocks of rock. Look for the turn-off marked "Borah Peak Access" and look to the left to see **Borah Peak.** This mountain monarch rises abruptly from the valley floor and leads the eye right to the summit, which, unlike many high peaks, isn't hidden behind lower interlopers.

Climbing the peak takes 8-12 hours round-trip, depending on your speed and physical condition. While the route isn't technical, it is very steep and strenuous, gaining almost a vertical mile in less than 3.5 miles. One short stretch involves third-class climbing (use of hands and feet) across "Chicken-out Ridge," a knife-edge ridge with serious exposure. Snow often lingers on a steep saddle near the summit well into midsummer. Use of an ice ax for insurance makes the necessary traverse across that saddle less scary. While the Forest Service brochure might lead you to think it's an easy walk to the summit, never underestimate the risks associated with climbing high peaks. If you're out of shape or don't have the proper equipment or clothing, don't attempt the hike. If you do attempt it, make sure to check in at the ranger station in Mackay first. Those who are prepared will find the climb exceedingly enjoyable.

A little south of Borah down U.S. 93, you'll get a glimpse of another Idaho giant. A roadside sign indicates the Matterhorn-like **Leatherman Peak** (12,230 feet), visible through a slot in the nearer ridgeline. Leatherman is the state's second-highest peak and a far more impressive sight than Borah.

MACKAY

Copper discoveries in the area led to the founding of **Mackay** (MACK-ee) in 1901. Ranching and recreation have since replaced mining as the mainstay of the local economy. The laid-back little town is the primary supply point for hikers heading up Borah Peak and for anglers trolling for trout in Mackay Reservoir and the Big Lost River. Basic accommodations and food are available.

RVing golfers will appreciate **River Park Golf Course and RV Campground** (717 Capitol Ave., Mackay, 208/588-2296, greens fees $15-20, RV sites $25). The RV sites lie right between the sixth and eighth tees. The course has nine holes, and the RV park has full hookups.

West of town, the White Knob Mountains rise to over 10,000 feet. They are home to rugged old mining roads that will surely chew up your wheel bearings, but it's a beautiful drive if you have a high-clearance vehicle, preferably with 4WD.

For recreation information, stop by the U.S. Forest Service's **Lost River Ranger District** (716 W. Custer St., Mackay, 208/588-3400).

North-Central Idaho

A s U.S. 95 unravels like a teased ribbon, north-central Idaho quickly goes from rugged peaks to rolling hills. This varied topography is what geologists and archaeologists dream about.

And what stuff are those dreams made of? Ponder all those massive mountains, myriad lakes, and dinosaur bone-filled prairies. Let's not forget the long mountain valleys that look like the set of *Bonanza*.

The western skirt of Idaho borders with Oregon and Washington, but Hells Canyon, the deepest river gorge in North America, even deeper than the Grand Canyon, makes crossing the border impossible for more than 70 miles. This is where the Snake River gets furiously funneled through an abysmal chasm en route to its confluence with the Columbia River in Washington.

Traveling north on U.S. 95, western Idaho's primary north-south arterial, the rough landscape starts to soften as it unfolds into the Camas Prairie near Grangeville. The landscape rolls out like a patchwork quilt to the west, while more impressive mountains and wild rivers dictate the scenery on the east side of the shadowy prairie.

PLANNING YOUR TIME

North-central Idaho encompasses a large portion of the state, from the McCall area all the way to the southern shores of Coeur d'Alene Lake. Much of it is wilderness, which requires travelers to clear their calendars for a week or two in order to fully enjoy what the region has to offer.

The high-walled gorge of Hells Canyon may look hellish, but it's pure heaven for white-water fanatics who come in droves for the unrelenting rapids. The Seven Devils, the most underrated mountain range in Idaho, hems the gorge to the east like a broken spine. Backpackers and mountain bikers will find miles of extreme backcountry untouched by human development. Remote trailheads lead to dramatic vantage points overlooking the gorge. Along the way, don't be surprised to see elk, bighorn sheep, cougars, black bears, and birds of prey; some say grizzlies roam these parts too.

Previous: barn in Moscow; dock at Lake Cascade. **Above:** ponderosa pines in the Payette National Forest.

Look for ★ to find recommended
sights, activities, dining, and lodging.

Highlights

★ **Ponderosa State Park:** The crown jewel of Idaho's park system is 1,000 acres of forested wonderland offering hiking, biking, fishing, camping, and cross-country skiing (page 282).

★ **The Seven Devils:** This unfettered mountain range skirts the east side of Hells Canyon. Seven devilishly named peaks offer outdoor enthusiasts unlimited wilderness opportunities (page 293).

★ **River Trips in Riggins:** Idaho's whitewater capital is located where the main Salmon and Little Salmon Rivers smash together in a spectacle of wild rapids (page 297).

★ **Nez Perce National Historic Park:** This park system has 38 historic sites in Idaho, Washington, Oregon, and Montana, but the park's headquarters near Lewiston serves as the nerve center for it all. Here you'll find an interpretive center and a wonderful picnic area next to the Spalding Mission site (page 309).

★ **Following the Lochsa River:** Follow the trail of the Lewis and Clark expedition along the steep grades of the Lochsa Face. This scenic river stretch along U.S. 12 is pure nirvana for anglers and white-water fanatics (page 318).

★ **University of Idaho:** The most beautiful college campus in the state boasts a variety of architectural styles and plenty of green space for picnicking (page 320).

North-Central Idaho

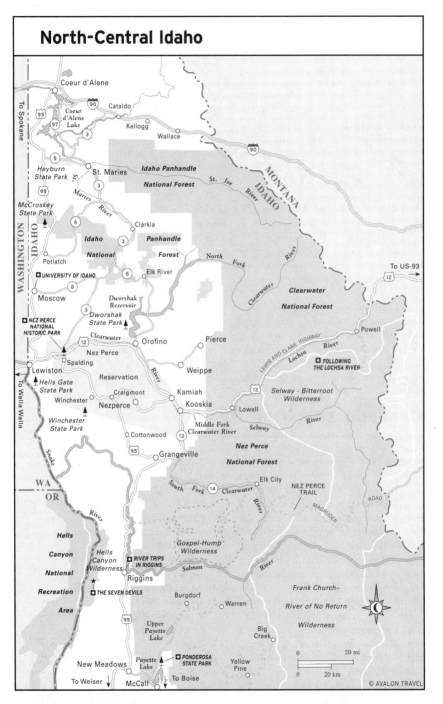

A few miles southeast of Hells Canyon, the West-Central Mountains run parallel with the Oregon border, creating two distinct Idaho valleys. Long Valley is a remote spread along Highway 55 fringed by high mountains to the west and east. The area is home to more than 130 lakes, including Payette Lake, a scenic waterway that's popular with boaters and anglers in summer. The burgeoning resort town of McCall lies on the lake's southern shores. Often outshone by the Ketchum-Sun Valley area to the east, McCall is hardly an ugly cousin. The spectacular high-country here offers outdoor enthusiasts a long list of year-round mountain fun: skiing and snowboarding at Brundage Mountain, backcountry hot springs, hiking, and mountain biking. Most hotels and lodges in Idaho's mountain resort towns offer special deals during the spring and fall months.

Just north of McCall is Riggins, a little hamlet along U.S. 95 where the main Salmon and Little Salmon Rivers come together in a wild exhibition of rapids. The town teems with activity in the spring and summer months when thousands of anglers and rafters show up for a piece of the action. Thirty-pound steelhead salmon run the rivers just a few feet from the downtown strip.

Lewis and Clark buffs will find much to do in this region, where the Corps of Discovery endured some of its harshest setbacks, namely at the Lochsa River (now U.S. 12) and its alpine hinterlands. These early explorers probably would never have made it to the mouth of the Columbia River had it not been for the help of the Nez Perce people, who still thrive here today.

The Clearwater and Snake Rivers meet near Lewiston, a city that boasts the only inland seaport in the West. Above the Clearwater River Valley lies the Palouse, a colorful quilt of fertile farms and undulating hills. Moscow is home to the University of Idaho. This friendly college town is an excellent place to chill for a few days, and possibly take an excursion to see ancient cedars and hemlocks, which stand majestic in the nearby forests. Summer is a great time to visit Moscow because the campus and town are a lot quieter when school is out for a majority of the students, who typically go away for seasonal jobs.

Cascade and Vicinity

North of Smiths Ferry, the steep canyons of the Payette River open up into Long Valley, a beautiful dell of scenic mountain vistas and lakes. Cascade is the first settlement you'll come to heading north on Highway 55. The town was named for some waterfalls on the North Fork Payette River that lost their thunder in 1948 to Cascade Dam. The resulting 30,000-acre Cascade Reservoir (now referred to as Lake Cascade) is one of the state's busiest fishing holes. Perch are the most numerous fish in the lake and are sought by both boating anglers in summer and ice-fishers in winter. But the lake also holds healthy populations of rainbow trout, Coho salmon, and smallmouth bass.

Cascade, the Valley County seat, is a bustling little hub for those who come for boating, fishing, hunting, mountain biking, camping, and skiing at nearby Tamarack Resort (Cascade is only about an hour and a half drive from Boise). There's a newish whitewater park that also keeps people flowing into town for a riot of river fun.

RECREATION
Lake Cascade State Park
Lake Cascade State Park (office 970 Dam Rd., at Lakeshore Dr., near Crown Point, Cascade, 208/382-6544) has 12 units around Lake Cascade's 86 miles of shoreline, including the Crown Point, Ridgeview, Sugarloaf, Buttercup, and Blue Heron units. Crown Point, the closest unit to town, is on the east

shore of the lake just north of the dam's spillway. You'll find 29 campsites ($12-21), some right on the lake, with nearby central water and vault toilets. These first-come, first-served sites (other park unit campgrounds are reservation-only) are adjacent to sandy alcoves and wave-smoothened rocks that make for great swimming holes, and the **Crown Point Railroad Grade Trail** runs right behind the campground. This 2.7-mile recreational trail, on a stretch of the old Oregon Short Line Railroad, is a mellow spot for a stroll or bike ride along the shore of the lake. Boaters will like the fact that the park system operates six boat ramps around the lake.

Kelly's Whitewater Park

The three-acre **Kelly's Whitewater Park** (www.kellyswhitewaterpark.com, 10am-7pm daily Memorial Day-Sept., free but donations are appreciated) is a white-water playground on the North Fork Payette River that boasts several water features for kayakers of all skill levels. Boaters can hone their rolling skills and work on other technical kayaking maneuvers. It has a visitors center with kayaking exhibits, restrooms, and a changing area. There's even an amphitheater where the park hosts live music during the warmer months. The park

is just south of Cascade at mile marker 114 on the east side of Highway 55. You can just show up with your boat, and on-site river rangers will help you out.

Golf

The nine-hole **Cascade Golf Course** (117 Lakeshore Dr., Cascade, 208/382-4653, Apr.-Oct., nine holes for $17) lines the east shore of Lake Cascade. You'll also find cart rentals and a small pro shop. After hitting the links, grab a burger and a beer in the bar and grill, which offers spectacular views of the lake and looming West-Central Mountains.

ACCOMMODATIONS

The **Ashley Inn** (500 N. Main St., Cascade, 208/382-5621, www.theashleyinn.com, from $132), right along the highway north of downtown Cascade, is probably the nicest lodging option in town. Expect to find an indoor pool and fireplaces in each of the 67 guest rooms. Rates include a breakfast buffet featuring fresh fruit, eggs, biscuits and gravy, pastries, and coffee.

CAMPING AND RVING

The beautiful ★ **Water's Edge RV Resort** (620 N. Main St., Cascade, 208/382-3120,

Lake Cascade

www.watersedgervpark.com, spring-fall), at the north end of town along Highway 55, lies on the banks of the Payette River. Amenities include bathroom and laundry facilities, beach volleyball courts, horseshoes, free kayaks and canoes for guest use, and evening campfires. The resort has 120 RV sites with full hookups ($29-36), 20 tent sites ($21-23), and two camping cabins ($65-99).

FOOD

Head to **Grandma's Homestead Restaurant** (224 N. Main St., Cascade, 208/382-4602, breakfast, lunch, and dinner daily, $8-20), on the main drag, for homespun diner fare served with a smile. The dining room looks like Granny's living room with lots of knickknacks and cutesy artwork. Sit in a large booth and enjoy a chicken-fried steak with all the fixings. Standard breakfast dishes are the norm in the morning, while later in the day it's all about sandwiches, burgers, and finger steaks.

INFORMATION

You can get updated information about the area at **Cascade Chamber of Commerce** (101 S. Main St., Cascade, 208/382-3833). For recreation information, stop by the **Cascade Ranger District** (540 N. Main St., Cascade, 208/382-7400).

WARM LAKE

East of the highway, Warm Lake Road leads up into the mountains to the South Fork of the Salmon River and the community of Warm Lake. This is wild country, near the west edge of the Frank Church-River of No Return Wilderness. The owner of Warm Lake Lodge once saw a wolf investigating his dumpster, and the Forest Service has recorded wolf sightings in this area since the early 1980s, well before their reintroduction.

Hot Springs

Hot springs lovers could spend a whole weekend exploring the many hot pools in the Warm Lake area, among them **Molly's Tubs, Vulcan Hot Springs, Penny Hot Spring,** and **Trail Creek Hot Spring.** Molly's Tubs and Vulcan lie along or just off Forest Road 474, south of Warm Lake Road 1.3 and 6.5 miles, respectively. Penny Hot Spring is 4.5 miles north of Warm Springs Road off Forest Road 474, across from the former Penny Campground. Trail Creek is west of Warm Lake, 0.5 mile east of mile marker 61 on Warm Lake Road.

Accommodations

Warm Lake's two mountain lodges are both open year-round. In winter, either would make a good base camp for cross-country skiing in Boise National Forest. **Warm Lake Lodge** (15 Lodge Rd., Warm Lake, 208/632-3553, $59-159) has been around since 1911. Its rustic cabins line the shore of Warm Lake and range in size from a small unit with one double bed to a hot tub-equipped unit that sleeps 10. Some units have kitchenettes. Campsites ($15) are available, and other facilities at the resort include a restaurant and lounge, a store, a post office, and a boat dock. Pets are discouraged.

North Shore Lodge (175 N. Shoreline Dr., Warm Lake, 208/632-2000, www.northshorelodgeidaho.com, $75-135) offers cabins of various sizes, all with kitchenettes. Other facilities include a restaurant and lounge, a store, gas and oil sales, canoe and boat rentals, horseshoe pits, volleyball courts, and docks. Pets are allowed but must be leashed.

Forest Service Campgrounds and Cabins

Boise National Forest campgrounds in the Warm Lake area include **South Fork Salmon River** (14 sites, $15), **Shoreline** (25 sites, $15), and **Warm Lake** (12 sites, $15). In addition, the **Stolle Meadows Guard Station** (May-Mar., $50), which sleeps up to five, is available for rent; winter access is by cross-country skis or snowmobiles only. For reservations, call 877/444-6777.

a historic church near Donnelly

YELLOW PINE

Out past Warm Lake, past Landmark, past Halfway Station, and past Johnson Creek, you'll finally come to Yellow Pine, one of the state's most remote communities. The tenacious outpost once supplied the Big Creek mining district. Today, it's home to the **Yellow Pine Harmonica Festival** (www.yellowpinemusicandharmonicafestival.org) in early August, an annual blow that draws reasonably large crowds, considering the effort it takes to get out here.

Camping

North of Yellow Pine and north of Wapiti Meadows on Forest Road 340, the U.S. Forest Service **Big Creek Campground** (4 sites, $10) lies between two trailheads providing access into the Frank Church-River of No Return Wilderness.

DONNELLY

This little hamlet along Highway 55, near the north shore of Lake Cascade, serves as an

outpost of sorts for Tamarack Resort and all the summer camps in the area. The downtown strip has a row of mainstay restaurants and bars that thrive on a seasonal basis.

Tamarack Resort

The all-seasons resort, between Cascade and Donnelly near the western shore of Lake Cascade, opened with high aspirations in 2004, only to go into foreclosure in 2008 after the economy went into the dumpster. The resort had completed its first phase of development, including the ski runs and chairlifts on Tamarack Mountain, a main lodge, a banquet and convention facility modeled after a small town, vacation homes and rental cabins, and a world-class golf course overlooking the lake. The second phase, a little district with condominiums, retail shops, and restaurants called Village Plaza, sat unfinished on a hillside next to a collection of temporary Sprung structures that house the resort's ski operations and services.

After the resort lay dormant for a couple of years, the local homeowner's association managed to get the resort open for limited winter operations, and they even reopened the Lodge at Osprey Meadows and the rental cottages so people could spend the night at the resort after skiing all day. To the relief of many folks, it was announced in 2014 that a new ownership group had purchased the resort and would take over operations immediately, with the goal of finishing Village Plaza (by 2016) and keeping the resort open for years to come.

For alpine skiing, **Tamarack Resort** (311 Village Dr., Tamarack, 208/325-1000, www.tamarackidaho.com, 9am-4pm daily Dec.-March, full-day pass $52 adults, $43 ages 13-17, $25 ages 7-12), with a vertical drop of 2,800 feet, has 39 well-designed runs spread out over 900 acres, with a base elevation of 4,900 feet. The runs are serviced by six high-speed lifts.

The resort also offers Nordic skiing and snowshoeing on its 15 kilometers of groomed trails that meander through the tamaracks and aspens above the lake. You can buy a $9 day pass at the **Nordic Center** (208/325-1030).

Spend the night at the **Lodge at Osprey Meadows** (208/325-1009, $99-149), which has an outdoor swimming pool and hot tub, a fitness center, and a spa. There's also a restaurant and bar where you can get Northwest-inspired cuisine and cocktails by a roaring fireplace. Discovery Square, an array of fabric domes near the ski lifts, has a grab-and-go eatery, a small pub with microbrews, and a coffee shop, as well as ski and snowboard rentals (208/325-1015).

In summer, golfers should check out the resort's **Osprey Meadows** (208/325-1000, May-Sept. greens fees $39-74, make reservations online). The par 72, 18-hole course, designed by Robert Trent Jones Jr., is certainly challenging, and you would be hard-pressed to find more beautiful golf links in this part of the state. A clubhouse and lessons are available.

Gold Fork Hot Springs

Getting to hot springs in the Cascade-McCall area usually requires a short hike, but you can drive right up to **Gold Fork Hot Springs** (1026 Gold Fork Rd., Donnelly, 208/890-8730, noon-9pm Sun.-Mon. and Wed.-Fri., noon-11pm Sat. year-round, $8 adults, $6 children, cash or check only), a commercial operation that offers soakers a variety of man-made pools and tubs fed by mineral-rich springs that bubble up from deep within the earth. And you'll need to relax after driving the bumpy six-mile dirt road that leads to the pools. The turnoff, Davis Creek Lane, is about three miles south of Donnelly on Highway 55; look for a blue-and-white sign.

Accommodations and Food

Boulder Creek Inn & Suites (629 Hwy. 55, Donnelly, 208/325-8638, www.thebouldercreekinn.com, from $79 d), on the west side of the highway right before you come into town, is a standard hotel that offers 43 clean and cozy guest rooms. It'll cost you a little more for a suite with a hot tub. Amenities include cable TV, Wi-Fi, guest laundry rooms, and free continental breakfast.

★ **Buffalo Gal** (319 N. Main St., Donnelly, 208/325-8258, www.buffalogali-daho.com, 5pm-9pm Wed.-Sun.) seems out of place in this land of steaks and domestic long-neck brews. The dinner-only restaurant serves contemporary fare with global flair. Expect to see entrées like Argentinean-style beef brisket

an old barn near Donnelly

(braised in red wine and espresso) and a delicious roasted vegetable Napoleon. The libations list includes lots of regional wines and microbrews.

Across the way, you'll find **Flight of Fancy** (282 N. Main St., Donnelly, 208/325-4432, 7am-4pm Tues.-Sat.), a funky little bakery and espresso bar in an old house. The kitchen turns out yummy baked goods such as scones, pastries, cookies, and lemon bars.

McCall and Vicinity

With an ideal location on the shore of beautiful Payette Lake surrounded by millions of acres of national forest land, it's not surprising that McCall (population 3,000) is a hub for recreation. More than that, however, it's one of the state's most unabashedly fun towns and knows how to have a good time. Its young, outdoor-oriented populace enjoys practically out-the-back-door skiing at Brundage Mountain, boating on the lake, and hiking in expansive backcountry. When the locals aren't outdoors, you'll find them having a good time with friends at the bars and restaurants downtown. Tourism drives the economy, vacation homes dot the lakeshore, and thousands of visitors pour in on summer weekends and for Winter Carnival, the town's biggest annual event.

© AVALON TRAVEL

★ PONDEROSA STATE PARK

Considered by many the crown jewel of Idaho's state park system, Ponderosa State Park occupies a 1,000-acre peninsula jutting into **Payette Lake,** two miles northeast of downtown McCall. The peninsula was never logged in the early days, so the old-growth ponderosa pines (some up to 400 years old and 150 feet tall) are big and abundant. Lodgepole pine, Douglas fir, and grand fir tower over the park, and wildflowers brighten the meadows and forest floor. Besides conifer forest, marshes and arid sagebrush flats provide habitat for a wide variety of species, including woodpeckers, muskrats, ducks, foxes, ospreys, and in summer, big hungry mosquitoes. Summer visitors can hike or bike through the park, or head for the park's beaches to play in the waters of Payette Lake. In winter, the park becomes especially quiet and serene under a blanket of snow. Cross-country ski trails lead to views overlooking frosty Payette Lake and the mountains beyond.

Visitors Center

Most of the **visitor facilities** (208/634-2164) are on the south and west sides of the peninsula. Immediately upon entering the park and paying the usual $5 per vehicle state park entry fee, you'll come to the **visitors center.** Rangers are on hand to answer your questions, provide you with a park map, and fill you in on the park's schedule of interpretive programs. Something takes place at the park amphitheater just about every night all summer long, and rangers lead guided hikes on many mornings. Also ask about the junior ranger program, designed to keep youngsters happy in the great outdoors.

Hiking, Biking, and Skiing

Pick up a park trail map from a ranger at the visitors center. Road bicyclists will enjoy the scenic paved loop road down the peninsula to Osprey Cliff, which affords great views of Payette Lake and McCall. Hikers and mountain bikers will find a seven-mile system of dirt trails more to their liking. The off-pavement trails also lead from the visitors center out to the tip of the peninsula, offering loops of several different lengths. All the trails are open to hikers, and two are open to mountain bikers as well.

In winter the trails lie beneath a blanket of snow, over which easy- to intermediate-level cross-country ski trails ($5 pp per day, annual pass $35) are set. Most of the trails are

Payette Lake

skiing at Brundage Mountain

year-round, $75-165) available to rent that are especially nice for ski-in overnights in winter. All cabins have heating and air-conditioning, full kitchens, and sleep up to six. A nonrefundable $10 reservation fee is required.

OTHER SIGHTS AND RECREATION
Central Idaho Historical Museum
The **Central Idaho Historical Museum** (1001 State St., at Lake St., McCall, 208/634-4497, 11am-3pm Wed.-Sat. June-Aug., donation) comprises several restored Civilian Conservation Corps buildings that house local logging history exhibits and offices of community organizations. It's a nice spot for a picnic.

Fish Hatchery
The kings of their genus, chinook salmon can grow to be five feet long and weigh well over 100 pounds, but unfortunately, the number of these anadromous fish has drastically declined in the last half decade or so. To help compensate for the shrinking chinook populations, the Idaho Department of Fish and Game raises these kings at the **McCall Fish Hatchery** (300 Mather Rd., McCall, 208/634-2690, self-guided tours 8am-5pm daily year-round). Hatchery personnel trap spawning fish near Warm Lake on the South Fork and then perform massive artificial insemination at the hatchery. More than two million juvenile salmon are raised and released annually, hopefully to make their way downriver to the sea.

Brundage Mountain
Brundage Mountain (208/634-4151, snow report 208/634-7669, www.brundage.com, lifts 9:30am-4:30 pm daily, full-day lift tickets $60 adults, $37 ages 12-17 and seniors, $23 ages 7-11, free under age 7) is a first-rate ski and summer resort just outside town. Here you can enjoy 1,300 acres and a 1,800-foot vertical drop, served by a high-speed quad chair, two triple chairs, and two surface lifts. From the top of the mountain at 7,640 feet,

groomed and include skating lanes where trail width allows. **Lighted night skiing** (6pm-11pm daily) is available on the wide and relatively flat Northern Lights trail. Snowshoeing ($5 pp per day) is permissible at the park, but you must stay on the fringe of the cross-country ski trails.

Camping and Cabins
Ponderosa has 137 campsites in three loops just west of the visitors center. Each loop includes restrooms and showers, and in the vicinity you'll find a volleyball court, beaches, boat docks, and a day-use picnic area with a boat ramp.

The park offers single-vehicle tent sites ($12-21) and serviced RV and camper sites ($24-31). **Northwest Passage Campground,** which has a waterway connecting Payette Lake to Upper Payette Lake, is first-come, first-served; the **Peninsula and RV Campgrounds** (888/922-6743) are reservation-only end of May-Labor Day.

The park has five cabins (888/922-6743,

you'll enjoy sweeping views of the Payette Lakes, Salmon River Mountains, and the impressive Seven Devils Range.

Powder hounds might want to check out the resort's snowcat skiing ($279 pp per day) as well, which will take them to untracked runs far from the crowds. And parents will appreciate Brundage's Kids' Center, which offers the finest kids' programs and facilities of any ski resort in Idaho. Reduced-price lift tickets are offered after 1pm, and both ski and snowboard rentals and lessons are available.

In summer, the resort runs a chairlift (Fri.-Sun. late June-Labor Day, full-day pass $32 adults, single ride $16 adults, $9 ages 7-14 and over age 69) to the top of the mountain for mountain bikers. From the top, bikers can access a 15-mile singletrack trail system built especially for mountain bikes. Mountain-bike rentals are available; one package includes a bike, a helmet (required), and a full-day lift pass for $99.

Also in summer, the resort's amphitheater becomes an alpine concert venue extraordinaire. Look for shows throughout the season. Bring a lawn chair and your picnic basket.

To reach the resort, take Highway 55 east toward New Meadows, and watch for the signed turnoff to your right about eight miles outside town.

Little Ski Hill

A dual alpine and cross-country area, **Little Ski Hill** (208/634-5691, www.littleskihill.org, lifts 3:30pm-8:30pm Tues.-Thurs., 3:30pm-9:30pm Fri., 12:30pm-9:30pm Sat., extended hours during Christmas holidays, $15 adults, $12 ages 5-17) is about three miles northwest of town on Highway 55. A nonprofit operation run by Payette Lakes Ski Club, it began in 1937, making it the second-oldest ski hill in Idaho after Sun Valley. Although the alpine area (one T-bar serves one hill) is humble, it's also cheap. The grooming is excellent, and the slope facing the highway is just steep enough to entertain intermediate skiers.

The cross-country area (dawn-dusk daily, full-day $10 adults, $5 ages 5-17) is one of the best in the state. The longest loop in the 31-mile system passes several side trails, some climbing a ridge to offer speedy descents on the way back. The main trail meanders south through a string of valleys far from the highway. Both skating and traditional tracks are set, and you don't have to share them with snowmobiles. No rentals are available, but you can arrange lessons by appointment.

A small day lodge along the highway includes a snack bar and some picnic tables for sack lunches.

Ice Skating

McCall's pride and joy is the year-round **Manchester Ice & Event Centre** (200 E. Lake St., McCall, 208/634-3570, www.manchestericecenter.com). The indoor facility is a great place to skate ($7.50 adults, $5.50 under age 13, skate rental $2.50), with huge windows that look out on Payette Lake. Public skating sessions are held at least once daily; call for current hours. The Idaho Steelheads pro hockey team occasionally trains here, and many hockey clinics and camps are held throughout the year. A snack bar (from 10am daily) is available for both skaters and spectators.

Day Hikes near McCall

The Payette National Forest surrounding McCall is full of trails, allowing you to plan hikes of just about any length you want, from a couple of hours to a couple of weeks. Stop in at the **McCall Ranger District** (102 W. Lake St., McCall, 208/634-0400) for trail suggestions and a list of the topographic maps you'll need for the hike you choose.

Duck Lake Trail begins up Lick Creek Road (Forest Rd. 48), just past Lick Creek Summit. An overlook at the summit provides panoramic views of the glacier-carved landscape. The trail climbs ever so slightly for about a mile to Duck Lake, making for a pleasant two-mile round-trip jaunt. Those looking for a slightly longer hike can try Trail 083 from Duck Lake up and over a steep ridge to Hum Lake. From Hum Lake the trail loops back to Lick Creek Road; then it's about a two-mile walk down the road back to the car.

Closer to McCall, don't forget the beautiful trails at Ponderosa State Park.

Fishing

Between the Payette Lakes and the numerous streams around McCall, the intrepid angler can catch cutthroat, rainbow, lake, and brook trout, as well as kokanee, kamloops, and bass. Anglers who are also backpackers should know that the Payette National Forest surrounding McCall contains some 300 mountain lakes and 1,400 miles of streams.

Golf

At **McCall Golf Club** (925 Fairway Dr., McCall, 208/634-7200, May-Oct., greens fees $29-41), on the east side of town, you can choose between three different nine-hole courses or combine them as you wish. The scenic course also has a pro shop and a restaurant.

The 18-hole, par-72 **Whitetail Club Golf Course** (501 W. Lake St., McCall, 800/657-6464) was designed by Roger Packard and two-time U.S. Open winner Andy North. The lovely course is mostly private, but you can play here if you stay at Shore Lodge. Call for greens fees and information about package deals.

Outdoor Outfitters

Gravity Sports (503 Pine St., McCall, 208/634-8530, www.gravitysportsidaho.com) rents canoes, kayaks, and mountain bikes in summer and cross-country touring skis, telemark skis, skating skis, snowboards, and snowshoes in winter.

Mile High Marina (1300 E. Lake St., McCall, 208/634-8605) rents ski boats, pontoon boats, fishing boats, canoes, and Jet Skis in summer, as well as snowmobiles in winter.

ENTERTAINMENT AND EVENTS
Nightlife

Rock-and-rollers usually wind up at **The Yacht Club** (203 E. Lake St., McCall, 208/634-5649, until late daily) for loud live music and dancing. Expect a small cover charge when bands are playing. Across the street is the **Foresters Club** (306 E. Lake St., McCall, 208/634-8529, 4:30pm-late Tues.-Sun.), a longtime watering hole that has a dozen microbrews on tap and live music on weekends.

Events

McCall's **Winter Carnival** is the biggest and best winter fest in the state, and it's not uncommon for more than 20,000 people to pack in on opening day. Motel rooms are booked a year in advance for this party. Fanciful snow sculptures line the streets, and an ice-carving contest brings out world-class artists. Sled dog races, a sledding hill, and an ice-skating rink draw devotees, while everyone enjoys the Mardi Gras-themed parade, fireworks, food, and fun. It runs for 10 days at the end of January and beginning of February.

For its size, McCall boasts a rich and diverse music scene. All summer long, Brundage Mountain hosts concerts and other events. In mid-July the **Summer Music Festival** (www.thesummermusicfestival.com), held in front of a big red barn in historic Roseberry, brings in people from miles around for an impressive lineup of folk, bluegrass, and Americana bands.

ACCOMMODATIONS
$50-100

★ **Scandia Inn** (401 N. 3rd St., McCall, 208/634-7394, www.thescandiainn.com, $60-85 d) has some of the best rates in town. This mountain-style motor inn (it's made out of pine logs) is within walking distance of downtown and the lake. It has 16 nonsmoking guest rooms with cable TV and high-speed Internet. Pets are not allowed. Speaking of made-from-logs motor inns, there's another one right across the way. The **Rustic Inn** (400 N. 3rd St., McCall, 208/634-7671, $55-70 d) also has budget rates for its alpine-inspired guest rooms. Amenities include in-room refrigerators and microwaves, Wi-Fi, and cable TV.

Just west of town, on the way to Brundage Mountain, **Brundage Inn** (1005 W. Lake St., McCall, 208/634-2009, www.brundagevacations.com, from $79 d) is a two-story hotel with 22 standard guest rooms. It's owned and operated by Brundage Vacations, a property management company that also rents out cabins around town.

$100-150

★ **Hotel McCall** (1101 N. 3rd St., McCall, 208/634-8105 or 866/800-1183, www.hotelmccall.com, $135-150, suites from $300 d) has been in operation since 1904. This beautiful hotel recently underwent a major renovation, adding more guest rooms and large suites, many of which boast spectacular views of Payette Lake and Brundage Mountain. Amenities include a lake-view garden patio, an infinity indoor pool, and milk and cookies at night. The hotel also houses Rupert's, one of the finest restaurants in town.

Bear Creek Lodge (3492 Hwy. 55, McCall, 208/634-3551, www.bearcreeklodgemccall.com, from $99 d) lies a few miles northwest of town at mile marker 149 on Highway 55. While this makes it slightly less convenient than in-town lodgings for enjoying McCall's lively social scene, the location is closer to Brundage Mountain and the Little Ski Hill and farther from McCall's noise and bustle. The beautiful modern lodge lies alongside Bear Creek on a scenic 65-acre spread. Accommodations include nine guest rooms equipped with fireplaces and refrigerators, as well as separate duplex cabins featuring king beds and in-room hot tubs. In the gorgeous dining room you'll be served a complimentary gourmet breakfast spread. In the evening you can hang out in the comfy wine bar area.

Brundage Bungalows (308 W. Lake St., McCall, 208/473-2894, $99-199) features cute separate bungalow cabins with microwaves, refrigerators, and cable TV. Pets are allowed; smoking is not allowed indoors.

$150-250

It's hard to miss the grand ★ **Shore Lodge** (501 W. Lake St., McCall, 800/657-6464, www.shorelodgemccall.com), sitting regal on the south shore of Payette Lake. This family-friendly resort was built in 1948, but it recently received an extensive remodel. It has something for everyone, including a fine-dining restaurant, a game room, a movie theater, an outdoor swimming pool, a marina, and a private golf course. Expect to find standard guest rooms as low as $129, the most extravagant suites topping out at $600, and everything in between. The lodge offers special rates during the fall and spring months.

For more lodging options in this price range, contact **Mountain Lakes Realty** (805 N. 3rd St., McCall, 208/634-2728, www.mountainlakesrealty.com), which lists short-term condo and cabin rentals in the McCall area.

FOOD

McCall is known for its mountain cuisine, so don't be surprised to find lots of elk, trout, huckleberries, and hand-foraged morels on menus around town.

Upscale Fare

★ **Rupert's** (Hotel McCall, 1101 N. 3rd St., McCall, 208/634-8108, www.rupertsathotelmccall.com, 5pm-9pm Thurs.-Mon., dinner entrées $19-32) is the place to go in town for inventive regional cuisine. Chef Gary Kucy, a semifinalist for a James Beard Award, changes his fusion menu with the season, usually featuring local wild mushrooms and huckleberries in summer. Start things off with smoked elk carpaccio with huckleberry reduction and baked Brie with peach chutney. The restaurant has the best wine list in town, pairing well with dinner entrées such as miso-glazed salmon with quinoa pilaf and ginger-scallion pesto.

The Narrows (501 W. Lake St., McCall, 800/657-6464, from 5pm daily, dinner entrées $24-47) at Shore Lodge serves contemporary fare in its beautiful dining room that overlooks the lake. Expect to see starters like Idaho trout chowder and duck meatballs with orange-fennel sauce. Larger plates include dishes such as lobster linguine and pan-seared chicken with black truffle risotto. The wine list, with lots of Washington, Oregon, and Idaho labels, is hardly an afterthought.

For an old-school steakhouse experience, head to **The Mill** (326 N. 3rd St., McCall, 208/634-7683, from 5:30pm daily, cocktail lounge from 5pm daily), on the west side of Highway 55 up the hill from the lake. Here you can score big steaks, slow-roasted prime rib, classic seafood dishes, and pork chops, most priced in the $20 range.

Casual Dining

★ **Salmon River Brewery** (411 Railroad Ave., McCall, 208/634-4772, www.salmonriverbrewery.com, 11am-11pm daily, entrées $8-13), next to Hotel McCall, is a microbrewery and restaurant that handcrafts a dozen or so seasonal and flagship brews. Enjoy a pint of stout and a black-and-blue elk burger. Other noteworthy picks are the deep-fried pickle spears, ale-soaked bratwurst, smoked salmon tacos, and macaroni and cheese.

Bistro 45 (1101 N. 3rd St., McCall, 208/634-4515, www.bistro45mccall.com, 8am-10pm daily, small plates $8-12), a venerable downtown wine bar and café right below Salmon River Brewery, has a great patio and bocce ball courts. This place pours a large array of wines by the glass to go with small bites like goat cheese tapenade, steamer clams and mussels, and hummus. You can also get panini sandwiches, salads, and quiche, and the small retail wine shop stocks good labels from around the globe.

International Cuisine

Downtown, you can get raw fish at **The Sushi Bar** (414 Railroad Ave., McCall, 208/634-7874, dinner from 4pm Tues.-Fri., lunch and dinner from 11am Sat.-Sun., $8-20). Besides fusion rolls, nigiri, and sashimi, the upstairs restaurant also serves hot Japanese items like miso soup, tataki, inari pockets, and noodle dishes from various parts of Asia. Of course there's plenty of sake and rice lager on hand to wash everything down.

Chapala (317 E. Lake St., McCall, 208/634-3905, lunch and dinner daily, $8-12), situated right on the lake, turns out standard Mexican fare in a festive environment. The lakeside deck is a great spot to hang out and drink margaritas. Good picks include carne asada, pork carnitas, chicken mole, and enchiladas suiza, splashed with zesty tomatillo sauce.

Breakfast and Coffee

The Pancake House (209 N. 3rd St., McCall, 208/634-5849, 6am-2pm daily, breakfast $6-10), a local dining institution since 1949, is where just about everyone in these parts goes for breakfast, so it can get extremely busy at times. As the name suggests, the restaurant specializes in pancakes, but also expect to find Belgian waffles, omelets, eggs Benedict, and "Those Potatoes," a pile of crispy spuds with gooey cheese and bacon. The lunch menu has everything from burgers to entrée salads and club sandwiches.

For freshly baked goods and a damn fine cup of coffee, head to ★ **Stacey Cakes** (136 E. Lake St., McCall, 208/634-2537, 8am-4pm Thurs.-Sun.) near the ice-skating arena. Owner Stacey Kucy, wife of chef Gary Kucy at Rupert's, puts out deliciously flaky croissants, berry tarts, quiche, cinnamon rolls, cakes, and cookies. Get there early, though, because this place is popular with the locals and the baked goodies go fast, especially on weekends.

Mountain Java (501 Pine St., McCall, 208/634-2027, from 6:30am daily), next to Gravity Sports, is a fun little coffeehouse that also sells cookbooks (my favorite reading material). Sit on the patio with your steamy espresso drink and watch boats buzz by on the lake, or cross-country skiers in winter.

INFORMATION

McCall Chamber of Commerce (301 E. Lake St., McCall, 208/634-7631, www.mccallchamber.org) can hook you up with more information about the town. For Payette National Forest recreation information, try the **McCall Ranger District** (102 W. Lake St., McCall, 208/634-0400).

Foraging for Morel Mushrooms

morel mushroom

Soon after the snow melts away in Idaho's mountains, morels pop up on the forest floor. These coveted edible mushrooms are a tasty harbinger that summer is on its way. Morels grow in great numbers in the McCall area, but you must know where to look.

First off, morels have a distinct conical cap with a honeycomb design. Most morels that grow in Idaho are western blonds from the yellow morel family *(Morchella esculenta)*. The color changes from white to beige to darker brown as the mushroom ages.

Morels love that perfect combination of moist and hot, so a spring rainfall in the mountains followed by a warm spell usually yields a harvestable crop. Morels have a symbiotic relationship with trees, especially broadleaf trees like aspen and ash. They don't typically thrive in acidic soils around cedars and other conifers, but morels seem to do all right in Idaho's ponderosa pine and tamarack forests, as long as a few deciduous trees are there to help balance the soil. Around old stumps and fallen trees are great places to look for these wild mushrooms. It's permissible to forage for morels on Forest Service land, unless you're doing it for commercial purposes; in that case you need a permit.

If you do encounter some morels, don't be a little piggy and take them all, and never pull the mushroom (stem and all) out of the ground, because that kills the fungi (the mycelium lives underground; the cap is the fruit). Just cut off the mushroom cap at mid-stem with a sharp knife, allowing another cap to grow later in the cycle.

Most locals aren't willing to give up their prized morel spots, or their favorite fishing holes, but they will generally offer you some advice at the pub, especially if you buy them a pint. Morels have a deliciously nutty, creamy taste with a meaty texture. If you don't feel like combing the forest on your hands and knees, just head to **Rupert's** or **The Narrows,** two restaurants in McCall that use morels in creative ways in the spring and summer months.

GETTING THERE AND AROUND
Getting There

Salmon Air (800/992-6559, $175 one-way, $325 round-trip) flies daily between Boise and McCall Municipal Airport (MYL, Hwy. 55 and Deinhard Ln., McCall). You can get reduced fares with 14-day advance purchase.

Northwestern Trailways (Old Town Shell Station at 507 N. 3rd St., McCall, www.

northwesterntrailways.com) offers daily bus service to and from Boise and points north.

Getting Around

McCall Air (300 Deinhard Ln., 208/634-7137 or 800/992-6559, www.mccallaviation.com) flies rafters, backpackers, anglers, and guest-ranch customers into the backcountry just about anywhere in Idaho. It's at the airport south of town along Highway 55.

EXPLORING THE BACKCOUNTRY

McCall is surrounded on three sides by the Payette National Forest, which offers some 2,000 square miles of prime hiking, biking, and horseback-riding country. Pick up a map at the McCall Ranger District, and the friendly rangers will mark it up for you with a highlighter pen.

Burgdorf Hot Springs

Burgdorf Hot Springs (208/636-3036, www.burgdorfhotsprings.com, $7 adults, $5 ages 17 and under), a natural hot springs resort, makes a scenic and relaxing day trip from McCall. Take Warren Wagon Road off Highway 55 at the west end of McCall and follow it north, past Payette Lake and past Upper Payette Lake. The U.S. Forest Service **Upper Payette Lake Campground** (20 sites, $10) is on the shore of the lake and offers a boat-launching ramp. Continuing up the highway, you'll pass thousands of acres of lodgepole pines charred in the fires of 1994. Eventually you'll come to the end of the pavement at the junction with Forest Road 246, the road in to the hot springs. In winter, the snowplows clear no farther, so you'll have to ski or snowmobile the rest of the way. Turn left on Forest Road 246 and follow it two miles to the hot springs.

The resort has been around since 1865, and there's an ongoing effort to restore many of the buildings on the property. The cabins ($35 per adult, $15 per child) are very rustic. Don't expect to find any electricity. The large, beautiful 50- by 75-foot hot-springs pool has rustic log sides and a sand bottom. It's about five feet deep and fed by a constant flow of 104°F spring water. A bonus for wildlife watchers: Across the road from the resort is a big open meadow where a large herd of elk comes to graze in the early evening in summer. If you're lucky, you might spy a moose here as well.

Camping is available right next door at the U.S. Forest Service **Burgdorf Campground** (5 sites, $10).

Warren

Dedicated explorers can continue farther east on Forest Highway 21 to the old gold-mining town of Warren, which in the boom days supported more than 2,000 people. According to the Payette National Forest's walking-tour guide to the historic town, "except for occasional bar fights, Chinese tong wars, highway robberies, and a huge 1904 business-district fire, Warren was considered a relatively calm mining camp." Today a handful of century-old buildings still stand, including a former hotel, saloon, and assay office.

East of Warren on Forest Road 340 is the remote U.S. Forest Service **Shiefer Campground** (4 sites, free), a great place for isolated fishing on the South Fork Salmon River. At this point you are 77 road miles from McCall.

Camping

In addition to the Payette National Forest campgrounds already listed, several others lie to the east and northwest of McCall. **Kennally Creek Campground** (12 sites, $10) offers a horse-unloading ramp and hitching rails at the Kennally Lakes trailhead. Take Highway 55 south from McCall a little over 10 miles, then turn east on Forest Road 388 and follow it 19 miles to the campground.

Three more campgrounds are accessed via Lick Creek Road (Forest Rd. 48), which begins east of Ponderosa State Park. **Lake Fork Campground** (9 sites, $10) is nine miles east of McCall, **Ponderosa Campground** (14 sites, $10) lies along the Secesh River 31 miles from McCall, and **Buckhorn Bar Campground** (10 sites, $10) is on the South Fork Salmon River beneath Sixmile Ridge. To get there, continue past Ponderosa Campground and bear right at two forks, first following Forest Road 48, then turning off onto Forest Road 674.

Northwest of McCall, take Highway 55 past the turnoff to Brundage and turn right on Forest Road 453 to reach **Last Chance Campground** (23 sites, $10). Alternately, turn up toward Brundage and continue past it to **Grouse Campground** (21 sites, $10) on Goose Lake, or a dozen miles farther on a washboard road to **Hazard Lake Campground** (12 sites, $10), which is near good hiking on the Lava Ridge National Recreation Trail.

The Hells Canyon Corridor

HELLS CANYON NATIONAL RECREATION AREA

Between Pinehurst and White Bird, U.S. 95 parallels the eastern edge of Hells Canyon National Recreation Area (NRA), a 652,488-acre preserve straddling the Snake River in Idaho and Oregon. For some 71 wild and scenic miles, the Snake carves its way northward through Hells Canyon, the deepest river gorge in North America. A few roads lead down to it in places, but none dare run through it.

Below Hells Canyon Dam, the Snake River's raging rapids and placid pools make for a recreational haven for rafters and jetboaters. Hikers can follow trails along the water's edge, beneath towering walls of crumbling black basalt, or climb out of the canyon to explore the high country along its rim (most notably the Seven Devils Mountains). This range of high peaks has some of the state's most magnificent alpine scenery and offers great views of the canyon floor more than a vertical mile below.

The 215,000-acre **Hells Canyon Wilderness** makes up a large portion of the national recreation area; motor vehicles and mountain bikes are prohibited. Although the majority of this wilderness lies across

Hells Canyon

Hells Canyon National Recreation Area

the river in Oregon, Idaho's share includes most of the Seven Devils Range as well as 18 river miles between Hells Canyon Creek and Willow Creek.

History

The canyon has long been popular with people, thanks to its mild winters, abundant game, and fish-filled river. Some 1,500 Native American archaeological sites have been found in the canyon, including evidence of human habitation going back 7,100 years. At **Upper Pittsburg Landing** you can look at petroglyphs (rock etchings) and pictographs (rock paintings) created by the canyon's first residents.

Before nonnatives came to the area, Chief Joseph's band of Nez Perce made an annual migration from their summer home in Oregon's Wallowa Mountains to warmer winter quarters here in the canyon. Shoshone, Northern Paiute, and Cayuse people also inhabited the region from time to time. Wilson Price Hunt's fur expedition of 1811 explored the upper reaches above today's Hells Canyon Dam but turned back before seeing the heart of the gorge.

The first population influx occurred in the 1860s, when the West's mining frenzy reached the area. Some placer mining took place along the river, and hard-rock mines soon riddled the southern Seven Devils. Copper was the big find; today you can drive to what's left of **Cuprum,** an aptly named copper-mining center. Later, homesteading farmers and ranchers made their way into the area. The farmers planted orchards and row crops on the fertile alluvial terraces, supplying both themselves and local miners with high-quality fresh produce. Ranchers grazed cattle and sheep on whatever relatively level areas they could find. A good example of an early sheep ranch is preserved today at **Kirkwood Ranch,** an interpretive site along the river accessible by foot, bicycle, or boat.

After World War II the Army Corps of Engineers suddenly found itself with nothing to do and latched onto dams as its new raison d'être. The Corps dammed its way inexorably up the Columbia River before casting eyes on the Snake. Hells Canyon, with its narrow width and steep gradient, looked like a prime target. In 1964 the Federal Power Commission gave the green light for development of a dam in the canyon. The proposal drew protest from canyon conservationists and eventually ended up before the U.S. Supreme Court. After years of legal wrangling, Congress created the Hells Canyon National Recreation Area in 1975, ensuring that no more dams would be built. The Snake is now undammed from Hells Canyon Dam at the south end of the canyon to Lower Granite Dam just beyond Lewiston, a distance of more than 100 miles.

Plants and Animals

Hells Canyon is a unique biome thanks to the extreme elevation changes that occur within its narrow boundaries. The land rises from 1,500 feet along the river to above 9,000 feet in the Seven Devils, all within about 10 miles as the crow flies. Each altitude zone supports a particular plant and animal community. Expect to see cacti and rattlesnakes on the canyon floor and lupines and marmots up high. And since those zones are horizontally compressed, you'll find many species living in abnormally close proximity.

The Snake River is one of the few remaining strongholds of the **white sturgeon,** a huge, primeval-looking monster that can reach lengths of 10 feet or more. If you catch one, the law requires you to put it back. Other fish in the river include steelhead, salmon, rainbow trout, bass, crappie, and catfish. On land, you'll find deer, black bears, elk, mountain goats, and bighorn sheep. Finally, the skies over the NRA are home to more than 100 species of birds, among them hawks, owls, and even bald and golden eagles.

The canyon's unique flora includes rare flowers such as Snake River phlox, rough harebell, the endangered MacFarlane's four-o'clock, and the bartonberry, found only in Hells Canyon. Also expect to see pockets of ponderosa pines and deciduous trees like hackberry, cottonwood, and alder.

Pittsburg Landing

Just south of White Bird on U.S. 95, signs mark a turnoff to Hammer Creek Recreation Area and **Pittsburg Landing.** Cross the Salmon River and make a quick left onto Deer Creek Road (Forest Rd. 493). Deer Creek Road winds up to Pittsburg Saddle and drops steeply down the other side to Pittsburg Landing, a total distance of 17 miles.

This important Native American archaeological site is also the only place south of Hells Canyon Dam on the Idaho side where you can drive right down to the river. Naturally, that makes it a popular launch and takeout point for rafters. At the end of the road you'll find an **NRA campground** (28 sites, $10), a boat-launching ramp, a dock, and a small ranger information booth. Nearby, a short spur road leads to another boat-launch area at Upper Pittsburg Landing, passing a gallery of Native American rock art on the way. The numerous pictographs and petroglyphs here mark the site as a favored studio for ancient Picassos. Upper Pittsburg Landing also marks the trailhead for the Hells Canyon National Recreation Trail. It can be extremely hot and dry in summer, and there's little shade. Campers will want to bring big floppy hats, plenty of sunscreen, and ice chests full of cold beverages.

★ The Seven Devils

Second only to the Sawtooths for spectacular alpine scenery, the **Seven Devils Range** rises steep and crag-like between the Salmon River on the east and the Snake River on the west. From the lofty summit of He Devil Peak (9,393 feet)—highest point in the NRA—it's a dizzying drop of nearly 8,000 feet in just over five miles down to the Snake at the bottom of Hells Canyon.

You can access the heart of this spectacular mountain range via Squaw Creek-Papoose Creek Road (Forest Rd. 517), which turns west off U.S. 95 on the south side of Riggins

at the Hells Canyon NRA Headquarters. A 19-mile drive up the gravel road leads you to **Heaven's Gate Lookout** (8,429 feet), where you'll be treated to possibly the most magnificent view in all of Idaho. The 360-degree panorama takes in four states: Idaho, Oregon, Washington, and Montana. To the northeast, the Camas Prairie spreads out all the way to the Clearwater River. To the southwest, Hells Canyon frames the foreground for the snow-capped Wallowa Mountains of Oregon, Chief Joseph's homeland. To the southeast, the Salmon River Mountains roll across the horizon. And practically right in front of you, the Devils' own cathedrals of granite tower over Seven Devils Lake and the U.S. Forest Service **Seven Devils Campground** (7 sites, free). A notice posted here warns visitors not to get too close to the mountain goats that occasionally wander into camp.

A number of trails open to hikers and horse-packers start from the Windy Saddle trailhead, between the lookout and the campground. The most popular, the Seven Devils Loop Trail, encircles the range's highest peaks while leading past sapphire-blue lakes and verdant wildflower-painted meadows.

Unlike the low country of Riggins or Hells Canyon, up here it's relatively cool and comfortable even in the scorching days of August. Snowfields linger right through summer in places.

Sawpit Saddle

Another off-pavement route leads to two canyon viewpoints but does not descend to the river. The three-hour loop follows **Bean Creek Road** (Forest Rd. 241) from its junction with U.S. 95, north of Riggins 0.25 mile, west to Iron Phone Junction. A loop farther west from Iron Phone Junction on rougher roads (Forest Rd. 2060 and Forest Rd. 1819) leads to views at Sawpit Saddle, Low Saddle, and Cold Springs. From Sawpit Saddle you can glimpse the Snake River, glimmering in the sun far below. The route returns to Iron Phone Junction, and then back the way you came.

Boating

In 1865 a Portland riverboat company tried to run the first steamboat up through Hells Canyon as a route to the south Idaho goldfields. After 4.5 days of slowly chugging up the canyon, the vessel reached the mouth of Oregon's Imnaha River. There the captain discovered an eight-foot-long gash in the bow and decided to beat a hasty retreat. The swift current carried the boat back out of the canyon in less than four hours. Four years later, the steamboat *Shoshone* successfully ran the Snake River downstream through Hells Canyon. It was followed in 1891 by another steamboat, the *Norma*. It's unclear how much was left of those boats when they reached Lewiston. In 1925, Amos Burg became the first bold adventurer to canoe down the Snake River through Hells Canyon. He was accompanied by perhaps the first river guide, a man named John Mullins. Before the trip, Mullins told Burg "he knew every rock in the river." After the trip, Burg added, "he ought to, since he hit them all."

The Snake is a big river. Its dam-controlled flow rates range anywhere from 5,000 cubic feet per second in low water to an incredible 80,000 cubic feet per second or more during spring runoff. Both jetboats and rafts are allowed on the river, but certain nonmotorized periods have been reserved for rafters who want to paddle in peace and quiet.

The **Hells Canyon Creek Visitors Center,** on the Oregon side of the river just below Hells Canyon Dam, is the most common put-in point for commercial raft trips. Pushing off from here, you don't have much time to prepare yourself for **Wild Sheep Rapids,** just 5.8 miles downstream. Wild Sheep, the river's longest rapids, is Class IV most of the time, Class V at high flows. Once you make it through that one, you'll barely have time to catch your breath before **Granite Creek Rapids** comes into view. This one's another Class IV-V monster with huge waves and a raft-eating hole at river center. More Class II-IV rapids lie ahead,

but the trip gets gradually less terrifying as you continue downstream.

Besides rapids, you'll find a few sandy beaches, a few bits of shade, a slew of campsites, and a few historic sites. It's a 2-3-day trip from the put-in at Hells Canyon Creek to the takeout at Pittsburg Landing, a distance of 32 miles. Add another 2-3 days to continue down to the confluence with the Grand Ronde at Heller Bar, 79 miles from the put-in.

While some jetboat tours also leave from Hells Canyon Creek, more of them leave from Lewiston and head upriver.

Among the commercial guide services (south of Lewiston) offering guided raft and jetboat trips down the Snake are **Hells Canyon Adventures** (Oxbow, OR, 541/785-3352 or 800/422-3568, www.hellscanyonadventures.com) and **Exodus Wilderness Adventures** (Riggins, 800/992-3484).

For just rafting, contact **Mountain River Outfitters** (Riggins, 208/628-3733, www.mtnriveroutfitters.com); **Hughes River Expeditions** (Cambridge, 208/257-3477, www.hughesriver.com); and **Idaho Afloat** (Grangeville, 800/700-2414, www.idahoafloat.com).

Private parties planning a float or powerboat trip through Hells Canyon must obtain a **permit** from the U.S. Forest Service. For information, contact the **Hells Canyon NRA Riggins Office** (1339 U.S. 95, 208/628-3916), just south of town across the highway from the Little Salmon River.

For daily **river flow levels,** you must call **Idaho Power Company** (800/422-3143) to find out how much water they intend to let out of Hells Canyon Dam during your trip.

Hiking and Horse-Packing

The U.S. Forest Service maintains some 900 miles of hiking and equestrian trails in the NRA, most on the Oregon side of the river. Some of the lower-altitude trails remain open year-round; in winter, snow closes the mountain trails up on the rim. Water sources at lower elevations are few and far between, and it gets hot down there; carry plenty of water with you. Also be alert for three common pests in the area: rattlesnakes, ticks, and poison ivy.

The **Hells Canyon National Recreation Trail,** a 31-mile footpath along the banks of the river, leads from Pittsburg Landing south right into the river. Sheer walls of rock block the last two-mile stretch just above Hells Canyon Dam; as a consequence, hikers generally take this trail south to north, paying one of the jetboat operators at the Hells Canyon Creek boat launch to drop them at the beginning of the trail on their way downriver. Note that portions of this trail may be submerged when the river rises above 40,000 cubic feet per second.

Up in the high country, the **Seven Devils Loop Trail** forms a 27-mile circle around the range's highest peaks, passing by or near some 30 alpine lakes along the way. This popular multiday backpack trip offers spectacular vistas looking down into Hells Canyon and up to the summits of He Devil, She Devil, Devils Tooth, and the Tower of Babel, among others. Main access to the loop is at Windy Saddle, but you can also hike in on Trail 214 from Black Lake, to the south, accessed through the small town of Council. This nine-mile trail follows upper Granite Creek north for a time, eventually meeting the Seven Devils Loop at Horse Heaven Junction, the loop's southernmost point.

For those looking to hike from rim to river, four different trails follow the snowmelt down to the Snake. From south to north, trails descend from the Seven Devils along Devils Farm Creek-Granite Creek, Little Granite Creek, Bernard Creek, and Sheep Creek. You can get the appropriate maps at the NRA office in Riggins. Don't forget that down in the canyon it's usually 15-20 degrees warmer than up on the rim.

Access Points

In addition to the eastern access points (Pittsburg Landing, Seven Devils, and Sawpit Saddle), there are several southern access points listed below. Paved Highway 71 (to Hells Canyon Dam) and gravel Deer Creek Road (to Pittsburg Landing) are usually open year-round. The other routes are unpaved and generally open mid-July-October. For current conditions and more information about these access points, call the **Riggins NRA office** (208/628-3916). A summary of all access routes are covered in this guide:

- **Hells Canyon Dam:** The approach from the south is via Highway 71, off U.S. 95 at Cambridge. If your vehicle is too wimpy for one of the other routes, don't despair, because the views of the canyon from along the pavement here are outstanding.

- **Kleinschmidt Grade:** An alternative off-pavement route to Hells Canyon Dam from Council.

- **Black Lake:** An off-pavement route from Council to a southern Seven Devils trailhead, which leads over Purgatory Saddle to Emerald Lake.

- **Windy Saddle:** A road from Riggins leads to a viewpoint and trailhead high in the Seven Devils.

- **Bean Creek Road:** Rough off-pavement loop to good views of the canyon; begins 0.25 mile north of Riggins.

- **Kirkwood Ranch:** From Lucile, Cow Creek Road (Forest Rd. 242) climbs toward Kirkwood Bar, but it's a rough road and ends prematurely. You'll need an all-terrain vehicle, horse, or backpack and sturdy boots to make it down to the ranch. You can also hike in to the ranch from Pittsburg Landing.

- **Pittsburg Landing:** A road from just south of White Bird leads to the Snake River, where you'll find a boat ramp, a campground, a trailhead, and Native American rock art.

NEW MEADOWS

At New Meadows, U.S. 95 meets Highway 55. Go north on U.S. 95 for Riggins; head east on Highway 55 to reach McCall. The original town of Meadows was a thriving burg west of the present town, but when the Pacific & Idaho Northern Railroad arrived from Weiser in 1911, the company pulled a typical railroad shenanigan. Rather than bring the tracks into town, they brought the town to the tracks. The company bought a large tract of land outside town, built a lavish $30,000 depot, and then sold lots around it. The population made the shift. New Meadows grew, very profitably for the railroad, and old Meadows faded away. The railroad hauled Meadows Valley cattle and lumber to market until 1979.

Today, the railroad grade has been turned into the Weiser River Trail (www.weiser-rivertrail.org), a meandering 85-mile recreational path that runs south of town along the Weiser River and U.S. 95. Mountain bikers, hikers, and horseback riders will enjoy this newly developed trail, which goes from pine tree-studded mountains to wide-open canyon lands at its starting point in Weiser. Along the way, you'll pass through the small burgs of Council, Cambridge, and Midvale. You can download a map of the trail at the website.

Zim's Hot Springs

The biggest attraction in the New Meadows area is **Zim's Hot Springs** (2995 Zims Rd., New Meadows, 208/347-2686, 9am-11pm daily Memorial Day-Labor Day, 10am-10pm Tues.-Sun. Labor Day-Memorial Day, $7 adults, $6 seniors and ages 3-17), which draws a sizable crowd of regulars up from McCall for nighttime après-ski soaks. The developed hot springs resort lies west of U.S. 95 in Meadows Valley, four miles north of town; watch for signs along the highway. An artesian well pumps sulfur-free hot water continuously through the 90-96°F swimming pool and 105°F soaking pool. You can also camp at Zim's, which has RV sites ($25) with water and electricity hookups as well as basic tent sites ($10).

Accommodations

The ★ **Hartland Inn and Motel** (U.S. 95 and Hwy. 55, New Meadows, 208/347-2114, www.thehartlandinn.com, $59-115) offers 11 motel units and five B&B guest rooms in a beautiful 1911 mansion. The inn also has a small wine and beer bar, **Stein & Stirrup,** where you can grab a libation and a light snack before bedding down.

Camping and RVing

Meadows RV Park (3278 Hwy. 55, New Meadows, 208/347-2325, spring-fall), 2.5 miles east of town on Highway 55, features 37 RV sites ($24) with full hookups as well as tent sites ($12). The quiet, tidy park includes showers and a laundry.

Information

For information about the area, check in at the Payette National Forest's **New Meadows Ranger District** (3674 U.S. 95, New Meadows, 208/347-0300) just west of downtown.

RIGGINS

While Salmon and even Banks also compete for the title of "Idaho's white-water capital," Riggins takes the prize. The Salmon River flows right through town on the last legs of its run down from Redfish Lake. The Little Salmon River joins it here, and the Salmon flows another 60 miles through Lower Salmon Gorge to the Snake River. The Snake River's Hells Canyon stretch lies just over the Seven Devils to the west. In short, Riggins is surrounded by a lot of big water. You can feel a buzz of excitement as soon as you enter town. Guide shops and outfitters line both sides of the highway, and packs of river rats linger outside local pubs and coffeehouses, planning the next trip.

Get out on the water as soon as the area's short spring begins to wilt away. Riggins sits at the narrow bottom of Salmon River Gorge, whose walls trap the heat like an oven. It bakes in summer; shade is at a premium, and local ice-cream vendors dish out the sundaes nonstop.

Entertainment and Events

The best entertainment in town can be found

at the **Seven Devils Steakhouse and Saloon** (312 N. Main St., Riggins, 208/628-3558), which hosts live music on weekends. Like the nearby river, the dance floor gets pretty wild at times.

On the Riggins events calendar, the town's annual **Salmon River Jet Boat Races** are held in mid-April; the boats roar up the main Salmon River between White Bird and Riggins in an international competition, the first leg of the U.S. Championships. The first weekend in May, the venerable **Riggins Rodeo** kicks up its heels, bringing Western fun and the obligatory parade. For more information on these and other events, call the Salmon River Chamber of Commerce (208/628-3778, www.rigginsidaho.com).

★ River Trips

Riggins is considered by many to be the best place for white water in Idaho; it's home to several guide services offering float trips on either or both the main Salmon run above town and the Salmon River Gorge stretch downstream from Riggins. Among the many are **Epley's Whitewater Adventures** (Riggins, 208/628-3586, www.epleys.com); **Exodus Wilderness Adventures** (Riggins, 800/992-3484, www.riverescape.

com); **Brundage Whitewater Adventures** (Riggins, 208/628-4212, www.brundage.com); and **Wapiti River Guides** (Riggins, 208/628-3523, www.doryfun.com), which uses wooden dories on its trips.

Rates for float trips generally range around $75 for a half-day trip, $100 for a full day, and $325-375 for two-day trips.

Fishing

If you'd rather float and fish than paddle white water, call **Mountain River Outfitters** (Riggins, 208/628-3733, www.mtnriver-outfitters.com), which leads fishing trips on the Salmon River near Riggins. **Exodus Wilderness Adventures** and **Wapiti River Guides** also offer guided fishing.

If you want to go fishing on your own, remember that steelhead season is in the spring and fall, and you'll need a special permit in addition to a fishing license. Stop by **Hook, Line, & Sinker** (112 N. Main St., Riggins, 208/628-3578) to pick up a steelhead fishing permit ($12.75 residents, $25.75 nonresidents) and a little advice, to which you'll reply, "A cork, some yarn, and a what?" For more information about steelhead fishing, contact the Idaho Department of Fish and Game (208/334-3700).

a bridge leading into Riggins

Hiking

Riggins is surrounded by great backcountry full of hiking trails. To the west lies Hells Canyon National Recreation Area. About 20 miles east is the Gospel-Hump Wilderness. Access the Gospel-Hump at the Wind River Pack Bridge trailhead, on Salmon River Road (Forest Rd. 1614) east of town.

Accommodations

Around half a dozen mom-and-pop places line either side of the highway through town, most with rates near the middle of the $50-100 category. The friendly ★ **Riggins Motel** (615 S. Main St., Riggins, 208/628-3001 or 800/669-6739, from $69 d) has good shade along with a hot tub, cable TV, a barbecue, and picnic tables. The motel is in the middle of town on the west side of the highway. On the south side of Riggins is **Salmon River Motel** (1203 S. Main St., Riggins, 208/628-3231, $39-91), a clean little motor inn with cable TV and coin laundry; pets are allowed.

Salmon Rapids Lodge (1010 S. Main St., Riggins, 208/628-2743, from $90 d) enjoys prime real estate at the confluence of the Salmon and Little Salmon Rivers. All 55 rooms have refrigerators, cable TV, and high-speed Internet. Amenities include an indoor pool and a fitness room, an outdoor patio and a hot tub, and complimentary breakfast.

Camping

River Village RV Park (1434 N. Main St., Riggins, 208/628-3443, year-round) has 20 RV sites ($20) with full hookups and a few tent sites ($15). It has cable TV and laundry facilities.

Salmon River Road (Forest Rd. 1614) follows the river 28 miles east from town to Vinegar Creek, a popular boat-launch site. Along the way, you'll pass Ruby Rapids, a good place to look for garnets along the shore, as well as **Allison Creek Picnic Area,** the U.S. Forest Service **Spring Bar Campground** (14 sites, $12), and the **Van Creek Picnic Area and Campground** (2 sites, free).

Backcountry Guest Ranch

Shepp Ranch (208/866-4268, www.sheppranch.com, $300 pp per day) is 45 miles east of Riggins on the north bank of the Salmon River at the mouth of Crooked Creek. The ranch's backyard is the 206,000-acre Gospel-Hump Wilderness, and outdoor recreation in the midst of this wild solitude is the main attraction. Available activities include jetboating, rafting, trail riding, fishing, hiking, and

white-water fun in Riggins

and saucy ribs at night. The restaurant also sells boxed lunches to go (around $10).

Information
For recreation information, contact the **Hells Canyon NRA Riggins Office** (1339 U.S. 95, 208/628-3916) just south of town.

NORTH OF RIGGINS
Slate Creek
Ten miles south of White Bird on the highway is the U.S. Forest Service's Slate Creek Ranger Station, home of the Nez Perce National Forest's **Salmon River Ranger District** (304 Slate Creek Rd., White Bird, 208/839-2211). Out front, a small 1909 log cabin that once housed the head ranger now serves as a Forest Service museum.

Slate Creek, now a ghost town, formerly supplied the booming mining camp of Florence. Heading east, Slate Creek Road (Forest Rd. 354) runs up past the Bureau of Land Management (BLM) **North Fork Campground** (5 sites, free) and up to the boundary of the Gospel-Hump Wilderness, where you'll find the Forest Service **Rocky Bluff Campground** (4 sites, free). Just south of Slate Creek Road on the river is the BLM's **Slate Creek Campground** (6 sites, $10), which has good wheelchair accessibility.

Hammer Creek
The BLM's **Hammer Creek Recreation Area** is a popular put-in point for rafters heading down the Lower Salmon Gorge. Here you'll also find a campground (8 sites, $10) with good wheelchair accessibility. To get to the area, turn off U.S. 95 at a well-marked turnoff just before the White Bird exit. The sign is marked Hammer Creek-Pittsburg Landing. Cross the Salmon River, turn right, and follow the road to the campground. For more information, contact the BLM's **Cottonwood Field Office** (1 Butte Dr., Cottonwood, 208/962-3245).

White Bird
Just past the turnoff to the little town of

historic White Bird Grade

soaking your cares away in the hot tub. The family-style meals are made with fresh garden vegetables, local berries, and trout from the river. No roads lead into the ranch, so you have to come by trail, boat, or plane.

Food
Back Eddy Grill & Alehouse (533 N. Main St., Riggins, 208/628-9233, 11am-10pm Sun.-Thurs., 11am-11pm Fri.-Sat., $8-10) is on the north end of town, and it has about a dozen microbrews on tap. Need I say more? The back patio is a good spot to hang out at night and quaff ale as the wild river stories become more and more epic with each downed pint. The pub grub menu features burgers (beef, elk, bison), nachos, panini sandwiches, pizza, and fried ravioli.

The menu at **River Rock Cafe** (1149 S. Main St., Riggins, 208/628-3434, breakfast, lunch, and dinner daily, dinner entrées $12-24) literally has something for everyone, with delish omelets in the morning, focaccia sandwiches and calzones for lunch, and big steaks

White Bird, U.S. 95 climbs White Bird Grade. This hill was long a major stumbling block in the effort to link the north and south halves of the state. Road construction began here in 1915 using convict labor and wasn't completed for regular traffic until 1921. That old road is east of today's U.S. 95, the White Bird Grade portion of which wasn't completed until 1975.

As you drive up the highway today from White Bird onto the Camas Prairie, you'll pass one of the most important battlefields in the history of the West, **White Bird Battlefield,** on the expansive hillside to the right, where the opening battle of the Nez Perce War took place in 1877. A turnout along the highway toward the top of the hill describes the battle in detail, but to get the best feel for the history of the event, continue to the top of the hill and take the drive down the old road, where there are several trailheads leading into the battlefield area. An excellent National Park Service pamphlet, *White Bird Battlefield Walking Tour,* brings the battle to life, moment by moment, as you hike through the canyon. For a copy of the pamphlet or more information about the site, contact **Nez Perce National Historic Park** (208/843-7001).

Grangeville and Vicinity

After climbing out of White Bird Canyon, you'll top out onto the Camas Prairie, where Native Americans once harvested the roots of the camas plant that grew profusely here. There's another Camas Prairie in the southern part of the state near Fairfield, but that's a rather contentious issue with folks around here. Anyway, Grangeville began in the mid-1800s as the site of a grange hall and gristmill built by local farmers and ranchers. Later it became a major supply center for miners working in the nearby mines. Today, the town of about 3,100 is the seat of enormous Idaho County, an area bigger than New Jersey. The county spans the width of Idaho from Oregon to Montana.

Grangeville is still a hub for Camas Prairie agriculture; the prairie's fertile volcanic soil produces bumper crops of wheat, barley, canola, peas, clover, and hay. The town also serves as a base camp for recreation trips to Hells Canyon National Recreation Area; the Frank Church-River of No Return and Gospel-Hump Wilderness Areas; and the Clearwater, Lochsa, Salmon, Selway, and Snake Rivers.

SIGHTS
Tolo Lake Mammoth Replica

In 1994 an excavating crew working on an Idaho Department of Fish and Game project at nearby Tolo Lake unearthed a large fossil bone and tusk. The subsequent archaeological dig, conducted by Idaho State University, yielded more than 400 specimens, many of which were complete mammoth skeletons from the Pleistocene era. To commemorate this massive find, a group of citizens in Grangeville purchased a life-sized, plastic **Tolo Lake Mammoth Replica** and had it housed in a glass-walled structure for all to see. The free exhibit is especially impressive at night when it's all lit up. The replica is in **Eimers Park** (U.S. 95 and Pine St., Grangeville), just north of town next to the chamber of commerce visitors center (208/983-0460).

Bicentennial Historical Museum

Catch a glimpse of local history at the small **Bicentennial Historical Museum** (305 N. College St., Grangeville, 208/983-2573, 1pm-5pm Wed.-Fri. June-Sept., donations appreciated) near downtown, which has old toys, flapper dresses, early mining exhibits, and Nez Perce artifacts. Most impressive is the displayed mammoth tusk from Tolo Lake.

RECREATION
Alpine Skiing

Snowhaven Ski & Tubing Area (208/983-3866, 10am-4pm Sat.-Sun. and holidays mid-Dec.-mid-Mar., full-day $17 over age 6, $15 seniors, free under age 7) is seven miles south of Grangeville on the Grangeville-Salmon Road (Forest Rd. 221). The road starts on the east end of town opposite the national forest headquarters; follow it straight up the hill and don't turn left at a junction just outside town. Snowhaven is a small area with one T-bar and one rope tow serving a 40-acre hill with a 400-foot vertical drop. Half-day passes are available, and lessons are offered for all levels as well as for telemarkers, snowboarders, and cross-country skiers. There's also a lift-serviced tubing hill (one hour $8, two hours $12, full-day $20) that blasts riders down an 850-foot-long stretch of the mountain. Ski and tubing combination passes cost $25.

The small day lodge has a grill that serves burgers, nachos, and the likes, but no booze. The south-facing deck, complete with picnic tables, is a sunny and pleasant spot to chillax after hitting the slopes. Snowhaven's peak elevation of just 5,600 feet means the season here is short.

Cross-Country Skiing

Two miles farther up the road is the **Fish Creek Meadows Park N' Ski Area.** The 10 miles of cross-country trails are groomed only once a week, and be prepared to share them with snowmobilers. The area offers a small ski-in cabin with a woodstove, picture windows, and views toward the Gospel-Hump Wilderness. If you've had enough of Fish Creek and want to practice your tele-turns, you can take an ungroomed but marked seven-mile ski trail over to Snowhaven.

ACCOMMODATIONS AND FOOD

Gateway Inn (700 W. Main St., Grangeville, 208/983-2500, $49-70) is a locally owned hotel with 26 recently remodeled guest rooms. Amenities include an outdoor pool, cable TV, and a free breakfast spread. For no-frills lodging, head to the **Downtowner Inn** (113 E. North St., Grangeville, 208/983-1110, from $49 d), a small motel with 16 relatively clean rooms.

★ **Whitebird Summit Lodge** (2141 Old White Bird Hill Rd., Grangeville, 208/983-1802, www.whitebirdsummitlodge.com, from $120 d) is a comfy guest ranch at the top of the White Bird Grade. Room rates include a great view, a big breakfast, and easy access to the area's recreational activities. The lodge, owned by Frank and Terri Schmitz, doubles as an outfitter, offering package deals on rafting and fishing trips.

Get a little history with your meal at **Oscar's** (101 E. Main St., Grangeville, 208/983-2106, breakfast, lunch, and dinner daily, dinner entrées $12-26), a venerable downtown eatery on the property of the city's first grange hall, thus the name "Grangeville." The restaurant dishes up standard breakfast and lunch fare during the day, and expect to see lots of hand-cut steaks and seafood at night. The recently remodeled bar is a great spot for a cocktail after dinner.

ACROSS THE CAMAS PRAIRIE
Cottonwood

Cottonwood began in 1862 when a Mr. Allen, first name unknown, lopped down a couple of cottonwood trees and used them to build a way station. The outpost eventually included a hotel and saloon, a store, and a stage stop. Today, Cottonwood still offers services to travelers, especially along the attractive main drag.

North of town, **Dog Bark Park Inn** (2421 U.S. 95, Cottonwood, 208/962-3647, www.

dogbarkparkinn.com, $92 d) is one of the strangest places to call it a night in Idaho. "Sweet Willy," a 30-foot-high beagle, disguises a studio apartment that can sleep up to four (two in the main room in the beagle's belly and two in a loft in the mutt's muzzle). Rates include a refrigerator and pantry stocked with all the makings for a hearty continental breakfast.

For recreation information about the area, contact the Bureau of Land Management's **Cottonwood Field Office** (1 Butte Dr., Cottonwood, 208/962-3245). If you want to pass some time when you're driving, tune into **National Public Radio** in the area at station KNWO (90.1 FM).

Keuterville

The "big" towns of the Camas Prairie (Grangeville and Cottonwood) aren't big by anything other than rural Idaho standards, but a highway runs through them and you'll find them on the map. Keuterville Road, on the other hand, doesn't go anywhere you need to be. It makes a long lazy loop out around the back of Cottonwood Butte, connecting farms and wooded ranches and eventually entering a maze of lonely gravel roads between the butte and Winchester. Out here, road signs are minimal, road forks are frequent, and many of the forks dead-end. You may get lost, which is exactly why you drive out Keuterville Road in the first place.

Near the turnoff from U.S. 95 and visible from the highway, **St. Gertrude's Monastery** is impressive enough to pull even pagans in for a gander. The twin-towered Romanesque priory was built of locally quarried stone and has been home to the Benedictine Sisters since 1920. It's now on the National Register of Historic Places. Adjacent to the monastery, the **Historical Museum at St. Gertrude** (465 Keuterville Rd., Keuterville, 208/962-2050, 9:30am-4:30pm Tues.-Sat., $6 adults, $3 ages 7-17) has a potpourri of historical artifacts, including pioneer and mining gear, a mineral collection,

and utensils handcrafted by legendary Salmon River mountain man Sylvan Hart.

Continuing down the road, you'll enjoy distant views of the Seven Devils Range, a roadside collection of antique tractors, and finally Keuterville itself. The town, such as it is, was founded around a sawmill in 1883 and named after settler Henry Kuther. Unfortunately for Henry, the Post Office Department needed glasses back then, and what should have been "Kutherville" came out Keuterville instead. Rafters have been known to float Grave Creek, a tributary of a tributary of the Salmon River, which starts just south of town.

Winchester

Winchester Lake State Park (1786 Forest Rd., Winchester, 208/924-7563, day-use $5) occupies a woodsy area at the foot of the Craig Mountains. Its centerpiece is 103-acre Winchester Lake, a **fishing** hole popular with warm-weather anglers in summer and ice-fishers in winter. The lake is stocked with rainbow trout and also has largemouth bass and bullhead catfish. A boat ramp is available, and there are some canoes and kayaks available for rent. When enough snow falls, a small **cross-country skiing** trail system is set up. Two beginner-intermediate groomed trails skirt the lake and loop around Craig Mountain. Another 0.75-mile, ungroomed trail is more difficult. The elevation is only about 4,000 feet, so the snowpack is vulnerable to rain and warm spells. Call for conditions before coming to ski. The park's campground offers the usual state-park amenities: clean restrooms and showers, campsites ($12-21), and picnic tables and grills. There are also three yurts ($50-70) available year-round, each heated and able to sleep up to six.

Winchester Lake is named for the adjacent small town of Winchester, which in turn is named for the rifle that won the West.

About a mile past the park (follow signs) is the **Wolf Education & Research Center** (1721 Forest Rd., Winchester, 888/422-1110, www.wolfcenter.org, 9am-5pm daily summer, donations suggested), a joint project with the Nez Perce tribe. Inside the visitors center you'll find exhibits on wolves and their place in the ecosystem as well as information on Nez Perce culture. Interpretive trails and an observation platform surround the facility. The center is open for self-guided tours, and guided tours are available as well.

Lewiston and Vicinity

Lewiston (population 32,000) lies at the confluence of the Snake and Clearwater Rivers, in the traditional homeland of the Nez Perce and a pivotal point for Lewis and Clark on their journey west in 1805. At an elevation of just 738 feet above sea level, it's also Idaho's lowest city. The resulting mild winters allow golfers to enjoy the sport year-round and make for a lovely spring season that turns the city into a riot of blooming trees.

Amazing as it may seem, considering it is 470 miles from the Pacific Ocean, Lewiston is a seaport, Idaho's only seaport. Barge traffic comes up the Columbia and Snake Rivers to serve the Port of Lewiston, which is an important rail-and-road connection for shipped goods. The city's largest employer is the big Potlatch mill perched on the south bank of the Clearwater River. The town also likes its jetboats, those nimble aluminum speedsters that hammer up through the rapids on the Snake and Salmon Rivers. Several manufacturers in town make Lewiston the jetboat capital of the West.

Like Pocatello in southeast Idaho, Lewiston feels blue-collar to the core, which isn't to say it lacks in culture. Lewis-Clark State College regularly brings the arts to town; a venerable community-theater troupe draws audiences for live drama; and the historic downtown has made some modest attempts at a facelift. But Lewiston, at the end of the day, is a sleepy town for the most part.

Early History

When gold was discovered up the Clearwater River in 1860, the site of today's Lewiston was transformed from a Nez Perce horse pasture into a port and mining supply camp. Steamboats cruised up the Columbia and Snake Rivers, dropping off thousands of hopeful prospectors. The community that soon sprouted around the steamboat docks was squatting illegally on the Nez Perce Reservation, but the cooperative Nez Perce agreed to give nonnative merchants one square mile where they could sell their goods to the miners. The earliest buildings were simple wood frames covered with canvas, which gave the settlement its early nickname, "Ragtown." Lewiston was formally founded on the site in May 1861.

The miners were just passing through, not looking to acquire land and settle down, but soon farmers showed up to grow crops to supply the mines. The farmers did need land, and lots of it. As the early mining strikes up the Clearwater River turned into a full-fledged boom, Lewiston grew exponentially. When Congress created Idaho Territory in 1863, Lewiston was named territorial capital, but the city was still trespassing on the Nez Perce Reservation. In typical fashion, the U.S. government "renegotiated" the original treaty, vastly reducing the reservation's size and moving its boundaries well outside of Lewiston.

The city's capital status lasted just a year and a half. By the end of 1864 the Clearwater mines were in decline. Down south, however, the Boise Basin mines were booming, and Boise sought the coveted capital crown. In April 1865, territorial secretary and Boise supporter C. DeWitt Smith rode into Lewiston with a contingent of federal troops from Fort Lapwai, stealing away the territorial seal and

Lewiston and Vicinity

archives under threat of force. Smith delivered the purloined goods to Boise, and Lewiston's governmental glory days came to an end.

SIGHTS
Lewis-Clark State College

Founded in 1893, **Lewis-Clark State College** (500 8th Ave., Lewiston, 208/792-5272 or 800/933-5272, www.lcsc.edu), a four-year state college, offers undergraduate degrees in about 20 fields as well as two-year associate degrees in a variety of vocational programs. The school's Warriors men's baseball team is legendary, having won the National Association of Intercollegiate Athletics (NAIA) World Series numerous times. As a matter of fact, the NAIA World Series is held in late May at Harris Field on campus. Home field advantage, perhaps? The

school's 4,500 students attend classes in one of the most beautiful parts of Lewiston. This hilltop neighborhood is full of stately homes and towering trees overlooking the city and rivers below. Even if you're not a student, the small campus (covered with green lawns and tidy brick buildings) makes a nice place for a picnic or an impromptu round of disc golf.

Lewis-Clark Center for Arts and History

Affiliated with Lewis-Clark State College, **Lewis-Clark Center for Arts and History** (415 Main St., Lewiston, 208/792-2243, 11am-4pm Tues.-Sat., free) presents rotating shows of local and regional artists as well as other exhibits of artistic or historical interest. A permanent historical display at this downtown museum and gallery remembers Lewiston's early Chinese community. The gift shop sells jewelry, crafts, books, and assorted CDs by past performers in the center's concert series.

Nez Perce County Historical Museum

The little **Nez Perce County Historical Museum** (0306 3rd St., at C St., Lewiston, 208/743-2535, 10am-4pm Tues.-Sat. Mar.-mid-Dec., donation) covers all aspects of the area's history, both its Nez Perce and Euro-American heritage. Among the highlights are a fantastic collection of old photographs and a huge, stunning triptych of Chief Joseph in three stages of his life, painted by Dan Piel, a former art professor at Washington State University.

Spiral Highway

The **Spiral Highway** is an "old road" to Moscow that snakes back and forth up some 64 switchbacks to the top of Lewiston Hill, nearly 3,000 feet above the city, thus earning its name. Up on the canyon rim you'll get impressive views of Lewiston, Clarkston, and the two rivers. The old road joins the new U.S. 95 at the top. From town, turn left at the second exit north of Clearwater Memorial Bridge, and then soon make a right onto the old road, following the signs.

RECREATION
Hells Gate State Park

Tenters and RVers passing through town will surely like **Hells Gate State Park** (5100 Hells Gate Rd., Lewiston, 208/799-5015, $5 per vehicle). The 200-acre park, just four miles south of downtown, is right on the river; swimming, boating, and fishing are steps from your campsite. It offers interpretive programs, lots of green grass and trees, picnic tables and barbecue grills, and clean restrooms with showers. Here you'll also find boat-launch ramps and trails for hiking, biking, or horseback riding. Thanks to Lewiston's mild, low-elevation winters, the park and marina are both open year-round.

The park's **Lewis and Clark Discovery**

Center contains a wealth of information on Lewiston's natural history and the exploration and settlement of Hells Canyon, including a 32-minute film about the Lewis and Clark expedition.

Of the park's 93 campsites ($12-31), 64 have water and power hookups. Eight camping cabins ($50-60) can each sleep up to five.

Clearwater and Snake River National Recreation Trail

Urban hikers and bicyclists will appreciate this 25-mile-long trail system, which runs along both the Idaho and Washington riverbanks. On the Idaho side, the trail begins at Lewiston's Clearwater Park. It crosses Memorial Bridge, turns west past Locomotive Park, Clearwater Landing, West Pond, and the Lewis and Clark Discovery Center, then continues south down the popular **Lewiston Levee Parkway** to Hells Gate State Park. On the Washington side of the Snake, the trail connects Looking Glass Park on the south with Swallows Park and the Clarkston Greenbelt on the north. Southway Bridge provides the connection for the two halves of the trail system. The trail is wheelchair accessible.

Hells Canyon Jetboat Tours

Several companies run jetboat tours up the Snake River through Hells Canyon. Unlike propeller-driven craft, jetboats move forward by shooting a jet of water out the back. Their inboard automobile engines turn powerful turbine pumps. The advantage of this design is its shallow draft; jetboats can navigate shallow rocky rapids that would destroy a standard inboard or outboard motor.

Unlike rafts, jetboats can go both up and down the river. Also unlike rafts, they pound through the rapids with a deafening roar, to the dismay of some folks.

The marina at Hells Gate State Park serves as the departure point for two commercial jetboat operators: **Snake River Adventures** (800/262-8874, www.snakeriveradventures.com) and **Riverquest Excursions**

(800/589-1129, www.riverquestexcursions.com). Half-day trips typically cost around $110 adults, $55 children.

Steelhead Fishing

In fall, the Clearwater River comes alive when the steelhead season opens. The river draws anglers from all over the country for a chance to hook one of these brawny fighters. Many angling guides lead trips on the Clearwater during fly-fishing season (late Aug.-Nov.) and drift-tackle season (Nov.-Apr.). Plan on spending about $550 per day for two people. Contact **FishHawk Guides** (888/548-8896, www.fishhawkguides.com) to arrange a trip.

Golf

Bryden Canyon Golf Course (445 O'Connor Rd., Lewiston, 208/746-0863, www.brydencanyongolf.com, greens fees $17-26), south of the airport, offers a public 18-hole course, a driving range, a pro shop, lessons, a putting green, and a restaurant serving breakfast and lunch as well as beer and wine.

ENTERTAINMENT

Lewiston Civic Theatre (805 6th Ave., Lewiston, 208/746-3401, www.lctheatre.org, Sept.-June) has presented community-based productions in Lewiston since 1961. Productions take place at the company's Anne Bollinger Performing Arts Center, and the performance season runs concurrently with the academic year. The **Lewis-Clark State College Artist Series** regularly brings touring opera, ballet, concert music, and drama productions to the city. For more information, call the **Lewis-Clark Center for Arts and History** (415 Main St., Lewiston, 208/792-2243).

ACCOMMODATIONS
$50-100

The ★ **Cedars Inn** (1716 Main St., Lewiston, 208/743-9526, www.cedarsinnlewiston.com, from $69 d) is a friendly, clean, and affordable hotel on the east side of town. Plus there's an outdoor pool, a laundry facility, and free continental breakfast. It's a good place for those traveling with children.

For about the same price, you can check into the **GuestHouse Inn** (1325 Main St., Lewiston, 208/746-3311, from $69 d). Here you will find 75 guest rooms, some with balconies and views of the river. Amenities include an outdoor pool and hot tub, a fitness room, high-speed Internet, and an on-site restaurant and lounge.

For a little more money, **Comfort Inn** (2128 8th Ave., Lewiston, 208/798-8090 or 800/228-5150, www.comfortinn.com, from $79 d) can put you up in one of its 52 guest rooms, all of which have cable TV, refrigerators, and microwaves. Other amenities include an indoor pool, a business center, a free morning newspaper, and breakfast. Pets are allowed.

$100-150

The nicest place in town, with guest rooms often available in a lower price range, is the **Red Lion Hotel** (621 21st St., Lewiston, 208/799-1000 or 800/232-6730, www.redlion-lewiston.com, from $99 d). The bright and modern inn offers 130 guest rooms, including 43 suites. Expect amenities like two heated pools (one indoor, one outdoor), a jetted tub, a full-size health club, and a few restaurants.

FOOD
Casual Dining

★ **Seasons Bistro** (301 Main. St., Lewiston, 208/798-4994, www.seasonsbistroandcatering.com, lunch and dinner Tues.-Sat., dinner entrées $17-34), downtown in Morgan's Alley, is the hottest new place to wine and dine in Lewiston. Start things off with some grilled oysters with chipotle remoulade and a flaky smoked gouda-portabello tart, washed down with a glass of local wine. Larger plates include pan-roasted duck breast with balsamic-blackberry reduction, hearty cioppino, and various seasonal pasta and risotto dishes.

Main St. Grill (625 Main St., Lewiston, 208/746-2440, 10:30am-9pm Mon.-Fri., 8am-9pm Sat.-Sun., sandwiches around $9, dinner

Wine in the Lewis Clark Valley

It wouldn't be entirely accurate to call the grape-growing scene in the Clearwater Valley a new one, considering the first vineyards in Idaho were planted here in 1872 (many years before it even became a state). The south-facing steps, profusion of water, and temperate climate make for excellent conditions to grow vinifera grapes, and a few early French and German settlers figured this out quickly. Unfortunately these vineyards didn't stand the test of time, mostly because they weren't maintained over the years.

In recent times, a handful of wineries in the Lewiston and Clarkston area have helped to define this burgeoning wine region. As a matter of fact, there's an effort underway to turn it into a government-approved American Viticultural Area (AVA). This would make the Lewis Clark Valley the second AVA in Idaho. (A petition was submitted in 2011 and it's expected to be approved any day now.) Wines sales and growth have soared in the Snake River Valley since it became an official AVA in 2007, and experts are predicting the same for the Lewis Clark Valley. Expect lots of wineries to pop up here in the coming years.

Head to these wineries for a taste of what this up-and-coming wine region has to offer. A small tasting fee may apply.

Clearwater Canyon Cellars (1708 6th Ave. N., Lewiston, 208/816-4679, www.clearwatercanyoncellars.com, 1pm-5pm Sat.) is Lewiston's first commercial winery since Prohibition days. The winery mostly grows red varietals. Stop by the tasting room and try some velvety syrah, cabernet sauvignon, and merlot.

In nearby Juliaetta, **Colter's Creek Winery** (308 Main St., Juliaetta, 208/276-3342, www.colterscreek.com, 2pm-5pm Fri., noon-5pm Sat.-Sun.) turns out several remarkable wines, including merlot, syrah, off-dry riesling, and oak barrel-aged chardonnay, to name a few. The tasting room also offers small plates of wine-friendly food, making it a great spot for an al fresco lunch on the patio.

Across the Snake River, in Clarkston, Washington, **Basalt Cellars** (906 Port Dr., Clarkston, 509/758-6442, www.basaltcellars.com, noon-5:30pm Mon.-Sat.) is known for its big cabernet sauvignon, sangiovese, crisp sémillon, and fruity riesling. The winery often pairs up with **Beamers Hells Canyon Tours** (509/758-4800, www.hellscanyontours.com) for a wine-tasting jetboat cruise (around $100 pp) that features a five-course dinner at Heller Bar Lodge.

entrées $12-16) is a lively place downtown with a sidewalk patio and retro lunch counter. The walls in the dining room chronicle the successes of Lewis-Clark State College's baseball team with a profusion of newspaper articles and photos. The expansive menu has everything from burgers to wraps to big salads and hot sandwiches. Especially tasty are the Philly cheese steak and Reuben. At night, you can get grilled steaks, pork ribs, and pasta dishes, and breakfast is served on weekends.

Barbecue and Brew

Got a hankering for barbecue? If so, stop by ★ **Hells Canyon Smokehouse** (145 Thain Rd., Lewiston, 208/816-1709, lunch and dinner Tues.-Sat., $8-23) for some smoky goodness. This funky little barbecue joint dishes up slow-smoked brisket, pulled pork sandwiches, saucy baby back ribs, chicken, and sausages. Make sure to add on some sides of spud salad, slaw, and macaroni and cheese. They also sell tangy Kansas City-style barbecue sauce by the quart.

M. J. Barleyhoppers Sports Bar and Brew Pub (621 21st St., Lewiston, 208/799-1000, daily), at the Red Lion Hotel, brews up about a dozen flagship and seasonal microbrews right on the premises, and it also carries a multitude of other microbrews and imports on tap. The bar serves typical pub grub, like hot wings, nachos, and gut-busting burgers. It's an excellent place to watch a game, thanks to the profusion of televisions that adorn the walls.

International Cuisine

When you need your fix of pad Thai, garlic prawns, or eggplant tofu, head to **Thai Taste** (1410 21st St., Lewiston, 208/746-6192, lunch and dinner daily, entrées $9-14). Dishes can be prepared as spicy as you'd like, from "For Those Who Hesitate" to "Dragon Fire." Put out the fire in your belly with a cold Thai beer.

For Mexican eats, check out **El Sombrero** (629 Bryden Ave., Lewiston, 208/746-0658, lunch and dinner daily, entrées around $10), a popular chips-and-salsa place that serves fajitas, pozole (hominy soup), chiles rellenos, tamales, enchiladas, and tacos. The restaurant keeps a cooler full of Mexican beers and sodas.

Breakfast

Waffles N' More (1421 Main St., Lewiston, 208/743-5189, 6:30am-2:30pm daily, most dishes under $10) is the spot to go for, you guessed it, waffles and more. Besides waffles served in about every conceivable form, you also can get omelets, biscuits and gravy, and other traditional breakfast fare. The small restaurant can get extremely busy on weekends.

Groceries

The **Lewiston Farmers Market** (5pm-8pm Sat. June-Sept.) sets up in the D Street parking lot across from Brackenbury Square. Here you can score locally grown produce (some organic), meat products, eggs, honey, baked goods, and seasonal preserves. The market offers cooking demonstrations from local chefs as well.

INFORMATION AND SERVICES
Information

For more information about Lewiston, visit www.beautifuldowntownlewiston.org. The *Lewiston Morning Tribune* (505 Capital St., Lewiston, 208/743-9411, www.lmtribune.com) is one of the state's best daily newspapers.

Services

Emergency medical services are available at **St. Joseph Regional Medical Center** (415 6th St., Lewiston, 208/743-2511).

GETTING THERE

Lewiston-Nez Perce County Regional Airport (LWS, 406 Burrell Ave., Lewiston, 208/746-4471, www.golws.com) offers commercial air service. **Alaska Airlines/Horizon Air** (800/252-7522) offers several daily flights to Seattle and Boise, and **Delta Airlines** (800/221-1212) provides twice-daily nonstop flights to Salt Lake City. Car-rental companies at the airport include **Budget** (208/746-0488, www.budget.com) and **Hertz** (208/746-0411, www.hertz.com).

GETTING AROUND

The **Lewiston Transit System** (208/298-1340), part of the greater **Ride the Valley** (www.ridethevalley.org) bus system that also serves Clarkston, provides fixed-route bus service around town. It costs $1 to ride. Go to the website to see the routes and schedules.

Clearwater Country

As U.S. 12 heads east from Lewiston, it stays close to the banks of the Clearwater River on its way to Montana. Traditionally this has always been part of the homeland of the Nez Perce people, who fished for the Clearwater's then-abundant salmon; hunted deer, elk, and other wild game in the Clearwater Mountains; and regularly crossed Lolo Pass into Montana on buffalo-hunting trips. Native American history abounds in this scenic stretch of the state.

In September 1805 the Nez Perce encountered nonnatives for the first time when the ragtag Lewis and Clark expedition staggered into Nez Perce Chief Twisted Hair's camp on the Weippe Prairie. The Nez Perce nursed the explorers back to health, sent them off down-river, and tended their horses until the expedition's return trip the following spring.

The Nez Perce and the Lewis and Clark expedition form the historical foundation for the area. Interesting are the roadside markers along U.S. 12 (known as the Lewis and Clark Highway) that point out one historic site after another. A portion of the route from Lewiston to Kooskia has also been designated by the state as the **Clearwater Canyons Scenic Byway.** As it climbs slowly up the steep-walled gorge, the vegetation gradually changes from arid grass- and brush-covered hills near Lewiston to lush green pine forests around Kooskia and points east.

NEZ PERCE RESERVATION

Thirteen miles east of Lewiston you'll enter the Nez Perce Indian Reservation, home to many of the 3,300 or so enrolled Nez Perce tribe members. The Nez Perce homeland once spanned from eastern Oregon all the way across Idaho into Montana. In 1855, enough white settlers had moved into the area to cause Washington Territory's governor to clamor for a treaty. The "deal" he negotiated, to which the peaceable Nez Perce reluctantly agreed, established the Nez Perce Reservation across a 5,000-square-mile area. But just five years later, white prospectors discovered gold on the reservation, and the deal was off. In 1863 a new treaty reducing the size of the reservation to just 500 square miles was drawn up. Some bands of the Nez Perce signed the treaty, while others refused. The nontreaty Indians kept to their traditional lands, and the government looked the other way until 1867, when it demanded with threats of force that the nontreaty Nez Perce move onto the pocket-size reservation. Seeing no choice but to comply, most of the nontreaty Nez Perce agreed to live this restricted way of life. But on June 13, 1877, three disgruntled Nez Perce braves took revenge on nonnatives in the Salmon River Canyon. General Oliver O. Howard

was called on to put down the Nez Perce once and for all, and the Nez Perce War began.

After holding off the Army on a 1,500-mile, 3.5-month flight, the Nez Perce finally surrendered at Bear's Paw, Montana, just 42 miles from the Canadian border and freedom. After the war, the nontreaty Nez Perce were exiled first to Kansas, then to Oklahoma, and the remaining Nez Perce were subjected to the "allotment" of their lands. In the process, the size of the Nez Perce Reservation was further reduced. Today it encompasses 88,000 acres (137.5 square miles), less than 3 percent of its original size under the 1855 treaty and a microscopic fraction of the land the Nez Perce once roamed. Lapwai, just down U.S. 95 from the Nez Perce National Historic Park's visitors center, is the seat of the Nez Perce government.

★ Nez Perce National Historic Park

A brief detour from U.S. 12 onto U.S. 95 leads to the headquarters of **Nez Perce National Historic Park** (39063 U.S. 95, Lapwai, 208/843-7001, www.nps.gov/nepe, free). This "concept" park consists of 38 separate historic sites in Idaho, Washington, Oregon, and Montana. Taken together, the sites tell the story of 11,000 years of Nez Perce culture, from their pre-Lewis and Clark days to the present. To visit them all entails a 400-mile drive.

The park's **visitors center** (daily year-round, hours change with the season, free) is a large facility on the hill next to the site of Henry and Eliza Spalding's old Lapwai Mission. Inside you'll find an auditorium screening a film on Nez Perce history and a bookstore selling books about the Nez Perce and Northwest history. In the exhibit room you'll find a copy of the 1855 Nez Perce Treaty signed by President James Buchanan as well as the Spalding-Allen collection of Nez Perce artifacts, which includes gorgeous beaded hide clothing, ornate cradleboards, porcupine quillwork, elk-tooth accessories, and more.

The park headquarters is the nerve

Nez Perce Reservation

center for the other sites comprising Nez Perce National Historic Park. Of the 38 sites, 29 are in Idaho, some of which are described below.

SPALDING MISSION

The **Spalding Mission** is within walking distance of the visitors center, and it was originally called the Lapwai Mission. Established by Presbyterian missionaries Henry and Eliza Spalding in 1836 and originally located a bit farther south, it was moved to this site

at the mouth of Lapwai Creek in 1838. The Spaldings were the first nonnative family to reside in Idaho and produced a number of "firsts" during their tenure, including the first gristmill, first sawmill, first printed literature, and first nonnative child born in the state. A sense of history pervades this grassy, tree-shaded flat along the riverbank. You can easily imagine how wonderful it must have been for the Spaldings when they first arrived more than 160 years ago. The alluvial bar provided fertile ground for the mission gardens, and salmon filled the Clearwater River then.

The site is well aligned along the beaten path, but it's still an amazingly peaceful place with lots of grass, picnic tables, and big shade trees, making it an ideal spot for lunch.

SOUTH ON U.S. 95

Continuing south from the visitors center on U.S. 95, you'll see a marker pointing out the general vicinity where the Spaldings' first home once stood, built soon after their arrival in the area in November 1836. At today's town of Lapwai, you'll find the site of **Fort Lapwai,** the first military fort in Idaho, built in 1862 to keep the Indians from messing with the miners who were flooding into the area. Also here is the site of the **Northern Idaho Indian Agency,** created by the government to monitor compliance with the Indian treaties. Continuing south, you'll come to a sign marking the **Craig Donation Land Claim.** Mountain man William Craig was a friend of the Nez Perce; he served as an interpreter for them and married a Nez Perce woman. His 1846 claim was the first by a nonnative settler in what is now Idaho. A little farther on is the turnoff to **St. Joseph's Mission.** It was the first Roman Catholic mission among the Nez Perce, built by Father Joseph Cataldo of Old Mission fame and dedicated in 1874.

Much farther south, outside the reservation, U.S. 95 passes five more park sites. Just south of Cottonwood, a sign marks the site of the **Cottonwood Skirmishes,** a couple of early engagements in the Nez Perce War. Small parties of Chief Joseph's band attacked various Army detachments and volunteers in this area on July 3 and 5, 1877. The diversionary attacks allowed the main band of Nez Perce to cross the Camas Prairie unnoticed and link up with Chief Looking Glass's band on the Clearwater River. A turnoff here leads seven miles to **Weis Rock Shelter,** a habitation site used by indigenous people for more than 8,000 years. West of Grangeville is **Tolo Lake,** where the Nez Perce bands of Chiefs Joseph and White Bird were camped

when a few angry braves touched off the Nez Perce War.

EAST OF SPALDING ON U.S. 12

Just east of the U.S. 95 turnoff on U.S. 12 are **Ant and Yellowjacket.** According to Nez Perce legend, the two insects were fighting over the right to eat salmon. Coyote tried to settle the dispute, but they paid no attention to him. To make an example of them, Coyote turned Ant and Yellowjacket to stone. Look up on the hill and you'll see the two creatures, with their backs arched and jaws locked in combat, now frozen there for all eternity.

Farther east, at the **Lenore Archaeological Site,** evidence indicates that this good fishing hole along the Clearwater was used by the ancestors of the Nez Perce some 10,000 years ago. Continuing east, you'll come to **Canoe Camp** near Orofino. On their westward journey in 1805, the Lewis and Clark expedition stayed here for 10 days, recuperating from a harrowing crossing of the Bitterroots. Up until this point, they had traveled by horseback; here they left their horses with the Nez Perce and continued downriver by canoe. The dugout canoe you'll see is an example of the sort of vessels the expedition fashioned.

Several sites are found around Kamiah. At mile point 67.6, two signs mark the sites of Lewis and Clark's **Long Camp** and the **Asa Smith Mission.** On their return trip from Astoria to St. Louis in spring 1806, Lewis and Clark camped here for a month while waiting for the snow to melt in the Bitterroots. By all accounts it was an idyllic time, spent in the good company of the Nez Perce. In 1839, missionary Asa Smith tried to start a mission here among the Nez Perce, but the pioneer life proved too much for him, so in 1841 he moved to a mission in Hawaii. At mile point 75.9, a sign memorializes **Looking Glass's 1877 Campsite,** up near Clear Creek. The great Nez Perce war chief Looking Glass tried to remain neutral in the conflict between the U.S. Army and the nontreaty Nez Perce. He told the Army, "Leave us alone. We are living here peacefully and want no trouble," but the Army nevertheless destroyed his village and stole his horses. He then joined Chiefs Joseph and White Bird in the fight and flight for freedom.

According to their legend, the Nez Perce people originated at the **East Kamiah-Heart of the Monster** site. Once again Coyote plays the leading role in the story. Before human beings inhabited the earth, a monster went on a feeding frenzy here, devouring all the creatures in his path. Coyote saw this and came to the rescue. He tricked the monster into devouring him too, but the monster didn't know that Coyote had a stone knife with him. Once inside, Coyote slashed the monster open, cut it into little pieces, and flung the pieces far and wide. Each piece became a different Native American tribe. Coyote then wrung the blood from the monster's heart, and the Nez Perce people sprang from the drops. What was left of the monster's heart is still visible here today.

OTHER SITES

South of Kooskia on Highway 13 is the **Clearwater Battlefield,** scene of one of the hardest-fought battles of the Nez Perce War. On July 11, 1877, Army general Oliver O. Howard tried a surprise attack on the Nez Perce encampment, but his plan failed. Twenty-four Nez Perce warriors managed to hold off Howard's 600 troops until 100 more warriors could get into position to keep Howard pinned down. Behind the fighting, the rest of the Nez Perce withdrew northward toward Kamiah.

North of Kamiah, up on the **Weippe Prairie,** just west of Weippe on Highway 11, a marker commemorates the first meeting of the Nez Perce with Lewis and Clark. The explorers must have been a scraggly, scrawny bunch at that point. They were near starvation when they stumbled upon the Nez Perce encampment; the Native Americans revived them and sent them on their way. You'll also want to check out the historical marker at **Musselshell Meadow,** due east of Weippe

on the Lolo Trail, which marks the last active camas-gathering grounds of the Nez Perce.

East of Kamiah on U.S. 12, a **Lolo Trail** marker shows the spot where Lewis and Clark picked up their old trail on their return trip in 1806. The Nez Perce also came this way in 1877, with General Howard hot on their heels. The sign at **Lolo Pass** also commemorates the Nez Perce trail. It was here in 1805 that Lewis and Clark reentered Idaho after an aborted attempt to negotiate the Salmon River Canyon far to the south.

OROFINO AND VICINITY

The seat of Clearwater County, Orofino's name essentially means "pure gold" in Spanish, a tribute to the first gold strike in Idaho at nearby Pierce in 1860. The town straddles the banks of the Clearwater River, and logging is the linchpin of the economy in these parts.

Recreation also brings in the dollars. In summer, anglers fish the Clearwater, boaters and campers flock to Dworshak Reservoir, and backcountry explorers head up the North Fork of the Clearwater to the Mallard-Larkins Pioneer Area. In winter, snowmobiling and cross-country skiing dictates people's days around here. You'll find a few hotels, some eateries, and basic services in the downtown area.

Dworshak Dam and Reservoir

In 1971 the Army Corps of Engineers stopped the flow of the North Fork of the Clearwater River with the construction of **Dworshak Dam.** At 717 feet high, only two dams in the country are higher.

Before the dam was built, the North Fork was used for log drives out of the forests upriver. The dam put an end to the log drives but allowed water access for loggers into previously inaccessible areas. Logs are still towed across the river and hauled out at several locations. In summer, 90-minute tours of the dam are available at the visitors center on the dam's north end (208/476-1255).

Dworshak Reservoir is a favorite spot for boaters, anglers, and water-skiers. Anglers probe the lake in search of introduced ko-kanee salmon, stocked rainbow trout, and plump smallmouth bass.

The lake spreads its long, skinny tendrils 54 miles back upriver. Boat ramps are available at Bruce's Eddy on the dam's east side, at Big Eddy marina and day-use area on the west side, and at several other locations. Big Eddy marina offers the only fuel dock on the lake. Boaters can also take advantage of more than 120 "minicamps" scattered around the lake's 184 miles of shoreline. Each of these primitive campsites has a tent pad, an outhouse, a picnic table, and a grill. The sites are free, and most are accessible only by boat.

The Bureau of Reclamation operates **Dent Recreation Area** on the shore of the lake just over Dent Bridge off Elk River Road (Wells Bench Rd.). Here you'll find a boat-launch area, restrooms, and a fish-cleaning station as well as the large **Dent Acres Campground** (reservations 877/444-6777, all sites $18). The campground features 50 grassy sites on a slope overlooking the lake and offers picnic shelters with tables and grills and a playground. RV sites with full hookups are also available.

Dworshak State Park

Although the small **Dworshak State Park** (reservations 208/476-5994, $5 day-use fee) lies just four miles from Dworshak Dam as the osprey flies, humans have to make a 45-minute drive around the west of the lake to get here. The park is 26 miles northwest of Orofino; head downriver from downtown to Ahsahka and follow the signs up County Road P1 through Cavendish, then east on Freeman Creek Road to the park. You'll find 105 campsites ($12-29), some with hookups, surrounded by trees and open meadows. Amenities include a shower house and restrooms, a boat ramp, a fish-cleaning station, and a sandy beach. There also are four cabins ($50-55) available that can sleep up to five.

The Bridges of Clearwater County

Two spectacular bridges cross Dworshak Reservoir far out along its eastern reaches. You'll cross **Dent Bridge** to get to Dent Recreation Area or Elk River. The 1,050-foot-long suspension-span bridge is a smaller version of San Francisco's Golden Gate Bridge, sans the bright orange paint. **Grandad Bridge** is way up the North Fork and connects the town of Headquarters with Elk River. It's a three-span cantilever-deck design, and you'll probably need a Forest Service map to find it.

Information

The U.S. Forest Service's **Clearwater National Forest Supervisor's Office** (12730 U.S. 12, Orofino, 208/476-4541), just west of town, has lots of brochures, maps, and advice for exploring the nearby backcountry.

NORTH FORK CLEARWATER RIVER
North Fork-Superior Adventure Road

This scenic cruise takes you some 160 miles up the North Fork Clearwater River and over Hoodoo Pass to Superior, Montana. The Civilian Conservation Corps built the primitive but well-graded road in 1935. Wildlife abounds back here, and you might even spy a moose or two along the way. Bring your camera and binoculars, and don't forget to fill your gas tank and load up the emergency gear before you go, because no services are available along the way.

From Orofino, take Grangemont Road to its intersection with Highway 11 and turn left. Soon the highway becomes a narrow corridor through dense forest, leading to the old Potlatch company town of **Headquarters.** During its logging heyday, some 170 million board feet of cut timber was transported here via the Beaver Creek flume. Logging is still going strong in these parts, so you should watch for trucks. Active logging roads are usually flagged with bright ribbons every few miles.

Past Headquarters, Highway 11 becomes Forest Road 247. The road crests a small saddle and then follows babbling Beaver Creek down to its confluence with the North Fork Clearwater River. A few miles east up the North Fork, the pavement ends. From here, the dirt road is narrow and occasionally washboard. At **Bungalow Ranger Station,** Forest Road 247 splits off across the river and winds its way up Orogrande Creek, over French Mountain Pass, and down French Creek to Pierce. This allows you to make a nice loop trip from Orofino.

Beyond Bungalow, Forest Road 250 continues east to Kelly Forks Ranger Station. You can continue straight up Forest Road 250 through Black Canyon, a scenic but rough stretch through old-growth cedar groves beneath steep canyon walls, or turn right and take the longer loop on Forest Road 255 through the old Moose City mining area. This road, the better choice for RVs, joins up with Forest Road 250 again at Deception Gulch, farther east. East of Deception Gulch, Forest Road 250 climbs to the headwaters of the North Fork on Long Creek and hops the Continental Divide over to Superior, Montana, and I-90.

Recreation

The North Fork and its tributaries are popular with anglers hoping to catch westslope cutthroat trout, rainbow trout, and whitefish. One of the tributaries, **Kelly Creek,** is classified a blue-ribbon trout stream. Kelly Creek and the waters that feed it are restricted to catch-and-release fishing. The North Fork is also a favorite for easy **rafting and kayaking** trips. The water level isn't very high; the most fun and challenging floating trips usually take place in May-June.

Many hiking trails leave from Forest Road 250 and wind through thick forests up into the mountains. Of particular interest is the **Mallard-Larkins Pioneer Area,** a 30,500-acre roadless area on the high divide between the North Fork and St. Joe watersheds. Inhabiting the Mallard-Larkins is one of the state's largest mountain goat populations. You might also see some of the region's resident moose, elk, deer, black bears, or cougars. Access to the Mallard-Larkins is gained via Isabella Creek (Forest Rd. 700, at the Beaver Creek-Clearwater confluence) or Avalanche Ridge; the trailhead is on Forest Road 250 three miles east of Canyon Ranger Station.

Camping

A number of U.S. Forest Service campgrounds line the North Fork. From west to east: **Aquarius** (7 sites, $10), at the Beaver Creek-Clearwater confluence; **Washington Creek** (23 sites, $10); **Weitas** (6 sites, $10); **Noe Creek** (6 sites, $10); **Kelly Forks** (14 sites, $10); and **Hidden Creek** (13 sites, $10).

WEIPPE

To get to the historic Weippe (WEE-ipe) prairie from Orofino, head south on U.S. 12 for eight miles, and then go east on Highway 11 for about another 12 miles. The story goes that Captain William Clark first saw the Weippe Prairie from high up on the east. The Lewis and Clark expedition had been picking its way along the Lolo Trail's steep terrain, and the sight of this relatively level prairie must have given Clark renewed hope. He pulled together an advance party and rode ahead to check it out. Arriving on the prairie on September 20, 1805, he surprised three young Nez Perce boys, who tried to hide in the grass. Clark managed to corral two of the boys and convince them he wasn't a danger. Soon Clark and his men were enjoying salmon steaks and camas roots at the Nez Perce village.

The prairie today isn't too terribly different than it was back then. The wide-open vistas remain, and at nearby Musselshell Meadows, the camas bulbs still bloom profusely in spring. In summer, Weippe makes a good base camp for hiking or horseback riding along the Lolo Trail. In winter, this rolling prairie makes for great cross-country skiing.

THE LOLO MOTORWAY

Even though U.S. 12 roughly follows the route of the Lewis and Clark expedition, in terms of highway markers, the expedition's actual route followed the Nez Perce's Lolo Trail, up on the highlands north of the river.

The Lolo Trail marked the most difficult conditions the expedition had yet faced on their trip west. Crossing the trail in September 1805, they encountered an early fall snowstorm that not only left them wet and cold but drove the wild game down to lower elevations. The expedition's hunters found little or nothing to kill, and the explorers were forced to eat their own horses to survive.

In the 1930s the Civilian Conservation Corps built the 150-mile-long Lolo Motorway (Forest Rd. 500) on or near the original Lolo Trail. The route runs from Lolo Creek south of Pierce over Lolo Pass into Montana. It's a primitive road not suitable for trailers and RVs and is usually covered by snow from sometime in October until early July.

Access Guide

From Weippe, head east where Highway 11 makes a 90-degree turn. After about 10 miles is a T intersection and Forest Road 100. Turn right and follow that road about nine miles farther to the junction with Forest Road 500.

From Kamiah, take Forest Road 100 east out of town through Glenwood and follow it another 10 miles to the intersection with Forest Road 500. Heading east to west, the most commonly used access to the trail corridor is Parachute Hill Road (Forest Rd. 569), which turns north off U.S. 12 just east of Powell.

Campground and Cabin

At the junction of Forest Roads 100 and 500 is the primitive **Lolo Creek Campsite** (9 sites, free). Heading farther east on Forest Road 500, you'll pass the **Castle Butte Lookout** (mid-July-mid-Sept., $45, sleeps four, reservations www.recreation.gov), a fire lookout cabin with breathtaking views of the nearby wilderness.

KOOSKIA

Kooskia (KOO-skee) got its name from the Nez Perce word *kooskooskia*, which Lewis and Clark translated as "clear water." Historians now believe the explorers didn't get it quite right, and that it should have been "where the waters join." Either translation proves appropriate for the town, which lies at the confluence of the Middle and South Forks of the Clearwater River. History buffs will want to check out the renovated 1912 **Old Opera House Theatre** (208/926-0094) along the downtown strip. The performance hall has year-round productions and a throwback sarsaparilla bar.

Accommodations

Western Motor Inn (6 Main St., Kooskia, 208/926-0166, www.westernmotorinn.com, $49-79) is a recently remodeled motel in downtown Kooskia with 20 nonsmoking rooms, all of which have microwaves, refrigerators, and coffeemakers. Other amenities include cable TV and wireless Internet. The motel has a giant white elk on the roof, meaning that hunters are welcome.

Reflections Inn (6873 U.S. 12, Kooskia, 208/926-0855, www.reflectionsinn.com, $97-139) is 11 miles east of Kooskia on 10 acres off U.S. 12, between mile markers 84 and 85. It offers seven guest rooms, each with a queen bed, a private bath, and a private entrance, and there's a hot tub on the deck. The inn also has a common room outfitted with a full kitchen and a lounge area. Rates include a full breakfast and afternoon refreshments.

Information

The U.S. Forest Service's **Lochsa Ranger District Kooskia Office** (502 Lowry St., Kooskia, 208/926-4275) can provide local recreation information.

Lewis and Clark Highway

LOWELL

At the small town of Lowell, the Lochsa and Selway Rivers meet to form the Middle Fork of the Clearwater River. The name Lochsa (LOCK-saw) is a Native American word meaning "rough water." The Selway, also far from smooth, was likely named after Montana sheepman Thomas Selway, who ran his herds here around the turn of the 20th century and had a cabin along the river. Lowell is supported almost entirely by recreation. In summer, its motels and campgrounds fill up with rafters, kayakers, anglers, bicyclists, and backpackers.

Accommodations and Camping

Three Rivers Resort (115 Selway Rd., Lowell, 208/926-4430, www.idaho3rivers.com) has been the happening spot in little Lowell for more than 35 years, but it's become a little run down in recent times. Enjoying prime real estate right where the Lochsa and Selway come together to form the Clearwater River, the resort gets jam-packed with river rats in summer. It even runs a busy guide service. Rafters aren't the only ones who enjoy this place, though: Three Rivers has something for every kind of camper, including 40 RV sites ($25) with hookups, tent sites ($10-25), a variety of cabins ($135-165) including some on the river, and seven small motel rooms ($59-69). There's also a pool, three jetted tubs, a grocery store, and a restaurant and bar. (Note: Plumbing problems seem to be an ongoing issue at the resort. I don't think I've ever had a hot shower here, and the toilet flooded during two visits.)

Just a few miles west of Lowell, back down U.S. 12, the U.S. Forest Service **Wild Goose Campground** (8 sites, $14) is right on the north bank of the Clearwater.

UP THE SELWAY RIVER

Forest Road 223 (Selway Rd.) crosses the Lochsa River at Lowell and follows the Selway River southeast. It dead-ends at a trailhead about 25 miles later, just past the 1912 Selway Falls Guard Station. The road is paved as far

Selway Falls

Three Rivers Resort in Lowell

Lookout Butte (mid-June–late Sept., $40) is a 60-foot-high tower south of the Selway River above Goddard Creek that sleeps four. Small children are discouraged because of the tower's height.

Across the road from Fenn Ranger Station, **Selway Pond** (also called Fenn Pond) is a stocked trout pond with fishing piers, a picnic area, and an encircling wooden plank walkway that's wheelchair friendly.

Selway Falls

Twenty-one miles up the road from Lowell, you'll come upon awesome **Selway Falls.** It's not a high, graceful waterfall but a low, wide, awesomely powerful man-eater. Here the Selway River pounds down in a thundering drop between house-size granite blocks. Woe to the unfortunate paddler who misses the warning signs strung across the river upstream; this white water would undoubtedly be his or her last.

Hiking

The Forest Service has laid out a one-mile **interpretive trail** at O'Hara Bar Campground, explaining the agency's efforts to rehabilitate the salmon-spawning grounds. Road-building and logging at one time clogged O'Hara Creek with silt, and the fish populations declined. The interpretive sites are situated along the road, so you could even drive to them. Along the way you might spot one of the area's resident ospreys, beavers, or belted kingfishers.

Two National Recreation Trails make for longer, more strenuous day jaunts or casual overnighters. The **East Boyd-Glover-Roundtop National Recreation Trail,** a U-shaped 14.5-mile trail, climbs the east side of Boyd Creek up to Roundtop Mountain, then descends the east side of Glover Creek farther east. You can loop back to the car along the main Selway Road, a scenic little stroll. The **Meadow Creek National Recreation Trail** is part of the Idaho State Centennial Trail. It leaves from Slim's Camp and follows Meadow Creek south. The first four miles are relatively

as the O'Hara Creek Bridge; after that it can turn washboard.

Amazingly enough, the road up the Selway seems *under*used. The river can be jammed down at Three Rivers Resort, but in a few minutes' drive up here you might find a great spot all to yourself. Deer feed in the grasslands along the riverbank, adding to the idyllic landscape.

Fenn Historic Ranger Station and Forest Service Cabins

Four miles down Forest Road 223 (Selway Rd.) you'll find this trim green-and-white building housing the Nez Perce National Forest's **Moose Creek Ranger District Fenn Ranger Station** (208/926-4258), which handles reservations for two Forest Service rental cabins in the area; you can also reserve them through the National Recreation Reservation Service (877/444-6777, www.recreation.gov). The **Meadow Creek Cabin** (mid-May–mid-Sept., $40) is 15 miles up the Meadow Creek National Recreation Trail and sleeps eight.

level, winding through lush cedar and fir forest along the creek bottom. The trail then begins to climb and continues south as far as you want to go; all the way to the Sawtooths, or even to its southern starting point in Murphy Hot Springs near the Nevada border.

Big Fog Saddle (at the end of Forest Rd. 319), **Race Creek** (at the end of the main Selway Road, Forest Rd. 223), and **Indian Hill** (at the end of Forest Rd. 290) are just some of the trailheads that provide hiker access into the Selway-Bitterroot Wilderness.

Camping

A string of U.S. Forest Service campgrounds line the Selway up as far as Selway Falls. From northwest (Lowell) to southeast (Selway Falls), these include **Johnson Bar** (9 sites, $6); **O'Hara Bar** (32 sites, $14), with good wheelchair access; **Rackliff** (6 sites, $5); **Boyd Creek** (6 sites, $5); **Glover Creek** (7 sites, $5); **Selway Falls** (7 sites, $5); **Race Creek** (3 sites, free); and, south up Forest Road 443, **Slim's Camp** (2 sites, free).

For more information, contact the Forest Service's **Moose Creek Ranger District Fenn Ranger Station** (208/926-4258).

★ FOLLOWING THE LOCHSA RIVER

From Lowell, U.S. 12 follows the Lochsa River northeast to its headwaters, then continues over Lolo Pass into Montana. Keep in mind that it's 64 miles up the highway to the next services at Powell.

The Lochsa Face, a steep 73,000-acre strip of land between the river and the Selway-Bitterroot Wilderness, runs parallel to the Lochsa's south bank. Elk, moose, and mountain lions inhabit this wild paradise of stark cliffs, steaming hot springs, and crystalline trout streams.

Lochsa Historical Ranger Station

Spring 1934 was wet, cool, and green in central Idaho, but a long heat wave began in June that turned the lush vegetation into a tinderbox.

On August 10 a dry lightning storm hit the Clearwater River area, sparking a number of blazes, including the disastrous Pete King fire just downstream from the ranger station. Thanks to abundant ladder fuels, the Pete King blaze turned into a crown fire that rapidly spread and burned out of control for 44 days before a heavy, prolonged rain arrived and extinguished the flames. At one point, fire surrounded the ranger station and threatened to incinerate it, but the 200 firefighters who had gathered here valiantly fought it off, and the structures were saved. Unfortunately two firefighters died in the blaze. In the end, the fire charred some 375 square miles.

Today the **Lochsa Historical Ranger Station** (208/926-4274, 9am-5pm daily summer, free) serves as tribute to both the Pete King crews and all of Idaho's forest firefighters. A self-guided tour leads from a museum building, full of historical photos, around the grounds to several outbuildings that contain old tools of the firefighting trade as well as the humble 1930s-era furnishings once used by the fire crews. The site is 48 miles east of Kooskia on U.S. 12.

Powell

★ **Lochsa Lodge** (115 Powell Rd., Lolo, MT, 208/942-3405, www.lochsalodge.com, year-round, $45-125), at milepost 163 on U.S. 12, is a high-mountain retreat alongside the upper Lochsa River just a short distance from the Selway-Bitterroot Wilderness boundary. Although the lodge has been here since 1929, it burned to the ground in 2001 and was entirely rebuilt a short time later. The lodge offers both motel rooms and private log cabins along with a store with gas and a restaurant. Favorite winter activities include cross-country skiing and soaking in the nearby hot springs.

Just a little farther down the road past the lodge, you'll find the U.S. Forest Service's **Powell Ranger Station** (208/942-3113).

Elk Summit Road (Forest Rd. 360) leaves U.S. 12 just east of Powell and leads south to a trailhead into the

Selway-Bitterroot Wilderness. At the trailhead is the Forest Service's primitive **Elk Summit Campground** (15 sites, free).

DeVoto Memorial Cedar Grove

Students of Idaho history remember Bernard DeVoto as a statesmen and editor of the annotated *Journals of Lewis & Clark*. A sign here explains:

> This majestic cedar grove is dedicated to the memory of Bernard DeVoto (1897-1955), conservationist, author, and historian. He often camped here while studying the journals of Lewis and Clark. At his request his ashes were scattered over this area.

The grove is truly magnificent. Towering cedars on either side of the highway shade the cool forest floor covered with bracken ferns, maidenhair ferns, sword ferns, and dogwoods. Short loop trails wind through the woods, and the one on the south side of the highway offers interpretive signs and leads to picnic tables by the rushing river.

Lolo Pass

Atop the Continental Divide on the Idaho-Montana state line is **Lolo Pass** (5,233 feet). A visitors center tells the tales of the Nez Perce and of the Lewis and Clark expedition. Outside, a 0.25-mile interpretive trail circles a restored wetlands area in warm weather. In winter, snowmobilers and cross-country skiers will find a warming hut.

Running the Lochsa River

White-water enthusiasts from around the world seek out the Lochsa River, considered to be one of the country's most difficult. Lewis and Clark took one look at it and decided to struggle along the steep canyon walls rather than attempt to float downstream. The Lochsa tumbles furiously off Lolo Pass in a swirling, crashing torrent. Among its more than 60 rapids are nine rated either Class IV+ or V-, including Ten Pin Alley, Bloody Mary, the Grim Reaper, and Lochsa Falls. Although U.S. 12 runs right alongside the river, wide-eyed rafters will be far too panicked trying to read the water ahead to even notice the cars going by.

Three Rivers Rafting (208/926-4430, www.idaho3rivers.com) charges around $120 for a one-day white-water run on the Lochsa, which includes lunch, a wetsuit, a paddle jacket, a helmet, a life jacket, shuttle service, and hot tubs and showers after the trip.

Fishing

As with the Selway River, chinook salmon, steelhead trout, and Pacific lamprey come up the Lochsa River to spawn. Cutthroat trout, mountain whitefish, and bull trout are also resident. Bull trout fishing is prohibited along the entire river. All waters of the main Lochsa, and Lower Crooked Fork Creek from White Sand Creek to Brushy Fork Creek, are restricted to artificial flies and lures, single barbless hooks, and no bait. All other tributaries have no bait restrictions. The main Lochsa above Wilderness Gateway Campground is catch-and-release only, as is the section of Crooked Fork Creek from White Sand Creek to Brushy Fork Creek. For opening dates and other information, contact **Idaho Department of Fish and Game** (208/334-3700).

Camping

Numerous U.S. Forest Service campgrounds line the Lochsa. From Lowell heading east are **Apgar Creek** (7 sites, $14); **Knife Edge** (5 sites, free); the humongous **Wilderness Gateway** (89 sites, $14), with wheelchair access; **Wendover** (26 sites, $14); and **Lewis & Clark** (17 sites, $14).

Moscow and Vicinity

Leaving Lewiston and heading north, U.S. 95 climbs steeply out of the Clearwater River Valley and onto a vast tableland of mostly treeless rolling hills called the Palouse. This rich agricultural land produces large crops of wheat, barley, canola, chickpeas, and lentils. Each spring when the dryland crops sprout from the furrowed hills, the landscape becomes a sea of green and yellow stretching as far as the eye can see.

The Palouse extends north from Lewiston virtually all the way to Coeur d'Alene, spreading west across the border into Washington and east of U.S. 95 about 30 miles before giving way to mountains. Plopped down in the middle of the Palouse, Moscow (population 24,000) is a cultural oasis in this wide-open, sparsely populated area. It's home to the University of Idaho, so expect to find plenty of coffeehouses, pubs, used-book stores, nightlife, and restaurants.

Early on, the town was called Hog Heaven thanks to the abundance of hog food (camas roots) covering the prairie. When the town took on a more permanent character, the self-respecting townsfolk sought a name with a bit more panache. They tried Paradise for a while but ended up with Moscow (MOS-coe) when an early postmaster decided the area reminded him of a northeastern Pennsylvania town by that name.

SIGHTS
★ University of Idaho

As a bone thrown to north Idaho to convince it not to become part of Washington, the Idaho Territorial Legislature established the **University of Idaho** (208/885-6111, www.uidaho.edu) here in 1889. Idaho's oldest university, the school has about 12,000 students in 10 colleges. The main 320-acre campus, on the west side of downtown, climbs a small hill overlooking the Palouse. The buildings reflect a variety of architectural styles, ranging from the centerpiece Gothic administration building to the **Kibbie Dome,** a big bloated bubble hosting indoor sporting events, concerts, and conventions. The school also boasts the state's largest **library,** which houses 1.6 million volumes and government documents, and the **University of Idaho Press,** a superb resource publishing an extensive catalog of books on the history, natural history, geography, art, and literature of Idaho and the Northwest.

Concerts, lectures, stage productions, and other events take place at the school's modern and acoustically superior **Hartung Theater.** Gardeners and outdoor lovers will enjoy a walk through both the **Shattuck Arboretum,** a 14-acre forest plot planted with evergreens and hardwoods, and the **University of Idaho Arboretum and Botanical Garden,** a 63-acre living laboratory featuring trees and shrubs from around the world. Spring is an especially beautiful time for a visit, when the lilacs, crabapples, and cherry trees come into bloom.

Campus tours are available at the **Student Union Building** (208/885-4636) next to the Idaho Commons. Visitors may park on campus at metered spaces any time, subject to the restrictions posted on each meter. Visitors can obtain free short-term parking permits at the information desk in the Student Union Building. The permits are required for non-metered parking year-round, including all vacation periods.

Appaloosa Museum

Known as the Dalmatian of the horse world, the spotted Appaloosa was prized by northern Idaho's Nez Perce people as a rugged and hardy breed. Early pioneers called this horse "a Palousey" due to its prevalence on the Palouse Prairie. That slang moniker morphed into "Appaloosa" over the years. The Appaloosa Horse Club celebrates the

Moscow

© AVALON TRAVEL

historic breed at the **Appaloosa Museum** (2720 W. Pullman Rd., Moscow, 208/882-5578, 10am-5pm Mon.-Fri., 10am-4pm Sat. year-round, suggested donation $3 pp, $5 family), right at the Washington state line. Inside you'll see Appaloosa-related historical artifacts, photos, and paintings as well as the Appaloosa Hall of Fame. In summer you'll likely find a corral of these beautiful horses out back.

McConnell Mansion

On the east side of downtown Moscow is the Fort Russell Historic District, a jewel box of gorgeous 19th-century homes presiding over quiet, tree-lined streets. One such gem is the 1886 **McConnell Mansion** (110 S. Adams St., 208/882-1004, 1pm-4pm Tues.-Sat., donation), the former home of William "Poker Bill" McConnell, Idaho's third governor. The Latah County Historical Society has turned the Victorian Gothic house into a museum, featuring period-furnished rooms and changing historical exhibits.

Prichard Art Gallery

The university's downtown art gallery, **Prichard Art Gallery** (414 S. Main St., Moscow, 208/885-3586, seasonal hours), showcases student, faculty, and regional art throughout the year. Expect to find everything from modern installment works to smaller multi-media pieces. The gallery also hosts lectures, readings, and workshops.

Camas Prairie Winery

Camas Prairie Winery (110 S. Main St., Moscow, 208/882-0214, www.

camasprairiewinery.com, tasting room noon-6:30pm Mon.-Sat, small fee) is north Idaho's oldest winery, in business since 1983. The winery produces and sells an array of red and white varietals, and it's known for its sparkling wines and various honey meads.

RECREATION
Parks

Moscow boasts nearly a dozen city parks. **Ghormley Park** (W. 3rd St. and Home St., Moscow), adjacent to the University of Idaho campus, includes a municipal swimming pool, softball fields, tennis courts, barbecues, and horseshoe pits. **East City Park** (E. 3rd St. and S. Hayes St., Moscow) provides a basketball court, a sand volleyball court, horseshoe pits, playgrounds, and picnic areas. **Mountain View Park,** a big, open space clear out on the east edge of town (take F St. east to Mountain View Rd.), offers plenty of space for you and your pooch to get some exercise. In addition to the usual park facilities, you'll find a bike path along Paradise Creek.

Latah County's **Robinson Park** (2094 Robinson Park Rd., Moscow) encompasses almost 55 acres of open space, including picnic areas, two softball diamonds, a sand volleyball court, horseshoe pits, a nature trail, and an ice-skating rink.

For a complete list of parks or more information, contact the **Moscow Parks and Recreation Department** (208/883-7085, www.moscow.id.us).

Recreation Center

University of Idaho's **Student Recreation Center** (1000 Paradise Creek St., Moscow, 208/885-7529, daily year-round), on the north side of campus, has a 55-foot freestanding climbing pinnacle, the largest of its kind on any college campus in the United States. Other amenities include a running track, free weights, circuit training, and locker rooms with saunas. Nonstudents can use the center for $7 per visit.

The **Outdoor Program Office** (208/ 885-6170, 10am-4:30pm Mon.-Fri.) is also in the rec center. Stop by to rent a wide range of equipment or to learn about upcoming classes and trips, which are often open to nonstudents.

Bill Chipman Trail

The **Bill Chipman Trail,** a paved seven-mile trail, links Moscow with Pullman, Washington. Built on a former railroad bed, it has a nice gentle grade, making it popular with cyclists, strollers, joggers, and in-line skaters. Find it on the north edge of the University of Idaho campus or anywhere south of Pullman Road, which it parallels.

Mountain Biking

The city's fat-tire fanatics consider **Moscow Mountain,** five miles north of Moscow, the premier mountain-biking destination. To get here, you can take either U.S. 95 north to Lewis Road then Lewis east to Foothill Road, or take D Street east to Mountain View Road, and Mountain View north to Moscow Mountain Road. Most of the Moscow Mountain trails are on private land, so camping is prohibited and you should be on your best behavior.

Other worthwhile biking areas in the region include McCroskey State Park and Palouse Divide Adventure Road.

Golf

The **University of Idaho Golf Course** (1215 Nez Perce Dr., Moscow, 208/885-6171, Apr.-Nov., greens fees $26-28), on the west side of campus, is open to the public. The hilly, often windy 18-hole, par-72 course offers a pro shop, refreshments, a driving range, cart rentals, and lessons.

Outfitters

For specialized outdoor gear, check out **Hyperspud Sports** (402 S. Main St., Moscow, 208/883-1150, open daily), which carries a great selection of mountaineering and climbing equipment, tents, backpacks, and extreme sports gear.

ENTERTAINMENT AND EVENTS
Nightlife

If you want to throw back some beers and listen to live music, head to **John's Alley** (114 E. 6th St., Moscow, 208/883-7662, www.alleyvault.com), a popular bar that hosts a bevy of touring bands. Expect to see acts like Tony Furtado, Luau Cinder, and burgeoning indie superstar Josh Ritter, who grew up in Moscow.

The **Garden Lounge** (313 S. Main St., Moscow, 208/882-8513, open late daily) is an intellectual dive bar downtown. Average joes, college professors, and other cerebral types come for stiff drinks and stimulating conversation, like whether or not Bukowski was a misogynist or just a true admirer of women.

Performing Arts

The **Idaho Repertory Theater** (tickets 208/885-7212) has presented summer stock productions in Moscow for half a century. Affiliated with the University of Idaho's Department of Theater Arts, the troupe's home stage is the E. W. Hartung Theater on campus.

Lionel Hampton Jazz Festival

The annual **Lionel Hampton Jazz Festival** (tickets 208/885-7212, www.uidaho.edu/jazzfest) is considered by many to be one of the best in the country. Hosted by the University of Idaho's Lionel Hampton School of Music in late February, it draws many of the biggest names in jazz to a four-day blowout of concerts, clinics, and student competitions. It's a rare opportunity to see lots of the masters all in one place. Headliner concerts are presented in Kibbie Dome on the university campus. Tickets go on sale in early December.

Off-Campus Events

Spring is in the air when the **Moscow Renaissance Fair** (www.moscowrenfair.org) comes to town. On the first weekend in May, bold knights, fair maidens, and tankards of grog will take thee back to the days before silverware and indoor plumbing. Music fills Moscow's East City Park during **Rendezvous in the Park,** the third weekend in July. The festival features various styles of music, from blues to bluegrass, and plenty of kids' activities to keep everyone happy.

SHOPPING

Bookpeople of Moscow (521 S. Main St., Moscow, 208/882-2669, www.bookpeopleofmoscow.com, 9:30am-8pm daily) is an independent bookstore that stocks its shelves with lots of new and used titles, making it a great spot to lollygag for an hour or so.

Cowgirl Chocolates (428 3rd St., Moscow, 208/882-4098, www.cowgirlchocolates.com) is a fun little chocolate shop with a bent on merchandising. Besides dark chocolate truffles, assorted seasoned bars, and caramels, the place has T-shirts, hats, and shoulder bags emblazoned with a cowgirl silhouette.

Highway 8 westbound to Pullman is also called Pullman Road, and it's where you'll find **Tri-State** (1104 Pullman Rd., Moscow, 208/882-4555, www.t-state.com), which bills itself as "Idaho's Most Interesting Store." That claim is debatable, but the large store does stock all things outdoors, including gear for camping, backpacking, kayaking, fishing, and snowshoeing. It also sells name-brand shoes and clothing alongside shelves filled with gardening, hardware, and kitchen supplies.

ACCOMMODATIONS

Most of Moscow's motels cluster along one of two strips. The older, established motels are along Main Street (U.S. 95), in or close to downtown, while the newer budget chains and a few fancier places are a few blocks away from downtown along Pullman Road (Hwy. 8), which runs west from downtown to Pullman, Washington. The Pullman Road lodgings are convenient to the University of Idaho campus, the big shopping mall, and a gauntlet of fast-food establishments. Tucked away downtown, you'll find a few quaint lodging options without all the hotel amenities.

If you can't find a room through the usual channels, contact **Moscow/Pullman**

Bedfinders (208/882-9716, www.moscowpullmanbedfinders.com), which lists vacation homes and rooms for rent on a short-term basis.

$50-100

Downtown, the no-frills **Royal Motor Inn** (120 W. 6th St., Moscow, 208/882-2581, from $40 d) has some of the most affordable rooms in town. All 38 rooms have cable TV and high-speed Internet. Pets are allowed.

Best Western University Inn (1516 W. Pullman Rd., Moscow, 208/882-0550, www.uinnmoscow.com, from $89 d) offers 173 guest rooms, an indoor pool, a jetted tub, a sauna, a fitness area, and a restaurant and bar.

Behind the Palouse Mall, the **La Quinta Inn** (185 Warbonnet Dr., Moscow, 208/882-5365, from $89 d) is a pleasant place to stay, with an indoor pool and hot tub, a fitness center, and a big breakfast spread.

$100-150

For those who prefer quieter, more private lodging, why not rent an entire house? It may not be big, but the **Little Green Guesthouse** (1020 S. Adams St., Moscow, 208/669-1654, www.littlegreenguesthouse.com, $100-130) has its charms. This one-bedroom cottage is in a mellow neighborhood within walking distance of downtown. Amenities include a full kitchen, a queen bed, satellite TV, free Wi-Fi, and a hammock in the shade. Pets are not allowed.

Another good choice in this price range is the ★ **Browne Block Guest House** (112 S. Main St., Moscow, 208/883-3661, www.browneblockguesthouse.com, $125), a private downtown apartment above **Camas Prairie Winery** in an 1890 brick building. This one-bedroom suite is decked out with antique furniture and a full kitchen. Other amenities include a queen bed, free Wi-Fi, cable TV, a laundry room, and a parking permit.

FOOD
Upscale Fare

Downtown, you'll find ★ **Nectar** (105 W. 6th St., Moscow, 208/882-5914, www.moscow-nectar.com, from 4pm Mon.-Sat., entrées $9-26), a stylish little eatery with exposed brick walls and a long wood bar. This place assuredly serves food designed with wine in mind. Order a bottle of Washington or Idaho wine and some artisanal cheeses with honeycomb while perusing the seasonal menu, which has upscale dishes like trout amandine and grilled lamb chops with couscous. Or you could go really decadent with the bacon-wrapped meatloaf and macaroni and cheese (made with Cougar Gold white cheddar produced at the nearby Washington State University Creamery).

Gambino's (308 W. 6th St., Moscow, 208/882-9000, www.gambinosmoscow.com, lunch and dinner daily, entrées $10-16) is definitely where to go for American-Italian comfort food and big glasses of Chianti. The dining room is classy and casual in one fell swoop. Sink into a deep booth and enjoy classic dishes such as spaghetti and meatballs, chicken Parmesan, and lasagna. The restaurant also serves Chicago-style stuffed pizzas and excellent gelato.

International Cuisine

★ **Patty's Mexican Kitchen** (450 W. 6th St., Moscow, 208/883-3984, www.pattysmexicankitchen.com, 9am-8pm Tues.-Sat., around $8) near the university is the spot to go for Mexican grub. Sit on the deck next to the *barbacoa* pit and devour a big burrito and a cold *cerveza.* The menu also has torta sandwiches, tamales, fish tacos, and enchiladas. The freshly made salsa is particularly good.

If you're craving Japanese and Korean food, head to **Red Bento** (215 W. 3rd St., Moscow, 208/596-4041, lunch and dinner daily, entrées $9-15) near downtown. Expect to find everything from chicken katsu to sushi rolls to beef bulgogi, a spicy Korean-style stir-fry served with steamed rice. The teriyaki (chicken, beef, salmon, and pork) is what keeps the masses coming back.

Locals have filed into **Mikey's Gyros** (527 S. Main St., Moscow, 208/882-0780,

Moscow's Organic Farming Revolution

Moscow Farmers Market

The Palouse has long been a bastion of traditional farming. Dryland (no irrigation) farmers here produce some of the largest lentil and chickpea crops in the United States. But in recent years, an unparalleled organic farming scene has taken hold in the Palouse, anchored by the vibrant **Moscow Farmers Market** (8am-1pm Sat. May-Oct.), the oldest of its kind in the state. Organic farmers set up booths at this popular public market held downtown in Friendship Square. Moscovites come in droves for spring onions, garlic, asparagus, raspberries, pattypan squash, heirloom tomatoes, eggplant, and other impeccably fresh produce. The market also has vendors who sell organic meats, dried beans, and eggs. When folks around here are not shopping at the farmers market, many of them hook up with local community-supported agriculture (CSA) farmers, who provide a weekly larder of organic produce and eggs for their consumer members.

11am-8pm Sat.-Wed., 11am-9pm Thurs.-Fri., around $5) for more than 30 years. Tucked away in an old mall downtown, this restaurant counter puts out various gyro sandwiches, falafel, hummus platters, spinach pie, and verdant tabbouleh.

Pizza and Brew

★ **Maialina Pizzeria** (602 S. Main St., Moscow, 208/882-2694, www.maialinapizzeria.com, 11:30am-10pm daily, pizzas $12-16) puts out delicious Neapolitan-style pies that get blister
ed in a scorching brick oven. Here you'll find everything from classic Margheritas to pesto pizzas to one topped with aromatic white sauce, Taleggio cheese, marinated shiitake mushrooms, and fresh thyme. The wine list has lots of good, affordable Italian labels.

Moscow Brewing Co. (130 N. Almon St., 208/874-7340, www.moscowbrewing.com, taproom from 4pm Wed.-Sat.) is a nano-brewery (meaning it's smaller than a microbrewery) that produces around a dozen handcrafted brews, including pale ale, amber ale, porter, oatmeal stout, and cedar-smoked IPA. The taproom has become a popular hangout for professors looking to escape academia with a few pints of ale.

Breakfast and Coffee

The Breakfast Club (501 S. Main St., Moscow, 208/882-6481, 6am-2pm Mon.-Fri., 7am-2pm Sat.-Sun., $8-10) serves traditional morning fare with a twist. Try the huckleberry zucchini bread, French toast Benedict, or a chicken-fried steak biscuit. You also can get omelets, flapjacks, and inventive egg scrambles. The restaurant serves lunch to boot.

For coffee and conversation, check out ★ **One World Cafe** (533 S. Main St., Moscow, 208/883-3537, 6:30am-11pm Mon.-Fri., 7am-11pm Sat.-Sun.). Relax in one of the comfy chairs and sip an espresso drink made from locally roasted organic beans, or a cup of loose-leaf tea. The small kitchen turns out freshly baked scones, cinnamon rolls, brownies, biscotti, and quiche. The coffeehouse features live acoustic music and other performances at night.

Groceries

For organic veggies, fresh juices, ginseng ginger ale, whole-grain breads, and more, head to **Moscow Food Co-op** (121 E. 5th St., Moscow, 208/882-8537, 7:30am-9pm daily), which also has a great beer and wine selection.

On Saturdays, almost everyone in town shops at the **Moscow Farmers Market** (8am-1pm May-Oct.), held in Friendship Square on Main Street.

INFORMATION

You can learn more about the town at the **Moscow Chamber of Commerce** (411 S. Main St., Moscow, 208/882-1800, www.moscowchamber.com). Moscow has a **National Public Radio** affiliate station, KRFA (91.7 FM).

GETTING THERE

Most people come by car to the Moscow area, but some fly into **Pullman-Moscow Regional Airport** (PUW, 3200 Airport Complex N., Pullman, WA, 509/338-3223), just across the state line. The airport is served by **Alaska Airlines/Horizon Air** (800/654-5669), which has daily flights to and from Seattle. Rental cars are available at the airport, and most of the major hotels offer free shuttle service to guests.

Across the Palouse

Outside Moscow in every direction, two-lane roads wind through pastoral countryside, making lazy curves over and around the scenic, gently rolling hills of the Palouse. It's great for road biking. Dotting the farmland are tidy villages and hamlets, many left over from the logging days. They're commonly tucked away in the draws between the hills, which helps give most of them a pleasant, cozy feel. Time seems to slow down out here, measured not so much by the ticking of the clock as by the turning of the leaves, the first snowfall of winter, foals in the pasture, or laughter at the swimming hole.

U.S. 95 TO COEUR D'ALENE
McCroskey State Park

Moscow mountain bikers probably make the most use of odd, little **McCroskey State Park** (day-use $5). The reserve was the brainchild and labor of love of eastern Washington resident Virgil McCroskey, son of homesteaders who came west from Tennessee after the Civil War. He wanted to create a park dedicated to his mother, Mary Minerva McCroskey, and indirectly dedicated to all the Northwest's pioneer women. He bought 4,500 acres, built the roads, cleared viewpoints, and put in picnic areas and campsites, envisioning an end result similar to the Skyline Drive route through Great Smoky Mountains National Park in his native Tennessee. He attempted to donate the park to the state, only to have the state refuse it because there was no money for maintenance. In 1955 a deal was worked out where the state would accept the park if McCroskey would maintain it for 15 years. In 1970 his obligation came to an end and McCroskey promptly died. Since then, the state has taken responsibility for the area but has kept it minimally developed. You'll never run into crowds, even in midsummer.

The park is about 20 miles north of Moscow along a tall, wooded ridgetop with great views of the Palouse. Coming up U.S. 95, watch for the turn onto Skyline Drive at the crest of the hill on the west (left) side of the highway. It's a terrible blind turn across the highway, although there's not much you can do except make the turn as fast as possible and hope for the best.

Skyline Drive makes a long run down the ridge past viewpoints, a trailhead, and a nice picnic area, then swings north, giving you a choice of either dropping west into Washington or north and east to DeSmet.

If you're coming from Coeur d'Alene instead of Moscow, turn in at DeSmet, continue for about six miles, and turn left on King Valley Road, just past the cemetery. Follow that road through the valley and up the mountain, eventually reaching signs marking Skyline Drive.

DeSmet and Tensed

Heading north on U.S. 95, just before you come to DeSmet you enter the **Coeur d'Alene Indian Reservation.** DeSmet, Tensed, Plummer, and Worley are all reservation towns. Other than the route to McCroskey State Park, there's nothing in **DeSmet** for the casual visitor, although photographers might appreciate the rolling farmland and open vistas.

The town was named after an early Jesuit missionary, Father Pierre Jean de Smet. The Belgian-born de Smet arrived in north Idaho in 1842 and began a mission near today's town of St. Maries. He became a good friend to the Coeur d'Alene people and succeeded in converting many of them to Christianity. The original mission was built on the St. Joe River floodplain. After being inundated on several occasions, the mission was moved to Cataldo and again in 1876 to present-day DeSmet to keep the Indians out of the way of the Silver Valley miners. A new mission was built, and the town that grew around it was named in the missionary's honor. The mission is no longer standing.

Tensed was originally a "suburb" of DeSmet, but when it grew big enough to get its own post office, it needed its own name. The residents applied for the name Temsed, which is DeSmet spelled backwards. The postal service misprinted it, and the town became Tensed.

Plummer and Worley

Plummer is the commercial center of the Coeur d'Alene Reservation. Although small, it offers sufficient visitor services to make it a good base camp for exploring Heyburn State Park (six miles east on Highway 5) and the northern Palouse country. Farming and logging are two important mainstays of the area's economy, and Plummer supplies those industries and their workers.

Worley, named for a onetime superintendent of the reservation, is home to the tribe's major cash cow, the **Coeur d'Alene Casino** (27068 S. U.S. 95, Worley, 800/523-2464, www.cdacasino.com). The glitzy venture entices passersby with high-stakes bingo, video pull-tab machines, and virtual card tables. The casino also has a hotel, restaurants, and a golf course.

After passing through Worley, the highway bends around Lake Coeur d'Alene (out of sight to the east) through more beautiful rolling farmland interspersed with wooded hillocks. You won't see the lake until just before you drop down across the Spokane River and into the city of Coeur d'Alene.

HIGHWAY 6: THE WHITE PINE SCENIC BYWAY

Seventeen miles north of Moscow up U.S. 95, you'll come to the turnoff for Highway 6, which leads east 35 miles to its junction with north-south Highway 3. This stretch of Highway 6 is part of the state-designated White Pine Scenic Byway and passes most of the white pines that gave the route its name. You'll go through a string of small towns along this stretch, including Potlatch, Princeton, and Harvard.

Palouse Divide Nordic Ski Area

The hard-core cross-country skier can tour the entire Palouse Divide Adventure Road, a 31-mile semicircle ending at Laird Park. For less of an epic trek, stay on one of two other marked and periodically groomed loops in **Palouse Divide Nordic Ski Area** that keep you closer to the downhill ski area. Grooming here is sporadic. The forest roads are skiable when ungroomed, but the narrow loop trails really aren't. Views of the surrounding mountains are panoramic. Park in one of two lots: One is along Highway 6, the other at the North-South Ski Bowl.

Palouse Divide Adventure Road

The off-pavement **Palouse Divide Adventure Road** leaves Highway 6 at the North-South Ski Bowl and follows Forest Road 377 down the Palouse Divide. Along the way you'll get great views of the Palouse, particularly from the Forest Service's **Bald Mountain Lookout Tower** (5,334 feet). After 17 miles, the road reaches a T intersection with Forest Road 447. Turn right (west) and loop back to Highway 6 (14 miles farther), or turn east and follow the Emerald Creek drainage 14 miles over to Clarkia and Highway 3. From late spring to late fall, a sturdy car or truck can negotiate the dirt roads; keep an eye out for both ripe huckleberries and rumbling logging trucks. The rest of the year, you'll need a snowmobile or cross-country skis.

HIGHWAY 3: CLARKIA TO ST. MARIES
Clarkia

About 20 million years ago during the Miocene period, the site of today's town of **Clarkia** was the bottom of a lake. More recently, Clarkia flourishes as a timber town. Passing through today, you'll see string after string of railroad cars, each loaded to the brim with milled timber products.

Grandmother Mountain Recreation Area

The Bureau of Land Management (BLM) manages the beautiful, 12,140-acre **Grandmother Mountain Recreation Area,** about 10 miles east of Clarkia on Forest Road 301. The trailheads are well marked. Four moderately easy trails loop through peaceful meadows and old-growth hemlock forests en route to a string of high-mountain fishing holes, including Fish Lake and Lost Lake. The only downside to hiking here is that most of the trails are mixed-use, meaning you'll probably encounter all-terrain vehicles along the way. Regardless of all that noise, wildlife is abundant in the Lund Creek drainage, home to elk, moose, deer, and black bears.

Primitive campsites (free) are available at **Crater Lake Saddle, Crater Peak,** and **Orphan Point Saddle.** For maps and more information about Grandmother Mountain, contact the BLM's **Coeur d'Alene Field Office** (3815 Schreiber Way, Coeur d'Alene, 208/769-5000).

Hobo Cedar Grove Botanical Area

If you can visit only one of the several old-growth cedar groves sprinkled through northern Idaho, try to make it the **Hobo Cedar Grove Botanical Area.** The 500-year-old cedars here escaped the saws, axes, and forest fires of the early 20th century. Today they are protected as a National Natural Landmark. The 240-acre grove lies on a gentle slope traversed by a 0.5-mile interpretive nature trail and a longer one-mile loop trail. The easy trails wind through the cool, shady forest, past brooks and lacy beds of lady ferns. In addition to the western red cedars, grand fir, western larch, Pacific yew, and Engelmann spruce also flourish in this mystical spot. Chances are good you'll have the area all to yourself, particularly on weekdays.

To get to the grove, take Forest Road 321 northeast from Clarkia for 10 miles. Continuing up the road, you'll crest Hobo Pass (4,525 feet) and almost immediately bear right onto Forest Road 3357. Find trailhead parking about two miles down the road.

St. Maries River

From Santa to St. Maries, the highway follows the **St. Maries River,** a placid watercourse that was once used as a log-drive highway. Floaters will find it a slow, relaxing paddle. Anglers can drop a line for a cutthroat or rainbow trout; note that the river is stocked between Clarkia and Santa, and that Alder Creek, which joins the St. Maries at the Lotus railroad crossing, is closed to all fishing.

St. Maries

A timber town clinging to life in the wake of the forest-products slowdown, **St. Maries** (pronounced "St. Mary's"), the Benewah County seat, has a gritty blue-collar feel. A small visitors center and museum occupy the historic **Hughes House** (S. 6th St. and Main Ave., St. Maries, 208/245-3212), a log cabin on the east end of town.

HEYBURN STATE PARK

Heyburn State Park is the largest of Idaho's state parks, encompassing more than 5,500 acres of land and 2,300 acres of water and offering 132 campsites ($12-31). Boating and fishing are major draws, and hiking and biking trails wind along the forested lakeshore. The park is home to one of the largest concentrations of nesting ospreys in North America, and deer, elk, bears, and wild turkeys also inhabit the woodlands. Another odd twist: Wild rice is grown and harvested in the shallows of the lake.

The park's several segments are strung one after the other along Highway 5. The biggest segment and the park's "main entrance" is located on Chatcolet Road, six miles east of Plummer or 12 miles west of St. Maries on Highway 5. Here you'll find the large **Hawley's Landing Campground** as well as the park headquarters (there is no visitors center) and hiking trails. The **Lakeshore Loop Trail** is an easy 0.5-mile-plus trail connecting Hawley's Landing Campground and the Plummer Creek Bridge. Along the way, amateur botanists can spot larch, grand fir, and western red cedar trees as well as bunchberry, oceanspray, and thimbleberry. Look for ospreys, wood ducks, and great blue herons

Heyburn State Park

out on the marsh. The **Plummer Creek Trail,** about 0.5 mile, is also easy and passes through groves of cedars, grand firs, ponderosa pines, western hemlocks, and cottonwoods. The **Indian Cliffs Trail** forms a three-mile loop lined by wildflowers like syringa, heartleaf arnica, and buttercup. The trail takes you up out of the forest to panoramic ridgetop views.

A mile east of the main park entrance along the highway is the park's **Rocky Point** area, where you'll find a park-managed **marina** with a small store, a gas dock, and restrooms as well as an interpretive center with exhibits on local natural history and Native American arts and artifacts.

Continuing east another mile, you'll find a picnic area and public docks at **Cottonwood Point.** Just east of Cottonwood Point on the highway is a turnout offering views of **a river flowing through a lake.** Before Post Falls Dam backed up the Spokane River in 1904, the water level of Coeur d'Alene Lake was significantly lower. The St. Joe River flowed down through the lowlands now underwater in Heyburn State Park and was flanked on either side by natural tree-lined levees. The dam raised the lake's water level enough to flood these southern lowlands, but not enough to crest the levees along the river. As a result, the levees now appear as island strips separating the water of the river from the water of the lake. Eventually, the downsloping topography of the riverbed reaches the surface elevation of the lake, and the phenomenon disappears. Before the dam was built, the four lakes at Heyburn State Park (Chatcolet Lake, Hidden Lake, Round Lake, and Benewah Lake) were four separate bodies of water. Today they're separate in name only; the waters flow together to make up the southern reaches of Coeur d'Alene Lake.

At the park's eastern end is a turnoff to the **Benewah Use Area** (day-use $5), where you'll find another campground, more docks, and some of the best sunsets in Idaho.

Out on the Water

Fishing at the park is excellent. That tug on the end of your line will most likely turn out to be a bass, kokanee, cutthroat trout, perch, or submerged log. Note that at the east end of the lake, **Benewah Creek** is closed to all fishing; the bull trout need their privacy while they're doing their spawning. Just about any other water-based form of recreation is a sure bet at the park as well; **waterskiing, swimming, kayaking, sailing,** and **canoeing** are all popular pastimes.

Rental Cabins

Three cottages ($115-132) and two cabins ($50-55) are available year-round for overnighters in the park.

Information

For campground or cabin reservations, marina rates, or other information, contact **Heyburn State Park** (57 Chatcolet Rd., Plummer, 208/686-1308).

The Panhandle

Look for ★ to find recommended
sights, activities, dining, and lodging.

Highlights

★ **Tubbs Hill:** This gorgeous 120-acre nature preserve on Coeur d'Alene Lake is a Frisbee fling away from downtown Coeur d'Alene (page 337).

★ **Old Mission State Park:** This state park in Cataldo boasts a beautiful Greek Revival-style mission, the oldest existing building in Idaho (page 350).

★ **Wallace:** Old mining towns don't get any funkier than Wallace, which is so historic that the entire town is on the National Register of Historic Places (page 353).

★ **Silverwood Theme Park:** People from across the Northwest flock here for wild rides like the 55-mph wooden roller coaster aptly named Timber Terror (page 357).

★ **Schweitzer Mountain Resort:** This all-season resort near Sandpoint has remarkable skiing and snowboarding—and the most stunning views in the Panhandle (page 366).

★ **Priest Lake State Park:** Idaho's northernmost state park has three units, two of which are on Priest Lake's pristine east shore (page 369).

This stovepipe-shaped section of the Gem State is a mere 45 miles wide at its skinniest swath, but what the Panhandle lacks in landmass, it more than makes up for with a multitude of large glacial lakes and densely forested mountains.

Idaho's Panhandle is shimmed like a log wedge between Montana, Washington, and British Columbia. The booming resort towns of Coeur d'Alene and Sandpoint bring in the lion's share of local tourism thanks to their prime real estate on Idaho's two largest lakes: Coeur d'Alene and Pend Oreille. But much of the region is remote and unpopulated, just a few miles on either side of the busy I-90 and U.S. 95 corridors.

People in the Panhandle are unabashedly independent, and friendly to boot. The state capital in Boise seems like a world away, and many folks here don't think that secession is such a bad idea. Why do you think they call it "north Idaho" instead of northern Idaho? Independent sovereignty probably won't happen anytime soon, but the Panhandle is definitely far removed from other parts of the state.

PLANNING YOUR TIME

The Panhandle is the state's smallest region in terms of square miles, but it offers some of the best resorts and recreational opportunities in Idaho, most of which are easily accessible from I-90 and U.S. 95. Allow yourself at least a week to explore the area. Coeur d'Alene and Sandpoint are good base camps, and expect to find good lodging deals in these places during the winter months.

Outdoor recreation abounds in north Idaho. White-water rafting near Bonners Ferry; hiking and mountain biking in the Selway-Bitterroot Wilderness; shredding morning powder at Silver Mountain; and cruising the sky-blue waterways in old wooden boats keep locals busy year-round, and they don't mind sharing their wondrous playground with others.

Historic sights are intertwined along the trodden pathways. The old mission in

---

Previous: Coeur d'Alene Lake; moose in the wetlands near the Cataldo Mission. **Above:** boardwalk on Coeur d'Alene Lake.

The Panhandle

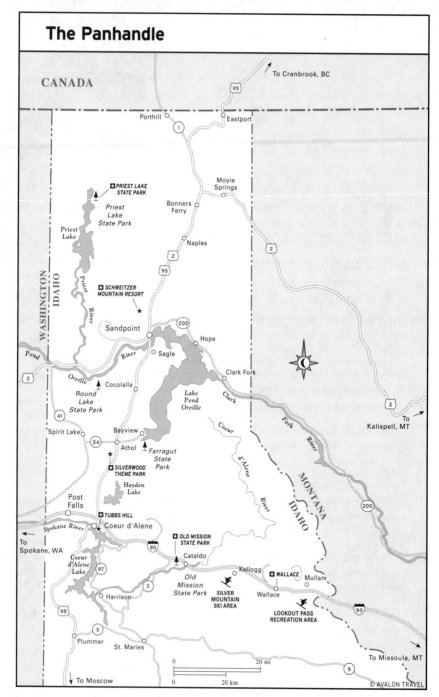

CANADA

To Cranbrook, BC

Porthill

Eastport

Moyie Springs

PRIEST LAKE STATE PARK

Priest Lake State Park

Bonners Ferry

Priest Lake

Naples

Priest River

SCHWEITZER MOUNTAIN RESORT

WASHINGTON

IDAHO

Sandpoint

Hope

Sagle

Pend

Clark Fork

Oreille River

Cocolalla

Lake Pend Oreille

Round Lake State Park

Clark

Coeur

Fork

41

Spirit Lake

Bayview

River

54

Athol

Farragut State Park

d'Alene

MONTANA

SILVERWOOD THEME PARK

Hayden Lake

River

IDAHO

Post Falls

TUBBS HILL

Coeur d'Alene

Spokane River

To Spokane, WA

OLD MISSION STATE PARK

Cataldo

Kellogg

WALLACE

Mullan

Coeur d'Alene Lake

97

Old Mission State Park

SILVER MOUNTAIN SKI AREA

Wallace

LOOKOUT PASS RECREATION AREA

Harrison

3

95

Plummer

5

St. Maries

To Moscow

To Kalispell, MT

To Missoula, MT

0   20 mi

0   20 km

© AVALON TRAVEL

Cataldo, just east of Coeur d'Alene in Silver Valley, offers glimpses into Idaho's early Catholic culture, which sought to bring Coeur d'Alene Indians into its fold in the mid-1900s. Nearby, travelers will marvel at the Victorian architecture and sheer funkiness of Wallace, a lovingly restored mining town with a taste for debauchery. A multitude of antiques shops, old saloons, and strange museums make this place one of the most interesting stops in the Panhandle, or in Idaho, for that matter.

To the far north, Priest Lake shimmers like a bright diamond below sharp mountain peaks. Ancient cedar and hemlock forests line the shore, and huckleberries are just about everywhere you look, including on local menus in late summer. For those looking to escape the hustle and bustle of Coeur d'Alene and Sandpoint, tranquil Priest Lake is where you'll want to go.

Coeur d'Alene and Vicinity

Shortly after the Mullan Road opened the Panhandle to miners and settlers, U.S. Army general William Tecumseh Sherman came through scouting locations for a new fort. The Army wanted a north Idaho base to protect the burgeoning white populace from Native American attack and to make sure the Brits didn't push their way south of the 49th parallel. In 1878, construction of Fort Coeur d'Alene began.

The fort, and the town that grew around it, were named for the local Native Americans. The French fur trappers who frequented this area called the local inhabitants the *coeur d'alène,* meaning "heart like an awl." Authorities agree the name arose from the Native Americans' shrewd trading abilities but argue whether the trappers coined the phrase first or adopted it after hearing the Native Americans use it to describe the French. In any case, the name stuck. After Sherman died, the fort's name was changed to honor him, but the town that grew around the fort kept the moniker Coeur d'Alene. In the 1880s the town became the lake's biggest steamship port; ships carried passengers and supplies to and from the booming Coeur d'Alene Mining District and communities around the lake.

Today, Coeur d'Alene (population 46,000) ranks as the top summer resort town in the Inland Northwest. The city, which is centered near the scenic beach areas, teems with recreational activity during the warmer months, when droves of people show up for boating, swimming, and a healthy dose of beachside relaxation. At night, Sherman Avenue comes alive with a profusion of restaurants, bars, and ice-cream shops.

In winter, the crowds disappear, and a quiet, intense beauty descends with the first snowfall. Skiers make the morning commute out to one of the region's three downhill resorts, while bald eagles make their annual pilgrimage to Wolf Lodge Bay to fatten up on kokanee salmon. It's a great season to relax at one of the town's numerous bed-and-breakfast inns.

SIGHTS
North Idaho College and Old Fort Sherman
The campus of **North Idaho College** (1000 W. Garden Ave., Coeur d'Alene, 208/769-3300, www.nic.edu) occupies the grounds of **old Fort Sherman,** one of the major military installations in the Northwest from 1878 to 1901. It was from here that troops were dispatched up the Silver Valley to quell the mining wars of 1892. Today only a few structures from the fort remain, scattered among the modern school buildings of this two-year junior college. The campus is a scenic place with prime lakefront real estate, expansive lawns, and big evergreens, making it a good spot for a picnic.

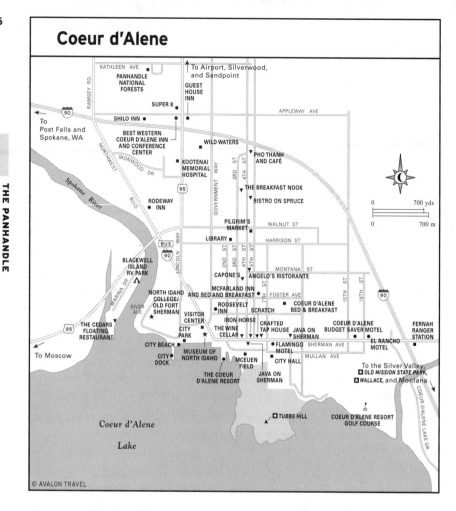

Coeur d'Alene

Museum of North Idaho

Take in some of Kootenai County's history at the **Museum of North Idaho** (115 Northwest Blvd., Coeur d'Alene, 208/664-3448, www.museumni.org, 11am-5pm Tues.-Sat. Apr.-Oct., $4 adults, $1 ages 6-16, $10 families), in front of City Park. Exhibit topics include the Mullan Road, Fort Sherman, early transportation, and local industry, especially logging and mining.

An annex, the **Fort Sherman Museum,** on the North Idaho College campus (W. Garden Ave. and N. College Dr., Coeur d'Alene, 1pm-5pm Tues.-Sat. May-Sept.), has exhibits including a 1924 smoke-chaser's cabin, a model of old Fort Sherman, and a lifeboat from the *Miss Spokane,* a passenger boat that plied Coeur d'Alene Lake in the 1920s. The museum provides a walking-tour brochure to the several Fort Sherman structures that have been preserved. A single admission of $4 adults, $1 ages 6-16, and $10 for families is valid at both museums.

On Guard for Human Rights

Idaho's Panhandle region has long had a reputation as a haven for racists, but events in recent years show that perceptions and reality may both be turning.

From 1973, Richard Butler ruled the white-supremacist Aryan Nations organization from a compound in Hayden, Idaho, a few miles north of Coeur d'Alene. The ultraright-wing racist and his followers were an unending source of embarrassment to the vast majority of north Idahoans. Groups including the Kootenai County Task Force on Human Relations and the Human Rights Education Institute spoke out strongly against the Aryan Nations' presence in their backyard.

Finally, in 2000, Butler was forced into bankruptcy by a $6.3 million civil judgment resulting from a suit filed by the Southern Poverty Law Center on behalf of an Idaho woman and her son who said Butler's group shot at them in 1998. Philanthropist Greg Carr, an Idaho native, purchased Butler's compound and donated it to the North Idaho College Foundation, which plans to turn the Hayden Lake site into a peace park in the coming years. Meanwhile, the **Human Rights Education Institute,** again aided by a donation from Carr, opened an **educational center** (414 Mullan Rd., Coeur d'Alene, 208/292-2359, www.hrei.org) in a historic building in downtown Coeur d'Alene's City Park. The center features permanent and traveling human rights exhibits, educational programs, and community outreach.

Sightseeing Tours

SIGHTSEEING CRUISES

Lake Coeur d'Alene Cruises (208/765-4000, www.cdacruises.com) offers 90-minute tours of the lake (daily late Apr.-late Oct., $22.75 adults, $20.75 seniors, $14.75 ages 6-12). Sunday brunch cruises and seasonal dinner cruises are also available. All public cruises leave from City Dock at Independence Point, next to the Coeur d'Alene Resort.

FLIGHTSEEING

Brooks Sea Plane (208/664-2842, www.brooks-seaplane.com) takes passengers aloft on 20-minute sightseeing flights around the lake ($60 adults, $30 under age 12). You'll fly aboard either a float-equipped Cessna 206 or a gorgeous seven-passenger De Havilland Beaver, the bush pilot's workhorse. The planes leave from City Dock on Independence Point, next to the Coeur d'Alene Resort. Longer flights are also available.

RECREATION

★ Tubbs Hill

One of the city's highlights, the beautiful **Tubbs Hill** (free), a 120-acre wooded preserve, juts out into the lake right next to the Coeur d'Alene Resort. Trails loop around the peninsula through groves of Douglas fir and century-old ponderosa pine. Some paths climb up the hill for panoramic views, while others drop down to hidden coves and beaches. It's all a city park, open to foot traffic only and within easy walking distance of anywhere downtown. It's definitely where you want to be for sunsets.

Biking and Skating

The **North Idaho Centennial Trail,** a 23-mile hiking, biking, and skating trail, stretches west from Higgins Point on Coeur d'Alene Lake's northeast shore through the cities of Coeur d'Alene and Post Falls to the Washington state line. Ambitious folks can continue west on the abutting Spokane River Centennial Trail; it's another 22 miles to Spokane. For most of its length, the trail is either completely separated from traffic or off on a big, wide shoulder. Animals on leashes are allowed, and interpretive signs mark many points of interest along the way. You can pick up the trail at City Park, downtown, or on Coeur d'Alene Lake Drive.

Swimming and Sunbathing

When those sunny summer days roll around, everyone heads to **City Beach.** The water warms up enough for swimming and splashing, and the beach, boardwalk, and adjacent **City Park** fill with skaters, Frisbee-throwers, joggers, swimmers, and other frolicking vacationers.

Parasailing

Coeur d'Alene Parasail (208/765-2999, www.cdaparasail.com, 10am-7pm Sun.-Fri., solo $60, tandem $100) can tow you 400 or more feet in the air behind a speedboat for a 10-minute ride over the lake. And thanks to the specially designed boat and hydraulic winch system, you won't even get wet.

Boat Rentals

Boardwalk Marina at the Coeur d'Alene Resort (208/415-5600) rents 22-foot runabouts for $99 per hour with a two-hour minimum. Tax and fuel are additional, and you'll have to leave a credit card for a deposit.

You can rent canoes and paddleboats at City Beach's dock during the summer months.

Fishing

Coeur d'Alene Lake has hungry populations of kokanee, chinook salmon, and northern pike. **Fins & Feathers** (1816 Sherman Ave., Coeur d'Alene, 208/667-9304), a tackle shop and guide service, can help you find the biggest ones and provide the boat and all equipment as well. The going rate for a party of two is $375 for a half-day trip, $595 for a full day.

While the big lake is the obvious centerpiece of the area, don't forget 300-acre **Fernan Lake,** east of I-90 at the Sherman exit, where you can fish for wild cutthroat trout and stocked rainbows as well as warmwater species like largemouth bass, crappie, perch, and catfish. In winter you can probe beneath the frozen crust, primarily for perch. Boat ramps and docks are found at either end of the lake.

Golf

The star attraction for Coeur d'Alene linksters is **Coeur d'Alene Resort Golf Course** (900 Floating Green Dr., Coeur d'Alene, 208/667-4653, www.cdaresort.com, nonguest greens fees from $200). The beautiful lakeside course boasts a great gimmick: The 14th hole features a movable floating green. A cute little putt-putt boat ferries you out to it, assuming your ball actually made it to the green and isn't on its way to the bottom of the lake.

All the golf magazines rave about the 6,804-yard, par-71 course, designed by Scott Miller and extensively renovated in 2003 with 500 new

A tour boat cruises around Coeur d'Alene Lake.

yards to play. Guests of the resort get a major price break and a free water-taxi ride from the hotel to the course. Rates include a cart and caddie. Clubs and golf shoes can be rented. Make sure to wear your nicest golf duds.

For much less money, head to **Ponderosa Springs Golf Course** (1291 N. Galena Dr., Coeur d'Alene, 208/664-1101, greens fees $12), a nine-hole course with an air-conditioned tenth hole where you can get a cocktail after hitting the links.

Backcountry Hiking and Mountain Biking

The U.S. Forest Service's **Coeur d'Alene River Ranger District Fernan Ranger Station** (2502 E. Sherman Ave., Coeur d'Alene, 208/664-2318) is on the east side of I-90. Stop by for information on nearby backcountry hiking and biking opportunities. The Forest Service publishes descriptive flyers on several hiking trails, primarily found deep in the Coeur d'Alene Mountains between Hayden Lake, Lake Pend Oreille, and the upper North Fork of the Coeur d'Alene River.

CANFIELD MOUNTAIN TRAIL SYSTEM

The **Canfield Mountain Trail System** offers 32 miles of single- and double-track trails, open to hikers, equestrians, motorcycles, and mountain bikes. Several access points are available along Forest Road 1562, which links Nettleton Gulch Road with Fernan Lake Road in a meandering, roundabout fashion. Nettleton Gulch Road intersects 15th Street 1.1 miles north of I-90 Exit 14, becoming Forest Road 1562 farther east. On the east side, Forest Road 1562 intersects Fernan Lake Road 5.5 miles east of I-90 Exit 15. Pick up a map to the trail system at the Fernan Ranger Station.

Outfitters

Vertical Earth (1323 E. Sherman Ave., Coeur d'Alene, 208/667-5503, www.verticalearth.com, 10am-6pm daily) rents out mountain bikes, road bikes, and other outdoor gear.

ENTERTAINMENT AND EVENTS
Nightlife

The **Iron Horse** (407 E. Sherman Ave., Coeur d'Alene, 208/667-7314, nightly) in downtown Coeur d'Alene is the place to go for drinks and dancing. This venerable nightspot features live music (usually rock and blues) on weekends. The Iron Horse also has a full-service restaurant serving breakfast, lunch, and dinner daily.

Performing Arts

North Idaho College sponsors the bulk of the area's concerts and dramatic performances, like the Coeur d'Alene Summer Theatre. For current listings, call the college's **Boswell Hall Schuler Performing Arts Center** (208/769-7780). The **Citizens' Council for the Arts** (208/667-9346, www.artonthegreen.org) has lots of information on the region's fine performing arts scene.

Events

Art on the Green (www.artonthegreen.org) is a vibrant arts festival that sets up at North Idaho College in early August, and fans of vintage lake cruisers will surely want to check out the **Coeur d'Alene Wooden Boat Festival,** held the second weekend in August at Coeur d'Alene Resort.

ACCOMMODATIONS

Sherman Avenue runs between Coeur d'Alene Resort and I-90 on the east side of town. A number of mostly inexpensive-moderate older independent motels are along this strip. The area has the advantage of being surrounded by quiet old residential areas and being near funky, character-filled shops and restaurants. On the west end, the lodgings are within easy walking distance of downtown; on the east end, you'll be near I-90.

The other motel district is along Appleway Avenue, which parallels I-90 to the north. This area is close to I-90 and a blur of modern shopping malls and fast-food joints. Most of the major chain motels are here.

$50-100

The **Budget Saver Motel Coeur d'Alene** (1519 Sherman Ave., Coeur d'Alene, 208/667-9505, from $50 d) doesn't look like much from the outside, but it has some of the lowest rates in town. The rooms are decent, and some even have two bedrooms. In the same area, you can also get budget rooms at **El Rancho Motel** (1915 Sherman Ave., Coeur d'Alene, 208/664-8794, from $40 d), which allows pets.

If you want to be a few blocks from the lake, try the ★ **Flamingo Motel** (718 Sherman Ave., Coeur d'Alene, 208/664-2159, www.flamingomotelidaho.com, from $90 d), a fun, retro, Miami-looking motor inn with impeccably clean rooms, kitchenettes, and a pool.

A few miles north of town on U.S. 95 is **Silver Lake Motel** (6160 Sunshine St., Coeur d'Alene, 208/772-8595, www.silverlakemotel.com, from $59 d), with amenities like an outdoor pool, a lounge, and free continental breakfast.

$100-150

Among the plushest places in town are the **Shilo Inn** (702 W. Appleway Ave., Coeur d'Alene, 208/664-2300 or 800/222-2244, from $100 d), which offers suites with kitchenettes, and the **Best Western Coeur d'Alene Inn** (506 W. Appleway Ave., Coeur d'Alene, 208/765-3200 or 800/251-7829, from $100 d), a full-service hotel with an indoor pool and spa. Both hotels sometimes offer guest rooms for under $100.

Coeur d'Alene is the bed-and-breakfast capital of Idaho; about a dozen are sprinkled throughout town, with a half-dozen more in the outlying areas. Unless specified, the B&Bs below serve a full breakfast and don't allow smoking indoors. Note that B&B prices vary widely with the particular guest room rented, and some places have guest rooms that exceed this price category. For more listings of area B&Bs, visit the **North Idaho Bed and Breakfast Association**'s website (www.nibba.com).

East of town, off the lake's north shore,

★ **Katie's Wild Rose Inn** (7974 E. Coeur d'Alene Lake Dr., Coeur d'Alene, 208/765-9474 or 800/371-4345, www.katieswildroseinn.com, $89-250) sits high on a promontory overlooking Bennett Bay. Wild roses grace the grounds, and a rose motif runs throughout the interior. The inn sits alongside the Centennial Trail bike path. Of the four guest rooms, two have private baths, while the others share a bath.

★ **The Roosevelt Inn Bed & Breakfast** (105 E. Wallace Ave., Coeur d'Alene, 208/765-5200 or 800/290-3358, www.therooseveltinn.com, $89-319) occupies the redbrick 1906 Roosevelt School, which was converted in 1994. All guest rooms have private baths and are furnished with antiques; some guest rooms have a lake view. Common areas include a small exercise center and two parlors. Rates include a gourmet full breakfast.

The **McFarland Inn Bed & Breakfast** (601 E. Foster Ave., Coeur d'Alene, 208/667-1232, www.mcfarlandinn.com, $100-175) offers five guest rooms in a graceful turn-of-the-20th-century home furnished with both elegant antiques and modern amenities. A gourmet breakfast and afternoon tea are served daily, and fresh coffee and goodies are always available. Each guest room has a private bath with a claw-foot tub and a shower. Children over age 14 are welcome.

Just west of town in a tranquil country setting is the **American Country Bed & Breakfast** (705 Zircon Ln., Coeur d'Alene, 208/651-2191, www.americancountrybedandbreakfast.com, $125-215). This Americana-inspired inn offers a big deck, a big breakfast, and big smiles from its hosts Brian and Shar Scott. The B&B has four guest rooms and a cottage in a tree out back. Children and pets are not allowed, and smoking is permitted outside.

Over $200

By many people's standards, **The Coeur d'Alene Resort** (115 S. 2nd St., Coeur d'Alene, 208/765-4000, www.cdaresort.

com), owned by publishing magnate Duane Hagadone, is the grandest hotel in Idaho. It definitely ranks high in terms of location and elegance, rising into the sky over the shores of beautiful Coeur d'Alene Lake, and it offers a mind-boggling array of extravagant amenities. Standard guest rooms usually run $200 or more in summer. The high-end guest rooms can fetch as much as $500 in summer. Lower prices are offered in the off-season. Spa, ski, golf, and other packages are available.

Vacation Rental Companies

Coeur d'Alene Vacation (800/679-3661, www.cdavacation.com) lists year-round vacation home rentals, some on the lake. **Resort Property Management** (2120 N. 3rd St., Coeur d'Alene, 208/667-6035, www.resort-propertiesidaho.com) has listings for more than 75 summer cabins in the $125-500 per night range.

CAMPING AND RVING

Blackwell Island RV Park (800 S. Marina Dr., Coeur d'Alene, 208/665-1300 or 888/571-2900, $40-55 with full hookups) is a large park with boat docks and grassy pull-throughs just across the Spokane River from town: Take U.S. 95 south one mile from I-90 and turn left on Marina Drive.

River Walk RV Park (1214 Mill Ave., at Northwest Blvd., Coeur d'Alene, 208/765-5943 or 888/567-8700, $30-58) offers 30 sites with full hookups. Some tent sites ($24) are available. The park has showers, restrooms, and a laundry room.

FOOD
Upscale Fare

Beverly's (115 S. 2nd St., Coeur d'Alene, 208/765-4000, www.cdaresort.com, lunch and dinner daily, entrées $26-55) is the Coeur d'Alene Resort's premier dining room, on the hotel's 7th floor overlooking the lake. On the menu, you'll find seasonal offerings done up in a contemporary manner. The restaurant maintains the largest wine cellar in this part of the state.

For fine Italian dining, make a reservation at ★ **Angelo's Ristorante** (846 N. 4th St., Coeur d'Alene, 208/765-2850, www.angelosristorante.net, dinner 5pm-10pm daily, $16-28). Here you'll find an elegant dining room and upscale preparations of antipasto, pasta, risotto, scampi, steaks, and rack of lamb. The wine list boasts lots of Italian and Washington labels.

The Cedars Floating Restaurant (208/664-2922, www.cedarsfloatingrestaurant.com, dinner from 4pm daily, $24-42), also affiliated with Coeur d'Alene Resort, is popular with tourists, so expect it to be crazy-busy during the peak of summer. Seafood is the order of the day at this place. Expect to see a variety of fish entrées, depending on availability, which may include wild salmon, swordfish, halibut, or ahi; some are grilled, others cooked on a cedar plank. Roasted chicken, pasta dishes, and steaks round out the menu. To get here, head south on U.S. 95 toward Moscow. On the edge of town, turn left onto Marina Drive immediately after crossing the Spokane River. This takes you out onto Blackwell Island, an area of working boat shops and boat storage yards. The restaurant is all the way out at the tip of the island, moored where the Spokane River flows out of Coeur d'Alene Lake.

Casual Dining

★ **Scratch** (501 E. Sherman Ave., Coeur d'Alene, 208/930-4762, lunch 11am-3pm Mon.-Fri., dinner 3pm-10pm daily, dinner entrées $18-40) is a global fusion restaurant and lounge downtown that uses local foodstuffs well. The inventive menu changes with the season and availability of products. The dinner menu looks toward Asia and the Mediterranean for inspiration.

Bistro on Spruce (1710 N. 4th St., Coeur d'Alene, 208/664-1774, www.bistroonspruce.com, lunch and dinner Mon.-Sat., brunch Sun., entrées $14-24) is a favorite with the locals. Expect to find dishes like Guinness onion soup, mushroom risotto, seafood paella, and pan-roasted duck breast with Marsala reduction. Oh, yeah, there are lots of microbrews and wines by the glass.

Wine Bars and Pubs

The Cellar (317 Sherman Ave., Coeur d'Alene, 208/664-9463, from 4pm Tues.-Sat., appetizers $8-12) is a venerable downtown wine bar that features live jazz several nights a week. The wine list has at least 250 labels from around the globe, which play well with the wine-friendly small plates that come out of the jewel box-sized kitchen. The sidewalk patio is a great place to people-watch while sipping syrah and noshing on tapas.

★ **Crafted Tap House** (523 Sherman Ave., Coeur d'Alene, 208/292-4813, www.craftedtaphouse.com, 11am-late daily, entrées $11-17) has become a popular place to quaff ale ever since it opened in 2013 along a bustling stretch of Sherman Avenue. The pub gets hopped up on weekends when droves of beer geeks show up for the seemingly endless array of handcrafted brews on tap (about 50 regional microbrews, to be exact). The gastropub menu features fun twists on pub classics, like crawfish chowder, garlic fries, a big pretzel with fontina cheese sauce, and upscale burgers.

Capone's Pub & Grill (751 N. 4th St., Coeur d'Alene, 208/667-4843, www.caponespub.com, lunch and dinner daily, $9-14) entices beer drinkers with more than 20 brews on tap. The decor is vintage sports, with old baseball mitts, skis, golf clubs, and ice skates hanging from the ceiling. Whatever game you're looking for, you'll probably find it on one of the many TVs connected to two satellite dishes. Capone's serves an extensive menu of first-class pub grub, including fat subs and made-from-scratch gourmet pizzas (try the Thai chicken pie). Live entertainment draws a fun crowd on weekends.

International Cuisine

If you're craving a bowl of pho (Vietnamese beef noodle soup), head to **Pho Thanh Café** (2108 N. 4th St., Coeur d'Alene, 208/665-9903, lunch and dinner daily, $6-9), a little Vietnamese restaurant near I-90. The servers can be gruff at times, but the kitchen pumps out decent Southeast Asian standards such as pho, crispy spring rolls, and vermicelli noodle dishes.

For tasty Mexican eats, check out **Toro Viejo** (117 N. 2nd St., Coeur d'Alene, 208/667-7676, lunch and dinner daily, around $10). This festive downtown eatery dishes up enchiladas, tostadas, tacos, burritos, and fajitas. The restaurant also serves margaritas and Mexican beers.

Breakfast and Coffee

The Breakfast Nook (1719 N. 4th St., Coeur d'Alene, 208/667-1699, 6am-2pm Mon.-Sat., 7am-2pm Sun., under $10) is known for its big American-style breakfasts. The menu has steak and eggs, French toast, eggs Benny, pancakes, and omelets galore.

Downtown, ★ **Java on Sherman** (819 Sherman Ave., Coeur d'Alene, 208/667-0010, 6am-8pm Sun.-Thurs., 6am-9pm Fri.-Sat.) puts out the best coffee in town, and it's a wonderful spot to kill some time. Try the Bowl of Soul, a delicious espresso drink made with steamed milk, chocolate, and cinnamon. The pastries are baked on the premises. Bigger breakfasts are available too. Both the atmosphere and the help are young, hip, and friendly.

Groceries

Pilgrim's Market (1316 N. 4th St., Coeur d'Alene, 208/676-9730, www.pilgrimsmarket.com, 9am-9pm daily) is a natural food store that specializes in organic local produce, meats, and bread. The market also has bulk foods, dietary supplements, and earthy beauty products.

Kootenai County Farmers Market (5th St. and Sherman Ave., Coeur d'Alene,

4pm-7pm Wed. May-Sept.) is the place to go for impeccably fresh local produce and meats, honey, salsa, eggs, and artisanal bread. You also can get hot food like wood-fired pizzas and lamb burgers, plus there's live music and a good vibe here.

INFORMATION AND SERVICES

Coeur d'Alene Chamber of Commerce's **Visitors Bureau** (105 N. 1st St., Coeur d'Alene, 208/664-3194, www.coeurdalene. org) is conveniently located downtown across from City Park. It's well stocked with maps and brochures on lodging, restaurants, and recreation.

Recreation information for most of north Idaho is available from the **Idaho Panhandle National Forests Supervisor's Office** (3815 Schreiber Way, Coeur d'Alene, 208/765-7233). The **Idaho Department of Parks and Recreation** (2885 Kathleen Ave., Coeur d'Alene, 208/769-1511) maintains its north region headquarters in Coeur d'Alene.

National Public Radio listeners can pick up Spokane's **KPBX** (91.1 FM). Another station, featuring a great jazz repertoire, is **KEWU** (89.5 FM), the radio station of Eastern Washington University in Cheney.

If you need emergency medical services, head to **Kootenai Medical Center** (2003 Kootenai Health Way, Coeur d'Alene, 208/625-4000), just off Lincoln Way near I-90.

GETTING THERE AND AROUND
Getting There
Spokane International Airport (GEG, 9000 W. Airport Dr., Spokane, WA, 509/455-6455) is about 35 miles away. It's served by several major airlines, including Alaska Airlines, Southwest, United, and Delta. The airport has a variety of rental car agencies inside the main terminal.

Getting Around
Parking in downtown Coeur d'Alene can be challenging, especially during the peak summer months. If you don't feel like riding a bike, jump on one of the free **Citylink** (www.idahocitylink.com) buses that run around town. See the website for schedule and route information.

POST FALLS
Frederick Post planted the seed for the city of Post Falls when he built a sawmill along the Spokane River in 1871. He needed permission

Kootenai County Farmers Market in Coeur d'Alene

from the locals to take advantage of the falls for his mill, so he negotiated a land-use deal with Coeur d'Alene Chief Seltice. Today, the riverfront city between Coeur d'Alene and Spokane is one of Idaho's fastest-growing towns, with a population that has more than doubled since 1990 to more than 29,000.

Parks

Legend has it that Post and Chief Seltice signed their deal on **Treaty Rock,** today preserved as part of a small four-acre park near the corner of Seltice and Compton Streets, two blocks west of Spokane Street. Short trails wind through the park and lead to the historic granite outcropping. Post's name is indeed carved on the rock, and below it are some Native American pictographs. But as the interpretive information at the site notes, no concrete evidence exists that this rock is actually the "contract" between Post and Seltice.

At **Falls Park,** visitors can walk to overviews of Post's famous falls and the narrow Spokane River gorge. Interpretive signs illuminate early area history; picnic tables, a playground, and a small fishpond make the 22-acre park a pleasant place for a lunch break. To get to the park, head south on Spokane Street from I-90 and watch for a posted right turn at 4th Street.

Q'emiln Riverside Park was once the site of a Coeur d'Alene Indian village. Q'emiln (ka-MEE-lin) means "throat of the river" in the Coeur d'Alene language. This 90-acre park on the south side of the Spokane River has five miles of beautiful hiking trails through steep, rocky gorges. Also here are boat ramps, horseshoe pits, playground areas, and picnic shelters. A parking fee ($4 cars/$6 boats) is charged Memorial Day–Labor Day. To get to the park, take I-90 Exit 5 for Spokane Street, follow Spokane Street south across the river, and turn right on Park Way Drive just on the other side.

Corbin Park is named for early Post Falls railroad developer D. C. Corbin. The 24-acre park lies on the riverbank on the west side of town and offers a softball diamond, a volleyball court, a boat ramp, and picnic areas. To get here, take I-90 Exit 2 for Pleasant View Avenue and head south to Riverbend Avenue; take Riverbend east (left) to Corbin Park Road and follow it into the park.

Centennial Trail

From Post Falls, you can follow the **Centennial Trail** bike and hiking path all the way to Higgins Point on Coeur d'Alene Lake, or west to Spokane and beyond. The 63-mile-long interstate trail system is a favorite of hikers, cyclists, and skaters in summer and cross-country skiers in winter. Access the trail at Falls Park.

Boating

Rent a boat for fishing or cruising the Spokane River or Coeur d'Alene Lake at **Red Lion Templin's Hotel** (414 E. 1st Ave., Post Falls, 208/773-1611). The hotel's marina rents out gas-powered pontoon boats for $79-99 an hour, with a two-hour minimum.

Rock Climbing

The city's **Q'emiln Riverside Park** offers dozens of single-pitch bolted climbs on reasonably solid river-canyon granite. It's a beautiful spot and seldom gets crowded. If you drive into the park, you'll have to pay a parking fee. Most climbers park their rigs just outside the gate on Park Way Drive and walk in; from the entrance gate it's just a short hike to the climbing areas.

Accommodations and Food

Red Lion Templin's Hotel (414 E. 1st Ave., Post Falls, 208/773-1611 or 800/283-6754, www.redlion.com, from $149 d) sits right on the banks of the Spokane River, offering spectacular views of the happening riparian scene. Ospreys and mallard ducks are among the hotel's neighbors. Amenities include an indoor pool, a sauna, a spa, a fitness center, tennis courts, a marina, guest laundry, and a restaurant overlooking the river. Wheelchair-accessible rooms are available, as are suites with jetted tubs, family suites, and parlor suites.

The River Cove B&B (212 Parkwood Pl., Post Falls, 208/773-1014, www.therivercove.com, from $129) bills itself as "a scenic waterfront retreat." From the back deck you can look past the pines to the water's edge below. Each of the guest rooms has a private bath, and rates include a gourmet breakfast. In winter, you can enjoy cross-country skiing right on the premises. Smoking is allowed outside only, and small children are not allowed.

In town, the **White House Grill** (712 N. Spokane St., Post Falls, 208/777-9672, www.whitehousegrill.com, lunch and dinner Mon.-Sat., $10-17) dishes up Greek food with a whole lot of attitude. The employees are zany at this little restaurant, which serves everything from deep-fried feta and hummus to gyro sandwiches and lamb kebobs. Let's not forget the flaky baklava and retsina wine.

WOLF LODGE DISTRICT
Eagle-Watching

A short distance east of Coeur d'Alene on I-90, Exit 22 is marked "Wolf Lodge District," where Wolf Lodge Creek empties into Wolf Lodge Bay. Wolves aren't as abundant as they used to be, but the bay's kokanee salmon population attracts a sizable population of bald eagles each winter. The eagles migrate down from the Canadian northlands to escape the harsh arctic winter. Here they find a relatively mild climate and easy food (the kokanee congregate to spawn and die at just about the same time the eagles begin arriving in late November). The eagle population peaks in late December, and by March most of them have moved on. The best viewing time is in early morning, when the eagles do most of their feeding. The best viewing locations are at the Mineral Ridge Boat Ramp on the south side of the bay and at the Mineral Ridge trailhead, a little farther down the road on Beauty Bay.

Hiking

The **Mineral Ridge National Recreation Trail** leaves from the Mineral Ridge Recreation Area, which you'll come to just after rounding the corner from Wolf Lodge Bay into Beauty Bay on Highway 97. The 3.3-mile nature trail loops past an abandoned mine with some outbuildings. The **Caribou Ridge National Recreation Trail** makes a nice day hike, running 4.6 miles from Beauty Creek Campground up to the Mount Coeur d'Alene Picnic Area. You'll find huckleberries in season along the way, and there are great views of the lake. The trail is moderately difficult, climbing 1,800 vertical feet in four switchbacks up onto the ridge. Beauty Creek Campground is less than a mile down Forest Road 438, which turns off Highway 97 along the east shore of Beauty Bay.

Camping

Lake Coeur d'Alene Camping Resort (10588 E. Wolf Lodge Bay Rd., Coeur d'Alene, 208/664-4471 or 888/664-4471, www.campcda.com) is on the south side of I-90. Among the plethora of amenities: lake access with free small-boat moorage for guests, a heated pool and spa, a playground, hiking and bike trails, laundry and shower facilities, and boat and canoe rentals. The resort has 47 RV sites ($35-45) with hookups, 45 tent sites ($27), and 20 cabins ($56-135).

Along the I-90 frontage road 1.7 miles east of the Wolf Lodge exit (north side of I-90) is **Wolf Lodge Campground** (12329 E. Frontage Rd., Coeur d'Alene, 208/664-2812). The RV park offers 55 grassy sites ($30-35) with hookups on a large, pleasant flat along Wolf Lodge Creek. Tent sites ($20) and cabins ($40-115) are also available.

Also in the area is the U.S. Forest Service **Beauty Creek Campground** (20 sites, $20), just up Forest Road 438 from Beauty Bay.

Food

Folks come from miles around for the juicy steaks at **Wolf Lodge Inn** (11741 E. Frontage Rd., Coeur d'Alene, 208/664-6665, dinner Tues.-Sun., entrées $20-44). Here you can choose from a selection of hand-cut

Bountiful Bike Trails

Over the past few years, north Idaho has become one of the best bicycling destinations anywhere, thanks to the Route of the Hiawatha and the Trail of the Coeur d'Alenes, two unforgettable biking experiences.

ROUTE OF THE HIAWATHA

The 15-mile **Route of the Hiawatha** is a rails-to-trails conversion on the old Milwaukee Road. The main trailhead (accessible via I-90 Exit 5 at Taft, Montana) begins just outside the 8,771-foot St. Paul Pass Tunnel, which means you start and end your ride by cycling through the 1.8-mile tunnel. It's dark in there, so make sure to bring a headlamp or bike light with you. The packed gravel trail includes eight other tunnels and seven railway trestles, the highest 230 feet off the valley floor. Guardrails and a gentle downhill grade make the Route of the Hiawatha an easy and enjoyable ride for nearly everyone. A **shuttle** ($9 adults, $6 ages 6-13) runs from the end of the trail back to the first tunnel several times each day late May-early October.

Bike rentals, including lights and a rack, and **trail passes** ($10 adults, $6 ages 6-13) are available at the trailhead and at **Lookout Pass** ski area (I-90 Exit 0 on the Montana-Idaho border east of Wallace, 208/744-1301, www.skilookout.com).

TRAIL OF THE COEUR D'ALENES

The **Trail of the Coeur d'Alenes,** now an Idaho state park, spans 72 miles across the Idaho Panhandle from Mullan in the east to Plummer in the west. The fully paved trail sits on a former Union Pacific rail bed that's co-managed by the state of Idaho and the Coeur d'Alene Tribe. Since it runs through an old mining district, signs along the way warn users to stay on the trail and eat at designated waysides, which may make some cyclists feel squeamish about riding the trail at all, but state and tribal officials say casual users need not worry about contamination from the mounds of tailings that are still visible.

The best and most scenic part of the mostly flat, free-access trail lies between Pinehurst (milepost 48.7), where it leaves the I-90 corridor, and the old Chatcolet Bridge south of Harrison (near milepost 8). Avid cyclists may want to tackle this section in a long day, but most riders will want to savor shorter out-and-back rides that can be done along any stretch of it. Be sure to carry your own water and snacks, since services are limited in most areas.

Bike rentals and **shuttle service** are available at **Excelsior Cycle & Sport Shop** (21 Railroad Ave., Kellogg, 208/786-3751) and **Pedal Pushers** (101 N. Coeur d'Alene Ave., Harrison, 208/689-3436). Maps and brochures are available at all trailheads, or contact the trail office at **Old Mission State Park** (31732 S. Mission Rd., Cataldo, 208/682-3814).

---

porterhouses, rib eyes, and filet mignon, to name a few. All steaks are flame-broiled over an open-pit cherrywood and tamarack fire and served with salad, bread, and buckaroo beans. Also expect to find tiger shrimp, salmon, lobster and, yes, Rocky Mountain oysters. Reservations are recommended.

LAKE COEUR D'ALENE SCENIC BYWAY

If you continue south from the Wolf Lodge exit around the east shore of the lake, you'll be traveling on the state's designated Lake Coeur d'Alene Scenic Byway. Keep your eyes peeled for ospreys; this area has the largest concentration of them in the western United States. The beautiful birds love the wetlands around the lake's east shore.

Arrow Point

About nine miles south of Beauty Bay en route to Harrison is the **Arrow Point Resort** (4502 S. Arrow Point Rd., Harrison, 877/525-3232, www.arrowpointresort.com, around $200), which occupies a finger of land jutting into the lake. The secluded, upscale resort offers furnished 2-3-bedroom condo units, a marina, beaches, and an indoor pool.

Bell Bay

At the south end of Powderhorn Bay, Highway 97 turns inland briefly before crossing the Coeur d'Alene River and rolling into Harrison. This inland stretch cuts off the nose of a peninsula sticking out into the lake. Here East Point Road turns off the highway and leads west some three miles across wide-open private property to the U.S. Forest Service **Bell Bay Campground** (26 sites, $18, day-use fee $6) on the lakeshore.

Harrison

Until 1889 the southeast shore of Coeur d'Alene Lake was part of the Coeur d'Alene Indian Reservation, but then timber companies cruising the area decided that the shore would be a perfect spot for a sawmill, so they planted a bug in then-president Benjamin Harrison's ear. Harrison "withdrew" a narrow strip of land from the reservation to accommodate the loggers.

The town of **Harrison** was founded in 1891 and named after the president who made it happen. By the turn of the century, Harrison was home to 2,000 people, 11 lumber mills, a dozen saloons, and a thriving red-light district. Steamboats plying Coeur d'Alene Lake made Harrison a major port of call, and at one point it was the largest population center on the lake. But fire devastated the town in 1917, and shortly thereafter the arrival of railroads rendered the steamboats obsolete. The local timber industry dwindled, and Harrison's glory days were over.

Today the town's 300-some residents rely on tourism to feed the coffers. Fishing and boating were long the primary draws, but increasing numbers of cyclists are using Harrison as a base camp for the Trail of the Coeur d'Alenes. Sunsets are stupendous here too. If you're looking for a refuge from the hectic tourist scene on the north shore of the lake, Harrison offers it.

If you're here to ride, **Pedal Pushers** (101 N. Coeur d'Alene Ave., Harrison, 208/689-3436, www.bikenorthidaho.com) is the place to get bike gear and other information. The shop rents bikes (road bikes $10 per hour, two-hour minimum) and related equipment like helmets and such. It also offers repairs and runs a seasonal shuttle service for the Trail of the Coeur d'Alenes.

Cyclists and other travelers congregate at the **Osprey Inn** (134 Frederick Ave.,

Chain of Lakes near Coeur d'Alene

Harrison, 208/689-9502, www.ospreyinn. com, $80-120). Built in 1915, the bed-and-breakfast inn was originally a boardinghouse for lumberjacks. Each of the five reconstructed guest rooms has a private bath with a shower. Rates include a full breakfast.

Chain of Lakes Route

South of Harrison, Highway 97 runs into a T intersection with Highway 3. If you turn right, you'll end up in St. Maries. Turn left to stay on the designated scenic byway, which takes you up the South Fork Coeur d'Alene River past 10 lakes. Most of the wetlands in this Chain of Lakes area are included in the **Coeur d'Alene River Wildlife Management Area,** a favorite stopover for migratory waterfowl.

The Silver Valley

East of Coeur d'Alene, I-90 climbs Fourth of July Pass and drops down the other side into the valley of the South Fork Coeur d'Alene River. In 1859, Jesuit missionary Pierre Jean de Smet described this valley as a verdant paradise: "Imagine thick, untrodden forest, strewn with thousands of trees thrown down by age and storms in every direction, where the path is scarcely visible." But this almost primeval scene was not to last. In 1885, prospector Noah Kellogg discovered a huge vein of a lead-silver-zinc ore called galena near the present-day town of Wardner. The find brought miners and mining companies flooding into the area, burrowing into the hills like mad, money-hungry moles. Over the next 100 years, more than $5 billion in precious metals would be taken from the earth, making "The Silver Valley" one of the most lucrative mining districts in world history, while at the same time turning it into a toxic waste dump. Portions of the once verdant forests of the South Fork were cut down for houses, mine timbers, and railroad ties. But that was just the beginning. In 1917 the first lead smelter was built near the Bunker Hill mine so that ore could be processed on-site. The U.S. Environmental Protection Agency's Superfund site description tersely outlines the consequences:

During the majority of time the smelters were operating, few environmental protection procedures or controls were used. As a result, there is widespread contamination of soil, water, and air from lead and other heavy metals.

The smelters belched toxic plumes into the air, and the sulfur dioxide fallout killed what vegetation was left on the hillside. Water pollution was an even greater problem. Until 1938, all residues from the Bunker Hill's mine tailings were discharged directly into the Coeur d'Alene River. Thereafter, the wastes were diverted into an unlined settling pond that leaked toxic effluent into the groundwater. In addition, spring floods routinely washed heavy metals from tailings piles into the river and on downstream. Between the 1880s and the 1960s, an estimated 72 million tons of contaminated tailings ended up in the Coeur d'Alene River system; today scientists debate the potential health threat of the heavy-metal sludge coating the bottom of Coeur d'Alene Lake.

Meanwhile, in the mid-1970s, it was discovered that lead had found its way into the blood of the valley's children in alarming concentrations. A class-action suit brought by a number of parents against Gulf Resources and Chemical Corporation, then-owner of the Bunker Hill mine, ended in an out-of-court settlement. But the lead problem persists here today, as evidenced by the Panhandle Health District's publication *Coeur d'Alene River*

the old Cataldo mission

System and Heavy Metal Exposure, A Public Awareness Message. Among other precautions, the pamphlet advises local residents:

> Clean shoes and change soil-stained clothes before going home. Keep soiled clothing in a plastic bag and launder it separate from the rest of your wash. Don't can whole fish caught from the lower Coeur d'Alene River system. Don't eat large amounts of fish, water fowl, or aquatic plants.

The Bunker Hill smelters shut down in 1981, pulling the rug out from under the local economy and leaving behind one of the country's largest Superfund toxic-cleanup sites. A 1992 report by the U.S. Geological Survey called the Coeur d'Alene River drainage the worst example of heavy-metal pollution in the world. Gulf conveniently declared bankruptcy, sticking taxpayers with the cleanup tab.

The towering smokestacks of the Bunker

CATALDO AND VICINITY
★ Old Mission State Park

Old Mission State Park (31732 S. Mission Rd., Cataldo, 208/682-3814, 8am-6pm daily summer, 9am-5pm daily in other seasons, $5 fee) is at I-90 Exit 39. Even from a distance the old Cataldo mission, visible from I-90, is powerful and striking. The Greek Revival-style structure sits atop a grassy hill that slopes down to the placid waters of the South Fork of the Coeur d'Alene River. It fits naturally into its surroundings, a tribute to the man who designed and helped build the mission and served as its first spiritual leader, Father Antonio Ravalli, born May 16, 1812, in Ferrara, Italy. Ravalli was ordained as a Jesuit priest in 1843 and sent to work with the Coeur d'Alene Indians alongside Father Pierre Jean de Smet. When Ravalli arrived, de Smet's mission was located on the St. Joe River near present-day St. Maries, but the regular floods (a phenomenon that persists today) caused de Smet to look for a higher and drier spot. Ravalli was assigned the task of supervising the relocation.

The park's literature calls Ravalli a Renaissance man, a title that seemed to fit him perfectly. By the time he reached Idaho at the age of 31, Ravalli had studied literature, philosophy, theology, mathematics, science, medicine, art, and architecture. The Native Americans and missionaries began building the mission in 1847, following Ravalli's plans, out of hand-hewn timbers held together with wooden pegs. The foot-thick walls were made of woven straw and river mud. The result, formally called the Mission of the Sacred Heart, is the oldest building still standing in Idaho.

The exterior is beautiful, but Ravalli's artistic handiwork and creativity really shine inside. Out on the wild frontier, with no budget to speak of, Ravalli became a master at decorating on the cheap. See that marble altar? It's actually made of wood, carefully painted by Ravalli to simulate marble. And what about those cast-iron chandeliers? They're tin, cut into elegant patterns by the artistic priest. The ceiling was dyed with huckleberry juice.

Ravalli also painted the side altars with scenes depicting heaven and hell and carved the statues of the Virgin Mary and Saint John the Evangelist standing on either side of the altar.

The mission opened for worship in 1853 and operated for 23 years. During that time it served as a welcome resting place for Native Americans, pioneers, John Mullan's road-building crew, and military contingents. Father Joseph Cataldo, a strong and popular leader of Idaho's Roman Catholics, took the reins in 1865; the nearby town is named in his honor. In 1876, mission activities were relocated to DeSmet in a political move that was heartbreaking for the mission's Native American congregation.

Today, the mission serves as the centerpiece of an outstanding state historic park. A modern interpretive center screens a short film illustrating the mission's history and offers exhibits about the Coeur d'Alene Indians and the Jesuits. Self-guided interpretive trails lead across the grounds to natural features and points of historical interest.

KELLOGG AND VICINITY

In attempting to rise anew from the ashes of its mining industry, Kellogg took two major steps: It replaced the narrow winding road up to the local ski hill with the world's longest gondola, which whisks skiers up some 3,400 vertical feet in 3.1 miles to the snowy slopes, and it gave the town a partial face-lift, turning it into a Bavarian-themed village. Uptown Kellogg is a charming historic district, but some of the storefronts now sit vacant as most of the attention is given to the area surrounding the burgeoning Silver Mountain Resort.

Silver Mountain

There has been a ski area on the slopes of Kellogg and Wardner Peaks since the late 1960s. First called Jackass (for Noah Kellogg's famous donkey), then Silverhorn, the resort struggled because many people didn't want to drive the steep, circuitous road leading to the base area from Kellogg. When the mines shut down in the early 1980s, developing **Silver**

skiing at Silver Mountain in Kellogg

holidays, $20 adults, $18 youth and seniors) for two-hour sessions. Scenic gondola rides ($18 adults, $14 youth and seniors) are possible year-round.

In summer, the resort is open weekends and holidays only and hosts concerts and other events in its mountaintop amphitheater. Other summertime draws include gondola-served hiking and mountain biking on an extensive, newly expanded trail system (same rates as above apply).

The resort also has an indoor water park connected to the main lodge. **Silver Rapids Water Park** is an expansive year-round aqua playground featuring a continuous surf wave, a flowing river, waterslides, private cabanas, and a small restaurant with hot tubs, but you must be a guest of the resort's Morning Star Lodge to partake in the fun. Packages start at around $200 for four people, which include a studio suite in the lodge and a two-day pass to the water park. Day-use for nonguests can be arranged for parties of 15 or more.

Mountain into a tourist destination represented the city's best hope for economic recovery. The late city councilman Wayne Ross envisioned an aerial tramway that would bypass the road and take visitors directly from town to the mountaintop. He successfully negotiated funding, and in 1990 the new, improved **Silver Mountain Ski Resort** (610 Bunker Ave., Kellogg, at I-90 Exit 49, 866/344-2675, www.silvermt.com, 9am-4pm daily late Nov.-late Mar., lift tickets $53 ages 18-61, $38 ages 7-17, $43 over age 61, free under age 7), with the world's longest single-stage gondola (3.1 miles), opened.

The area gets around 300 inches of snow per year on average. The resort has 1,500 acres with a 2,200-foot vertical drop and a longest run of 2.5 miles. Intermediate runs are most prevalent, but 40 percent of the runs are either advanced or expert. Besides the gondola, the mountain is served by one fixed-grip quad, two triple chairs, two double chairs, and a surface lift. The gondolas also take people up to the four-lane tubing hill (Sat.-Sun. and

Bunker Hill Staff House Museum

Otherwise known as the Shoshone County Mining and Smelting Museum, **Bunker Hill Staff House Museum** (820 McKinley Ave., Kellogg, 208/786-4141, 10am-6pm Tues.-Sun. late May-Sept., small entrance fee) occupies the former staff house for resident and visiting bigwigs of the Bunker Hill & Sullivan Mine Co. The house was built in 1906 for a manager of the Bunker Hill mine. Exhibits cover the town's mining history, with an emphasis on Bunker Hill itself. A great collection of old photos includes one of a burro, supposedly Noah Kellogg's famous sidekick. Another display lists the Bunker Hill's staggering statistics: 1,900 tons of ore mined daily; 400 tons of waste rock removed daily; 3,500 gallons of water expelled per minute; 160,000 cubic feet of air circulated each minute. During the mine's 96-year life span, 37 million tons of ore were excavated, yielding more than 165 million ounces of silver, as well as copious amounts of lead and zinc. Don't forget to check out the ingenious 3-D model of Bunker Hill mine's enormous underground labyrinth in the basement.

Wardner

To see where it all began, take Kellogg's Division Street up the hill into Milo Gulch to the town of **Wardner** (population 185). Just 1,000 yards up the gulch from today's Wardner City Hall, Noah Kellogg found the gleaming rock that sparked the Silver Valley's mining boom. In "downtown" Wardner, locals keep the memories of the mining days alive at **Wardner Gift Shop and Memorabilia Museum** (625 Main St., Wardner, 208/786-2641). The free museum has a fascinating collection of photographs and mining artifacts.

Noah Kellogg's Grave

On the way up Division Street heading toward Wardner, you'll spot signs directing you east (left) up the flanks of the mountain to the local cemetery. Here you'll find **Noah Kellogg's grave,** marked by a fence and a modern monument that seems out of place. It's a poignant spot to ponder the dead miners who couldn't take their wealth with them, and the costs of their obsession on the scarred valley below.

Sunshine Mine Memorial

The Sunshine Mine is recognized as the world's all-time greatest silver producer. But on May 2, 1972, extraction of that bounty exacted a horrific price. Sometime after 11am, a fire broke out more than 3,000 feet down in the mine's depths. Warnings spread as soon as the first smoke was noticed. Those among the 173 miners at work that day who got word of the blaze bolted for the hoists that would take them toward the surface. Failure of a mine-wide alarm system prevented others from getting the warning until it was too late. Smoke and carbon monoxide soon asphyxiated the hoist operators, trapping the miners left beneath them. Despite the valiant efforts of local, national, and even international rescue workers, 91 miners died in the tragedy.

Just east of Kellogg, off I-90 Exit 54, is the **Sunshine Mine Memorial,** a huge sculpture of a miner at work dedicated to those who died in the disaster.

Accommodations

On the low-priced end of the spectrum, you'll find the **Trail Motel** (206 W. Cameron Ave., Kellogg, 208/784-1161, from $45 d) on the north side of I-90. This no-frills motor inn allows pets.

GuestHouse Inn & Suites (601 Bunker Ave., Kellogg, 208/783-1234, from $89 d) is especially noteworthy for its convenient location adjacent to the Silver Mountain gondola. Amenities at the newish 61-room hotel include an indoor pool and spa, free continental breakfast, cable TV with HBO, a guest laundry, and ski and bike storage. Another good choice in this price range is the **Silverhorn Motor Inn** (699 W. Cameron Ave., Kellogg, 208/783-1151 or 800/437-6437, www.silverhornmotorinn.com, from $89 d). It offers an on-site restaurant, laundry services, and a big hot tub. Pets are allowed.

Silver Mountain Resort's ★ **Morning Star Lodge** (610 Bunker Ave., Kellogg, 208/783-1111 or 866/344-2675, www.silvermt.com, $139-349) offers plush condo-style suites ranging from studio units to lavish loft suites. The resort has several skiing and water-park packages as well as cheaper off-season rates. Amenities include kitchens, decks, and preferential treatment at the resort's facilities.

Food and Drink

Down at the gondola base, **Noah's Canteen** (610 Bunker Ave., Kellogg, 208/783-2440, lunch and dinner daily, entrées $12-29) serves upscale pub fare in a casual dining room with a roaring fireplace. The menu has lots of steaks, seafood, burgers, wraps, and pizza, and the adjacent bar pours around a dozen microbrews on tap.

Silver Spoon Restaurant (699 W. Cameron Ave., Kellogg, 208/783-1151, 6am-9pm daily, under $10), at the Silverhorn Motor Inn, offers goopy cinnamon rolls, big egg breakfasts, huckleberry pancakes, and other homespun fare throughout the day.

In Uptown Kellogg, you'll find ★ **Moose Creek Grill** (12 Emerson Ln., Kellogg, 208/783-2625, www.moosecreekgrill.com, dinner from 4pm Wed.-Sun., $12-29) in an old blue house. This casual restaurant serves excellent burgers, steaks, salads, pork chops, fish tacos, and freshly made pasta. Try the delish dark chocolate turtle cake for dessert. Lots of regional microbrews and wines by the glass are available to wash everything down.

Information

The **Historic Silver Valley Chamber of Commerce** operates a **visitors center** (10 Station Ave., Kellogg, 208/784-0821, www.silvervalleychamber.com) where you can get brochures and general information about the area.

★ WALLACE

East of Kellogg, I-90 climbs through Osburn to Wallace. Of all the towns in the Silver Valley, Wallace feels most like the quintessential mining town. It is a compact place where the valley narrows into a tight canyon, forcing the town to creep off the canyon floor and up the steep forested slopes. In the small

downtown, you'll find a multitude of well-preserved 19th-century buildings. As a matter of fact, the entire town is listed on the National Register of Historic Places. This colorful yet checkered downtown corridor is packed with antiques shops, old saloons, restaurants, and weird museums, making it a great place to get lost in time.

Up on the lofty wooded hill are old miners' cabins and newer homes. This is where Hollywood starlet Lana Turner spent her early years, in a house overlooking the rough-and-tumble town. Sometimes after a storm, when the mist hangs over the hillsides and raindrops drip off the rooftops and pines, the town takes on an almost tangible tranquility. Walk up the rickety wooden stairs, past the small clapboard houses, and you'll half expect to find a grizzled old prospector sitting on his front porch, plucking the melancholy strains of "My Darling Clementine" on a banjo. It's almost enough to make you want to trade in the Lexus for a pickax and mule.

Museums

Three museums downtown commemorate Wallace's three greatest industries. The **Wallace District Mining Museum** (509 Bank St., Wallace, 208/556-1592, 10am-5pm

winter in downtown Wallace

daily May-Labor Day weekend, 10am-5pm Mon.-Sat., 10am-3pm Sun. Apr. and Sept.-Oct., 10am-5pm Mon.-Fri., 10am-3pm Sat.-Sun. Nov.-Mar., $3 adults, $1 ages 6-17, $7 family) offers exhibits about mining, miners, and the hard-rock life they led during the valley's boom days. You can ponder historical photos and artifacts and watch two different videos on the valley's mining history. More than one billion ounces of silver were mined in the region over the course of a century. That's 62.5 million pounds, or 31,250 tons.

The **Northern Pacific Depot Railroad Museum** (6th and Pine St., Wallace, 208/752-0111, 9am-7pm daily summer, reduced hours spring and fall, closed Oct. 31-Mar. 15, $2 adults, $1.50 over age 59, $1 ages 6-16, $6 family) occupies the beautiful château-style 1901 Northern Pacific Depot. Bricks used in the building's construction were imported from China and destined for a fancy Tacoma hotel, but that project never got off the ground and the bricks ended up here. Until 1980, the Northern Pacific's Yellowstone Park Line stopped at this depot on its run between Chicago and Seattle. In 1986 the depot was carefully moved to its present site after the new I-90 threatened to run right over it. Old railroad photos and paraphernalia fill the museum. One of the most interesting exhibits is a huge glass route map that once hung in another Northern Pacific depot.

Perhaps the most interesting of the three museums is the **Oasis Bordello Museum** (605 Cedar St., Wallace, 208/753-0801, 10am-5pm Mon.-Sat., 11am-3pm Sun. May-early Oct., tour $5). Mining towns have historically been populated with a far higher percentage of men than women, and this imbalance created numerous business opportunities for enterprising women of questionable virtue. The Oasis was just one of several brothels that once lined this end of town. Interestingly enough, the Oasis remained in business until 1988, which was 15 years after Idaho's governor officially proclaimed prostitution illegal in the state and 93 years after the first

brothel opened. The workers apparently left in a hurry, and the rooms have been preserved as they were when abandoned.

The 20-minute upstairs tour offers many interesting anecdotes, like the fact that in 1982 the Oasis women bought the town a new police car with money saved from their earnings. Their relatively recent departure takes this museum out of the realm of a charming Western anachronism and into the somewhat seedier reality of the modern world. Nothing on the tour is particularly graphic or offensive, but it's probably better suited for adults. Entry is free to the ground-floor store, which sells assorted brothel souvenirs such as shirts, hats, and beer koozies.

Sierra Silver Mine Tour

Rarely can someone not drawing a paycheck from a mining company go down the shafts for a look around. The 75-minute **Sierra Silver Mine Tour** (420 5th St., Wallace, 208/752-5151, www.silverminetour.org, every 30 minutes 10am-4pm daily May-early Oct., $15 adults, $13 seniors, $8.50 ages 4-16, $47 family of two adults with two or more kids) allows you to do just that. The mine you'll explore was once an operating silver mine. From Wallace, you'll board a trolley for the short ride to the mine, then don hard hats and make your way down into the cool, dark depths. Guides explain the mining process, history, and various techniques.

Recreation

The Route of the Hiawatha mountain bike trail goes right through Wallace along its 15-mile run to the Montana border. In summer, the trail brings to town an endless flow of Lycra-attired bicyclists, who mingle with leather-clad Harley riders at the sidewalk cafés.

For information on the local backcountry and trail maps for the areas on both the North and South Forks of the Coeur d'Alene River, contact the U.S. Forest Service's **Coeur d'Alene River Ranger District Silver Valley Office** (Smelterville, 208/783-2363).

Entertainment

Sixth Street Melodrama (212 6th St., Wallace, 208/752-8871, www.sixthstreetmelodrama.com, tickets $15-18) is a long-running local thespian troupe. In summer, the players present old-fashioned melodrama with plenty of audience participation. In winter and spring, the company offers more serious performances and musicals. Check the website for a current playbill and schedule.

Accommodations

The Brooks Hotel (500 Cedar St., Wallace, 208/556-1571, www.thebrookshotel.com, from $70 d) is the grande dame of the old Wallace hotels, but she's getting a little scruffy behind the ears. Off the lobby is a good family restaurant serving three meals a day. **Stardust Motel** (410 Pine St., Wallace, 208/752-1213, $50-90) is a retro motor inn that's also hit or miss in the cleanliness department, but the place is affordable, and you could easily stumble back to your room from the saloons thanks to the motel's close proximity to downtown.

Wallace Inn (100 Front St., Wallace, 208/752-1252 or 800/643-2386, from $129 d) is the most modern and upscale lodging option in town. Amenities include a heated indoor pool and jetted tub, a sauna and steam rooms, and a restaurant. The inn offers free shuttle service to Lookout Pass Recreation Area.

The ★ **Beale House Bed & Breakfast** (107 Cedar St., Wallace, 208/752-7151 or 888/752-7151, from $170) occupies a 1904 Victorian residence in a quiet residential neighborhood. The house has a long and distinguished history, well documented in a collection of old photographs available for perusal. A crackling fireplace inside and a bubbling hot tub outside combine to take the chill off those après-ski evenings. Four of the five guest rooms share baths. Rates include full breakfast. Children and pets are not allowed.

If you're really into privacy, why not rent an entire house? **The Bungalow at 214 Cedar** (214 Cedar St., Wallace, 208/512-7686) is a Victorian-era home near downtown with three bedrooms and a full kitchen. You can rent the house for $105 per night per couple, $15 for each additional person up to eight guests. You'll have to leave a $500 deposit, all of which is refundable except for a $50 cleaning fee.

Camping and RVing

Wallace RV Park (108 Nine Mile Rd., Wallace, 208/753-7121), just across I-90 from downtown, offers 43 RV sites ($30) with hookups, cabins ($40), and a few tent sites ($20). Amenities include showers, restrooms, a laundry room, a game room, and a saloon.

Food and Drink

Smoke House Barbecue & Saloon (424 6th St., Wallace, 208/659-7539, 11am-9pm daily, entrées $9-27), a historic bar along the main drag, dishes up applewood-smoked pork ribs, pulled pork sandwiches, bison, wild Alaskan salmon, and brisket. Sides include red beans and rice, coleslaw, and macaroni and cheese. Service here can be spotty, but the beer is cold and the food is good enough to make up for a little forgetfulness.

Locals call Wallace the "Center of the Universe," which might help to explain why the **Red Light Garage** (5th St. and Pine St., Wallace, 208/556-0575, breakfast, lunch, and dinner daily, breakfast under $10) has a spaceship in its parking lot. This funky little restaurant and junk store, in a former service station, serves burgers, burritos, wraps, and a damn good huckleberry milkshake. You can also get breakfast items in the morning, like one big huckleberry pancake, egg-filled burritos, and freshly baked cinnamon rolls, but the coffee could peel the chrome off your Harley's tailpipe. If you're in a hurry, this might not be the place for you, because the servers and cooks appear to have lead in their pants.

★ **The Fainting Goat** (516 Bank St., Wallace, 208/556-1650, www.faintinggoatwinebar.com, lunch and dinner daily, $7-14) has drastically changed the dining scene in town since it opened in 2013. This hip wine bar and restaurant offers high-end cuisine as far as Wallace goes. The menu has standout dishes like Cornish game hen brushed with pumpkin seed pesto, duck tacos, and meatloaf with balsamic glaze and chunky tomato jam. You also can get a rustic board with assorted cheeses and cured meats, to go with a glass of vino poured from the 16-bottle wine-dispensing machine. If wine is not your thing, the place also has regional craft beers and hard ciders.

Wallace Brewing Company (610 Bank St., Wallace, 208/660-3430, www.wallacebrewing.com, 1pm-6pm Sun.-Thurs., 1pm-8pm Fri.-Sat.) is the place to go for locally handcrafted beers. The delicious array of flagship and seasonal brews includes Jack Leg Stout, Vindicator IPA, and Red Light, a honey wheat lager that pays homage to the town's former ladies of the night.

Information

Wallace Chamber of Commerce (10 River St., Wallace, 208/753-7151, www.wallaceidahochamber.com) operates a visitors center right off I-90 Exit 61. Next door you'll find the **Mining Heritage Exhibition,** a free park with a collection of old mining equipment and some picnic tables.

LOOKOUT PASS

Lookout Pass Ski and Recreation Area (208/744-1301, www.skilookout.com, 9am-4pm daily mid-Dec.-New Year, 9am-4pm Thurs.-Sun. the rest of the season, closed Christmas Day), at I-90 Exit 0, right on the state line, may be small in stature, but it's big in heart. The state's second-oldest ski area, Lookout has been faithfully serving the Silver Valley since 1938. Over much of its life, the area owed its existence to the volunteer efforts of the Idaho Ski Club and others. It is famous

for its family-friendly atmosphere and offers skiing, snowmobiling, and other winter activities as well as summer fun like mountain biking. It's the main outfitting point for the Route of the Hiawatha cycling trail.

Alpine Skiing

Although this is a humble mountain in some ways, the snow quality and quantity (a whopping 387 inches per year average) are excellent, and the sweeping views into two states provide a real "high mountain" feeling, despite a peak elevation under 6,000 feet. Lookout Pass recently expanded a bit and now has about 18 runs (the longest is 1.2 miles) and 1,150 feet of vertical drop served by a rope tow and two double chairs. The mountain's backside sports a snowboard and ski terrain park.

Lift tickets (weekend $40 adults, $29 juniors and seniors) won't break your budget, and midweek rates are a few bucks less. Half-day tickets and various special promotional tickets are available too. You can also find ski and snowboard rentals, lessons, and day care services.

The day lodge is cozy and clean, offering both food and drink. The bar's lively social scene is especially friendly and intimate, since most of the patrons are locals who know one another. The season here generally runs mid-November-late March or early April.

Cross-Country Skiing

A 16-mile system of cross-country ski trails, ranging in difficulty from beginner to advanced, is accessible from the resort's base area. Some are shared with snowmobiles. Cross-country skiers can purchase a single-ride lift ticket ($10) and ski their way back down to the base area on the trails.

U.S. 95 to Lake Pend Oreille

ATHOL AND VICINITY
★ Silverwood Theme Park

Silverwood Theme Park (27843 N. U.S. 95, Athol, 208/683-3400, www.silverwood-themepark.com, Sat.-Sun. early and late in the season, daily in peak season, early May-Oct., $46.99 ages 8-64, $23.99 ages 3-7 and seniors), a 700-acre amusement park, is literally a scream. Let's see you keep your mouth shut on that upside-down corkscrew roller coaster, or on Tremors, a coaster that plummets into the bowels of the earth, or on Timber Terror, a 55-mph wooden ride sure to please even the most obsessed roller-coaster buff. Monster, Roundup, Scrambler, Skydiver, and other "high-intensity" rides will scare the living daylights out of you, and the park recently added Aftershock, a new coaster that drops 177 feet at 65 mph into three upside-down loops. Don't miss the magic show or the ice spectacular. There's even a Wild West train ride that runs around a wooded section of the park, simulated gunfight included. Silverwood also operates **Boulder Beach** water park, with waterslides, a wave pool, a lazy river, and a tree house-themed kids area. Admission is included in the Silverwood rates.

Those wanting to make a week or weekend of it will find the park's own 132-site RV park ($39) right across the street. Amenities include full hookups, shaded sites, showers, picnic tables, volleyball courts, horseshoe pits, barbecue grills, a laundry, and a small store with propane. Tenters are welcome, with a maximum of two tents per site ($30). Guests receive discounted admission to the amusement park.

Farragut State Park

During World War II the 4,000-acre **Farragut State Park** (13550 E. Hwy. 54, Athol, 208/683-2425, day-use $5), on the southern shores of Lake Pend Oreille, had a large U.S. Naval Training Center. The site was supposedly "discovered" by Eleanor Roosevelt on a flight from Washington, DC, to Seattle. FDR was looking for an inland body of water to train submariners in safety, away from the eyes and ears of the enemies. Eleanor saw Lake Pend Oreille and described it to her husband, who deemed it perfect for the task. Construction of the base began in 1942. By the fall of that year, the base's population of 55,000 military personnel made it the second-largest naval training facility in the country and the largest "city" in Idaho. At war's end the base was decommissioned, and in 1964 Farragut State Park was established, named after Civil War hero Admiral David Farragut (1801-1870), whose important victories on the Gulf Coast and Mississippi River allowed the Union Army to capture and control the region.

Today the sprawling park, with its many long loop roads and open areas, still retains a military-base ambience. Four separate campgrounds have a total of 135 sites ($14-40) plus several camping cabins ($50-55) that can sleep up to five; the Whitetail Campground ($16-18) is closest to the lake, the park's prime recreational attraction. Sunbathing and splashing are favorite activities, and a concessionaire rents pedal boats, rafts, and beach chairs. A boat-launching area is available for those hauling their own vessels. Those who prefer terra firma fun can explore the park's hiking, biking, and horseback-riding trails, and you can rent horses at the Thimbleberry Group Area, off Highway 54 toward the west end of the park. The north-side trails wind through beautiful woods, while the south-side trails skirt the lakeshore. In winter, the park sets and grooms 10 miles of mostly flat cross-country ski trails. Unusual offerings here include a model-airplane flying field and a shooting range often used by black-powder enthusiasts (watch for the occasional cannon shot). To get to the park, take Highway 54 four miles east from U.S. 95 at Athol.

Bayview

The little fishing village of **Bayview** is an uncrowded hideaway. Docks, boats, and fishing resorts ring the calm waters of Scenic Bay, and the views across the lake are superb. Front and center on the water is friendly **Boileau's Resort and Marina** (208/683-2213), where you can walk out on the dock to the marina bar and grill for a sandwich, a can of beer, and an earful of fish stories. The campground has RV sites ($30-40) with full hookups.

Although the Naval Training Center has disappeared, the Navy still makes good use of Lake Pend Oreille for submarine research and development. On the south edge of Bayview is the **Naval Surface Warfare Center, Acoustic Research Detachment,** where the Navy develops stealth technology for submarines. Lake Pend Oreille is the ideal spot for such work for a number of reasons, including its deep, still water; flat bottom contour; isothermal temperature profile; low ambient noise; low echo interference; and large, unobstructed operating areas.

To get to Bayview, continue on Highway 54 from Athol through Farragut State Park. Coming from the north, turn east off U.S. 95 at Careywood.

COCOLALLA, SAGLE, AND VICINITY
Cocolalla Lake

Stretching between the towns of Cocolalla and Westmond, 800-acre **Cocolalla Lake** attracts anglers all year. They come to round up the usual suspects: rainbow, cutthroat, brown, and brook trout; channel catfish; largemouth bass; crappie; and perch. In winter, you'll see the diehards out on the lake bundled up in their snowsuits, drilling holes through the ice to sink a line. In summer, you can launch a boat onto the lake from a ramp at the northeast end.

Round Lake State Park

Small **Round Lake State Park** (208/263-3489, day-use $5) is two miles down Dufort Road, which turns west off U.S. 95 four miles north of Cocolalla. You'll find 53 wooded campsites ($12-29) ringing beautiful, 58-acre Round Lake. The shallow lake warms up in summer, making for pleasant swimming. Drop a line for brook and rainbow trout, largemouth bass, sunfish, perch, bullhead, and crappie; ice fishing is popular in winter. Hikers and cross-country skiers enjoy seven miles of trails that follow the lakeshore or head off into the forest through lush stands of western red cedar, western hemlock, ponderosa pine, Douglas fir, and western larch. Keep your eyes peeled for some of the park's abundant resident wildlife. Winter also brings out ice skaters and sledders; areas are specifically maintained for both activities.

Sagle and Garfield Bay

Another goofy postal story explains **Sagle**'s name. Back in 1900, the first resident to apply for a post office applied for the name Eagle. That name was already taken, so he changed it to Sagle. The town marks the turnoff to **Garfield Bay,** a great out-of-the-way spot with a couple of character-laden bar and grills, some campgrounds, and a small golf course.

Just as you come into Garfield Bay from Sagle, a road branches left and climbs the hill to the north. A short distance down that road, Forest Road 532 branches off to the right and leads to the **Mineral Point Interpretive Trail** (Trail 82), a short and pleasant nature trail winding through groves of Douglas fir, ponderosa pine, Pacific yew, and western red cedar. Along the way you'll find benches where you can sit and enjoy superb views of the lake. This peaceful spot is perfect for a picnic, and chances are good you'll have it all to yourself. The trail connects with another that leads down to the water at the U.S. Forest Service **Green Bay Campground** (11 sites, free).

Bottle Bay

This major bay opening onto the northern arm of Lake Pend Oreille is a favorite stopoff of cruise boats and anglers. **Bottle Bay Resort & Marina** (115 Resort Rd., Sagle,

208/263-5916) has a restaurant and a collection of vacation cabins (from $139 d). The resort also rents out canoes, kayaks, and paddleboats.

Bottle Bay can be reached via Bottle Bay Road (accessed from Sagle or from just across the long bridge from Sandpoint) or via a cutoff from Garfield Bay Road. Bottle Bay Road leads around the lakeshore, approaching Bottle Bay from the north; Garfield Bay Road winds around Gold Mountain and finds its way up to Bottle Bay from the south.

Sandpoint and Vicinity

Sandpoint and Lake Pend Oreille seem to sneak up on you traveling north on U.S. 95, thanks to the dense woods on either side of the highway. Then the road rounds the last bend and the striking panoramic view of this mountain-ringed, brilliant-blue lake comes into sight. To get to downtown Sandpoint from Sagle, you have to drive right across the water on an aptly named long bridge.

The town perches on the lake's northwest shore, on a "sandy point" first noted by Canadian fur trapper and geographer David Thompson in 1808, the same year that the first nonnative settlement was established. When the railroads and timber companies found their way here, the town took root. It's still a mill town, but a couple of other elements add to the economic and cultural mix.

Back in the 1970s, artists discovered the town's cheap rents and stunning surroundings, and thus began a thriving arts community that's still going strong today. Then recreation-minded visitors latched on to the area's great skiing, fishing, and other outdoor activities. Today, the logger, artist, and outdoor recreationist are all part of a pleasantly diverse cultural tapestry.

Sandpoint is full of decent restaurants and lively pubs, and it offers a full calendar of performing arts events.

SIGHTS
Bonner County Historical Museum

A good place to start your study of Sandpoint is the **Bonner County Historical Museum**

Long Bridge leading into Sandpoint

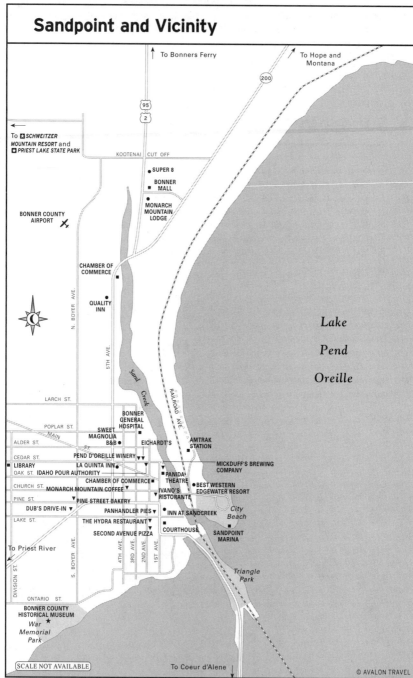

Sandpoint and Vicinity

To Bonners Ferry

To Hope and Montana

200

95
2

Kootenai Cut Off

To ✚ SCHWEITZER
MOUNTAIN RESORT and
✚ PRIEST LAKE STATE PARK

SUPER 8

BONNER
MALL

MONARCH
MOUNTAIN
LODGE

BONNER COUNTY
AIRPORT ✈

CHAMBER OF
COMMERCE

N. BOYER AVE.

QUALITY
INN

5TH AVE.

Sand Creek

RAILROAD AVE.

Lake

Pend

Oreille

LARCH ST.

POPLAR ST.

BONNER
GENERAL
HOSPITAL

SWEET
MAGNOLIA
B&B

EICHARDT'S

AMTRAK
STATION

MAIN ST.

ALDER ST.

CEDAR ST.

LIBRARY

OAK ST. IDAHO POUR AUTHORITY

PEND D'OREILLE WINERY

LA QUINTA INN

MICKDUFF'S BREWING
COMPANY

CHAMBER OF COMMERCE

MONARCH MOUNTAIN COFFEE

PANIDA
THEATRE

CHURCH ST.

PINE ST.

PINE STREET BAKERY

IVANO'S
RISTORANTE

BEST WESTERN
EDGEWATER RESORT

DUB'S DRIVE-IN

PANHANDLER PIES

INN AT SANDCREEK

City
Beach

LAKE ST.

THE HYDRA RESTAURANT

SECOND AVENUE PIZZA

COURTHOUSE

SANDPOINT
MARINA

To Priest River

S. BOYER AVE.

4TH AVE.

3RD AVE.

2ND AVE.

1ST AVE.

Triangle
Park

DIVISION ST.

ONTARIO ST.

BONNER COUNTY
HISTORICAL MUSEUM

War ★
Memorial
Park

SCALE NOT AVAILABLE

To Coeur d'Alene

© AVALON TRAVEL

(Lakeview Park, 611 S. Ella Ave., Sandpoint, 208/263-2344, 10am-4pm Tues.-Sat., reduced hours in winter, $4 adults, $1 ages 6-18, free under age 6). Exhibits explain the region's history, beginning with the indigenous Kootenai peoples and continuing through the days of steamboats and railroads. You also can ask the friendly volunteers about the Pend Oreille Paddler, a supposed lake creature that pops its head up every now and then.

LAKE PEND OREILLE RECREATION

Largest of the state's lakes, **Pend Oreille** is 43 miles long and more than 1,100 feet deep in places. In summer, swimmers splash along the shores, sailors glide silently across the clear waters, water-skiers skim over the surface, and anglers troll the depths searching for some of the 14 species of resident game fish.

City Beach

As soon as the hot summer sun arrives, it seems the whole town heads for **City Beach.** On a July weekend you'll find blankets covering nearly every square inch of this relatively small spit of sand extending out into Lake Pend Oreille. Besides the beach itself, the recreation area includes a playground; areas for basketball, volleyball, and picnicking; and docks from where the lake cruise ships depart. In winter, City Beach takes on a quieter, more contemplative air, but it's still a great place to watch the whitecaps on the water. The beach is at the foot of Bridge Street, off U.S. 95 downtown.

Boat Rentals

Sandpoint Marina (120 E. Lake St., Sandpoint, 208/263-1535) at Dover Bay rents ski boats and pontoon boats ($375-650 per day). Hourly rentals with a two-hour minimum are available too. The marina also rents kayaks, canoes, and water-ski equipment.

Scenic Boat Cruises

To get a duck's-eye view of Sandpoint, hook up with **Lake Pend Oreille Cruises** (208/255-5253, www.lakependoreillecruises.com) for 1.5-hour sightseeing cruises (2:30 pm daily mid-June-mid-Sept., $22 adults, $20 seniors, and $15 under age 12) aboard the custom-designed *Shawnodese* from the dock at City Beach. Also offered are dinner cruises, eagle-watching cruises, and other seasonal trips.

marina along Lake Pend Oreille in Sandpoint

OTHER RECREATION
Golf

The Lower Pack River meanders through the golf links at **The Idaho Club** (151 Clubhouse Way, Sandpoint, 208/265-8600 or 800/323-7020, greens fees $80-145), creating periodic water hazards on 15 of the course's 18 holes. This semiprivate golf resort gives first dibs to its members, who have vacation homes on the property, but the 6,923-yard, par-71 course is open to the public. Greens fees for nonmembers vary by season and include a cart. Your tee shots might be critiqued by some of the area's abundant wildlife, including elk, deer, bald eagles, and ospreys. The moose play through. Traversing the fairways of the scenic course, you'll play past stands of cedar and birch, the latter glimmering gold in fall. To get to The Idaho Club, take Highway 200 east from Sandpoint about seven miles and turn left just past mile marker 37.

Hiking and Biking

One of the best places for a hike, run, or bike ride in town is also one of the easiest to get to. The **Long Bridge** that you drove into town on has a pedestrian and bike path along the east side of it. To access the trail from downtown, follow signs from the foot of Lake Street. **Outdoor Experience** (314 N. 1st Ave., Sandpoint, 208/263-6028) rents cruiser bikes for $35 per day, $20 for two hours.

South of town across the lake, the 3.7-mile one-way **Gold Hill Trail** (Trail 3) climbs the northern flanks of Gold Hill, providing panoramic views of the city and the lake. The lower trailhead is on Bottle Bay Road, about five miles north of Sagle. To get to the upper trailhead, take Sagle Road six miles to Contest Mountain Road (Forest Rd. 2642) and follow that road six more miles to the trailhead.

North of town, the easy 0.5-mile one-way **Caribou Lake Trail** (Trail 58) leads to a small lake in the Selkirks north of Schweitzer Mountain Resort. Take U.S. 95 north from town 13 miles to Pack River Road. Follow that road five miles to Caribou Creek Road (Forest Rd. 2684) and continue down that rough road seven miles to the trailhead.

East of town, the long **Round Top-Bee Top Trail** (Trail 120) is especially popular among mountain bikers. The route traverses a long, high divide linking Trestle Peak, Round Top, Cougar Peak, and Bee Top. It's about 20 miles long and provides many great views from its 6,000-foot heights. The northwest trailhead is on Forest Road 275, which leaves Highway 200 at Trestle Creek between Sandpoint and Hope. Look for the trailhead at a hairpin turn in the road about 15 miles in. The southeast trailhead is off Lightning Creek Road (Forest Rd. 419), about five miles north from Clark Fork.

Fishing

Kamloops, kokanee, whitefish, perch, crappie, bluegill, largemouth bass, and rainbow, brown, and brook trout—this lake has it all. You can rent a boat and head out on your own, but it probably makes more sense to avail yourself of local expertise. Fishing guides in the area include **Pend Oreille Charters** (208/265-6781, www.pocharters.com) and **Diamond Charters** (208/265-2565, www.diamondcharters.com).

Outfitters

For backcountry gear, head to **Outdoor Experience** (314 N. 1st Ave., Sandpoint, 208/263-6028). The full-line adventure-gear store sells packs, mountain bikes, and backcountry duds, and also rents cross-country skis, snowshoes, telemark skis, and kayaks. Schweitzer Mountain Resort (10000 Schweitzer Mountain Rd., Sandpoint, 208/255-3081) is the best place to rent alpine skis and snowboards.

ENTERTAINMENT AND EVENTS
Entertainment

The **Panida Theatre** (300 N. 1st Ave., Sandpoint, 208/263-9191, www.panida.org) is the focus of Sandpoint's flourishing entertainment scene. The beautiful Spanish Mission-style theater hosted vaudeville and movies after its construction in 1927. Age took its toll over the years, but in 1985 the city purchased the theater and has since restored it to its former glory. Today, the Panida is on the National Register of Historic Places and stages local drama productions, an art-film series, concerts by touring and local musicians, and many other special events. The theater's name is a combination of *pan* from Panhandle and *ida* from Idaho, but nevertheless it's pronounced "PAN-idda."

Events

In early August, the big 10-day **Festival at Sandpoint** (www.festivalatsandpoint.com) concert series takes place at Memorial Field. The 2014 lineup included big-name acts like Cake, Steve Miller Band, and Rosanne Cash, to name a few. That same week, the **Pend Oreille Arts and Crafts Fair** brightens City Beach with a bevy of locally produced paintings, photography, jewelry, and pottery.

Art Galleries

Sandpoint enjoys a reputation as an art colony, and some 15 galleries are scattered throughout the downtown area. A couple of favorites are **First Light Gallerie** (302 N. 1st Ave., Sandpoint, 208/263-7148) and **Art Works** (214 N. 1st Ave., Sandpoint, 208/263-2642), a local artists' co-op gallery offering an eclectic collection of paintings, sculpture, pottery, jewelry, wood and glass works, and more.

Many local galleries, restaurants, and shops participate in **Artwalk,** a self-guided art tour of the town. You can pick up a list of the featured artists, their respective media, and the locations of their works at the chamber of commerce or many of the galleries around town.

ACCOMMODATIONS

Summer is peak season in Sandpoint (summer rates are listed below), so don't expect to find much in the $50-100 range. The winter rates here are significantly lower.

$50-100

GuestHouse Lodge (476841 U.S. 95 N., Sandpoint, 208/263-2210, from $59 d) has 60 guest rooms, a hot tub, and free breakfast, and it allows pets. **Quality Inn** (807 N. 5th Ave., Sandpoint, 208/263-2111 or 800/635-2534, from $69 d) is in a hectic location right on U.S. 2/95, but it's got an indoor pool, a decent restaurant, and 62 guest rooms.

$100-150

The 1907 ★ **Sweet Magnolia Bed and Breakfast** (502 N. 4th Ave., Sandpoint, 208/263-2425, $129-149) is a cozy inn within easy walking distance of downtown. The creaky, character-filled Victorian is full of antiques, and each guest room has its own bath, cable TV, and phone. Rates include a full breakfast featuring freshly baked breads.

Best Western Edgewater (56 Bridge St., Sandpoint, 208/263-3194 or 800/635-2534, from $109 d) enjoys a prime piece of lakefront real estate overlooking City Beach, just a block from downtown. All 54 guest rooms face the water and offer either a private balcony or a private patio. The resort has an indoor pool, and rates include continental breakfast. The hotel's restaurant is a great place for dinner or a sunset cocktail.

La Quinta Inn (415 Cedar St., Sandpoint, 208/263-9581 or 800/282-0660, from $129 d) is right in the heart of downtown. Amenities include a heated pool, a whirlpool tub, and an adjacent restaurant open for breakfast, lunch, and dinner daily.

$150-250

Western Pleasure Guest Ranch (1413 Upper Gold Creek Rd., Sandpoint, 208/263-9066, www.westernpleasureranch.com, $125-265) sits on a 960-acre spread about 16 miles northeast of town. The working cattle ranch has been around since 1940. Summer trail rides through forest inhabited by deer, elk, bears, moose, and wild turkeys lead to views of Lake Pend Oreille and the Selkirks. Horse-led sleigh rides in the winter pull guests through the snowy woods on a 45-minute ride culminating in hot drinks and popcorn. Cross-country ski trails are also set up and groomed in winter.

Accommodations are in either modern log cabins or a new lodge building. Each of the cabins has a full kitchen and woodstove and can accommodate up to six people. The 10,000-square-foot lodge sports a massive river-rock fireplace and has six guest rooms. In summer season, late June-mid-September, package stays are offered that include daily rides, evening entertainment, lodging, and all meals with a three-night minimum. Packages without the trail rides and packages with breakfast only are also available.

Vacation Rentals
North Idaho Property Solutions (877/223-0345, www.nivacationrentals.com) lists rentals of float homes, cottages, and condos in a variety of price ranges.

CAMPING AND RVING
On the south side of the long bridge, Lakeshore Drive leads west around Murphy Bay to the Corps of Engineers' **Springy Point Recreation Area** and its **campground** (reservations 877/444-6777, mid-May-Labor Day, 38 sites, $18, no hookups).

FOOD AND DRINK
Upscale Fare
Trinity at City Beach (58 Bridge St., Sandpoint, 208/255-7558, www.trinityatcitybeach.com, breakfast, lunch, and dinner daily, dinner entrées $16-29), in the Best Western Edgewater, has a stylish dining room with killer views of the lake. During the day, the menu focuses on breakfast and typical lunch fare. At night, the restaurant gets serious with high-end entrées like trout amandine, slow-roasted prime rib, and lobster ravioli. The wine list boasts lots of European and Washington labels.

Ivano's Ristorante (102 S. 1st Ave., Sandpoint, 208/263-0211, lunch and dinner daily, $12-28) is an excellent Italian joint with an elegant yet comfortable dining room. The upscale menu offers appetizers, various pasta dishes, and Mediterranean-inspired entrées of chicken, veal, and seafood. As expected, the restaurant pours plenty of good Italian wines.

The Hydra Steakhouse (115 Lake St., Sandpoint, 208/263-7123, lunch Tues.-Fri., dinner daily, entrées $12-32) is Sandpoint's venerable steak and seafood restaurant. This is where everyone around here goes for special occasions. The rambling interior is done up with lots of wood tones, and subdued lighting adds to the aura of cool tranquility. The menu offers classic steakhouse and seafood entrées and pasta dishes.

Wine Bars and Pubs
One of the best boutique wineries in Idaho happens to be in Sandpoint. ★ **Pend d'Oreille Winery** (301 Cedar St., Sandpoint, 208/265-8545, www.powine.com, 10am-7pm daily) boasts a recently remodeled tasting room and wine bar downtown. Here you can sample the offerings of winemaker Steve Meyer, who produces an array of varietal red and white wines, blends, and a few off-dry wines, like Huckleberry Blush. Most of his wines are made from Columbia Valley grapes. The winery's small bistro puts out tasty, wine-friendly fare.

MickDuff's Brewing Company (312 N. 1st Ave., Sandpoint, 208/255-4351, www.mickduffs.com, lunch and dinner daily, $8-15) is a great spot for a burger and a handcrafted beer. This downtown brewpub dishes up appetizers, burgers, hot sandwiches, and other pub grub. Expect to find a rotating selection of ales, porters, and stouts.

Idaho Pour Authority (203 Cedar St., 208/597-7096, noon-8pm Mon.-Sat.) is a newish hotspot downtown that focuses on pouring lots of craft beers from around the Northwest, thus the name. The taproom and bottle shop keeps around a dozen microbrews on tap and stocks more than 300 bottled beers in its coolers. They also serve artisanal cheeses, cured meats, and crusty bread.

McManus Muses About the Selkirk Mountains

Outdoor humorist **Patrick McManus,** who hails from Sandpoint in Idaho's Panhandle, has made a living out of adding levity and wit to potentially fatal situations associated with outdoor fun. He has written 13 books about the lighter side of the great outdoors, including *Never Sniff a Gift Fish, How I Got This Way,* and *They Shoot Canoes, Don't They?* Besides penning nonfiction books (he admits to some fictional embellishment), McManus has also been an editor at *Field & Stream* magazine and a longtime columnist for *Outdoor Life* magazine, in which he wrote the hilarious kicker "The Last Laugh." In recent years, he has tried his hand at writing mystery novels and even a children's book. McManus, who now lives in nearby Spokane, Washington, offers this humorous recollection about the mountains near his hometown:

When I was a boy camping in the Selkirk Mountains, the range contained at least one grizzly bear. I know this because our rural postman was once treed by it. He was a large and flabby man, so it was hard for me to imagine him scurrying up a tree, but he explained that the sight of a grizzly headed your way can virtually flood you with such energy and enthusiasm for climbing that you could zip up a dozen such trees, if any of them proved unsatisfactory. I explored the Selkirks from the time I was 12 until I went off to college and can report there was not a single dark night our postman's grizzly did not populate my thoughts.

International Cuisine

Jalapeño's (314 N. 2nd Ave., Sandpoint, 208/263-2995, lunch and dinner daily, dinner entrées $9-14) is the local favorite for Tex-Mex food. The large menu is packed with tamales, flautas, tacos, enchiladas, and burritos galore. The green chile burger and chicken flautas are good picks.

Get your Thai fix at **Bangkok Cuisine** (202 N. 2nd Ave., Sandpoint, 208/265-4149, lunch Mon.-Fri., dinner Mon.-Sat., dinner entrées $8-14), where you'll find a profusion of spicy noodle dishes, wok-fried rice, and coconut milk-infused curries, many of which are vegetarian.

Pizza

Second Avenue Pizza (215 S. 2nd Ave., Sandpoint, 208/263-9321, lunch and dinner Mon.-Sat.) is known for its big pizzas and cold microbrews. Try a Schweitzer Ski Flakes pie made, as the menu states, with "fresh spinach, tomatoes avalanched with feta cheese, garlic, moguls of mushrooms, black olives, and at the peak, it's knee deep in asiago cheese."

Burgers and Sandwiches

Dub's Drive-In (U.S. 2 W. and Boyer St., Sandpoint, 208/263-4300, lunch and dinner daily, under $10) is a Sandpoint institution that pumps out artery-clogging burgers in sizes suitable for big and little tykes alike. Cool your head with some soft-serve ice cream or a tasty butterscotch milkshake.

You also can clog your arteries downtown at ★ **Joe's Authentic Philly Cheesesteaks** (102 Church St., Sandpoint, 208/263-1444, 10am-8pm daily, under $10). This little sandwich shop serves several variations of the City of Brotherly Love's most famous sandwich, as well as hoagies, burgers, and Reubens.

Breakfast and Coffee

The best place in town for a big breakfast is at **Panhandler Pies** (120 S. 1st Ave., Sandpoint, 208/263-2912, 6:30am-10pm Mon.-Sat., under $10), which offers a full menu morning, noon, and night. Of course, it also bakes 23 different kinds of pie.

Speaking of yummy baked treats, make

sure to check out ★ **Pine Street Bakery** (710 Pine St., Sandpoint, 208/263-9012, 7am-5pm daily). This friendly bakery turns out flaky croissants, sweet pastries, cookies, tarts, and loaves of rustic bread. You also can get espresso drinks and loose-leaf teas.

On the edge of downtown, you'll find **Monarch Mountain Coffee** (208 N. 4th Ave., Sandpoint, 208/265-9382, 6am-6pm daily). It's a spacious, bright, and shiny place great for writing that postcard to the folks back home. Plus the coffeehouse roasts its own beans and serves freshly baked goods and light breakfast items.

Groceries

The **Farmers Market at Sandpoint** (9am-1pm Sat. and 3pm-5:30pm Wed. May-Oct.) fills Farmin Park (3rd Ave. and Oak St.) with fresh produce, honey, eggs, prepared food-stuffs, fresh-cut flowers, and crafts.

Foodies definitely need to check out **Pend Oreille Pasta and Wine** (476534 U.S. 95, Sandpoint, 208/263-1352, www.pendopasta.com, 9am-6pm Mon.-Sat.). This specialty food store and wine shop carries cured meats, artisanal cheeses, freshly baked breads, olives, and prepared pasta dinners. Finding that perfect bottle of vino for the picnic basket is not a problem here.

INFORMATION

Recreation information is available at the U.S. Forest Service's **Sandpoint Ranger District** (1500 U.S. 2, Sandpoint, 208/263-5111). Sandpoint's **public library** (1407 Cedar St., Sandpoint, 208/263-6930) offers free Internet access and a relaxing space to peruse periodicals (a ski magazine, perhaps?).

GETTING THERE

To reach the **Amtrak** station (450 Railroad Ave., Sandpoint, 800/872-7245), turn left off Bridge Street, which is just across Sand Creek on your way toward City Beach. Amtrak's *Empire Builder* stops at this beautifully restored depot on its run to and from Chicago and Seattle or Portland. Eastbound trains leave at 2:35am daily, westbound trains leave at 11:49pm daily (both times PDT).

★ SCHWEITZER MOUNTAIN RESORT

High in the Selkirk Mountains, a short 11-mile drive north of town, is **Schweitzer Mountain Resort** (10000 Schweitzer Mountain Rd., Sandpoint, 208/263-9555, snow report 208/265-9562, www.schweitzer.com). One of Idaho's top ski areas, Schweitzer offers a vertical drop of 2,400 feet, two massive bowls, and outstanding base-area lodging and dining. In summer, you can come up the hill for hiking and lift-served mountain biking.

Alpine Skiing and Snowboarding

Seemingly underused, Schweitzer's lifts seldom have any appreciable lines. The resort's high-speed "six-pack" chair (the first in Idaho, nicknamed "Stella") plus a single detachable quad, four double chairs, and two handle tows serve 2,500 acres of terrain and 59 named runs rated at 20 percent beginner, 40 percent intermediate, 35 percent advanced, and 5 percent expert. More than half the runs are groomed, including some of the steep upper slopes, by means of winch cats. The longest run measures a quad-burning 2.7 miles. Racing enthusiasts can try out the NASTAR course, while snowboarders enjoy the resort's terrain park.

Full-day lift tickets cost $72 adults, $50 ages 7-17, free under age 7. Two lifts are lighted for night skiing Friday-Saturday and holiday evenings until 9pm. Lessons and a wide range of rental equipment such as skis, snowboards, tele-gear, and snowshoes are available at the base area. The resort offers day-care services (208/255-3038) and discounted beginner packages including rentals, lessons, and lift tickets.

Cross-Country Skiing

Schweitzer sets and grooms 19 miles of cross-country trails just to the north of the base area. The trails are better groomed than any Park N' Ski area and offer great views and pleasant, rolling terrain. The well-marked trails leave the busy lodge area and climb around the ridge to the north. Both a wide skating lane and traditional tracks are set up. An all-day trail pass costs $15 adults, $10 seniors and ages 7-17.

Mountain Biking

Schweitzer maintains 20 miles of mountain-bike trails on the resort property, and those trails connect with many more miles of logging roads that wind through the Selkirks. You can rent top-notch bikes at Schweitzer for about $50 per half day, $85 per full day. Those who love the downhill but loathe the uphill can load their fat-tire friend onto the resort's quad chairlift and get a ride to the top ($22 for an all-day pass). For more information, call the activity center at 208/255-3081.

Hiking

In summer, the hills around Schweitzer are bursting with berries and wildflowers. Add panoramic views of Lake Pend Oreille and you've got ideal hiking country. Ten miles of trails meander through the hills. Those who want the mountaintop views without the toil can ride the resort's quad chair to the summit for around $10, then enjoy a downhill stroll. Free trail maps are available at the base area.

Accommodations

Schweitzer Mountain Bed & Breakfast

(110 Crystal Court, Sandpoint, 208/263-7117, $135-310) is up Crystal Springs Road from the main Schweitzer parking lot. This mountain-top B&B has five guest rooms, each with a private bath. Amenities include a hot tub, a TV room, and ski-in, ski-out access. Rates include breakfast, as well as tea, coffee, and beverages throughout the day.

The resort has two slope-side lodges and condos in the base area. The **Selkirk Lodge** (10000 Schweitzer Mountain Rd., Sandpoint, 877/487-4643, $210-293 peak season) sits right at the base of the lifts, its tall gabled roof giving it the air of a Bavarian château. Some guest rooms have jetted tubs, and there's an outdoor heated pool and hot tub complex. The newer **White Pine Lodge** (10000 Schweitzer Mountain Rd., Sandpoint, 877/487-4643, $330-578 peak season) has 1-3-bedroom accommodations, plus outdoor hot tubs and a shopping and dining village.

Highway 200:
Pend Oreille Scenic Byway

HOPE AND VICINITY

East of Sandpoint, Highway 200 skirts the north shore of Lake Pend Oreille, soon coming to Hope, East Hope, and even Beyond Hope. On a warm summer's day, this area of big trees and big water is sublime. Perhaps that's why famed Canadian geographer and explorer David Thompson built the very first fur-trading outpost in Idaho, Kullyspell House, on the Hope peninsula way back in 1809. Today, Thompson is commemorated here with the David Thompson Game Preserve. Also on the peninsula are posh homes hidden away in the woods, a superb national forest campground, and great views of the lake at every turn.

Accommodations

Pend Oreille Shores Resort (47390 Hwy. 200, Hope, 208/264-5828, www.posresort.com, $170-255) is an upscale condominium development on the lake. Each of the 51 condos has a kitchen, a washer and dryer, a stereo, cable TV, and a fireplace. An on-site athletic club features an indoor pool, hot tubs, racquetball and tennis courts, a sauna, and a weight room.

Camping and RVing

Out on the Hope peninsula, you'll find an RV park and a superbly located national forest campground. To get to the peninsula, continue east two miles past Hope and watch for the Sam Owen Road turnoff on the right. Especially appealing here is the area's status as a game refuge. In the early morning and evening hours, large numbers of tame deer feed on the grassy hills.

Island View RV Resort (1767 Peninsula Rd., Hope, 208/946-1374, year-round) has 60 sites ($35-40) with full hookups. The resort also has a marina with gas and boat rentals, a small store, and hot showers.

Also on the Hope peninsula, the Forest Service's sprawling **Sam Owen Campground** ($18-20) offers million-dollar lakefront property. Head straight for the Skipping Stone Loop; units 32, 33, and 35 are among the choicest, just steps from the water. To make reservations, log onto www.recreation.gov.

Food

Right next door to Pend Oreille Shores Resort, you'll find the **Floating Restaurant** (Hwy. 200, East Hope, 208/264-5311, lunch and dinner daily, brunch Sun. Apr.-Oct., dinner entrées $17-28), located on a dock at Hope Marine Services. The menu features traditional seafood and steak preparations. It's a great spot to kick back with a microbrew and watch the sunset.

CLARK FORK AND VICINITY

Clark Fork is the last outpost of civilization you'll pass through before crossing into Montana. The town enjoys a scenic location in the shadow of the Cabinet Mountains, at the confluence of the Clark Fork River and picturesque Lightning Creek. The downtown area has a couple of stores and taverns but not much else.

Cabinet Gorge Dam

Virtually at the Idaho-Montana border, this is the last point of interest along Highway 200 before you leave the state behind and venture into Montana. **Cabinet Gorge Dam** is 208 feet high and 600 feet long and backs up the 20-mile-long Clark Fork Reservoir, almost entirely in Montana. The spectacle of the water surging through narrow Cabinet Gorge is powerful indeed. Imagine what it must have looked like when ancient glacial Lake Missoula broke through to carve out the gorge in the first place.

Hiking

A popular and strenuous trail starts outside Clark Fork and leads to the top of **Scotchman Peak,** a 7,000-foot sentry watching over Lake Pend Oreille to the west and the lofty Montana ridgeline to the east. The views from the summit can't be beat. The trail is only seven miles round-trip but climbs some 3,700 vertical feet in less than four miles. To reach the trailhead, follow Clark Fork's Main Street north. It soon turns into Forest Road 276. Continue past the turnoff to the University of Idaho's Forestry Field Campus. When the road forks about a mile farther down the road, bear right, following signs to Trail 65. One mile farther, turn left on Forest Road 2294A, then turn left again 0.5 mile down that road. After a little over two miles, make one last left and proceed 220 yards to the trailhead. If all that seems too confusing, ask the rangers at the Sandpoint Ranger District office in Sandpoint to draw you a map.

Huckleberry Tent & Breakfast

Huckleberry Tent & Breakfast (180 Thunderbolt Dr., Clark Fork, 208/266-0155, www.huckleberrytentandbreakfast.com, Apr. 15-Nov. 15) specializes in chic camping among the huckleberry bushes. Stay the night in one of the three decked-out canvas tents (from $135 d), all of which have fire rings, wonderful mountain views, and no TVs or other modern devices to distract you from the great outdoors. Wake up to a big homespun breakfast, huckleberry pancakes included.

U.S. 2 WEST

West of Sandpoint, U.S. 2 follows the lazy and scenic Pend Oreille River down to the town of Priest River and on to the Washington state line. In the town of **Laclede,** named after a French engineer on the Great Northern Railway, is the Corps of Engineers-built **Riley Creek Recreation Area,** where you'll find a campground (reservations 877/444-6777, mid-May-Labor Day, 67 sites, $25 with hookups). Laclede is also well known to **rock climbing** enthusiasts for Laclede Rocks, right off the highway two miles west of town. The area has a couple of easy routes, but most are in the 5.8-5.10 range. One 5.12 top-rope problem challenges the very skilled. Come in summer when it's hot and you can end your climb by jumping into the nearby Pend Oreille River.

Like Priest Lake, the town of **Priest River** was named in honor of Jesuit priest and early area missionary Father John Roothaan. Logging has long been its lifeblood; great log drives down the Priest River once fed the big mills here. Today the town is in the process of sprucing itself up for tourists.

Priest Lake

Surrounded by the dense forests and lofty, snowcapped peaks of the Selkirks, Priest Lake is a secluded, off-the-beaten-path gem. There are no cities along the lakeshore, and the biggest towns on the lake, Coolin and Nordman, are not much more than small supply stations for anglers, campers, and the few hardy souls who live up here.

The area is a haven for wildlife. Black bears are common at the lake, and a few grizzlies roam the high country around the periphery. Deer and moose are plentiful, mountain goats inhabit rocky crags near the east shore, and a small herd of endangered woodland caribou survives tenuously in the wildest reaches of this northern realm.

The lake is also a favorite of anglers, who fish for lunker mackinaw in forest-shaded coves along the lake's edge. Campers looking for solitude camp on one of several islands in the lake, or they boat or hike north to Upper Priest Lake. The upper lake—connected to the much larger lower lake by a two-mile-long narrow and shallow channel called the Thorofare—is preserved for the wilderness experience. Waterskiing and Jet Skiing are prohibited on the upper lake, where canoes are the vessels of choice. Trails through cool, dense forest lead between the lower and upper lakes to campgrounds reached only by boat or on foot.

Around the shore of the lower lake you'll find numerous resorts, lodgings, and campgrounds of varying degrees of luxury as well as several marinas and a couple of villages offering convivial contact with members of your own species. Many of the restaurants feature huckleberry dishes of every description. Priest Lake is huckleberry country, and people come from all over the region in mid-late summer to pick the delectable fruit.

★ PRIEST LAKE STATE PARK

Historic sites, natural-history interpretive information, and abundant recreation opportunities make **Priest Lake State Park** (day-use $5) an outstanding destination. Two of the three units of the park are found along the lake's east shore.

Park headquarters is at the **Indian Creek Unit,** 11 miles north of Coolin on East Shore Road. Once a logging camp for the Diamond Match Company, the site displays an old flume that once floated logs into the lake from up to three miles away.

The campground's broad, sandy beach attracts swimmers and sunbathers; others prefer to hike one of the two easy hiking trails meandering through the woods, or play volleyball or basketball on the campground's courts. A boat-launching ramp lets you float your boat. Throughout summer, the interpretive center presents a full slate of events, including educational campfire programs, guided walks and bike rides, and junior ranger activities. In winter, the park offers easy access to more than 300 miles of groomed and marked snowmobile and cross-country ski trails.

Some of the Indian Creek Unit's 93 campsites ($12-31) have hookups. Two cabins ($50-55) are also available. Other on-site facilities include a camp store, showers, toilets, and an RV dump station. The campgrounds are popular and fill up in summer. Make reservations by contacting the Priest Lake State Park **office** (314 Indian Creek Park Rd., Coolin, 208/443-2200).

Twelve miles farther north along the east shore, at the mouth of Lion Creek on the lake's northern tip, is the park's **Lionhead Unit** (open summer-fall only). Canadian-born silent-film actor and filmmaker **Nell Shipman,** who many consider to be the country's first independent filmmaker, operated a movie studio on this site 1922-1925, producing wildlife and outdoor-adventure films

and maintaining a movable zoo of 70 animal actors used in the films. Although several of the shorts and features filmed here were successful, the studio's high-overhead operation eventually drove it into bankruptcy. The animals were shipped off to the San Diego Zoo, and Shipman returned to Los Angeles where she continued to work behind the scenes in the film industry. She died there in 1970. Most of her films have been rediscovered, restored, and assembled in a collection at Boise State University.

Also at the Lionhead Unit is the sunken shell of the *Tyee II* lying in the shallow waters of Mosquito Bay just offshore. The vessel was a steamer tug used to haul large booms of logs from the Diamond Match flume site to the lake's outlet, where the logs were ferried down the Priest River to the sawmill. Towing a full load of logs, the tug managed just 0.5 mph and took some 60 hours to reach the end of the lake. On such a trip, the tug would typically burn 10 cords of wood. The operation lasted until 1959, when the *Tyee* was stripped of its iron and scuttled where you see it today.

The Lionhead Unit campground (47 sites, $12-21) is smaller than the one at the Indian Creek Unit and less developed; the sites don't have hookups. Hiking trails wind through

Priest River at Priest Lake

the woods, across Lion Creek, and out to the beach, where you just might find moose tracks in the sand. The park is also an excellent launching place for boaters heading to Upper Priest Lake.

The **Dickensheet Unit** is the most primitive of the state park's three units, on the Priest River south of the lake between Coolin and the road junction with Highway 57. The campground (11 sites, $12) has minimal facilities. It's a great place to kick back with a fishing pole, away from the crowds up on the lake.

OTHER SIGHTS AND RECREATION
Priest Lake Museum and Visitors Center

The informative **Priest Lake Museum and Visitors Center** (208/443-2676, 10am-4pm Tues.-Sun. Memorial Day-Labor Day, free), just north of Hill's Resort on Luby Bay, is a good place to begin your exploration of the area. The museum occupies a log cabin built by the Civilian Conservation Corps in 1935. It was originally a residence and office for the Kaniksu National Forest's first ranger. Inside you'll find exhibits on the threatened grizzly bear and woodland caribou, and on rare area plants such as the northern beechfern, deerfern, black snakeroot, and salmonberry.

The most entertaining fact you'll learn here is how the name of the local national forest came to be changed from Priest River National Forest to Kaniksu National Forest. It seems the Forest Service wanted a fresh start after the antics of Priest River National Forest's first supervisor, Benjamin McConnell, gained public attention. McConnell was dismissed for "public drunkenness, habitating with a newly divorced woman, and shooting his pistol in the middle of town." The new name, Kaniksu, was the local Native American term for the Jesuit missionaries in the area. Friendly volunteer docents at the museum are on staff to answer your questions.

Vinther-Nelson Cabin

You'll need a boat to get to the historic **Vinther-Nelson Cabin** (10am-3pm Wed.-Sun. summer, free) on Eightmile Island, which was built in 1897 by the Crenshaw brothers, who tried their hand at mining on the island. After a year with no luck, the Crenshaws gave up and sold the cabin to W. J. Anders and family. Anders cleared the land and planted crops but couldn't make a go of it. In 1900 he sold out to two cousins (Sam Vinther and Nels Nelson) who intended to revive the mine and make a fortune, but they never struck pay dirt either. Nevertheless, the two men and their families continued to live on the island. In 1967 the U.S. Department of Agriculture ordered that all private buildings on Priest Lake's federally owned islands be demolished. The descendants of Vinther and Nelson negotiated an agreement to allow the log cabin to remain standing as a historic site open to the public. Inside the cabin you'll find a restored kitchen and a small museum. Outside, trails lead to great views and the old mine site, long since caved in.

Hanna Flats Cedar Grove

Hanna Flats Cedar Grove, the small area just south of the Priest Lake Ranger District office in Nordman (look for signs marking the turnoff to the west), offers a short nature trail in summer, cross-country ski trails in winter, and a soggy, mosquito-infested bog in spring. Pick up the interpretive trail brochure at the ranger station; it explains that one reason these cedars survived is because they weren't considered valuable by early loggers. An interesting subplot dates from the settler days when a man named Gumpp built a cabin here. He moved away for the winter, and when he returned found Jim Hanna and family living in his house. They had come upon the cabin, assumed it was abandoned, and moved in. Gumpp didn't raise a stink; he just moved on.

Beaver Creek Recreation Site

The **Beaver Creek Recreation Site** is the main jumping-off point for hiking, mountain biking, and canoeing to Upper Priest Lake Scenic Area. Once the site of the Beaver

Creek Ranger Station, the area offers a campground ($20), a picnic area (day-use $8), a boat launch into the main lake, trailhead parking for the hiker-biker Navigation and Lakeshore Trails, and a 1,600-foot canoe-portage trail directly to the Thorofare. The site is on the lake's northwest shore; turn east on Forest Road 2512 at Nordman and follow it north 12 miles.

Granite Falls and Roosevelt Grove

Actually just over the border in Washington, but reached only via Idaho, the short Granite Falls Trail (Trail 301) leads to views of upper and lower **Granite Falls** and continues to the **Roosevelt Grove of Ancient Cedars.** To get to the trailhead, continue north on Highway 57 past Nordman; the road eventually becomes Forest Road 302. Most of the old-growth cedar grove went up in flames in 1926, but about 22 acres are left. These ancient cedars are impressive, but it's lower Granite Falls that steals the show. The roaring water rounds a corner at the top of the falls and plummets down a huge granite dihedral. Clever Forest Service engineers have constructed a truly scary viewpoint right out over the cliff edge.

Also at the trailhead is **Stagger Inn Picnic Area** (free). The area was named by firefighters who used it back in the 1920s as a base camp. At that time, the road up the west shore ended at Nordman, and the firefighters had to hike in to the spot from about 14 miles away. By the time they got here, they were exhausted, and many had to "stagger in."

Hiking and Biking

A favorite for hikers and mountain bikers alike is **Navigation Trail** (Trail 291). It begins at Beaver Creek Recreation Site and first enters a dense, fern-filled cedar forest. The trail can be mucky in places, but it's always beautiful. You'll pass an abandoned trapper's cabin before arriving at Plowboy Campground on the southwest shore of Upper Priest Lake. It's an easy three-mile hike to this point. You can picnic and head back from here, or continue north another three miles to Navigation

Campground at the upper end of the lake. Between the two campgrounds the trail traverses a wooded lakeside slope, offering great views of the water and mountains at many points along the way. This portion of the trail is also easy. Fit hikers will have no problem hoofing it all the way from Beaver Creek to Navigation Campground and back (round-trip 12 miles) in half a day.

Beaver Creek is also the trailhead for **Lakeshore Trail** (Trail 294), which heads south along the western edge of the lake for 7.6 miles. It's an easy and popular trail open to both hikers and bikers. Along the way you'll cross five streams, pass numerous campsites, and get great views of the lake.

Probably the most popular and heavily used trail at Priest Lake is the nine-mile **Beach Trail** (Trail 48), which runs right by Hill's Resort, Luby Bay Campground, and several summer cabins. It's open to hikers only (sorry, no mountain bikes) and runs between the Kalispell Bay boat launch on the north and Outlet Bay on the south. Along the way it meanders through woods and along the beach, jumping back to Lakeshore Road for two short stretches.

Mountain bikers can make best use of the east side of the lake, particularly the northeast shore north of Priest Lake State Park's Lionhead Unit, where numerous gravel roads have been closed to motor vehicles, making ideal mountain-biking country. For starters, try Caribou Creek Road, right out of the Lionhead campground.

To pick up a map of the area, stop by the **Priest Lake Ranger District office** (32203 Hwy. 57, Nordman, 208/443-2512).

Floating the Priest River

The 44-mile stretch of the Priest River between Priest Lake and the town of Priest River makes a relatively easy float trip, taken either in segments or one long 14-hour day. The toughest rapids, Binarch and Eight Mile, are rated Class III. You'll also encounter three other Class II rapids along the way. In periods of high water (spring and early summer) the Class III rapids are unsuitable for novices. Later in the summer, the river's average depth decreases to three feet or less, and the slow, lazy stretches dominate; after mid-July, plan on dragging the bottom in places.

Fishing

Priest Lake holds large populations of kokanee, cutthroat trout, rainbow trout, and mackinaw. The Idaho Parks and Recreation Department suggests trying the following not-so-secret fishing spots: off East Shore Road about 5-6 miles south of Indian Creek; off the end of Pinto Point; and, for deep trolling, off the Kalispell-Papoose-Bartoe Island group (try a chartreuse crocodile as a trolling lure).

Boating

The west-shore resorts all have marinas with boat rentals. In and around Coolin you'll find **Coolin Marine** (2148 Cavanaugh Bay Rd., Coolin, 208/443-2469) and **Blue Diamond Marina** (958 Blue Diamond Rd., Coolin, 208/443-2240) about five miles from town, both of which rent boats.

Free **boat-launching ramps** are available at Coolin and at the U.S. Forest Service Luby Bay Campground on the west shore. Ramps that charge a fee can be found on the east shore at Cavanaugh Bay Marina and on the west shore at Priest Lake Marina (Kalispell Bay), Elkins Resort (Reeder Bay), and Grandview Resort (Reeder Bay).

Note: The Thorofare is a no-wake zone, and waterskiing and Jet Skiing are prohibited in Upper Priest Lake.

Huckleberry Picking

The Priest Lake area is loaded with huckleberries, and the menus of many local restaurants boast huckleberry pies, milkshakes, pancakes, cocktails, and more. Berry-picking season runs mid-July-Sept. The berries like the sun, so the best places to find them are in open areas along logging roads and trails, mostly west of the lake. You can pick up a berry-picking map from the U.S. Forest Service's Priest Lake Ranger Station, on Highway 57

just south of Nordman. Remember, bears love huckleberries too. If you hear something big thrashing around in the bushes nearby, it's best to yield dibs on the area.

Cross-Country Skiing

In winter, cross-country skiers and snowmobilers take advantage of the hundreds of miles of groomed and marked trails in the area. About five miles of mostly easy ski trails wind through the Indian Creek Unit of **Priest Lake State Park** on the lake's east shore. Across the lake, **Hanna Flats Cedar Grove** just south of Nordman tracks about four miles of easy loops as well. Heading south toward Priest River, the **Chipmunk Rapids Trail System** offers another 10.5 miles of trails.

ACCOMMODATIONS
Resorts

Several resorts dot the lake's west side. The biggest, plushest, and most popular with the tourist set is the venerable **Hill's Resort** (4777 W. Lakeshore Rd., Priest Lake, 208/443-2551, www.hillsresort.com, year-round, $1,750-4,900 weekly summer) on beautiful Luby Bay. The Hill family has run the resort since 1946 and offer accommodations in either private cabins or condo-like housekeeping units, most with fireplaces. Amenities include a marina; swimming areas; tennis and volleyball courts; hiking, biking, cross-country skiing, and snowmobiling trails; a gourmet restaurant; and a lounge with live entertainment in season. In summer, bookings are taken only for stays of a week or longer. Summer rates are in effect from the last Saturday in June until the Tuesday after Labor Day weekend. The rest of the year, rates are about 15 percent lower, and nightly rates are available. Units vary in size, sleeping 2-12 people.

★ **Elkins on Priest Lake** (404 Elkins Rd., Nordman, 208/443-2432, www.elkinsresort. com, year-round) is another full-service resort. Accommodations are in individual log cabins, most with fireplace and all with kitchens, full baths, and separate bedrooms; you need to bring your own soap and towels. The lodge restaurant, overlooking the lake and nicely landscaped grounds, serves top-notch Pacific Rim-inspired cuisine daily in summer and between Christmas and New Year's, with a limited schedule the rest of the year. The Trapper Creek Lounge is one of the west shore's social hubs. Other amenities include a marina, beaches, volleyball, and recreation trails. You must book for a week or longer in peak summer season (early July-late Aug.). Peak season weekly rates range from around $1,500 for a creek-side cabin that sleeps four to $4,600 for a lakefront cabin that sleeps 14. The rest of the year, rates are about 15 percent lower, and a two-night minimum (three nights on holiday weekends) is in effect.

Grandview Resort (3492 Reeder Bay Rd., Priest Lake, 208/443-2433) offers cottages, lodge rooms, and suites with, yes, grand views of Reeder Bay. Amenities include a small swimming pool, a marina with boat rentals, and a bright dining room overlooking the lake. It's open year-round. Peak season rates range from around $100 for a lodge room with one queen bed up to $350 for a private lakeview cottage that sleeps 10. Weekly rates are available, and pets are not allowed.

Inns

The **Inn at Priest Lake** (5310 Dickensheet Rd., Coolin, 208/443-2447, $85-150) is a short distance from the lake and offers little in the way of views. The big hexagonal structure looks something like a stone fort dropped incongruously into the woods. But the inn's modern amenities are welcome and include a year-round heated pool and spa, a restaurant, and a lounge. Spa suites and kitchenettes are available. The inn has a nicely landscaped backyard and is within walking distance of Coolin. Pets are allowed for a few extra bucks. The inn's year-round RV park offers 12 nice pull-through sites ($35) with full hookups. Restroom and shower facilities are available.

In Coolin, the ★ **Old Northern Inn** (220 Bay View Dr., Coolin, 208/443-2426, www.oldnortherninn.com, $115-175) occupies the former Northern Hotel, a turn-of-the-20th-century haven for travelers to the secluded shores of Priest Lake. The restored two-story wooden structure has antique furnishings and first-class modern amenities. The atmosphere is one of rustic elegance. The beautiful cedar-paneled living room features a stone fireplace and picture windows looking out on the lake. Old photographs and newspaper clippings provide a historical accent. The lake is just a short walk down a wooded slope to the private dock and beach. The four standard guest rooms and two suites all have private baths. Rates include a full breakfast (expect huckleberry pancakes) and afternoon wine and cheese. Children over age 12 are welcome, but pets aren't. Smoking is permitted outdoors only. The inn is on your left just before you come to the Coolin Marina.

CAMPING

Priest Lake State Park offers 151 campsites at its three units. For information and reservations, contact the state park office (314 Indian Creek Park Rd., Coolin, 208/443-2200).

Forest Service Campgrounds

Forest Service campgrounds ring both lower and upper Priest Lake. Many more are found on two islands out in the lake. All campsites are open mid-May-end of September, weather permitting. Camping is limited to 14 days.

From south to north on the west shore, the campgrounds (all $20) are **Outlet** (31 sites); **Osprey** (18 sites); **Lower Luby Bay** on the lakefront, and **Upper Luby Bay,** across the road in the woods (54 sites total), with an RV dump station; **Reeder Bay** (24 sites); **Beaver Creek** (41 sites). Reeder Bay, Beaver Creek, and the two Luby Bay campgrounds accept reservations (877/444-6777).

Four more campgrounds (free) on Upper Priest Lake are accessible only by boat or on foot. On the west side of the upper lake are **Plowboy Campground** (4 sites) at the south end of the lake and **Navigation Campground** (5 sites) on the lake's north end. Along the east shore of the upper lake are **Geisinger's Campground** (2 sites) and **Trapper Creek Campground** (5 sites).

Island Camping

In addition to the mainland campgrounds, the Forest Service maintains extremely popular boat-in campgrounds on **Kalispell Island** (12 campgrounds and two day-use areas), **Bartoo Island** (five campgrounds and two day-use areas), and **Fourmile Island** (one campsite). All are first-come, first-served ($10). Island campers are permitted to stay 14 days maximum.

Some of the campgrounds have vault toilets; others don't. Because of the heavy summer use, the Forest Service now requires campers staying at campgrounds without vault toilets to carry and use their own portable toilets while on the island. When they return to the Kalispell boat launch (the most commonly used public boat launch for trips to the islands), a free sanitizing machine there will clean their portable toilets. The machine works like a giant coin-operated dishwasher, flushing the waste into the mainland sewage system and sterilizing the container.

A Safety Reminder

This is bear country, so keep a clean camp. Dispose of all trash properly and promptly, and don't leave food out on picnic tables.

FOOD

The resort restaurants are safe bets for tasty grub around Priest Lake. On the west shore, **Hill's Resort and Elkins Resort** both serve excellent food.

For good comfort food, go to **Ardy's** (205 Cavanaugh Bay Rd., Coolin, 208/443-4086, breakfast and lunch daily, under $10), on the east side of the lake in Coolin. In late summer, this classic diner makes good use of local huckleberries, putting the plump little buggers in pies, pancakes, milkshakes, and more.

North to Canada

BONNERS FERRY AND VICINITY

Heading north from Sandpoint on U.S. 95, you'll pass through a string of small logging towns en route to Bonners Ferry, and farther on toward the Canadian border. This friendly and attractive town is a mellow place to spend a few days.

In 1834, 24-year-old New Yorker Edwin Bonner came west, intent on using his already considerable experience in the retail trade to establish himself as a successful frontier businessman. After opening a department store in Walla Walla, Washington, he passed through Idaho's northernmost reaches and noted that the well-traveled ford of the Kootenai River (used by miners stampeding north to British Columbia's goldfields) needed a ferry. By 1864 he had built his ferry and begun to operate it successfully. Eventually Bonner left the area and settled in Missoula, Montana, where he became a wealthy and powerful merchant and political leader. Despite his departure, the town that grew up here stuck with its original name.

Boundary County Museum

A repository of regional history, the small **Boundary County Museum** (7229 Main St., Bonners Ferry, 208/267-7720, 10am-4pm Tues.-Sat. summer, donation appreciated), across from City Hall, holds a wealth of historical photos and artifacts.

Kootenai National Wildlife Refuge

Before the building of dikes and Montana's Libby Dam tamed the Kootenai River, annual spring floods washed over the valley floor, creating prime wetlands for migratory waterfowl. The dikes made for flood-free farming but took away the wildlife habitat. The 2,774-acre **Kootenai National Wildlife Refuge** (Riverside Rd., 5 miles west of Bonners Ferry, 208/267-3888, sunrise-sunset daily, office 8am-4:30pm Mon.-Fri.) was created to mitigate that loss. The refuge is kept flooded with water diverted from the Kootenai River and two local creeks. Today, tens of thousands of waterfowl pass through the refuge every year. A 4.5-mile loop road circles the refuge, and several hiking trails (one is wheelchair accessible) lead to good photo vantage points.

In spring, look for mallards, northern pintails, American wigeon, and tundra swans. In late summer and early fall, the refuge attracts large numbers of Canada geese. Bird-watchers might also catch sight of bald eagles and ospreys. Among other wildlife occasionally seen are black bears, white-tailed deer, moose, and elk. In all, 230 bird species and 45 mammal species have been observed here.

Lookout

Up in the Selkirks, about four miles south of the Canadian border, is the rentable U.S. Forest Service **Shorty Peak lookout** (July 1-Sept. 30, $25). It's a 2.5-mile hike to the 15-by 15-foot cabin, perched at an elevation of 6,515 feet. The tower sleeps two and offers panoramic views of Creston Valley and the surrounding peaks. This lookout is in grizzly country, so take all appropriate precautions. For reservations, directions, and more information, contact the **Bonners Ferry Ranger District** (6286 Main St., Bonners Ferry, 208/267-5561, reservations 877/444-6777 or www.recreation.gov).

Rafting

Northeast of Bonners Ferry, the **Moyie River** provides Panhandle rafters with a one-day white-water stretch during its high-water season (Apr.-June). Lots of rock gardens among the Class II-III rapids can make it an interesting ride. **ROW Adventures** (Coeur d'Alene, 208/765-0841 or 800/451-6034, www.rowadventures.com) runs guided Moyie day

trips ($100-125) that begin and end in Moyie Springs.

The lazy **Kootenai River** isn't in a hurry to do much of anything. It eases out of Montana into Idaho, wanders aimlessly back and forth up the Purcell Trench, and then crosses the border into British Columbia to feed Kootenay Lake. The Class I float is perfect for leisurely canoeing and wildlife watching, particularly west of town where the river flows past Kootenai National Wildlife Refuge.

Cross-Country Skiing

The northernmost of the state's Park N' Ski areas, **Snow Creek Park N' Ski** lies 14 miles west of Bonners Ferry. Turn west off U.S. 95 south of town just before the golf course. The turnoff is marked with a sign for the Park N' Ski area. Follow the road west for a short distance and watch for Snow Creek Road 402 on the right. Snow Creek Road heads north up the valley a couple of miles before branching west once again and beginning its climb into the Selkirks. You'll probably need chains to make it to the trailhead; the road is steep and very icy in places. Parking at the trailhead may consist of no more than one small plowed slot, depending on the good graces of the plow driver.

The well-marked trail system provides a variety of interesting routes. On the Hemlock trail, you'll see numerous examples of the trail's namesake, the delicate mountain hemlock. Although these trails are high in the mountains, most of them are not high enough to offer any panoramic views. The trail system here is not extensive: The longest loop will take you just over an hour, about the time it takes to drive to the trailhead from Bonners Ferry in all but the best conditions. Grooming is minimal, and on weekends, snowmobilers will be buzzing about the vicinity.

Accommodations and Food

On the north end of town, two miles north of the Kootenai River on the west side of U.S. 95, is the ★ **Bonners Ferry Log Inn** (43 Tobe Way, Bonners Ferry, 208/267-3986,

Border Crossing Regulations

As of 2009, **U.S. citizens** must have a passport or similar document to enter Canada and to reenter the United States after their visit. The U.S. Department of Homeland Security's Western Hemisphere Travel Initiative requires all American citizens returning from Canada, Mexico, and the Caribbean to present one of the following documents: a valid passport, a passport card, an enhanced driver's license, or a Trusted Traveler Program Card (NEXUS, SENTRI, or FAST). To apply for these documents, contact the **U.S. Department of State** (877/487-2778, www.travel. state.gov). **Canadian citizens** now need a passport or similar documentation to enter the United States. **Citizens of all other countries** need passports and appropriate visas to enter Canada and the United States.

   Customs regulations for both countries are extensive. Generally, you can transport a limited dollar amount of foreign-bought goods across the border duty-free. Above that limit, you must declare your purchases and pay duty on them.

   Some items may require a **permit** to transport them between the two countries. Red flags immediately rise with firearms and other weapons, pets, agricultural products, and drugs (prescription or otherwise).

   For customs regulations and information pertaining to the Idaho border crossings, contact the **U.S. Customs** office in Eastport (208/267-3966, www.cbp.gov), or the **Canadian Customs** offices at the Idaho border: Kings Gate (250/424-5391) for Eastport and Rykerts (250/428-2575) for Porthill.

THE PANHANDLE
NORTH TO CANADA

---

www.bonnersferryloginn.com, $78-100). Even though the inn is right along the highway, it's farther away from the hustle and bustle than the motels on the south side of town. The beautifully landscaped grounds, warm, comfortable guest rooms, and toasty hot tub make it a good pick.

   The largest and swankiest lodging in town is the **Best Western Kootenai River Inn and Casino** (7169 Plaza St., Bonners Ferry, 208/267-8511 or 800/346-5668, from $109 d). The inn is owned and operated by the local Kootenai tribe, and gambling is the name of the game here. Expect to find a sea of slot machines and bingo, and all the finest amenities. Besides wonderful views of the Kootenai River, the inn's **The Springs Restaurant** (breakfast, lunch, and dinner daily, dinner entrées $14-26) offers a full-service menu of standard fare throughout the day.

   For burgers and craft beer, head to ★ **Kootenai River Brewing Company** (6424 Riverside St., Bonners Ferry, 208/267-4677, 11am-9pm daily, $7-13), a newish microbrewery that puts out a variety of handcrafted beers with names like Osprey Pilsner and Grizzly IPA. The brewpub serves above-average pub fare. Don't be surprised to find potato-chip nachos, saucy wings, salmon cakes, and big burgers.

Information

The **Bonners Ferry Visitors Center** (U.S. 95, 208/267-5922, www.bonnersferrychamber.com) is in the parking lot across the highway from the Kootenai River Inn. It's usually closed in winter, though. The U.S. Forest Service's **Bonners Ferry Ranger District** office (6286 Main St., Bonners Ferry, 208/267-5561) is on the south edge of town. They can hook you up with recreation information.

U.S. 95 TO EASTPORT

U.S. 95 leaves Bonners Ferry heading north, following the Kootenai River for a time. Then it branches east, winding its way through the Purcell Mountains to the Canadian border crossing at Eastport. For much of the way you drive through a veritable tunnel of trees.

Several nice lakes line the route, but they're all sheltered from view.

Camping

At **Smith Lake,** anglers will find a boat ramp and a small lake full of rainbow trout, bass, and catfish as well as the Forest Service **Smith Lake Campground** (7 sites, free). To get here, take Smith Lake Road (Forest Rd. 36) off U.S. 95, seven miles north of Bonners Ferry. Another 12 miles down U.S. 95 is Brush Lake Road (Forest Rd. 1004), which leads to **Brush Lake** and a campground (4 sites, free).

Nineteen miles from Bonners Ferry is Robinson Lake Campground Road (Forest Rd. 449), which leads into large **Robinson Lake** and a campground (10 sites, $8). A two-mile interpretive trail points out the intricate interactions within the forest ecosystem. Boaters note: The boat-launching ramp at Robinson Lake is on the lake's north side, accessed a little farther down the highway. No gasoline motors are permitted on Robinson Lake.

Copper Falls

Take time to stretch your legs at this exquisite spot just a short distance off the highway. Turn east at the Copper Creek Campground sign and head down Forest Road 2517 a couple of miles past the campground (16 sites, $8). Be careful of logging trucks along this road. A pullout on the right and a sign on the left mark the trailhead. The easy trail climbs briefly, and then traverses a beautiful slope of mixed conifers before descending slightly to **Copper Falls.** The falls make a beautiful 80-foot cascade, perfectly proportioned to allow you an up-close look without getting soaked. After crossing the creek, the trail loops back to the trailhead a little lower down Copper Creek (a total distance of less than a mile). Benches are well placed at particularly tranquil spots. Bring a picnic lunch and enjoy an alfresco repast in the cool clean air by the rushing waters.

Eastport

The **Eastport border station** marks the international boundary between the United States and Canada. It's open 24 hours. Those interested in cultural differences will note that canary-yellow Union Pacific locomotives rub elbows with their cherry-red Canadian Pacific cousins, while the Yankee-sharp U.S. Customs and Immigration building contrasts nicely with its older, more civilized Canuck counterpart. The Moyie River knows no border, however. It flows past unimpeded on the way to its confluence with the Kootenai, some 20 miles to the south as the Canada goose flies.

HIGHWAY 1 TO PORTHILL

From its junction with U.S. 95, Highway 1 continues up the Purcell Trench, past fertile farmland and the Kootenai River on the west and the abruptly steep Purcell Range on the east. The Purcells continue on into British Columbia, Canada. The Porthill border crossing is open 7am-11pm daily.

Background

The Landscape

Idaho has more than 83,000 square miles of land within its borders, making it the 14th-largest state in the nation in land area. Most of the state's population is concentrated along the Snake River Plain in the south and along the state's western fringe, leaving vast amounts of land either sparsely settled or uninhabited.

MOUNTAINS

Virtually the entire state is covered with mountains. Even on the wide grin of the Snake River Plain, which arcs across the width of southern Idaho, mountains rim the horizon in most directions.

Southern Ranges

The mountains rising up right behind Idaho's capital city of Boise are, appropriately enough, the **Boise Mountains.** Their lower slopes mirror the brown desert that spreads out along the Snake River Plain, while the upper slopes are home to Boise's backyard ski resort, Bogus Basin. Across the Snake River, in the state's southwest corner, are the **Owyhee Mountains.** Silver City, high in the Owyhees, was once one of the West's richest little towns, thanks to the vast seams of silver and gold found nearby.

East of the Owyhees, still on the south side of the Snake River, a string of north-south-trending ranges leads, one after the next, to the Wyoming border. This incredible procession of peaks is a prime example of basin-and-range topography, caused by the slow stretching apart of the earth's crust. Just across the Wyoming border rise the impressive granite spires of the Teton Range.

Central Ranges

The Wood River Valley is the most common gateway to the lofty ranges of central Idaho: the **Smoky Mountains** (home of Sun Valley's famous ski hill), **Pioneer Mountains,** the **Sawtooth Range,** and the **White Cloud Peaks.**

All of these ranges are high and wild, but the state's highest point, the 12,662-foot summit of **Borah Peak,** is farther east in the **Lost River Range.** Experienced mountaineers who make it to the top of Borah will also have a great view to the east of the lofty **Lemhi Range.**

In the very center of the state, the **Salmon River Mountains** make up most of the Frank Church-River of No Return Wilderness, south of the Salmon River. Farther west, the **Seven Devils Mountains** tower over Hells Canyon, providing spectacular views to hikers and horseback riders.

On the other side of the state, running north-south along most of Idaho's eastern border, is the **Bitterroot Range,** the towering rugged peaks that helped make Idaho the last of the Lower 48 states to be explored by nonnatives. The **Beaverhead** and **Centennial Ranges** are subranges of the Bitterroots on the Idaho-Montana border.

Northern Ranges

North of the Salmon River, the **Clearwater Mountains** extend north all the way to the St. Joe River. Across the St. Joe are the **St. Joe Mountains.** North of I-90, the **Coeur d'Alene Range** extends north to Lake Pend Oreille. Finally, way up in the Panhandle, you'll see the **Selkirk, Cabinet,** and **Purcell Ranges.** The Selkirks are home to small numbers of rare woodland caribou, and both

---

An Idaho Almanac

- **Birthday:** The 43rd state, Idaho joined the Union on July 3, 1890.

- **Capital:** Boise

- **Dimensions:** 483.5 miles long at its tallest point, varies from 45 miles wide at the tip of the Panhandle to 310 miles along the southern border. Area is 83,557 square miles, making it the 14th-largest state in area.

- **Population:** 1,567,582, according to the 2010 census

- **High point:** Borah Peak (12,662 feet), in the Lost River Range near Mackay

- **Low point:** Lewiston (738 feet), where the Snake River flows into Washington

- **State motto:** *Esto Perpetua,* meaning "It Is Forever." The motto adorns the state seal, which was designed in 1891 by Emma Edwards Green. It's the only state seal in the country designed by a woman.

- **State song:** "Here We Have Idaho," written in 1931 by Albert J. Tompkins, McKinley Helm, and Sallie Hume Douglas

- **State flower:** the syringa, which explodes into bloom like delicate white fireworks

- **State tree:** the western white pine, once abundant north of the Clearwater River. You can still see specimens of the hulking trees along the White Pine Scenic Byway (Hwy. 6 between Potlatch and St. Maries).

- **State bird:** the mountain bluebird, found throughout the West

- **State fruit:** the huckleberry

- **State gemstone:** the star garnet, which is found only in Idaho and India. The "star" is the rays within the garnet—normally four, sometimes six.

- **State horse:** the Appaloosa, proud horse of the Nez Perce. Horse lovers will want to visit the Appaloosa Museum in Moscow.

- **State folk dance:** the square dance

- **State insect:** the monarch butterfly

- **State fish:** the cutthroat trout, named for a red or orange slash on the bottom of its lower jaw

- **State fossil:** the Hagerman horse, discovered in the 1920s near Hagerman

---

the Selkirks and Cabinets remain grizzly bear country.

RIVERS AND LAKES
Along the Snake and Salmon

From its abundance of famous white-water rivers to its more than 2,000 lakes, Idaho is rich in water resources. Start with the mighty **Snake River,** which begins in Wyoming and then traverses the entire southern width of Idaho. The Snake enters Idaho at **Palisades**

Reservoir, a popular lake with boating anglers; below Palisades Dam, it's commonly called the **South Fork of the Snake** to differentiate it from the Snake's **Henrys Fork** tributary, which begins in a massive spring near Island Park. Both rivers are revered for fly-fishing.

As the Snake makes its way west across southern Idaho, it is dammed in many places (major turn-of-the-20th-century irrigation projects made Idaho the breadbasket it is today), forming reservoirs used for both water storage and recreation. Evel Knievel once tried to leap a rocket-powered cycle across the famous **Snake River Canyon** at Twin Falls, about 500 feet deep.

After passing through rapids-ridden Hells Canyon along the state's western border, the Snake rolls into Lewiston and then to its confluence with the Columbia River in Washington, which works its way to the Pacific Ocean near Astoria, Oregon.

The state's other famous river is the **Salmon River,** one of the country's longest free-flowing watercourses. It begins high in the Sawtooth Valley and flows through the Frank Church-River of No Return Wilderness before joining the Snake River in Hells Canyon. The Salmon was nicknamed the River of No Return early in the history of Euro-American exploration; because of its powerful rapids, explorers could float down the river but they could never boat back up. Today, jetboats defy this rule on parts of the main Salmon. The Salmon's largest tributary, the **Middle Fork Salmon River,** is another prime white-water run, even more remote and wild than the main Salmon.

South Idaho Waters

Other rivers beginning in and around the high peaks of the Sawtooths flow into southwest Idaho. The **Boise River** and **Payette River** both offer water recreation very near Boise, making them chock-full of boaters in summer. On the South Fork Payette you'll find some of the most spectacular white water in the state—a kayaker's heaven. Farther west, the **Weiser River** irrigates the farmlands of Hells Canyon rim country.

In the far southwestern corner of the state, the **Bruneau, Jarbidge,** and **Owyhee Rivers** cut deep, rugged canyons into the desert far from civilization. The rivers draw rafters and kayakers to their remote reaches in spring along with a few hardy canyon hikers year-round.

In south-central Idaho, the **Big Wood River** flows down from the heights north of Sun Valley to rendezvous with the Snake at the bottom of Malad Gorge. Along the way it's joined by the **Little Wood River,** which is fed by **Silver Creek.** All three draw anglers; Silver Creek is among the state's three most famous trout streams. East of the Little Wood, the **Big and Little Lost Rivers** and **Birch Creek** flow down from high valleys and disappear into the lava of the Snake River Plain, later to emerge at **Thousand Springs** along the Snake River in Hagerman Valley.

Down in the state's southeastern corner, **Bear Lake** boasts surreal turquoise-blue waters well used by water-skiers and anglers.

North Idaho Waters

Two of the finest white-water rivers in the country, the **Lochsa** and **Selway,** begin high along the Continental Divide and race their way down in furious rapids, coming together to form the more placid **Clearwater River,** an important spawning ground for anadromous salmon and steelhead. Farther north, through the southern reaches of Idaho's Panhandle, the **St. Joe River** and **St. Maries River** flow through big-timber country into the south end of **Coeur d'Alene Lake,** also fed by the **Coeur d'Alene River,** a historic waterway through the heart of Silver Valley mining country. It is drained by the **Spokane River,** which flows west into Washington State.

Sandpoint, farther north up the Panhandle, lies on the shores of **Lake Pend Oreille,** the state's largest body of water. The lake is so deep that the U.S. Navy uses it to test submarines. Others prefer to boat on the surface of the water, and marinas dot the shoreline. The lake is fed by the **Clark Fork River** and drained by the **Pend Oreille River.** A tributary of the Pend Oreille, the **Priest River** flows south out of **Priest Lake,** the state's most northerly major lake and one of its most beautiful. Tall mountains ring the shore, and wildlife is abundant in the area.

The **Kootenai River** and **Moyie River** drain the northernmost reaches of the state along the Canadian border.

the deep and majestic canyon cut by the Bruneau River in southwest Idaho

CLIMATE

Idaho's varied topography, ranging in elevation from 738-12,662 feet, and large size (the state spans seven degrees of latitude and six degrees of longitude) make for a complicated climate. Generally speaking, the state enjoys a relatively temperate, maritime-influenced climate that is drier than Washington and Oregon and milder than Montana and Wyoming. Also generally speaking, the north half of the state is lower, warmer, cloudier, and wetter than the south half.

Humidity is not much of a problem anywhere in the state. In the hottest months, humidity is generally a comfortable 25 percent or lower. Other weather woes you'll seldom see in Idaho include dense fog, tornadoes, and hailstorms, but high winds are common along the Snake River Plain.

Boise

Boise's climate is warm and dry in summer, cold and dry in winter. In July, highs average around 90°F, and overnight lows drop to around 59°F. Hot spells with temperatures over 100°F usually occur every summer but are short-lived. About 90 percent of July days are sunny, and the city usually gets only about 0.25 inch of rain that month. Fall in Boise offers stable, pleasant weather. Average high temperatures are around 78°F in September, 65°F in October, and 50°F in November, with average overnight lows of 50°F, 40°F, and 30°F, respectively.

In winter, temperatures remain relatively mild. January is the coldest month, with an average high temperature of around 37°F and an average overnight low around 22°F. Extended cold spells with high temperatures of 10°F or lower are not uncommon. Sunny days drop to around 40 percent in December-January. January is also the city's wettest month, although Boise is a dry place; average January precipitation is around 1.5 inches. Winds are relatively calm in winter, keeping windchill problems low.

The winds generally pick up in the spring, and this time of year has the most changeable weather and the biggest temperature swings. Daytime high temperatures average around 50°F in March, rising to 61°F in April and 71°F in May. Spring is also a relatively wet season in Boise and in southwest Idaho in general, with precipitation averaging more than one inch per month all season.

Southwest Idaho

Most of this region's sizable population lives in the relatively low-lying areas along the Snake River Plain and the valleys of the Boise, Payette, and Weiser Rivers. As in the southwest Idaho city of Boise, summers are toasty and winters are mild. Winter brings freezing temperatures only a couple of months of the year, in December-January. The state's reporting station at Swan Falls, on the floor of the Snake River Canyon south of Boise, has recorded the highest annual mean temperature in Idaho, 55°F.

At **Parma,** along the Boise River, at an elevation of 2,215 feet (about 600 feet lower than Boise), July days run around 93°F on average, while January days come in around 38°F.

Magic Valley

This part of the state also shows a wide range in elevation. Its lowest stretches along the Snake River are the warmest year-round. In **Twin Falls** (3,690 feet), July daytime highs average around 90°F, while overnight lows drop to around 55°F. January in Twin Falls brings daytime highs around 40°F and lows around 20°F.

From Twin Falls east up the Snake River Plain, freezing temperatures generally last December-February. Daytime high temperatures in **Burley,** about 500 feet higher than Twin Falls, average 88°F in July and just 36°F in January. Precipitation in south-central Idaho is heaviest in May, followed in no particular order by December, January, April, and June.

Southeast Idaho

Eastern Idaho may have the most complex weather in the state. Farthest from the reaches of the Pacific maritime storms, this region is influenced partially by pooped-out westerlies, partially by southerly storms pushing north from the Gulf of Mexico, and partially by disturbances from every other direction as the surrounding mountains swirl and break storms into any number of tracks. Precipitation patterns are the opposite of what you'd expect in the west and north parts of the state. Rainfall is heaviest in spring and summer, when thunderstorms are common. The region also has the widest temperature variations from season to season. Winter storms are among the coldest in the state, so it's no surprise that Grand Targhee Ski Area, in the Tetons just outside of Driggs, offers the state's lightest powder.

Pocatello (4,454 feet), on the Snake River Plain, sees July highs averaging 89°F and January highs around freezing, 32°F. In July, **Idaho Falls** (4,730 feet) stays just a couple of degrees cooler than Pocatello, but its January highs average a frigid 28°F. Both

cities are wettest in May-June. The **Island Park** area (6,300 feet) can see brutal cold: On December 17, 1964, the mercury dipped to -51°F. Temperatures aren't usually that severe, however; January highs average 25°F and July highs a pleasant 79°F.

Sun Valley and the Sawtooths

High altitudes mean lower temperatures, which makes the high country a great place to be in summer and a bitterly cold spot in winter. The National Weather Service reporting station near **Stanley,** at an elevation of 6,780 feet, holds the record for the state's lowest annual average temperature: a nippy 35.4°F. Much of the high country's precipitation comes as snow, a great boon to Sun Valley's reputation as a premier ski destination. December and January are the wettest months in Sun Valley, with high temperatures right around freezing. Spring comes late to the mountains; snow covers the high peaks and meadows until well past summer solstice. Look for wildflowers in June at the earliest, and not till July in many places. In summer, Sun Valley enjoys high temperatures in the 70s and low 80s with minimal precipitation.

East of Sun Valley in the rain shadow of the high peaks, the Lost River, Pahsimeroi, and Lemhi Valleys are among the state's driest regions, receiving an average of just over eight inches of precipitation annually.

North-Central Idaho

North-central Idaho is unique for its deep canyons, namely Hells Canyon of the Snake River, Salmon River Gorge, and the canyons of the Clearwater River and its tributaries. Towns on the floors of these canyons have the lowest elevations in the state and are sheltered from the wind, giving them the state's warmest temperatures. In summer, you'll definitely want air-conditioning in places like **Lewiston, Riggins,** and **Orofino,** where average temperatures hover around 90°F and periods of 100°F temperatures are not uncommon. On the plus side, in winter, none of these cities has a mean temperature below freezing.

Lewiston golfers play year-round, and a lush spring comes to town in March-April, when blossoms explode into color.

Up out of the canyons, on the prairies of north-central Idaho, higher elevations and increased wind make for cooler temperatures year-round in places like Moscow and Grangeville. Daytime high temperatures in **Moscow** (2,660 feet) average 84°F in July and 35°F in January. Precipitation in Moscow averages 23 inches annually, with winter the wettest season.

The Panhandle

North Idaho's maritime-influenced climate derives from prevailing westerlies that carry warm, wet storms from the Pacific and Gulf of Alaska across the Northwest. The Washington Cascades wring some of the moisture from these storms, but the Columbia River Gorge ushers other storms right on through to drop rain and snow on the Panhandle's mountains. Consistent with maritime weather patterns, winters here are cloudy and wet, while summers are clear and relatively dry. July is the prime travel month in the Panhandle, with precipitation reliably lower than in other months. Temperatures are more moderate year-round than at corresponding latitudes on the east side of the Continental Divide.

In the Silver Valley town of **Kellogg** (2,290 feet), look for July highs in the mid-80s, January highs in the mid-30s, and about 30 inches of rainfall per year. Farther north in **Sandpoint** (2,100 feet), July highs generally average 80°F, and January brings highs right down to freezing. Sandpoint receives an average of 34 inches of precipitation per year.

Plants

Syringa was designated as Idaho's state flower in 1931. This flowering wild shrub comes to life during the springtime all over the Gem State with clusters of snowy white flowers that put off a strong, sweet aroma.

DESERT AND SHRUBLAND
Sagebrush Country

Before the arrival of settlers and their irrigation practices, southern Idaho was largely an arid desert covered in heat- and drought-tolerant grasses and shrubs. Dominant among them is **sagebrush** (genus *Artemisia*), which comes in at least 23 different species in Idaho. One of the most common is big sage *(Artemisia tridentata).* Most sage species are small shrubs, but one variety, basin big sage, can grow to the size of a small tree.

In sage-dominated areas, you'll likely also encounter **antelope bitterbrush,** a favorite browse of antelope, deer, elk, and domestic livestock. Occasional particularly alkaline soils in the sagebrush zone support a number of salt-loving shrubs, including **greasewood, winterfat,** and **shadscale.**

Alongside the streams and rivers that slice benevolently through this barren landscape, larger, lusher vegetation flourishes. The *bois* that gave the Boise River its name were magnificent stands of **black cottonwood.** These impressive trees can grow to more than 100 feet tall and eight feet in diameter, and they light up bright yellow in fall. Black cottonwood is the state's largest native broadleaf tree, found along every major river in the state. Another native species, **narrowleaf cottonwood,** grows principally in southeast Idaho; look for it along the South Fork of the Snake River, downstream from Palisades Reservoir.

Another common plant along Idaho riverbanks is **willow.** About 30 species inhabit the state, making *Salix* the largest genus in Idaho. Willows range in size from shrubs to large trees. Their bitter bark is the source of salicylic acid, a proven headache remedy. Perhaps this explains why the bark is a favorite food of the perennially busy beaver. In winter, the yellows and oranges of the plant's leafless stems brighten drainages across the state. While shrub-size willows are most common in the wild, the large **golden weeping willow** (*Salix alba* Tristis) is a popular tree-size ornamental.

Juniper Highlands

In the high-desert areas of southern Idaho, you'll find occasional tracts of juniper. These evergreens are too small for commercial lumber production but are widely used across southern Idaho for fence posts and firewood. The tiny, spherical, pale-blue cones are frequently called "berries," and they're responsible for giving your gin its just-so flavor. The berries, along with the tree's scaly leaves, make the juniper easy to identify.

Near the Utah border on I-84 you'll pass through a large area of **Utah juniper** that supports a population of ferruginous hawks. To the east are occasional woodlands of **Rocky Mountain juniper,** the most common species in the state, while to the west stretch vast areas dominated by **western juniper,** the largest of the three species found in Idaho. The Owyhee County Backcountry Byway passes through a particularly large and absolutely stunning forest of western juniper.

A couple of pines are commonly found growing in and around juniper woodlands, primarily in the southern reaches of the state. The hardy **limber pine** ordinarily prefers higher elevations but has established a community among the juniper woodlands around Soda Springs as well as atop the lava fields of Craters of the Moon National Monument. **Singleleaf piñon** also enjoys the company of junipers in and around south-central Idaho's City of Rocks. The piñon is an anomaly in many ways. It is a Great Basin species most commonly found farther south in Nevada (the City of Rocks area is the northernmost tip of its range and its only foothold in Idaho). It's also the world's only species of pine growing

syringa, Idaho's state flower

single needles akin to a fir; all other pines grow needles in bundles of 2-5. And unlike other pines, the piñon bears extra-large seeds called pine nuts, a food enjoyed and often relied on by Native Americans.

Mountain Shrub Zone

As you head up into Idaho's southern hills, the sagebrush-dominated desert vegetation gives way to a habitat of predominantly broadleaf shrubs. The most common species of this zone is **curlleaf mountain-mahogany.** It's no relation to the exotic Southeast Asian mahogany prized for fine woodworking, but its dark wood is similar. Deer and elk love the stuff and tend to keep it trimmed down to shrub size. You can identify mountain-mahogany by its narrow and leathery one-inch-long green leaves, and by the unique 2-3-inch-long feathery tails emerging from its seedpods. Other common shrubs in this zone include **black chokecherry,** found throughout the state in warm, relatively low-altitude locations; **antelope bitterbrush,** whose range extends down into the sagebrush zone; and **western serviceberry,** one of Idaho's most ubiquitous plants.

A number of relatively small native trees also inhabit this zone, including **interior box-elder** and **bigtooth maple.** The latter lights up like a blowtorch in fall, all dark reds and oranges. It's the state's largest color-changing tree.

FORESTS

Botanists classify Idaho's forests under the umbrella heading of **Rocky Mountain montane,** a biome that includes most of the forest lands of the Rockies, extending from British Columbia in the north, through Idaho, and on down to New Mexico in the south. Several different specific forest types make up this biome.

Ponderosa Pine Forest

On sunny slopes at lower elevations (1,000-3,500 feet), the ponderosa pine is king. It's the widest-ranging and most common pine in North America and one of the grandest as well. A large ponderosa can reach over seven feet in diameter and be as tall as an 18-story building.

Mature ponderosas have thick, platelike bark that provides protection from forest fires; the bark is colored so intensely golden-orange it seems to glow in the sunshine. As a result, many foresters call them "pumpkins." The tree's thirsty root system sucks up nutrients to such a degree that no other trees or even shrubs of consequence can grow within a wide radius of the trunk. This makes the ponderosa look like a solitary loner and accentuates its magnificence.

Ponderosa pine needles are 4-8 inches long and grow three to a bundle, but unless you're looking at a young tree that hasn't developed its characteristic bark or size, you probably won't need to get up so close for identification. The best place in Idaho to see these beautiful trees is, not surprisingly, along the state's **Ponderosa Pine Scenic Byway,** Highway 21 between Boise and Stanley.

Douglas Fir Forest

Above the ponderosas at a cooler and wetter altitude is the Douglas fir zone. Douglas fir is named after David Douglas, a 19th-century naturalist who named and cataloged many of the trees found in the Pacific Northwest. This tree is a little harder than ponderosa pine to identify from a distance. No particular distinguishing features are apparent until you get up close and personal. Look at the cones. Odd paper-thin bracts protrude from behind the normal woody cone scales. Most of central Idaho is covered with Douglas fir. It's the most important fodder for Idaho's timber industry, and you can find it across the state. The biggest one, a 209-foot-tall skyscraper nearly six feet in diameter, rules the woods southeast of Clarkia.

Cedar-Hemlock Forest

Given an even cooler, wetter environment than the Douglas fir zone, things start to get interesting. Where the ponderosa pine rules essentially alone, and the Douglas firs have but one or two interlopers keeping them company, the cedar-hemlock zone is shared by three climax species and several other prominent hangers-on. Here the woods can take on the dark, wet, fecund feel of a rain forest.

The three climax species in this zone are **grand fir, western red cedar,** and **western hemlock.** Southern Idaho is too dry to support these trees, so this zone is found primarily in maritime-influenced west-central and northern Idaho. Grand fir prefers the zone's drier ranges, usually equating with either lower altitudes or lower latitudes. Like all true firs, its cones stand upright on the branches and its needles grow singly from the twigs.

Western red cedar is generally a little thirstier, growing higher within the zone or hunkering down near streambeds. Western red cedars have a different family tree, so to speak, than pines and firs. They're in the juniper family (Cupressaceae), and like junipers their leaves are scalelike rather than needlelike. Their foliage looks distinctly ferny from a distance. They're the giants of this zone in terms of bulk, growing to more than 18 feet in diameter.

The western hemlock thrives in the wet and stormy high-altitude end of the zone. Forests dominated by this tree have an enchanted, primeval quality, giving the impression that if you took a short nap on the forest floor, you might awaken covered by a blanket of lush ferns and mosses. Head for Priest Lake State Park to see what the western hemlock forests are all about.

Another prominent inhabitant of this zone is **western white pine,** Idaho's **state tree** and the battleship of the state's arboreal fleet. Its hulking gray trunk rises straight as an arrow off the forest floor, reaching heights of nearly 200 feet. The biggest white pine in Idaho is nearly seven feet in diameter. The species is very valuable to the timber industry. Between the chainsaws and the dreaded white pine blister rust (a fungus lethal to these leviathans), it's lucky Idaho has any specimens of its state tree left standing.

One more resident of the cedar-hemlock zone is worth mentioning. Scattered throughout the wetter areas of the Panhandle and densely concentrated in the mountains around Elk City is the **Pacific yew.** This tree has attracted a lot of attention in recent years since the discovery that its bark contains taxol, a compound that slows the growth of cancerous tumors. The yew is a relatively small tree with flat, one-inch-long leaves and thin, reddish bark.

Subalpine Forests

The highest forests of Idaho—ranging in elevation from around 5,000 feet right up to the timberline—are the airy realm of **Engelmann spruce, subalpine fir,** and **mountain hemlock.** Both Engelmann spruce and subalpine fir have steeply peaked crowns; the latter is especially pointy on top, looking almost surreally cartoonish. The two trees are usually found growing together as neighbors. If you can't tell them apart by their shape, look at the cones: the fir's stand up on the branches, while the spruce's hang down.

The third climax species of the subalpine forests is the exquisitely elegant mountain hemlock, John Muir's favorite tree. You'll have no trouble recognizing this one—just look for the graceful, droopy crown. These trees require a cool, wet climate, and as a result are found only in the high mountains of Idaho's Panhandle, and then usually on the wettest north-facing slopes.

Several other trees also prefer life in the subalpine zone. **Limber pine** is found at subalpine heights in the sunny east-central and southeast portions of the state, and it has been known to grow occasionally at lower elevations. Look for it in the lava fields at Craters of the Moon National Monument. **Whitebark pine** is a gnarly denizen of the craggy timberline reaches, ranging from the high country of central Idaho north to the Panhandle. It's almost never found lower than the subalpine zone. Grizzly bears like to chow down on whitebark pine nuts in fall, so it's not a bad idea to know what the tree looks like if you're hiking in bear country. Both the limber and whitebark pines have short needles that come five to a bundle. Male whitebark cones are easily recognizable because they're purple. **Subalpine larch** is another high-altitude habitué. It requires a cold but sunny climate and is found above 8,000 feet in the Sawtooths, above 7,000 feet in the Selkirks. Like all larches, its needles turn brilliant gold in fall.

Two More Ubiquitous Trees

A prolific deciduous tree counts as one of the regulars in Idaho's forests. The splendid **quaking aspen** provides a delicate counterpoint to the deep green of surrounding conifers. Aspens have albino bark and shimmering leaves that are light green in spring and turn brilliant gold in fall.

Another tree found widely across Idaho is the **lodgepole pine.** It's easy to identify: Its long, straight trunks, once used by Native Americans as lodge poles, are covered with a thin, pale, distinctively pebbly bark. The lodgepole's clever reproductive strategy has led to its ubiquity. The tree produces two types of cones. Some of the cones open and drop normally, allowing the tree a chance to reproduce in any openings in the understory. Others remain closed and tightly sealed with resin until fire sweeps through. The flames melt the resin, freeing the seeds and allowing them to get started on the open, sunlight- and nutrient-rich burned-out slopes. Thanks to this unique trait and a fast-growing nature, lodgepoles tend to come back first and dominate forests charred by fire. The lodgepole isn't too picky about its habitat. It'll grow anywhere from the Douglas fir zone up to the subalpine zone, but it does prefer cold temperatures. You'll find good examples of lodgepole forest at Harriman State Park near Island Park, a very cold place in winter that was burned out many summers ago.

Animals

THREATENED AND ENDANGERED SPECIES
Wolves

Largest of the wild dogs, the wolf stands close to three feet tall at the shoulder, stretching as long as six feet from nose to tail tip. An average adult male weighs around 100 pounds. Wolves are intelligent, playful, social animals with one unfortunate character trait that has made them pariahs in their homeland. Although wild deer and elk form the mainstay of their diet, they've also been known to eat livestock. The wolves' taste for domesticated animals has caused some of the most heated debates in the Northwest and probably more than a few fistfights over the years in saloons across rural Montana, Wyoming, and Idaho.

For many years, ranchers killed the animals with abandon. Once the most numerous large predator in the United States, wolves were virtually exterminated from the American Rockies by the 1930s, when they were trapped, shot, and poisoned by ranchers and bounty hunters. In 1988 the gray wolf population in Boise National Forest was estimated at between four and nine.

In 1973, Congress passed the Endangered Species Act, designed to identify and protect endangered species and nurse their populations back to self-sustaining levels. As originally written, the act required the U.S. Fish and Wildlife Service to take positive action to reintroduce endangered species to their former habitat, at the same time placing severe penalties on anyone attempting to harm those species in any way. When it came the wolves' turn for protection under the law, it set off a major political battle in the West, pitting ranchers against the government and environmentalists, who pushed for the act's full implementation on behalf of the beleaguered wolf.

More than a decade of political wrangling ensued, as powerful Western ranching interests and their allied representatives in Washington (both elected and nonelected) attempted to overthrow the Endangered Species Act. At last a deal was reached that seemed to please no one—probably the sign of a good compromise. The act was not overturned, and the U.S. Fish and Wildlife Service proceeded with efforts to reintroduce wolves to the West. But the Act was amended to allow reintroduction of the wolves as "nonessential, experimental" populations south of I-90, which removes the strictest protective measures of the federal government from such populations. (North of I-90, where there isn't much ranching, the wolves received regular endangered species status.)

The compromise appears to have worked. Fifteen gray wolves were released into central Idaho in 1995, and by 2002 the state's wolf population had climbed to more than 250 in an estimated 19 packs. In the broader Northern Rockies region, including Idaho,

Montana, and Wyoming's Yellowstone National Park, where wolves were reintroduced in the mid-1990s, there were an estimated 664 wolves in 44 packs by 2003. These numbers helped lead the U.S. Fish and Wildlife Service in March 2003 to reclassify gray wolves as a "threatened" species.

The controversy and contention about wolves rages on in Idaho. In 2008, to the dismay of environmentalists and the delight of ranchers and hunters, the federal government delisted wolves from endangered species protection. This action paved the way for wolf hunting in Idaho and Montana. The Idaho Department of Fish and Game allocated a quota of 220 wolves to be taken during the 2009 hunting season; approximately 134 wolves were killed legally in Idaho, and 72 were taken in Montana.

In 2010, the 9th U.S. Circuit Court of Appeals overturned the ruling, which once again gave wolves protection under the Endangered Species Act, to the consternation of Idaho's top elected officials. But the very next year, the federal government began to allow states to regulate their own wolf populations, which paved the way for wolf hunting to become an annual event in Idaho. Activists and wolf advocates are not giving up the fight, though.

Grizzly Bears

At one time this biggest and most powerful of North American mammals was widespread across the West, but that was before Lewis and Clark set the stage for human devastation of the grizzly population, which were reduced to around 1,200 in the Lower 48 over the years. In 1975, grizzlies were given threatened status under the Endangered Species Act, and today Idaho is one of only four states where *Ursus arctos* still lives (the others are Washington, Montana, and Wyoming).

Wildlife biologists believe there are as many as 100 grizzlies living in Idaho at any given time. But unless you go backpacking in a few specific areas of the state and get extremely lucky, you'll probably never see a grizzly. They roam the northern tip of the Panhandle north of Sandpoint, particularly in the Selkirk Mountains; the Bitterroot Range from the Clark Fork River south to the headwaters of the St. Joe River; and along the Wyoming border from near Henrys Lake south to Alpine.

The grizzly is immense. A full-grown adult male averages 450 pounds and can weigh up to 500 pounds. Just coming across a fresh grizzly print in the mud is enough to set the adrenaline flowing as the scale of this beautiful beast becomes apparent. Grizzlies are far larger than black bears, but at a distance, it might be difficult to gauge an animal's size. You can't tell a black bear from a grizzly by color alone, because grizzlies can appear black and black bears can be brown. Look for the dish-shaped head profile and the telltale shoulder hump.

Salmon

Idaho was once home to literally millions of anadromous fish, meaning they are born in freshwater, migrate downstream to the sea, grow into adults there, and then return upriver to their birthplace to spawn. Idaho is at the headwaters of the great Columbia River drainage; historically, the total run of adult fish to the Columbia River has been estimated at 8-16 million fish, of which the Snake River may have produced 1.5-3 million. Salmon and steelhead once made their way annually from the Pacific up the Columbia to the Snake River, and up the Snake River to prime spawning grounds on the Salmon and Clearwater Rivers and their tributaries, a journey of up to 900 miles. Redfish Lake in Idaho's Sawtooth Mountains gained its name from the area's first settlers, who found the lake colored red with the bodies of thousands of sockeye salmon that spawned here each season. Idaho's Native Americans relied on the salmon as a staple in their diet for centuries.

Then the newer human transplants built dams to harness the waters of the Columbia for cheap electricity. Twelve dams were constructed on the Columbia, Snake, and

Clearwater Rivers between 1938 and 1973. The main-stem dams were equipped with fish ladders to help adults get upstream to spawn but provided no help for offspring making their way back to the sea. The fish were sucked into dam turbines and killed, died of disease exacerbated by the warmer temperature of the slower-moving water, or succumbed to increased predation during the journey. Before the dams, the young smolts made it to the Pacific in 7-10 days. After the dams, it took two months or more for those who made it at all.

Three species of salmon (the coho, chinook, and sockeye) once spawned in Idaho waters, along with the steelhead, an anadromous rainbow trout. The coho was officially declared extinct on the Snake River in 1986. The sockeye population has struggled over the years. All sockeye that return are captured and placed in a captive-breeding program in an effort to save the species. Wild chinook salmon were declared a threatened species when returns declined to a few thousand adults in the early 1990s, and wild steelhead were listed as threatened under the Endangered Species Act in 1997. Although artificial production (hatchery) programs produce millions of smolts every year and provide some surplus fish for fishing, the once-abundant wild and natural runs remain at a tiny fraction of the historical numbers. None of the mitigation measures attempted, including capturing smolts above the dams and barging or trucking them to the sea, has worked to restore natural spawning and wild salmon runs.

Environmentalists have urged the breaching of four dams on the Lower Snake River, but the idea hasn't gained political traction, and the salmon issue remains mired in legal maneuvering.

Bull Trout

Back in 1949, a world-record 32-pound bull trout was pulled from Lake Pend Oreille. But the bull trout (actually not a trout at all, but a char) hasn't been doing so well in recent years,

and it's now listed as threatened. A predator fish that prefers the coldest waters, bull trout are also sometimes called Dolly Varden.

Woodland Caribou

Two small herds of Selkirk Mountains woodland caribou cling to a precarious existence in the Panhandle's Selkirk Range and neighboring eastern Washington and British Columbia. Populations had declined to around 25 animals in the early 1980s. Today, after extensive management efforts to strengthen populations, there are still only around 35-40 animals left. Habitat loss and low birthrates have inhibited their comeback. Wildlife biologists have proposed establishing a third herd, hoping to keep the gene pool strong and avoid catastrophic loss of animals from disease. The caribou, a medium-size member of the deer family, has a broad muzzle, large hooves, and impressive antlers with shovel-like brow tines.

OTHER ANIMALS
Mammals
BLACK BEARS

Common and numerous throughout Idaho and the West, the black bear (Ursus americanus) is much more likely to be encountered by Idaho hikers and backpackers than its larger cousin, the grizzly. The black bear was once a shy, nervous creature of little threat, but continued human-bear encounters have left it less afraid of humans and more likely to be trouble. Black bears are smaller than grizzlies, have straight (as opposed to dished) head profiles, and lack the grizzly's trademark shoulder hump. Also note that unlike grizzlies, many black bears are adept at climbing trees.

WILD DOGS AND CATS

The wolf's little cousin, the **coyote** (Canis latrans), is alive and well in Idaho. This survivor plays a leading role in many Nez Perce legends; he's a cagey prankster who always seems to have a lesson to teach. **Mountain lions** inhabit remote parts of Idaho but are so shy and elusive they are seldom seen by humans.

Other cool cats found in Idaho include the **bobcat** and the **Canada lynx.**

HORNS AND HOOVES

Elk were found across the country when European explorers first arrived. By 1900 the New World's new residents had killed off 99 percent of them. The rest were found almost entirely in Yellowstone National Park. Today, healthy elk populations can be found all over the state.

White-tailed deer and **mule deer** are plentiful, as is the largest member of the deer family, the **moose.** Priest Lake in the Panhandle is a possible spot to see a moose, as are the Caribou-Targhee National Forest of southeast Idaho and along the North Fork of the Payette River near McCall.

Mountain goats can often be seen on the high cliffs of central Idaho, while **bighorn sheep** share the arid southwestern deserts and highlands with **pronghorn.** Owyhee County is also home to relatively large herds of **wild horses.**

SMALL MAMMALS

Beavers have become popular helpers in restoring rangelands eroded by cattle. Dams built by the 50-pound, paddle-tailed rodents create wetlands, slow fast-moving storm water before it can do erosion damage, and catch eroded topsoil before it's washed downstream. **River otters** also inhabit many of the state's waterways. **Marmots** and **pikas** inhabit rocky areas, usually above the timberline. The pika's sharp whistle is familiar to high-country backpackers.

Life isn't so good these days for the **Northern Idaho ground squirrel,** a species found only in a 20- by 61-mile area in Adams and Valley Counties. In the mid-1980s there were about 5,000 such squirrels; today there are fewer than 500, and they're listed as threatened. Ground squirrel populations have declined mainly due to habitat loss and fragmentation.

Birds
RAPTORS

Southwest Idaho provides the focal point of human efforts to preserve raptors, or birds of prey. On the outskirts of Boise you'll find the World Center for Birds of Prey, and, farther south, the Birds of Prey National Conservation Area. The latter preserve protects a stretch of the Snake River and the surrounding cliff tops where, in spring, the world's densest concentration of nesting

elk in a meadow

raptors can be found—more than 700 pairs of 14 different species.

A cruise down just about any rural road in the region will provide close-up looks at big birds of prey perched on power lines or soaring on thermals. But Idaho's incredible cast of raptors, including red-tailed hawks, Swainson's hawks, ferruginous hawks, goshawks, northern harriers, peregrine falcons, prairie falcons, bald eagles, golden eagles, short-eared owls, great horned owls, ospreys, and others, aren't just found in southern Idaho. For example, **bald eagles,** whose populations have recovered from near extinction and have been down-listed from endangered to threatened status under the Endangered Species Act, can be found in winter across the state, from Boise to Coeur d'Alene, fishing in open waters. **Ospreys** seem to particularly like the southeast shores of Coeur d'Alene Lake around Harrison, while **ferruginous hawks** congregate in the Juniper Valley near the Utah border. And the ubiquitous **vulture** will carry on wherever there's carrion.

WATERFOWL

Eastern Idaho lies along a major avian migratory route, and its lakes and wetlands become mass staging areas for hundreds of thousands of **ducks** and **geese** in spring and fall. **Sandhill cranes** flock to Gray's Lake National Wildlife Refuge in some numbers; if you're lucky, you might catch a glimpse of the endangered **whooping crane** there as well. The largest of all North American waterfowl is the rare **trumpeter swan,** which weighs 30-40 pounds and has a wingspan of up to eight feet. Hunting and habitat loss had reduced their numbers to as few as 200 at the turn of the 20th century. Though they are still rare, the trumpeter population is now about 3,000. Trumpeters migrate through the Henrys Fork area; look for them at Harriman State Park in winter.

Fish
TROUT

Many consider the anadromous steelhead trout to be the state's premier game fish. Adult steelhead can weigh 10-15 pounds and are found in the Snake, Salmon, and Clearwater Rivers and their tributaries.

True trout species in Idaho include **rainbow, cutthroat, brook, brown,** and **lake trout,** this last also known as mackinaw. Also in the trout family are Idaho's **kamloops** and **kokanee.**

a hooked trout as it is reeled to shore in the Snake River

STURGEON

For sheer size, the king of Idaho's piscine population is the bottom-feeding white sturgeon. These giants live about as long as people—100-year-old individuals have been reported, although the oldest fish officially documented by state biologists was 65. Today, these fish grow to lengths of over 11 feet and weigh upward of 300 pounds. In the old days, before commercial fishing and the construction of the Snake River dams, individuals up to 20 feet long and weighing more than 1,000 pounds were reported (and yes, photographed for posterity). But populations have declined steadily since the turn of the 20th century. Commercial sturgeon fishing has been banned since 1943, and today all sport sturgeon fishing is catch-and-release only. In 1995, sturgeon fishing on the Kootenai River was closed completely. The strongest remaining sturgeon populations are found today on two stretches of the Snake River: between Bliss Dam and C. J. Strike Dam, and between Hells Canyon Dam and Lewiston.

WARM-WATER FISH

Idaho's lakes harbor a number of species prized by anglers, including largemouth and smallmouth **bass,** three different species of **catfish,** and **perch, crappie,** and **tiger muskie.** The **Bonneville cisco** is a rare sardine-like fish that lives only in the waters of Bear Lake, in Idaho's southeastern corner.

History

THE EARLIEST INHABITANTS

The earliest people to roam the state on a more-or-less continuous basis probably came into the area some 14,000 years ago. Luckily not yet clear on the concept of no-trace camping, these nomadic hunters left remnants of their existence behind. At the bottom of Wilson Butte Cave near Dietrich in south-central Idaho, archaeologists have discovered bones of a prehistoric horse, camel, and sloth dating from 13,000 BC and a spear point dated to 12,500 BC—one of the oldest conclusive bits of evidence of human habitation in the country.

Native Americans

Before the arrival of the Lewis and Clark expedition in 1805, the Northwest was inhabited by numerous tribes of indigenous peoples. The **Kootenai** tribe roamed the territory now comprising southern British Columbia, northeastern Washington, the Idaho Panhandle, and northwestern Montana. They fished for salmon and sturgeon in the rivers; hunted deer, elk, and caribou; and gathered wild vegetables, roots, and berries. The **Coeur d'Alene** tribe lived around Coeur d'Alene Lake. They too hunted deer and fished in the lake and its feeder rivers. To catch salmon, they trekked to Spokane Falls, which blocked salmon migration to Coeur d'Alene Lake and the upstream rivers.

Eastern Oregon's Wallowa Valley, parts of southeastern Washington, and Idaho's Clearwater River Valley were once the home territory of the **Nez Perce** tribe. They fished for salmon in the Clearwater River; hunted deer, elk, moose, bighorn sheep, and bears; and gathered camas roots from the vast field on the Camas Prairie around Grangeville.

Southwestern Idaho was part of the territory wandered by the **Shoshone** and **Paiute** tribes of the Great Basin, a vast area spanning parts of southeastern Oregon, northeastern California, southwestern Idaho, and northern Nevada. Tribal cooks in this desert landscape had an entirely different list of ingredients to choose from; hunters brought in pronghorn, sage grouse, squirrels, rabbits, and prairie dogs as well as deer. Some bands found pine nuts; some searched for seeds and berries. Bands were small, and the people were peaceful.

The Shoshone people coexisted in south-central and southeastern Idaho with the **Bannock** people; the two tribes had distinct languages but shared similar hunter-gatherer lifestyles.

The Spanish introduced horses to North America in their forays into Mexico and today's southwestern United States, and by around 1700 the horse reached the Native Americans of Idaho. Soon many tribes made forays across the Continental Divide into what is now Montana and Wyoming. There they found great herds of buffalo that would sustain them until the nonnatives came and wiped out the herds. The trails blazed by the Idaho tribes crossing east to the buffalo-hunting grounds were the same trails later used in the opposite direction by explorers, fur trappers, and pioneers.

THE ADVENTURES OF LEWIS AND CLARK
The Corps of Discovery

Even before the April 1803 brokering of the Louisiana Purchase gave the United States title to most of the West, President Thomas Jefferson secretly began planning an exploratory expedition to find a viable northern route between the Mississippi River and the Pacific Ocean. Jefferson looked to his personal secretary, a young Virginian named Meriwether Lewis, to lead the mission. Lewis had been a captain in the Virginia state militia. Much of his duty had been west of the Alleghenies, and he had considerable experience dealing with indigenous Native Americans.

Lewis chose fellow Virginian William Clark as his co-commander. Clark also had considerable military experience. He was known as a skilled negotiator with Native Americans as well as a qualified mapmaker. He also recruited many members for the expedition. By the winter of 1803-1804, Lewis and Clark and their party of about 40 men were camped at the confluence of the Missouri and

Mississippi Rivers near St. Louis. Lewis was 29; Clark, 33.

In May 1804, the expedition, known as the Corps of Discovery, set out west. Their mission: to follow the Missouri River to its headwaters in the Rocky Mountains, cross the Rockies, and find the nearest navigable waterway to the Pacific Ocean. The first summer was marked by several meetings with Indian nations and by Lewis and Clark's careful recording (via their journals and sketches) of many plants and animals unknown in the eastern United States.

By October 1804, the expedition had reached North Dakota. They wintered there near a village of Minnetaree (Hidatsa), Mandan, and Amahami people and picked up their famous guide, a teenage Shoshone woman named Sacagawea. As a girl, Sacagawea had lived with her people in the Lemhi Valley near present-day Salmon, Idaho. But on a hunting expedition into Montana, her band had been attacked by the Minnetarees. Sacagawea, about age 12, was captured and taken east to be traded among the Indians like legal tender. She ended up as the property and wife of French trapper Toussaint Charbonneau. When Lewis and Clark reached the Minnetaree village, they hired Charbonneau as an interpreter, at least in part with the hope that Sacagawea might be able to help them find her people and negotiate for horses to cross the Rocky Mountains. When the Corps of Discovery resumed its westward journey in May 1805, Sacagawea, Charbonneau, and the couple's two-month-old baby joined the expedition.

Scouting the Bitterroots

A small advance party led by Lewis crossed the Continental Divide on August 12, becoming the first nonnatives to lay eyes on the land that would become Idaho. It was the last piece of the American jigsaw puzzle to be filled in and the beginning of the end for the region's Native American inhabitants. The explorers' route across the Continental Divide is today commemorated by the **Lewis and Clark**

National Backcountry Byway, which connects Montana's Highway 324 with Idaho's Highway 28 at Tendoy. It can be negotiated in summer by a sturdy passenger vehicle or a trusty Appaloosa.

The party continued down the western side of the pass and soon surprised a small group of Shoshone women. After being assured of the party's peaceful intentions, the women led the group back to their main encampment, where they were received with open arms. In a twist of fate, Sacagawea and a Shoshone woman saw each other and gleefully embraced. It seems Sacagawea had found her people at last—the Shoshone woman was a childhood friend. Later that night, the two groups celebrated with a reunion feast. But it was a bittersweet reunion for Sacagawea, who learned that most of her family was dead.

Lewis told the Shoshone chief, Cameahwait, of his plan to navigate the Lemhi River downstream, eventually to the Columbia. The chief advised against it, telling Lewis that not far to the north, past a major confluence (with the Salmon River), the river cascaded through steep, impassable canyons. Lewis suspected the chief was exaggerating and decided to forge ahead with the plan.

Continuing West

On the morning of August 17, Clark and a small party began to scout a route down the Lemhi River. Not far past the confluence of the Lemhi and Salmon Rivers, the steep route along the Salmon was judged impassable, exactly as Chief Cameahwait had told Lewis. Clark dispatched a messenger relaying the word to Lewis, who agreed that the expedition should abandon the Lemhi-Salmon Rivers route and instead attempt the Nez Perce route (the Lolo Trail) that crossed the Bitterroot Mountains far to the north. Lewis and the rest of the expedition set out immediately, crossing Lemhi Pass and catching up with Clark once again. Sacagawea bade a sad farewell to her people and, along with the rest of the corps, headed north.

They doggedly worked their way up the

Continental Divide, first along the west side via the North Fork of the Salmon, then across to the Montana side near **Lost Trail Pass** (U.S. 93 today) and down into the Bitterroot River Valley, where they camped with a party of 400 Salish people.

Over the Bitterroots, Barely

After camping for a few days at the junction of the Bitterroot and Lolo Creek, the party proceeded west up the creek along a traditional Nez Perce hunting trail. On September 13 they crested **Lolo Pass** and dropped back into Idaho. They camped in present-day Packer Meadows near Lolo Pass and along the Lochsa River near what's now the Powell Ranger Station. Game was scarce, and they had to kill a horse for meat. On September 15, the party set off up Wendover Ridge to gain the Nez Perce trail to the north. It began to snow, obscuring the trail and slowing progress even further. Clark was "as wet and as cold in every part as I ever was in my life, indeed I was at one time fearful my feet would freeze in the thin moccasins which I wore." It's a wonder they didn't lose anyone to hypothermia. The early-season storm had driven the game out of the mountains to lower, warmer elevations, making food scarce for the expedition. They shot another horse for dinner and huddled around campfires trying to get warm.

By September 18, the expedition had run out of spare horses to fricassee. (Picture yourself on a remote mountain trail in 1805, in stormy weather, with no Gore-Tex, no road, no car, no ready-made food, and no idea what lay ahead. It's safe to say that the expedition was running on hope at this point.) Clark and a party of six hunters went on ahead to find, kill, and bring back food. Two days out, they sighted the Weippe Prairie—a welcome, easily traversable bench unlike the steep canyons they'd been crossing, and also where they met the Nez Perce. Although some discussed killing the strangers, Nez Perce oral history says they were stopped by a woman named Watkuweis who, like Sacagawea, was kidnapped when she was younger and had been helped by white people. The agreeable Nez Perce gave Clark's party dried salmon and camas flour, some of which Clark sent back to Lewis and the rest of the expedition with one of his men. Clark and his hunting party accompanied the Nez Perce to their main encampment farther downriver at present-day Orofino. Lewis and the rest of the corps straggled in later.

Among the Nez Perce

Safe and in good hands with the friendly Nez Perce, they established their own camp, called Canoe Camp, just west of the Nez Perce camp, near today's Ahsahka, where they recuperated from their difficult mountain crossing. Besides being a place to recuperate, Canoe Camp was important for another reason. When Lewis and Clark saw the Nez Perce paddling up and down the river, they knew that they could now safely do the same. The expedition members began cutting down ponderosa pines to fashion into canoes, and by October 6, five canoes were finished and preparations were made to get under way. Under cover of darkness, the expedition members dug a secret hole and buried all their saddles. Then they branded their remaining horses and left them with the Nez Perce, intending to pick them up on their return trip the following spring.

The next day they floated and loaded their canoes and said goodbye to their hosts. Nez Perce Chief Twisted Hair gave Lewis and Clark a map of what lay downriver, and a couple of Nez Perce offered to come along as guides. At last they shoved off. The river's rapids proved difficult, and twice canoes were damaged. But the expedition reached the confluence of the Clearwater and Snake Rivers (site of present-day Lewiston, Idaho, and Clarkston, Washington) on October 10, and paddled on into Washington.

Epilogue

The expedition continued down the Snake to the Columbia River and then down the Columbia to the Pacific Ocean in mid-November. They built Fort Clatsop near present-day Astoria, Oregon, and stayed for the winter. On March 23, 1806, they began their return journey by essentially the same route they had come. They picked up the horses and saddles they'd left with the Nez Perce at Orofino. The Indians once again treated them warmly, and the explorers camped near present-day Kamiah for nearly a month while they waited for the snow to melt from the Bitterroots.

Lewis and Clark arrived in St. Louis to a hero's welcome on September 23, 1806. Most people had long since given them up for dead. The expedition had been a success on many fronts. It had carried out its mission while losing only one man—Charles Floyd, whose appendix ruptured three months into the trip. It had proved an overland route to the Pacific was possible, mapped the land and cataloged its flora and fauna, and established friendly relations with the indigenous peoples. But all those accomplishments contributed to the subsequent flood of white emigrants to the West, an unstoppable wave that would greatly diminish Native American culture and have a profound effect on the land and resources of the Northwest.

THE FUR TRAPPERS
David Thompson

Two years after Lewis and Clark passed through Idaho on their way back home, British fur trappers began working their way into the territory from Canada. One of the first to arrive was geographer David Thompson, an Englishman working for Britain's venerable Hudson's Bay Company. Thompson—today widely considered one of the greatest geographers in history—was an explorer at heart who used fur trapping as a convenient way to fund his true passion. He had come to Canada as a teenage apprentice for Hudson's Bay, and by the time he arrived in Idaho in 1808 he had vast experience in mapmaking and dealing with indigenous peoples. He had also jumped ship, so to speak, leaving Hudson's

Bay Company for its Montreal-based British archrival, the **North West Company.**

In 1809, Thompson and his crew built a log house, the first permanent structure built by nonnatives in Idaho, near the present-day town of Hope on Lake Pend Oreille. They named it Kullyspell House after the area's Kalispel Indians—a goodwill gesture guaranteed to grease the wheels of trade with the locals. In the four years Thompson stayed at Kullyspell House, he and his colleagues sent bushel upon bushel of beaver pelts back to England, where beaver-fur hats were all the rage. Also during that period, Thompson explored and mapped much of the Panhandle, established good relations with the Native Americans, and surveyed the passes that would later allow railroads into the area. In doing so he set the stage for further nonnative expansion into the Panhandle.

Andrew Henry

Not to be outdone by the Brits, American interests soon raced west to reap their share of the wealth. First to the scene were members of the St. Louis-based **Missouri Fur Company.** In 1809, Pennsylvania native Andrew Henry, a former lead miner, became a partner in the enterprise. In the fall of the following year, Henry led a party of the company's trappers across the Continental Divide into southern Idaho. There he discovered a big, beautiful lake and encouraging prospects for trapping. Deciding to settle in the area for the winter, Henry headed downstream from the lake several miles and built a fort. What he didn't know was that the area sees some of the coldest, most severe winter weather in the West. The winter of 1810-1811 was no exception. The local deer and antelope hightailed it out of there early to go play on a warmer range, leaving little for Henry's party to hunt and eat. The men were forced to fry up their own horses to survive. As soon as the first spring thaw came, Henry decided Missouri wasn't such a bad place after all and returned home posthaste. While the trip hadn't yielded much in the way of beaver pelts, Henry did get immortality out of it: The big beautiful lake and the river below it are now called **Henrys Lake** and **Henrys Fork,** respectively.

Wilson Price Hunt

The same winter that Andrew Henry huddled shivering and homesick in eastern Idaho, 28-year-old greenhorn Wilson Price Hunt was holed up in South Dakota, leading an expedition for John Jacob Astor's **Pacific Fur Company.** After winter let up, Hunt's party continued west. That fall they made it to Jackson Hole, where they came upon three impressive mountain peaks stacked against the horizon. The sight inspired a couple of French Canadians to name the impressive peaks Les Trois Tétons: "The Three Breasts." Today we know the beautiful mountains as the Grand Tetons.

The party continued over Teton Pass into Idaho, arriving in October 1811 at abandoned Fort Henry, where they made the mistake of leaving their horses behind and attempting to ride the Snake River west. The eastern Snake is a relatively placid affair, today floated by novices, but the flat waters become cantankerous downstream. The expedition portaged around Idaho Falls and American Falls with little difficulty, but then they came to the Milner Reach, a section that even today is run only by experts and fools.

The Hunt party lost a man and equipment on the upper Milner Reach, but the worst was yet to come: a spot so ferocious, so impossibly unforgiving that they named it **Caldron Linn,** or Witch's Caldron Falls. From a safe vantage point today, you can feel some of what Hunt and his men felt. The innocuous river rounds a corner and far too suddenly funnels down a tight rocky gorge, thundering into frothing white madness. The falls spark respect, if not outright fear. And remember, today the flow is regulated by Milner Dam upriver. When Hunt's party first saw Caldron Linn, the water was racing unbridled down from the Continental Divide. It must have been horrifying. The expedition abandoned thoughts of floating to the Columbia River and began an overland trek along the banks of the Snake. They pressed on forlornly, reaching Fort Astoria at the mouth of the Columbia River in mid-February 1812.

The Woods!

It may sound like something out of *Fantasy Island,* but it was actually the men of an 1832-1834 expedition led by **Captain Benjamin Louis Eulalie de Bonneville** who famously said, *"Les bois! Les bois!*—"The woods! The woods!" Bonneville was from a Parisian family that came to the United States in 1803 after Napoleon took control of their homeland. Young Bonneville graduated from West Point and became an Army officer. When he decided to mount his own expedition to the West, the Army graciously gave him some time off to do so.

In 1832, the 110-man expedition left Fort Osage, Missouri, and made it to the Salmon River headwaters before winter set in. The following spring they moved to southeast Idaho, and the year after that, in 1834, they followed the dry and dusty north bank of the Snake River west. After miles and miles of this desert landscape, they topped a small rise and saw to the west a river valley filled with trees, lush and verdant in the distance. The French Canadians could hardly contain themselves.

Today you can drive to the site where they saw the trees (it's just north of I-84) and read a plaque that will tell you that it was the ecstatic Bonneville expedition that gave the Boise River its name. It's a nice story, but some historians believe that the river was given its name by fur trappers more than 20 years before.

Bonneville got an Idaho county, a prehistoric lake, and a modern-day Utah salt flat named for him, but he never really amounted to much as a trapper. You can read all about him in Washington Irving's book *The Adventures of Captain Bonneville,* published in 1837.

The Fur Forts

The year 1834 also saw the establishment of two permanent fur-trading forts on the Snake River: **Fort Boise** in the west, at the confluence of the Snake and Boise Rivers near present-day Parma; and **Fort Hall** in the east, near present-day Blackfoot. Both forts were successful and important for two reasons. First, they led to the eventual end of the rendezvous system by creating what were essentially permanent year-round rendezvous sites. Their strategic placement at either end of the Snake River Plain would make them important way stations along the emigrant trails soon to be established.

Fort Boise (not to be confused with the U.S. Army fort of the same name in today's city of Boise) was built by the Hudson's Bay Company and run by a jolly French Canadian trapper named **François Payette.** The portly Payette was well known for the hospitality he lavished on visitors to his fort, setting out feasts for his guests and regaling them with tales of his past adventures. The Payette River was named after him.

Fort Hall was built and run by **Nathaniel Wyeth,** a Boston entrepreneur who had been trying unsuccessfully to wring a profit out of the West for some years. The fort was christened with a raucous party on August 5, 1834. Wyeth must have had high hopes that day. Unfortunately, the venture proved only marginally lucrative. After just two full seasons, he sold the fort to the Hudson's Bay Company and moved back to Boston. One might suspect Wyeth's financial disappointments were caused by a lack of business acumen, but for this venture he just had bad luck and bad timing. Although Fort Hall remained in use by the Hudson's Bay Company until 1856, out West, the times were a-changing.

EARLY MISSIONARIES

When Idaho's indigenous peoples first encountered nonnatives, they must have been amazed at the odd things the pioneers carried with them: guns, medicines, Christianity. In 1831 the Nez Perce decided to send a party of emissaries back to St. Louis to visit their old friend William Clark. After the success of the Corps of Discovery expedition, Clark had taken an assignment with the U.S. government as head of Indian affairs for the West. The Nez Perce may have intended to ask Clark to send them someone to teach them reading, writing, and farming—or they may have sought spiritual assistance in exploring Christianity. Whichever their motivation, word soon spread of the Nez Perce sending representatives all the way to St. Louis in search of a Christian god, and the challenge was quickly taken up.

The Lapwai Mission

Henry and Eliza Spalding answered the call and ended up in Idaho, where they built a mission among the Nez Perce at the confluence of Lapwai Creek and the Clearwater River. By all accounts, the Spaldings were quite a couple. Eliza learned to read and write the Nez Perce language, and soon was teaching locals of all ages to do the same. Word of her successful school reached a Protestant mission in Hawaii, which sent Eliza a printing press so she could print her lessons. In 1838 Eliza had a baby, also named Eliza, the first nonnative child born in Idaho.

Henry was equally busy. First he built a cabin and outbuildings, then taught the locals farming. They got a sizable garden up and sprouting and built a gristmill, a sawmill, and a blacksmith shop. Soon they were up to their ears in corn and up to their eyes in potatoes. The Nez Perce were sufficiently intrigued by the idea of farming to settle around the mission and begin cultivating their own plots. In 1839, Henry put in an irrigation system, the region's first.

Things went well for a few years, but soon the novelty wore off for the Nez Perce. The Spaldings were unable to supply the Native Americans with much in the way of firearms or magic medicinal remedies, and Henry became a strict disciplinarian who was sometimes harsh with the locals. When word got to the Spaldings that Marcus and Narcissa Whitman had been killed, Henry and Eliza decided to leave Lapwai. With a friendly

Nez Perce escort to protect them from the Cayuse, they moved to the Willamette Valley and took up farming. Eliza died there in 1851. Henry moved back to Lapwai in 1863, where he died in 1874; both he and Eliza are buried there. The site of the Spaldings' Lapwai mission is today part of Nez Perce National Historic Park, easily visited off U.S. 12 east of Lewiston.

The Catholic Contingent

Protestants weren't the only ones actively attempting to convert Idaho's indigenous peoples. The first Roman Catholic missionary on the scene was the Belgian priest **Father Pierre Jean de Smet,** who arrived in Idaho's Coeur d'Alene country in 1841. De Smet laid the groundwork for the Mission of the Sacred Heart, which was constructed in its final form and location by **Father Antonio Ravalli** in the early 1850s. The mission was built entirely without nails and still stands today, the oldest extant public building in Idaho. It boldly crowns a hillock along the Coeur d'Alene River east of the city of Coeur d'Alene. The disastrous floods of early 1996 inundated much of the Panhandle, but the old mission stayed high and dry—a credit to Father Ravalli's site selection.

WESTWARD BOUND
South Pass:
Gateway to the West

By the 1840s the reports of Lewis and Clark, fur trappers, the Spaldings and Whitmans, and naval explorers off the Pacific coast all confirmed Oregon Country was not a desert wasteland; rather it was a bountiful region of good water and rich soil, ripe for cultivation and settlement. But how to get there? Lewis and Clark, following the Missouri River and its tributaries, had struggled over the Continental Divide at Idaho's Bitterroot Range. Clearly, settlers' wagons could never negotiate the passes that had almost defeated the Corps of Discovery.

The key that unlocked the West to settlers existed but had gone all but unnoticed.

In 1824 the great mountain man Jedediah Smith had led a party of trappers working for William Henry Ashley across the Rockies at Wyoming's South Pass. Unlike Idaho's paths across the Rockies, South Pass hardly seems a pass at all. It arcs gently up and over the Continental Divide like a rolling swell on a calm sea. South Pass was reached not by following the Missouri River to its headwaters in Montana, as Lewis and Clark had done, but by following the Missouri to its confluence with the Platte River (near present-day Omaha, Nebraska). From there, the emigrants followed first the Platte, then the Sweetwater River west to its headwaters in Wyoming's Antelope Hills, just east of South Pass.

However, it wasn't until 1841 that the first bold party of pioneers hell-bent on settling the West set out from Missouri. The group of 70 was led by Thomas Fitzpatrick, who had helped found the Rocky Mountain Fur Company in 1830, and John Bidwell, who split off with about half the settlers at Soda Springs and made his way to California. Among the 70 emigrants was Jesuit Father de Smet, the early Panhandle missionary. Their journey was successful.

The following year, one of the country's great explorers, **John C. Frémont,** headed to Wyoming as a member of an official government survey expedition. The survey party crossed South Pass, and Frémont's rich, prosaic reports made the crossing seem like a walk in the park. The following year, Frémont took the trail all the way to Oregon Country. With the benefit of an immensely talented ghostwriter—his wife, Jessie—Frémont described the whole route from St. Louis to Oregon in an enthusiastic and detailed report that was published by Congress and found its way into the hands of many an American contemplating the trek. The route Frémont described (one capable of being negotiated by settlers' wagons) came to be known as the **Oregon Trail.**

The Great Migration

In 1843 a combination of favorable reports from the West, malaria outbreaks in the Mississippi and Missouri River valleys, and perhaps a desire to participate in history prompted the first major wave of emigrants to pack their wagons. About 1,000 hopefuls set out from Independence, Missouri, that spring. The schedule for the crossing was tight. They couldn't leave the Midwest before the spring grasses had sprouted because they needed the new growth to feed their livestock. Yet they had to be safely across the mountains of Oregon before the first snowfall. The average trip took five months.

The "trail" the pioneers followed was seldom a single set of tracks but rather a braid of parallel trails. Only in the narrow passes and canyons did the various parties funnel into the exact path of their predecessors; in those places, even today, you'll find deep wagon ruts.

Along the way, the Oregon Trail emigrants crossed through the territories of many different indigenous nations between Missouri and Oregon. Some of the Native Americans were friendly, some more hostile. The emigrants were understandably worried about Native American attacks, but that proved the least of their worries. Most who died succumbed to accidents or disease.

Along the Snake River

After crossing South Pass, the original Oregon Trail entered today's southeast Idaho (at the time part of Oregon Territory) near Bear Lake and headed north to Fort Hall, Nathaniel Wyeth's old fur fort on the upper Snake River. In 1837, Wyeth had sold Fort Hall to the Hudson's Bay Company. The British managers, fearing they'd be driven out by Americans flooding into Oregon, customarily tried to discourage settlers from continuing west. They exaggerated the difficulty of the route, telling emigrants that the rest of the trail to Oregon was impassable by wagons. As a result, many pioneers traded their oxen and wagons for horses for the remainder of the journey.

Like bookends, Fort Hall in the east and Fort Boise in the west were the only two safe harbors along Idaho's stretch of the Oregon Trail. Leaving Fort Boise, the trail followed the south side of the Snake River west through hot, dry, and treeless desert and lava country. Occasionally, emigrants might sight the tantalizing waters of the river, usually out of reach at the bottom of steep, rocky canyons.

At **Three Island Crossing,** near today's Glenns Ferry, they were faced with a choice: brave the river crossing to easier going on a shorter route down the north side, or continue the long way down the hot and dry south side. Much of the decision depended on how high the Snake was running when they got there. The Snake's south side can be pretty miserable during the dog days of August, even for today's motorists. Imagine what the pioneers felt like, tromping through the dust day after day, with no air-conditioned car or motel room to offer respite. Reaching Fort Boise and the legendary hospitality of François Payette must have felt very good indeed, especially knowing that they were nearing Oregon.

Between 1841 and 1848, most westward-bound pioneers followed this route to Oregon; a far smaller number turned off the trail and headed south to California. Those proportions were reversed dramatically following the discovery of gold in California in 1848. Between 1849 and 1860, about 42,000 pioneers followed the Oregon Trail west to fertile farmland in Oregon's Willamette Valley, while some 200,000 others staked their future on easy money and headed to California, the "Golden State."

The California Trail and Hudspeth's Cutoff

Those pioneers choosing California as their destination followed the Oregon Trail west from Fort Hall only as far as the confluence of the Snake with the Raft River. There they turned south up the Raft River Valley, crossed the divide at City of Rocks, and continued south into Nevada and across the Sierras to the promised land. This route was used primarily until 1849. That year, a group of emigrants led by Benoni Hudspeth tried a shortcut similar to the original route followed by John Bidwell in 1841. From Soda Springs, they turned directly west, crossed four separate north-south-trending mountain ranges, and rejoined the California Trail midway up the Raft River Valley. This route turned out to be 25 miles and two days shorter than the previous route via Fort Hall.

Three Island Crossing State Park commemorates one of the most important sites on the Oregon Trail.

Other Routes

In 1859 the federal government commissioned engineer Frederick Lander to build a new wagon road from Wyoming's South Pass directly west to Fort Hall. The **Lander Road** took 100 miles off the length of the Oregon Trail. It also bypassed Fort Bridger, depriving the fort's great mountain-man proprietor, Jim Bridger, of a large chunk of business.

In 1862 another mountain man, Tim Goodale, pioneered a new route from Fort Hall to Fort Boise. Instead of following the hot, dry Snake River Plain west, **Goodale's Cutoff** headed northwest from Fort Hall to the base of the Pioneers. Hopping west from river to river at higher elevations than the routes to the south, Goodale's followers made their way across the Camas Prairie near present-day Fairfield before rejoining the Oregon Trail some 75 miles east of Fort Boise.

The Wood River Valley town of Hailey is named for John Hailey, who pioneered a stagecoach route from Salt Lake City to Boise City in 1869. The **Kelton Road** left Kelton, Utah, passed through the major pioneer-trail intersection at City of Rocks, continued northwest to the little oasis at Rock Creek, then crossed the Snake River and followed the north side of the river into Boise. This was the most important mail and freight route across southern Idaho until the Oregon Short Line Railroad was completed in 1883.

GOLD FEVER

Before 1848, the Oregon Trail was the major route, and the California Trail was a smaller spur. Then James Marshall discovered gold at Sutter's Fort, and the two trails swapped places in importance. Gold fever built throughout the West as strikes were made in British Columbia, Nevada, and Colorado.

The first find in Idaho was made by E. D. Pierce in 1860. Pierce was an Irish immigrant who had been a captain in the Mexican War. In 1852, while trading in north-central Idaho's Nez Perce country, he heard stories of gold in the area. He caught gold fever, but he didn't start prospecting there. News of Canada's

Fraser River strikes reached him, and he raced north, apparently meeting with little success.

In 1855 the Nez Perce signed a treaty with the U.S. government that created the Nez Perce Reservation. Pierce returned to Idaho's Nez Perce country in 1860 to find that whites were no longer welcome on the lands he had seen. He asked the tribe to let him do some prospecting on the reservation, but the Nez Perce understandably refused. Not to be deterred, Pierce and 10 other men snuck onto the reservation without permission and began searching for riches on the north fork of the Clearwater River. The Nez Perce eventually discovered the miners but restrained themselves from throwing the trespassers out. That fall, one of the Pierce-party miners, Wilbur Bassett, found some very fine gold in a shovelful of dirt. The Idaho gold rush was on.

The Clearwater Mines and Boise Basin

Soon the Orofino Mining District was formed, and miners rushed into the area. By the summer of 1861, some 3,000 nonnatives had moved in; by the following summer, 10,000. Pierce City and Orofino were founded as the Nez Perce looked on helplessly. The miners spread out, and new mining towns sprouted: Elk City, Newsome, and Florence. Some $3 million worth of gold dust was carried out of the area by the steamships plying the Snake and Columbia Rivers to and from Lewiston.

Named for Meriwether Lewis of Corps of Discovery fame, Lewiston became the rip-roaring supply center for the Clearwater District. Outlaws and vigilantes ran unchecked by any active judicial system. Idaho's first newspaper, *The Golden Age,* started up in Lewiston, and mail service was instituted; the mail was carried on foot between Lewiston and Pierce City, a 10-day trip.

In August 1862, a group of miners discovered gold in the Boise Basin, 30 miles north of today's city of Boise. Idaho City, Placerville, Centerville, and nearby Rocky Bar and Atlanta sprang up to support the hordes of money-hungry hopefuls. Because these communities supported a substantial population of nonnatives, the government decided it needed a fort in the area to protect the miners and their families from hostile Native Americans. The Army selected a site at the foot of the mountains along the Boise River and dedicated Fort Boise on July 4, 1863. (This fort was not connected with the Hudson's Bay Company's famous fur fort of the same name, at the confluence of the Boise and Snake Rivers some 40 miles to the west.) A town was platted around the Army post and grew quickly as the major supply center for the Boise Basin mines, which yielded an estimated $66 million in gold. Today, the basin's boomtowns are ghost towns, relying not on mining but on tourism to keep them alive. Idaho City on Highway 21 is the easiest to reach and the most developed; Atlanta, at the base of the Sawtooths, is the most ghostly.

The Owyhee Mines

Also in 1863, miners discovered gold along Jordan Creek in the Owyhee Mountains, about 50 miles southwest of Boise. The initial finds were streambed placer deposits that soon played out. But then rich seams of gold and silver were discovered up on War Eagle Mountain, and the focus shifted from placer to hard-rock mining. Ruby City was the first major settlement in the area but was soon replaced by Silver City, two miles farther upstream. In the mid-1860s, a constant stream of hopeful miners poured in, giving Silver City a peak population of 2,000. The mines turned out to be among the world's richest, and Silver City became one of southern Idaho's biggest boomtowns.

Unfortunately, it also became one of the most violent. When two competing mining companies discovered they were mining the same seam from opposite directions, an underground mining war broke out. One company's foreman was killed by gunfire deep in the shafts, while mining magnate J. Marion More died when an argument on the porch of the Idaho Hotel in Silver City got out of control and shots were fired. The territorial governor sent in troops from Fort Boise to quell the disturbance, which ended with no further bloodshed. The Owyhee unrest was a portent of even greater troubles to come in Idaho's mining industry.

Idaho Territory

During the Clearwater, Boise Basin, and Owyhee mining booms, this part of the country was part of Washington Territory, headquartered in Olympia. Fearful that the wealth and population explosion that mining was bringing to the eastern part of the territory would result in a shift of governmental power away from them, Olympians began lobbying to separate the mining districts in a new territory. On March 4, 1863, President Abraham Lincoln signed into law the act creating Idaho Territory. The western boundary of the territory corresponded to today's borders between Idaho on the east and Washington and Oregon on the west. The eastern reaches of the new territory took in parts of Montana and Wyoming.

The territory's name, Idaho, had no particular meaning. In 1859 it had been suggested as the name for a new territory being formed around the Pike's Peak Mining District. At that time, the head of the Senate Committee on Territories explained that Idaho was an Indian word meaning "Gem of the Mountains." When that was proved untrue, the name Colorado Territory was chosen instead. The name Idaho still appealed to some people, however, and was used as the name of a steamship on the Columbia River's Portland-Lewiston run. The steamship supplied the mines up the Clearwater River, which as a result came to be loosely referred to as the Idaho mines. Eventually, the name was applied to the new Idaho Territory.

Lewiston was the only readily accessible city in the fledgling territory, so it was chosen as the temporary territorial capital. The first territorial governor, William Wallace, was a close personal friend of Abe Lincoln. Wallace took office in Lewiston on July 10, 1863, and immediately faced his first crisis.

It seems Lewiston wasn't technically in Idaho Territory, but instead squarely on the Nez Perce Reservation, as delineated by the 1855 treaty. The Nez Perce had allowed the miners a primitive staging and supply camp at the site, located at the confluence of the Clearwater and Snake Rivers. But the inch given had turned into a mile taken, and Lewiston had become a full-fledged town in the process. Wallace and the federal government approached the Nez Perce, asking the Native Americans to once again negotiate away more of their land, which included Lewiston. To say the least, the Nez Perce people were divided. One group resigned themselves to a reduced reservation and signed a new treaty; the other group refused. The "non-treaty" Nez Perce didn't make trouble then but 14 years later precipitated the Nez Perce War of 1877.

Just five months after taking office as Idaho's governor, Wallace was elected as a territorial delegate. He resigned as governor and moved to Washington, D.C., in December 1863. His replacement, Caleb Lyon, arrived in Lewiston in August 1864. Lyon soon found himself in the middle of a heated debate over where to put the territory's capital. Since the formation of the territory, the mines served by Lewiston had begun to play out and most of the miners had moved south to the Boise Basin, where mines were beginning to boom. In December 1864, the territorial legislature met in Lewiston and voted to move the capital to Boise City, supply center for the Boise Basin mines and protected from trouble by the U.S. Army's Fort Boise. Lewiston's residents were furious, and Governor Lyon was on the hot seat. Under the pretense of going duck hunting, he fled across the Snake River to Washington and didn't return for a year. In the meantime, territorial secretary C. DeWitt Smith arrived in Lewiston and, with the aid of federal troops, forcibly took possession of the territorial seal and archives and took them south to Boise. From that point on, Boise was entrenched as the territorial capital and later as state capital.

THE IRON HORSE
Idaho's First Railroad

With the driving of the golden spike at Promontory, Utah, on May 10, 1869, the Union Pacific and the Central Pacific Railroads were linked, and a transcontinental rail line became a reality. The rail line passed north of Salt Lake City, but that was no problem for Brigham Young and the Mormons; they formed the Utah Central Railroad and built their own spur north to the Union Pacific Line at Ogden, completing the link in 1870. The following year, the Mormons organized the **Utah Northern Railroad,** planning to build a narrow-gauge line north from Ogden to the gold mines of western Montana. This rail line reached Franklin on May 2, 1874. Here it temporarily ran out of steam, but not before it had become the first railroad into Idaho Territory.

Franklin grew into a major freight center for wagons shipping goods back and forth from the Montana mines, which lay due north over Monida Pass (the route of today's I-15). With all this commerce on the route, it was inevitable that someone would succeed in pushing a rail line through. A new company loosely affiliated with Union Pacific, the **Utah and Northern Railway Company,** grabbed the honor, completing a connection between Franklin and the Northern Pacific line at Garrison, Montana, in 1884. This line had a profound effect on southeast Idaho, as settlements of predominantly Mormon colonists sprang up all along the route. Between 1879 and 1889, many new towns appeared in the region, among them Menan, Rexburg, Rigby, Sugar City, and Victor.

Tracks Along the Oregon Trail

Scouts for the Union Pacific had investigated possible railway routes along the Oregon Trail as early as 1867. By 1881 the company was ready to build the line. All it needed to do was sidestep government regulations that prohibited it from doing so. Another "loose affiliate" of Union Pacific was formed, and work on the new **Oregon Short Line Railway** began. Construction began off the main

Union Pacific line at Granger, Wyoming, and headed northwest to Montpelier, Pocatello, and Shoshone, where a spur was constructed up to the Wood River Valley mines. The line was completed through to Huntington, Oregon, on November 17, 1884, and hauled both passengers and freight. With transfers at Granger and Huntington, passengers could make an Omaha-Portland trip in three and a half days. The iron horse had made the country smaller.

The line also eased development of the Snake River Plain, as irrigation equipment, seeds, harvested crops, cattle, and laborers could now cross the plain easily and connect with markets across the country. Pocatello, junction of the Oregon Short Line and the Utah and Northern, became an important rail hub, and in 1893 was named the seat of Bannock County.

Northern Routes

Railroad builders in northern Idaho were also hard at work in the 1870s and 1880s. In 1883 the **Northern Pacific Railway** connected eastern Washington with Missoula, Montana, via Sandpoint, resulting in a through line from St. Paul, Minnesota, to Portland, Oregon. In 1887 a branch line was extended up the South Fork Coeur d'Alene River; by 1891 it had crested Lookout Pass and connected through to Montana along the route of today's I-90. This line was later taken over by the Northern Pacific. In 1892, the **Great Northern Railway** connected St. Paul and Seattle via Bonners Ferry, Sandpoint, and Spokane.

Finally, in 1909, the old **Chicago, Milwaukee, St. Paul, and Pacific Railroad** pushed into Idaho from Montana south of Lookout Pass. It was unusual because a 438-mile segment of the line over the Continental Divide was handled by electric-powered trains. Numerous tunnels and trestles were built to get the trains down from the pass to Avery, Idaho, on the St. Joe River. The now-abandoned railroad grade has become the Route of the Hiawatha, one of the West's coolest mountain-biking trails.

MODERN TIMES
Statehood

Oregon gained statehood in 1859, Nevada in 1864, Washington and Montana in 1889. By 1890, the movement was afoot either to make Idaho Territory a state or to apportion it among neighboring states. The rivalry between the former and the current capital

Oregon Trail near Glenns Ferry

cities, Lewiston and Boise, had continued unabated since C. DeWitt Smith had "stolen" the territorial books from Lewiston in 1865. Lewiston residents wanted nothing more than to separate from Boise. Nevada was looking to annex southern Idaho. Northern Idaho residents were split; Palouse farmers and many others wanted to annex the northern part of the territory to geographically and economically aligned Washington, while Silver Valley miners preferred annexation to Montana, which they perceived as a more mining-friendly state. Boise politicians fought to retain a unified Idaho with Boise as the capital. Finally, southern Idaho threw northern Idaho just enough of a bone to keep it from seceding: plans for a university in northern Idaho at Moscow. Northern Idaho agreed to the deal and got behind the push for Idaho statehood. President Benjamin Harrison signed the bill creating Idaho, the 43rd state, on July 3, 1890, and Idaho's star was officially placed on the nation's flag the following day, July 4. Emma Edwards Green designed the state seal in 1891, the University of Idaho opened in Moscow on October 3, 1892, and Idaho granted women the right to vote in 1896, becoming the fourth state to do so.

The Growth of Agriculture

Idaho's population nearly doubled between 1890 and 1900, and it more than doubled between 1900 and 1910. The reason was agriculture. First the timber barons came west and discovered the great pine forests of Idaho. The U.S. government had given much of Idaho's forestlands outright to the railroads, supposedly to encourage westward expansion. Given the cozy relationship between the era's politicians and business leaders, one suspects their motives were rather less principled and more self-serving. The timber companies snapped up this land for a song, since the railroads knew their trains would haul the logs out of the forests. It was a classic case of mutual backscratching. Loggers flooded into the state to partake in the conversion of green to gold.

Next, dry farmers turned the Palouse into a profitable sea of green. Between the fertile farmland there and the new university, the population of north-central Idaho swelled. But the biggest factor in increasing Idaho's population after the turn of the century was the development of irrigation on the Snake River Plain. A whole network of privately financed canals laced southwest Idaho by 1900, and settlers rushed in to try their luck at farming. These canals made use of the many tributaries of the Snake River. The mass volumes of water in the Snake River itself weren't fully exploited until the completion of major government-sponsored irrigation projects in the early 1900s.

In 1894 the federal government passed the Carey Act, which granted federally owned arid lands to the states if they would undertake and complete irrigation projects on those lands within 10 years. Private companies built the irrigation systems on the state land, and when those systems were completed, the lands were offered for sale. Farmers bought parcels of irrigated land from the state and bought water rights to that land from the irrigation companies.

Nowhere was this public-private partnership more successful than in south-central Idaho. Led by Twin Falls entrepreneur Ira B. Perrine, the region's movers and shakers completed Milner Dam in 1905 along with a network of canals that eventually irrigated 244,000 acres. Farms soon blanketed the once dry, desert region, which as a result of its incredible transformation was nicknamed the Magic Valley. Along with subsequent similar projects under the Carey Act, 850,000 arable acres were created, and Idaho's population increased by 50,000 as a result.

The Reclamation Act of 1902 brought the federal government in on the irrigation efforts in a big way. The U.S. Reclamation Service, forerunner of the Bureau of Reclamation, built huge, earth-filled Minidoka Dam near Rupert between 1904 and 1906. The dam included the region's first major hydroelectric power plant. Other federal Reclamation Act dams included Arrowrock Dam on the Boise

Famous Idahoans

Among famous natives or transplanted residents who have called Idaho home:

ARTS AND ENTERTAINMENT

- Matthew Barney – mixed media artist
- Gutzon Borglum – sculptor of Mount Rushmore
- Gene Harris – jazz musician
- Mariel Hemingway – actor
- George Kennedy – actor
- Lana Turner – actor
- Bruce Willis – actor

BUSINESS

- Joseph Albertson – founder of Albertson's supermarkets
- Nephi and Golden Grigg – founders of Ore-Ida Potato Products
- Harry Morrison and Morris Knudsen – cofounders of the Morrison-Knudsen civil engineering firm
- J. R. Simplot – potato king; was the richest man in Idaho

LITERATURE

- Edgar Rice Burroughs – creator of the *Tarzan* series

River and American Falls Dam. As a result of irrigation, nearly the entire Snake River Plain was rapidly settled, and Idaho became one of the country's premier agricultural states.

World War I and the 1920s

Following the outbreak of World War I in 1914, the state's agricultural potential was tapped to its fullest as farmers geared up to supply food for Allied troops. Nearly 20,000 Idahoans served in the armed forces during the war, and 782 of those lost their lives. Patriotism ran high, spawning occasional bouts of anti-German backlash. Interestingly, the state's governor during this period and his wife were German immigrants. Moses Alexander was elected in 1914 as the nation's first Jewish governor. Perhaps because he was Jewish, or because he was not especially sympathetic to other German immigrants enduring suspicion bordering on persecution in the state, Alexander's loyalties were considered above reproach.

At the end of the war, returning GIs brought home victory but also a particularly virulent strain of influenza dubbed the Spanish flu. The virus swept through the world's population; 500,000 Americans died from the disease, and Idaho was not exempt. The epidemic lasted until spring 1919.

The Roaring '20s didn't do much roaring in Idaho. After the war, agricultural exports tapered off as European farmers returned to their fields. The resultant farm-commodity surplus sent prices plummeting; many farmers suddenly found themselves struggling. In a prelude to the Great Depression, small independent banks that dealt virtually exclusively

- Vardis Fisher – novelist and director of the Works Progress Administration-era Federal Writer's Project

- Ernest Hemingway – Nobel Prize-winning novelist

- Patrick McManus – outdoor humorist

- Ezra Pound – poet

POLITICS

- Cecil Andrus – four-term governor (1971-1977, 1987-1994) and Secretary of the Interior in the Carter administration (1977-1980)

- William Borah – six-term senator (1907-1940)

- Frank Church – four-term senator (1957-1981)

- George Shoup – first state governor, 1890; resigned to become a U.S. Senator

- William Wallace – first territorial governor (1864-1865)

SPORTS

- Stacy Dragila – Olympic pole vaulter; 2000 gold medalist

- Walter Johnson – record-setting pitcher for the Washington Senators; played 1907-1927

- Harmon Killebrew – home run champ for the Minnesota Twins; played 1954-1975

- Picabo Street – Olympic skier; 1998 gold medalist

in loans to farmers began to go under as farmers found it increasingly difficult to make their loan payments. Labor groups like the radical socialist Industrial Workers of the World (IWW), cofounded by Big Bill Haywood of Coeur d'Alene Mining War fame, tried to take advantage of the economic downturn by organizing strikes and advocating labor control of industry. But conservative Idahoans would have none of it in light of Russia's Bolshevik Revolution of 1917 and its aftermath, and fearing that the Wobblies, as IWW members were known, were working to overthrow the U.S. government.

Highways and automobiles made steady inroads into Idaho during the 1920s. The Prohibition era came, along with talkies, but worsening economic conditions caused a population exodus from the state.

The Great Depression

No sooner had Idaho dug itself out from the economic trough of the 1920s than the whole country was thrown into the Great Depression of the 1930s, precipitated by the stock market crash of October 1929. With drought exacerbating dried-up markets, Idaho's farm economy crashed. Farm prices dropped to their lowest point in a century, and between 1929 and 1932 the state's total farm income dropped 65 percent. Farmers lost their farms to foreclosure; bank runs caused many banks to fail. Firefighters in southwest Idaho deliberately set fires to provide themselves with employment; Idaho's governor had to call out the National Guard and close off all public access to the forests. Drought had stricken the Midwest as well, bringing refugees into Idaho and other Western states in search of work and better conditions. But conditions weren't any better in Idaho, and the influx of economic refugees added to the burden of the state's relief agencies.

Soon after his inauguration in 1933, President Franklin D. Roosevelt initiated his New Deal program of federal spending in an effort to jump-start the nation's economy. Many of the New Deal programs greatly aided Idaho. The Civilian Conservation Corps (CCC) put young men to work in Idaho's expansive national forests.

In the meantime, some entrepreneurs found ways to succeed without federal help. Harry Morrison and Morris Knudsen started their famous civil engineering firm in 1912; it went on to become one of the biggest such companies in the world. And in 1936, railroad baron and sometime statesman W. Averell Harriman founded his Sun Valley Ski Lodge, which enjoyed immediate success as an escape from the tribulations of the era and spawned the world's first chairlifts for skiers.

World War II

Roosevelt's New Deal spent somewhere in the neighborhood of $24 billion over seven years in an attempt to bolster the American economy. But in the first year alone of its involvement in World War II, the United States spent more than double that amount. Defense spending skyrocketed, and Idaho benefited in several areas. The Defense Department kept Morrison-Knudsen busy building airfields and roads in the Pacific theater. The Navy built Farragut Naval Training Center on the shores of Lake Pend Oreille in the Panhandle and used it to train recruits for submarine duty. Construction of the base put 22,000 men to work nearly round-the-clock. Pocatello got an ordnance plant, Boise an airfield for bombers. Mountain Home's airbase was built, and Sun Valley Lodge was taken over by the Navy as a hospital.

Of the 60,000 Idahoans who served in World War II, nearly 1,800 died, eight were declared missing in action, and 31 were captured as prisoners of war. As it had in World War I, Idaho's agricultural industry provided much of the food the GIs ate during the conflict; the war started Idahoan J. R. Simplot on the road to riches when he began dehydrating potatoes and selling them to the military. In addition, as more high-tech armaments were developed, Idaho's supplies of strategic minerals were tapped. Cobalt, tungsten, and antimony mines worked overtime to satisfy defense-industry requirements.

A prisoner-of-war camp for German soldiers was established at Farragut Naval Base. And following the Japanese attack on Pearl Harbor, Japanese Americans living on the West Coast were rounded up and incarcerated at several concentration camps farther inland, including one near Minidoka. Between September 1942 and October 1945, this "relocation center" was the eighth-largest "city" in Idaho, holding about 10,000 internees. Morrison-Knudsen built the camp, the construction of which helped pull south-central Idaho out of the Depression.

The war had exacted a horrible price in human lives but, as elsewhere in the country, it had gotten the state's economy back on track.

Postwar Growth

Following World War II, mining for strategic metals continued to enjoy defense-industry support as the Korean, Cold, and Vietnam Wars raged on. Other industries that had fueled the war effort turned their knowledge and experience to civilian uses. J. R. Simplot went from selling dehydrated potatoes to the military to selling french fries to McDonald's.

In 1949 the U.S. Departments of Defense and Energy established the National Reactor Testing Station (now INL) in Idaho, where physicists and nuclear engineers developed the world's first nuclear power plant, EBR-1, and first sent fission-produced electricity through the wires to provide electricity for municipal needs, supplying the town of Arco for a couple of hours on July 17, 1955. The site also developed fission reactors for the U.S. Navy's nuclear needs.

Entering a New Century

The last part of the 20th century saw Idaho transitioning from its traditional natural resources-based economy. While agriculture remains strong and pockets of mining and timber activity continue today, technology and tourism have become increasingly important.

Idaho has embraced advanced technology in a big way. Hewlett-Packard established a Boise division in the 1970s, and Micron Technology (a semiconductor company that began in Boise in 1978) is now the state's largest private employer. Although the economic downturn in the early 21st century meant tech-industry layoffs, especially in Boise, Idaho's pro-business climate means good long-term prospects for the industry. The state's recreational riches, meanwhile, have proven a drawing card both for tourists and for entrepreneurs who like to mix business and leisure.

People and Culture

DEMOGRAPHICS

Idaho's population is 87 percent white, 8 percent Hispanic, 1 percent Native American, and 4 percent others.

Hispanics

Traveling through Canyon County and other parts of agricultural southern Idaho, you might think you are in Mexico. Some counties along the Snake River Plain are nearly 20 percent Hispanic, and the population is growing steadily.

Native Americans

After relegating Idaho's native peoples to reservations, the federal government gave them only minimal aid. Unemployment and poverty became epidemic, forcing the tribes to look for income in nontraditional places. When they hit upon gambling, they struck the mother lode. Today, revenues from bingo halls, casinos, and lotteries bring in large sums of money for the tribes, helping turn the tables on poverty. In 2003, Idaho voters approved a measure allowing expanded Indian gaming despite strong opposition that was rooted in south-central Idaho, a region closely aligned with the border-town destination of Jackpot, Nevada.

The **Coeur d'Alene** tribe is setting aside a percentage of the profits from its gaming operations to reacquire land that was first granted and then taken away by successive treaties with the nonnatives. The tribe is also putting substantial amounts into both remedial action and court fights to clean up and gain control of the waters and shores of Coeur d'Alene Lake that have been ravaged by heavy-metal pollution from a century of mining. The Coeur d'Alene Reservation is in north-central Idaho, surrounding the south side of Coeur d'Alene Lake.

Other Indian reservations in the state include the Shoshone-Bannock **Fort Hall Reservation** in southeast Idaho; the Shoshone-Paiute **Duck Valley Reservation,** straddling the Nevada border in southwest Idaho; and the **Nez Perce Reservation,** in north-central Idaho, home to the headquarters of Nez Perce National Historic Park.

The Kootenai tribe doesn't have its own reservation, but it owns the **Kootenai River Inn** in Bonners Ferry. You can support the descendants of Idaho's indigenous Kootenai and learn a little about their culture by staying at the inn on your way through the area.

Basques

Their homeland is in northern Spain, but many Basque immigrants make their home in Idaho. Boise has the largest Basque population in the United States and offers plenty of opportunities for the visitor to learn about this unique culture. You can eat Basque food

Say It Right

So many names of places and things in Idaho are pronounced differently than you'd expect that it sometimes seems as if there is a plot to confound the outsider. Here is a list of the most common odd pronunciations. Many result from their origins as Native American or French words, reflecting the state's multilingual history. Memorize them or risk being branded a tourist.

- Boise: "BOY-see," not "BOY-zee," and certainly not the French "bwah-ZAY"
- Coeur d'Alene: butchered French "core-duh-lane"
- creek: always rhymes with "sick"
- Dubois: "doo-BOYCE" (from Fred Dubois), not the French "doo-BWAH" ("from the woods")
- Kamiah: "KAM-ee-eye"
- Kooskia: "KOO-skee"
- Kootenai: "KOOT-nee"
- Lochsa: "LOCK-saw"
- Montpelier: "mahnt-PEEL-yer," never the French "moan-pale-YAY"
- Moscow: "MOS-coe"
- Moyie: "MOY-yay"
- Nez Perce: "nezz purse," never the French "NAY-pare-SAY"
- Owyhee: "o-WHY-hee"
- Pend Oreille: close to the original French, "PON-der-ray"
- root: always rhymes with "foot"
- Sawtooths: never Sawteeth
- Weippe: "WEE-yipe"

at a number of restaurants across the state. Try Boise's Bar Gernika, where chances are good you'll overhear the unusual Basque language being spoken while you eat. Boise is also the site of the annual Festival of San Inazio and Jaialdi, a weeklong festival that brings in Basque people from all over the world once every five years.

POLITICS

Idaho is one of the most Republican states in the country. Sixty-five percent of Idahoans voted for Mitt Romney in the 2012 presidential election. The Gem State is not an easy place for Democrats to win office. As a matter of fact, Idaho hasn't had a Democrat

for governor since Cecil Andrus in 1995. Even more remarkable, Idaho hasn't had a Democrat as a First Position U.S. Senator since Bert Miller in 1949, and a Second Position U.S. Senator since Frank Church in 1981. Idaho has recently had Democrats as U.S. Representatives, but currently they are both Republicans. The state legislature continues to be overwhelmingly GOP.

Former *Idaho Statesman* columnist Dan Popkey recalls that during the era of U.S. Senator Frank Church and Governor Cecil Andrus, the 1960s through the 1980s, Democrats "shared power in Republican Idaho through force of intellect and personality." But these days the only areas where Democrats prevail are Sun Valley, Pocatello, and Boise; the latter elected former Democratic state legislator Dave Bieter as mayor in 2003 in a four-way race in which Bieter polled more than 50 percent. Bieter still holds office as Boise's mayor.

Many Idahoans are firmly entrenched in the mind-set of the Sagebrush Rebellion: "It's our land to do what we want with, and the federal government should mind its own business." In other words, the Tea Party movement is alive and well in Idaho.

THE ARTS
Performing Arts

Boise is home to the excellent Boise Philharmonic, Boise Opera, Boise Master Chorale, and Ballet Idaho as well as the premier Idaho Shakespeare Festival. In addition to performances by those groups, live music venues and festivals keep the entertainment calendar busy enough to satisfy all but the most ardent city-dweller.

Most of Idaho's other major cities also offer community orchestras and theater groups, and many small towns have community theaters. The quality is usually first-rate, and what you lose in cutting-edge talent and training are more than made up for in down-home

heart, as people take pride in performing for their friends and neighbors.

Look for plentiful student performances and active nightlife scenes in Idaho's college towns: Boise, home of Boise State University; Moscow, home of University of Idaho; and Pocatello, home of Idaho State University.

Visual Arts and Crafts

Mountain landscapes, wildlife, and Western themes dominate the subject matter of much of the state's artwork. Native American crafts (primarily beadwork and leatherwork) are also widespread across the state. Visitors to the big Shoshone Bannock Indian Festival and Rodeo, at Fort Hall the second week in August, will be faced with an enormous array of craftworks.

The biggest art towns in the state are Ketchum, Boise, and Sandpoint, in that order. Ketchum is a gallery prowler's paradise; some blocks have several galleries, all filled with quality work. Boise's galleries run the gamut from traditional to avant-garde, while Sandpoint's venues display a delightful mix of regionally famous artists and local hopefuls. Boise Art Museum is the state's premier public art repository. The museum hosts traveling shows of merit and houses a respectable permanent collection.

Danny Edwards's bronze sculpture of a pioneer sheepherder in Hagerman

Essentials

Transportation

AIR
Major Airlines

No international flights serve Idaho directly. Boise has the state's largest airport, served by **Alaska Airlines/Horizon Air** (800/654-5669, www.alaskaair.com), with nonstop service to and from Seattle, Lewiston, and other western U.S. cities; **Delta Air Lines/SkyWest** (800/221-1212, www.delta.com), regionally based in Salt Lake City; **Southwest Airlines** (800/435-9792, www.southwest.com), which offers direct flights between Boise and many western U.S. cities; and **United** (800/241-6522, www.united.com), which flies direct to and from San Francisco, Chicago, and Denver.

Travelers headed into and out of southeast Idaho generally book flights through the airport in Salt Lake City, Utah, 161 miles south of Pocatello. Those headed for the Panhandle book flights into Spokane, Washington, 33 miles west of Coeur d'Alene.

Commuter Airlines

Once you've arrived in Idaho, you can avail yourself of smaller airlines of the turboprop sort to fly you to and among the smaller cities. **Alaska Airlines/Horizon Air** (800/654-5669) maintains an extensive route system across the Northwest and California. From Boise, Horizon flies to about a dozen cities around the West. Delta-affiliated **SkyWest Airlines** (800/221-1212, www.skywest.com) also serves Idaho Falls, Pocatello, Sun Valley, and Twin Falls with nonstop service from Salt Lake City. **Salmon Air** (800/992-6559) has weekday flights from Salmon to McCall and Boise.

Backcountry Charters

To fly into one of Idaho's many rural burgs, or to remote airstrips in the state's expansive backcountry, you'll need to hire an air taxi service. A number of companies do a booming business shuttling rafters, backpackers, and anglers into the wilderness. For starters, try **McCall Aviation** (800/992-6559, www.mccallaviation.com), which offers branches in McCall, Stanley, and Salmon.

TRAIN

Train service in Idaho is now limited to the *Empire Builder,* an Amtrak (800/872-7245, www.amtrak.com) route that runs between Chicago and either Portland or Seattle via Wisconsin, Minnesota, North Dakota, Montana, north Idaho, and Spokane, Washington. The train was named for the nickname of James Jerome Hill (1838-1916), a Canadian-born railroad magnate who founded the Great Northern Railway; the Great Northern's line between St. Paul, Minnesota, and the Pacific opened up the Northwest at the turn of the 20th century. Today's Amtrak train makes one run daily in each direction. Its only Idaho stop is in the Panhandle at Sandpoint, where it creeps through in the middle of the night (11:49pm westbound, 2:35am eastbound).

BUS

Greyhound (800/231-2222, www.greyhound.com) goes almost everywhere in this great country. **Northwestern Trailways** (800/366-3830, www.northwesterntrailways.com) connects Boise with McCall, Lewiston, Grangeville, and Spokane, Washington. **Sun Valley Express** (877/622-8267) offers service between Boise Airport and Sun Valley. **Rocky Mountain Trails/Salt Lake Express** (800/356-9796, www.saltlakeexpress.com)

---

offers daily van shuttle service between Salt Lake City and the Idaho communities of Rexburg, Rigby, Idaho Falls, Blackfoot, and Pocatello.

CAR

Driving is the easiest and most efficient way to travel around Idaho, but it's important to note that except near major cities and on the interstates (I-84, I-86, I-15, and I-90), all Idaho highways have two lanes and are undivided. So, be careful out there, especially at night when big animals feed alongside the highways.

All the major national car-rental companies are represented in Idaho, including at the major airports.

Traffic Laws

Here are a few of the common Idaho traffic laws you ought to know before you start the car. First, you'll need to possess and carry a valid driver's license from your home state or country, or a valid international driver's license. You must also possess and carry proof of liability insurance. Your vehicle must also be currently registered. Finally, before you turn the key, buckle up; Idaho has a seat belt law, and all children under 40 pounds must be strapped into a car seat. Motorcyclists aren't required to wear helmets.

Once out on the road, a couple of rules are worthy of special mention. First, in the United States, you drive on the right side of the road. Unless posted otherwise, you are permitted to make a right turn on a red light after coming to a complete stop. You can also make a U-turn at a controlled intersection if no sign specifically prohibits it, and then only if you can do so safely, in one continuous movement (no three-point turns). Unless posted otherwise, the maximum speed limit on city streets is 35 mph. And be careful of horses; horseback riders are permitted on most public roads.

A special note for RVers: Idaho law requires you to pull over if you are holding up three or more vehicles.

Driving is the easiest way to get around Idaho.

Drinking and Driving

The drinking age in Idaho is 21. If you're 21 or over, you're considered legally drunk if your blood-alcohol level is 0.08 percent or above. If you're under 21, you can't have any alcohol in your system while operating a motor vehicle on Idaho's roads. These laws are strictly enforced.

Winter Driving

Old Man Winter is always ready to get you if you don't watch out, so just keep it slow and between the fence posts. You'll see plenty of signs warning of **frost heaves,** places where water beneath the pavement has frozen and expanded, buckling the road. Hitting one of these at too high a speed on a rain- or snow-slickened road can throw you instantly out of control.

The weather in Idaho can be unpredictable, and much of the state gets at least some snow in winter. You'd be wise to carry chains in your trunk October-April. Also in the trunk should be a short-handled shovel, blankets, a sleeping bag, and extra food and drinking water just in case you get stranded. Winter and summer, carry emergency flares and a flashlight or headlamp. If you do break down in a snowstorm, stay with the car. Don't try to walk for help unless you can see that it's very close; many people have died of hypothermia in the attempt.

Summer Driving

Much of the state swelters in summer, particularly at low elevations on the Snake River Plain and in the canyons of western Idaho. Make sure your radiator is in good working order, and carry a couple of extra gallons of coolant in the trunk. As in winter, also carry extra food and water in the trunk, in case you get stuck out in the middle of nowhere. And even in summer, carry blankets. Idaho summer days may get hot, but nights can still get plenty cold in many parts of the state, even in mid-July. If you're renting a car, make sure it has a functioning air conditioner. As in winter, keep emergency flares and a flashlight or headlamp handy at all times.

As summer opens up many roads into high mountain country, roadside encounters with wildlife become more common. In your travels through the state, you'll see many dead deer and other animals on the roadsides. To avoid a collision with an animal, never outdrive your headlights at night, use your high beams whenever possible, and immediately slow down as soon as you spy any animal even remotely close to the road.

Getting Off the Pavement

Half the fun of exploring the state is leaving the highway behind and heading out into the desert or deep into the mountains. Special precautions apply, however, since often these roads will take you a day's hike or more away from the nearest fellow human being. Four-wheel-drive vehicles are really in their element here, but if you go slowly enough, most of Idaho's dirt roads are passable in the family minivan.

Southern Idaho's deserts are especially desolate. If ever a case could be made for carrying not one but two spare tires, this would be it. Make sure your jack works and you know how to use it. Two jacks could even come in handy. Carry a shovel to dig yourself out of the sand or mud, and some boards (two-by-fours or whatever you can fit in the trunk) to put under your stuck wheels for traction.

In the mountains, you'll have to contend with **logging trucks,** which often barrel down narrow one-lane roads and around blind corners at high speed with seeming disregard for everything in their path. The best advice is to just stay out of areas being actively logged; stop at the nearest ranger station to find out where these areas are.

Further Information

To find out the current status of the roads along your intended route, call the Idaho Transportation Department's 24-hour recorded **road conditions** report (511 or 888/432-7623, www.511.idaho.gov). RVers can obtain a list of RV **dump stations** in the state by contacting the RV Program Supervisor, Idaho Department of Parks and Recreation (5657 Warm Springs Ave., Boise, 208/334-4199).

ESSENTIALS
TRANSPORTATION

Sports and Recreation

STATE PARKS

Each of Idaho's 26 state parks highlights a different Idaho natural wonder, but they all feature well-kept facilities, and many offer outstanding interpretive programs. Most parks charge a $5 motor-vehicle entry fee (no charge for walk-ins or bike-ins). For $40, you can buy a calendar-year pass that provides unlimited entry to all the state parks that year (however, it doesn't include camping fees); a second vehicle can be covered for just $15 more. To purchase this pass, call 888/922-6743 or go to www.parksandrecreation.idaho.gov.

Many of the parks are designed for camping. You'll generally find RV-suitable campsites with water and electric hookups for $21-29 per night, or water only for $12-21 per night. The first-rate restroom facilities are kept clean, and most parks have showers as well; non-campers can use the showers for a small fee. Several parks have camper cabins that sleep up to six and rent for around $50-55 per night. The cabins have electricity and heat along with a cooking grill outside. You'll also find larger cabins at Harriman, Heyburn, and Ponderosa as well as year-round yurts at Harriman, Ponderosa, and Winchester State Parks. Pets are allowed on a leash at most parks but must be kept enclosed within your RV or tent at night.

Reservations are taken for some campsites and cabins for $10. Call the park of your choice, or go to www.reserveamerica.com. Some parks offer campsites on a first-come, first-served basis.

For more information, contact the **Idaho Department of Parks and Recreation** (5657 Warm Springs Ave., Boise, 208/334-4199).

NATIONAL FORESTS

Idaho encompasses all or part of 13 different national forests, which together cover most of the state, so it's no surprise that national forest campgrounds are the most numerous of any type in Idaho. At the larger campgrounds, you'll typically find a host who keeps the place picked up and collects fees from campers. Fees commonly run $10-20 per site per night for up to two vehicles. Some of these campgrounds

Some state parks in Idaho offer year-round yurts.

are on a **central reservation system;** make reservations at www.recreation.gov or 877/444-6777. A reservation fee is charged.

The Forest Service also operates many free campgrounds throughout the state. These are usually found in less popular or more remote areas either too small for practical fee collection or lacking potable water. At these campsites, you'll usually find a vault toilet, picnic tables, and fire rings or grills, but you'll often be on your own for drinkable water. As a good many of these campgrounds are found along lakes or streams, this is not much of a problem for anyone with a water filter.

One other Forest Service option is available: rental guard stations and lookout towers. Air surveillance today has largely replaced the staffed lookouts, so the Forest Service offers the buildings to the public as backcountry accommodations. Almost by definition, these will have terrific views and be ensconced in remote and wild landscapes. The rentals are by and large primitive and sleep anywhere from a pair of cozy friends to a whole college football team. Many are accessible only on skis or snowmobiles in winter.

BUREAU OF LAND MANAGEMENT LANDS

Most of the 12 million acres of Bureau of Land Management (BLM) land in Idaho are found on and around the Snake River Plain in the southern portion of the state. BLM campgrounds are generally free, primitive, minimally maintained, and minimally used. They tend to be near areas offering recreation opportunities such as rivers, lakes, and remote hiking areas. The BLM maintains a number of district offices in Idaho (see www.blm.gov/id for more information).

SUMMER SPORTS
White-Water Rafting and Kayaking

Idaho ranks as king of the Lower 48 when it comes to wild white water, boasting about 1,000 more white-water miles than runner-up California. The Snake River through Hells

Canyon, the Salmon River and its Middle Fork, and the Lochsa, Selway, and Payette are the state's most notorious rivers. The Snake and the main Salmon offer big-water thrills; the Lochsa and Payette offer challenging runs through narrower gorges; and the Middle Fork and the Selway provide a wilderness experience par excellence. Many more Idaho rivers await white-water enthusiasts, however, ranging from the remote desert canyon run of the Jarbidge near the Nevada border to the lushly forested run of the Moyie near the Canadian border.

If you go with a commercial guide service, you won't need to worry about a permit. Otherwise, you must obtain a permit from the U.S. Forest Service for private noncommercial trips on the Middle Fork of the Salmon, the main Salmon, the upper Selway, and the Snake River through Hells Canyon. Only a limited number of permits, awarded through the Four Rivers Lottery, are issued each season. You need to fill out an application form, available October 1 for the next summer, and submit it December 1-January 31 for the following season. You can specify your preferred rivers and launch dates. For Middle Fork permits, contact the **Middle Fork Ranger District** (U.S. 93 N., P.O. Box 750, Challis, ID 83226, 208/879-4101); for main Salmon permits, contact **North Fork Ranger District** (U.S. 93, P.O. Box 180, North Fork, ID 83466-0180, 208/865-2700); for Selway permits, contact the **West Fork Ranger District** (6735 West Fork Rd., Darby, MT 59829, 406/821-3269); for Snake permits, contact **Hells Canyon National Recreation Area** (P.O. Box 699, Clarkston, WA 99403, 509/758-0616). Applications can also be downloaded online at www.recreation.gov/permits.

Other Water Sports

With lakes and reservoirs scattered from one end of the state to the other, you'll never be too far from **waterskiing** and **windsurfing,** the latter of which is popular on the windy reservoirs of the Snake River Plain, notably American Falls Reservoir and Lake Walcott.

International Scale of River Difficulty

- **Class I: Very Easy.** Small regular waves and riffles. Few or no obstructions. Little maneuvering required.

- **Class II: Easy.** Waves up to three feet. Wide, clear channels that are obvious without scouting. Low ledges; small rock gardens. Some maneuvering required.

- **Class III: Medium.** Rapids with numerous high, irregular waves capable of swamping an open canoe. Strong eddies. Narrow passages that often require complex maneuvering. May require scouting from shore.

- **Class IV: Difficult.** Long difficult rapids with powerful, irregular waves, dangerous rocks, boiling eddies, and constricted passages that require precise maneuvering in very turbulent waters. Scouting from shore is necessary, and conditions make rescue difficult. Generally not possible for open canoes. Boaters in covered canoes and kayaks should be able to Eskimo roll.

- **Class V: Very Difficult.** Long, violent rapids with wild turbulence and highly congested routes that must be scouted from shore. Rescue conditions are difficult, and there is significant hazard to life in event of a mishap. Ability to Eskimo roll is essential for paddlers in kayaks and covered canoes.

- **Class VI: The Limits of Navigation.** Difficulties of Class V carried to the extreme limits of navigability. Nearly impossible and very dangerous. For teams of experts only, after close study and with all precautions taken. Rarely run and a definite hazard to your life.

If water temperature is below 50°F, or if the trip is an extended trip into a wilderness area, the river should be considered one class more difficult than normal.

Others take their boards up to Redfish Lake in the Sawtooths, where the winds can be erratic but the views are world-class. In the state's southeastern corner, Bear Lake is popular with water-skiers, as are Lakes Coeur d'Alene and Pend Oreille in the Panhandle and Payette Lake at McCall, all of which are also suitable for **sailing.**

Mountain Biking

For mountain bikers, Idaho is pure nirvana. Look at all that national forest land with all those national forest roads ripe for the pedaling. Yes, mountain biking is big virtually everywhere in the Gem State.

In Boise, the **Boise Front** is practically right behind the state capitol—just head out on 8th Street and keep going up the hill. At **Bogus Basin,** ride up the hill and take off on the forest roads.

If you're in southwest Idaho and ready for multiday solitude, head for the **Owyhee County Backcountry Byway;** if you'd rather go out for the day and come back to a brew, head up to McCall and explore the **Payette National Forest** or the lift-served trails at **Brundage Mountain.**

There are lots of choices in southeast Idaho. The **Mink Creek** trails outside Pocatello make for a good workout, or try the lift-served biking at **Grand Targhee.**

The high country is total mountain biker heaven. Just about anywhere in the **Wood River Valley** you'll find dirt roads heading off into the mountains. Or cross over Galena Summit and bike into the **White Cloud Peaks,** an airy realm of sheer craggy summits and wildflower-filled meadows.

In the north-central area, **McCroskey State Park** north of Moscow is a little-known state park used more by mountain bikers than by cars. The park offers sweeping views of the Palouse. When you're done, head east to Harvard and up into the **Palouse Range,** where you'll still see forests of white pine and ancient cedars.

For Panhandle biking, first try the **Route of the Hiawatha** near Lookout Pass, for thrills negotiating the tunnels and trestles of an abandoned railroad grade. After that, head for **Priest Lake,** where you can ride from the northwest edge of the lake all the way to Canada.

Road Biking

Although many Idaho roads are narrow, with little or no shoulder, paved trails are popping up all over. The **Boise River Greenbelt** offers a beautiful traffic-free path long enough to give the average cyclist a workout. The **Wood River Valley** makes the list for its extensive network of bike paths. The **Palouse,** east of Moscow, offers gently rolling hills through scenic farmland. But the best road-biking experience of all is the 72-mile **Trail of the Coeur d'Alenes,** a popular rails-to-trails conversion in the **Panhandle** with incredible views along the way.

Fishing

You'll need to purchase an Idaho state fishing license before you head out to try your luck. Idaho residents pay $25.75 adults, $13.75 ages 14-17. Nonresident anglers pay $12.75 for the first day, $6 for each additional consecutive day. You can get a license at sporting goods stores, many convenience stores, or any office of the Idaho Department of Fish and Game.

Fly-anglers will find pure bliss in Idaho at **Silver Creek,** in south-central Idaho, and at **Henrys Fork** and the **South Fork Snake** in the southeast. Fishing lodges in these parts are sometimes booked years in advance. Meanwhile, the hard-core types among the angling crowd prefer to wrestle the enormous, primeval-looking **sturgeon** (catch-and-release only), which inhabits the lower Snake River. Others find **steelhead** fishing on the Clearwater and Salmon Rivers to hold the biggest thrills.

To find out up-to-the-minute information about fishing conditions in various parts of Idaho, contact the **Idaho Department of Fish and Game** (600 S. Walnut St., Boise, 208/334-3700, www.fishandgame.idaho.gov).

Golfing

Idaho has around 100 golf courses. Some courses in southwest Idaho and south-central Idaho stay open year-round. Linksters will find many modest nine-hole courses in small towns throughout the state as well as several world-class courses. Among the most impressive are the Robert Trent Jones Jr. courses in

Boise River Greenbelt

the Sun Valley area and the luxurious Coeur d'Alene Resort course with its novel floating green. Statewide, prices range from around $12 to more than $200 per round.

Hiking and Backpacking

With all that public land at their disposal, hikers will find no shortage of trails to explore. Start with the wilderness areas for a pristine experience free from exhaust fumes and chainsaws. For sheer scenic beauty, it's hard to top the **Sawtooth Wilderness,** which offers peaks and lakes galore. Nevertheless, the **Hells Canyon Wilderness,** with its exquisitely beautiful Seven Devils Range, gives the Sawtooths a run for their money. If you really want to get lost for a couple of weeks, head out into the vast **Frank Church-River of No Return Wilderness** or the adjacent **Selway-Bitterroot Wilderness.**

Those looking for the ultimate Idaho trek can attempt the 1,200-mile **Idaho Centennial Trail,** which runs the length of the state, south to north. The trail starts near Murphy Hot Springs on the Nevada border and follows the Jarbidge and Bruneau Rivers north, crossing I-84 near Glenns Ferry. It works its way into the Sawtooths, and then traverses both the Frank Church and Selway-Bitterroot Wildernesses, crossing U.S. 12 near the Lochsa Historical Ranger Station. From there it bears east to the high Bitterroots, following the Continental Divide along the Idaho-Montana border for a time before sliding off the divide to head west into the Cabinet Mountains and over to Priest Lake. At Priest Lake, the trail makes a short hop, skip, and jump north to the Canadian border. Signage of the trail has been completed in recent years.

Hot Springs

Thanks to its geology, Idaho is blessed with more hot springs by far than any other state in the West. No matter what your style (developed or primitive, clothing mandatory or clothing optional, easy access or remote), you'll find a hot spring to suit you. Many of the springs taunt the nose with that characteristic sulfur smell; many do not. True hot-springs believers come to appreciate the smell and can follow their nose to hot-soaking delights.

The best-developed family hot springs in Idaho is the state-run **Lava Hot Springs** resort, in the laid-back little resort town of Lava Hot Springs, southeast of Pocatello. The facility is immaculate, the setting beautiful, and the fumes sulfur-free. Fans of developed yet rustic geothermal-pool facilities will surely like **Burgdorf Hot Springs** outside McCall. Here you can soak in a sand-bottomed pool, stay in a rustic old pioneer's cabin, and watch elk feed under the stars. For a personal spiritual retreat, head for **Murphy Hot Springs.** It's remote, quiet, and magical—out in the middle of nowhere in Owyhee County.

Idaho has so many undeveloped natural hot springs that it's beyond the scope of this guide to describe each and every one; whole books are devoted to the topic. A couple of favorites: **Chattanooga Hot Springs** in Atlanta and **Elk Bend Hot Springs** south of Salmon off U.S. 93. The award for the most social natural hot springs goes to **Jerry Johnson Hot Springs,** off U.S. 12 east of Lowell, where you'll just about always find good conversation with your soaking companions.

Rock Climbing and Mountaineering

Rock jocks will find world-class climbing centers at **City of Rocks/Castle Rocks** in south-central Idaho, a massive area of rock towers up to 600 feet high; in the **Sawtooth Range,** on sheer granite spires and big-wall faces; and in the Panhandle's **Selkirk Range,** which climbers share with grizzlies and woodland caribou.

Mountain ranges literally cover most of the state. There's no end to the peak-bagging possibilities. The highest peak in the state is **Borah Peak** (12,662 feet) in the Lost River Range near Mackay. It's an easy Class 2-3 climb, but airy in places; it makes a comfortable solo for the experienced mountaineer and a great place to take your neophyte partner for his or her first big summit. Borah isn't a particularly impressive peak to look at, but others in the range are sheer spectacles.

Ketchum, in close proximity to the Soldiers, Smokies, Pioneers, Boulders, Sawtooths, and White Clouds, is the hub of a strong mountaineering scene. The area has enough peaks to keep you busy well into your next life. Among the biggest: **Castle Peak** in the White Clouds tops out at 11,815 feet; **Hyndman Peak** in the Pioneers juts up into the thin air at 12,009 feet.

WINTER SPORTS
Alpine Skiing

In a state with so many mountains, ski resorts are understandably ubiquitous, with nearly 20 alpine ski areas from Pomerelle Mountain in the south to Schweitzer Mountain in the extreme north. Powder-hounds should take Idaho's climatology into consideration; for better powder, go higher or drier. The best powder skiing in the state isn't even in the state but just across the border in Wyoming at **Grand Targhee,** accessible only through Driggs, Idaho. Here, continental weather patterns produce colder, drier storms than the maritime-influenced storms of the more northerly and westerly resorts.

Sun Valley is the West's oldest, grandest ski resort, offering a zillion fast lifts up a big mountain and luxurious pampering at every turn. It's also the state's priciest resort. **Schweitzer Mountain** outside Sandpoint, **Silver Mountain** at Kellogg, **Brundage Mountain** near McCall, and **Bogus Basin** outside Boise are medium-size areas offering lots of fun skiing at reasonable prices. Schweitzer has a beautiful base lodge and hotel; Silver Mountain boasts the world's longest gondola; Brundage offers some of the best

facilities for kids in the state and the liveliest ski-town atmosphere; and Bogus Basin has killer night skiing.

Idaho also has lots of smaller ski hills, like **Soldier Mountain, Pebble Creek, Kelly Canyon,** and **Lookout Pass,** where prices are substantially less than the glitzy resorts.

Cross-Country Skiing

Across the state, from Boise to Bonners Ferry, you'll find **Park N' Ski areas** established by the Idaho Department of Parks and Recreation. To use the Park N' Ski areas, you must first buy a permit ($25 for an entire season, $7.50 for three days). Theoretically, this is supposed to get you plowed trailhead parking and groomed trails, but grooming can be sketchy in some areas. For more information on the Park N' Ski areas, contact the Idaho Department of Parks and Recreation (5657 Warm Springs Ave., Boise, 208/334-4199, www.parksandrecreation.idaho.gov).

In a class by themselves are the **Wood River Valley** trails. Two separate systems in the lower and upper parts of the valley offer a vast network of meticulously groomed trails. The lower valley system is free, courtesy of Blaine County. The North Valley trails require a $17 daily permit, which is easily worth three times as much. The North Valley system culminates in the trails at Galena Lodge, the ultimate intimate cross-country ski chalet.

Snowshoeing

Most of the state's cross-country ski areas welcome snowshoers too, but try to stay away from the groomed tracks. The great thing about snowshoeing is you don't need a trail; you can set off across any snowy patch of land. Some ski areas and other parklands offer guided snowshoe treks, which can be a great way to learn animal tracks and other winter ecology.

Festivals and Events

Something is going on somewhere in Idaho every weekend year-round. If you're traveling through an area of the state and want to find out what's happening, consult the travel chapters of this guide; many major events have been listed in the city sections.

If, on the other hand, you're planning a trip to Idaho around a big event, here's a list of some of the biggest and best.

CULTURE

- **Festival of San Inazio** (Boise, last weekend in July): Boise's Basque community pulls out all the stops for this cultural celebration; look for food, dancing, and contests of strength and skill.

- **Shoshone Bannock Indian Festival and Rodeo** (Fort Hall, second week of August): One of the biggest powwows in the West, drawing Native Americans and visitors from all over the continent for dancing, drumming, rodeo, and arts and crafts.

MUSIC

- **Lionel Hampton Jazz Festival** (Moscow, late February): How can this many jazz masters show up in one place at the same time? Don't miss it.

- **National Oldtime Fiddlers' Contest** (Weiser, third full week of June): The finest fiddlers in the country compete, and a party atmosphere prevails day and night.

- **Festival at Sandpoint** (Sandpoint, early August): Expect performances by many big-name rock and jazz musicians.

RODEO

- **Snake River Stampede** (Nampa, mid-July): A venerable southwest Idaho institution and one of the country's top 25 rodeos, this one draws upward of 40,000 spectators.

- **Caldwell Night Rodeo** (Caldwell, mid-August): The Snake River Stampede may be bigger, but this one is the most rip-roarin' fun.

SPORTS

- **Boulder Mountain Nordic Ski Classic** (Ketchum, early February): Idaho's biggest Nordic ski race held on the Wood River Valley's magnificent Boulder Mountain Trail.

- **Race to Robie Creek** (Boise, mid-April): Thousands of legs thrash madly up and over Adalpe Summit in the Northwest's toughest half marathon.

- **Sun Valley Ice Show** (Sun Valley, mid-June-September): All the big names perform on the ice at the ritzy Sun Valley Lodge.

- **Payette Whitewater Roundup** (Banks, July): Idaho's largest kayak competition features scores of brightly colored boats and competitors from all across the country.

GENERAL FUN

- **Winter Carnival** (McCall, late January-early February): This wintery bash includes snow monsters, ice sculptures, sleigh rides, and a Mardi Gras-inspired parade.

- **Teton Valley Balloon Rally** (Driggs, July 4 weekend): Brightly colored balloons speckle the sky with the Tetons in the background. How scenic can you get?

Accommodations and Food

ACCOMMODATIONS

Idaho has every kind of hotel and motel chain possible. If you're looking for your favorite one, just call its toll-free number, or check the website for a location finder.

Generally, peak-season accommodation rates are listed in this guide. Peak-season rates can run rather high in Idaho's resort towns, but many of these places offer great deals in the off-season or the in-between seasons. For example, many hotels in the Sun Valley area (during spring and fall slack) and McCall (during spring and fall shoulder) offer discounted rates when things slow down, sometimes up to 30 percent off peak-season rates. Coeur d'Alene's peak season is summer, so look for big discounts there during the winter months.

Guest Ranches and Fishing Lodges

Most of Idaho's 20 or so guest ranches provide a bit of Old West adventure with their accommodations. Typically rustic and remote, these lodgings put an emphasis on outdoor activities such as fishing, hunting, swimming, and horseback riding. Rates are usually based on stays of a week and generally include all meals and recreation. Some are working ranches; some operate in summer only while others are open year-round.

Also usually offering weeklong packages but replacing horseback activities with guided fishing are Idaho's numerous fishing lodges. Most of these are found along the Henrys Fork and the South Fork Snake River in southeast Idaho.

Many guest ranches and fishing lodges are members of the **Idaho Outfitters & Guides Association** (208/342-1438, www.ioga.org) in Boise.

Bed-and-Breakfasts

Idaho's bed-and-breakfast inns basically fall into two camps. Many are converted residences, where you'll be sharing a family's home and living space with them. Others are more like small hotels, designed as guest accommodations from the ground up and generally offering more privacy at higher prices. Breakfast is included in the rates, but if it makes a difference to you, be sure to inquire what sort of breakfast is served; a few B&Bs offer only a light continental breakfast, while others serve a big homespun breakfast. It's also important to remember that many B&Bs don't allow children, at least young ones.

The Panhandle has the majority of Idaho's bed-and-breakfast inns, especially in the Coeur d'Alene area. To check listings, visit the **North Idaho Bed & Breakfast Association**'s website (www.nibba.com).

FOOD AND DRINK

Idaho is a meat-and-potatoes state. Steakhouses are standard, and particularly in rural areas, vegetarians will make good use of grocery stores. The larger cities all provide a range of fare. In Boise you can get nearly every ethnic food imaginable, and in nearby Canyon County you'll find some of the best Mexican restaurants this side of Los Angeles. As Idaho has a large Basque population, many towns, particularly in the southwest, have Basque restaurants. And cowboy cooking is dear to the heart of many Idahoans; Dutch-oven cookouts and grilled steaks are the prime offerings of many tourist resorts and excursion providers. Chefs in mountain resort towns make good use of hand-foraged foodstuffs such as morel mushrooms and huckleberries as well as farm-raised elk and trout.

Idaho has several excellent farmers markets where shoppers can score impeccably fresh organic produce, natural meat products, alfalfa honey, eggs, and more. Among the best are the Boise Farmers Market, the Kootenai County

Farmers Market in Coeur d'Alene, and the Moscow Farmers Market, the oldest of its kind in the state.

Southwest Idaho holds the state's best vineyards and wineries, in the Snake River Valley American Viticultural Area, and there are microbreweries all over the state that put out tasty handcrafted beers.

Travel Tips

TRAVELING WITH CHILDREN

State parks, national parks and monuments, and Forest Service ranger district offices all have a multitude of resources for children. Interpretive centers with interesting exhibits and short films, outdoor programs, travel brochures, and free Smokey Bear coloring books and other fun swag can help keep kids happy while on the road.

Rest stops also are a saving grace when traveling with kids. The main interstates (I-84, I-86, and I-15) have relatively clean rest stops with some green space about every 40 miles or so. The two-lane highways (U.S. 20, U.S. 95) also have rest stops, but these are fewer and farther between. Most convenience stores don't have a problem letting travelers use their restrooms, especially if you buy something, and nearly every town you'll pass through has a city park with restrooms and picnic areas.

TRAVELERS WITH DISABILITIES

While resources are getting better for disabled folks in Idaho, it still falls below the national average for accessibility for those with mobility issues. Wheelchair ramps and wheelchair-accessible restrooms aren't always where you need them to be, especially in older districts and in small towns. But Idaho has made great strides to improve accessibility in its state park system. For general information and resources about accessible travel, go to **Access-Able Travel Source**'s website (www.access-able. com).

SENIORS

Elderhostel (800/454-5768, www.road-scholar.org), also known as Road Scholar, is a nonprofit organization that focuses on worldwide recreational and cultural programs for travelers age 55 and over. In Idaho, Elderhostel offers white-water rafting trips on the Salmon River and skiing adventures at Sun Valley Resort. Contact the organization for a free catalog of its global destinations and programs.

GAY AND LESBIAN TRAVELERS

In Boise, especially downtown and in the city's North End, a progressive attitude prevails about gays and lesbians. But as you get farther out into the small towns and even larger cities in southeast Idaho, the feeling can quickly change to one of intolerance. Thankfully physical violence toward gays and lesbians is not the norm, but public displays of affection with your partner could result in having some Bible verses shouted at you, or worse, some f-bombs. Smaller towns where this likely wouldn't happen are the liberal bastions of Ketchum and Moscow—both have big out gay and lesbian communities.

An excellent travel resource for gay and lesbian sojourners worldwide is www.purple-roofs.com, which has some Idaho listings.

EMERGENCIES

For extreme emergencies, **dial 911** to summon medical or law enforcement help. The 911 system is installed universally throughout Idaho.

PLANTS TO AVOID

A few plants in Idaho can cause discomfort if they come into contact with your skin. **Poison ivy** is common in the state; look for small white-to-yellow berries and large, waxy, ternate (three to a bunch) leaves. Poison ivy likes water, so be especially careful on overgrown trails around creek beds. **Stinging nettle** has broad, coarse-toothed leaves and also grows near water. Unlike poison ivy, you'll know you've encountered stinging nettle soon after contact. Yes, it stings. If any of these plants contact your skin, wash the area with soap and water and try not to scratch. Once the area is thoroughly washed, you can't spread the rash by scratching, but you can scratch the skin open, inviting infection. Calamine lotion or mudpacks may offer some relief.

PARASITES
Giardia

The *Giardia lamblia* intestinal parasite has spread throughout the backcountry of the West in the past 20 years, lurking in streams and lakes, just waiting for the thirsty, unsuspecting hiker to come along. You should assume *all* water in the backcountry is contaminated, no matter how crystal clear and pure it may appear. Once inside you, the giardia parasite attaches itself to the intestinal wall, causing symptoms including severe fatigue, cramps, nausea, diarrhea, and gas. To ensure that none of the little buggers gets inside you, you'll have to boil (10 minutes minimum at sea level; longer at altitude), chemically treat (iodine, halazone, or other water-purification tablets), or filter your water. If you go with a filter, be sure to get one with a pore size of less than one micron (one millionth of a meter) in diameter. That's the maximum width that will safely filter out *Giardia*.

Schistosomes

Shallow waters at the edges of lakes commonly harbor the larvae of these parasitic flatworms. The larvae can penetrate human skin, and after doing so will die, but not before causing **swimmer's itch.** The itchy red spots or welts will go away after about a week. To avoid the possibility of contracting the bug, swim in water away from the shore and towel off as soon as you get out of the water.

INSECTS
Ticks

These creepy crawlers cling to brush and hop a ride on any warm-blooded animal that happens by. Inserting their barbed mouthparts into the skin, the ticks clamp on tight and begin sucking merrily away. Contrary to the commonly held misconception, you do not remove a tick by unscrewing it, burning it out, or covering it with nail polish or petroleum jelly in an attempt to suffocate it. Instead, get a pair of tweezers and grab it as close to the head as possible, then pull it out with slow, steady pressure. Wash the area with soap and water and check to see if any part of the tick broke off under the skin. If so, best check with your doctor or at least monitor your condition closely for any signs of illness. Ticks have been linked to the spread of Lyme disease and Rocky Mountain spotted fever, but such cases are rare in Idaho. Ticks are most prevalent in late spring-early summer. To avoid them, tuck your shirt into your pants and your pant legs into your socks or boots. Wearing a DEET-based insect repellent is an additional safeguard. Check your clothes often during your hike, and do a thorough body check when you get back to your home base.

Mosquitoes

The joke about mosquitoes being the state bird could apply in some parts of Idaho, although the dry Snake River Plain doesn't seem to get as many. With lots of wild backcountry with lots of water, Idaho grows 'em big and bountiful. Summer is prime time for skeeters; a hike in the woods in mid-July-August will invite a bloodthirsty bombardment. Repellents containing DEET work the best.

Mosquitoes infected with **West Nile virus** have been detected in Idaho, and many cases of the virus have been reported in humans and horses since it first hit the state in 2004. Most of the human cases have involved older people with compromised immune systems, but younger folks have contracted it too. Luckily the infection rate is going down as the awareness level rises. To avoid being bitten, especially around dusk and dawn, take these precautions: Apply DEET or another Environmental Protection Agency-approved insect repellent; wear a long-sleeved shirt, long pants, and socks; and always cover infant carriers with mosquito netting.

Yellow Jackets

The picnickers' pariah, these unwelcome intruders will inevitably crash your outdoor party, buzzing around your soda can, your sandwich, and you. They're incredibly persistent, and the more agitated you get, the more persistent they seem to become. The best advice may be just to ignore them. Or you can try creating a "sacrifice area" by opening a couple of cans of soda and making a really gooey ham sandwich with lots of mustard, then setting it all out at some distance from your table. If you're lucky, the yellow jackets will go for the easy grub and leave you alone. Of course, if you're allergic to their sting, you should just retreat to the safety of the car rather than risk anaphylactic shock. In the end, you just can't win with these buggers.

BEARS

While bear attacks are extremely rare in Idaho, they do happen from time to time, especially in grizzly country on the state's east side. Black bears, which are prevalent throughout Idaho, generally are smaller than grizzlies, and they have tall, pointed ears, whereas grizzlies tend to be larger and have a pronounced shoulder hump. Some experts say that attacks from black bears can be just as vicious as grizzly attacks, since the latter often bluff-charge people. Either way, keep your distance from these beautiful but

Know your bears and keep your distance.

powerful animals. Follow these general rules when hiking or camping in bear country: Never hike between dusk and dawn when bears are most active; keep a clean campsite, and don't put food in your tent; make loud noises along the trail and by streams; and never mess with a dead animal (like a deer or elk carcass) that you might encounter—this could be a bear's dinner. It's a good idea to carry bear spray if you're backpacking in Idaho. If a black bear attacks, use bear spray, throw rocks at the animal, or shout commands with a loud, firm voice. In other words, fight back. It's the opposite for grizzly attacks, though, where you should not try to fight the animal. It's recommended that you drop to the ground, lay flat on your stomach, and clasp your hands behind your neck. In other words, play dead.

COUGARS

Cougar attacks are extremely rare, but keep your wits and your kids close to you when hiking in big cat country, which is the entire state. Like bears, cougars are highly active at night and in the early morning, so pay close attention on hiking trails during these hours. Cougars are incredibly fast and stealthy, and if one does attack, fight it with every available weapon, like a hiking stick or a big rock. Pepper spray works well on cougars.

RATTLESNAKES

These venomous pit vipers inhabit Idaho, generally at elevations below 5,000 feet, but you'll probably never see one. They crawl into cool places under rocks and logs in the heat of day, and even if they're out and about, they'll generally avoid humans if possible. Your greatest chance of encountering one along the trail would be in early morning or evening, or in turning over the wrong rock. Scrambling up rocks is also risky, as you tend to grab above your head in places you can't see. If you do get bitten, the current medical consensus seems to be to get to a doctor as soon as possible, rather than trying the incision-and-suction method formerly recommended. It seems many people did more damage than the snake by slicing themselves or their friends open incorrectly. The best advice is to be cautious and avoid contact in the first place. If you come around a bend in the trail to find one staring you down and rattling at you, just back off a safe distance and wait for it to crawl away. And never invite trouble by poking at a rattler with a stick or otherwise harassing it.

MINES

One place you might indeed encounter a rattlesnake at midday is a place to be avoided for other reasons as well. Idaho is full of old abandoned mines. Rattlers come in for the cool darkness. You come in to explore and wind up getting bitten by the snake, falling down a hidden shaft, getting knocked unconscious by a falling rotten timber, and being buried alive in the ensuing cave-in. It's probably best just to stay out of old mines.

HANTAVIRUS

This nasty virus attracted a lot of attention a few years ago after a major outbreak in the Four Corners area of the Southwest. It's worth mentioning because the virus (spread by deer mice and other rodents common to Idaho) can be fatal in some cases. The virus is found in the animals' urine, saliva, and feces. You can get it by handling contaminated materials, being bitten by a rodent, or, most commonly, by breathing in the virus in contaminated dust or airborne mist from urine. Household disinfectants such as bleach and alcohol will kill the virus. If you rent a backcountry cabin and find telltale signs of rodent habitation, the safest course of action would be to spray the area down with bleach, then mop it up. Don't sweep mouse droppings up without spraying them with disinfectant first. And don't invite rodents into your camp by leaving food out carelessly or intentionally attempting to feed them.

CRIME

Idaho's relatively small population makes for a relatively low crime rate. Homicides and other violent crimes are thankfully rare and still make front-page news, even in Boise. Part of this can be attributed to Idaho's overall strong sense of community. People know their neighbors more than in many other parts of the West. But car burglaries and other property crimes do happen in Idaho, so don't leave valuables in plain sight on the front seat of your parked car.

Information and Services

TOURIST INFORMATION

If, heaven forbid, you can't find the answer to your question somewhere in this guide, contact the **Idaho Department of Commerce/ Idaho Division of Tourism** (700 W. State St., Boise, 800/847-4843, www.visitidaho.org).

MAPS AND GUIDES

National Forest Maps

The U.S. Forest Service publishes detailed maps to each of Idaho's national forests, which are a must for backcountry users. The maps cost $6 each. You can obtain a particular national forest's map from the office for that forest, but if you're interested in several different forests, it's easier to deal with the Forest Service regional offices. For maps of the forests in the southern half of the state, including the Boise, Caribou, Payette, Salmon-Challis, Sawtooth, and Caribou-Targhee National Forests, contact the Forest Service Intermountain Region office (324 25th St., Ogden, UT 84401, 801/625-5306).

Idaho Atlas and Gazetteer

DeLorme Mapping (P.O. Box 298, Yarmouth, ME 04096, 800/452-5931, www.delorme.com) publishes detailed atlases to many western states, including Idaho. These are not detailed city street maps, à la Thomas Bros., but rather partially topographic maps that show Forest Service roads, campgrounds, and natural features across every inch of the state. They are indispensable for off-the-beaten-path travel in Idaho.

State Publications

Ever notice how all those many roadside historical markers you pass in your travels through Idaho are numbered? The handy catalog *Idaho Highway Historical Marker Guide* describes them all. It's available for $5 from the Idaho Transportation Department, Office of Communications (P.O. Box 7129, Boise, ID 83707-1129, 208/334-8000).

The state's tourism folks put out the *Idaho Official Travel Guide,* a lush and lovely guide to the state, every year. It's got a wealth of information on sights, lodgings, and recreation opportunities, accompanied by stunning color photography. Best of all, it's free. Request a copy from the Idaho Division of Tourism, Administrative Office, Idaho Department of Commerce (700 W. State St., P.O. Box 83720, Boise, ID 83720-0093, 208/334-2470).

MEDIA

The best of the state's mainstream daily newspapers are Boise's *Idaho Statesman* (www.idahostatesman.com), the largest-circulation paper in the state, and Lewiston's *Lewiston Morning Tribune* (www.lmtribune.com). The Spokane-based *Spokesman-Review* (www.spokesmanreview.com) also offers comprehensive coverage of north Idaho.

Also in the state capital, the *Boise Weekly* (www.boiseweekly.com) stands out as a highly credible liberal rag featuring excellent reporting and writing. The paper is available for free all around the Boise area.

National Public Radio junkies will find affiliates in Boise at KBSU (90.3 FM),

KBSX (91.5 FM), and KBSU (730 AM); in Cottonwood at KNWO (90.1 FM); in McCall at KBSM (91.7 FM); in Moscow at KRFA (91.7 FM); in Rexburg at KRIC (100.5 FM); and in Twin Falls at KBSW (91.7 FM).

MONEY

Automatic teller machines (ATMs) are found at most Idaho banks and at many grocery stores and other locations. If you need to deal with a human, you'll find that most banks are typically open 9:30am-5:30pm Mon.-Fri., with some open on Saturday as well.

TELEPHONES

Here's a relief to visitors from other areas of the country where new telephone area codes seem to be spawning faster than cockroaches. The area code for all of Idaho is **208.** On cell phones, that means when you're calling someplace in Idaho distant from where you are, there's no need to dial 208 in order for the call to go through. For telephone **directory assistance,** call 208/555-1212.

Cell phone coverage can be spotty in Idaho, especially deep in the mountains and far out in the desert, but coverage is clear most everywhere else.

TIME ZONES AND SYSTEMS

Idaho is shared by two different time zones. Northern Idaho is on **Pacific Standard Time.** Down around Riggins, the time zone changes to **Mountain Standard Time,** an hour ahead of Pacific time. As with most places in the country, Idaho follows the daylight saving convention. In spring (the second Sunday in March) daylight saving time goes into effect, and everyone sets their clocks an hour ahead. In fall (the first Sunday in November) the clocks go back an hour to standard time. Remember the ditty: "spring forward, fall back."

Resources

Internet Resources

STATE SERVICES AND INFORMATION

State of Idaho
www.accessidaho.org
State of Idaho
Idaho's official website has all the usual links to state agencies, plus some truly useful and fun stuff. Here you can check road conditions, get fishing license information, and more.

Idaho State Travel Planner
www.visitidaho.org
A handy itinerary planner, calendar of events, and lodging guide are among the features of the state's official tourism site.

Idaho Transportation Department
www.itd.idaho.gov
One of the most practical sites for visitors, where you can check winter road conditions in Idaho and neighboring states, learn about road closures and detours, and get forecasts from the National Weather Service.

Idaho State Library
www.lili.org
Use this site to find a local library and search catalogs statewide.

ACCOMMODATIONS

In Idaho Reservations
www.inidaho.com
This private McCall-based company is a handy place to research and book accommodations and activities throughout the state. It features good package deals too, including some you won't see on the official state website.

North Idaho Bed-and-Breakfast Association
www.nibba.com
The website offers information and links to bed-and-breakfast inns in the Panhandle.

CULTURE AND HISTORY

Idaho Commission on Hispanic Affairs
http://icha.idaho.gov
Idaho's growing Hispanic community can look to this site for information on Spanish-language media, upcoming events, job postings, and more.

Idaho Tribal News
www.shobannews.com
The online edition of the tribal newspaper for the Fort Hall Reservation near Pocatello offers a glimpse into modern Native American life as well as links to other Indian news sources.

Lewis and Clark in Idaho
www.lewisandclarkidaho.org
Look here for information on the famous expedition's travels through Idaho, where it crossed the rugged Lolo Trail in fall 1805 and returned to camp among the Nez Perce on the way home in 1806.

MEDIA

Idaho Statesman
ww.idahostatesman.com
The online edition of this Boise-based newspaper, Idaho's largest, is a great place to learn what's going on in the state, especially in the Boise metro area. There are also links to the paper's superb entertainment section and its archive of restaurant reviews.

Boise Weekly
www.boiseweekly.com
For an irreverent, informative look at life in and around Boise, check out this alternative weekly's site.

RECREATION

Idaho State Parks and Recreation
www.parksandrecreation.idaho.gov
Learn about Idaho's state parks and make online camping reservations.

National Park Service
www.nps.gov
The website has links to such Idaho attractions as Craters of the Moon National Monument and City of Rocks National Reserve, along with Yellowstone National Park, a small part of which is in Idaho.

U.S. Forest Service
www.fs.fed.us
Search for Idaho on the main page, then follow the links to all of Idaho's dozen national forests. The agency administers more than 20 million acres throughout the state. This is also a good place to get forest fire information.

Bureau of Land Management
www.blm.gov/id
The BLM manages 11,836,481 acres in Idaho—close to one-quarter of the state's total land. This site has information on BLM-related recreation sites as well as a list of field offices throughout the state.

Idaho Outfitters and Guides Association
www.ioga.org
Plan an outdoor Idaho adventure on this site, which showcases the state's licensed outfitters and guides in hunting, fishing, river running, trail rides, mountain biking, and more.

ReserveUSA
www.recreation.gov
Reserve campsites, cabins, and fire lookout stays in nearly 100 U.S. Forest Service and U.S. Army Corps of Engineers locations across Idaho. As with the state parks' online reservations, the only drawback is a fairly stiff reservation fee—though it's a small price to pay for a guaranteed campsite on busy holidays and weekends.

OTHER WEBSITES

Idaho Conservation League
www.idahoconservation.org
Of the many environmental groups working in Idaho, this homegrown organization ranks among the oldest and best. Its website has regularly updated information on every major environmental issue facing the state, from salmon runs to forest health and efforts to preserve such places as the Boulder-White Cloud Mountains, Owyhee Canyonlands, and even the Boise Foothills.

Digital Atlas of Idaho
http://imnh.isu.edu/digitalatlas
This is a wonderful compendium of knowledge about all the natural sciences in Idaho. Whether you're trying to identify a bird or learn more about the state's weird geology, you'll find it here.

Index

N

XYZ

List of Maps

Photo Credits

Also Available

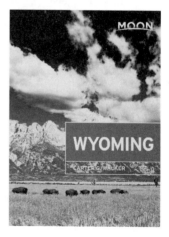